The Wilder Shores of Dylan Thomas

Booksellers are not known for their engagement with the literary world. They are usually out the back checking in stock or doing the accounts. Jeff Towns might be the big exception. Long an invited member of that august organisation the Welsh Academy he has now proved himself by producing a collection of literary essays that encompass not just 5his long-term specialism of Dylan Thomas but RS, Allen Ginsberg, Ted Hughes, Peter Blake, Cerys Matthews and Taylor Swift as well. Who knew that DT was once a runner or that RS liked the horses.

This new book is a bibliophile's joy, celebrating a world that if the digitisers get their way will soon vanish. Jeff has met everyone still around, visited the great collectors, rambled the States, sought the missing and found the lost. His stories of the literary hunt can read like Agatha Christie. These essays are certainly the wilder shores. Long may Jeff Towns celebrate them.

Peter Finch Cardiff 2024

A found American beer advert featuring an Ape reading Dylan Thomas' Poems

The Wilder Shores of Dylan Thomas

18 Essays by Jeff Towns

Foreword By Jon Gower

H'MM
12th ANNIVERSARY

Other books by Jeff Towns

DYLAN THOMAS LETTER TO LOREN. Salubrious Press. 1993.

DYLAN THOMAS WORD AND IMAGE. Exhibition Catalogue. 1995.

4 DYLAN THOMAS TRAIL BOOKLETS for the City and County of Swansea.

1. *Swansea City Centre*. 1999. (reprinted 2006).

2. *Uplands*.

3. *Mumbles and Gower*.

4. *West Wales*.

"Salzburg-on-the-Tawe" VERNON WATKINS' SWANSEA. Ty Llên Publications. 2006.

DYLAN THOMAS / THE PUBS. Y Lolfa. 2013.

VERNON WATKINS: OF POETS AND POETRY. Parthian. 2013. With Gwen Watkins.

A PEARL OF GREAT PRICE, Dylan Thomas' Letters to Pearl Kazin. Parthian. 2014.

DYLAN THOMAS AMONG THE BOHEMIANS. Parthian. 2014. With G. & L. Summers.

EDWARD THOMAS AND WALES. Parthian. 2018.

THE TWO DYLANS. McNidder & Grace. 2022. With K.G. Miles.

Dedication

To Rosie Aslett – Long May She Bloom

"Dylan Thomas is by now as much a case history as a chapter in the history of poetry. Mention of his name is enough to turn on a multi-channel set of associations. There is Thomas the voice, Thomas the booze, Thomas the debts. Thomas the jokes, Thomas the Wales, Thomas the sex, Thomas the Lies – in fact there are so many competing and revisionist inventions of Thomas available, so many more or less corrective, reductive, even punitive versions of the phenomenon that it is with a certain tentativeness that one asks whether there is still a place on the roll-call for Thomas the Poet."

Seamus Heaney – the opening paragraph of
his lecture DYLAN THE DURABLE. 1992

I could never have dreamt that there were such goings-on in the world between the covers of books, such sandstorms and ice blasts of words, such slashing of humbug, and humbug too, such staggering peace, such enormous laughter, such and so many blinding bright lights breaking across the just-waking wits and splashing all over the pages in a million bits and pieces all of which were words, words, words, and each of which were alive forever in its own delight and glory and oddity and light.

Dylan Thomas *Notes on the Art of Poetry*

First published in 2025 by the H'mm Foundation

The H'mm Foundation is: c/o Bevan Buckland, Langdon House, Langdon Road, Swansea SA1 8QY.

ISBN 978 1 0685053 1 7
A CIP catalogue record for this book is available from the British Library.

Design: Andy Dark
Typeset in Freight
Printed and bound by Gwasg Gomer, Llandysul, Ceredigion, Wales

www.thehmmfoundation.co.uk

Contents

Foreword *Jon Gower*

Enthusiasm for a subject can be a power source and this captivating collection of essays flickers, fizzes and crackles with a real enthusiast's energy. Here Jeff Towns shares tales of fifty years of dedicated book-dealing, ferreting out fine and first editions, locating lost letters and seeking out long-sought-for memorabilia. It includes the highlight of his life as a bibliophile businessman when he holds his nerve in the auction rooms of Sothebys and, courtesy of a steely final bid, brings a valuable trove of Dylan Thomas poems home to Swansea. There is a colourful account of the Thomas bibliography and the cover art adorning the many volumes as well as a surreal road trip to Sedona, Arizona.

With his customary humility Jeff avers that he is no scholar, critic or biographer and yet anyone who had ever had the good pleasure to spend more than five minutes in his company knows that here is a real expert, a self-taught literary scholar and a diligent and dedicated detective, making a myriad connections between writers and their work, hunting down clues, interrogating expert witnesses.

The essays range very widely, taking in subjects such as sex and gender as Jeff ponders how Dylan is attracted to the word "hermaphrodite" or considers the erotic and scatological elements in Under Milk Wood without ever sounding a bum note. There is a fascinating account of Dylan's appeal to both Sylvia Plath and Ted Hughes and, of course there is plenty here about the successes and skullduggeries of buying and selling books. Thus we have plenty of fine, vivid vignettes of other sellers and their disappearing shops and personal dispositions. We also find out why Dylan is so very coveted and dedicatedly collected by both huge institutions and passionate individuals and learn why Jeff has often cornered the market, or found a literary gem among the silverfish and dust of the bottom shelves. In a sense the book is an account of single-minded, sometimes bloody minded dedication to bibliolocating in many cities, towns and continents, but never without a sense of joy in the seeking and delight in the finding

Dealing is a word one often associates with street drugs but The Wilder Shore suggests that book-dealing has similar highs and habituations, derangements and occasional, searing visions.

In taking us to The Wilder Shore Jeff proves himself to be a brilliant companion, the sort of raconteur you'd sorely need should you be stranded on a desert island, one where the very last thing either of you would wish to do is burn any of the books that have washed in with the tide. For as you'll find out in these pages, books are works of art, repositories of learning, sacred objects and valuable commodities. Here's to them all. Here's to this fine one in your hands.

Our First Bookshop. This is a council photograph and comment, taken shortly after we had moved on. This whole row of Georgian buildings has since been demolished.

Introduction

We opened our first bookshop in 1970, at 75, High Street, Swansea. I had settled in Swansea after four years of further-education in Cardiff, but I had been born and raised in the East End of London. Now, aged 22, I was about to be married to a Swansea girl I had met in college in Cardiff a few years before.

I had always been a voracious reader and spent my teens devouring any interesting paperbacks I came across by fair means or foul, and in college I studied English Literature. I was also well aware that Swansea's most celebrated literary son was Dylan Thomas, who was born here in 1914, and that he wrote much of his published work while he lived here. He was already one of my most favourite authors. I had trained to be an English and P.E. teacher, but at that time a strong vein of nepotism permeated South Wales teacher-recruitment and nobody seemed to want to employ an East-End lad. Thankfully my new father-in-law, John James, was a well-respected local antique-dealer and auctioneer and he was keen to lure me out of the class-room and into business. In partnership with his brother Penry, we hatched a plan to open a second-hand book shop. They held the lease on a small, empty, low-ceilinged, rather dilapidated, Georgian building on Swansea High Street, which they were happy to sub-let to me at a very manageable rent of 10 shillings per week. I couldn't believe my luck – I was to have a bookshop on Swansea's High Street! In the spirit of literary homage, laced with a heaped spoonful of commercial exploitation, we named our tiny shop *Dylans Bookshop*. Dylan Thomas became our house author of choice and, although the shop was to be a general second-hand bookshop, we proudly kept a range of new Dylan Thomas books on display in their current paperback format.

I was aware that Swansea already boasted a legendary used bookshop – RALPH THE BOOKS – run by the avuncular Ralph Wishart aided by his brother Bryn and sister Winnie.

1970. My wife Liz, pictured in the local paper in front of our Dylan Thomas display on our shop opening day

Ralph Wishart and Winnie at their open newsagent section

Ralph was very kind helpful and generous to me when I opened and his bookshop really was 'Dylan's Bookshop' as Dylan was a regular customer and nuisance to Ralph, who was just as generous to the poor young poet. There is even a section about Ralph's bookshop in Dylan's radio script *Return Journey*[1]. A Minister recalls;

> A bookshop. Yes. I knew it well ... A young man like you... used to rub shoulders with me ...you see poetry and theology was next door to each other... His pleasure was to read to me ... some Babylonian lines from a man called Ezra Pound.
> Tried to shock me he did, but I was not shocked...

After Ralph died I bought his copy of Dylan's second book, 25 POEMS, warmly inscribed by Dylan to Ralph and as I was writing

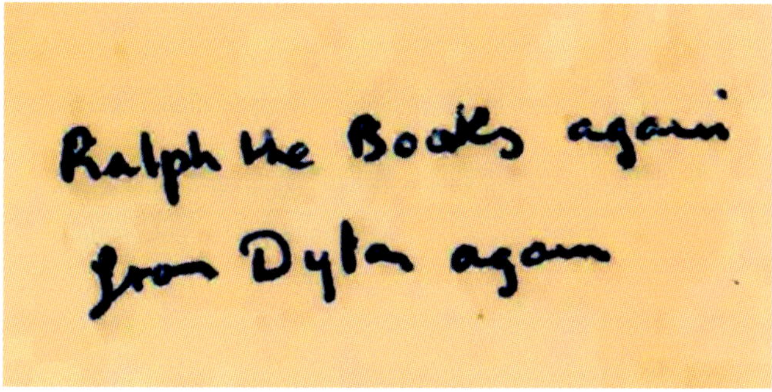

It was priced arounds £15 thousand and appears to have been sold

this book a Californian dealer offered a copy of Dylan's rare first book *18 POEMS* inscribed by Dylan to Ralph.

Apart from some general advice from my in-laws and Ralph, my naïve vision for the business was that I would buy used academic text-books from graduating students and sell them to the next year's intake. I quickly realised that this was the road to ruin – when leaving students came in to sell their text books they wanted half the cover price; when new students arrived they wanted to buy used text books at half the new price. I quickly realised this was a flawed business model. Not only that, students were already going off text-books in favour of beer and duplicated handouts from their lecturers.

Luckily one of my first regular customers was a Pontypridd man named Malcolm Parr. He was a passionate Iberophile, librarian, bibliophile, published poet & translator, and brilliant raconteur. Oh, and he loved the pub. He was a lecturer in Spanish and the librarian at the local College of Further Education.

We very soon became good friends, and he came into the shop one day, waving an advert for an Antiquarian Book Fair to be held in Bath, about which he was extremely excited, and very keen for us to visit. I quickly fell in with his plan, even though I did not have the faintest idea what an 'Antiquarian Book Fair' was. Most of my stock came from boxes dropped into the shop by people on the move, a very few local house calls usually after a family bereavement and Friday/Saturday local Church, Scout & Guide jumble sales, which I diligently queued up for on a regular basis. So on the following Saturday my wife opened the shop and Malcolm and I set off to Bath.

The Bath Book Fair was my first bookselling epiphany. The venue was the elegant *Octagon* in the centre of Bath, and on either side of each of the eight sections was a stand of three, ingenious, tall folding shelves full of books of a richness and wonder I had never imagined, and the dealers were a colourful bunch too! Malcolm and I browsed the stands together, me pretending to know what I was doing, with Malcolm advising and instructing me. I was totally smitten. I made a couple of small nervous purchases; a late, posthumous Dylan Thomas first edition and a Swansea local history book, but I was more interested in hunting out the organiser. I was directed to a middle-aged, bohemian-looking, but less than well-dressed chap, Gerry Mosdell,[2] who ran a book-shop called *Porcupines*, in Barnstable (indeed the West Country provided many of the dealers).

Gerry Mosdell was very laid-back and easy to get on with. He informed me that there was to be another Fair in a couple of months in Bristol and I immediately signed up to exhibit. So, Gerry waved his wand and I became a 'Book Fairy'. I cobbled

The Bath book fair after a move to equally grand Assembly rooms

together some folding shelves (they were tragic, I am neither shoe mender nor carpenter but they just about worked). When the fair date arrived, I packed my van with a dozen boxes with what I thought were my best books, strapped my makeshift shelves to the roof rack and drove over the bridge to Bristol. As soon as I began to set up my stand I was surrounded by a pack of the other dealers, all grabbing at the books as soon as I placed then on my rickety shelves; some were even reaching into my boxes and demanding to buy what they discovered (I was later to discover that this was very bad form). But I felt I had arrived; I had found my tribe and my calling. And, by the end of the two-day fair, I had also sold a great many books.

Before long, I too was a regular exhibitor at Book fairs across the UK. (Malcolm came with me to the first Liverpool book fair and we had a fine time). After much pleading, I finally started exhibiting at the Monthly London book fair at the *Kenilworth Hotel*, located near the British Library as it was then.

Inside a few years of this development I added yearly fairs in Canada and America to my roster, with side-trips to exhibit at book fairs in Amsterdam and Malta for good measure. I was immediately at home in this itinerant version of the book trade and quickly made a group of new-found bookish dealer friends and colleagues. I learned fast and quickly and picked up, what I now realise was a very superficial knowledge of the tricks of the Second-hand and Antiquarian Book Trade – I now know that one never stops learning about books and bookselling and every day I add some one-new-thing or another to my bibliographic knowledge. However, superficial as my early book-knowledge was, I now realise that I learned more at one weekend bookfair in a provincial town or city, especially the monthly London book fairs, than I would have learned sitting in my Swansea bookstore for a whole year.

One other factor added to this; money was tight and overnight accommodation, even of the most basic level, ate up capital I did not have, and profit that I badly needed to buy books and food (often in that order). So, I joined the small and wonderfully eccentric, band of itinerant and impecunious booksellers who dispensed with Hotels or Guest-houses and chose instead, to unroll sleeping bags on the floors of the exhibition spaces, amongst all the books, and bed down for the night. We were notionally acting as extra overnight security, but for me it gave hours and hours of quiet time to browse a vast array of fine books – unhampered by noisy customers or pushy dealers.

I think that this was when and where I really began to learn my chosen trade. I soon began to specialise in areas other than just Dylan Thomas and one of these became books about women. It was then still a subject largely unexplored by booksellers, but I became aware of the growing Women's Liberation Movement and intrigued by books such as Germaine Greer's, *The Female Eunuch* and Valerie Solanas' *S.C.U.M (Society for Cutting Up Men) Manifesto*, both of which featured arresting cover designs.

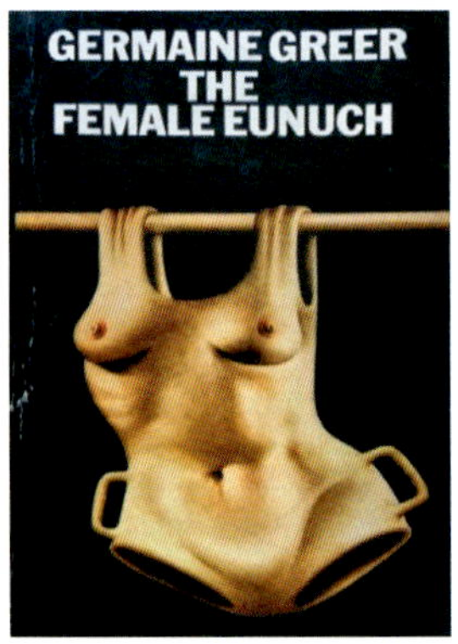

These two books sparked my interest – and led to my second bookselling epiphany – my meeting with Lisa Baskin, an American, who was the most passionate and dedicated book-collector I had ever encountered. She collected 'girl books', as she was allowed to call them. We met in the mid-seventies at the first ever one-day Tiverton book fair, where amongst the stock I was exhibiting, was a shelf or two of books by and about women.

My good and generous friend, the late, Len Kelly,[3] a bookseller with a shop in the town and the book fair organiser, had advised me to bring 'Women's Books' as there was a keen local collector;

Virginia Woolf's desk.

Len even brought this lady, Lisa to my stand and introduced us. We immediately got on well; Lisa bought a good many of my selection of 'girl books'. We chatted some more about what else I had in stock back in Wales, and then she invited me back to have tea after the fair closed, with her and her husband, Leonard,[4] a sculptor, artist, fine printer, and also a mad obsessive book-collector. Lisa had moved from America to Devon with her artist husband Lenny, as he liked to be addressed. I found him pretty scary to begin with, older than Lisa; and at first encounter, gruff and taciturn, but that soon softened and he was as generous and kind as Lisa. Leonard was an incredible artist across all mediums, sculpture, drawing, painting, printmaking and he also founded and oversaw a fine private press – *The Gehenna Press*. They chose to move to Devon so they could be nearby to their close friends, the poet Ted Hughes and his wife Carol. Leonard and Ted collaborated on fine Gehenna editions of Ted's poetry illustrated by Leonard who also made illustrations for the dust-jacket designs of many of Ted's collections of poetry.

The first of many books Leonard inscribed to me

I knew I was in a very special library when I admired and commented on, an unusual painted desk in a corner of the room, only to be informed that it had once belonged to Virginia Woolf! Furthermore, it was hand-painted by Quentin Bell in the Bloomsbury/Charleston manner.

If that wasn't enough, sat on top of the desk was a colourful beadwork cushion enclosed in a Victorian glass Victorian dome. It was inscribed on the frame;

SAMPLER By CHARLOTTE BRONTE

These two non-book historic artefacts were surrounded by Lisa's collection of books about women – starting with an incunabulum printed by nuns, and early books on women's costumes with dazzling woodcut illustrations and on through the centuries: books by Elizabeth Elstob, Mary Wollstonecraft, Phillis Wheatley, and historic works by women scientists, travellers, poets, artists and bookbinders; original letters by The Ladies of Llangollen and Emma Goldman, and on into the more

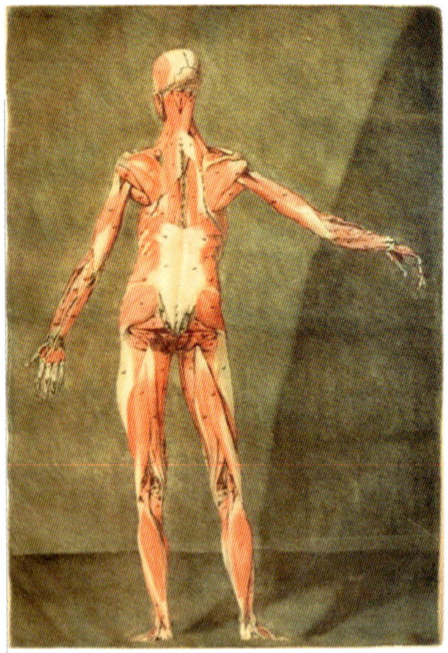

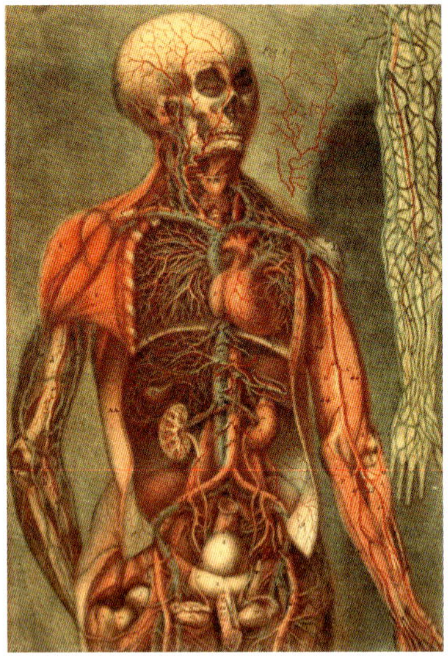

modern period with a huge suffragette and Women's Rights collection.

And then there were Leonard's books – shelf after shelf of 16th, 17th and 18th century books in all shapes and sizes and subjects; books on decorative arts, illustrated medical and anatomical books, natural history, portrait books and bibliographic curiosities, which included a 17th century book bound in human skin (which I later bought and sold), and a set of the incredible, early colour printed, life-size anatomical illustrations charts by the great French 18th century anatomist, Gautier d'Agoty.

Subsequently I have only ever visited one better private library and that was the incredible library of the late, mega-wealthy collector, John Paul Getty Jr.[5]

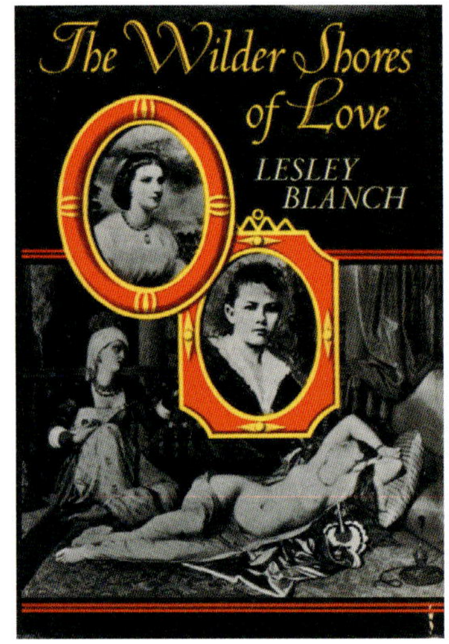

Lisa and Leonard became very good customers, and better still, great and generous friends. Eventually Lisa's magnificent collection out-grew the huge library housed in her attached New England barn. Lisa is very proud that her great collection is now getting very well used by scholars and students at the David M. Rubenstein Library at Duke University in North Carolina. It was also the subject of a major exhibition both at the Rubenstein Library and at The Grolier Club in New York. I am very proud to have supplied a good number of books and ephemera to the collection over the years, a good few of which are illustrated in the sumptuous catalogue that accompanied the exhibition.

One of the 'girls books' which used to turn up on a regular basis when I first looked out for books on women was Lesley Blanche's 1954 book – *The Wilder Shores of Love*, which was a best seller and has hardly been out of print since.

Lesley Blanch was a remarkable woman; a traveller, journalist and biographer, who died in the south of France aged 103. In this, her most famous book, she writes about four remarkable women who all travelled east: Isabel Burton (who married Richard Burton the explorer of Arabia and translator of the Arabian Nights), Jane Digby el-Mezrab (Lady Ellenborough, the society beauty who ended up living in the Syrian desert with a Bedouin chieftain), Aimée Du Buc de Rivery (a French convent girl captured by pirates who ended up in the Sultan's harem in Istanbul) and Isabelle Eberhardt (a Swiss linguist who felt most comfortable in boys clothes and lived among the Arabs in the Sahara). I've read and always kept a copy of the book on my shelves and the title stuck in my head, so now I have appropriated a part of it for the title[6] of this collection of essays, short pieces, lecture notes and transcribed talks and lectures, which often go where previous Dylan Thomas scholars, critics, and biographers have not gone before. The reason for this is that I am neither scholar, critic, nor biographer but an antiquarian & second-hand bookseller who, for fifty years has pursued Dylan Thomas (and his friends and cohorts) around the world, buying, selling, and collecting Dylan Thomas curiosa and it is these activities that begat or prompted the writings gathered here in this book.

1. This section however was not written by Dylan! The producer Philip Burton (Richard Burton's surrogate father) found his programme was a few minutes short; Dylan refused to write more; so Burton recalled Dylan talking about Ralphs Bookshop and he wrote it up and added into the script. This section was not included in the first publication of the Script in the 1954 *Quite Early One Morning*, but it is included in Ralph Maud's edition of *The Broadcasts* (Dent 1991).

2. Sadly, I recently attended Gerry Mosdell's funeral up in Llandudno Junction, where his partner Glenda, another book trade old-timer, still runs their shop. Gerry, into his 80's, was still exhibiting at a few fairs; he was a remarkable man and pretty much dragged the book-trade into the twentieth century. After those early fairs in the early 70's he Founded/Established the P.B. F. A. – The Provincial Booksellers Fairs Association, which grew and grew to a membership of some hundreds of booksellers in the UK and abroad and ran over fifty fairs a year. To begin with there were no paid officers – Gerry established it as a 'workers co-operative'. No payments were given – If you ran a fair as Fair manager you got a free stand and I believe that holds good today.

3. Len Kelly became a close friend. A Londoner, he was an autodidact who had been a London bus conductor before joining The Epworth Press, a Methodist publishing house with a second-hand book department. He then left for Canada where he opened a successful bookshop in Toronto. He returned to the UK in the sixties and settled in Tiverton and opened another bookshop and began an imaginative specialization in books on the technical and social history of broadcasting. It was Len who suggested we exhibit at the Toronto book fair – my first fair in North America and we also went together to the first ever Malta book fair. He was a good man, a good friend and a good bookseller. He died in 2008.

4. Leonard had also known Sylvia Plath when she was in Northampton Mass, when she was at Smith University. In her first collection of poems is a poem; *Sculptor; For Leonard Baskin*. It is the first poem Sylvia ever dedicated to a specific person.

5. I had heard there was to be a cricket match between two 'rival' bookselling Associations; the A.B.A. and the P.B.F.A. to be played at Getty's sumptuous private cricket pitch at Wormsley, his Oxfordshire estate. But what persuaded me to Blanco my boots and wash my flannels was the added note that after the match we would be offered a special private viewing of his legendary book collection. I played competent but unremarkable cricket for the PBFA and we won but, more importantly, the library did not disappoint; untold bibliographic treasures; to mention just a couple; a stunning small 16th century prayer book, in an elaborate and intricate needlework binding with gold, silver and coloured threads which belonged to Mary Queen of Scots which she clutched when she was executed in 1587; a copy of the first edition of Marx's *Das Capital*, at first sight in a rather surprising Guild of Women Bookbinders binding, but less surprising when on opening one saw it was inscribed by Karl Marx to William Morris! AND more on this in Chapter 17.

6. It appears I'm not the first – I just got a copy of Lesley Blanch's *Memoirs* edited by her goddaughter, Georgia de Chamberet, who wrote in her forward of how her godmother was delighted that her 'title coined a phrase which I still hear people use, or see it in the press – *the wilder shores of Westminster* in a piece on stormy politics, or the wilder side of romanticism on a fashion'. She goes on to note that the chanteuse, Marianne Faithfull, wrote a song called *The Wilder Side of Love* and that the great American abstract painter, Cy Twombly, called one of his most important works *The Wilder Side of Love*, which the Tate Modern recently used to promote his major retrospective in 2008 – so I'm in good company.

DYLAN THOMAS AND HIS WELSH BACKGROUND

ディラン・トマスの風景

○松浦 直巳著

愛 育 社

1.

My First Dylan Thomas Collection & Naomi Matsurra of Kyoto, Japan

I hold a book-dealer, a book-collector and a madman in me, and my enquiry is as to their working, and my problem is their subjugation...

I often ruminate on, and explain to anyone who will listen, that I believe I am a book-collector *manqué*, trapped in the body of an inveterate book-dealer. Dylan Thomas wrote in an early letter to his first critic Henry Treece:

> I hold a beast, an angel, and a madman in me, and my enquiry is as to their working, and my problem is their subjugation...

In my case – for 'beast' use 'book-dealer', and change 'angel' to 'book-collector' ('madman' can stay for us both). My main method of subjugation has been to build collections. Early in my bookselling days I always tried to have two or three collections on the go at the same time; both author collections and subject collections. In most cases it's a long game, but it satisfies my need to collect. It also means that when scouring bookshops and book fairs, I can usually find at least one book to buy and add to a collection (known in the trade as a *Courtesy Purchase*).[1]

For over fifty years of book dealing, I have built, catalogued and sold, many large and varied collections. The first was a great Mervyn Peake collection – pretty much complete in terms of his printed books, but it also contained some great original art by him too. It went to a private collector in Bath who came into some money just as I was ready to part with it. Next came the British avant-garde and experimental writer B. S. Johnson, a large collection comprising almost all his published stuff, original letters and the odd concrete poem. I eventually sold it to the Library at London University, his alma-mater.

Then an extensive Gypsy collection that went to a bookseller even madder than me in Vancouver. My Edward Thomas collection went to the great Cheltenham book-seller Alan Hancox; it must have been good for him to reach for it – such was his passion for Edward Thomas.

Two collections were sold quite recently; Bruce Chatwin went to Harvard and my Tattoo books went to another American University, as yet unknown to me. In the late 70's my

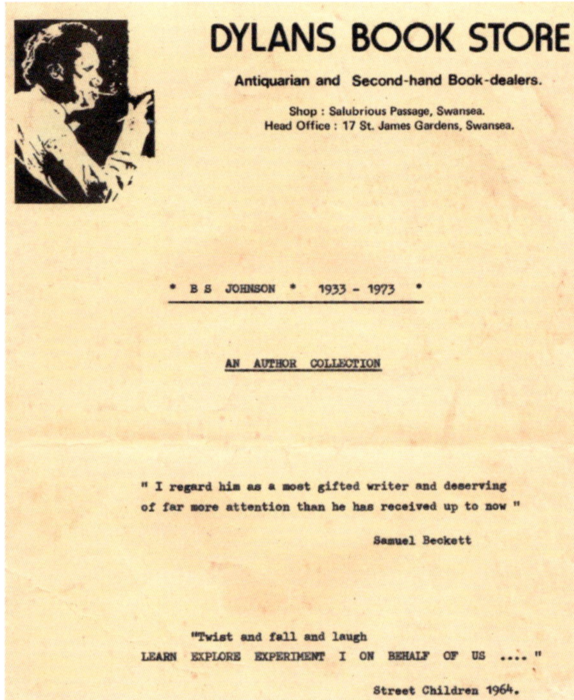
DYLANS BOOK STORE

Antiquarian and Second-hand Book-dealers.

Shop : Salubrious Passage, Swansea.
Head Office : 17 St. James Gardens, Swansea.

• B S JOHNSON • 1933 - 1973 •

AN AUTHOR COLLECTION

" I regard him as a most gifted writer and deserving of far more attention than he has received up to now "

Samuel Beckett

"Twist and fall and laugh
LEARN EXPLORE EXPERIMENT I ON BEHALF OF US .... "

Street Children 1964.

room full of Rock and Roll and Modern Music books went, to my astonishment, to Japan. A dealer I was friendly with, who knew I had this collection phoned me and said she had a client for them in Japan. It was to be my introduction to a new bookselling phenomena.

Around this time Japan's economy was booming and the small Private Universities across the country suddenly began to hoover up collections, in fierce competition with each other so as to attract wealthier students by the calibre of their library. They were hungry for quality, but also quantity; so they wanted established 'common' rare books – *Blackstone's Laws, Smith's Wealth of Nations*, early editions of *Shakespeare* and *Dickens, Kelmscott Press*; in fact they wanted any bookish cornerstone of

Western Culture. This phenomena spawned a group of clever and astute booksellers who saw what this new potential market had to offer and made it the lynchpin of their business to exploit this new demand.

Armed with printouts of lists, catalogues and often photographs, of collections they had assembled or had the sale of on consignment, these new travelling book salesmen would fly out to Tokyo and then do the rounds trying to win over librarians. But the clever ones saw that Japanese business culture was different, more restrained and subject to much stricter protocols than in the West, so they courted the biggest Japanese booksellers and worked with them rather than against them, and it seemed there was enough money for both parties to make handsome profits.

Around this time one of the rare book- trade magazines carried a profile of me and my book business. It was written by a pal of mine, who happened to mention in his feature that I enjoyed building book collections and always had a few on the go. Shortly after the article appeared one such bibliographic Sinophile, who had read the article, introduced himself to me at a London book-fair and gently asked if I had any collections for sale. I liked Johnny Boyle, as I came to know him, he was an easy-going old-school bookseller; an upper-class chap, who still played Real Tennis. His main business specialised in serious antiquarian philosophy and economics books. His avuncular manner and winning smile caught me at a good time. I told him about my Dylan Thomas collection and suggested that maybe he could do something with it.

Very soon after getting into more serious bookselling I had begun to collect Dylan Thomas. Why wouldn't I? He was a favourite writer, I lived in his home town; I had named my bookshop *DYLANS* as a gentle homage to him and I stocked a range of his works both new and used. But the better and more unusual Dylan Thomas material that came my way I kept for myself and began to build my first Dylan Thomas Collection. Some fifteen years on, the key books in the collection filled a small Edwardian glazed bookcase in my home. I enjoyed looking through the glass door, proud of what I had gathered. However, I was finding it hard to add to the collection and when that happens the collection begins to get a tad stale. I always felt that the best book in any collection was the last book you bought.

Also by then I had two young children, and I needed an injection of capital for them and my expanding business. So I agreed to catalogue the books and let my new colleague try and place it in Japan. John had little or no knowledge, or interest in this Welsh poet, but he was eager to try and place it.

I knuckled down to cataloguing my collection; it took longer than I expected because this was before even the Amstrad Word Processor; I typed the catalogue up manually onto stencils on an old typewriter but it was a slow process (I was, and still am a fat-fingered Luddite). I then printed off a few copies on the big old Gestetner duplicating machine which I kept upstairs in my shop.[2] I had bought this beast of a machine second-hand, with a view to cataloguing books and printing off catalogues and lists to increase my sales by postal bookselling.

I still have a copy of the original catalogue which I had bound in maroon leather (for posterity), which I stumble across in my office every so often. I can't resist wistfully flicking through; it stands up pretty well and I'd love to have a good few items back again. The first item was an original, manuscript worksheet for one of his most famous poems; *Deaths and Entrances*, the titular poem of his fourth book published in 1946. The second item was a rare pamphlet by a New York poet, one of Dylan's close American friends, Oscar Williams, on which Dylan had written *Dylan His Book* on the cover, doodled characteristically on the title page, and then scrawled three lines of rough notes for his final finished poem, the *Prologue* to his 1952 *Collected Poems*. The third item (and the final piece of original manuscript) was a long gushing letter from Edith Sitwell to Dylan Thomas. It was the first letter addressed to Dylan Thomas I had ever seen. I bought it at a New York Book Fair but since then I have only encountered one or two other letters sent to Dylan. He wrote some thousand plus letters, many replying to letters he received, but it seems his untidy and itinerant lifestyle, maybe coupled with an element of wilfulness, have made the other side of his correspondence vanish.

Here is the original introduction I wrote for the catalogue: I priced the collection at £10,000, which was a tidy sum in those days. I printed off a few copies and sent one off to Johnny and pretty much forgot about it. Time passed and then, out of the blue, Johnny rang and informed me he had sold the collection. I was pleased and saddened at the same time, but I had set the process in motion so I had to accept the outcome. I was shortly to exhibit at a book fair at the Commonwealth Institute in London and we arranged that I should take the collection, roughly packed in a few boxes, up to the fair, where Johnny would pick them up. We duly met and transferred the boxes from my car to Johnny's and he gave me a cheque for ten grand, and as was his style, it came with a fine magnum of champagne to celebrate with. A short while after I put together another smaller collection of scholarly and academic books about Thomas and a further gathering of periodicals containing Thomas contributions, which John also sold in Japan.

Naomi of Kyoto Women's University, Japan

In 1977 a Japanese professor of English, whose anglicised name was Naomi Matsuura, came to Swansea for a year as a visiting Professor at Swansea University, in the English Department. His sabbatical to Swansea was to enable him to further his studies into the life and work of Dylan Thomas and develop and improve his translations of Dylan Thomas' works into Japanese. This passion swiftly led him to search out my Bookstore which, by then, had moved from High Street down to Swansea's old docks area, where I rented a suite of ground floor rooms in a large and run-down building (the owner, my landlord was the local Tory politician Sir Michael Heseltine). Before long, this small quietly spoken oriental man, dressed plainly in a three-quarter length black leather coat and polished shoes, would visit almost every Friday afternoon to browse through and most often buy something from my Dylan Thomas holdings. We became friends and after he had browsed and bought books, I

DYLAN THOMAS 1914 - 1953

AN AUTHOR COLLECTION

Although his flamboyant and bohemian life style tended to over shadow his work and estrange many critics, since his tragic death in New York his reputation as a major Poet and innovative prose writer has been confirmed. His poetry is remarkable for its lyrical power, surrealistic, compact imagery, puns and intricate patterns of sound and meaning. It expresses his personal 'religion' which celebrates the wonder of procreation, growth and death, and conveys his joy of childhood, in which he himself seemed to be trapped. His earlier prose work consisted of strange surrealistic short stories but his exposure to radio broadcasting led him into writing his more popular humourous poetic prose - mainly about his childhood and youth, which culminated in his dramatic masterpiece 'Under Milk Wood'.

Writing of Thomas' Collected Poems, Cyril Connolly said, 'At his best he is unique...' and Philip Toynbee wrote of the same book, that Thomas was 'The greatest living poet'. Thomas was obsessed with his vocation as a poet, and his painstaking and intricate method of writing, which involved constant alterations, deletions and corrections is evident from the manuscript worksheet, which is the cornerstone of this collection. Although Thomas must have produced hundreds of such worksheets they are now of great rarity, many having been destroyed whilst the remaining specimens have found their way into institutions most often in America. Such items rarely appear on the market.

Bibliographicly Thomas' work is very interesting as most of his poems and stories go through at least three stages of publication, appearing first in one of the proliferation of literary magazines of the thirties and forties, then being anthologised in some annual or collection, before finally being published in one of his own books. Throughout this process minor alterations are plentiful and radical changes often occur. This collection is quite rich in this periodical and ephemeral material, whilst also containing all his English trade editions, some American editions, and one or two key rarities - the 1947 proof of 'Doctor and the Devils' being of great scarcity and interest. Alongside the manuscript worksheet and two presentation copies are several items from the library of Vernon Watkins, himself a fine poet and according to Fitzgibbon (Thomas' official biographer) 'A very close friend and in every sense one of Dylan's most loyal helpers'.

would take him across the road to one of Swansea's most wonderful and infamous pubs – *The Queens*.

In earlier times, in the late nineteenth/early twentieth century, during the heyday of the Swansea docks, the pub had doubled as a brothel; the higher ranking officers were entertained in the upstairs rooms while the deckhands and engineers would take the 'shilling ladies'(as Dylan Thomas described them in one of his short stories), out into the night and utilise the nearby darkened museum[3] steps or the graveyard to conduct their transactions. Naomi was fascinated by these snippets of local lore and loved to hear stories of the Swansea Dylan grew up in. He particularly liked the story of how the more common 'ladies of the night' would sit at the pub's long bar with their scruffy shoes up on the brass foot-rail so would-be punters could see their scale of charges which they chalked on the soles of their shoes!

Such human interaction is, thankfully, no longer apparent but the pub is still a proper old-style *Boozer*; a real local, full of warmth, character and characters. I would help the tiny Professor up onto the high bar stool, get us both pints of bitter, which, I assured him, was Dylan's tipple of choice, and spend an hour talking about our mutual favourite poet, as he glowed with contentment. He really felt that he has immersed himself into the little-changed milieu of his favourite poet.

As I got to know Naomi, I learned that he was a serious Zen Buddhist, steeped in ancient Zen philosophy, and that he was Professor of English at Kyoto Women's University. He spent a busy year in Wales, engaging with the Dylan Thomas Society, exploring Laugharne and West Wales and enjoying a classic performance of *Under Milk Wood* staged by Swansea Little Theatre, the amateur company that Dylan had joined in the early thirties and had acted with to great acclaim.

Naomi would later write about his memorable evening watching them perform;[4]

> ...hardly had the performance started when I was absorbed in it and transformed into the visibly "flying" voices of the characters of the play...
>
> I can safely say that the Anglo-Welsh speech as well as the

An illustration of a loose lady from the *Queens* by Wyn Thomas from my Book *Dylan Thomas the Pubs*

Thursday, February 16, 1978

PROFESSOR MATSUURA with one of his translations of the work of Dylan Thomas in his Swansea Japanese garden.

Welsh Language is musical and witty and even comical in quality and character...

At the end of his sabbatical year Naomi came to see me one last time. It was my last chance to question him on a matter that had been troubling me since we met. I broached my question gently:

Naomi, I can understand and am familiar with translations of Dylan's poetry into other Romance languages like French or German but please, how do you translate, *The Force that through the green fuse drives the flower/ Drives my green age* into the Japanese language?

Naomi thought for a while and then replied:

Jeff, in Japan we go for the spirit of the poem.

He then gifted me a warmly inscribed a copy of D.T. Suzuki's classic text WHAT IS ZEN, and, when I read it, I think I understood what he was getting at. The local paper gave him a fine send-off.

Back in Kyoto, Naomi would spend his next year writing a book in Japanese describing his year in Wales, illustrated with some

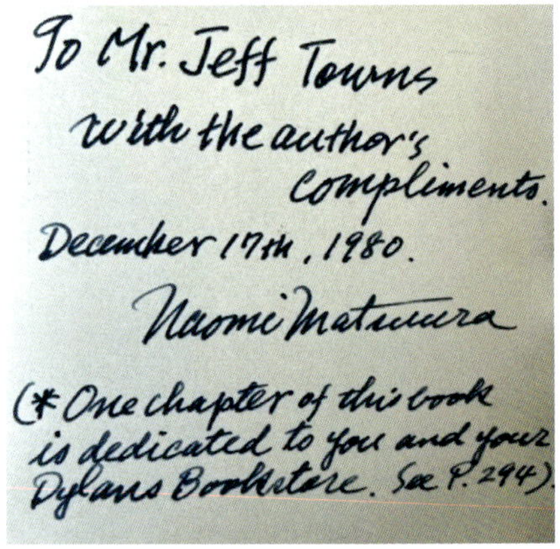

To Mr. Jeff Towns
with the author's
compliments.
December 17th, 1980.
Naomi Matsuura
(* One chapter of this book
is dedicated to you and your
Dylans Bookstore. See P. 294).

Naomi's warm inscription to me in his book about Dylan

colour plates, a few facsimiles and a great many grainy-grey photographs that he took during his stay. In due course a copy of *Dylan Thomas and His Welsh Background* arrived in the mail. A fine hardback copy, complete with a bold inscription on the endpapers and Naomi had also marked the index, guiding me to the chapter on my bookstore.

I went to these pages, and I found this image which I had taken with Naomi's camera on his first of many visits to my bookstore.

And that, I thought, was that, until a year or so later when a Japanese Air mail letter arrived in my shop from Naomi. In it he proudly and triumphantly informed me that his University had bought the Dylan Thomas Collection that I had consigned to a John Boyle some years previously.

Naomi's excitement and joy was so tangible as I read his letter;

I asked the Dean could recommend our library to buy the Dylan Thomas Collection and to my great surprise I found it the one you sold to a certain bookstore in London... Now I think it

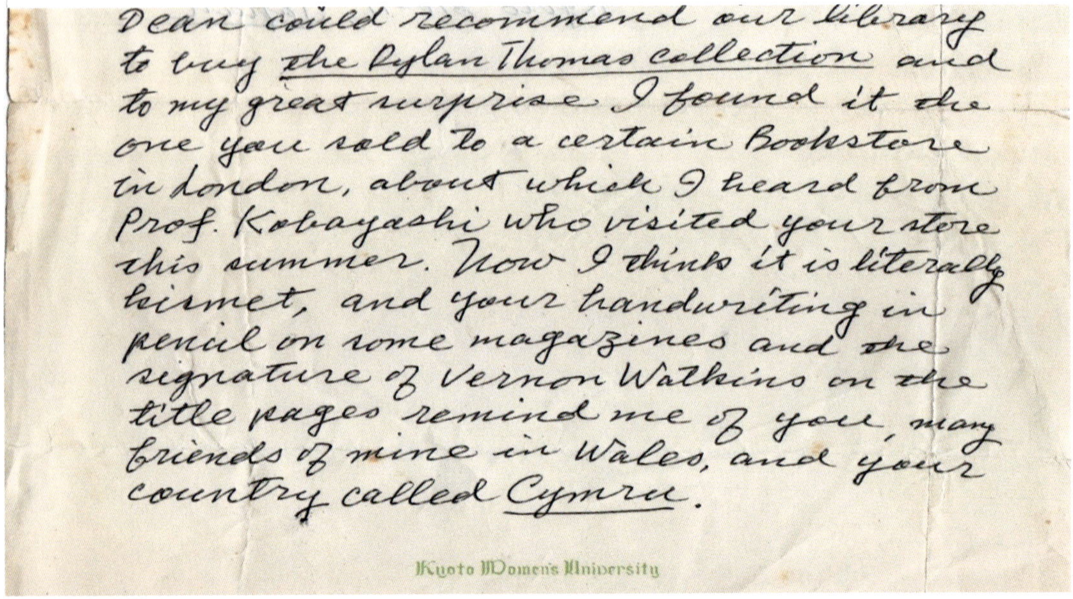

Dean could recommend our library
to buy the Dylan Thomas collection and
to my great surprise I found it the
one you sold to a certain Bookstore
in London, about which I heard from
Prof. Kobayashi who visited your store
this summer. Now I thinks it is literally
kismet, and your handwriting in
pencil on some magazines and the
signature of Vernon Watkins on the
title pages remind me of you, many
friends of mine in Wales, and your
country called Cymru.

Kyoto Women's University

is literally Kismet, and your handwriting in pencil on some magazines... remind me of you... Anyway, the collection now belongs to our library and are my treasure.

And an element of *Kismet* for me too. A very pleasing conclusion, and I was very content to know my first collection of Dylan Thomas materials were safe and being well used in such a deserved institution under the charge of such a dedicated and knowledgeable custodian.

ディランズ・ブック・ストア

1. I did a lot of book scouting both in the UK and U.S.A. with my long-time friend and bookselling colleague, the remarkable Eric Korn (Michael Frayn described him as 'the cleverest man I ever met'). In the wilds of America we often landed up in huge ill-lit book barns full of energetic scampering mice and very creaky bowed shelves full of dull and decrepit books. We browsed hard to be the one who found the 'get out' book so as to gleefully whisper in the ear of the other our secret acronym "C P sorted" which got us out the door and back on the road ASAP.

2. I can remember but cannot communicate the pride and joy I experienced when, on my first visit to San Francisco, I made my obligatory pilgrimage to *City Lights Books* – the legendary home of Beat Literature. I met and engaged with the poet and owner Lawrence Ferlinghetti, that was exciting enough but, that was surpassed when down in the poetry basement I found a thin green paper-wrappered, stencil-printed and stapled poetry book published by *The Galloping Dog Press*. And on the verso of the title page it said *Printed at Dylans Bookstore, Swansea, and Wales*. Back then my part-time shop-assistant was Peter Hodgkiss; a big player in the Small Press Poetry scene in the U.K. Peter was in Swansea reading English at the University. As a perk I was happy for him to use the shop printer to produce one of his books. And here was a copy in one of the world's most legendary bookshops.

3. Swansea Museum, aka The Royal Institution of South Wales, is the oldest museum in Wales, which Dylan described in his radio piece *Return Journey* as:
The museum which should have been in a museum.
I wrote at length about this establishment in my book Dylan Thomas the Pubs.
Jeff Towns: *DYLAN THOMAS THE PUBS*. Y Lolfa. 2013.

4. *Dylan Thomas and Wales: A Japanese Perspective*. Publisher's Offprint. 1979. The text of a lecture that Naomi delivered in Wales. Naomi also published an article; *My 'long friend' Dylan through his awareness of word and being* in a Dylan Thomas Society Publication *The World Winding Home*.

MODERN LITERATURE AUCTION

FIRST EDITIONS • SIGNED & INSCRIBED COPIES • DRAWINGS
MANUSCRIPTS & LETTERS • RELATED MATERIAL
INCLUDING THE MIRIAM J. BENKOVITZ COLLECTION

AT SWANN GALLERIES, NEW YORK CITY
THURSDAY, DECEMBER 11, 1986 AT 11 AM & 2 PM

An Important Collection of the Work of Ronald Firbank
First Editions, Manuscripts, Typescripts, Autograph Letters, Specially-bound volumes, Photographs, and related material: a fine portrait sketch of Firbank by Augustus John; Albert Rutherston's design for the dust jacket of *Inclinations,* and an unusual painting by C. R. W. Nevinson related to his designs for the endpapers of *Sorrow in Sunlight.*

Illustrated Autograph Letters by Important British Artists
Augustus John, Albert Rutherston, Will Rothenstein, Charles Ricketts, William Nicholson, Nina Hamnet, William Orpen, and Laura Knight.

Autograph Letters, Typescripts, and Photographs
An 11 page Autograph letter in verse by Dylan Thomas; several corrected typescripts and letters of Tennessee Williams; a fine group of autograph letters of Paul Valery; a large collection of Hours Press–Nancy Cunard letters and manuscripts; Pino Orioli's heavily annotated copy of his *Adventures of a Bookseller;* Cecil Beaton's photographic portrait of Brigit Patmore, signed; an important Richard Aldington collection, comprising typescripts, letters, signed and inscribed copies and first editions.

First Editions • Signed and Inscribed Books
W. H. Auden, James Joyce, Ian Fleming, Sylvia Plath, John Galsworthy, Ellery Queen, Siegfried Sassoon, John Steinbeck, Norman Douglas, Harold Acton, Max Beerbohm, The Sitwells, Cecil Beaton, Derek Patmore, W. B. Yeats, Iris Tree, and others.

ILLUSTRATED CATALOGUES $15 or £10 (PPD) in the UK from
BERTRAM ROTA LTD, 30 & 31 LONGACRE, LONDON WC2E 9LT

OTHER CATALOGUE ORDERS AND INQUIRIES TO

SWANN GALLERIES, INC.

104 East 25 Street, New York, N.Y. 10010 ■ (212) 254-4710

The Auction Catalogue containing *An 11 page autograph letter in verse by Dylan Thomas*

2.

Dylan Thomas: Letter to Loren.

I am a bookseller, but I cannot control a collector's interest in the life and works of Dylan Thomas.

Some 45 years ago, I was about to leave the office of my good friend Richard Landon, the accomplished head-librarian at the great Thomas Fisher Library at the University of Toronto. I had just enjoyed a successful Toronto Book Fair. I had also eaten well a few times with Richard and, shared a bottle of whisky with him, and moreover, I had also sold Richard a good few books! As I leant across to his book-strewn desk to shake hands farewell, I glanced down and saw the flyer advertising a New York book auction pictured above. When my gaze hit upon the 'An 11 page letter in verse by Dylan Thomas' I gasped and grabbed at it.

'Oh yeah, I was gonna' mention that' drawled Richard in his slow, Montana cowboy accent.

This chance encounter led to me buying the Thomas letter they were offering, visiting the recipient in New York on two occasions and finally publishing the book as an elegant hand-printed, limited edition designed and printed by Michael Mitchell at his Marlborough, *Libanus Press*, with a frontispiece photomontage of Dylan Thomas, Lloyd Frankenberg and Loren MacIver, and with a fine pen-and-ink drawing of Dylan by Leonard Baskin.[1]

Herewith is the original introduction I wrote to the edition:

Letter to Loren. Introduction.

Lot. 123.

I am a bookseller, but I cannot control a collector's interest in the life and works of Dylan Thomas. I first heard about the manuscript that is published here some ten years ago, at a book fair in Los Angeles. A Californian friend and colleague, Peter Howard (of Serendipity books), knowing of my weakness, casually asked if I could use a long and apparently unpublished letter written by Dylan Thomas to an American lady friend, adding that, if I was interested, I should speak with his associate Burton who was their man in pursuit. Burton and I did talk on several occasions; and each time he whetted my appetite with more details; it was eleven pages long; it was written in verse; it discussed fellow writers; it was somewhat indecent; but Burton was only just getting close to his quarry, and I was to be kept informed of his progress.

For several months I heard no more, but then something karmic occurred. I had exhibited at a book fair in Toronto. On the day of my departure, I went to say goodbye to a librarian friend. As I shook his hand across his busy desk, piled high with papers, offprints, pleading catalogues, incunabula, Canadiana and all topped off with that day's mail, I glanced down and

The frontispiece illustration to *Letter to Loren*

scanned a flyer for a forthcoming New York Auction. Beneath a doleful drawing of Ronald Firbank by Augustus John and under the heading, 'Autograph Letters, Typescripts and Photographs', I read 'An Eleven Page Autograph Letter in verse by Dylan Thomas...' It had to be the same letter, my West Coast colleagues had lost it to an auction house. Back in Wales I promptly sent for the catalogue. It arrived; tasteful, elegant, well-illustrated, and obviously heralding a big and glamorous sale. Lots of Auden, Eliot, Firbank and Rolfe, Cunard and Joyce, and sandwiched between some inscribed Allen Tate and 'James Thurber Inscribed Twice' was Lot 123:

> **A SUPERB LETTER IN VERSE: THOMAS, DYLAN. Autograph letter in verse, signed 'Dylan,' to Loren MacIver. 11 pages 4to, minor creases and tears at edges...**

The letter was given reasonable coverage; almost a page of quotations and facing these, two pages, the first and last, were reproduced in facsimile. The lines quoted were very interesting, and a short note added:

> **This superb letter presents Thomas's views, in verse, on Hollywood, American writers (especially poets), American college girls, etc!**

However, nothing was said about the background to the letter or its recipient, and although this intrigued and puzzled me, my immediate priority was dealing with the forthcoming auction. The estimate for Lot 123 was aggressive; \$8000-\$12000 (the highest estimate in the entire sale). When I called the saleroom, their attentive and helpful cataloguer was even more bullish in his expectations. I began to feel that this item was out of my league, but I was unable to just ignore it. I circulated the details to all the libraries and clients who had purchased significant Dylan Thomas materials from me in the past, with a view to acting for them; at least then I would still be involved and would get to handle the letter. I got very little response, but The National Library of Wales expressed some interest and I sent them all the details. Although they gave it careful consideration, just prior to the day of the sale they informed me that they did not have sufficient funds available to make a serious bid.

By now I was in too deep and I decided that I should at least leave a covering bid. Stretched to my limits and with no real hope of success, I rang Serendipity, who were to act for me, and gave them my bid; it was out of my hands. Late on the day of the sale I could wait no longer; I rang the auction house in New York, trepidation filling the transatlantic spheres: they picked up and I babbled;

'Yes, please, could you tell me what Lot 123 made?'

A Bronx-bred voice quickly recited a string of numbers, but I was too anxious to make sense of them. I dropped into the vernacular:

'Could you run that by me one more time please?' She did; and I realised that my bid had been successful! A record price for a single Dylan Thomas letter, but I had bought it.

I rang Peter, full of nervous and excited thanks and, after a little discussion, we decided that he should hold the 'letter', pending my scheduled visit to California in the coming February. It was already December. I envisioned them sending the letter and it being caught up in the Christmas mail, ending up in the Swansea sack of tired, indolent, un-civil, no-good boyo of a temporary postman, who chooses to tip the last of his round into the muddy waters of the River Tawe – the eleven pages would float to the surface and glide through the town, on out to sea, all the while being bleached by unknown pollutants, only to be washed up round the coast in Laugharne, back again where they had started from, after some thirty-five years. No, I would wait. It was safer and I could occupy myself over the ensuing weeks finding out about the letter, its background and its recipients.

Loren MacIver and Lloyd Frankenberg

> **...for the pleasure of dying with loren l(hullo!) and long (thank you!) lloyd,**

The auction catalogue had provided just one name to work on, 'Loren MacIver', but neither of the two biographies of Dylan

Thomas, the official biography by Constantine Fitzgibbon (1965) and Paul Ferris's apparently exhaustive, *Dylan Thomas a Biography* (1977), made any reference to her. I turned to the recently published and massive, *Collected Letters of Dylan Thomas* (1985 edited by Ferris). Here, in the index, I found two references one to 'Loren McIver' (sic) and one to' Loren McIver (Mrs Lloyd Frankenberg)'(sic). The recipient of the letter referred to was John Malcolm Brinnin, the American writer, responsible for arranging Dylan's first reading tours to America. Dylan is writing to him in April of 1951, after his first visit to the States and in the course of the letter asks Brinnin to relay best wishes to a whole group of his new American friends:

'Give my love, if ever you see
them or believe it, to Pearl, Lloyd & Loren...'

A footnote to the letter adds: *The poet Lloyd Frankenberg and his wife, the painter Loren McIver* (sic).

I looked in the index for 'Frankenberg' and found one other reference to an earlier letter, also to Brinnin, written in 1949. This letter is Dylan's response to Brinnin's initial suggestion that he should tour America giving readings and lectures, with Brinnin acting as organiser and agent. Dylan informs Brinnin:

Lloyd Frankenberg has written to me, saying that he is to be in charge of a series of Poetry Readings at the Museum of Modern Art and wanting me to give one. He said that when he knew the dates and the fees he would get in touch...

It would appear that Lloyd Frankenberg was one of the first people to recognise Dylan's potential as a live performer; to suggest the idea to him; and to offer him such an opportunity. I was becoming more intrigued and began to look in less obvious sources. Bill Read's *The Days of Dylan Thomas* (1965) is subtitled *A Pictorial Biography*, and is known for its wealth of illustrations, mainly splendid photographs of Dylan by Rollie McKenna. In this book I learned that Lloyd Frankenberg was responsible for another 'first' in Dylan's life. In a section dealing with Dylan's 'Recording Career', Read explains how:

In the summer of 1949 he [Dylan] recorded his own *Poem in October* and *In My Craft and Sullen Art* for Lloyd Frankenberg's Colombia record *Pleasure Dome*.

These recordings were the first ever recordings of Dylan reading his own poetry (Dylan was later to meet Barbara Holdridge and Marianne Mantell, who were so impressed with his reading that they founded a record company, Caedmon, just to issue records of him reading). Read also has this to say about Dylan's visits to America, and the people he encountered there:

'But for all the hundreds of those who merely felt themselves friends, there were many who actually became real friends...'

He goes on to list eight names. This short list includes both Lloyd Frankenberg and Loren MacIver. Next, I checked in J. Alexander Rolph's *Dylan Thomas: A Bibliography*, (1956). In his section F. on 'Gramophone Recordings'. F.1 is:

'Pleasure Dome. A Collection of Phonograph Records of various Poets Reading Their Own Works. Ed. Lloyd Frankenberg.'

However, it was only when I consulted Ralph Maud's encyclopaedic *Dylan Thomas in Print: A Bibliographical History* (1970) that I discovered that the record had been issued in conjunction with a book of criticism by Lloyd Frankenberg, *Pleasure Dome: On Reading Modern Poetry* (Boston 1949). Although

The album sleeve to Lloyd's spoken-word L.P

it was reissued as a paperback by Dolphin in 1968, the book has never been published in the UK, but once I knew of its existence it did not take long to find a copy.

The front jacket of Lloyd's book designed by Loren

The rear panel of the book's dust-jacket has a photograph of a young lean writer and below this the blurb offers a short resume of Lloyd's career; 1938, won the Spenser Award; 1939, first book of poems, *The Red Kite* published; 1940, Guggenheim Fellow, and so on. This is followed by an impressive list of literary periodicals and anthologies which had included his work. The text contains essays on a number of poets – T.S Eliot, Auden, Marianne Moore, Elizabeth Bishop, e. e. cummings, and an eight-page study of Dylan Thomas. From Maud's bibliography I also learned that Lloyd had reviewed, for The New York Times, Dylan's *In Country Sleep* (1952, but issued only in America). He had edited another anthology – *Invitation to poetry: A Round of Poetry from John Skelton to Dylan Thomas* (1956); and in June 1958 Harper's Magazine had included Lloyd Frankenberg's poem about Dylan – Refusal to Mourn, Etc., which was later to be included in the anthology of poems inspired or occasioned by Dylan's life and death, *A Garland for Dylan Thomas* (1963 ed. George Firmage). Lloyd's poem, of sixteen three-line stanzas, ridicules those who sought to exploit Dylan and are boastful of superficial friendship, but it does not overlook or romanticise Dylan's faults, describing him as a 'lover of ale' and,

> 'Roisterous, roaring, rantical...
> Lusty indeed and verbally, Master of all hyperbole
> Whether of joy or death.'

But the final tone of the poem is one of deep admiration and loss. Slowly a picture of Lloyd was beginning to emerge. I turned finally to John Malcolm Brinnin's *Dylan Thomas in America* (1955). Here Brinnin gives an account of Dylan on his first trip to New York, exhausted but still eager and able to attend:

> 'a small party at the apartment of Lloyd Frankenberg and his wife Loren MacIver and later to drink through the long night at the itinerary of Village bars that would shortly become standard.'

He writes of Loren and Lloyd taking Dylan to a Marx Brothers movie and, later how on Dylan's second trip, when he was accompanied by his wife Caitlin and looking for a place to stay:

> 'Loren ... and Lloyd ... came by. We all went out together then, bought half a dozen newspapers in which to peruse classified advertisements, and stopped at a bar on Sixth Avenue. Taking turns on phoning to inquire about advertised possibilities, we turned up discouragingly few. Finally, someone remembered that the Hotel Chelsea had one room kitchenette apartments. Loren went along with Caitlin to inspect one of them, and they returned shortly to say that it looked like just the thing. Dylan said they could move in that very evening.'

Just as Lloyd had been instrumental in bringing Dylan to America, and first recording Dylan reading his poems, so Loren was instrumental in introducing Dylan to the Hotel Chelsea, which he came to love and which was to provide the dramatic backdrop during the few weeks prior to his death in New York in 1953.

It was becoming apparent that Lloyd and Loren were more than mere bit-part players in Dylan's life. A footnote in *The*

Collected Letters recorded that Lloyd Frankenberg had died in 1975, but what of Loren MacIver? So far, I knew little more about her than I had gleaned from Brinnin and Read. I had also noticed that Lloyd's book *Pleasure Dome*, as well as being dedicated to 'Loren – the first reader', had a rather Bauhaus like dust-jacket design, primary colours geometrically set on a black background, which was 'Designed by Loren MacIver'. From Serendipity I got yet more invaluable help. They found for me a copy of an art book on Loren and another New York artist.[2] The book was published in conjunction with a major exhibition of the works of these two painters, being held at the Whitney Museum of American Art. It has, as a frontispiece, a fine photographic portrait of Loren MacIver at work in her studio, looking more Quant-like sixties than fifties, and many reproductions of her pictures. Most are painted in a very individual style combining semi-figurative and abstract-expressionist techniques. In the text, I read of her travels to Europe with Lloyd; of her interest in the circus, particularly in clowns; of the important galleries that had acquired her work; of her portrait of her friend, the poet e e cummings; 'which stands out as a sensitive tour de force'; and that: no one but a Japanese artist has painted rain so successfully as MacIver. In the picture titled after a line of poetry by e. e. cummings 'the streets turn young with rain, it falls with the impetuous freshness of a spring shower.

Apart from the book on Loren, Serendipity also provided me with the address of the New York bookseller who could take me to see Loren herself. Howard Frisch[3] is a real Greenwich Village character in his own right: one-time bookshop owner, sometime publisher, and a respected book scout for major reprint publishers. He had been helping and acting for Loren in the sale of some of her not inconsiderable literary property (a subsequent New York auction contained a fine group of letters to Loren from Alice B. Toklas).

I wrote to Howard and started what was to grow into a fine friendship. He was immediately more than helpful and arranged for me to 'visit with' Loren, who still lived in the same Greenwich Village apartment studio that she and Lloyd had lived in when Dylan visited New York in the early fifties. Howard met me in the 'White Horse Tavern', one of Dylan's favourite New York bars. We had a quick memorial drink before taking a short walk to Loren's apartment, but I was still nervous, like a teenager going on his first date, as I climbed the stairs to her studio. I was greeted first by Aurora, a young artist who acted as a general assistant and companion to Loren. Aurora was young and very attractive; Loren was old and very attractive. I thought immediately of Dame Freya Stark, although I didn't know then what she really looked like. Loren looked how I imagined Dame Freya should look. Pale smooth skin, like translucent vellum, stretched tight over high prominent cheek bones; straight heavy grey fair hair, cut in a shoulder length bob and falling out of a wide-brimmed straw hat; colourful ethnic clothes juxtaposed with the austerity of the bare wood of her uncluttered and undecorated studio; an easel holding a work in progress was turned to the wall. I was mesmerised.

Loren was wonderful. We greeted each other and Howard effected ebullient introductions. Then Loren beckoned to Aurora, and they whispered in a conspiratorial manner. Aurora left the room but quickly returned and smuggled a small object into Loren's hand, who then began to tell me of Dylan's first visit to the apartment. How, on being shown into the drawing room, he had gazed around, sighed, and exclaimed with contentment 'How glad I am that Miss Tiggy is here.' As she spoke Loren slowly uncurled her long artistic fingers and revealed a small ceramic figurine of Beatrix Potter's character, which she still kept on her mantelshelf, from where, some thirty years previously it had gazed back and set a displaced Welsh poet at ease.

Over good coffee and apple pie Loren answered my questions, and told me more stories; of how Dylan had been so exhausted that he had fallen asleep at the Marx Brothers movie, and of his deep disappointment when they woke him, and he realised he had missed the film, of Dylan's near debilitating stage-fright before his reading at the Museum of Modern Art, but how, once Lloyd had introduced him, – 'Ladies and Gentlemen – Mr

Thomas', he read, 'like an angel'; of taking Dylan to smart tailors for a new suit, and of Dylan emerging from the fitting room and clowning before the mirror, with trousers at least 12 inches too long, enquiring of the bemused tailor with mischievous naivety,

'Is this the way trousers are worn here?'

Loren went on to tell me of the poets and writers to whom she and Lloyd had introduced Dylan: Ted [Theodore] Roethke and e e cummings; too many anecdotes for me to take in but I remember one involved Roethke arriving with a well packed brown paper parcel which proved to contain a whole fish! She ended by describing afternoons of creative madness in their apartment, with Lloyd at his desk writing, Loren at her easel painting and Dylan, of all things, seated at the grand piano (which still occupies the same corner of the studio), attempting to entertain his hosts by vamping and singing wild invented songs! It was a wonderful visit for me, and Loren seemed to have enjoyed a chance to remember and re-live her earlier life. She urged me to return and inscribed a copy of Dylan's 'Letter to Loren' which I had brought with me:

'How happy I am we have met with Dylan.

With all my best Salutes, Loren.'

Over the next year we corresponded and eventually arranged my second visit. Once again, after I arrived at Loren's apartment, it was apparent another conspiracy was afoot. I heard Loren whisper to her new companion and helper, a young artist called Bud, 'Go, fetch the cloth.' I was bemused, but Bud was quickly back with a folded rough linen tablecloth. Loren took it and ceremoniously unfolded it across the top of the grand piano. The cloth, Turin-shroud-like, was covered with images! The first one I recognised was a competent caricatured profile of Dylan, which I was sure had been drawn by Dylan's wife Caitlin – I had seen an almost identical sketch drawn on an opened-out cigar box, reproduced in Rollie McKenna's book, *Portrait of Dylan*.[4] The sketch on the tablecloth was inscribed, 'Mio Marito', Italian for 'My Husband'. At the other end of the cloth was a group of child-like doodles. These too were familiar; I had encountered

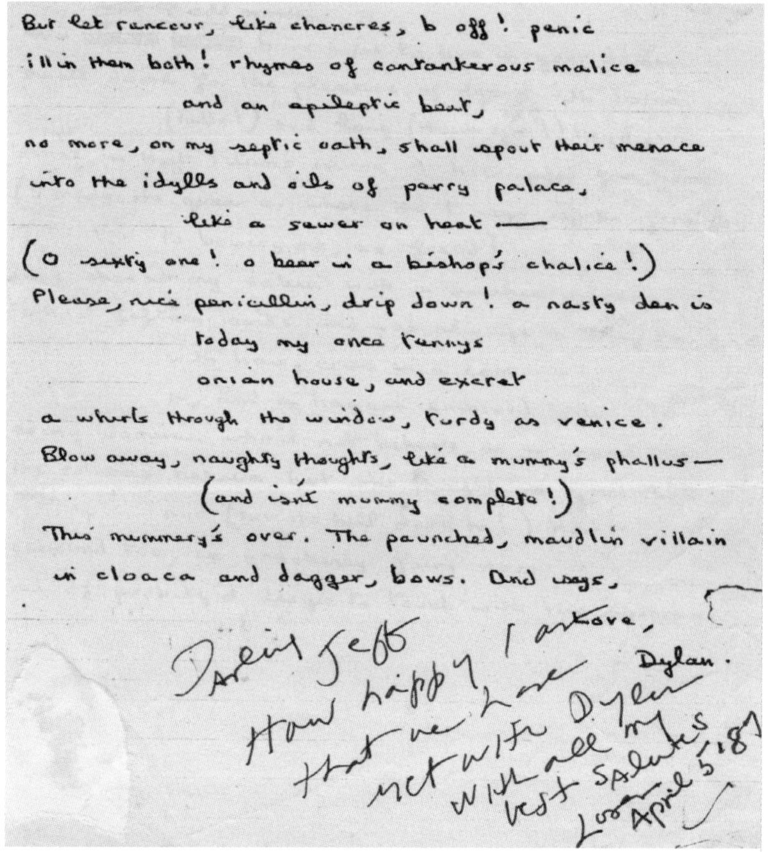
But let rancour, like chancres, b off! penic
ill in them both! rhymes of cantankerous malice
and an epileptic beat,
no more, on my septic oath, shall spout their menace
into the idylls and oils of parry palace,
like a sewer on heat —
(o sexty one! o beer in a bishop's chalice!)
Please, nice penicillin, drip down! a nasty den is
today my once funnys
onion house, and exeret
a whirls through the window, turdy as venice.
Blow away, naughty thoughts, like a mummy's phallus —
(and isn't mummy complete!)
This mummery's over. The paunched, maudlin villain
in cloaca and dagger, bows. And ways,
I am Love,
Dylan.

Dear Jeff
How happy I am that we have met with Dylan
with all my best Salutes
Loren April 5 '81

Loren's warm inscription on the last page of my facsimile of Dylan's Ms

similar drawings, scrawled by Dylan, across the endpapers of presentation copies of his books. The middle section of the cloth was taken up with what was obviously the most accomplished of all the drawings. This was a portrait sketch of Lloyd, drawn by Loren.

As I puzzled over the cloth, Loren began to explain how, on Dylan's second trip to America, when Caitlin was with him, the two couples had gone out in a foursome for dinner. During the course of their wine-filled supper, in a small Italian restaurant in the Village, they had begun to deface the tablecloth with their varying degrees of artistic skill. On settling the bill, Loren begged the obliging maître d' to be able to keep the cloth as a memento of a fine evening. It was a wonderful story, and the tablecloth was a remarkable icon, still stained with Bolognese sauce, encrusted with tomato pips and decorated with Caitlin's sketch[4] of her Dylan, Loren's drawing of Lloyd and Dylan's spirited doodles, depicting their eventful evening; waiters running with trays of drinks, couples dancing on the table and a body lying stuporous under it!

Dylan's spirited doodle depicting the events of the lively evening...

Loren meant for me to have the cloth; she felt it belonged with Dylan's poem and we quickly struck a deal. As I flew back to Wales with the cloth in my baggage, I imagined indulging in a kind of gastronomic necrophilia; spreading the cloth out across my desk; chipping off coagulated vegetables – and chewing on them, as I read the poem again.

When Peter received the manuscript from the auction house he telephoned and soothed me with assurances of its safety, but excited me by expressing his opinion, having read the 'letter' in its entirety, that it was even better than the catalogue description had suggested. By February I was charged with an almost debilitating excitement and anticipation. I finally got the manuscript in my hands at a very crowded pre-bookfair party in Serendipity's cavernous book shop. I hunted around until I found a quiet niche, hid myself away, and began to read. I read it through once, not making much sense: I read it again: I stopped and puzzled by its intricate density, I called colleagues for help, and slowly I began to form some idea of the shape and meaning of the poem, for I had begun to see it, not so much as a letter in verse, but as a highly wrought poem that had been sent as a letter. I also found myself agreeing with Peter's comments on

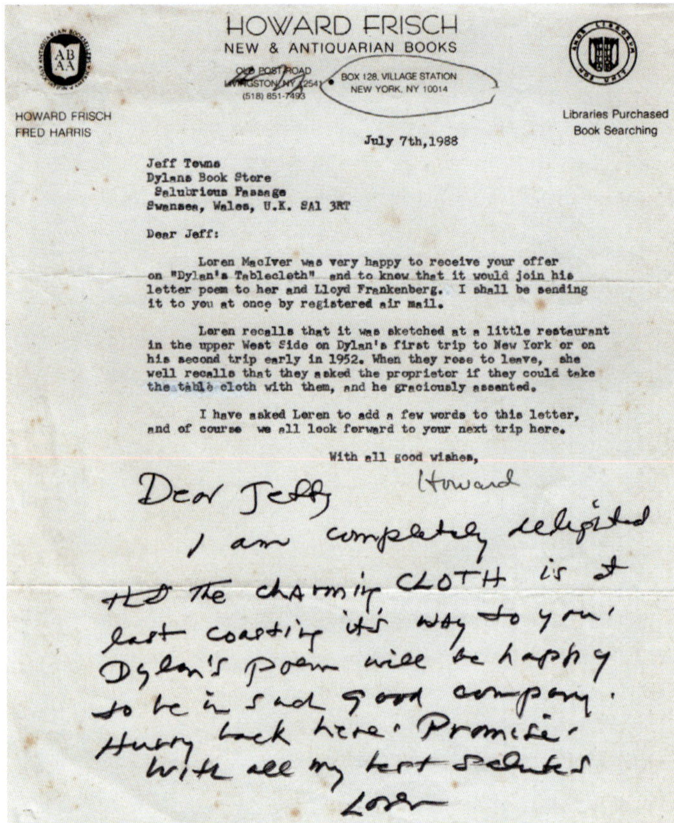

HOWARD FRISCH
NEW & ANTIQUARIAN BOOKS

OLD POST ROAD
LIVINGSTON, NY 12541 • BOX 128, VILLAGE STATION
NEW YORK, NY 10014
(518) 851-7493

HOWARD FRISCH
FRED HARRIS

Libraries Purchased
Book Searching

July 7th,1988

Jeff Towns
Dylans Book Store
Salubrious Passage
Swansea, Wales, U.K. SA1 3RT

Dear Jeff:

Loren MacIver was very happy to receive your offer on "Dylan's Tablecloth" and to know that it would join his letter poem to her and Lloyd Frankenberg. I shall be sending it to you at once by registered air mail.

Loren recalls that it was sketched at a little restaurant in the upper West Side on Dylan's first trip to New York or on his second trip early in 1952. When they rose to leave, she well recalls that they asked the proprietor if they could take the table cloth with them, and he graciously assented.

I have asked Loren to add a few words to this letter, and of course we all look forward to your next trip here.

With all good wishes,

Howard

Dear Jeff
I am completely delighted
the charming CLOTH is at
last coasting it's way to you!
Dylan's poem will be happy
to be in such good company.
Hurry back here. Promise.
With all my best salutes
Loren

The letter of provenance from Howard & Loren for the embellished table cloth

the inadequacy of the catalogue description. As the letter was to be sold in America the cataloguer had focussed, rather superficially, on its American content – 'Hollywood, American writers ... American college girls etc!' – and done this at the expense of so much else.

Looked at as a letter, it is like so many of the thousand-plus letters that make up *The Collected Letters of Dylan Thomas*, in that it is basically a 'bread and butter' letter, a 'thank you for having me' letter. As John Ackerman says, in his book *A Dylan Thomas Companion* (1990), in the section on Thomas as a letter writer, 'he enchants not without calculation', and he goes on to describe Dylan as 'unwittingly laying up treasure for others both literally and metaphorically'.

Dylan begins this 'poem/letter' to his friends and some-time hosts in New York by describing his voyage home aboard the

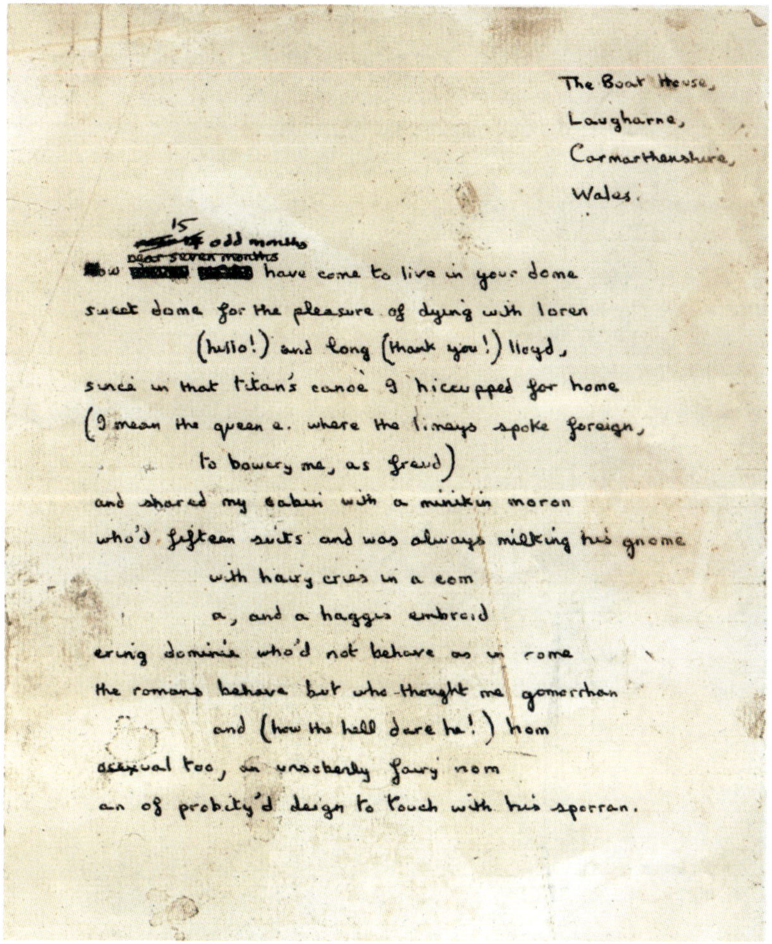

The Boat House,
Laugharne,
Carmarthenshire,
Wales.

15 odd months
~~Dear seven months~~
How [illegible] have come to live in your dome
sweet dome for the pleasure of dying with loren
(hullo!) and long (thank you!) lloyd,
since in that titan's canoe I hiccupped for home
(I mean the queen e. where the limeys spoke foreign,
to bowery me, as freud)
and shared my cabin with a minikin moron
who'd fifteen suits and was always milking his gnome
with hairy cries in a com
a, and a haggis embroid
ering dominie who'd not behave as in rome
the romans behave but who thought me gomorrhan
and (how the hell dare he!) hom
osexual too, an unsoberly fairy nom
an of probity'd deign to touch with his sporran.

The first page of the letter – the corrections at the start are the only corrections in the whole of the manuscript

liner Queen Elizabeth, adding some scurrilous details about some of his fellow passengers. He tells Loren and Lloyd how much he misses them and their home – 'the fankenberg eyrie' – in New York, and he bemoans the people and the place – 'this cockles and mussels town' – of Laugharne, that he has returned to. All the impressionable townsfolk want to know about is the famous personalities they imagined (and hoped) he might have met, they cared nothing for his 'odyssey' of readings. They only want to hear of film stars and celebrities; to be titillated by tales of Dylan's loose living, and to sneer (with envy) at American excesses. The only person Dylan can think of whom he met and who might, just, impress them, is the playwright Tennessee Williams. His name at least causes the 'pig vents' to 'sizzle!'. Dylan goes on to paint an even more grim and macabre picture of his Welsh home. He ends with wishing again to be back in America with them, but he invents a series of improbable hypotheses, mainly involving dramatic changes in the personalities, politics, and sexual proclivities of their mutual literary friends, that will have to occur before he can escape from Laugharne and return. He ends on a note of gloomy resignation, describing his poem as ' rhymes of cantankerous malice' and himself as a 'paunched maudlin villain'. Dylan is being deliberately melodramatic and playfully excessive in his descriptions of his life in Laugharne and its inhabitants, (Lloyd was to describe him as 'master of all hyperbole'), in an attempt to amuse and flatter his American friends. It is interesting to compare the sentiments expressed in this poem with the letters he sent from America to his wife Caitlin, back in Laugharne. In these he depicts himself as a 'country cousin' overwhelmed and unhappy in a 'titanic dream world'; a 'monstrously rich ... soaring Babylon'; 'a nightmare, day and night; there never was such a place'. Dylan was not averse, in his letters, to writing what he thought people would like to hear. There is no doubt that his poem for Loren and Lloyd is an attempt 'to enchant' and that it is 'not without calculation', but it is, even by Dylan's standards, one of his most elaborate efforts.

The Collected Letters is rich in long, rambling, witty and surreal texts, many carefully constructed, with evidence of revisions and re-writing. Thomas obviously spent much time and trouble over their composition. However, almost all of them are written in prose, albeit a very poetic and florid prose. Thomas himself spoke of 'prose with blood pressure'. There are just a few exceptions where Thomas chose to write letters in verse, or partially in verse. Most of these are little more than doggerel, like the lines interspersed in his early letters to Pamela Hansford Johnson, and there are humorous doggerel verses in letters to Henry Treece, Trevor Hughes and Marged Howard-Stepney, but amongst the others there are few more intricate examples which bear a closer resemblance to *Letter to Loren*. One such lucky recipient was Tommy Earp[5] a hard-drinking art critic and writer, whom Dylan met in London in the mid-thirties. He became one of Dylan's favourite drinking companions; they shared the same sense of humour, based on smart anagrams, surreal fantasies, double-meanings and elaborate puns. There are eighteen letters to Earp in *The Collected Letters*, (the originals are now in Ohio University). Many of these are just brief notes, but of the more substantial five are in verse. Written in the early forties, Ferris refers to them as 'cross-word-puzzle poems', because of the clue-like allusions and dense cross references. A typical example, written in 1943, begins:

> When next shall we stumble to the stutter of our Lewis-gun carols?
> From bombazine-bosomed bars to bliss of barrels ...

The pun on the Lewis machine-gun and the writer Lewis Carroll, which also involves a pun on 'carols', which they 'stumble and stutter' instead of sing, and the phrases 'bombazine- bosomed' and 'a bliss of barrels'; these are very similar to the type of conceit found in *Letter to Loren*. In one of the other verse letters to Earp, Thomas invents a series of strange mutations in nature:

> Poison is dropped from the sky in the shape of hip flasks and cheque books. Pigs can be taught to firewatch and hens to lay hand grenades.

Thomas uses this device again in *Letter to Loren*, where he has 'fish that taste like feet'. 'cow pouncing owls', and 'scraggy swans' that 'deathsing' like an operatic tenor! Thomas seems to have had a certain style and vocabulary that he slipped into when writing this kind of verse letter.

The other recipient of this kind of verse letter was Dylan's boss and employer at Strand Films, Donald Taylor. A mutual friend, Ivan Moffat (the son of the actress Iris Tree), had introduced them to each other in 1940 when Dylan was desperate for a job to see him through the war years, and as Fitzgibbon says they 'took an immediate liking for one another which grew stronger with the years'. Film-struck Dylan loved the idea of working in the movie industry and admired and respected Taylor's skills. They began to collaborate on many projects, and Taylor provided the storyline for Dylan's script *The Doctor and the Devils* and contributed an afterword to the text when it was published in 1953. The group of fifteen letters that Dylan wrote to Taylor (now to be found in the Buffalo Collection) includes two in verse, which are very similar in style and tone to the letters to Tommy Earp, and one of them also bears remarkable similarities to *Letter to Loren*. Writing to Taylor in 1944, Dylan is complaining of his poverty, and particularly bemoaning the fact that 'a bunch of letters from the US' contained no money. These lines from this letter:

> 'Shall we arrange a personal Lease-Lend
> From Betty Hutton. Or will you play for me
> An Air on my G. string? Signed Gypsy Lee.'

Are resonant with stanza 4. of *Letter to Loren:*

> '...and act like betty manhutton?
> Did you pluck the g strings (how your plectrum pawed!)
> ... and put in their belly button
> holes whole bowls and pink bord
> ers of gypsy lee roses? ...'

Apart from these quite striking similarities, the earlier verse letters all have one thing in common: they are, and are supposed to be funny. Almost without exception, the same cannot be said of his published poetry, which is intense and almost devoid of humour. For Thomas, 'Poetry' is 'Serious Business'. That many readers regard him as a humorous writer is largely due to his prose output; the stories from *Portrait of the Artist as a Young Dog*; the broadcast anecdotes and the radio drama *Return Journey*, and of course *Under Milk Wood*. These amuse us and make us laugh; poetry is for weightier matters. Indeed, even when giving his public readings, the humour was in his introductions and casual asides.

The poetry he chose to read, whether his own or by other favourite writers, is almost entirely serious in tone. A glance at the contents of the anthology of these poems *The Colour of Saying* (1963, edited by Ralph Maud and Aneirin Talfan Davies) will reveal little light and humorous verse. Yet we know that all his life Dylan was constantly inventing droll and facetious verses. From his earliest schooldays Dylan loved to play word without exception games with his erudite friend Daniel Jones. Between them, writing alternate lines, they produced a body of verse by the great 'Walter Bram'[6] (their joint pseudonym). Daniel Jones describes these poems thus:

> The poetic style of Walter Bram ... is bafflingly inconsistent ... fragile, furious ... Chinese, Greek and shocking.'

He goes on to quote such surreal gems as 'wilful moccasin' and 'innumerable bananas'. In his book, *My Friend Dylan Thomas* (1977), Daniel Jones devotes a chapter to these 'literary collaborations', which he describes as 'serious play'. He gives many examples and singles out one poem, Chameleon, as the one,

> 'which we considered our champion tongue twister, to be declaimed from the Acropolis by an orator with his mouth full of pebbles, like Demosthenes'.

A sample verse goes:

I am still oracular,
Something with a phalanx male,
Down the date vernacular,
Pedal tail.

A little later, on moving onto secondary school, Dylan began to contribute to his school magazine, *The Swansea Grammar School Magazine*, (his father D.J. Thomas was Senior English Master at the school). It was here that his first ever poem was to be published – *The Song of the Mischievous Dog* (in 1925) – and Thomas became sub-editor in 1929, and full editor in 1930. He was always a major contributor and the poems he published here, while being clever and precocious, were also for the most part light and humorous. The opening lines of one of them, *The Life Belt* (July 1928 issue), convey the typical style of most of Dylan's juvenilia:

'I can't say when Columbus sailed
To find the United States!
I don't know when the plague began
(I'll own I am not good at dates)

On leaving school in July 1931 Dylan became a journalist on the local paper, *The South Wales Daily Post*, and he soon stopped submitting this kind of light verse for publication, but he never lost his schoolboy enthusiasm for comic verse. It began to manifest in a passion for inventing limericks and rhymes, more often than not of an obscene and scatological nature. He shared this passion with another school friend, Wynford Vaughan Thomas, who went on himself to become a broadcaster, raconteur and bon-vivant. Wynford writes in his autobiographical book *Madly in All Directions* (1967), of Dylan's 'marvellous gift of almost spontaneous humorous verse'. Together they delighted in composing limericks, and they specialized in inventing challenging examples, based on the more unpronounceable (to their English drinking companions!) names of Welsh towns and villages. The more violently obscene and down-right filthy the limericks were, the better pleased were the two writers. Although Wynford goes on to say 'I only wish that I had noted down half of the songs, lampoons and the rest of them', I am fortunate to have in my collection Wynford's own, annotated, copy of the infamous Olympia Press edition of Christopher Logue's pseudonymous collection, 1962, *Count Palmiro Vicarion's Book of Limericks*. In this copy Wynford has filled the margins with many of the marvellous, but scurrilous rhymes, that he and Dylan delighted in, but which he said had been lost! He has examples based on such places as Llandysul, Abercwmboi, and even a limerick for, Llanfairpwllgwyngyllgogerychwyrndrobwllllantysiliogogogoch...! I will quote just one of the less extreme:

Daniel Rowland was charged at Llangeitho
With printing lewd pictures in litho
His greatest success
Was the Queen in undress
Being mounted by Hector Bolitho!

This tradition of humorous verse that we have seen developing from the early schoolboy and adolescent nonsense verse into adulthood and the more risqué verse letters and limericks, is quite different from *Letter to Loren* in a significant area. The juvenilia, the limericks, the verse letters to Earp and Taylor, while not without wit and invention, are written with a very basic rhyme scheme and verse structure. Their usual form is of simple straight couplets or unvarying alternate rhymes, which came easily and spontaneously to Thomas; he could reel them off. However, this is not the case with *Letter to Loren*, which is written with a much more elaborate structure and rhyme scheme. *Letter to Loren* is made up of eleven almost equal stanzas. Stanzas 1,2,3,6,7,8 and 9 all have fifteen lines; 4 and 11 have fourteen lines, and stanzas 5 and 10 have sixteen. The first two stanzas have identical rhyme schemes:

A.B.C, A.B.C, B.A.A.C, A.B.A.A.B.

All the following stanzas, bar stanza 9, begin with a pair of triplets, and then continue with various permutations of these three rhymes. The final stanza returns to the scheme of the first, but a fourth rhyme is introduced so that the poem ends with the couplet:

This mummery's over. The paunched, maudlin villain
in cloaca and dagger, bows. And says,
Love, Dylan.

To achieve this complex pattern of rhyme Dylan indulges in a novel breaking-up of common words to get the line ending he needs; in the first stanza 'coma' is written as 'com / a' and 'homosexual' as 'Hom / osexual'. This gives him the rhyme, 'com' with 'hom'. Together with this there is a series of less regular rhymes working at the start of the lines which also utilises theses unconventional typographical devices: in the first stanza four lines start with an 'o' sound; in the second stanza thirteen lines start with 'an', 'in' or 'en' sounds. This lends the poem a visual style similar to a poem by e. e. cummings, and Thomas's random disregard of capital letters adds to the cummings-esque appearance of the text.

Add to this Thomas's usual quota of half rhymes and internal rhymes; ('holes and bowls'), alliterations; ('nipple, nibble and nuzzle'), and compound words: ('bathwater sky' and 'bedpanoramas')' and you end up with a poem far more complex than the naive simplicity of the other humorous verse. Such a poem is (even) beyond the spontaneous skills of a poet with Dylan's ability, and for a poem such as this there would have been any number of worksheets and trial versions. The fact that the manuscript reproduced here bears just the one serious correction at the very start, (and this is necessitated by Dylan's tardiness in sending the poem), and is otherwise a 'final draft', also suggests that this is the final version of a well worked poem: a poem which combines humour with the kind of craftmanship that had previously been confined to Thomas's serious poetry.

There is however, one exception to this. Dylan's own choice of his poetry, *Collected Poems 1934-1952* does contain one humorous poem. The poem *Lament* describes the development of a lecherous 'windy boy and a bit' on his Rabelaisian journey through life. It is similar to *Letter to Loren* in that it is both a humorous and a carefully crafted poem – five twelve-line stanzas with nine or ten syllables to a line, and a regular rhyme scheme:

A.B.C.D, A.B.C.D, E.F.E.F.

(although for each stanza the refrain varies slightly). What is also of interest to us here is that *Lament* may also have begun life as a letter. Lament was written just after *Letter to Loren* (Lament was completed in March 1950), and one of the early worksheets for this poem (now in Texas) is dedicated to Henry Miller, another American writer and artist whom Dylan visited on his first reading tour. Dylan liked Miller the first time he met him at Lawrence Durrell's flat in London in 1939, and greatly admired his novel *Tropic of Cancer* (he would recommend it to friends as 'the best modern fucking book'). Thomas enjoyed his visit with Miller at Big Sur, and he described it warmly in a letter to Caitlin:

> ... stayed the night with Henry Miller ... He lives about 6,000 feet up in the hills, over the blinding blue Pacific, in a hut of his own making ... He is gentle and mellow and gay.

It could well be that *Lament* was originally conceived as a 'thank-you poem' for Henry Miller, similar to the one that Loren and Lloyd were lucky to receive.

Yet one more poem can be linked to this thread of verse

letters, and Dylan has described its development for us in a letter to Oscar Williams. Writing in 1953 Dylan says of it:

> It was going to be a piece of doggerel written to someone in the States on my return from there to Wales, but soon grew involved and eventually serious.

On an early worksheet for this poem (there are over 160 of them in the Houghton Library in Harvard), the working title appears as: '*Letter on Returning from the United States of America.1952*' Apart from the date, this title and much of Dylan's comments to Williams about this poem could be applied to Letter to Loren. However, in this instance the poem Dylan is referring to is the poem used to introduce his *Collected Poems – Prologue*. We are even given an indication as to who the original recipient was to have been; another early worksheet begins, (with a passage not unlike the end of *Letter to Loren*):

> At home sweet Christ at last.
> Wry, Welsh, and far from Scotch
> My pecker at half mast,
> This unamended potch
> Of poppycock and love
> I send dear Ruth

'Ruth' is believed to be Ruth Witt-Diament, who was a teacher at San Francisco College and Dylan's hostess in San Francisco. Dylan fell in love with the city, and Ruth let him use her home there as his West Coast refuge. On his second trip he and Caitlin stayed with her for a week or so, but she was never to receive her 'thank-you poem', for, as Dylan commented, it 'grew involved and eventually serious and the 'unamended potch' became one of the most elaborately constructed of all his poems. In an uncharacteristic moment of self-explanation, Dylan wrote to his editor, E.F. Bozman of J.M. Dent & Sons Ltd, and revealed to him the complexity of the poem's structure:

> I set myself, foolishly perhaps, a most difficult technical task: The Prologue is in two verses – in my manuscript, a verse to a page – of 51 lines each. And the second verse rhymes backward with the first. The first & last lines of the poem rhyme; the second and the last but one; & so on & so on. Why I acrosticked myself like this, don't ask me.

In this instance a 'thank-you poem' was transformed into the complex poem that sets the tone for what was to be Dylan's last collection (in his book 1965 *The Modern Movement*, Cyril Connolly describes it as 'the last port of call before we embark upon a sea of Legend'), and even Dylan had to admit that the structure of the poem presented 'a most difficult technical task'. Given the existence of the earlier verse letters to Tommy Earp and Donald Taylor and Dylan's life-long love of comic verse, as evidenced by Daniel Jones and Wynford Vaughan Thomas, it is possible to see Dylan returning to, or at least experimenting with, the form of the verse letter, in *Letter to Loren*, in *Lament*, and in the *Prologue*. This form of poem may have enabled him to lighten the tone of his poetry, and to make it more like his prose in its subject matter and levity. Indeed, it is almost as if to compensate for this lighter tone that Dylan deliberately makes his verse form, in all these poems, more artificial and complex.

Dylan was finding it hard to produce any new poems at this stage of his life and John Malcolm Brinnin makes the point that these verse letters may have been the kind of catalyst Dylan needed to get him writing poetry again. When Dylan told Brinnin that *Prologue*[7] had begun as a letter to him, Brinnin responded:

> I told him I was pleased, naturally, that the letter had proved such an inspiration, and suggested, a little caustically, that he write
> ... more often as a means of finding his way into new poems.

In the same conversation which occurred in the early fifties, Dylan also told Brinnin that in future he only intended to write 'happy poems' – was this Dylan himself suggesting that he wanted to write poems for publication closer in tone to the humorous verses he wrote for his friends? Unlike *Lament* and *Prologue*, *Letter to Loren* was actually sent as a letter. It is more structured and worked on than the earlier verse letters sent to Earp and Taylor, but like those letters, it was not being offered for publication, and as such it shares with them a frankness and an earthiness which is only present in his published poetry in a much more veiled and metaphorical manner. *Letter to Loren* is far more explicit and revealing; indeed, in this poem we are being drawn down into the seamy world of the limericks. Hardly a line or two goes by without some references to sexual mores, sexual perversions, bodily functions, in both a literal and metaphorical manner. *Letter to Loren* is far more explicit and revealing; bodily-parts, bodily-products (human and animal), undergarments, low-life's, venereal diseases and drugs! From the evidence in this poem, Dylan, though well into middle-age, still manifested a schoolboy's (and a particularly nasty and puerile schoolboy at that) baser obsessions. It takes a particular and peculiar intellect to see Tennessee William's *A Streetcar Named Desire* as A truck called fuck.[8]

Letter to Loren is not a great poem, it may not even be a very good poem, but it is interesting for the complexity and the almost too-clever virtuosity of its allusions and references to writers, writings, films and film-stars. But perhaps most of all, it is interesting for the picture it paints of Laugharne and its inhabitants.

In a letter (dated October 1951) to Princess Caetani, an American patron of the arts, who lived in Rome and financed and edited the literary periodical *Botteghe Oscure* in which a portion of *Under Milk Wood* was first published, Dylan describes the genesis of his play as an 'idea that I write a piece, a play, an impression for voices, an entertainment out of the darkness, of the town I live in'. He certainly dwells on the darker side of his hometown of Laugharne in *Letter to Loren*. One can imagine the trees in Milk Wood already swaying, when Dylan writes here of his 'cockles and mussels town'; his 'pretty as a stricture town by the eely oily, licking sea full of fish that taste like feet and feet that taste like fur'; where 'welcome is botched on the mat of the excrementious townhall with blood and spinach' and 'excreta whirls through the window, turdy as Venice'. Where 'under a bathwater sky' live 'goitered scraggy swans', 'cow pouncing owls' and 'a whiskey whiskered seal wet barking virgin with spurs on her teats' who 'gives birth to a mole in the main street'.

Dylan's crude but witty take on Tennessee Willimas' *A Street-Car Named Desire*

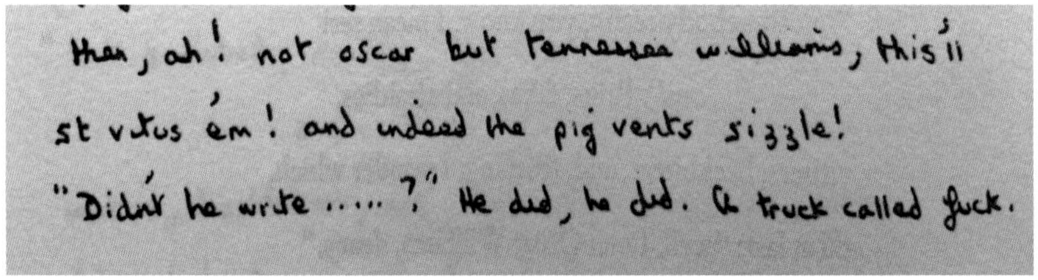
Then, ah! not oscar but Tennessee williams, this'll
st vitus 'em! and indeed the pig vents sizzle!
"Didn't he write .....?" He did, he did. A truck called fuck.

And where the inhabitants, all 'nine hundred gabies', enjoy a full and ordered life:

> Today we hunt babies ... Tomorrow's the day for the circumcision of birds ... And on 'cannibal Sunday' they all 'hope the vicar's sweet'!

It is not far from here to Llareggub. It is hard to imagine what Loren and Lloyd made of this when they opened the envelope and read this poem a little over forty years ago, but they treasured it enough to keep and preserve it (for some years it was kept in a bank vault), and now exactly forty years after the death of Dylan Thomas it is first published. But the last word should go to Lloyd, who must have had it in his mind when he wrote in his poem for Dylan:

> 'Gossip of titbit bodicey
> On your immodest Odyssey ...'
> Lusty indeed and verbally
> Master of all hyperbole.

Writing now some 40 years on there is not too much to add to this. Michael Mitchell[9] did an amazing job on the book. It garnered a couple of decent reviews, albeit both from friends and Dylan Thomas scholars – Ralph Maud and John Ackerman. I had 20 copies bound in quarter blue Morocco and signed by Loren McIver. I had 5 bound in blue Morocco with vellum tips to the corners that were signed by Loren and Leonard Baskin (and me as editor).

As a rare gift to myself I gave two fine designer binders[10] a set of unbound sheets of the book to do with as they deemed fit.

Paul Delrue, a Welsh-based designer binder, sent a back a beautiful full leather abstract creation. A fine American binder I had met in New England, Claudia Cohen, made my vision of the airmail letter that took the Ms poem from Laugharne to New York a reality, with her binding including stunning inlaid colour leathers.

I treasure them both. I sold just about enough copies of the regular original edition to persuade myself (and my wife) that I had covered my costs and had broken even on the project. I was left with a small pile of bright blue cloth copies that I gift, as and when, I encounter a person who I feel deserves one.

The text of the letter was included Paul Ferris' enlarged New Edition of *Dylan Thomas The Collected Letters* which Dent published in 2000, where it occupies 5 pages. And I am pleased that Paul utilized most of my footnotes and he gave me a warm mention in his acknowledgments. And it was again included in John Goodby's monumental new edition of *Dylan Thomas' Collected Poems* published by in 2016 Weidenfeld and Nicolson. However, I get scant acknowledgement and he re-titles the poem *Verse Letter to Loren McIver and Lloyd Frankenberg*.

Paul Delrue's binding

Claudia Cohen's binding

To conclude with a sorry tale…
An Untold story of Attempted Literary Skullduggery and Piracy

When I decided that I wanted to publish Dylan Thomas' letter-poem to Loren McIver as a book I knew that, although I owned the physical manuscript, I did not own the copyright to it, which remained in the charge of his literary agents David Higham Associates.[11] They in turn liaised with the Dylan Thomas Trust. And I would have to seek permission and pay a royalty fee before I could go ahead with publication.

A short history and background to the Dylan Thomas Trust; this trust was established on the day of Dylan's funeral in Laugharne. Dan Jones, seeing how distraught and unbalanced Caitlin was, approached David Higham, Dylan's friend and Literary agent, and Stuart Thomas, the Thomas family solicitor, who had been in school with Dylan, before joining his father's local law firm who acted for Dylan's parents and thenceforth for Dylan and Caitlin. Dan suggested the immediate establishment of a trust to care for Dylan's family and legacy over the long term. Andrew Lycett sums it up in his biography:

> The idea was that Dylan's best friend, literary agent and solicitor would oversee his posthumous affairs, assuming responsibility for, loosely, his texts, copyrights and finances.

All three agreed that Caitlin was in no fit state to deal with these complicated but important decisions. However, Lycett also sums the future up:

> They had no idea what they were letting themselves in for: Legal problems relating to the Trust were to drag on for almost half a century.

Although Dan's idea was well meant and made good sense, he soon realised just how much work it entailed and just how difficult Caitlin could be; so he quite promptly resigned from the trust, saying he wanted to concentrate on his life as a musician and composer. His place was taken by another of Dylan's good friends, Wynford Vaughan Thomas.

The Trust did the best they could, but Caitlin made things very difficult. Perhaps the worst incident was when in 1966 she instructed Stuart to sue for the return of the Manuscript of *Under Milk Wood* that Dylan had 'gifted' to the BBC producer of the radio play, Douglas Cleverdon. The action failed in a very public and expensive court case.

However, things became somewhat farcical when, a few years before the Wynford died in 987, he stepped had down from the Trust and Stuart insisted on replacing him with his long-time Swansea drinking pal, the novelist Kingsley Amis; who made no secret of his loathing of the Thomases, both man and wife, on a personal and literary level. What it did facilitate was occasional long and very bibulous and expensive lunches in Swansea for the two grand old topers to discuss 'Trust affairs'. Their restaurant of choice was on Swansea's Wind Street; my bookshop was in Salubrious Passage which led off the street. They were in the habit of dropping into my bookshop, late morning, shuffling around the shelves making a few grunted sober observations before going to dinner, and then returning in a much more lubricated state and being somewhat blunt, incoherent and unpleasant.

It was around this time that I started to work on publishing the Loren Letter manuscript. My first move was to visit Stuart and explain what I intended. I took a facsimile of the poem with me which he gave a cursory look and listened to what I proposed – a small, elegant hand printed edition which would include a facsimile of the manuscript as well as a printed version with introduction and notes supplied by me, as editor.

He concluded by saying that in principle he could see no objections, and that I should approach the agents to negotiate a fee. This I did, and we struck a deal, and I began working on the book with Michael Mitchell of the Libanus Press, Marlborough; one of the finest book designers and printers working in the UK at that time. Things were moving on well when I got a telephone call from Stuart asking me to send a fax copy of the manuscript 'so that Kingsley could examine it and confirm its authenticity as a Dylan Thomas original work'. Now being an acknowledged leading expert on Dylan Thomas and moreover, having paid a world record price for it at a bona fide New York Auction House, I was 100% confident of its integrity, but when I suggested this Stuart insisted, even making it a condition that I comply with this request if I wished to go ahead with its publication.

I duly faxed off a copy and awaited their response. But nothing came. I wanted to get on with publishing my edition so eventually I called Stuart. When I asked if I could go ahead with publication he quite bluntly said no. When I asked why he replied that he and the trust were going to control the publication of it themselves. I was stunned, flabbergasted and bemused. I responded along the lines:

'But I own it' I said 'you only own the copyright'

He replied nonchalantly but firmly but with a hint of cunning,

'Then you should not have sent us a copy'

I had been caught in a classic, mean and devious, 'Catch 22'. You utter crooked bastard I thought...

The I thought more sensibly, gathered myself together and rang my solicitor, a good book-collector and a very astute legal man, who ran a local second-generation law office. He was as appalled as I was, and immediately said he would give the case to a new, very bright, intern to deal with. And deal with it he did, compiling such a dossier of precedence and detail, that when it was sent over to Stuart's office they very quickly capitulated; but not without meanly saying they were keeping the serial rights for themselves. Edward, my solicitor was very pleased, but also very generously did not charge me, so I was very pleased to gift him and his intern two of the first copies of the book off the press. I had one more problem to sort out. Stuart had gone ahead and sold

The cover of the magazine publication of *Letter to Loren*

the UK serial rights to a literary periodical for a paltry sum. I of course wanted my book to be the first published printing ever of the poem.

The magazine that had bought the 'rights' was the long running and well-respected London Magazine.[12] I wrote to its legendary editor, Alan Ross and explained the situation and he very gallantly deferred publication in his magazine until after publication of my book; everything worked out in the end, but Stuart and I were no longer pals!

One further synchronistic addendum

Just recently the 2024 Annual New York International Antiquarian Book Fair took place – a very grand and prestigious event indeed. One English bookseller Sophie Schneideman Rare Books, issued a fine catalogue of her bookfair stock. Item 5 on the catalogue was this;

> The first printing of a Dylan Thomas manuscript, with a signed illustration by Leonard Baskin and an excellent designer binding by Welsh bookbinder Paul DELRUE.
> THOMAS, Dylan. BASKIN, Leonard. Letter to Loren. Swansea, printed by The Libanus Press for The Salubrious Press, 1993. With an introduction and notes by Jeff Towns. One of 200 numbered copies, signed by Loren MacIver, this copy is also signed by Leonard Baskin and Paul Delrue. Photographic frontispiece tipped in, reproduction of a portrait of Thomas by Leonard Baskin, signed by the artist in pencil, 2 further illustrations after drawings by Dylan and Caitlin Thomas, and a facsimile of Thomas's manuscript printed in blue. 19 × 26 cms., sm. 4to., bound by Paul Delrue in 2001 (signed on upper turn-in) in green, black and blue, red and yellow green dies roceed on laid in a remarkable patterned each section bordered with tan roceed strips tooled with circles in blind, the green roceed is tooled in blind and black with overlapping circles creating a remarkable textures, marbled endpapers, edges patterned in yellow, green and blue, housed in the original blue cloth solander box signed by Delrue with a reproduction of Baskin's portrait and roceed spine label. £2600.
> A remarkable publication by bookseller and 'Dylan Thomas expert' Jeff Towns. The Welsh binder Paul Delrue responded to the book with a remarkable binding. In the prospectus, included with the book, Jeff Towns explains: "Dylan Thomas returned to Laugharne after his first trip to America in June of 1950. Once established back in his cliff-top writing shed, one of the first things he did was to compose a long poem, complex in structure and humorous in content, for two of his new friends and sometime hosts in New York, painter Loren MacIver and her husband, the critic and poet Lloyd Frankenberg, (it did however take him over a year to actually get round to posting it!)...The couple had treasured Dylan's poem which was packed don't arcane references, wicked puns, cruel descriptions of Laugharne...and mischievous jibes at many of their mutual literary friends". Eventually it was sold and Jeff Towns bought it at auction and printed it here for the first time with a full facsimile of the manuscript.

I recalled that I had given Paul, in part payment for my binding, two sets of sheets one to bind for me And this the other set, bound up superbly, found a buyer and a new home...

Baskin's signed portrait of Dylan

The Book Box/Slipcase

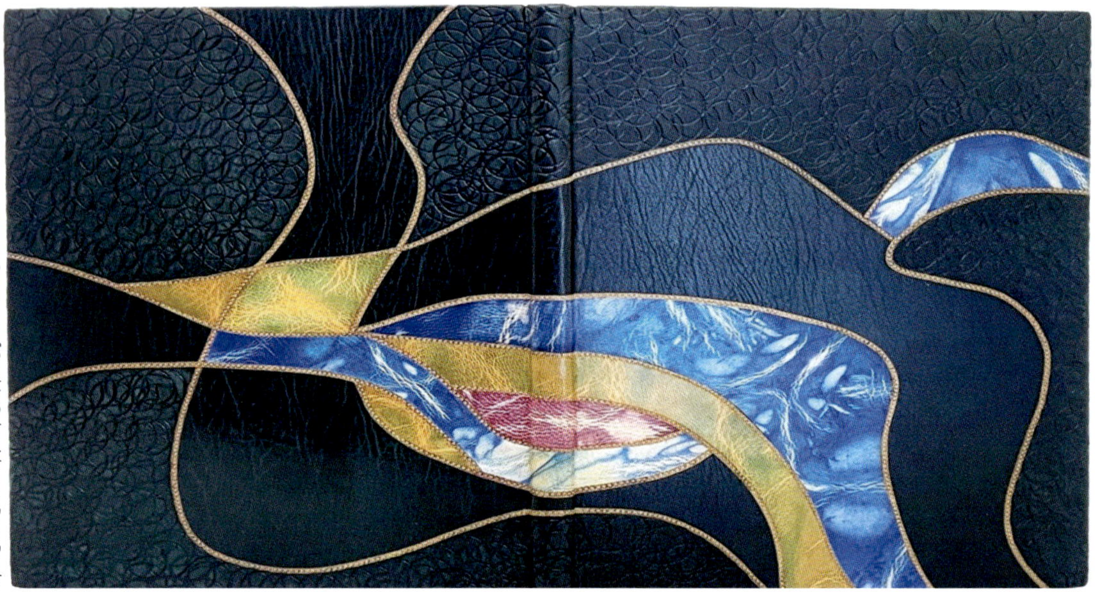

Paul Delrue's stunning binding

Images Courtesy of Sophie Schneideman Rare Books

1. Dylan Thomas: *Letter to Loren.* The Salubrious Press, Swansea. 1993. Published In an edition of 200 copies with 20 special bindings and 5 artists' copies which are Signed by Loren, Baskin and the editor.

2. *Loren MacIver & I. Rice Pereira* by John I.H. Baur.1953. Irene Rice Pereira, the other artist featured in the book, was also a member of Dylan's coterie of New York friends. In 1950 she had married the Irish poet George Reavey. Dylan had known Reavey in London in the thirties when Reavey had tried, unsuccessfully, to publish Dylan's early surrealistic stories (they eventually appeared in *The Map of Love* 1939). Reavey and his wife were among the group made up of close friends, and morbid hangers-on, who, in November 1953, were gathered at St Vincent's Hospital in New York, as Dylan lay dying. In his biography of Dylan, Paul Ferris quotes Reavey when discussing the circumstances of Dylan's death.

3. Howard Frisch was a remarkable character – a Greenwich village book- runner and book dealer of the old school, well known and used by many NYC publishers and collectors. We became good friends and he and his partner Fred eventually came and visited with us in Swansea.

4. *Portrait of Dylan. A Photographer's Memoir.* Rollie McKenna. Stemmer House 1954. In her book Rollie McKenna describes Caitlin's drawing habit: 'Finally, when dinner was already overdone [Caitlin] came downstairs, greeted our guests perfunctorily, then sat silent and detached in a far corner and began to draw cartoons of Dylan on the back of a 'Between the Acts' cigar box.'

5. Fitzgibbon has this to say about Earp: 'Tommy was an almost incredibly etiolated figure with the most exaggerated Oxford accent I have ever heard. When an undergraduate ... he had once been arrested for being drunk and disorderly in an enormous basket of strawberries at Covent Garden. Next morning the magistrate asked him why he had climbed into the basket and Tommy, in flutey tones, had replied; 'For valetudinarian reasons, purely valetudinarian reasons!' 'Don't address me as if you were the president of the Oxford Union,' the magistrate had snapped. 'But I am' wailed Tommy 'I am!' And he was.'

6. On the subject of schoolboy humour 'Bram' is a Welsh slang word for fart.

7. I have an original typescript of 'Prologue' inscribed by Dylan to John Malcolm Brinnin: 'To dear John from Cheap Dylan, with love'. Brinnin has subsequently added a note of his own: 'When I asked Dylan about some minor point in this poem he said '... in fact it began as a letter to you'. It appears that Dylan may have changed his mind at some point, as to whom he was intending to send this verse letter, before eventually reshaping it into the final poem as we know it. This manuscript is now in the National Library of Wales Aberystwyth.

8. Writer and critic John Walsh a former literary editor of *The Sunday Times* and editor of *The Independent* magazine declared in print that this was the best literary joke of the 20th century!

9. Sadly Michael passed away in November 2017 but I did have the pleasure of working with him again when we were both involved with Sir Peter Blake's magnificent illustrated Under Milk Wood exhibition and book in 2013/14.

10. See one further addendum below.

11. David Higham was born in 1895. After serving in the First World War, he took up a job in the books department at Albert Curtis Brown's literary agency. Then with a loan from Harold Macmillan he and two colleagues set up as, Pearn, Pollinger & Higham and began trading in 1935. In 1956 it became David Higham Associates. Dylan met him on one of his earlier trips to London in 1934. At first Higham as not convinced with his poetry but encouraged his Jarvis Valley prose stories.

12. *The London Magazine* is England's oldest literary periodical, with a history stretching back to 1732. In the modern era Alan Ross took over from editor and writer John Lehmann in 1961 and the Magazine became a pole star in the London literary firmament, developing a reputation for publishing the best fiction, poetry, criticism and essays from England and across the world, including work by William Burroughs, Harold Pinter, Ted Hughes, Sylvia Plath, Les Murray, and Paul Muldoon.

The Cover of *Word and Image Exhibition* Catalogue

3.

Dylan Thomas:
Word & Image Exhibition.

In 1995 Swansea hosted a year-long Literary Festival – known as The Year Of Literature. It was one of a series of 'Years'; each one in a different city around the U.K.; each one focusing on a different branch of the Arts.[1] Leading up to the millennium, there was a Year of Music in Birmingham in 1992, which kicked off this Arts Council Arts 2000, and a Year of Architecture in Glasgow. The Swansea Year of Literature got off to a rocky start with the first two appointed directors leaving after very brief stays before an Irishman – Sean Doran took the job (he went on to become artistic director of the English National Operas in Covent Garden). All three had decided to make Dylan Thomas a large part of the year's programme. Sean Doran quickly arranged to take a group of Swansea Councillors to Dublin to see how they promoted their great writers, especially James Joyce and W. B. Yeats.

Again after another couple of false starts, a substantial grant from European Funds allowed for the old and near derelict former Guild Hall of Swansea to be completely rebuilt, refurbished and repurposed to be the hub of the Festival and renamed with two names – a Welsh name; *Ty Llên* (*House of Literature*) and an English name; *The Dylan Thomas Centre*.

As one of the main booksellers in the city, with a reputation for pursuing Dylan Thomas in a somewhat obsessive fashion, I was called upon to provide a large exhibition to run throughout the year based on my own extensive collection of Dylan Thomas books, manuscripts, ephemera and iconography to be installed in the large ground floor exhibition space in the building (the building also had another large ground-floor space designated *Bookshop* on the initial plans and I ended up taking that on as well).

I worked on the exhibition with a good local artist, Paul Hughes and the exhibition we created turned out well and was very popular. We did not have a massive budget and I really had to work hard to persuade the Council to fund a decent illustrated printed catalogue but they did and it fell to me to write it and source the illustrations but a very good local design team, *Riddler Webster*, made a great job of it.

The introduction which I wrote was, I think, the first piece on Dylan Thomas I ever wrote and published. Here it is, unchanged, with the original of my text and the prelims which consist of a brief Foreword by Sean Doran and a supporting piece by a preeminent Welsh, Dylan Thomas scholar, John Ackerman, who was both a friend of mine, a customer of my bookshop. He was to be the official guest who declared the exhibition open.

Dylan Thomas Word and Image
FOREWORD

The UK Year of Literature and Writing 1995 is pleased to be the principal supporter of '*Dylan Thomas: Word and Image*'. This exciting new exhibition will form part of the festival's year-long retrospective of Swansea's famous son. It is an appropriate moment for the City of Swansea to celebrate the genius it has given the world at a time when it plays host to the world's largest and most ambitious literature festival ever.

Sean Doran Director UK Year of Literature and Writing 1995

INTRODUCTION

It is a delight, and indeed delightful learning, to read the Dylan Thomas story in picture, manuscript, book, model and image that this Catalogue and wide-ranging 'Exhibition' provides. Inevitably I was reminded it was in 1955 while an undergraduate that I published my first article on Dylan Thomas and began the first research on his Welsh background that led to *Dylan Thomas: His Life and Work*; later preparing the Catalogue and Exhibition Welsh Dylan to mark the Twentieth Anniversary of his death, and the book *Welsh Dylan*.

DYLAN THOMAS: WORD AND IMAGE takes on the Dylan journey and properly and illuminatingly begins with the poet's Welsh roots and background, and we move on to London, New

Quay, Laugharne, and America. It is a story with illustration, dramatic and literary narrative, both scholarly and moving, as well as legendary and with journalistic contributions, which depicts both the creative and sociable Dylan. In recent years attention has been focused on Thomas's career in broadcasting, films, his unique skills as a reader, even a brief television 'tour de force' *A Story*, and of course *Under Milk Wood*; and while writing *A Dylan Thomas Companion* and editing *Dylan Thomas: The Filmscripts* like many came to realise the great poet was also a popular and remarkable prose writer.

Jeff Towns's Exhibition offers a thoroughly researched and fascinating presentation of Dylan Thomas not only as poet but also as prose writer, actor, and comic genius. As this Catalogue demonstrates DYLAN THOMAS: WORD AND IMAGE provides a unique and varied collection of Dylan Thomas material for new and life-long readers and enthusiasts.

John Ackerman

INTRODUCTION TO THE COLLECTION

A common reaction from people who have been confronted by my collection is a somewhat puzzled, "Why?" Or "When?" or "How come Dylan Thomas? Answering these questions in some ways explains the thrust of this Exhibition. Although I have lived in Wales many years, (1995 is the 25th anniversary of Dylans Bookstore in Swansea) my accent still marks me out as a Londoner, and this makes my apparent obsession with a Welsh poet even more bizarre. This is my explanation and like many of the stories surrounding Dylan Thomas, some of it may be true.

Around 1962, and as a nascent hippie, developing a taste for Rock and Roll, I bought my first LP.[2] I can remember it well – Ilford High Road; The Record Den, then rushing back home to my bedroom placing the disc on my ancient *Dancette* record player and suddenly the nasal whine of Bob Dylan was. The Album sleeve pictured Bob and Susie walking huddled together, (I would later discover a similar picture of Dylan and Caitlin) and it may have been from the sleeve notes that I learned that my new hero had been born in Duluth Minnesota, as Robert Allen Zimmerman but eighteen year later had changed his name to Bob DYLAN in homage to a Welsh Poet. I guess that's when it all started. My mother was from South Wales. Not only that, she liked and read poetry. Freewheelin' around my bedroom, I was proud that she came from a small mining village with a name to marvel at, and, in East London play-grounds, to boast of;

Y N Y S D D U

There could be no such word; there could be no such place. But there was, and it was the birthplace of another Thomas, William Thomas, who, writing as the bard Islwyn, was one of the greatest Nineteenth-century Welsh poets. My mother had told me about her local poet William Thomas; now she told me about Dylan Thomas. She told his legend well, for already, less than ten years after his death, his life had already taken on many of the characteristics of folk-lore and legend. She eventually got me the recent official biography of Dylan Thomas by Constantine Fitzgibbon. Reading it I was immediately captivated by the romance of his life. I still listened to Bob Dylan's songs, but I also read Dylan Thomas's poems. I followed one Dylan's life in *MELODY MAKER* and read the other Dylan's life in Fitzgibbon's biography and in the books of his poems and stories. That these two Dylans were respectable adolescent cult heroes was absolutely confirmed to me a few years later when I was assiduously scouring Peter Blake's wonderful album cover for my recently purchased Beatles "Sgt. Pepper" album,[3] mainly so as one could impress girls by being able to name and claim familiarity with all the faces.

And there HE was – Dylan Thomas; peering over Marlon Brando's shoulder and around Tom Mix's Stetson. Dylan Thomas was one of the band; he was Lennon's hero too! (Much later when I got to meet Peter Blake he confirmed that Dylan was indeed Lennon's choice!). And full circle, there, in the top corner, Bob Dylan was there too. Along with Wilde and Beardsley, Crowley and Monroe, Lawrence of Arabia and William Burroughs – they were all members of an elite club; icons – famous as much for who they were, as what they were.

From then on it all has a kind of inevitable fatalism; college in

Cardiff, taught by Welsh poets named Jones and Williams about Welsh poets named Thomas and Thomas; seduced by a girl who could recite Dylan's And death shall have no dominion with Eisteddfod winning verve, and then, when she revealed she was from Swansea; Dylan's home town and that she lived in the Uplands; his very own stamping ground – Well, these seemed sound enough reasons for marriage. I settled in a Swansea no less ugly nor lovely than when Dylan grew up there – first the Luftwaffe and then a succession of very bad town planners had ensured this.

Eventually we bought a derelict old manse; only to discover that it was once the home of Dylan's Aunt Dosie and his uncle, the Rev. Rees and that Dylan had himself spent many of his childhood weekends in what has become our home. With the help of my antique-dealing in-laws we had opened a Bookshop in a town which seemed then, to almost deny the very existence of my hero-poet. We could begin the process of rehabilitation. As a simple act of celebration (and a hint of exploitation) we named the shop DYLANS BOOKSTORE.

Twenty-five years on and the town is beginning to tip its hat to its most famous son- a statue here, a plaque here; another statue there; a 'Dylans' pub; a 'Milk-Wood' Disco. And now this exhibition. For twenty-five years I have been part of a campaign fought on the poet's behalf. Almost daily some wizened and embittered local would enter the shop and uninvited, unprompted, begin abusing Dylan (and by inference, me) as a waster, a drunkard, a fornicator and a reprobate. Deep-rooted Welsh puritan Baptist ancestry would boil up and they would spew out vitriolic gobs of irrational disdain; and me; I rose to the bait and sprang to his defence with what I now realise was an equal dose of self-righteous pomposity;

READ HIS WORK

I would urge, and add;

THAT'S WHAT COUNTS!

Now I realise that "the rest" could not be ignored, for the locals had been, and were continually, subjected to a regular bombardment of media hype, which consistently reiterated and reinforced the negative stereotype of "hard-drinking" (perhaps the single most overworked cliché) bohemian poet, they were already so eager to disgrace. This did not stop them regularly offering me Holy Relics of the man – the carpet he walked on, his pocket watch, his shredded bow-tie, and his favourite armchair. I was even offered the hearse used to transport his body back to Laugharne. In most cases I would sneer, climb on my high horse, and send these temple thieves packing, but bought some (should I have bought them all?); a school cap, an inscribed table cloth, doodles, a phial of his sweat (?). But all the time from up astride my self-righteous steed I would proclaim his literary merit, and praise his writings.

NOW I HAVE DISMOUNTED THAT HIGH HORSE.

I still regard Dylan Thomas as a great poet, I still admire and recommend his short stories and sing (like the Rev. Eli Jenkins) the praises of Llareggub, but I now acknowledge that Dylan Thomas has become an Icon. I have come to realise that like James Dean, like Marilyn Monroe, Dylan Thomas exists beyond himself and his writing. He has entered our collective unconscious as the archetype of Bohemian, Romantic Poet and this exhibition seeks to celebrate both sides of the man; the poet and the icon; the words and the images of Dylan Thomas; *One of the Band*

Jeff Towns, 1995.

A Look Back: The Year In Hindsight

For me *The Swansea UK Year of Literature* was a very busy one and one of the most remarkable, and memorable year's in my many years of bookselling. I had provided a well-received and well visited exhibition and I got to show Prince Charles, U. S. President Jimmy Carter and Noble Prize winner, Seamus Heaney, around the Exhibition. There seemed to be world-class writers turning up to read, lecture and perform on a weekly basis; Allen Ginsberg and Rita Dove, two great American poets; Robertson Davies from Canada, Kenzaburō Ōe from Japan, another Nobel winner; great British jazz-men Stan Tracy and Jools Holland; Adrian Mitchell and Ralph Steadman; Sir George Martin and Sir

President Carter and I at the evening event – I was told it was 'informal'

Peter Blake.

Poets and writers from around the world came; Miroslav Holub, Paul Muldoon, African writers and, of course, Welsh poets; Peter Finch, Danny Abse, Nigel Jenkins and Swansea-based poet David Woolley, who programmed and ran the Festival. I was brought in to be his consultant for the Year, and the subsequent decades that the Dylan Thomas Centre, aka Ty Llên, functioned as an Arts venue. Our budget was not huge, but browsing back through the monthly brochures I think we can be quite satisfied with what we achieved. I am conscious of that old chestnut 'You can lead a horse to water but you can't make it drink.' We certainly offered up a rich cultural menu, but often audiences were hard to attract. I had also established a large bookshop in a ground floor space which eventually became one of the first bookshop cafes in the UK.

Addendum

Around 2012/2013 Swansea Council were under financial pressure and were looking to make cuts-backs[4]. and the Arts budget is often the first target. After enjoying the glory days of 1995 – The UK YEAR of LITERATURE and 2003, the fifty-year Commemoration of Dylan's death, they began to talk about making different use of some of Ty Llên building or perhaps selling it off completely. I got wind of this and was concerned about the future of my bookshop but also about the future of the exhibition and the whole Dylan Thomas Centre. Various schemes were rumoured some bizarre, some crazy, but it then narrowed down to doing some kind of deal with the University of Wales, which by then was a curious entity; all the regional component Universities; Cardiff, Bangor, Trinity in Lampeter, Aberystwyth and Swansea, were now independent and autonomous. So the new tenants were a University without a proper campus. But negotiations were ongoing and change was in the air.

Ty Llên, The Dylan Thomas Centre façade Swansea

I was invited and involved in a few 'stakeholder' meetings which were a bit of an eye-opener for me. The Dylan Thomas Centre was a fine building, recently refurbished at great cost, with the help of grants and some European money. The building had a very chequered past. Back in 1825 the corporation resolved to build a new guildhall, and a site was chosen for a new civic building in the Burrows, formerly a patch of sandy meadows between the town and the sea. It had been turned into a fashionable development with elegant terraces and assembly rooms, a fitting place for the imposing new building. Work started later on that year, and it was finally completed in 1829. It was an elegant-looking building with a well-proportioned façade. A grand double flight of steps led to the main entrance at first floor level. Inside there were two court rooms, along with various smaller rooms. However, it soon became clear that the new building was not big enough. The Municipal Corporations Act of 1835 more than doubled the size of the borough, bringing in the industrial parts along the Swansea Valley as far as Morriston. In 1848 the decision was taken to enlarge the building and give it a new façade. When finished, the building looked splendid with classical columns and much increased accommodation.

Later in the century it was embellished with the addition of a statue of John Henry Vivian, and two Russian canons, captured during the Crimean War. However by the beginning of the next century a striking Germanic Art Deco building was built in the more western salubrious area and in 1934 the New Guildhall opened. The old building went through a variety of uses; as secondary school; as a Juvenile Employment Centre; before finally being abandoned and left to rack and ruin, eventually becoming a derelict, unofficial shelter for local street people, down-and- outs and itinerant gentlemen of the road, who began to strip the interior fittings to fuel their bonfires. But when Swansea City was awarded the honour of hosting The UK Year of Literature, after much to-ing and frowing, it was this building that was chosen to be the new landmark, *National Literature Centre of Wales* aka, *Ty Llên*. It was extensively and expensively renovated at a cost of a good few millions and it re-opened with much pomp and ceremony in its new livery in 1995.

But, in Swansea in 2012, the council needed to make serious cutbacks to their Arts and Culture funding budget. A few meeting were held which I attended, but nothing firm seemed to be happening. I then encountered one of the senior council employees who I had worked with and, in the course of our conversation outside the Centre, he rather indiscreetly told me that if a local multi-millionaire property magnate, who already owned several big properties in the area, were to offer to buy the building for £400 grand, that they would sell!

A recently refurbished huge edifice, for just £400 grand? I mulled this over and at the next meeting with the council, in a lull before it closed I raised my hand, mentioned my recent conversation, without mentioning any names, and gently asked whether I might buy the building on the same terms. To say that the manure hit the air conditioning is an understatement! The room became a hub-bub of whispers and shock. I was immediately considered a dangerous and malicious citizen and within 24 hours, I unlocked my bookstore in town to find, pushed under the door, a single sheet of paper, no envelope, just a sheet printed on one side only. It was a swiftly and shabbily fabricated official eviction-notice from the Council, giving me just 28 days to empty and completely clear out, my full- to-bursting, very large used bookshop in the Centre, which I been running for some fifteen years, while also being the paid Dylan Thomas consultant in the building. Needless to say I felt more than a tad disgruntled after all I had done during those twenty years. I just about managed the task I had been set by first off having a huge half-price sale, then inviting a few Booksellers down who like to buy big quantities, before finally announcing in the local press and online, that on my final days in situ, all books left on the shelves were free to anybody who cared to come and take whatever they wanted away.

Since then I am no longer involved in any Council sponsored arts developments or events. The Building is still there, the exhibition is still there, and in 2013/4 it was totally re-vamped, updated and reinstalled at the cost of some £million from the Lottery Fund. But it no longer offers the year-round programme of literary and arts events. However, over the years the Centre has attracted some philanthropic folk to gift some interesting Dylan Thomas artefacts and ephemera, but even with these additions the exhibition still comprise some 90% of exhibits which came from me, and I must say they do look splendid in this new incarnation. But still the long-term future is unclear. All in all, it was a very unhappy denouement for myself and Dylans Bookstore.

But we picked ourselves up, dusted ourselves down and went out and bought a near-vintage, decommissioned Mobile Library Bus, complete with all original shelving and fixtures. We got local old-school sign-writers and they swiftly and rebranded it as DYLANS MOBILE BOOKBUS.

Our inspirations were manifold; This wonderful, unusual and compelling Book; The Night Mobile[5] And two great Heroes –

Ken Kesey

Iolo Morganwg

One Welsh and the other American; This wonderful 18th/ 19th century Welsh hero; Edward Williams aka IOLO MORGANWG – one of who's many occupations was itinerant pedestrian bookselling. And this modern day American hero – Ken Kesey and his Magic Bus which not only went Further – he brought it to Swansea too![6]

So we became bookselling Merry-Pranksters and squeezed another decade of huge fun and enjoyment, driving the lumbering vehicle from Festivals to Markets; from Arts Events to Eisteddfodau; we became true itinerant Welsh booksellers.

One of our early, occasional staffers, Joe, captured the early years in this account...

The old boy in the bar on Bourbon Street leant over, put his face near mine, leant in close to me, so close I could hear the whiskey in his voice, and smell the rhythm in his words...

"Im'a give you two piece of advice so you listen up real good now boy. Y'all ready. One. Let the city come to you. And two. Let the good times roll"

When I think about the BookBus, and I think about the BookBus quite a bit... I think back to the old boy in that New Orleans bar.

Shifting books the old way wasn't happening. The internet had taken down our pants while we weren't looking and Google, eBay, Kindle then Oxfam snuck up, and slowly shafted us from behind.

It wasn't pretty but there was no other way, we had to get out on the road. We had books, good books, and we knew there were people, good people, who still wanted to hold them, touch them, smell them and possibly own them.

Ken Kesey had the right idea. Buy a f **kin' bus.

We found our 'Bus, and promptly filled it with our Books,

thousands of them, and the BookBus was born. We launched as #DylansMobileBookstore. To this day no one other than us has ever used that hashtag.

We took the ‘Bus to the Uplands Market in Swansea. And something happened...YOU started buying books again. Stepping on the ‘Bus was like stepping back in time. But we were selling books like no tomorrow. The BookBus provides a doorway into something special. A sanctuary from the outside world and a store of limitless possibilities, its walls lined with escape routes to deserts, spaces and oceans. New worlds inside every cover, on every page.

Better still it was up to us where we parked the ‘Bus. The rules had changed. Our location wasn’t fixed. This felt like Gonzo Bookselling. Free-form, freestyle, free-love Bookselling.

Hunter had a mantra.
Find an event.
Immerse Yourself.
Become the Story.

That worked for us.

Before long we had a spiritual home. Laugharne. A village out on its own. Literally, geographically and psychologically. Dylan Thomas said Laugharne was the place where people ‘got off the bus and forgot to get back on again’. Until now. Now we were getting people back on the ‘Bus. The BookBus.

It might have had something to do with the bottle of absinthe we keep on one of the shelves. Buy a book, get a free shot. Not something you’re likely to see on Groupon but an excellent deal all the same. The BookBus staff and its customers need more oiling than the old ‘Bus itself.

We made a sign to hang outside the ‘Bus and asked people to leave a message. Trouble was the people leaving messages were so damn sweet and the messages they left were so incredible we had to keep buying new signs. ‘Homophobia Sucks’ wrote Paul Durden, ‘Onwards and Upwards’ from Molly Parkin, and Peter Blake left us this piece of wisdom ‘Living well is the best revenge” ...‘Vote Bez’ wrote Bez.

The BookBus was on a roll. It rolled east, coast to coast to *Latitude*. West to the Brecon Hills for *Green Man*. North to Portmeirion for *Festival No.6*. Anywhere in search of what Sir Clough William-Ellis described as ‘the possibility of pleasurable fantasy’. A never-ending-endless summer tour.

Further. Further was the name of Ken Kesey’s Magic Bus. Further, the lengths we remain willing to roll to find the good times.

‘Let us go then, you and I’ screamed the actor we hired and dressed as a bunny and gave a copy of ‘The Love Song of J Alfred Prufrock’ with the strict instructions to read aloud to our customers. And what customers...in our first six months we’d welcomed and sold books to most of our heroes...musicians, artists, film makers, comedians, poets... some of the best minds of our generation...Gruff Rhys, Cat Le Bon, First Aid Kit, Luke Wright, Mike Garry, Keith Allen, Arthur Smith, Kieran Evans, Joe Dunthorne, Pete Wylie, Tom Hollander, Gavin Turk, Pete Paphides, Simon Armitage, Rhys Ifans.

We are 27ft of fully shelved, fully loaded, wall to wall anachronistic, anarchistic, existentialist, surrealist bliss. We offer books to eat in or take away. We are a timeless and timely tide against the death of the high street, the loss of the libraries, the rise of the right and the curse of the Kindle.

Our ‘Bus moves with what Gerald Manly Hopkins might’ve called a ‘sprung rhythm’. You can’t inscape us. We’ll be coming your way soon, and as Frank Zappa once told you Don’t make a fuss, just get on the Bus.

And remember these two things:

Let the BookBus come to you. And Let the Good Times Roll.

1. I felt a tad queasy when I learned that this notion came to the then Tory arts Minister, Michael Portillo, as he lay sipping red wine in his bath...

2. The LP was Bob Dylan's first ever LP release. It was just titled *Bob Dylan* and it was recorded on the cheap and very quickly. The album cover features a reversed photo of Dylan holding his acoustic guitar. This was done to prevent the neck of the guitar from obscuring Columbia's logo.

3. More about this album and Peter Blake in Chapter 17.

4. This now seems to be an ongoing and constant problem for local councils the length and breadth of the UK.

5. The graphic novel, was first serialised in the Guardian newspaper. It was first published as book in 2010 by Jonathan Cape. Audrey Niffenegger both wrote and illustrated it.

6. In 1995 Ken Kesey brought his refurbished Magic Bus to the UK with a new bunch of Merry Pranksters and they visited Swansea as part of the UK Year of Literature Festival. I had been to a talk he gave at Riverside Campus of UCLA back in the late 70's, he was inspirational then and he did not disappoint when he staged a bizarre psychedelic happening here in Swansea. Her was a major inspiration for our BookBus, just as his novel, *One Flew Over the Cuckoo's Nest* was a BookBus favourite on the page and on the screen.

Tate Gallery London

Eileen Agar's, surrealist portrait of Dylan Thomas

4.

Sedona to the Max.
With a Postscript:
Dylan Thomas & Surrealism.

Sedona has always attracted artists, from the great Surrealist Max Ernst on...

This account of an American adventure was written after I got back from a Book Fair in San Francisco in the late nineties. It was an unusual trip because my wife came with me and, before the Fair, we went on a road trip into Arizona, where the following occurred...

Sedona 'to the Max'.

It was late and I was about to sleep when it hit me. I was stretched out on one of two raft-like beds; my wife was curled up on the other one, in the Desert Quail Inn, Oak Creek Village, Sedona, Arizona. We had to leave early in the morning. In an effort to avoid the adverts that pollute American TV, I had zapped around until I settled on the local 'Sedona Welcome' channel, which was made up entirely of local adverts. Up-market ads for up-market Bistros offering 'Buffalo Steaks with Biscuits 'n Gravy'; Boutiques offering 'The Finest Western Apparel and Boots'; Rock shops with Tarot readings and endless up-market Art Galleries.

Bored to somnambulism, a phrase that still managed to penetrate my near sleeping brain; the annoying voice of the programme host trilled;

Sedona has always attracted artists, from the great Surrealist Max Ernst on...

MAX ERNST. Of course: Max Ernst/Sedona; Sedona/Max Ernst.[1] I was in Sedona by chance not design. I am a bookseller from Wales specializing in Welsh History, Topography and Literature; in particular the works of Welsh Poet, Dylan Thomas. I was on a book-buying road-trip before exhibiting at a Book-Fair back in San Francisco. The best books I had found on the trip so far were *A History of Fox-Hunting in Canada*, signed by the author in bright red ink (fox-cub's blood for sure), and a diminutive little pocket-book designed for the forces, *The Americans Guide to Hindustani*, circa 1945, in the rare Stars & Stripes d.j.

Inside I found many essential and many useful phrases such as;

These eggs are bad – yeh ande kharab hain

I don't want gingerade – Ham gingerade naheen mangte

In fact, they were the only books I had found, but the trip had taken us by that great hole in the earth some 30 miles north called, with uncharacteristic restraint, *The Grand Canyon*. It had not disappointed. It was an enormous hole. But after walking a little way around it, stumbling some small distance down it, and finally getting the true measure of it by flying into its vast spaces by helicopter, we had reluctantly left and driven somewhat randomly southwards towards a place named Sedona which was full of 'awesome red rocks and great desert Art shops' of which we had been earnestly beseeched not to miss by waitresses named Jeannetta and Priscilla, backed up by pump attendants named Chuck or Lou. The giant red rock formations springing up out of even redder soil were indeed spectacular (reminding me of Uluru down under). However, the 'Art' on offer in *Desert Vista, Desert Moods, Desert Dreams*, type Galleries was less appealing.

Moreover, the place was full of *Mumbo-Jumbo*. Sedona, I was told, all too often, was on/or in a 'VORTEX'. This accounted for endless avenues of Crystal Shoppes, Tarot Tepees, *SHAMANS R US* stores, and other old age, new age outlets, offering psychic treats for the troubled soul. The 'Vortex' was also responsible for a strong magnetic force which apparently attracted UFO's and aged brain-fried hippies with the same unyielding force. But suddenly there was Max. Did I not have, back in my Swansea home, a great 12″ x 12″ photograph, framed and hung above my desk, of a giant Max Ernst laying his hand on the head of a midget Dorothea Tanning? Goliath and David in an Arizona desert; A great photograph, carefully crafted by the surrealist eye of Lee Miller, with her cunning use of perspective and depth of vision to produce such a witty image of two of the most enduring and popular Surrealist artists. Lee Miller took the photograph in 1949 when, with her husband, a leading British Surrealist artist, Roland Penrose, they had visited their old friends Max and Dorothea in their stunning desert hideaway.

But, even more importantly, I also had in my best bookcase a copy of Max Ernst's famous surrealist collaged graphic novel *Misfortunes of the Immortals*. It is one of a limited edition of just 620 copies, designed by Carese Crosby and issued by her 'Black Sun Press' in 1943. It is also inscribed in bold black ink on the front endpaper

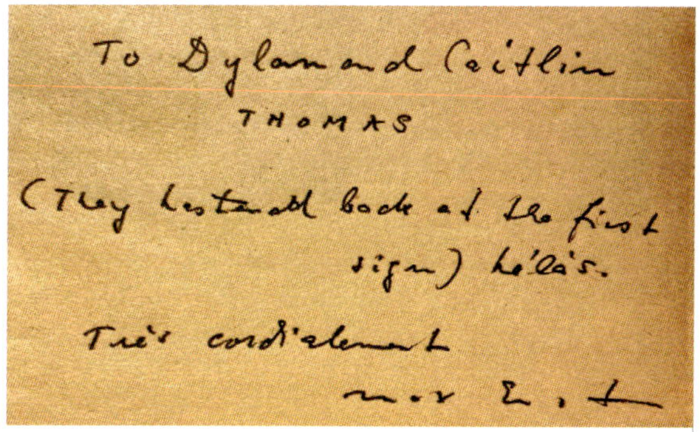

To Dylan and Caitlin THOMAS (They hastened back at the first sign) Helas. Tres cordialement Max Ernst

Lee's stunning David and Goliath image of Max Ernst and Dorothea Tanning in the Sedona Desert.

It was a precious and cherished holy relic which told the story of how Dylan and Caitlin Thomas had also joined the long list of artists and writers who had sought out Max and Dorothea in their remote desert hideaway.

How had I not remembered these treasures, so cherished but buried deep in my vacationing brain. Even the VORTEX had tried to help. The night previously Dylan Thomas had reared his head. I was enjoying a serious browse around the very seriously extensive liquor section of the Sedona all-night Supermarket. Nestled on the shelves among some 50 various whiskeys from around the world was a bottle of a home-grown variety, *Old Grand-Dad*, a Kentucky Bourbon which was allegedly Dylan Thomas' favourite tipple on his American binges. I had recently failed to procure just such a bottle when asked by some local theatre group to provide it as a stage prop for their imminent production of yet another Dylan Thomas bio-play. I have a bottle now should they decide to reprise the piece, but I drank the Whisky with great pleasure so they will have to fill it with cold tea.

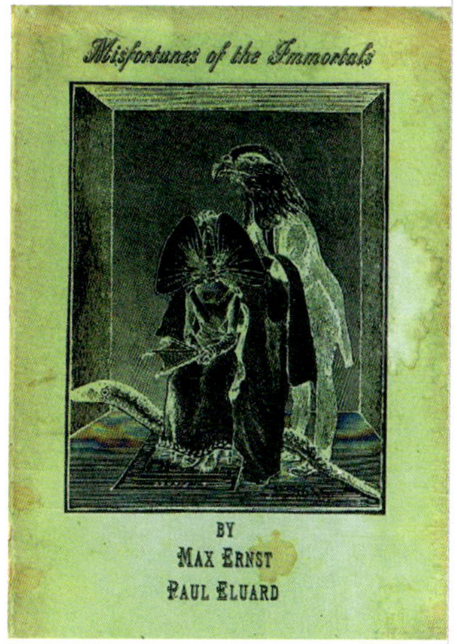

Max Ernst' Surrealist collage novel

But even *Old Grand-Dad* had not triggered off memories of Max. Now after the TV proclamation, I slept fitfully, angry with myself for my stupidity, for missing the chance of hunting out traces of this intriguing episode. And now I really had no time to back-track. In the morning, we had to get on the road, to get back to San Francisco in order to sell some books (especially the Fox-Hunting book, which was beginning to weigh on my conscience and glow green in my suit-case in this most eco-friendly of environments). In the morning, over breakfast, I explained my grave sin of omission to my wife. She feigned interest, but being sane and rational she was, as usual, unable to grasp my level of concern.

As planned we headed smartly south-west but we were interested in stopping at an intriguing nearby 'Ghost Town' called Jerome. It had been a thriving mineral centre until the fifties when the ore ran out followed by 90% of the population. A few die-hards, but deeply eccentric stalwarts had stayed on, and now it was in the process of being slowly revitalised as the poor overspill for the over-busy, up-market Sedona. On the drive I had just one thing on my mind; I had to get onto the Internet to masochistically satisfy myself as to what I might have missed back in Sedona. Jerome was entered up a steep hill. The road passed through clapped out suburbs. It was bright, dusty and deserted, resembling a set from a long finished 'Mad Max' movie. We pulled into the *Town Centre* and right across from the car park I spotted, up on a second-floor window a sign; *Java Internet*, and I was off and running, taking the stairs two at a time. I burst into the shop and realised it was a heady mix of – 1. Books, used, condition – scruffy – subject areas – alien abductions and hunting chakras; 2. Crystals; 3. U.P.S. Parcel Depot and 4. A bespoke Tarot Reading Service. It also contained two desks covered in ephemera and paper detritus on which were buries two computers. At one, a small elfin woman was sat working; dark-haired, dark-trousered, fine-featured, with a short, one length bob of striking maroon hair. If my sudden entrance had startled her she did not show it. She was calm personified. I pointed to the computers and gasped,

'Can I use the Internet please?'

She answered politely, to the effect that I looked or seemed harmless and that I could and should use her computer as the other one needed booting up, and she vacated her chair. All this was delivered in delightful accented English which sounded like Ingrid Bergman with a hint of Marlene Dietrich. Her calmness was captivating. I learned quickly that she was Ingrid; originally from Hungary but had been 40 years in L.A. Then two years in Sedona, before moving to Jerome and becoming the proud proprietor of the cutely rhymed and alliterated '*Ingrid's Mountain Top Shipping Shop*' [*Tarot readings optional extra*]. Ingrid lived behind the shop with her daughter who made the magical crystal charms and necklaces which were in cabinets amongst the esoterica. Introductions out of the way I began Googling frantically using searches combining numerous variations of Ernst/ Thomas/ Sedona/. As I typed I thought to ask Ingrid, who seemed to be a cultured expatriate Eastern European *intellectual*, if she knew anything of Max and Dorothea in Sedona. Her reaction suggested she has no idea whatsoever what I was babbling on about; a look of quite total incomprehension crossed her face and she offered nothing back to fuel my line of inquiry. My internet search had proved equally unproductive. Hugely disappointed, I gave up, logged off, got up and turned to leave; and there before me, hung on the wall, was a very large, very imposing, framed enigmatic surrealist poster for an art exhibition. It was by Max Ernst.[1]

For a moment I was struck dumb, and then I rounded on poor Ingrid exclaiming loudly;

But there! There! You have Max Ernst!

I struggled to make her comprehend, but she was unmoved;

Oh zat, she said nonchalantly. A friends gived it to me – I am not attached to it. Now I try all zer time to not attach myself to tings.

I interrupted; Then can I buy it? I'd really like too

sev-venty dollars maybe, – it is a wery nice frame I tink.

I pounced: Fine – I'll buy it for that.

And I began to fumble in my pockets for dollar bills. A longer pause ensued, that went on and on as Ingrid ruminated, then;

Noh. Noh, I vill not sell it, I vill have then a beeg, beeg empty Space. Noh I must keep it, maybe if I find another picture I vill sell.

I did not give up at once. I wanted that picture. If anyone

could prise it off that wall I could. I tried persuasion, I tried charm, and I played up to the synchronicity, the coincidence, the fatefulness of it all. I may even have used the V word – VORTEX. I offered to go and find her a like-sized replacement image. But she was firm in her refusal. So reluctantly I gave up, but I was disappointed. Inside I was very needful of that image. My wife joined us and Ingrid bade us both sit down, stay for a chat, but we had to get lunch and get on. Ingrid recommended a nearby Diner called *The Haunted Burger* – where else would she recommend in spooky Jerome? So, we said our good-byes and left.

The Diner should have been called *The Grand Burger* after the nearby Canyon. The burgers were the size of small UFO's. I looked down on tiny Aliens were disembarking onto my platter – but it was just a trickle of lumpy guacamole. I could not concentrate on the food. I was still thinking about Max's ghost back in Sedona and what I might have missed. Eventually I leapt up, told Liz to take her time with her meat spacecraft and then settle the bill, as I was going back to use Ingrid's computer one more time before we had to leave the area for good.

My magnificent hard fought for copy of the Ernst Exhibition poster[2]

If there was something to see I could still just about afford the time to go back to Sedona.

Ingrid seemed unphased by my return, even pleased to see me, but then she was not exactly overrun with customers for any of the services she offered. She indicated that this time I use the other computer which was directly below Max's poster. An omen, I thought, and went to work feeling sure that I would this time, discover if there were any tangible visitable remains of Max and Dorothea's time in Sedona. Nothing was forthcoming from some thousands of *Google* results, but I did get a phone number at the *Sedona Centre for the Arts* where someone was offering an Ernst lithograph for sale. I used Ingrid's phone. The lady who answered turned out to be one of the Centre's directors. I was obviously getting nowhere when suddenly Ingrid grabbed the phone from me with Teutonic forcefulness and began pounding in the numbers of the *Sedona Civic Centre and Chamber of Commerce*. She got me through to a person who finally put the lid on things. In a somewhat curt and direct tone I was informed that there was absolutely nothing to see or visit in Sedona for an Ernst/Tanning pilgrim. Max's legendary desert home had new owners who insisted on absolute privacy, as was their right, and thus Sedona had given up on promoting Max Ernst.

I was disappointed but also relieved – I had missed nothing and could journey on with no regrets. If I could buy the poster above me all would be kismet. I tried again Ingrid wavered. She asked a favour of me – would I take some of her original Occult postcard sized drawings back to 'Vhales' and slip them secretly into some of my books, secret bookmarks which meant some of her 'soul' would rest in a Celtic domain. Of course I could do this

I assured her. I would do anything for that poster.

'Then it is yours'

My spirits soared...

'Ven you return'

They crashed.

She repeated her offer – I was to consider the picture mine and I could buy it when I came back to Jerome. She was very convinced of this happening. I was less so. I tried reasoning with her about the unlikelihood of this occurring, evoking distance, pressures of work and life, but once again she was firm. The picture was mine but I could only have it when I returned. Devastated, I gave up yet again, and left clutching nothing more than a sheaf of her curious doodles and drawings – some of her soul for Wales.

Out on the streets Jerome had just been invaded by bigger Aliens. A chapter or three – maybe a whole volume, of weekend Biker-types, all too clean to be real Hell's Angels, with shiny new black leathers and even neater new black tattoos and even shinier huge new chromed Harley's; Bankers by day Bikers on the weekend. The narrow roads were filled with the noise and fumes of hundreds of well-tuned expensive engines. It made getting out of town difficult, but we got on the way and drove in silence back, we thought, towards San Francisco. After a good few miles winding down the mountain, the turn I was looking for was failed to appear, so I stopped for gas and directions. The gas was easy. The directions proved harder. Liz went inside where she managed to accost the resident desert drunk who insisted the road we wanted did not exist anywhere in the state of Arizona but that he would be very pleased to share his brown bagged beer with her. Outside I favoured a more promising looking young cowboy, filling his battered red flat-bed truck with diesel. He was somewhat challenged linguistically. I asked my question and he drawled;

Awe' Hell man yous are a-ways outa yur way.

Y'all gotta go ways back over the mountain.

He indicated the way I had just come. Incredulous, I asked,

You mean back up and out through Jerome?

He responded with cruel glee in his voice;

Yes- Sir-ree bouy! An' keep on goin' straight on 'till y'all see the sign for Needles!

I blamed those damn alien bikers. They had managed to further disorientate my already preoccupied brain. We got back in our dusty Chevy and headed back up the mountain. A long half-hour of travel passed with little conversation, but to a sound-track of mawkish Country & Western music (one song had the touching refrain sung by a bitter Tammy Wynette clone; "*Jesus may love you but I sure as hell don't*"; and another had a croaky-voiced good ole' boy crooning to his wife "*You're the reason our kids are so ugly*.") And then we were back in Jerome.

On the way in I had quickly formulated a selfish and cowardly plan that might well turn this negative into a positive. I pulled over on the hard shoulder a little up the road and below the *Mountain Top Shipping Stop* and I thrust a bundle of $20 notes at Liz and bade her to go buy the picture, instructing her that she was to demand it on the grounds that Ingrid had quite categorically offered it to me on my return to Jerome and here I was returned. I was, of course, scared to go myself, but had not Max written in the book he gave to Dylan,

(**They hastened back at first sign**)

Liz reluctantly but stoically climbed out of the car. She herself was not in any way as emotionally involved in this whole business as I was, but she was used to these grail-like quests of mine from past experience and knew only too well that any prevarication would be quite pointless. I watched her progress in the rear-view mirror until she was out of sight, but I did not take my eyes off it, as I tried to imagine the scene and soundtrack up in Ingrid's grotto. Time passed. More time passed. Then a small Welsh woman appeared in the mirror, coming my way, her progress slow and awkward on account of the large framed surrealist image she was lugging and hugging to her breast! Result!

I sheepishly got out of the car and took the picture from her silently, gently and gratefully, and slid it into the cavernous trunk, and gazed down on it, with awe and pride. I drove westwards, very satisfied and with an ever-so-slight smirk on my face. After the Book Fair which was busy and enjoyable, the large print was wrapped in layers of bubble wrap and joined my unsold stock to be air-freighted back to Wales. They all arrived and were back in my bookshop a week or so after our return. As promised, I carefully secreted Ingrid's drawings inside suitable volumes of Celtic Folklore, and I sent her a large poster printing of Thomas's poem *Fern Hill*, not as any kind of *quid pro quo* for the Ernst poster, but hopefully to fill the space on her wall. And the Ernst poster took pride of place on my wall in my Swansea study.

We do not have too much in the way of detail about Dylan and Caitlin's eight day stay in Sedona with the Ernst's, but we can get the gist of it from this short note on a postcard sent to Daniel Jones;

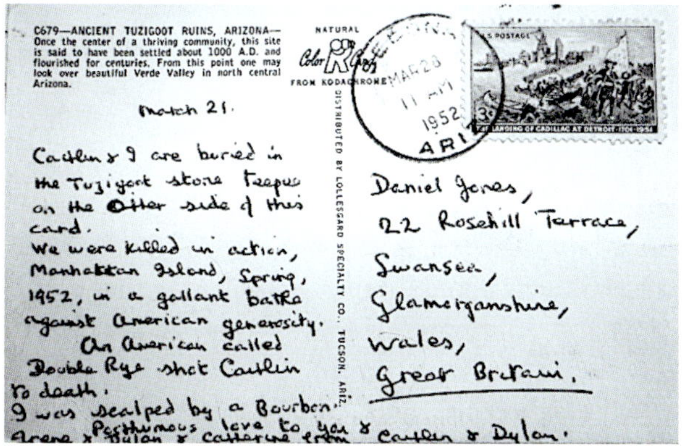

'Caitlin and I are buried in the Tuzigoot stone tepee on the other side of this card. We were killed in action, Manhattan Island, Spring 1952, in a gallant battle against American generosity. An American called Double Rye shot Caitlin to death. I was scalped by Bourbon Posthumous love to you and Irene...'

And Caitlin sent a postcard to David Lougee a New York, American friend of Dylan's, with another vignette of their desert adventure.

More puzzling is just what made them attempt such an out of the way stop in the first place. I originally assumed Dylan

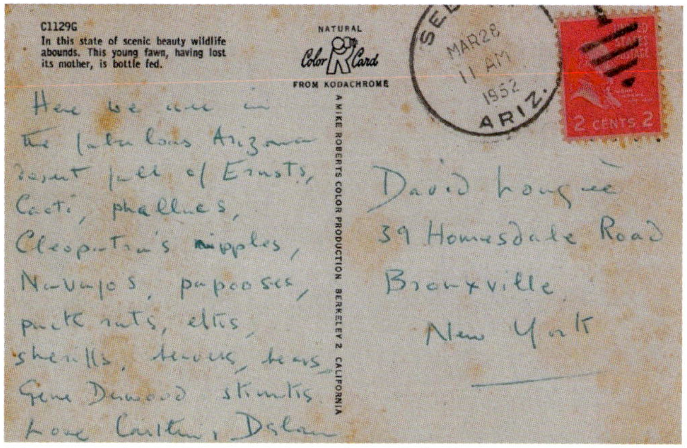

'Here we are in the fabulous Arizona desert full of Ernsts cacti, phalluses, Cleopatra's nipples, Navajos, papooses, pack rats ...sheriffs ...Love Caitlin + Dylan

Thomas had met Max at the 1936 Surrealist Exhibition but it appears that was wrong. In the most recent biography of Thomas by Andrew Lycett, he writes that in a letter from an aging Dorothea Tanning she states her husband, Max, had never met Dylan before the Sedona visit. Lycett suggests that it was Dylan's unofficial American editor and promoter, the New York poet Oscar Williams and his wife, the painter Gene Derwood, who, being good friends with Dorothea Tanning, put Dylan in touch with the Ernsts. A card sent from Sedona in March 1952 would seem to support this. It is written in Dylan's hand and just says 'Wild and Western Love to Gene and Oscar from' and then all four, 'Max Ernst, Dorothea, Dylan and Caitlin', signed it.

Whatever the truth Dylan and Caitlin left New York for San Francisco and Vancouver on March 17th 1952. This was during the second of Thomas's reading tours and the first and only time that Caitlin accompanied him. They were about six weeks into what had been an exhausting trip for all involved and John Malcolm Brinnin was pleased to send then off with all their tickets and expenses covered and a further $400 spending money on what was to be a short vacation between engagements.

But things did not go to plan. After a brief stop for Dylan to give a reading at Penn State University they travelled on to Chicago during which things started to go wrong, as Dylan later explained in a letter to Brinnin;

Caitlin was frightfully ill ...on the night train to Chicago.

Dylan and Caitlin en route in America

During the Chicago journey, my bottled-up bottle illness also grew severe; indeed, we were both so near to undignified death that, on reaching Chicago, we just *could* not go straight across the city to catch our next unrocking bed. So, we went to a cozy little hovel of a hotel and wept and sweated there until next day. The hotel was fabulously expensive; the Pullman reservation for Tuesday, the 18th. Fell out of date. I had to buy a new one so, we arrived at Flagstaff with less than a dollar.'

This accounts for the telegram sent to Brinnin from Flagstaff on March 21.

PLEASE URGENTLY WIRE ONE HUNDRED DOLLARS CARE OF ERNST CAPRICORN HILL SEDONA D.

This telegram however was too slow in reaching Brinnin in time for him to act on it and Dylan and Caitlin were stuck stony broke in Sedona. But they managed. Dylan goes on in his letter to Brinnin,

The Ernsts were lovely, charming and hospitable, but had no ready money and none to lend. We stayed absolutely penniless, for about 8 days, being unable to buy our own cigarettes, to post a letter, or stand with a beer at a Sedona's cowboy bar, or even wire you again. We stayed there, saying "Beastly John" until help came from San Francisco.'

As usual Dylan is exaggerating. As mentioned they had sent postcards to Dan Jones, Oscar Williams; and they sent others, – to Bill MacAlpine; 'tumultuously exhilarating & axe-splitting tour... sensational as the desert itself; to John Davenport; 'A killer-diller of a journey so far; and Caitlin's card to David Lougee'. Andrew Lycett, in his biography of Dylan, also quotes from an unpublished postcard to Ebie Williams the landlord of Brown's Hotel back in Laugharne and a big lover of Western films. Dylan writes of being in a Poker Flat saloon in Sedona surrounded by genuine cowboys in ten-gallon Stetsons and being treated to rye whiskey by a sheriff with two pearl handled revolvers in his belt.

And Dorothea Tanning herself tells the best story in her autobiography '*Between Lives*' (2001).

I can still see him, vibrant boomer, swaying down the main street of Cottonwood our nearest town, repudiating by his very existence any hint of mortality, any rent in the fabric of flesh and fantasy. We look in to a lively bar, called the Bridgeport Tavern. This delightful haven for the likes of Dylan Thomas was next door to a revivalist meeting house, with a neat lawn on which was a large signboard, bearing the words WHERE WILL YOU SPEND ETERNITY?

One evening after a few beers next door, Dylan and Max carefully placed beside it a reply they had cooked up that afternoon, a big sign that read,

IN THE BRIDGEPORT TAVERN.

After about a week, Dylan and Caitlin attempted to leave. Max presented Dylan with a finely printed catalogue for one of his American exhibitions. He inscribed it warmly urging his guests to return again. When Dylan and Caitlin got into Sedona they found

Dylan and Max outside their favourite bar[3] with their mischievous new sign in place. An original watercolour by Wyn Thomas

there was no money from Brinnin waiting for them to finance their onward travel so had to return sheepishly to Capricorn Hill. It was when they finally did arrive a back for a couple of days and they made ready to leave for a second time that Max gave them a copy of his iconic surrealist collage book *Misfortunes of the Immortals* with another warm inscription:

'(They Hastened back at first sign).'

POSTSCRIPT – DYLAN THOMAS AND SURREALISM

Dylan Thomas was no stranger to Surrealism. At first, as a young teenager, he might not have identified his work as surrealistic but the results often were, especially the collaborative poems he wrote in the late 1920's with his close schoolmate and friend, Daniel Jones. They would write alternate lines passing the paper back and forth like the children's game 'consequences' often ending up with startling results. Many of these poems (some 200 hundred have survived) have ended up in the vast Harry Ransom collection of literary manuscripts in the University of Texas. Daniel writes about them in his book *My Friend Dylan Thomas*; describing how he would write the odd-numbered lines and Dylan the even lines. Here is one quite remarkable example;

A coin burns my hand, and the street is dark;
You are propped at every bending lamp,
like flimsy dolls, dreaming with rotten lips,
A robe coiled, rent and heaving: I am dreaming,
with thoughts like shining fish in a silver sea: and you,
With lips and skin that will wither and pass.

As his writing career developed it became something of a problem especially when he was working on his second collection of poems, *Twenty-Five Poems* which a major publisher, J. M. Dent were to publish. Thomas's editor at Dent was the mystical and some-what straight-laced poet and critic, Richard Church and although impressed with Thomas's first collection *18 Poems*, some of the poems offered for this second collection troubled Church and he wrote a long letter to Dylan in November 1935 which included these strong opinions;

> ...I look upon surrealism in poetry with abhorrence...
> Surrealism is to me an anti-social activity, and therefore destructive. I am distressed to see its pernicious effect in your work...

Driven by a desire to see his poetic career progress Dylan is somewhat economic with the truth when he replies;

> I have not, never have been, and never will be, or could be for that matter, a Surrealist and for a number of reasons: I have very little idea what Surrealism is; until quite recently I had never heard of it; I have never, to my knowledge, read even a paragraph of Surrealist literature.

Reassured, Church went on to accept *Twenty-Five Poems* for publication and it came out in September of 1936. Unabashed, around the same time, Thomas published three somewhat strange short stories in Roger Roughton's left wing surrealist magazine and Church must have been taken aback if he was aware of Thomas' participation in the seminal 1936 International Surrealist exhibition at the Burlington Galleries which opened on 11 June and ran to 4 July 1936, in London's Mayfair. Its

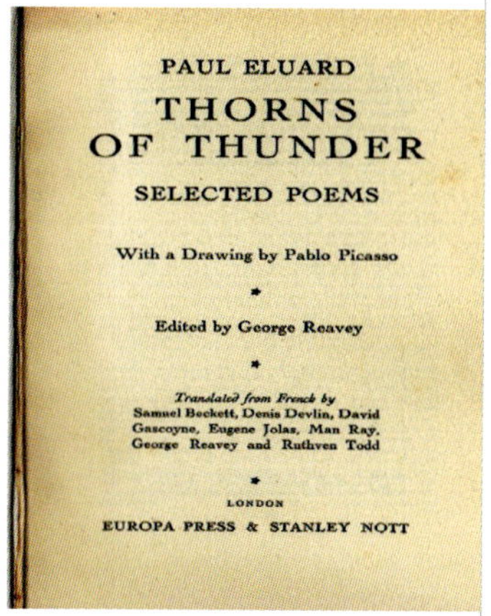

Eluard's First publication in English with Max Ernst cover design

In connection with the

INTERNATIONAL SURREALIST EXHIBITION

NEW BURLINGTON GALLERIES
Burlington Gardens, W. 1

Friday, 26th June,
at 9 p.m.

PAUL ELUARD
will recile his poems

English versions by Samuel Beckett, Denis Devlin, David Gascoyne, George Reavey.

Other Surrealist poems. Also poems by David Gascoyne, George Reavey, Dylan Thomas and others.

Admission 1/6d. - 2/6d. - 5s.
2/6d. and 5s. seats may be reserved from
G. Reavey, 1, Parton Street, W. C. 1

"Weak or strong?"

My reproduction of Dylan's concoction

organising committee consisted of the leading British and French Surrealists including, David Gascoyne, Roland Penrose, Humphrey Jennings, Andre Breton, Paul Eluard and Man Ray. Dylan became involved through the interventions of a London drinking pal – George Reavey a Russian-born Irish surrealist art collector poet, translator and sometime publisher.[4] Reavey had recently moved back from Paris where he got to know Samuel Beckett and many of the French Surrealists, including Paul Eluard. Reavey had his own press – The Europa Press, and he had published the first translation of Eluard in a limited edition with a frontispiece by Picasso, and a cover design by Max Ernst.

It was George Reavey who was asked by the organisers to stage a small poetry reading and he brought in Eluard and also asked Dylan Thomas to read with him.

Dylan appears to have been at the opening where he witnessed Salvador Dali delivering a lecture whist encapsulated inside a deep-sea diving suit, – including the heavy brass helmet, which got jammed and Gascoyne and Penrose had to use a wrench to free the artist before he was asphyxiated. Dylan could not resist getting into the spirit of the occasion and devised his own impromptu *art happening*, by crawling around the floor of the exhibition rooms tugging at legs of random visitors and proffering a cup of boiled string, while asking whether the bemused victim wanted it 'weak or strong'.

There is an uncorroborated story that Dylan went home that night with Shelia Legge, who had taken up a place in Trafalgar Square on the day of the opening in a white gown but with her head and face covered in red roses – another early example of performance art.

So, Although Dylan was at pains to distance himself from Surrealist attitudes to poetic composition he did read and contribute to some of the major Surrealist magazines, most notably Eugene Jolas' French based journal *Transition*. As early as 1934, Dylan was writing to Glyn Jones of, 'Some poets, like Gertrude Stein and the French-American Transitionists of Eugene Jolas...' Max Ernst's work was in almost every early number of *Transition* and his paintings were also reproduced in Connolly's Horizon. So, Dylan would have been well aware of Ernst's work. Dylan only contributed to one issue of *Transition* but as Dougald McMillan observes in his history of the magazine; His [Dylan's] respect for the magazine may be seen in the fact that he did send them *Then was my Neophyte*, the poem he thought of as his best work, and *The Mouse and the Woman*, the story that had occupied him longer than any of his prose pieces up until this time.'

Jolas obviously wanted more from him because a year later Dylan writes to Vernon Watkins about having been asked by Jolas;

> ...for a description of my most recent Trauma, with if possible, ancestral symbols, for 'Transition'

Max Ernst had some of his work in this exhibition but did not come over until a year later when Roland brought Max to

My copy of the exhibition issue of the *International Surrealist Bulletin*, with Rose-headed lady on the cover

England from Paris for his exhibition at the Mayor Gallery. We also know that Dylan watched and admired Luis Bunuel's and Salvador Dali's 1928 famous surrealist film *Un Chien Andalou.*[5] The film's famous image of an eye being razored seems to have entered Dylan's poem *'I in my Intricate Image'*, where he writes of;

Death Instrumental, Splitting the long eye open...

It is also likely then that Dylan watched Bunuel's second film *'L'age d'or'* made in 1928, in which Max Ernst plays a significant and striking role onscreen.

As mentioned, in England, Surrealism was expounded through the pages of Roger Roughton's magazine *Contemporary Poetry and Prose.* Dylan spent some time hanging out with Roughton and other Surrealists at David Archer's bookshop in Parton Street [the co-publishers of Dylan's first book *18 Poems* in 1934]. Opposite the bookshop was *The Arts Café*, from where Roughton compiled *'Contemporary Poetry and Prose'*. Dylan contributed four poems and three stories to the magazines short ten issue run. Ernst himself was not a contributor, but the 1936, *Double Surrealist Number*, issued to coincide with the exhibition at the Burlington galleries it did include Paul Eluard's poem, *Max Ernst.* Dylan met most of the leading British Surrealists such as David Gascoyne and Julian Trevelyan at *The Arts Café*, and it is not unlikely that Ernst and Penrose were sometimes around. Indeed, it had been the chance encounter in 1935 of Roland Penrose with David Gascoyne, who was strolling along the Rue de Tournon with Paul Eluard, that sparked the British awakening to Surrealism. As Roland recalled,

> We got talking, and he said to me 'It is extraordinary, but in London they don't seem to know anything about the excitement here in Paris – why is that? Let's do something about it'. 'So, I said 'Let's do something about it indeed'.

In London Dylan Thomas had also met and became friendly with the young David Gascoyne, and it was Gascoyne who took Dylan to a party at the home of the one of the few women surrealist artists, Eileen Agar, which eventually led to her painting a wonderful surrealist portrait of Dylan She describes the events in her 1988 autobiography *A Look at My Life*;

> It must have been around this time, 1933 or 1934 ...when in walked two delightfully refreshing youngsters. Both were poets: one was a shy sensitive plant, the other a ruddy-faced cherub with a snub nose and no chin...Dylan squatted on the floor with and in a jiffy was reciting limericks... then we greeted his companion, David Gascoyne who had brought Dylan along... While Dylan was deep in a flow of bawdy nonsense ...I managed to grab a pencil and paper and did some lightening drawings of this ugly suckling...Later on I worked from one of the drawings on a painting which was bought by the National Portrait Gallery in 1962.

However, even after all Dylan's prevarications with Surrealism, when Dylan's first serious critic, Henry Treece, a poet and writer who was a leading light in the New Apocalyptic movement, was writing the first critical book to be published on Dylan Thomas' work, which came out with the subtitle *Dog among the Fairies,* he sought to depict Thomas as a surrealist. Dylan responded, with even more conviction. Writing to him in March 1938 he declares that;

...the comparison [of my work] with the Surrealists should give you a lot of scope, especially if, as I'm sure you do, you think it little more than a highbrow parlour game. I haven't, by the way, ever read a proper Surrealist poem.

I had always assumed that Dylan had met Max through his friendship with Roland Penrose. Dylan met Penrose at the 1936 Surrealist Exhibition at the Burlington Galleries in London. Roland was one of the main organisers of this seminal event that introduced Surrealism to Britain.

In 1937 Roland was to meet and co-habit with the American photographer Lee Miller. They did not marry until 1947, the year that she was commissioned by American *Vogue* magazine to photograph Dylan Thomas. She took a wonderful series of photographs of Dylan, one of which was published when Vogue ran Dylan's radio piece, *Holiday Memory,* shown overleaf.

Curiously, the image *Vogue* used is not on this contact sheet. It is similar to the two images on the top right in which Dylan is rocked back in his chair, but the published image has him turning his head towards the camera. The image is printed large in the magazine, filling the whole page opposite the text. This feature was used in the American edition only and the magazines opening credits; Vogue's Eye View, this a jaunty note appears;

> DYLAN THOMAS. The author of the piece on page 37 is, at thirty-three one of the brilliant present-day British poets, a mainstay of BBC' "Third Programme"(and you'll find out more about *that* on page 40). He is short, brown haired, crumpled, Welsh...his strange gift is a wide-eyeing memory. He is married to the daughter of Francis Macnamara, the Irish poet and philosopher, and has two young children.

This is the only time have I seen Dylan's Irish father-in-law mentioned, and the next article did indeed big-up the BBC Third Programme. It was written by Eizabeth Bowen under the headline: *Britain's Wave-Length For Intellectuals.*

This day-long photo-shoot in the basement of London's *Vogue* offices occurred just a few months after Lee and Roland had returned from their visit with Max and Dorothea in Sedona. Lee took many great photographs of Max and Dorothea in their desert hideaway and she and Roland accompanied the painters to a nearby reservation to watch a Hopi rain dance which the dancers performed holding live rattlesnakes; experiences she could well have shared with Dylan during the photo-session.

One final episode involving Dylan with Roland and Lee occurred in 1951, just four days before Dylan left for his first reading tour of America. Roland Penrose had translated Picasso's only play *Desire Caught by the Tail*, based on his war time experiences in Nazi occupied Paris. It had been given several clandestine readings during the Occupation of Paris with a cast drawn from Picasso's literary friends such as Sartre, Camus, Simone de Beauvoir and Raymond Queneau. It was to be given a reading at the ICA on February 16th 1950. The evening consisted of a double bill. The first play was a dramatisation of Blake's '*An Island of the Moon*'. The programme tells us that Dylan played 'Obtuse Angle, the mathematician'. For the Picasso play Dylan is described in the programme as 'Stage Manager' but this is misleading for in this play the stage manager stands stage left and reads the stage directions throughout the play, and although the programme states that Randall Swingler was to play '*The Onion*' Roland recollects that Dylan took this role as well. The whole evening was recorded in a well-illustrated double-page spread in the March issue of '*Picture Post*', with pictures of Dylan in performance and Lee and Roland

Picture Post, 4 March, 1950

Dylan Thomas Acts as the Stage Manager Who Gives the Clues

e had the task of informing the audience of such imagined stage props as ". . . an immense ıth-tub full of soap suds. . . . After a piece for violin from 'La Tosca,' from the bottom of the ıth-tub rise the heads of 'Big Foot,' 'The Onion,' 'The Tart,' 'Her Cousin,' 'Round Piece,' he Two Bow-Wows,' 'Silence,' 'Fat Anxiety,' 'Thin Anxiety,' 'The Curtains.'" And the same ene closes with ". . . the bathers come out of the tub. 'The Tart' alone gets out stark naked. cept for her stockings. They bring in baskets of food, bottles of wine. . . . In come some underkers with coffins, into which they dump everybody, nail them down and carry them off

DESIRE CAUGHT BY THE TAIL'

Lee Miller's contact sheet for her 1947 Vogue shoot with Dylan Thomas

The Programme for the play

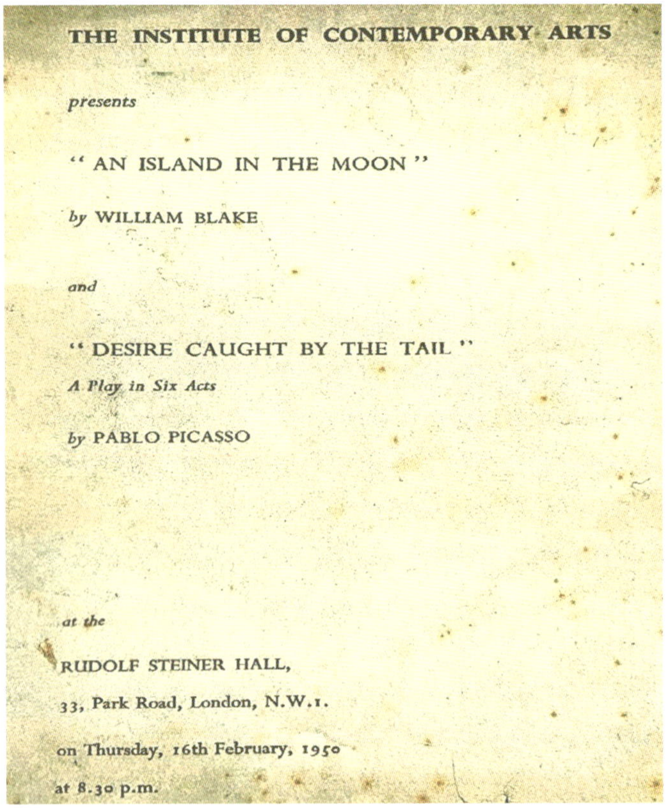
THE INSTITUTE OF CONTEMPORARY ARTS

presents

" AN ISLAND IN THE MOON "

by WILLIAM BLAKE

and

" DESIRE CAUGHT BY THE TAIL "

A Play in Six Acts

by PABLO PICASSO

at the

RUDOLF STEINER HALL,

33, Park Road, London, N.W.1.

on Thursday, 16th February, 1950

at 8.30 p.m.

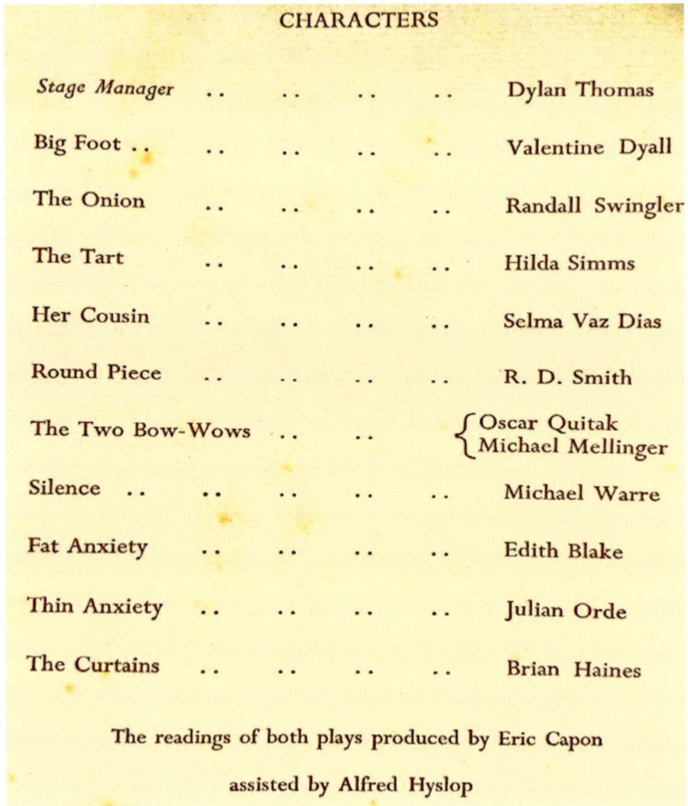
CHARACTERS

Stage Manager	Dylan Thomas
Big Foot	Valentine Dyall
The Onion	Randall Swingler
The Tart	Hilda Simms
Her Cousin	Selma Vaz Dias
Round Piece	R. D. Smith
The Two Bow-Wows	Oscar Quitak Michael Mellinger
Silence	Michael Warre
Fat Anxiety	Edith Blake
Thin Anxiety	Julian Orde
The Curtains	Brian Haines

The readings of both plays produced by Eric Capon

assisted by Alfred Hyslop

mingling with the audience. That Dylan was keen to participate is revealed in a letter he wrote to Caitlin sent two days before the performance;

> Here is 10 pounds. Will you please, my love, collect my suit from cleaners And send it *at once* to the above address. Then I can be in Picasso play.

Dylan Thomas also got involved with a curious mainstream Hollywood romantic drama; *Pandora and the Flying Dutchman,*[5] which had strong surrealist connections. The director of the film was an American, Albert Lewin, who Dylan knew and Albert was also a friend of Lee and Roland's, and visited them at their home, Farley Farm when Max Ernst was also there.

However, in spite of all of this, I was still unsure how Dylan and Caitlin had been invited to the Ernst's Sedona desert hideaway. Dylan's latest biographer, Andrew Lycett had written to the aging Dorothea Tanning, who wrote back that Max had never met Dylan before the Sedona visit. He goes on to suggest that it was Dylan's unofficial American editor and promoter, the New York poet Oscar Williams and his wife, the painter Gene Derwood, who, being good friends with Dorothea Tanning, put Dylan in touch with the Ernsts. A card sent from Sedona in March 1952 would seem to support this. It is written in Dylan's hand and just says,

> *Wild and Western Love to Gene and Oscar from–*

And then all four, 'Max Ernst, Dorothea, Dylan and Caitlin', sign it.

Whatever the truth Dylan and Caitlin left New York for San Francisco and Vancouver on March 17th 1952. This was during the second of Thomas's reading tours and the first and only time that Caitlin accompanied him. Although unplanned Dylan and Caitlin were destined to stay for a couple of weeks with Max Ernst and Dorothea Tanning in their spectacular desert hideaway.

Dylan Thomas and his friend, Oscar Williams in May 1953 on New York's Fifth Avenue.
Mr. Williams has dedicated THE POCKET BOOK OF MODERN VERSE, just published by Pocket Books Inc., "to the memory of Dylan Thomas, 1914-1953, Major Poet, Great Man and Immortal Soul." The anthology contains 28 pages of the poetry of Mr. Thomas, including the last four great poems he wrote just before his death.

1. Max Ernst(1891–1976) is one of my favourite Surrealist artists. He was a German (naturalised American in 1948 and French in 1958); a painter, sculptor, printmaker, graphic artist collagist. He was a prolific artist, Ernst was a primary pioneer of the Dada and Surrealist movement. He lived a long and rich life which he shared with three very interesting wives.

2. The painting is entitled *The First Clear Word*. It was painted in 1923 during his first French period. The painting was actually part of a series of murals in the house of the surrealist poet Paul Éluard (1895-1952) in Eaubonne, a few kilometres north of Paris. It was rediscovered in 1967 under layers of old paint and wallpaper. The title comes from one of Éluard's poems (each line is followed by a possible translation in parentheses): *Au premier mot limpide* = (*At the first clear word*). It was later used as an exhibition poster at the Guggenheim.

3. Wyn Thomas suggested that we collaborate on a book about Dylan Thomas' favourite pubs and bars. He made fine watercolour illustrations drawings of all the licenced establishments that I wrote about in *Dylan Thomas The Pubs*. Y lolfa. 2013.

4. George Reavey (1907–1976) was a Russian-born Irish whose poetry leant towards Surrealism. He was also a publisher, translator and art collector; and he was Samuel Beckett's first literary agent.
I have also written more about this interesting movie at the end of Chapter 8. Dylan was an extra on the film when they filmed it on the vast, flat beach at Pendine, the next beach west of Laugharne

5. This film is also discussed in Chapter 8.

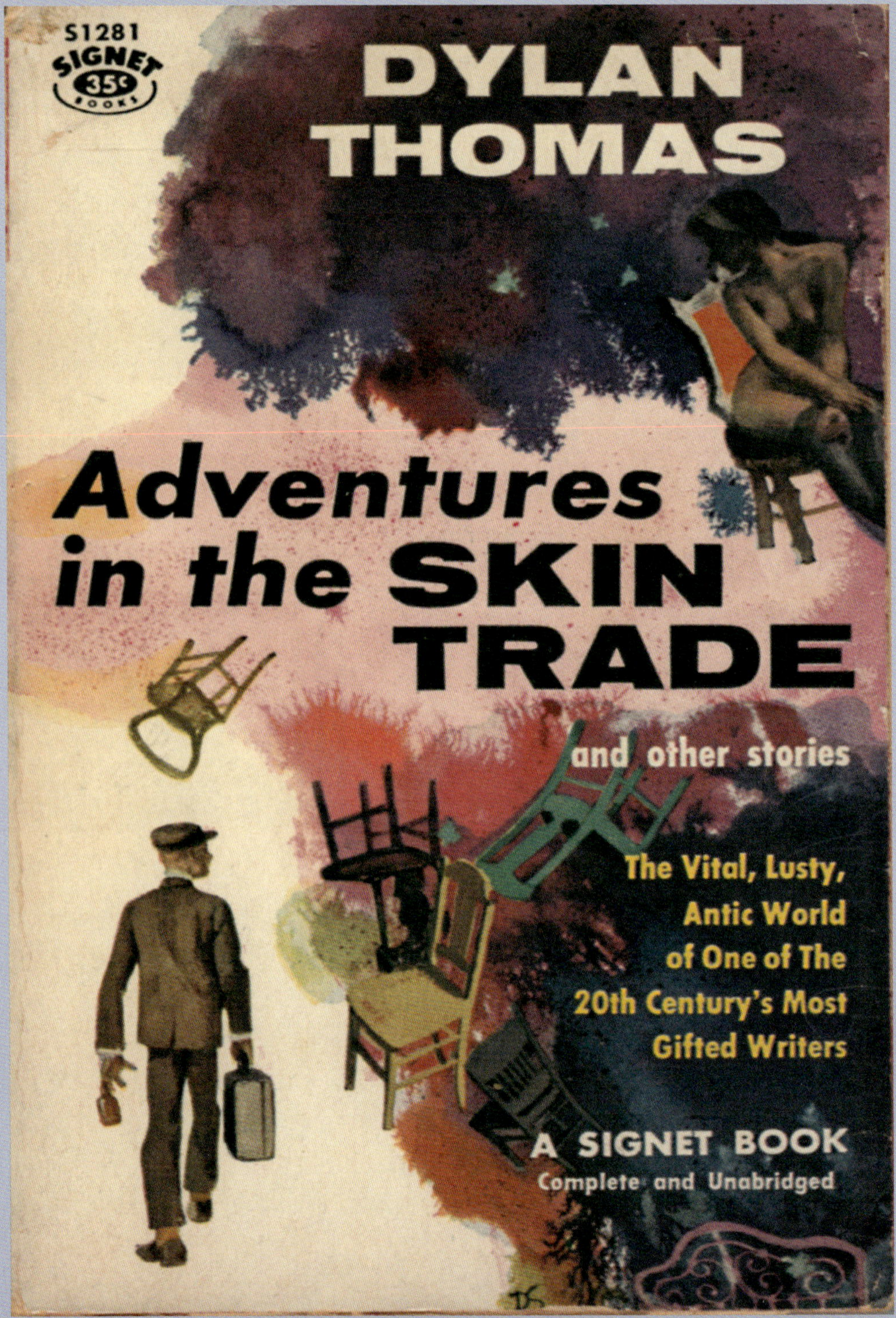

The 1956 pulp paperback edition of *Adventures in the Skin Trade* with the naked lady on the cover that Dylan wished for...

5.
Dylan Thomas & Hermaphroditism.

If a Hermaphrodite were a Schizophrenic,
which half would you take?
Dylan Thomas speaking in America

In 2013 I was asked by a curious long-running American online literary magazine, called *Ralph*, to contribute a long-form article for their 2014 Dylan Thomas Centenary tribute issue. I had free rein to write about any related topic and I decided to examine in detail Dylan's mild, but curious obsession with the word *Hermaphrodite*.[1] The editor seemed keen and sent his approval. I wrote the piece and transferred it to them to publish, which they did, but then it seems *Ralph* closed down, and it can no longer be found on the web. So here is the piece pretty much unchanged from the now disappeared, online version.

Dylan Thomas and Hermaphroditism

> If a Hermaphrodite were a Schizophrenic, which half would you take?
>
> Dylan Thomas' *joke*, often delivered in his introductions to poetry readings in America.

Dylan Thomas's was a practised and self-conscious bohemianism. Both his parents were first-language Welsh-speaking, country-folk from chapel-going families, who had only recently moved into the town of Swansea. There were no proclivities towards excess and debauchery, nor any traces of Absinthe or Hashish coursing through the veins of the boy who entered the world in the front bedroom of the brand new, suburban semi-detached house at number 5 Cwmdonkin Drive, Swansea, on October 27th 1914. Dylan would later offer us this self-portrait from his 1947 radio play, *Return Journey to Swansea*.[2]

> He worked on the Post and used to wear an overcoat, sometimes with the check lining inside out so that you could play giant draughts on him. He wore a conscious woodbine too... He'd be about seventeen or eighteen... and above medium height. Above medium height for Wales, I mean. Thick blubber lips; snub nose; curly mouse brown hair; one front tooth broken... speaks rather fancy; truculent; plausible; a bit of a shower-off; plus fours and no breakfast, you know... a bombastic adolescent provincial bohemian with a thick-knotted artist's tie made out of his sister's scarf – she never knew where it had gone – and a cricket shirt dyed bottle-green; a gabbing, ambitious, mock-tough, pretentious young man; and mole-y too.

Another passage from *Return Journey* describes what he and his close boyhood friends, all painters, musicians and would-be writers and poets, discussed in their favourite meeting place, Swansea's *Kardomah* Cafe;

> ...Music and poetry and painting and politics. Einstein and Epstein, Stravinsky and Greta Garbo, death and religion, Picasso and girls... Communism, symbolism, Bradman, Braque, the Watch Committee, free love, free beer, murder, Michelangelo, ping pong, ambition, Sibelius and girls... Oh, the hissing of the butt- ends in the drains of the coffee-dashes and the tinkle of the gibble-gabble of the morning young lounge lizards as they talked about Augustus John, Emil Jannings, Carnera, Dracula, Amy Johnson, trial marriage,

> pocket money, the Welsh sea, London stars, King Kong, anarchy, darts, T. S. Eliot and girls...

It is a pretty heady mix and it seemed to lead him into youthful excess, but as yet, there is no mention of Hermaphrodites. It is hard to decide whether this Swansea 'no-good boyo' had a regular boyish interest in sex or whether it spilled over into the 'unhealthy' and obsessional. The foremost and most prolific modern critic of Dylan Thomas writings, John Goodby, is prompted by aspects of them to declare;

> The hermaphrodite qualities of the embryo, like that 'polymorphous perversity' of desire that Freud attributed to the infant, are taken by Thomas to apply to the human condition generally.

Thankfully he then simplifies things by quoting Andrew Lycett, Dylan's most recent biographer, who refers to it as;

> ***Thomas's fascination with Hermaphroditism.***

> *THE TERM:*
>
> *HERMAPHRODITE: A person or animal or a plant having both male and female sex organs and other sexual characteristics, either abnormally or (in the case of some organisms) as the natural condition.*
>
> *HERMAPHRODITUS: The two-sexed child of Aphrodite and Hermes (Venus and Mercury) had long been a symbol of androgyny or effeminacy, and was portrayed in Greco-Roman art as a female figure with male genitals. Hermaphroditus's name is derived from those of his parents Hermes and Aphrodite. All three of these gods figure prominently among erotic and fertility figures and all possess distinctly sexual overtones. Sometimes, Hermaphroditus is referred to as Aphroditus.*

So where did Dylan's interest come from? The word first appears in his work as early as March of 1931, when he was just 16, and he wrote a poem into his second notebook (it is now in New York State University at Buffalo). This poem[3]. includes the word in its opening line:

You be my hermaphrodite in logic,
My avocado temptress out of magic –
For who can keep illusions up
Before such honest chemistry
As turns love like a ring
From tip to cavity –
And when, in tune with me,
You're lost to sense,
With what coincidence
I'll rip your kiss from me,
And force you to a different sex.
The change will do my conscience good,
Before it blunts my tongue
And hurts whatever knows the joy
Of such cerebral sodomy.
There's truth in every word, there's gaiety,
To germinate in each chaotic move
Beyond the region of the mouth,
There's truth for the voluptuary
Inside satiety, or out of hate.
How is the cynic cancerized.
He cannot laugh with me at me;
He laughs from him at me;
We laugh at him with words and blood
Or paint and wood,
Safe in our wise orgasm,
Mind after body to endeavour.

This is quite a precocious and remarkable use of a somewhat arcane word for a 16-year-old to use but he goes on to include, 'cerebral sodomy', 'different sex', and he ends this poem with;

> Safe in our wise orgasm
> Mind after body to endeavour

So he includes a few other unusual sexual terms that would not have been familiar to most of his contemporary school-mates for sure. Dylan does seem to be very aware of sex and gender issues at a very young age. A few years after writing this poem, Dylan began to send off his poems and stories to various magazines and newspapers for publication. He got his best responses from a national weekend newspaper, *The Sunday Referee*, which featured a weekly *Poets Corner* column edited by a curious cove, Victor Neuberg, who would become Dylan's literary god-father. Neuberg was an eccentric bisexual who had previously indulged in homosexual magic with the notorious

Aleister Crowley, (who was christened *The Great Beast* by the popular press of the day.) Neuberg published many of Dylan's early poems and eventually was responsible for the publication of Dylan's first ground-breaking collection, *18 Poems* in 1934. It was through this newspaper column in 1933 that Dylan first encountered Pamela Hansford Johnson, who was also sending poems to *The Referee*. Dylan reveals more about his somewhat confused, youthful attitudes to sex in his long epistolary courtship of Pamela Hansford Johnson, who would become his first serious girlfriend. She lived in London with her mother and went on to be a successful novelist and she eventually married C. P. Snow. Writing to her before they actually met, Dylan describes himself in one letter as being;

> ...small, chinless, and like an emasculate Eton boy.

In another he suggests he is not dogmatic about his own masculine sexual identity describing himself as:

> 'Sex– male, I think'.

In his second letter to her, sent around September 17 1933, he included two poems one of which was the poem *The Woman Speaks*. He explains that the poem;

> ...is, though complete in itself from an ...unfinished play. I think this needs mention; references in the poem would otherwise cast aspersions on the nature of my sex...
>
> P.S. The Woman poem is to be published in the *Adelphi*

This worry about his sexual orientation was indeed the case when, after the publication of the *Woman Speaks*, in Adelphi in March 1934, Dylan received an unsolicited fan letter from the Cardiff poet and novelist Glyn Jones,[4] who was a schoolmaster when he read Dylans poem. Dylan's reply indicates that Jones was obviously confused as to the gender of the writer, Dylan answers;

> Thank you for your appreciation of my *two* poems in the *Adelphi*.
>
> The 'Woman Speaks' but the young man writes, and your doubt as to my sex was quite complimentary, proving (or was it merely my uncommon name) that I do not employ too masculine a pen.

In the just published new biography[5] of Dylan Thomas by two long-standing, modernist critics, who both teach at Sheffield Hallam University, Messrs Goodby and Wiggington have this to say about Dylan's reaction to this gender confusion, concluding that it is;

> ... an indication of his interest in hermaphroditism and gender-switching that feature in his work.

Another long letter to Pamela(they were landing on her mat thick-and-fast)contains a paragraph headed The Arty Party, in which Dylan responds to Pamela's description of a London literary gathering with a blistering and scatological rant;

> The type of party you describe – and you describe it very well indeed – is a menace to art...but still they flourish, still do seedy things in their mothers' pyjamas... Neuter men and lady tenors rub shoulders with 'the shams and shamans, the amateur hobo and homo of Bloomsbury W.C.1.' whiles their Hostess, clad in scarlet corduroy, drinks to their health in methylated spirits. With a smattering of often incorrectly memorised encyclopaedia learning...with their men's breasts shaped with the aid of wadding, the young women speak on Sodom hipped young men, with the inevitable side-whiskers and cigarettes, the faulty livers and the stained teeth, reading Lawrence as an aphrodisiac and Marie Corelli in their infrequent baths, spew into paper cups and canvas their ignorance and perversions, wetting the bed of their brains with discharges of fungoid verse.

Is this the young Dylan trying yet again writing to impress with his gender-bending descriptions of the partygoers? Or are these his firmly held views – I tend to think the former. But Hermaphrodites stayed in his mind

In 1936, two years after his arrival in London, Dylan's second collection of poetry, *Twenty-Five Poems*, was published by a major London Publishing house, J.M. Dent. It contained the poem *Then was my Neophyte*, which was Thomas's favourite poem in the collection.[6]

The poem contains the only use of the word hermaphrodite in one of his published poems; it appears in the first stanza.

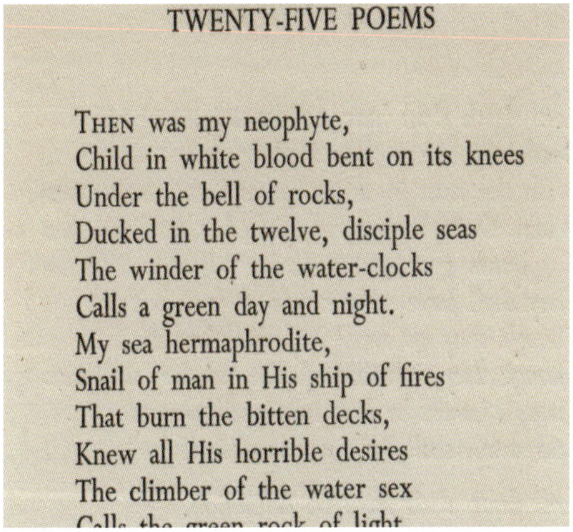
TWENTY-FIVE POEMS

THEN was my neophyte,
Child in white blood bent on its knees
Under the bell of rocks,
Ducked in the twelve, disciple seas
The winder of the water-clocks
Calls a green day and night.
My sea hermaphrodite,
Snail of man in His ship of fires
That burn the bitten decks,
Knew all His horrible desires
The climber of the water sex
Calls the green rock of light

Professor John Goodby, the Swansea-based academic who edited the most recent and certainly the most annotated edition of Thomas's poems glosses the line thus:

> sea hermaphrodite = the embryo is initially genderless;
>
> A hermaphrodite brig is a ship carrying two kinds of sail.

And he comments on the next line

> Snail of man = snails are hermaphroditic; ship of fires = the body consumed by passion.

I am happy to believe that Dylan was aware of the snail's complicated sexuality, however, even though Swansea had a thriving international sea-port, where Dylan loved to go slumming around the wilder dock-side pubs, I'm not sure he would have been up on such nautical minutiae concerning brig-rigging. I think he just loved using the word – for its sound and its curious and bizarre connotations.[7]

The 'word' turns up again a year later in his prose fragment *Prologue to an Adventure* – a draft of the opening passage of his only attempt at a novel. This Surrealist recasting of *The Pilgrim's Progress* only in reverse, ostensibly describing a young man's road to perdition, was first published as the leading item – with the title and first few words appearing on the cover of the first issue of Keidrych Rhys's modernist Welsh based literary magazine *WALES*[8] in the summer of 1937.

The extract is a riot of bizarre sexual references, as the two protagonists, Daniel and Dom, wended their way through a bizarre and nightmare urban landscape:

> I jostled the devil at my elbow but lust in his city shadows dogged me under the arches down the black blind streets. Now in the shape of a bald girl smiling, a wailing wanton with Handcuffs for earrings, or the lean girls that lived on pickings, now in the ragged woman with a muckrake curtsying in the slime, the tempter of angels whispered over my shoulder, We shall be naked but for garters and black stockings, loving you long on a bed of strawberries and cream, and the nakeder for a ribbon that hides the nipples...There is more than man's meaning in a stuffed man talking, split from naval to arsehole, and more in the horned ladies at your heels than a pinch of the cloven delights and the tang of sulphur.

The two travel on, their journey taking them through alleys and lanes, variously named '*Damaroid Alley*' (Damaroid were an early over the sleazy counter quack sex-aid drug; '*Pessary Court*', a Pessary is a medical device inserted into the vagina as a contraceptive procedure; and '*Gamarouche Mews*', (Gamarouche–an arcane word for cunnilingus or fellatio). Quite a sexually exciting route!

On their way they pass; 'Lucifer in a woman's shirt pissing from a window', 'the bishop of Bumdom, dressed like a ratcatcher', 'two weasels coupling on All Paul's alter', 'a Jew girl crucified to the bedposts', and eventually they are accosted by 'A negress' who,

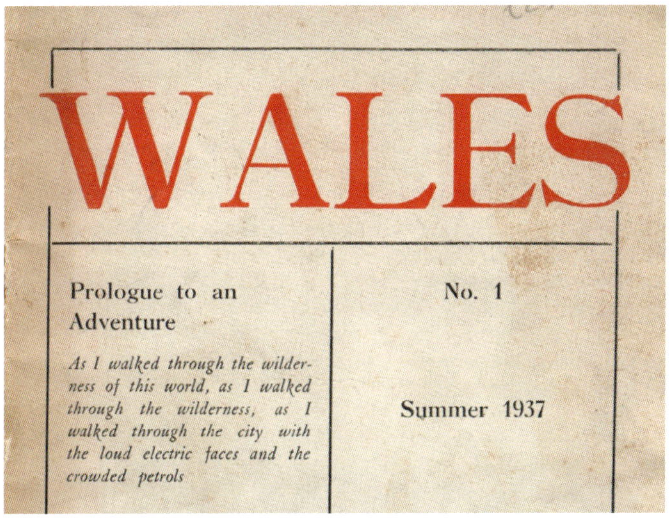
WALES

Prologue to an Adventure

As I walked through the wilderness of this world, as I walked through the wilderness, as I walked through the city with the loud electric faces and the crowded petrols

No. 1

Summer 1937

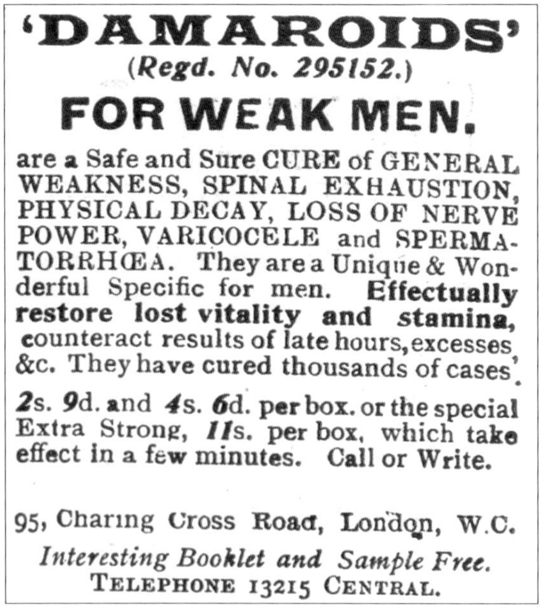

> loosened the straps of her yellow frock and bared a breast, holding a plate under the black flesh. Buy a pound, she said, and thrust her breast in Daniel's face.

The 'H' word is then deployed again when they arrive at a nightclub named *The Deadly Virtues*, where a kind of orgy ensues and Daniel ends up lamenting, with his 'hair-on-end', and here the androgynous creatures smell of hell too;

> There can be no armistice for the sexless singers and the sulphurous hermaphrodites, the flying beast and the walking bird that war about us, for the horn and the wing. I could light the voices of the fiery virgins winking in my glass, catch the brandy-brown beast and bird as they fumed before my eyes, and kiss the two-antlered angel.

The passage comes to a drug fuelled climax,

> No, not for nothing were these two intangible brandymaids neighbouring Daniel who cried, syringe in hand, Open your coke-white legs, you ladies of needles, Dom thunder Daniel is the lightening drug and doctor.

This is Dylan Thomas in fully extended, bravura, verbal flight, and this piece was aptly reprinted by Henry Miller's publishers, the *Obelisk Press* of Paris, which Thomas's biographer, Paul Ferris, describes as a Press that;

> 'specialised in erotica and avant-garde novels, (often the same thing) that weren't acceptable in London').

It appeared in the Christmas 1938 issue of the short-lived periodical, Delta, that Henry Miller edited. Dylan Thomas' only attempt at a novel – *Adventures in the Skin Trade*,[9] which he never finished, has a section in a similar vein, in which he does not use the *H* word, but it does have elements of louche sex and bizarre behaviour. Thomas described it to his friend Vernon Watkins in 1941;

> My novel blazes on. It's a mixture of Oliver Twist, Little Dorrit, Kafka, Beachcomber and good old 3-adjectives a penny belly-churning Thomas, the Rimbaud of Cwmdonkin Drive.

It is interesting to note that in the same letter Dylan takes a pop at an American Writer and translator Frederic Prokosch.[10] In an earlier letter, in 1939, to John Davenport, Dylan informs him he written a parody of Prokosch's poem *The Dolls* from his first collection *The Assassins* (1936). Dylan re-titled it as *The Molls*. In his somewhat saccharine poem, Prokosch writes at his musical best of the sweet, crescent-eyed shapes that, reaching into the poet's "secret night," become the "furies" of his sleep. Not to Dylan's taste; so he offers this cross-dressing version which would not be out of place on the pages of his novel;

> *The Molls*
> I found them lying on the Floor,
> Male shapes, girl-lipped, but clad like boys
> Night after night their hands implore
> Emetic Percies for their joys
>
> Gently they sigh to my behind
> Wilde words, all buttered, badly bred,
> And when I dream of them I find
> Peacockstein poems on my bed

Thomas's American publishers described *Adventures in the Skin Trade* thus;

Adventures is the story, written in a shrewd, sly, deadpan vein of picaresque comedy, of young Samuel Bennet, who runs away from his home in Wales to seek his fortune in London. These adventures see him enduring an embarrassing first sexual experience in a cold bath, before going off meandering through low-life London all the while with a beer bottle stuck on his little finger! His new found 'friends' take him out drinking and they go into two pubs or drinking clubs. The first is a pub called *The Antelope*, where their conversation turns to;

Sex, said Mr Allingham
Sex, sex, sex, it's always sex with you, Donald.
You must be repressed or something
Sex, whispered the young woman by the fire
ex is all right Mrs Dacy said You leave sex alone

Their next port of call? The Gayspot! Dylan's regular publishers, J.M.Dent, were not enamoured of the book as this reader's report makes clear so the book was eventually published by Putnam in 1955 with an introduction by Vernon Watkins.

Dylan Thomas's recent biographer, Andrew Lycett in his *Dylan Thomas: A New Life*[11] draws attention to Dylan's obsession with hemaphroditism and offers us yet another clue when he writes of Dylan's work in the film business when he joined Strand Films as a script-writer in the early 1940's, when he worked mainly with his work-colleague, the writer and somewhat eccentric but very companionable drinker, Julian Maclaren-Ross;

Apart from drinking they shared a passion for art-house cinema classics. They dreamt of producing a film called *The Whispering Gallery* or *The Distorting Mirror* in the style of *The Cabinet of Dr Caligari*. Dylan suggested a plot... involving fairgrounds and stately homes. When they were unable to decide whether the villain should be male or female, Dylan suggested the character should be both – or should have a sex change halfway through. (Dylan's fascination with hermaphroditism may have come from his father-in-law Francis Macnamara who had retired to his sick bed, convinced he was both male and female).

Prologue to an Adventure appears to be the last time Dylan uses the

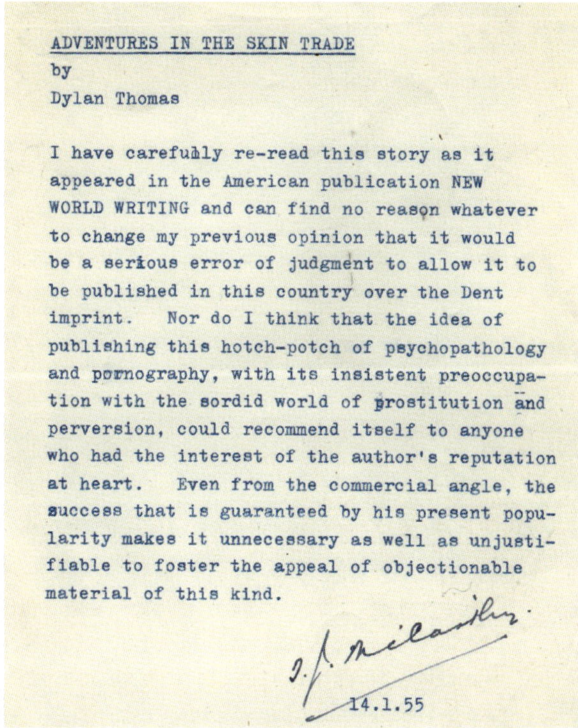
ADVENTURES IN THE SKIN TRADE
by
Dylan Thomas

I have carefully re-read this story as it appeared in the American publication NEW WORLD WRITING and can find no reason whatever to change my previous opinion that it would be a serious error of judgment to allow it to be published in this country over the Dent imprint. Nor do I think that the idea of publishing this hotch-potch of psychopathology and pornography, with its insistent preoccupation with the sordid world of prostitution and perversion, could recommend itself to anyone who had the interest of the author's reputation at heart. Even from the commercial angle, the success that is guaranteed by his present popularity makes it unnecessary as well as unjustifiable to foster the appeal of objectionable material of this kind.

14.1.55

The damning opinions of a J.M.Dent's publisher's reader on Dylan's would-be-novel

word hermaphrodite in print, however, it remains in his vocabulary and becomes more of a rhetorical tool. In the early fifties, when Dylan began to embark on reading tours of America, the word hermaphrodite would litter his reported speeches. In one of his facetious introductions to his American readings at Massachusetts Brandeis University, in the spring of 1950, he ended with this explanation of why he hoped no one would ask questions:

I'd like to be able to answer anybody's question fluently, but always as soon as I try to start, as soon as gauchely and inarticulately I bog, bury, and bitch myself in a sentence which can never, I know, come to an end, such as the sentence I am now bogged in, I find myself thinking of certain other subjects, all almost as interesting as the subject supposedly under discussion. You know the sort of subject that comes into one's head when one's asked these odd questions, subjects such as: '*Rilke and the Gold Standard*,' or '*Charles Morgan, My Favourite Character in Fiction*', or even the very awful thing that occurs to one occasionally;

If a Hermaphrodite were a Schizophrenic, which half would you take?

I once owned an eleven-page manuscript (now in The National Library of Wales), written in Dylan's neatest and best hand. It was his frequently used prompt notes for use at any such event and it included the 'schizophrenic hermaphrodite' joke, so many audiences at his prolific readings across the States were asked to ponder that strange choice.

John Malcolm Brinnin in his 1956 book *Dylan Thomas in America* reports the following incident, (with some censorship, as befitted the time);

In California [Dylan] had suffered through an intolerably long and dull dinner party with a group of male professors. When cigars were passed around, Dylan, refusing to sink into the general stupor, addressed the company:

Gentlemen, I wish we were all hermaphrodites!

'Why?' said one of the professors politely, 'Why do you wish that Mr Thomas?

Dylan roars;

Because, Gentlemen, then we could all ** ourselves!**

Only one word fits the asterisks with any sense in Dylan's scandalous riposte and it provided a powerful cinematic moment when the Welsh actor Celyn Jones, playing Dylan Thomas, against Elijah Wood's Brinnin, in the 2014 biopic, *Set Fire to the Stars*.[12] The film version was far less constrained by respectability and Celyn delivered the line in full, with huge and powerful gusto;

Because, Gentlemen, then we could all FUCK ourselves!

To conclude – it seems to me to be very difficult to decide whether all this amounts to an extreme outpouring of what Goodby describes as;

...ghastly gothic anti-blazon of skin, eyes, teeth, ribs, bone, hair, blood, brain, nerves, womb, cock, nails, breast, heart,

The Poster for the movie

'manseed', sweat and other bodily fluids. That was ...central to Thomas's Welsh gothic -grotesque modernism...

Or is it closer to what the Welsh critic (and editor of the Welsh periodical *Planet*), John Barnie, describes thus;

All [Thomas's] ...stuff about sex and death and so on, was part of growing up in a world where sex was a taboo subject. It seemed daring to refer to it obliquely in modernist or symbolist imagery. But it's really the worst kind of provincialism masquerading as international modernism.

Dylan Thomas's major biographer, Paul Ferris, who also wrote a biography of Dylan's wife Caitlin, but more importantly, edited the monumental edition of Thomas's correspondence, has this to say in his introduction to the enlarged second edition:

Sexual themes and statements abound, the strident sexual imagery of the earlier poems has always been evident; he liked to dwell on the biological machinery and this taste spread over into his letters...Thomas was more honest than most in making no secret of the fact that he had a dirty mind. The letters offer evidence of what he thought not what he did. Hints and winks suggest an improbable sexual boldness.

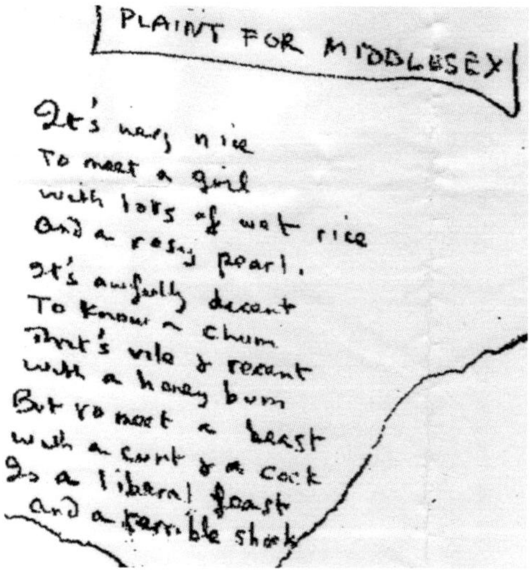
PLAINT FOR MIDDLESEX

It's very nice
To meet a girl
With lots of wet rice
And a rosy pearl.
It's awfully decent
To know a chum
That's vile & recent
With a honey bum
But to meet a beast
With a cunt & a cock
Is a liberal feast
And a terrible shock

Dylan's hand-written poem

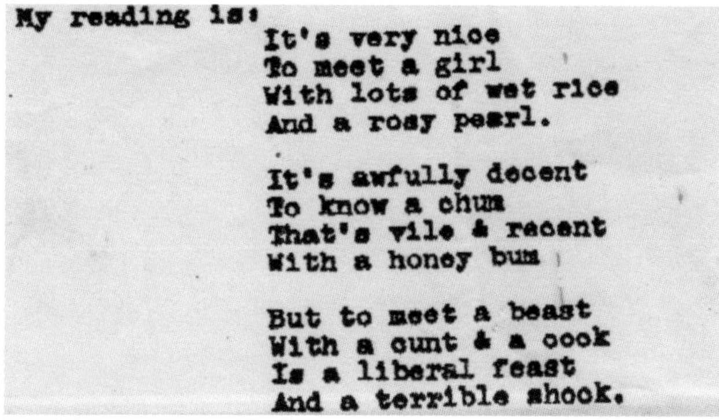
My reading is:
It's very nice
To meet a girl
With lots of wet rice
And a rosy pearl.

It's awfully decent
To know a chum
That's vile & recent
With a honey bum

But to meet a beast
With a cunt & a cook
Is a liberal feast
And a terrible shook.

Brinnin's transcription of Dylan's poem

I think we should let Dylan have the last words. It was from between the pages of a book held in the *John Malcolm Brinnin Papers* in Delaware University that this scrap of paper, bearing this little dirty poem by Dylan, fluttered to the floor...
Dylan appears to have pre-empted Jeffrey Eugenides epic novel[13] of 2002, with this wildly scatological poem...

Yet one more hermaphrodite!

I was recently cataloguing some early Dylan Thomas original typescripts, one of which was and early version of his bizarre, gothic and surrealistic short story *The Holy Six*. It was first published in Roger Roughton's Surrealist magazine *Contemporary Poetry and Prose*, no. 9 (Spring 1937), but it was first published in a book in America, in his first book published there by New Directions', *The World I Breathe*, in 1939. The story was not published in book form in the UK until 1971 in the posthumous Dent collection, *Dylan Thomas Early Prose Writings*, edited and introduced by Walford Davies who summarises it in his intro;

> 'The Holy Six' lets loose, and makes concretely active, anti-life forces anagrammatised as Rafe (fear) Lucytre (cruelty), Stul (lust), and so on.

Towards the end of the story *hermaphrodite* appears yet again in this bizarre episode;

> Touching Mr Stul on the ankle, his ghost who laboured – now he was three parts ghost, and his manhood withered like the sap in a stick under a scarecrow's tatters – leapt out to marry Mary; all sexed and nothing, intangible hermaphrodite riding the neuter dead, the minister of God in a grey image mounted dead Mary.

1. Since I wrote this piece back in 2013, *Gender* has become a new and often contentious issue, which our society is trying to come to terms with – as I imagine Dylan Thomas was. It would appear the word *Hermaphrodite* has been dropped and replaced by the word *Intersex*.

2. Return Journey was first printed in Vogue Magazine in 1954 and published in the same year in *Quite Early One Morning*, a posthumous collection(but not the full text). The full text and notes are published in Ralph Maud's *Dylan Thomas The Broadcasts*. Dent 1993.

3. First published in *Poet in the Making: The Notebooks of Dylan Thomas* edited by Ralph Maud (USA 1967, UK 1968), and reprinted in a new edition Maud, Ralph: *The Notebook Poems 1930-1934*. Dent 1989. The poem was never given a title and never published by Dylan Thomas.

4. Glynn Jones (1905–1995) was a poet and novelist writing in English although brought up in a Welsh-speaking household. He was a Cardiff schoolmaster when he read Thomas's poem '*The Woman Speaks* in the *Adelphi* in 1934. Jones wrote to Dylan straight away (Collected Letters of Dylan Thomas p120). Both men were relatively unknown in that period, but the correspondence led to a long-lasting friendship between the two. They met at Whitsun 1934; Jones, who had a car, drove the two of them to Laugharne and Aberystwyth to visit Caradoc Evans. Thomas later described Jones to his girlfriend, Pamela Hansford Johnson, as "a nice, handsome young man with no vices". Glyn would later publish a seminal history of Welsh writing in English; *The Dragon Has Two Tongues*. Dent 1968.

5. *Dylan Thomas Critical Lives*: John Goodby & Chris Wiggington. Reaktion Books 2024

6. An earlier version of the poem was published in *Purpose* magazine in October and this version was also printed in *Transition* magazine around the same time. There are minor differenced in the two versions. See Rolph p. 19. for details.

7. Two recent critics have applied themselves to these issues of gender and sexuality in Thomas's writings. Jean Michael Rabate tackles Thomas' use of the word bisected in the poem *My World is Pyramid*, in his 1991 book *Joyce upon the Void: The Genesis of Doubt*. Katie Gramich addresses gender and other related issues in her essay '*Daughters of Darkness*'; *Dylan Thomas and the Celebration of the Female* in Goodby & Wiggington: *Dylan Thomas: New Casebook* 1991.

8. Dylan Thomas was Keidrych Rhys's co-conspirator in this literary venture and contributed to many of the first ten issues and co-edited one of them.

9. *Adventures in the Skin Trade and Other Stories* was first published in 1955 by New Directions in America in a collection containing most of Dylan's other prose. Later in the same year it was published in the UK by PUTNAM as a stand-alone novel albeit unfinished, but with an introduction by Vermon Watkins which contains a brief outline of its tortured publishing history. I had an unpublished letter circa 1951, from Dylan Thomas to Professor Cecil Price of Swansea University after he had given a reading there. He ends the letter by announcing that Skin Trade was soon to be published as a U.S. pulp-paperback with a naked lady on the cover and that it would sell millions selling off racks in Drug stores. It didn't happen for 5 years by when he was 3 years dead. The letter is now in the National Library of Wales. An earlier draft was sold at auction a while back which contain this Dali-esque fragment;

   'Thinking to be witty I stabbed her through the titty with a hard-boiled egg.
   She is dead. I cracked. I split, I made an omelette out of her.'

10. Late in his life Prokosch took up literary forgery! He carefully produced very small fake Private Press books, including a Dylan Thomas book. He produced the books in Paris in the late sixties but he faked, aged them, dated them decades earlier and tried to pass them off as great rarities. He was exposed by a bookseller, Arthur Freeman in 1972, who worked at the leading London Booksellers' *Quaritch*.

11. Lycett, Andrew; *Dylan Thomas A New Life*. Weidenfeld and Nicholson. 2003.

12. The film *Set Fire to the Stars* takes its title from Dylan Thomas' poem *Love in the Asylum* and the production company take their name *Mad as Birds* Films, from the same poem. This was their first ever film and I was privileged to work on this film in an advisory capacity. I was on set for the Gower and Swansea Town shoots, and was used as an extra in a bar scene. I was honoured to have an official credit as *Poetry Advisor* on the film. It is one of the better Thomas biopics.

13. *The recently Discovered Memoirs of a Nineteenth-century French Hermaphrodite. Middlesex.* Farrah Straus & Giroux. 2002. A Pulitzer Prize-winning novel by Jeffrey Eugenides which sold over a million copies since its publication. Its characters and events are loosely based on aspects of Eugenides' life and observations of his Greek heritage however it is not an autobiography; unlike the protagonist, Eugenides is not intersex. The author decided to write *Middlesex* after reading the 1980 memoir, *Herculine Barbin* and finding himself dissatisfied with its discussion of intersex anatomy and emotions. Herculine Adélaïde Barbin, later known as Abel Barbin (1838–1868), was a French intersex person who was assigned female at birth and raised in a convent, but was later reclassified as male by a court of law, after an affair and physical examination. She is known for her memoir, *Herculin Barbin*, Her birthday is marked as Intersex Day of Remembrance Intersex Day of Remembrance. Her Memoir, first published in French in 1872 was discovered by Michel Foucault in the 1970's while conducting research at the French Department of Public Hygiene. He had the journals republished in 1980 by Pantheon as *Herculine Barbin: Being the Recently Discovered Memoirs of a Nineteenth-century French Hermaphrodite*. Pantheon Publishers, 1980.

74

THE SONG OF THE MISCHIEVOUS DOG.

There are many who say that a dog has its day,
  And a cat has a number of lives ;
There are others who think that a lobster is pink,
  And that bees never work in their hives.
There are fewer, of course, who insist that a horse
  Has a horn and two humps on its head,
And a fellow who jests that a mare can build nests
  Is as rare as a donkey that's red.
Yet in spite of all this, I have moments of bliss,
  For I cherish a passion for bones,
And though doubtful of biscuit, I'm willing to risk it,
  And love to chase rabbits and stones.
But my greatest delight is to take a good bite
  At a calf that is plump and delicious ;
And if I indulge in a bite at a bulge,
  Let's hope you won't think me too vicious.

D. M. THOMAS 3A.

Dylan Thomas' first published poem in *The Swansea Grammar School Magazine*. December 1925
He had just turned 11 years old

6.

Dylan Thomas: Borrowed Plumes – Requiem for a Plagiarist.

Immature poets imitate: mature poets steal.
T. S. Eliot

In 2013 I was asked to contribute a chapter to a book of essays; *DYLAN THOMAS A CENTENARY CELEBRATION*. It was to be edited by Hannah Ellis, Dylan Thomas' granddaughter (her mother was Aeronwy Thomas). It was published in 2014 in an elegant hardback edition by *BLOOMSBURY*. It contained essays by most all the usual suspects in the posthumous world of Dylan Thomas. My essay did not get flagged up in the publishers pre-publication publicity but it did get a significant and positive response in Michael Caines' review of the book in the *Times Literary Supplement*.[1] The start of my title is a title Dylan used for some parodies he contributed to the Swansea Grammar School magazine.

Borrowed Plumes:
DYLAN THOMAS – REQUIEM FOR A PLAGIARIST

'Immature poets imitate: mature poets steal.'
T. S. Eliot

Much has been written about Dylan Thomas's childhood; his life was tragically short – he lived for just 39 years, forcing his many biographers to look very closely at each and every precious year, in order to fill their hefty volumes. Critics too, especially those who came at exegesis from a psychoanalytical position, have examined the poet's boyhood to help them in their attempts to explain his poems. And for Dylan Thomas himself his childhood memories were a constant source of material for his prose and an inspiration for many of his greatest poems. Dylan wrote his radio piece, *Reminiscences of Childhood* twice. He often 'plagiarised' his own works, or recycled his back catalogue, in order to rinse a second fee out of them – or a third, fourth and fifth! His famous radio script, *A Child's Christmas in Wales*, first saw the light of day as *Memories of Christmas* and was first broadcast in 1945 on the BBC Children's Hour programme and published in *The Listener*. It subsequently reappeared and was resold in various guises – *Conversation about Christmas, A Child's Memories of Christmas* and was finally recorded on his first ever LP recording for Caedmon, where it became known as '*A Child's Christmas in Wales*'. At the New York recording in 1952 Barbara Holdridge and Marianne Mantel, who had founded Caedmon just to record Dylan, discovered they needed something to fill up side two of the LP. Desperate, someone recollected a recent *Harper's Bazaar* piece by Dylan, *A Child's Memories of Christmas in Wales*, and a copy of the up-market, *New York* magazine was hastily sourced. That recording secured the longevity of the LP, which went on to sell millions of copies world-wide and to be illustrated by great illustrators here in the UK, (by Mervyn Peake in 1954 and then Edward Ardizzone in 1978), and in America (by Fritz Eichenberg and many others).

It has since been filmed, animated, and adapted more than once for the stage. The second version of *Reminiscences of Childhood* printed in '*Quite Early One Morning*' (1954), begins:

> 'I like very much people telling me about their childhood, but they'll have to be quick or else I will be telling them about mine.'

And it ends:

> 'The memories of childhood have no order, and no end.'

Dylan Thomas would draw on his own early 'memories of childhood' in six of the short stories that make up the collection, '*Portrait of the Artist as a Young Dog*' (1940). One of the best known is *The Fight*, Dylan's account of his first meeting with Daniel Jones, who became his life-long friend, his sometime collaborator, the musician who provided the music for *Under Milk Wood*, and later his editor. But it is also the story in which Dylan makes his only reference to his youthful predilection for what his most recent biographer, Andrew Lycett, refers to as 'discreet plagiarism'. In the story Dylan gives us a detailed description of his 'bedroom by the boiler' and describes how,

'A poem I had printed in the *Wales Day by Day* column of the *Western Mail* was pasted on the mirror to make me blush, but the shame of the poem had died. Across the poem I had written with a stolen quill and in flourishes: 'Homer Nods'. I was always waiting for the opportunity to bring someone into my bedroom – 'Come into my den; excuse the untidiness; take a chair. No! not that one it's broken' – and force him to see the poem accidentally. 'I put it there to make me blush.' But nobody ever came in except my mother.

His mother Florence would later tell her Swansea friend Ethel Ross that she and D. J. (Dylan's father) were so proud of their son's early poetic achievement that they gave Dylan the ten shillings in cash so they could treasure forever this first remunerative postal order, sent by the paper as payment for the poem. But Dylan's embarrassment was caused by something other than the mawkish sentimentality of the poem. His comments in *The Fight*, are his only nod to an incident which only came to light some forty five years later and then only by chance and one man's remarkable powers of observation and recall.

In 1971, the same Daniel Jones that Dylan fought with in *The Fight*, edited and introduced a new edition of Dylan's poetry. Up until that point readers were content with the 1952 Dent, *Collected Poems 1934–1952*. This was Dylan's own edition of his poems. Daniel Jones new edition *The Poems* enlarged upon this by adding extra poems and he also attempted to arrange the work chronologically.

The second 'Appendix' to the book comprises a group of 26 'Early Poems' gathered from various sources – Dylan's early notebooks, and the poems published in the pages of the *Swansea Grammar School Magazine*. The section starts with a poem *His Requiem*. This is Daniel's note to *His Requiem*:

1926– early 1927. Thomas, born on 27th October 1914 wrote this poem when he was twelve or just over twelve years of age. It was published in the *Western Mail*, 14th January 1927.'

All true – apart from the 'Thomas... wrote' bit! This was the poem

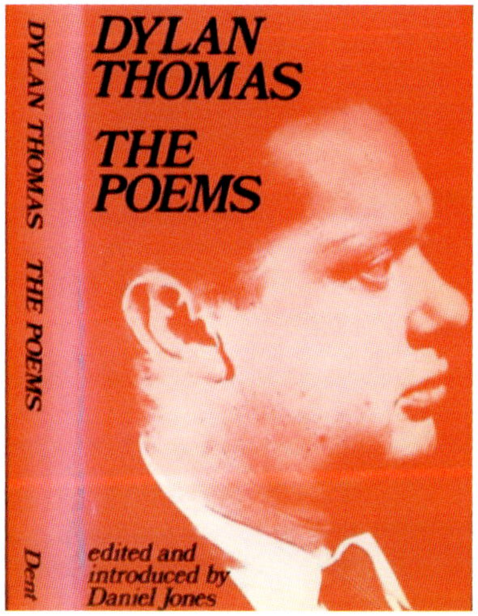

Dan Jones' edition of Dylan's poems

that Dylan was referring to in his short story, *The Fight*, the poem he, 'had printed in the "Wales Day by Day" column of the *Western Mail* ... pasted on the mirror to make me blush.'

The history of this poem came out in a curious fashion. A diligent and observant reader of the *Sunday Telegraph* saw the poem reproduced in that paper's review of Jones's edition and recognized it as being published in *The Boys Own Paper* some four years earlier, where the author was given as Miss Lillian Gard. Although Dylan had made four or five very small changes, the poem is otherwise identical.

The newspaper article that revealed the details of this literary theft ends with a bold statement:

'Daniel Jones who edited 'Dylan Thomas: 'The Poems' discounts the possibility of other borrowings but he is to replace "His Requiem" in the next edition with another early poem – presumably of cast-iron authenticity.'

That last comment, presuming 'cast-iron authenticity' of the replacement poem, should actually have haunted Daniel Jones. In his introduction to his edition, he writes quite categorically, about Dylan's 'fondness for collaboration' and he seemingly gloats about how many of these collaborations – mostly

His Requiem.

NOBODY cared a bit, folks said,
When that wicked old man at
the farm lay dead.

He had no kith and he had no kin—
And nobody cared his love to win.
Nobody thought of him kindly—none,
For many a cruel harsh thing he'd done ;
And many a bitter and angry word
From those thin hard lips had the neigh-
bours heard.
He had lived alone—he had died alone,
With never a friend he could call his own ;
Or so folks thought.
And the cortège grim,
With never a mourner mourning him,
Passed through the gate of the garden-
ground !

But hush ! A requiem's softened sound
Stole over the silence.
And someone said :
" 'Tis the little brown linnet the old
man fed ! "

LILLIAN GARD.

The original by Lillian Gard in *Boys Own Paper*

HIS REQUIEM.

Nobody cared a bit, folks said,
When the wicked old man at the gate lay
dead.

He had no kith, and he had no kin,
And nobody cared his love to win:
Nobody thought of him kindly, none,
For many a cruel thing he'd done;
And many a bitter and angry word
From those thin lips the neighbours heard.
He had lived alone, he had died alone,
With never a friend he could call his own,
Or so folks thought;
And the coffin grim,
With never a mourner mourning him,
Passed through the gate of his garden
ground.

But hush! a requiem's softened sound
Stole over the silence,
And someone said:
" 'Tis the little brown linnet the old man
fed."

Swansea. D. M. THOMAS.

D. M. THOMAS *Western Mail* January 13th 1927

DYLAN'S POEM WAS NOT HIS

By RICHARD BENNETT

DYLAN THOMAS, the Welsh poet, began his literary career with a poem which was another person's work, it was disclosed last week.

" His Requiem " until now thought to be his first published work, is to be removed from the next edition of a new volume, " Dylan Thomas: The Poems."

It was published under Thomas's name in the *Western Mail* on January 14, 1927, when the embryo poet was 12. It is included among his contributions to periodicals in J. Alexander Rolph's " Dylan Thomas: A Biography."

The long memory of a reader, Mr. Richard Parker, of Torridon Road, Catford, London, started off inquiries by *The Sunday Telegraph* which have shown that the poem was first published in November, 1923, in the *Boys' Own Paper*, under the name of the actual writer, Miss Lillian Gard.

" His Requiem " was reproduced in our review last week of " Dylan Thomas: the Poems " and Mr. Parker remembered seeing it in the *Boy's Own* Paper.

FOUR SMALL CHANGES

Thomas had apparently made four small verbal changes, but the poem he claimed as his own was otherwise identical. Its opening lines read:

Nobody cared a bit, folks said
When the wicked old man at the
gate lay dead

Lillian Gard contributed a number of poems to the magazine in the 1920s. The Lutterworth Press, which published the *Boys' Own Paper* bought the sole rights in everything that appeared in it.

It is understood that Lutterworths is unlikely to take action unless it is proved that Thomas raided other treasures from the journal. There is no guarantee that this one poem was the sole source of his youthful inspiration.

Mr. Daniel Jones, who edited " Dylan Thomas: The Poems," discounts the possibility of other borrowings but he is to replace " His Requiem " in the next edition with another early poem—presumably of cast-iron authenticity.

Dylan Thomas's agent and estate trustee, David Higham, and his publishers, J. M. Dent, have been informed.

The *Sunday Telegraph's* exposure of Dylan's chicanery

involving Dan and Dylan – had even hoodwinked some experts. They had, wrote Dan smugly,

> 'created a trap into which many students of his work, including commentators and bibliographers have fallen'

He goes on to describe how:

> 'This collaboration extends even to three or four poems that appeared in the *Swansea Grammar School Magazine* above the initials D.M.T.'

He then firmly declares that:

> 'Poems written in collaboration are excluded from this book.'

Thus it was with some surprise that I noticed that Jones did not include in this first edition the important poem which has always been considered and cited as Dylan's first ever published poem, – *Song of the Mischievous Dog* – which had appeared in the school magazine in December 1925, when Dylan had just turned eleven.

However, when the true authorship of *His Requiem* had been established, the publishers first inserted a small tab at the start of the remaining copies of the original print-run, identifying the poem as being the work of Lillian Gard and explaining that it would be removed in subsequent re-printings. Thus I was even more surprised and perplexed when the first reprint appeared and I discovered that Daniel Jones, having to fill the void left on the page by the removal of *His Requiem* inserted in its place The *Song of the Mischievous Dog*! A poem that by his statement that he wrote in his introduction to the first edition of the book which declared 'Poems written in collaboration are excluded from this book'. Jones had led us to believe that this poem was, by its initial exclusion, 'a collaborative' poem, which had suddenly become 'un-collaborative'. I found it hard to see this cobbled together solution to the problem of an empty half page offered little evidence of the 'cast iron authenticity' Dr Jones had promised us.

This discovery, back in 1971, of a plagiarised poem was down to one man's remarkable observation and memory, but just recently it happened again, and this time the discovery was due to a bizarre coincidence and the new and mighty powers of Google. This has led to other discoveries that make the *Sunday Telegraph*'s bold assertion made by Daniel Jones '...discounts the possibility of other borrowings', seems somewhat wide of the mark. It would appear that during his early teens, Dylan Thomas was a serial plagiarist.

Dylan's first official biographer, Constantine Fitzgibbon[2] gave us some measure of forewarning of this particular trait in his Life of Dylan Thomas which came out in 1965. Fitzgibbon chooses to include this long episode within parenthesis and he gives us a detailed an account as 'told' to him by E.F. McKinery, another Swansea Grammar schoolboy who wrote poems and edited the school magazine. He told Fitzgibbon that Dylan submitted a poem to him while he was editor that he recognised as being from *Arthur Mee's Children's Encyclopaedia*, a ubiquitous ten-volume shelf-filler in middle class households (and a curse to booksellers!) The poem, simple and short, was called *Sometimes* and was written by Thomas S. Jones:

> 'Across the fields of yesterday
> He sometimes comes to me,
> A little lad just back from play –
> The lad I used to be.
>
> And yet he smiles so wistfully
> Once he has crept within,
> I wonder if he hopes to see
> The man I might have been.'

Despite his Welsh sounding name Jones was an American poet born at Boonville, New York on November 6th 1882 (he died in 1932). Jones graduated from Cornell University in 1904 and became a journalist on The New York Times from 1904 to 1907. He went on to be the associate editor of *The Pathfinder* in 1911. He published several volumes of poetry and the titles give us some indication of his metier; *Path of Dream*, 1904; From Quiet Valley, 1907; *Interlude*, 1908; *Ave Atque Vale* (In Memoriam Arthur Upson), 1909; *The Voice in the Silence*... ... The internet also provided this testimonial:

'Mr Jones was a poet of rare delicacy and fineness whose work has gathered to itself a discriminating group of readers.'

Dylan Thomas was obviously a proud member of that 'discriminating group'. McKinery considered it his duty as editor to report this attempted deception to the master in over-all charge of the School magazine who also happened to be the perpetrator's father, D. J. Thomas. Although he reported his findings, McEnery's own final judgment was that it was a not a case of literary theft but more an incident of 'total unconscious recall' on Dylan's part. However this appears to be a very lenient judgment if one considers the trouble and care which Dylan showed in his selection of this poem. It is just the kind of poem that would lie easily on the pages of S.G.S.M and also consciously dug out from a reasonably good hiding place, buried deep within ten fat volumes. Moreover, Thomas Jones was not widely read in the UK, and Arthur Mee's encyclopaedia was a didactic work, not known for poetry, and this all seemed to me very similar to young Thomas's usual 'modus operandi'.

Subsequent biographers provide more details: Paul Ferris, Dylan's second biographer gives us chapter and verse. Dylan found the poem in Volume 8 of the *Encyclopaedia*, on 'page 5669, where it is one of the "*Thousand Poems of All Times and All Countries*." Ferris adds more detail: on being made aware of the discovery of another example of his son's plagiarism by his colleague McInerny, D. J. Thomas exclaimed,

'After this, everything he writes is suspect.'

In his revised, '*New Edition*' of his biography Paul Ferris offers new details: it was the magazine's co-editor, H. M. V. Thomas who found the original printing, and that McInerny had changed his original charitable 'unconscious recall' opinion when he learned of the western Mail incident, and concluded that it was Dylan,

'in an anti-social, devil-may-care mood, like a secret agent
Fingering a false and superfluous moustache.'

Andrew Lycett in his, the most recent, life of Thomas, introduces the incident lightly,

'...Dylan was not above discreet plagiarisation'. But he too finds it hard to explain. Why did a bright boy, who clearly knew how to write verse, resort to such deceit? The answer is that this was his way of dealing with the various pressures on him... It showed Dylan's need to demonstrate his poetic ability to his parents partly to his indulgent mother...but rather more to his remote father whose laissez-faire attitude to learning in the home belied his firm ambition for his son'.

James A. Davies, in his *Reference Companion to Dylan Thomas* (1998), writes of Dylan's other less than attractive childhood traits, – petty theft, outrageous foul- mouth, wild behaviour, but then he adds, 'Even more serious and puzzling were two clear instances of plagiarism. Davies then writes of both *His Requiem* and Sometimes, and of the latter he adds 'When D. J. was informed, he was furious'. He then adds his own comment, 'Oddly, both poems were trifles: Thomas's own light verse of the time is more vigorous and interesting.'

My personal involvement in this complicated tale began earlier this year when I acquired yet another large collection of Dylan Thomas materials – books, photographs, letters and ephemera. Amongst all the papers was a file of letters and photocopies concerned with a group of Dylan Thomas's juvenile poems, in particular a clutch of poems that Dylan's mother, Florence, found when clearing out a cupboard in the family cottage, Blaen Cwm, after Dylan's death. I was led to believe that there was nothing original amongst the quantity of papers I acquired were copies and some original holograph poems one of which was written over two sheets a curious hand and was entitled *It Can Be Done* but I did not single it out in any way.

Florence was being helped in this by a long-standing friend and her sometime companion, Hettie Owen who, with her husband Ken, lived at Blaen Cwm. Earlier, Hettie, who was from Port Talbot, had Dylan's 'Uncle Arthur' (D. J. Thomas's brother) staying with her, as both a friend and as a lodger, in her home in Arthur Street, Port Talbot. When Florrie announced that she was going to burn the papers and manuscripts Mrs Owen asked if she could have them and Florrie gave them to her. A decade later Kent Thompson, the first of what was to become a continuing stream of American post graduate students, who arrived in Swansea and entered the University to further his research on the city's greatest poet.

In the Hettie Owen file were numerous letters from him Kent to her husband Ken. It was apparent from these letters that Kent had visited the couple and been shown the original manuscripts that Hettie had preserved. The earliest letter is dated 22nd November 1966, and Kent writes,

> 'First and foremost, thank you once again for your kind assistance and hospitality...As the saying goes, you have 'contributed to scholarship' and filled in those dark gaps in knowledge which slip so ridiculously easily into history.'

Further on in the letter we get the first mention of the original juvenile poems,

> 'The University definitely wants to buy the manuscripts'

The other letters in the file provide a paper trail of how the group of poems get photographed and offered around to potential purchasers. Swansea University is quickly out of the running. In January 1965 the then Prof of English Cecil J. L. Price, (who another decade on was to become one of my first and best customers – almost the patron of the city's new fledgling Dylans Bookstore), writes Hettie a rather dismissive letter and offers her just,

> 'fifty pounds for the manuscripts of the nine poems'

Various parties get involved, Kent Thompson suggests 'Sotheby's London' but he also tells Hettie that he has mentioned the manuscripts to Bill Read – an American academic, and the partner of John Malcolm Brinnin, who in 1964, had published an early and very well illustrated biography of Dylan – *The Days of Dylan Thomas.*

Kent tells Hettie that,

> '...through Bill Reed I have learned of several of those rich Americans who are interested?'

Argh!– the scourge of 'those rich Americans', so often the bane of my bookselling life! Eventually Dylan Thomas's literary agents, David Higham Associates, get involved and they broker a cosy deal with their near neighbours, Bertram Rota, a famous London bookselling institution that specialized in Modern Literature in First Edition, Literary Archives, Letters and Manuscripts. Back in 1941 a 26 year old Dylan Thomas had taken into Rota's five of his early manuscript notebooks crammed with his early poems, both published and unpublished, which they bought. Rota sold them on to the Lockwood memorial Library of the State University of New York at Buffalo for $140! (that would have been around £70.) Ferris writes 'whatever Thomas received it was far less than that'. Dylan was then the same age as his literary hero John Keats was when he died, which may have some significance. Dylan had set the deal up earlier in a letter, which ended,

Bill Read's Biography

> 'Will you let me know soon? I should like to sell them, if possible, as I am in need of money'.

Rota's ended up buying Hettie's group of poems for £200.

But that is not the end of the Trail. Rota completed the purchase in May of 1965. Later in the same year one of the leading, and most legendary and prestigious American Booksellers, the New York based, HOUSE OF EL DIEFF INC., issued one of their elegant and sumptuous catalogues. The title page has a dazzling brief alphabetical list of the literary treasures they have on offer; the penultimate line reads:

> 'Steinbeck; Stendhal; Stevenson: **Thomas**; Tolstoy'

The catalogue has three Thomas items each given a double page

56

Unpublished and Unrecorded Juvenile Poems by Dylan Thomas

THOMAS, Dylan. *Autograph Manuscripts of Five Unpublished Early Poems* (two signed "Dylan," in his mother's hand), 8 pages, 4to, written in ink on ruled exercise paper, with one correction and two marginal notes in pencil, presumably in another hand; *Autograph Manuscripts of Four Unpublished Early Poems,* in fair copies written by his mother and signed by her "Dylan Marlais," with a Swansea address, 7 pages, 4to, written in ink on ruled exercise paper, with some minor corrections; with two family photographs and two letters relating to the manuscripts, v.p., v.d. $2500.00

This important group of hitherto unknown and unpublished juvenilia by one of the major poets of our time was given to a friend during the Second World War by Dylan Thomas's mother. They remained in her possession until early this year. Thomas's extraordinary influence and importance have served to bring to light the greater portion of his existing manuscripts, and the appearance of new work is an event of major significance for collectors and students of the Welsh bard.

The poems in the present collection would appear, on the basis of internal stylistic evidence, to have been written over a considerable period of time. Three of those in Mrs. Thomas's hand might be the work of any youthful poetaster. *Little Dreams* is a moralistic sermon, and *My Party* a wistful day-dream. *The Mishap*, a humorous tale, exhibits a wry point of view. *The Secret Whisky Cure*, also in his mother's hand, is a satirical look at the marriage of a couple who may have been among the Thomas's circle of acquaintances. Written in a romping ballad meter it is sustained for 48 lines and shows a surprising insight into the psychology of the drinker, a subject with which the poet became painfully familiar in later years. The five autograph poems in his own hand are revealing glimpses into the influences and models of his apprenticeship. *The Maniac* is a romantic echo of Keats' *La Belle Dame Sans Merci*, and *Decision* is Tennysonian. *Inspirations* and *La Danseuse* sound most clearly the distinctive note we associate with the poet in his prime. The striking delight achieved by unusual juxtapositions, the beginnings of that richness of vocabulary, the faintly heard Biblical echoes, and the famed verbal complexity. The *Five Limericks* are a delightful romp in an old and honored form.

These poems are decidedly the work of a young man trying out his talents and seeking to find his own inimitable and personal voice, and offer much fruitful study for the development of his style.

The two photographs included show a family group, consisting of the poet's parents, grandparents, two uncles, an aunt, and his sister Nancy as a young child. The other is a small photograph of Dylan's grandfather, in a miniature decorative frame. The two letters provide a record of the provenance and early history of this unusual discovery.

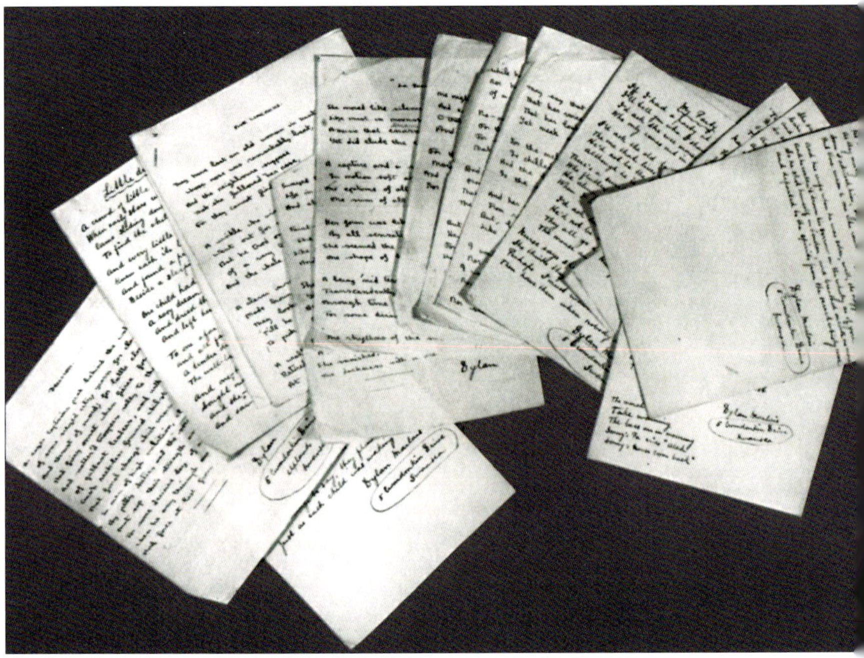

spread but it is the first that is of interest to this story – Item 56 *Unpublished and Unrecorded Juvenile Poems by Dylan Thomas.*

Dylan's childhood scribblings, rescued from a cupboard and the threat of bonfire in rural Carmarthenshire, had found their way to the plush cabinets of a swish bookstore on East Sixty-Second Street, New York City! And they are now priced at $2500.00! Two Thousand Five Hundred Dollars! And they sold! They were bought by The Harry Ransom Humanities Research Centre at the University of Texas, and added into the largest collection of Dylan Thomas manuscripts in existence in where they can be seen and studied today.

The group of manuscripts were described in great detail but I slowly realised that they made no mention or reference to a poem entitled *It can be Done*. I began to realise that by some quirk, I had acquired an original holograph manuscript of an unknown and unrecorded Dylan Thomas juvenile poem! What a discovery! I could not explain why it had not gone to America with the others, but that was my good fortune; or so I blindly thought. Herewith my original hand written (by young Dylan Thomas), "**I can be done**".

But then things took a strange turn. Fast forward just a few weeks, during which time I had carefully transcribed the poem, scanned it and printed it. During the course of his I also decided that is was written by Dylan himself in his young school-boy handwriting. I had even begun to mention my new discovery to whomever I met who might be vaguely interested, or be a potential customer.

And then I was home alone one evening, mooching about, reading, shuffling papers in a desultory fashion, but with the TV on in the background, to which I was paying scant attention. It was the night of the marathon, live, annual BBC Sports Personality of the Year programme,[3] and I was only taking any interest when a favourite sport of mine was being covered.

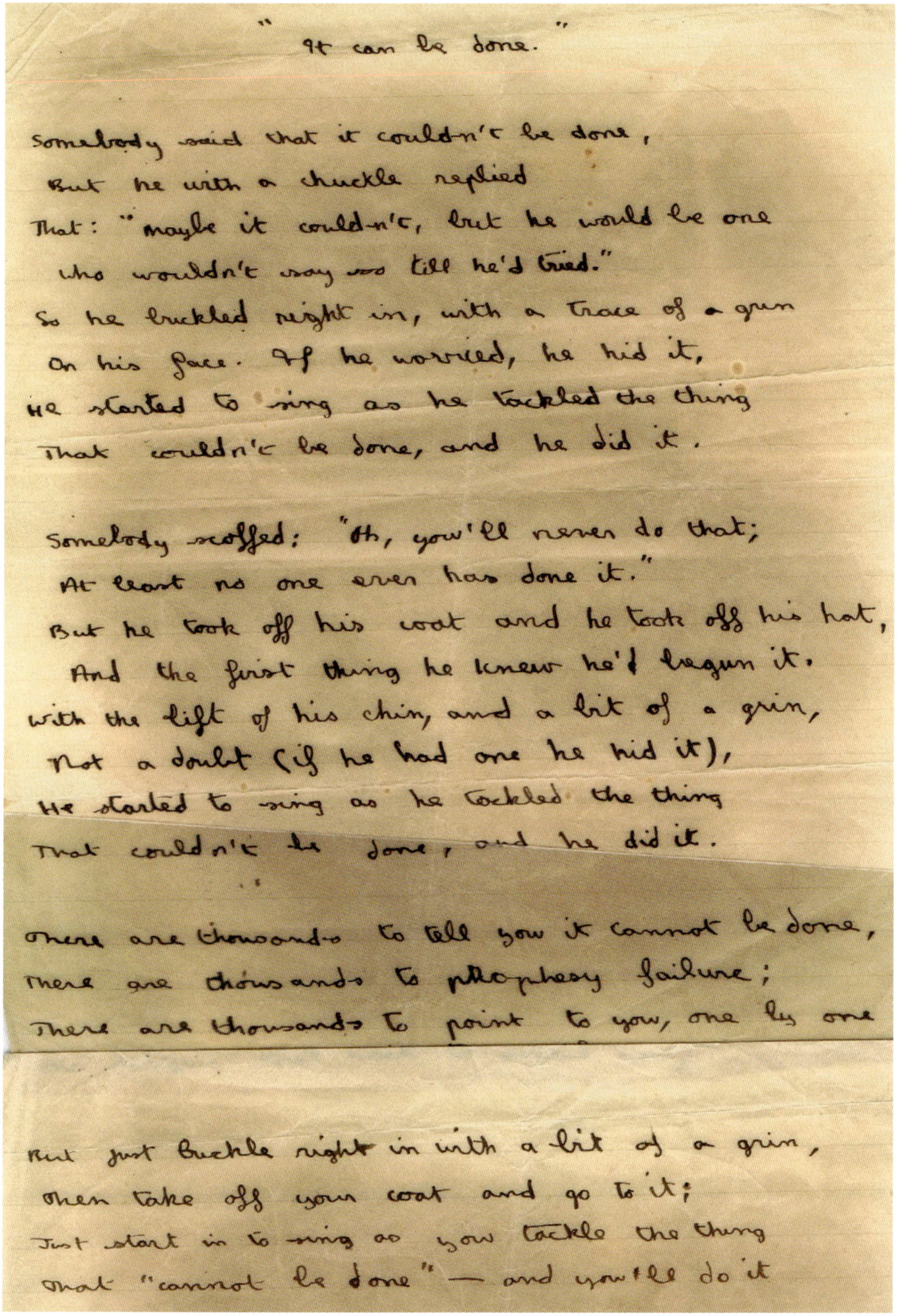
"It can be done."

Somebody said that it couldn't be done,
But he with a chuckle replied
That: "maybe it could-n't, but he would be one
who wouldn't say so till he'd tried."
So he buckled right in, with a trace of a grin
On his face. If he worried, he hid it,
He started to sing as he tackled the thing
That couldn't be done, and he did it.

Somebody scoffed: "Oh, you'll never do that;
At least no one ever has done it."
But he took off his coat and he took off his hat,
And the first thing he knew he'd begun it.
with the lift of his chin, and a bit of a grin,
Not a doubt (if he had one he hid it),
He started to sing as he tackled the thing
That couldn't be done, and he did it.

There are thousands to tell you it cannot be done,
There are thousands to prophesy failure;
There are thousands to point to you, one by one

But just Buckle right in with a bit of a grin,
Then take off your coat and go to it;
Just start in to sing as you tackle the thing
That "cannot be done" — and you'll do it

The original manuscript of "It can be done" in Dylan's schoolboy hand

About half way through the epic proceedings, the presenter, Sue Barker came centre stage and said something like;

'...and now a poem 'It Couldn't be Done'....

I suppose that just might have caught my ear, and I turned to the screen to see a lone figure come into frame, a somewhat familiar fine looking black actor. He began to recite a poem with gravitas and passion. A poem which began to nudge the nerve ends in my synapses. I tried to ignore the words but they did sound somewhat strangely familiar. The actor's stirring, impassioned performance came to an end to tumultuous applause and Sue Barker thanked the actor, who I learned was Idris Elba, the star of a very highly rated American police drama *The Wire* Then she acknowledged the author of the poem as being one Edgar Guest.

'Who he?'

I thought, but I tried to banish this stuff from my head and go back to reading *my* book. But the poem kept bothering me, I kept hearing the words and about an hour later I could not stop myself from going to my office, finding one of my transcripts of my new Dylan Poem and heading for my computer.

Oh to the power of Google. I typed in Edgar Guest and was offered a choice of 'About 2,690,000 results'! As ever the first result was the Wikipedia bio, where I began to read;

> Edgar Albert Guest (August 20, 1881, Birmingham, England. August 5, 1959, Michigan) (aka Eddie Guest) was a prolific English-born American poet who was popular in the first half of the 20th century and became known as the People's Poet. In 1891, Guest came with his family to the United States from England. After he began at the Detroit Free Press as a copy boy and then a reporter, his first poem appeared December 11, 1898. He became a naturalised citizen in 1902. For 40 years, Guest was widely read throughout North America, and his sentimental, optimistic poems were syndicated in newspaper columns. From his first published work in the Detroit Free Press until his death in 1959, Guest penned some 11,000 poems which were syndicated in some 300 newspapers and collected in more than 20 books, including A Heap o' Livin' (1916) and Just Folks (1917). Guest was made Poet Laureate of Michigan, the only poet to have been awarded the title...

That was quite enough, in a state of incredulous disbelief, another search got me to a printing of Edgar's poem with its original title '*It Couldn't be done*'. The game was up: this was another '*Requiem*'. Dylan had copied the poem. A quite extraordinary co-incidence. Would I ever have discovered this original otherwise. I'm not a huge fan of the programme and I wasn't giving it my full attention, but it led to the discovery of yet another incidence of obvious plagiarism.

I then did a close comparison, and saw that, apart from slightly changing the title from negative to a positive, Dylan has made a few other subtle changes, and these are highlighted below. (Shown here in Red)

Edgar Albert Guest (1881-1959)
It Couldn't Be Done [Thomas "It can be done"]
Somebody said that it couldn't be done,
But, he with a chuckle replied
That "maybe it couldn't," but he would be one
Who wouldn't say so till he'd tried.["]
So he buckled right in with the trace of a grin
On his face. If he worried he hid it.
He started to sing as he tackled the thing
That couldn't be done, and he did it.
Somebody scoffed: "Oh, you'll never do that;
At least no one has done it"; [.]
But he took off his coat and he took off his hat,
And the first thing we knew he'd begun it.
With a lift of his chin and a bit of a grin,
Without any doubting or quiddit, [Not a doubt (if he had one he hid it)]
He started to sing as he tackled the thing
That couldn't be done, and he did it.
There are thousands to tell you it cannot be done,
There are thousands to prophesy failure;
There are thousands to point out to you one by one,
The dangers that wait to assail you.

But just buckle it in with a bit of a grin,
Just take off your coat and go to it;
Just start to sing as you tackle the thing
That "couldn't be done," and you'll do it [That "cannot be done" – and you'll do it]

So my great discovery turned out to be some kind of fake, and definitely not an original juvenile poem by Dylan Thomas. A poem in his hand: Yes. But written by him: No. He had copied the poem out but he had cunningly made significant small alterations which subtly changed it; by changing the title from negative to positive and by removing the arcane American phrase 'quiddit', which might have aroused suspicions. I could only conclude that this was in preparation for an attempt to pass the poem off as his own. Whether he tried and offered it to his school magazine or some other outlet we do not know but it does not appear to have been published anywhere under Dylan's name.

It was a huge disappointment on many levels, not the least being that it was now hard to see the manuscript having any real monetary value.[4] Although on one level I marvelled at and was captivated by the synchronicity of the whole evening, I felt angry with myself for being duped. Should I not have known of such a prolific versifier as E. A. Guest? Should I have been familiar with

Edgar Albert's cannon? In an attempt to convince myself that I was not at fault for the next week or two I challenged each and every literate person I encountered, from well-read customers to Professors of English, demanding of them to confess if they had ever heard of Edgar Albert Guest. I was feeling better when all my questioning brought nothing but blank, incredulous and negative replies. But then I was on the phone to a very smart young American rare bookdealer,[5] who immediately said yes, he knew of such a poet. But I felt less inadequate when he explained he had never read a word of his poetry but knew him through a particular and wonderful Dorothy Parker rhyming aphorism, which totally disparages any merit in his poetry; the sharp-tongued satirist wrote,

"I'd rather flunk my Wasserman test/ Than read the poetry of Edgar Guest."

[The Wassermann test is an antibody test for syphilis, named after the bacteriologist August Paul von Wasserman who discovered it].

Louche Dorothy would rather be struck down with Syphilis than read a poem by Guest! At least my smart bookseller friend's revelation put a smile on my face.

There this story could have ended had I not been concurrently finishing up a book[6] about Dylan's love of the Pub and the place of drink and drinking in his life. When I was going through the Hettie Owen file, I had carefully read all the poems therein and been struck by one of the other early photocopied poems in the file entitled, *The Secret Whisky Cure*, a three page epic ballad, written out by Dylan's mother.

The cataloguer at El Deiff obviously had a similar reaction to me and had signalled this poem out for special attention when describing the manuscripts;

The Secret Whisky Cure...in his mother's hand, is a satirical look at the marriage of a couple, who may have been among the Thomas's circle of acquaintances. Written in a romping ballad meter (sic) it is sustained for 48 lines and shows a surprising insight into the psychology of the drinker, a subject with which the poet became painfully familiar in later years.

The poem ends with a startling and shocking penultimate stanza wherein the whisky drinker, poisoned by his wife so as cannot drink anymore, finds his only respite in a brutal suicide;

'And his wife, when he was sober?—Well, she nagged him all the more!
And he couldn't drown his sorrow in the whisky as of yore
So he shot himself in London, and breathed earth no more
And found rest amongst the spirits from the Secret Whisky Cure'

I thought straight away that I could certainly use the poem in my book on Dylan and drink; a little known gem that was evidence of Dylan's youthful knowledge of the perils of alcohol. At least *That could be done*, would be giving me some small recompense for my disappointment and loss.

But it was not to be. I had scanned and typed (and hyped) the poem into the manuscript of my book but it was making me wary and I could not stop myself going back to Google. Slowly, and with trepidation mounting, I typed in 'Secret Whisky Cure' in the box, my hand gingerly moved the mouse, the cursor edged towards the 'search' tab – I double clicked; the first result showed on the screen;

> The Secret Whisky Cure – Australian Poetry Library http://www.poetrylibrary.edu.au/poets/lawson-henry/the-secret-whisky-cure-0108042 TIS no tale of heroism, 'tis no tale of storm and strife, / But of ordinary boozing, and of dull domestic life– / Of the everlasting friction that most husbands must ...

Young Dylan Thomas – the *Demon Plagiarist* – had struck again and I had been caught again! But at least I discovered the theft before unwittingly including it, with great hype, in my book. Even I had heard of Henry Lawson. Again I found myself transcribing a poem and highlighting Dylan's few devious and cunning alterations – he leaves out two stanzas from the Lawson original, including the concluding stanza, probably because the opening couplet is too misogynistic, brazen and distasteful to ever have ever come from the head and hand of a young boy:

> 'And the moral? – well, 'tis funny–or 'tis woman's way with men–
> She's remarried to a publican who whacks her now and then,'

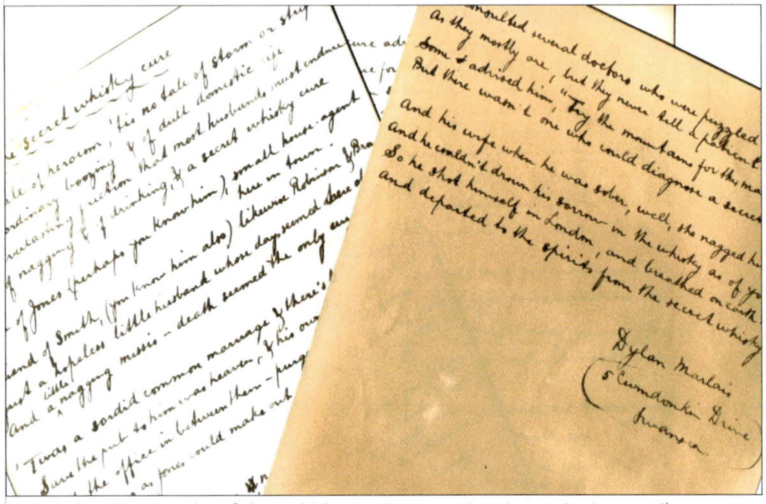

The photographs of the '*Whisky Cure*' Manuscripts in Hettie Owens File

The most pertinent changes are his blatant efforts to re-locate the poem and remove its Australian elements; the 'Sidney Bulletin' becomes the 'Monthly Magazine'; the final dramatic act of the suicide takes place in 'London' not on Manly, a beach just outside Sidney, and the dropping in of some curious *strine* words or Australian usages –such as 'coalised' and 'Woore' (which I still cannot find a meaning for)[7] Dylan's changes highlighted in Red.:

> The Secret Whisky Cure
> by Henry Lawson From book: When I Was King
> 'TIS no tale of heroism, 'tis no tale of storm and strife,
> But of ordinary boozing, and of dull domestic life—
> Of the everlasting friction that most husbands must endure—
> Tale of nagging and of drinking—and a secret whisky cure.
> Name of Jones—perhaps you know him—small house-agent here in town—
> (Friend of Smith, you know him also—likewise Robinson and Brown),
> Just a hopeless little husband, whose deep sorrows were obscure, [whose days seemed here obscure]
> And a bitter nagging Missis—and death seemed the only cure. [a little nagging missis]
> 'Twas a common sordid marriage, and there's little new to tell—
> Save the pub to him was Heaven and his own home was a hell:
> With the office in between them—purgatory to be sure—
> And, as far as Jones could make out—well, there wasn't any cure. [was not any cure]
> 'Twas drink and nag—or nag and drink—whichever you prefer—
> Till at last she couldn't stand him any more than he could her.

Friends and relatives assisted, telling her (with motives pure)
[no brackets]
That a legal separation was the only earthly cure.
So she went and saw a lawyer, who, in accents soft and low,
Asked her firstly if her husband had a bank account or no;
But he hadn't and she hadn't, they in fact were very poor,
So he bowed her out suggesting she should try some liquor
cure.
She saw a drink cure advertised in the Sydney Bulletin—
[Monthly Magazine]
Cure for brandy, cure for whisky, cure for rum and beer and
gin,
And it could be given secret, it was tasteless, swift and sure—
So she purchased half a gallon of that Secret Whisky Cure.
And she put some in his coffee, smiling sweetly all the while,
And he started for the office rather puzzled by the smile—
[and Jones started]
Smile or frown he'd have a whisky, and you'll say he was a
boor—
But perhaps his wife had given him an overdose of Cure.
And he met a friend he hadn't seen for seven years or more—
It was just upon the threshold of a private bar-room door—
And they coalised and entered straight away, you may be
sure— [agreed and entered]
But of course they hadn't reckoned with a Secret Whisky
Cure.
Jones, he drank, turned pale, and, gasping, hurried out the
back way quick,
Where, to his old chum's amazement, he was violently sick;
Then they interviewed the landlord, but he swore the drink
was pure—
It was only the beginning of the Secret Whisky Cure.
For Jones couldn't stand the smell of even special whisky
blends,
And shunned bar-rooms to the sorrow of his trusty drinking
friends:
And they wondered, too, what evil genius had chanced to lure
Him from paths of booze and friendship—never dreaming of
a Cure.
He had noticed, too, with terror that a something turned his
feet,
When a pub was near, and swung him to the other side the
street,
Till he thought the devils had him, and his person they'd
immure
In a lunatic asylum where there wasn't any Cure. [This whole
stanza omitted]
He consulted several doctors who were puzzled by the case—
As they mostly are, but never tell the patient to his face—
[but they]
Some advised him 'Try the Mountains for this malady
obscure:'
But there wasn't one could diagnose a Secret Whisky Cure.
[who could]
And his wife, when he was sober?—Well, she nagged him all
the more!
And he couldn't drown his sorrow in the pewter as of yore:
[in the whisky as of yore]
So he shot himself at Manly and was set upon by Woore,
[So he shot himself in London, and breathed earth no
more]
And found rest amongst the spirits from the Secret Whisky
Cure.
And the moral?—well, 'tis funny—or 'tis woman's way with
men—
She's remarried to a publican who whacks her now and then,
And they get on fairly happy, he's a brute and he's a boor,
But she's never tried her second with a Secret Whisky Cure.
[This stanza omitted]

Once again I had discovered another plagiarised poem, and again, as with *It can be Done*, I have not found it published anywhere above Dylan's name, although I am convinced that these two manuscripts are examples of poems that he was intending to offer out for publication as his own. This plagiarism also seems to be a trait belonging to Thomas's his mid-teens and there has never been any suggestion that any of the poems he included in his published collections was anything other than entirely his own work. But hold on – what about his prose? Quite recently I received a note from an old customer and friend, Kerith Trick. Kerith lived in Norwich and had been a top psychiatrist at St Andrews Hospital, which was earlier known as Northampton General Lunatic Asylum and was where the Victorian poet John Clare was incarcerated, and Kerith collected Clare's poetry. But Kerith had been born in Swansea, the son of Bert Trick, often referred to as Swansea's 'communist' grocer, and one of Dylan Thomas's most influential friends and his major political mentor during his final Swansea years. I invited Kerith to give a lecture on his father in the 2000 *Swansea Dylan Thomas Festival* and in it he put the record straight – Bert was never a Communist but was "always a member of the Labour Party, albeit on the extreme left". [and it was Dylan who had suggested that Bert call his son Kerith after the George Moore novel 'The Brook Kerith[7] that they both admired so much).

Kerith's note pointed me towards a remarkable similarity between a famous passage from one of Dylan's most popular stories, now known as *The Outing*, and a passage in an early Sherlock Holmes short story by Arthur Conan Doyle, *A Scandal in Bohemia. 1891*. Doyle was a favourite author of Dylan's, in particular the Sherlock homes stories as the appeared in *The Strand* magazine. *The Outing* was commissioned by the BBC as a television programme – one of only two TV appearances by Thomas – both now, sadly lost. It was originally called A Story and it dates from the very last year of Dylan's life. It was televised on the 10th August 1953 and subsequently published in the *Listener* in September of the same year. (Dylan was to die in New York in November). In *The Outing* Dylan writes in the voice of his younger self: a young boy forced to accompany his Uncle on a typical Welsh all male, annual, coach outing to the seaside, on a bus full of beer, with stops at every other pub passed, and all manner of shenanigans; destinations are rarely reached as the pubs become harder to leave.

The story begins,

'If you can call it a story. There's no beginning or end and there's very little in the middle. It's all about a day's outing, by charabanc, to Porthcawl, which, of course, the charabanc never reached, and it happened when I was so high and much nicer.'

And *The Outing* ends with this episode[8]. of typical drunken banter;

They stopped at the Hermit's Nest for rum to keep out the
cold.
I played for Aberavon in 1898', said a stranger to Enoch Davies
'Liar,' said Enoch Davies.
'I can show you photos,' said the stranger
'Forged,' said Enoch Davies
'And I'll show you my cap at home.'
'Stolen.'
'I got friends to prove it,' said the stranger in a fury.
'Bribed,' said Enoch Davies.'

And here is the passage that Kerith Trick[9] pointed out to me which occurs in

Doyle's A Scandal in Bohemia:

When I fail to follow your Majesty. If this young person should produce her letters for blackmailing or other purposes, how is she to prove their authenticity?

'There is writing.'
'Pooh, pooh! Forgery.'
'My private notepaper.'
'Stolen.'
'My own seal.'
'Imitated.' '
'My photograph.'
'Bought'.

There is little or no doubt that Dylan's bar-room exchange echoes profoundly and remarkably with the passage from Conan Doyle, but is it another example of plagiarism? – I think not. In this instance I am inclined to give Dylan the benefit of the doubt and to side with Fitzgibbon and agree that what we have here is;

'a case of total, unconscious recall'.

Or is Dylan again living up to Eliot's maxim,

'mature poets steal'

My juvenile literary delinquence...

Dylan Thomas speaking to an audience at M I T Boston July 1952

And what are we to make of all of this – is it terrible? Is it wicked? Should we think any the less of the perpetrator? I am not sure that in the light of these new examples we can dismiss them all as Fitzgibbon did when he chose to dismiss the poem taken from *The Children's Encyclopaedia* as an example of 'a case of total, unconscious recall'. Fitzgibbon adds, 'Dylan at that age was writing so many poems that he certainly had no need to steal one'. Paul Ferris concludes his account of the 'His Requiem' by seeing it as being provoked by Dylan's overwhelming desire to prove to his father in particular, but to his whole world in general, that he was a poet. Ferris writes:

'He would hardly have taken such a risk unless he badly needed to prove – to himself, to his father, to his friends – that he could write acceptable poetry; and unless he was uncertain of his ability to do so.'

Andrew Lycett's conclusion is similar:

'Why did a bright boy, who clearly knew how to write poems resort to such deceit? The answer is that it was his way of dealing with various pressures on him ... It showed Dylan's need to demonstrate his poetic ability to his parents, partly to his indulgent mother, who made copies of his work, but rather more to his remote father whose laissez-faire attitude to learning in the home belied his firm ambition for his son.'

But what of *His Requiem, Sometimes, It couldn't be done* and *The Secret Whisky Cure*. I would like to propose another explanation. Dylan wrote his first poem for the *Grammar School Magazine* in 1925 aged eleven. He was still publishing similar light verse in its pages in 1930, when he becomes editor, and on into 1931, by when he is fast approaching seventeen and has actually left the school to work on the local paper. However if we look at Ralph Maud's *Poet in the Making: The Notebooks of Dylan Thomas* (1967. New Edition 1989), we can see that by 1930 Dylan Thomas had already begun to compile the four notebooks (now in Buffalo) that were eventually to yield almost half of his published poems, including all the poems that made up his groundbreaking and reputation-building, first two books *18 Poems* (1934) and *Twenty-Five Poems* (1936). Maud writes in his *Introduction* that his study of these notebooks reveals;

'...for the first time the extent of Thomas's poetic output from his fifteenth to his nineteenth year. It also confounds previous assumptions about the poet's later development by showing, also for the first time, how much of the poetry printed up to his twenty-sixth year was really a reworking of early poems.'

And he adds later:

'Indications are that up to this point [1930] Thomas's poems had been derivative, the borrowed forms dictating the subject and keeping the compositions essentially, albeit enthusiastically, artificial. The poems of this self-assigned homework appeared in the school magazine from 1925, first as precious buddings, later as deftly turned parodies. In April 1930, at the same time as he began the extant Notebooks with *Osiris, Come to Isis*, a serious poem in the Yeatsian manner, Thomas was actually ribbing Yeats in the school magazine with a parody entitled *In Borrowed Plumes*.'

We can see his considerable preconscious skills at poetic parody in this rendition of the nursery rhyme, *Little Miss Muffed* as written by W.B. Yeats.

My final thoughts are that this massive, never-to-be-repeated, testosterone-fuelled, outpouring of searing poems, that occurred as Dylan entered his later teens: poems fixated on Dylan's major themes of birth, sex and death, took him away from, and moreover, made repulsive, the business of writing anything but these new visceral poems. It was this that drove him to plagiarizing poems of this unchallenging kind of lesser work that he was still required to offer, and felt compelled to have to hand to give to the school mag. He was bored of writing what he knew was inferior doggerel rubbish, so why not pinch it ready-made? And he knew where to look – to the popular folk poets and poetasters from faraway lands, in America and Australia, or buried within the thick pages of the *Boys Own Paper*, or *Arthur Mee's Children's Encyclopaedia*, making discovery very unlikely.

There is a striking similarity of tone in the poems of Messer's Guest, Lawson, Thomas J. and Miss Gard. He may well have found suitable examples in the anthologies on the shelves of his father's extensive library at 5 Cwmdonkin Drive. More might be sourced in the library at the Grammar School, and there was always his favourite local second-hand bookshop, Swansea's famous 'Ralph the Books', where his lifetime pal, Ralph Wishart, would let him have the run of the shelves and sold him books for pennies. Having to deal with this sudden explosion of serious poetic creativity, during that moment between Eliot's 'Immature' poet and 'mature' poet, Dylan Thomas seems to have felt the need for a little literary misappropriation, about which he displayed little or no conscience.

One final point, let us remember that Dylan Thomas had a very developed and mischievous sense of humour; you only have to look at the very Welsh-looking name he invents for the village where *Under Milk Wood* is set – LLAREGUBB – and then read it backwards, to see this in action. He was a joker, a 'trickster', a leg-pulling weaver of fantasies and fallacies. He would no doubt have enjoyed the wicked, guilty ('Homer Nods') pleasures obtained by hood-winking his readers with a few poems – not his own. As late as 1952 he was still giving us a few pointers. Herewith a couple of clues he threw into an introduction he gave to a reading at The Massachusetts Institute of Technology in Boston on July 3rd 1952.[10] First he expands on his poetic influence and methods when he was a very young reader and writer:

> 'I wrote endless imitations, though at the time of writing I never thought of them as imitations but rather colossally original...imitations of whatever I happened to be golloping then, Thomas Browne, Robert W. Service, Stevenson, De Quincy, *Eskimo Nell*, Newbolt, Blake, Marlowe, the Imagists, the *Boys Own Paper* ...'

The same *Boys Own Paper* from where, 25 years earlier he had

25

IN BORROWED PLUMES.

Little Miss Muffet
Sat on a tuffet,
Eating her curds and whey,
When up came a spider
And sat down beside her,
And frightened Miss Muffet away.

From the *Swansea Grammar School Magazine* April 1930

II.

W. B. Yeats:

There was a pearl-pale moon that slid
Down oceans of ambrosial sky,
Under the drooping of the day's dusk-lid
Where darkness and her wine-waves lie,
And at that full nocturnal hour
She twined her splendid, curving hair,
And bent her body like a flower,
And glided through the evening air
Light as a cloud, and petal-fair.
She gained the garlanded and leaf-green mound
That tapered like a dove-gray hill,
To sink upon the deep grass without sound,
To press her face upon the lilting ground,
And twine her yellow hair like daffodil.
She raised fine, luscious fruit up to her lips,
Tasted the round grape in full-throated sips,
Smoothed upon her mouth the lovely pear,
When through the darkness coiled about the place,
The terror-scented darkness passion-dim,
A silver spider crawls, and weaves his web about her hair,
And weaves his silken rapture everywhere,
And looks into her wave-wild face,
And wonders why she weeps at him.

D.M.T.

misappropriated *His Requiem*. And later in his preamble he admits to his audience that whenever he likes he,

> '...can summon my juvenile literary delinquence before me and give it a long periodic sentence.'

What would strengthen this theory would be the existence of some poems known to be by Dylan, that bridge these two extremes but nothing of the sort seems to exist. Fitzgibbon offers another aside, unique to his biography, which concerns this and it also has a coincidental element. He writes:

> 'I cannot, in the school magazine, find any trace of the poems that were to come, though his notebooks show that he was beginning to write "Dylan Thomas poems" before he left the school.

Then he adds this:

> 'A German scholar, who researched lengthily in Swansea, did unearth one unsigned poem in the school magazine which gave a transitional clue between Dylan-the-boy and Dylan-the poet. I understand he had to scrap a whole thesis he was writing around this poem. Unfortunately it turned out to have been written by E.F. McInery.

The whistle-blower was almost mistaken for a culprit. And it is not just the general reader, but experts too, have been hood-winked, and in some instances still seem to be. The current Penguin Books *DYLAN THOMAS Selected Poems,* (2000), edited and introduced by Walford Davies has a 'Table of Dates' at the start, where the fifth entry states:

> *1927 14 January*: His first poem to be published nationally: *His Requiem* in the *Western Mail.*

And deep in the heart of Texas at *The Harry Ransom Humanities Research Centre*, they still seem to believe that *The Secret Whisky Cure* originates from Wales and not Australia! The catalogue of the collection describes the poem thus:

> *Also notable among the poetry in this collection is a selection of juvenilia, representing some of Thomas's earliest poetic output. There are four fair copies in the hand of his mother Florence – "Little Dreams," "The Mishap," "My Party and "The Secret Whisky cures"!*

Perhaps someone should run a check on all these early poems...

Addendum

The Times Literary Supplement December 19 & 26, 2014, Poetry and Biography. MichaelCaines Review of; Hannah Ellis, Editor; Dylan Thomas A Centenary Celebration.

He was also, in the beginning, another kind of imitator. The teenage Thomas filled notebook after notebook with visions and revisions, out of which much of the published work of the 1930s was to emerge: a "massive, never-to-be-repeated, testosterone-fuelled outpouring", as Jeff Towns enthuses in his contribution to *Dylan Thomas: A centenary celebration*. But the outpouring was to be contained and reworked for years to come. Towns's "'Borrowed Plumes' – Requiem for a Plagiarist" considers a subject Goodby does not dwell on. Thomas plagiarized what was thought to be his first published work, "His Requiem", published in the *Western Mail* in 1927 when he was about twelve. The subterfuge was only uncovered, remarkably, when somebody read the poem in 1971 and recalled that it had previously appeared in the *Boy's Own Paper*. Likewise, "Sometimes", submitted to the school magazine, turned out to be the work of the American Thomas.S. Jones, nabbed this time from Arthur Mee's *Children's Encyclopedia*. Last year Towns thought he had found an "unknown and unrecorded" poem – then he happened to turn on the television and heard something impossible: Idris Elba reading it out on the BBC *Sports Personality of the Year* programme. How could that be? It was, of course, another borrowed plume plucked from the works of another cannily chosen, unsung source, the sometime Poet Laureate of Michigan, Edgar Guest. Towns takes Eliot's maxim about immature poets imitating and mature poets stealing as his rueful epigraph.

Why steal, when you have talent? In their biographies, Ferris and Lycett suggest that Thomas felt the need to impress others (and in particular, Lycett suggests, "his remote father") when he made off with these competent but conventional works. Towns offers an alternative theory: Thomas was already, before his twenties, disgusted by the idea of writing anything except for his "new visceral poems" but, "compelled" to show up with something, mischievously offered up these inferior works instead. Buying himself time, perhaps, already obsessed with those fatal fundamentals – but courting popularity. And there you have the Dylan Thomas paradox *in nuce*, as reflected in the bifurcated centenary celebrations of 2014, blithe walking tours proceeding around Swansea and south Oxfordshire unperturbed by the fist-shaking of an irate editor of the *Collected Poems*.

Extract from the TLS review of *Dylan Thomas a Centenary Celebration*

1. See the Addendum at the end of this essay.

2. Paul Ferris gives a slightly different account of this event in his more recent biography.

3. You can still watch this on YouTube: It Couldn't Be Done – Edgar Guest – YouTube http://www.youtube.com/watch?v=tIhbAKL3EzE Jan 7, 2013 ... It Couldn't Be Done – As seen on BBC Sports Personality Of The Year 2012.

4. The original poem and all the supporting papers and ephemera are now in Swansea University.

5. Hosie Baskin, Cumberland Rare Books, Northampton, Mass. USA.

6. *DYLAN THOMAS: THE PUBS*. Jeff Towns. Illustrated by Wyn Thomas. Y LOLFA. 2013.

7. Woore – this word really puzzled but thanks to my editor David Cowell, who, using AI, discovered that the coroner who conducted the inquest was named Woore – John Chadwick Woore, who was the Sidney Coroner between 1889 and 1903.

8. *The Outing* began life with the title A Story and it was published in the American edition of *Quite Early One Morning*. New Directions 1954. It had previously (Sept. 1953) been published with an illustration by Charles Keeling in *The Listener*.

9. It is also worth noting that once while visiting with Bert, Dylan heard his daughter Pamela ask him 'What colour is glory? The question so intrigued and beguiled Thomas that he later used it in his note-book poems and finally it appears in *My World is a Pyramid*, the penultimate poem in Dylan's first collection, *18 Poems*. In this instance Eliot gets it right – Mature Poets Steal:
Who blows death's feather? What glory is colour? blow the stammel feather in the vein.

10. Published as *I Am Going to Read Aloud*. An Introduction to a reading at M I T Boston. Published in *The London Magazine* Sept.1956.

The rarest of all Dylan Thomas publications

7.

O Rare Dylan Thomas; A Book-Dealers View

I first addressed this subject in 2002, when my friend, one of the foremost Dylan Thomas scholars, editors and bibliographers, Ralph Maud, invited me to Vancouver, where he was Professor of English at Simon Fraser University. I was to give a lecture on some aspect of Dylan Thomas' life and work to the English Society. My memory was that it was around St. David's day and I was also asked to give another talk at the fine old Cambrian Hall, to the thriving local Welsh Society.

I decided that my talk at the university was to be a close examination of the bibliography of Dylan Thomas' publications in all its minutiae. I gave it a title; *Not in Rolph; Not in Ralph*; a nod to the two foremost Dylan Thomas bibliographers – John Alexander Rolph and my host, Ralph Maud. I began my talk warmly acknowledging them both, especially as one of them was sat right in front of me:

> Thank you for inviting me here to talk to you. The title of my talk may seem a little impertinent in as much as one of the protagonists is here in the audience – indeed it is largely due to Ralph Maud that I am here today. I would like to think that this talk is in many ways a homage and tribute to the diligent work of both John Rolph and Ralph Maud. But is not a scholarly bibliographical lecture, it is rather the self-indulgent ramblings and selected memories of a bookseller who is approaching a half century in Wales, coupled with a specific, maybe obsessional pursuit of the original manuscripts, letters, books, ephemera and iconography of Dylan Thomas, across the Western World.

The talk went well – I had carried a few rarities with me so I could engage in some show-and-tell, and my basic tenet was that between them, Rolph and Ralph had done a pretty thorough job, with very few omissions and inaccuracies. But I had a few additions to talk up and I also talked in general about Thomas' publication history and how it lends itself to both collecting and studying.

Not long after I got back to Swansea I was asked by the committee of *The Dylan Thomas Society of Great Britain*, if I could contribute a chapter to a collection of essays which they were putting together. I offered them a transcription of my Vancouver talk which they were very happy to accept and they duly published it in their 2003 tribute publication: '*I Sang in My Chains*' to commemorate the 50th anniversary of Dylan Thomas' death.

In the years following, every so often some new publication would be discovered, more nuggets of bibliographic information arose, and a few more odds and ends of unseen Dylaniana turned up; a good few I discovered and others came to me via Thomas scholars and his biographers. Then, in 2013, a Cardiff literary philanthropist and some-time publisher, but full time successful businessman – the remarkable Ali Anwar, approached me with a publishing project. Ali runs a literary foundation in Cardiff – the *H'mm Foundation* (named after a collection of poems by R.S.Thomas, Ali's first love). He explained that he wanted to add a book to a series he was publishing.[1] It was to be called *Encounters with Dylan* and it would comprise of a collection of essays by various writers on different responses to Dylan Thomas and be ready for publication in 2014 – Dylan Thomas' Centenary Year. I was very keen to oblige, and even more so when I saw that Jon Gower[2] was to edit the book. Jon is a writer who I admire, an old friend and a prolific, but always readable writer across many genres, and he writes in both Welsh and English. I was delighted when I saw a provisionary list of my co-contributors, which included some other good friends; the biographer Andrew Lycett; actor and theatre director Guy Masterson; Laugharne bookselling colleague, George Tremlett, the first Dylan Thomas Prize Winner, Rachel Tresize and one of my best customer and a good friend; the theatre director Michael Bogdanov.

I had a free hand to choose a topic but I needed to come up with something distanced from the other essays and so, as a still functioning rare book dealer, with over forty years' experience, I decided to revisit the area I knew best; the printing history, bibliography and collecting of Dylan Thomas, which would incorporate the Vancouver talk, but with new additional materials and images. I had retitled my chapter O *Rare Dylan Thomas*.[3]

The book, a small paperback, came out in 2014. Now some ten years on I'm having another look, but this time I've also added a postscript detailing some of the most extraordinary rare and unique Dylan Thomas items that have passed through my hands.

O Rare Dylan Thomas – A Book Dealers View

Dylan Thomas has been well served by his bibliographers. The standard bibliography *Dylan Thomas: A Bibliography* was compiled by J. Alex Rolph (himself a bookseller). It was published by J. M. Dent (Dylan's publishers) in 1956, with a foreword by Dame Edith Sitwell.

Rolph had begun work on it in 1952, while Dylan was still alive

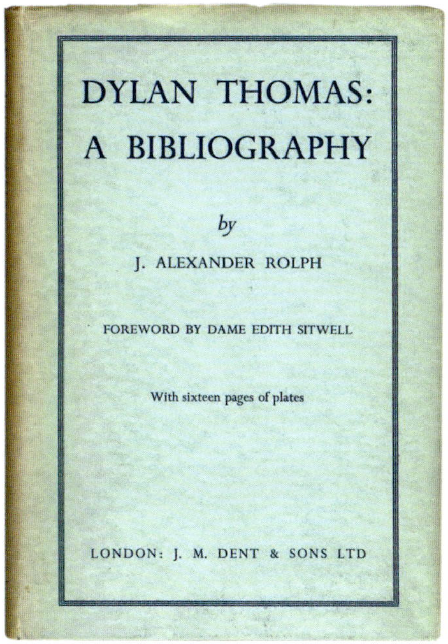

and the book reproduces a letter from Thomas in response to Rolph's request for his help and support, in which Dylan refers to the idea of the book as both a 'fantastic project' and a 'peculiar cause'. Needless to say Dylan was no great keeper of records and could offer scant assistance. He prophesies thus;

> 'I must warn you I can't remember much'

And indeed other letters from Dylan to Rolph have Dylan asking Rolph for his help in finding elusive printings of stories that Dylan needed to locate for inclusion in a projected new anthology. The great achievement of Rolph's bibliography is that it actually manages to be a good read. It is well laid out and clearly printed, has sixteen good plates, and offers a slightly eccentric methodology, in as much as Rolph's first section, his 'A' items, comprises of very detailed 'Literary biographies' of most all of Thomas's published poems written from September 1933, until 1956. This section in particular makes very interesting reading and the succeeding sections on the Books, Periodicals and Anthologies are full of useful information. The book ends with short sections on Translations and Gramophone recordings. All the entries are presented with very full bibliographical descriptions and details of dates, print runs, reprints and sales are also included wherever such figures were available.

More recently, but still over 40 years ago, Ralph Maud was one of the pathfinders of Dylan Thomas scholarship and exegesis having written published and edited many books about and by Dylan Thomas. His major work was in the editing of the four Dylan Thomas note-books that are now in the State University of New York (Buffalo). *The Poet in the Making The Notebooks of Dylan Thomas* was first published by Dent in 1968 but it was revised and updated in 1989 as *Dylan Thomas The Notebook Poetry*.[4] Ralph's *Dylan Thomas in Print; a Bibliographical History*, was first published in the States in 1970 and a year later it appeared in the UK. The book offers an encyclopaedic listing of books and magazines by and about Dylan Thomas. It does not attempt to provide the full bibliographical details that Rolph offers, but it is more than just a checklist, in that scattered throughout the listings, both in the main body of the text and in footnotes, it reprints interesting articles and reviews by and about Dylan, many of which had not been hitherto reprinted.

A few years ago Ralph Maud asked me to collaborate with him on a new edition of Rolph but the project came to nought, in many respects because Rolph and Ralph did such a good job between them, that these two pioneer bibliographers of Thomas did not miss very much at all.

The English edition of Ralph's bibliography

The only significant addition to these two works is the Author Checklist distributed by an American Bookselling company – *Quill and Brush*, run by Pat and Alan Aherne and their daughters who specialise in Modern First Editions. They would produce and offer their clients detailed duplicated Author Checklists. They recently approached me to help update their *Dylan Thomas Checklist* and much of what I write about here is contained in their most recent issue.

But before I begin my parade of Dylan Thomas rarities and curiosities a word about Dylan Thomas's bibliography in general. Dylan Thomas's canon is not vast – just seven or eight lifetime books and perhaps a dozen significant posthumous books. This is perhaps doubled by the James Laughlin's American *NEW DIRECTIONS* variant publications.

Dylan's *Collected Poems 1934-1952* contains under a hundred poems, but his juvenilia, fragments and notebook poems may just about double that number. Add to this a couple of dozen short stories, an unfinished novel, some thirty radio scripts, twenty film scripts and top this body of work off with *Under Milk Wood* – and there you have it – not too vast an output to trouble bibliographers about except for two related coincidences.

Firstly, Dylan was writing during the golden age of the literary periodical; the thirties and the forties – the two decades, which encompass most all of Dylan's publishing life. Maud lists over 100 little mags that published Dylan. So there existed for Dylan this vast opportunity and marketplace for poems and short stories which he endeavoured to exploit to the full; Connolly's *Horizon*, Eliot's *Criterion*, Desmond McCarthy's '*Life and Letters*', Grigson's '*New Verse*, Keidrych Rhys' *WALES*, Tambimuttu's *Poetry London*, Roger Roughton's surrealist and left-wing Contemporary *Poetry and Prose*; and short-lived curiosities like *Seven*, and *Yellow Jacket*, where the first issue (edited by Dylan's friend and future first biographer Constantine Fitzgibbon) actually sported a yellow cellophane over-wrapper!

These were all U.K. Publications; add to them their American equivalents: Harriet Munro's *Poetry* from Chicago, James Laughlin's *New Directions in Poetry and Prose*, *The Partisan Review* edited by Philip Rahv and William Phillips: plus numerous periodicals such as *The Kenyon Review* and *The Swanee Review*. And then there were the more exotic foreign publications – Henry Miller's '*Delta*' and Eugene Jolas' *Transition*, that featured surrealist, expressionist, and Dada art artists and writers. The Fall 1936 issue includes Dylan's poem, *Then was my Neophyte* and his short story *The Mouse and the Woman*, alongside reproductions of paintings by Piet Mondrian, Paul Klee, Henri Matisse and photographs by L. Moholy-Nagy, Francis Bruguiere, and Henri Cartier-Bresson; and Cover design by Joan Miró. It also contains the first part of Franz Kafka's *Metamorphosis*.[5]

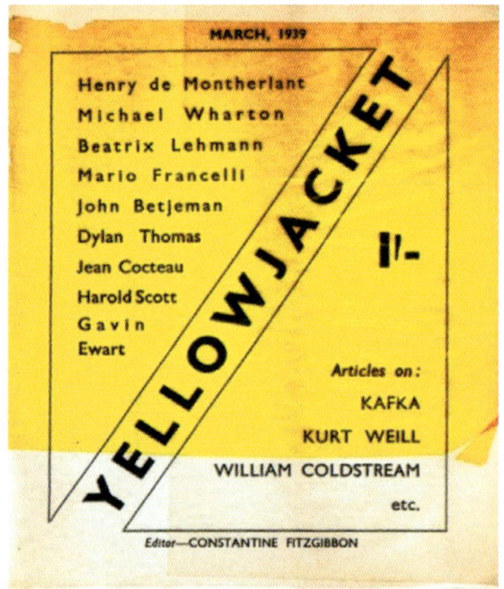

Secondly these decades, were for Dylan, marked by almost constant pecuniary embarrassment. Dylan Thomas was short of money his whole life through. This was in part due to his total lack of financial acumen but also because he rarely had a proper salaried job.[6] He lived by his pen, by royalties from his books and

payments for contributions to the literary magazine. He later added to this irregular income with fees for broadcasting at the BBC and other speaking engagements. Furthermore, some of these opportunities were coming under threat from the wartime paper shortage and the development of radio and television which were both contributing towards the eventual demise of most all these publications.

Living by his pen was a hard slog, and he was constantly short of money to keep himself and then, eventually, his wife and three children. He clutched at any source of income; he submitted poems and stories to many literary magazines and journals and constantly badgered editors for prompt payment. Moreover he was not beyond offering the same poem or story to more than one editor.

As a result almost all his individual poems or stories appear first in at least one periodical and often two, then in an anthology, before coming out in one of his own books; at least three bites of the cherry for Dylan and three bibliographical references for us. Throw into this mix the curious anomaly, in that, although Dylan described himself thus;

> I am a painstaking conscientious, involved and devious craftsman in words.

He was indeed a poet who constantly worked and re-worked his poems in draft after draft until he was satisfied, however, once he gave up his poems to an editor for publication he was quite cavalier about proofing and misprints. Thus the same poem often never appears the same way twice. Many of these variations may be minutia of punctuation – but even these can be crucial, and sometimes, whole words are mutated and changed. This makes for rich pickings for bibliographers, librarians, booksellers and collectors.

This can be shown quite deftly if we look closely at the publishing saga of one poem – his early and famous poem, *Light breaks where no sun shines*. It is poem A.8 in Rolph and Maud tells us, in his masterly editions of 'Dylan Thomas; The Notebook Poems' (1970 and 1989), that this poem was written in his fourth notebook in November of 1933. Dylan was obviously pleased with his notebook poem because we learn from Rolph that it was first published, without revisions, in *The Listener* in March 1934, entitled 'Light'. It is worth noting that this publication led to Dylan being noticed and approached by three of the doyens of the London Literary scene, Stephen Spender, Geoffrey Grigson and T. S. Eliot. Dylan also expostulated boastfully in a letter to Pamela Hansford Johnson, his first and current girlfriend, that the poem's sexual imagery provoked sack-full's of outraged and complaining letters and that this led to the BBC banning any future publication of his work. He writes;

> The little smut-hounds thought I was writing a copulatory anthem In reality ...it was a metaphysical image of rain and grief.

Although phrases such as 'Candle in the thighs', and 'the fruit of man unwrinkling in the stars' and 'gushers of the sky spout to the rod' are not devoid of sexual references, but his boasts are largely hyperbolic bravado for he was soon gracing the pages of '*The Listener*' again in October of the same year and he went on to become a regular contributor. The poem next appears in December in an anthology, *The Years Poetry 1934*, edited by Gerald Gould and John Lehman. Rolph describes this publication as constituting Dylan's first ever appearance in book form, and it is listed as D.1 in his section *Contributions by Dylan Thomas to books*.

Just a few days after the appearance of *The Years Poetry* in December of 1934, Dylan's first book, the monumental *18 Poems*, was first published by The Sunday Referee and Parton Street Bookshop. They printed 500 sets of sheets but only 250 copies were bound up as the first issue, the remaining sheets were bound up and published in 1936 and constitute the second issue. During these printings minor changes to the text occur, – 'glow-worms' loses the hyphen and 'fenced' gains a coma. The poem

next appears in Dylan's first American book *The World I Breathe*, published by James Laughlin's New Directions in 1939, in an edition of just 700 copies. In 1942 a rogue publisher Reginald Caton rather dubiously obtained the rights of *18 Poems* and offered a series of reprints bearing the imprint of his *The Fortune Press*, (each printing was dated 1934 and he went on issuing the book in variant bindings and colours until as late as 1954). The poem is finally included by Dylan in his *Collected Poems 1934-1952*, but by now the first line has become its title and 'glow-worms' has got its hyphen back! Along the way the poem also appears in a French translation in the magazine *Fontaine* in 1942, (only the second translation into French of a Dylan Thomas poem to appear), and later in 1957 it was released as a recording on a 7" 45 RPM, EP.

One poem,[7] a variety of different incarnations, and so it is with so much of Dylan's out-put. Much of the above – but not all, can be found in Rolph and Maud, but now to a few books, editions and curiosities that they missed.

Proof Copies

Proof copies are the advanced printings of books issued by publishers and are usually bound in drab paper covers for further editing and correcting of errors of spelling, grammar, punctuation, fact, or typography. They are usually marked *Proof* or *Proof-copy* and say *Not for Resale*. They may also be used as advance copies to be used for reviewers. Some Collectors see them as the earliest state of a text after the original manuscript or typescript. Sometimes they can differ significantly to the final edition which makes them even more desirable. In his Bibliography Rolph makes a generic comment regarding his attitude to 'Proof Copies' in his introduction to his *Section B. Books and Pamphlets by Dylan Thomas*;

> Proof copies are not mentioned except where some special significance attaches to them, but they may be taken to exist in the case of all bound books (trade edition) except *18 Poems*. The quantity of such proofs can be reckoned to be at about thirty copies before and during the war, and about double this figure, or even slightly more thereafter.

This makes these fragile little paper covered productions very scarce and I believe that in many instances Rolph was not in a position to examine certain proofs to decide whether or not they offered any 'special significance'. Herewith some observations on Dylan Thomas's Proof Copies I have handled which Rolph does not describe.

Twenty-Three Poems. 1936

An unrecorded Advance Proof copy for the book that was published as Twenty-Five Poems – Thomas's second collection of poems. Neither Rolph nor Maud makes mention of any proofs for *Twenty-Five Poems*, which was Dylan's first book with a major London Publisher, J. M. Dent. (who became and remain his major UK publisher). Rolph does describe Dylan showing his first publisher, Victor Neuberg, a sheaf of twenty-one poems. Neuberg was eager to cash-in on the responses to *18 Poems* and suggested that Dylan make up the number of poems to twenty-five, but at this point Dylan was taken on by a mainstream publisher and it was *Twenty-Five Poems* that Richard Church, of J. M. Dent & Sons, saw through the press in 1936 (Rolph tells us that only 700 copies of the first edition were printed, a very small edition for a

The rare proof

The published book

large commercial publisher like Dent).

Not strictly of Bibliographic interest, I can't resist sharing this spoof blurb which came up for auction recently. Dylan wrote this into the front a copy of *Twenty-Five Poems* for a lucky friend; Dylan was no fan of blurbs and cover puffs!

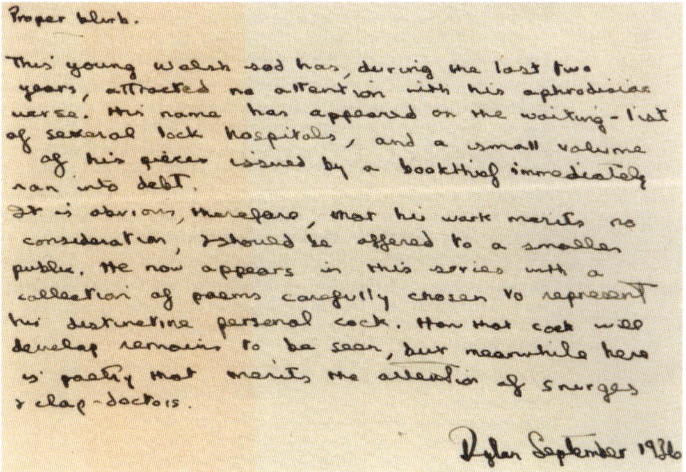
Proper blurb.

This young Welsh sod has, during the last two years, attracted no attention with his aphrodisiac verse. His name has appeared on the waiting-list of several lock hospitals, and a small volume of his pieces issued by a bookthief immediately ran into debt.
It is obvious, therefore, that his work merits no consideration, & should be offered to a smaller public. He now appears in this series with a collection of poems carefully chosen to represent his distinctive personal cock. How that cock will develop remains to be seen, but meanwhile here is poetry that merits the attention of smurges & clap-doctors.

Dylan September 1936

[A transcription of the above][8]

This young Welsh sod has, during the last two years, attracted no attention with his aphrodisiac verse. His name has appeared on the waiting list of several lock hospitals,* and a small volume of his pieces issued by a bookthief immediately ran into debt. It is obvious, therefore, that this work merits no consideration, and should be offered to a smaller public. He now appears in this series with a collection of poems carefully chosen to represent his distinctive personal cock. How that cock will develop remains to be see, but meanwhile here is poetry that merits the attention of smurges** & clap-doctors***. Dylan Thomas 1936.

*Lock Hospital; An establishment that specialised in treating sexually transmitted diseases.

** Smuges; A person who flirts "with intent". i.e. to talk to a member of the opposite sex with the express intent to have sex with that person

***Medical specialist in Venereal Diseases

Rolph makes no mention of the proof of this book, but close examination of my copy of a proof [Now in the national Library of Wales] shows that the first section of the book was entirely reset before publication. The proof copy has no dedication page, which in the published version is simply to Caitlin, this was, after all, Dylan's first book since his marriage.

In the proof copy, the second contents page, lists only six of the seven stories listed in the published book, – no mention of 'The Enemies'. However, this story is to be found in the text. Once into the text proper, in the proof, the first poem is entitled 'January 1939' with no number. In the published version this poem is number 1, with 'January 1939' below, and in parenthesis. In the proof the second poem – 'I make this warring absence' is poem number 1, but it is split so that poem number 2 begins with the line 'These Once Blind Eyes have breathed'. This is reflected in the contents page of the proof. In the published version of the book this poem has disappeared from the contents page and has become part of poem two, 'I make this Warring Absence'. From then on the poems and numbers are identical.

Collected Poems 1934-1952: An Unrecorded Proof Copy

In his bibliography Rolph writes:

> A few weeks prior to publication 68 proof copies were printed; these have the leaves which ultimately bore the 'Authors Prologue' blank except for the word 'Preface' on p. (v), also the Dedication and The 'Note' on its verso is lacking (pp. (v)-(vi) in the trade edition)

I once handled a later, unrecorded proof, almost certainly not one of the original 68 copies. This proof has an extra fascicle inserted after the preface which has the 'Authors Prologue' printed across a two page opening. On September 10th 1952, (just one month before publication of 'Collected Poems') Dylan writes a letter to E.F.Bozman, his editor at Dent in which he includes 'The Prologue', and tries to explain it,

'I intended to write...a more-or-less straightforward &

intimate Prose preface, and then funked it.
And then I began to write a prologue in verse
... To begin with, I set myself, foolishly
perhaps, a most difficult task: The Prologue is
in two verses in my manuscript, a verse to a
page of 51 lines each. And the second verse
rhymes backward with the first...Why I
acrosticked myself like this, don't ask me'

And he asks quite pointedly;

> I will have a proof of this, won't I?

In this later proof the printing of 'Prologue' follows Dylan's two page original typescript in which the central couplet spans the page break;

> sheep white Hollow farms
> To Wales in my arms

It is also printed with line numbers in the margins, in fives, advancing to 50 and then ascending from 50. All this helps the reader detect this complicated pattern. I am sure that after struggling with such a challenge, 'It has taken the devil of a time to finish', wrote Dylan, he wanted his readers to notice his achievement. Furthermore a new 'Note' in this proof explains this structure to us;

> 'it is in two verses of fifty one lines each,
> and the second verse rhymes backward with the first'

However this was not to be. To squeeze the poem across two pages a much smaller typeface was necessary, which was almost unreadable, and typographically unpleasant. In the published version it has become the 'Author's Prologue' and it is printed over four pages without line numbering, and we are left to fathom out the rhyme scheme by ourselves because the 'Note' from the proof is also scrapped. In the new note, we are given no clues as the Prologue's intricacies but we are told,

> These poems with all their crudities, doubts, and confusions, are written for the love of Man and in praise of God, and I'd be a damn' fool if they weren't.

In both proofs Paper and Sticks is still printed on page 116, but

Author's Prologue

This day winding down now
At God speeded summer's end
In the torrent salmon sun,
In my seashaken house
On a breakneck of rocks
Tangled with chirrup and fruit,
Froth, flute, fin and quill
At a wood's dancing hoof,
By scummed, starfish sands
With their fishwife cross
Gulls, pipers, cockles, and sails,
Out there, crow black, men
Tackled with clouds, who kneel
To the sunset nets,
Geese nearly in heaven, boys
Stabbing, and herons, and shells
That speak seven seas,
Eternal waters away
From the cities of nine
Days' night whose towers will catch
In the religious wind
Like stalks of tall, dry straw,
At poor peace I sing
To you strangers (though song
Is a burning and crested act,
The fire of birds in
The world's turning wood,
For my sawn, splay sounds),
Out of these seathumbed leaves
That will fly and fall
Like leaves of trees and as soon
Crumble and undie
Into the dogdayed night.
Seaward the salmon, sucked sun slips,
And the dumb swans drub blue
My dabbed bay's dusk, as I hack
This rumpus of shapes
For you to know
How I, a spinning man,
Glory also this star, bird
Roared, sea born, man torn, blood blest.
Hark: I trumpet the place,
From fish to jumping hill! Look:
I build my bellowing ark
To the best of my love
As the flood begins,
Out of the fountainhead
Of fear, rage red, manalive,
Molten and mountainous to stream
Over the wound asleep
Sheep white hollow farms

viii

To Wales in my arms.
Hoo, there, in castle keep,
You king singsong owls, who moonbeam
The flickering runs and dive
The dingle furred deer dead!
Huloo, on plumbed bryns,
O my ruffled ring dove
In the hooting, nearly dark
With Welsh and reverent rook,
Coo rooing the woods' praise,
Who moons her blue notes from her nest
Down to the curlew herd!
Ho, hullaballoing clan
Agape, with woe
In your beaks, on the gabbing capes!
Heigh, on horseback hill, jack
Whisking hare! who
Hears, there, this fox light, my flood ship's
Clangour as I hew and smite
(A clash of anvils for my
Hubbub and fiddle, this tune
On a tongued puffball)
But animals thick as thieves
On God's rough tumbling grounds
(Hail to His beasthood!).
Beasts who sleep good and thin,
Hist, in hogsback woods! The haystacked
Hollow farms in a throng
Of waters cluck and cling,
And barnroofs cockcrow war!
O kingdom of neighbours, finned
Felled and quilled, flash to my patch
Work ark and the moonshine
Drinking Noah of the bay,
With pelt, and scale, and fleece:
Only the drowned deep bells
Of sheep and churches noise
Poor peace as the sun sets
And dark shoals every holy field.
We will ride out alone, and then,
Under the stars of Wales,
Cry, Multitudes of arks! Across
The water lidded lands,
Manned with their loves they'll move,
Like wooden islands, hill to hill.
Huloo, my prowed dove with a flute!
Ahoy, old, sea-legged fox,
Tom tit and Dai mouse!
My ark sings in the sun
At God speeded summer's end
And the flood flowers now.

ix

COLLECTED POEMS 1934–1952
by Dylan Thomas

With a frontispiece portrait of the author
by AUGUSTUS JOHN, *and a ~~Preface~~ by the Author*

Demy 8vo. 12*s.* 6*d.* net Prologue in Verse.

Special edition of sixty-five numbered copies, signed by the author, of which sixty are for sale; mould-made paper, leather binding; £5 5s. net

Mr. Dylan Thomas is one of the most widely discussed poets of his generation, and the place of his work in the field of modern poetry is assured. This volume gathers together all his published poems, including those from books which have been out of print for a while, that is to say from *Eighteen Poems* (1934), *Twenty-five Poems* (1936), *The Map of Love* (1939), which contained sixteen poems as well as seven stories, and *Deaths and Entrances* (1946), which was among the few modern writings included in the Festival of Britain great books exhibition at the Victoria and Albert Museum. In addition the present volume includes ten new poems which have not hitherto appeared in book form, and the author has written a ~~preface~~ for it. Prologue in Verse

In 1939, Mr. Herbert Read, reviewing the poems in *The Map of Love*, wrote: 'They contain the most absolute poetry that has been written in our time, and one can only pray that this poet will not be forced in any way to surrender the subtle course of his genius.' Since then Dylan Thomas has still further increased his reputation, and his output to the present time is consolidated in this important volume.

★ *Probable publication date:* NOVEMBER 1952

4

in the letter to Bozman, quoted above, Dylan ends with this footnote;

> Proofreading the Collected Poems, I have the horrors of '*Paper & Sticks*' on page 116. It's awful. I suppose it's quite impossible to cut it out like it, somehow, to be omitted.

And in the final edition it was removed.

Dylan got his wish because this poem had to go to accommodate the four pages of '*Prologue*' and '*Do not go gentle into that good night*', is moved from page 174 in the proofs, to page 116, somewhat compromising the rough chronological order of the poems. My copy also has an interesting printed publicity blurb pasted to the verso of the front wrapper, which has two corrections in Dylan's hand that indicates the real importance he placed on this new poetic prologue. In both cases 'Preface' is crossed out and 'Prologue in Verse' is inserted. He has also inserted 10th into the publication date. I have never seen this advert anywhere else.[10]

New Poems 1942. An Anthology of British and American Verse. An Unrecorded Signed Limited Edition

Herewith the description of the recorded regular trade edition of this anthology *New Poems 1942. An Anthology of British and American Verse.* Edited by Oscar Williams. Mount Vernon, NY: Peter Pauper Press, 1942. 8 pages of poets' portraits in black and white photographs. Although the trade edition of this is volume is recorded in both Rolph and Maud This is my description of this Signed Limited Special issue, which is not mentioned in either Rolph or Maud's bibliography.

New Poems 1942. An Anthology of British and American Verse. Edited by Oscar Williams. Mount Vernon, NY: Peter Pauper Press, 1942. First edition, signed limited special issue, of 59 copies, comprising of 33 copies each printed with the name of the recipient and signed by all contributors.[9] With a further 26 copies lettered A-Z, all signed by all contributors. The 26 Lettered copies were offered for sale.

The contributing poets were: Conrad Aiken, Kenneth Allott, W. H. Auden, George Barker, John Peale Bishop, R. P. Blackmuir, Hugh Chisholm, Gene Derwood, Richard Eberhart, William Empson, Jean Garrigue, Horace Gregory, Alfred Hayes, Ruth Herschberger, Randall Jarrell, Robinson Jeffers, C. Day Lewis, Archibald Macleish, Louis Macneice, Marianne Moore, Howard Nemerov, Frederic Prokosch, Muriel Rukeyser, Delmore Schwartz, Winfield Townley Scott, Karl Shapiro, Theodore Spencer, Stephen Spender, Wallace Stevens, Dylan Thomas, Robert Penn Warren, and Oscar Williams.

I was first made aware of this extreme rarity when, in the early 80's I was offered this copy at a London book fair by a public school-educated, hot-shot young dealer. Not only had I never seen nor knew of its existence, but this copy was the copy with the printed name designating it as the copy for – DYLAN THOMAS. And not only that; the signatures were all on three leaves of lined pages at the start, with the signature running down the page. All were just scrawled straight forward signatures but Dylan's of course was different It was the last one so he added a typical flippant addition – he wrote

Uncle Dylan Thomas & All

A witty enough reference to a famous old English folk-song *Are you going to Widdecombe Fair*.[11] I really had to buy that book. The young dealer knew it was good and he could sense me trying to hide my excitement. He drove a hard bargain and I think I ended up paying around £450 for the book.

In those days that was a tidy sum and back then, that was a figure too high for me to hide the book away on my own shelves. I needed to turn books over, so I carefully packed it up and shipped it to New York, where I was about to exhibit at the next big International book fair.

I had recently made the acquaintance of a wealthy Californian book collector, Maurice Neville, who was building what would become one of the great Dylan Thomas Collections of all time. I planned to offer this unrecorded rarity to Maurie and priced it $1500 (around £1250). Maurie duly came by my booth and I showed him the book but he just looked bemused and confused when I kept going on about Tom Cobley and Widdecombe Fair, but of course he was puzzled; he was from Santa Barbara; he

The Trade Edition in Dust-wrapper

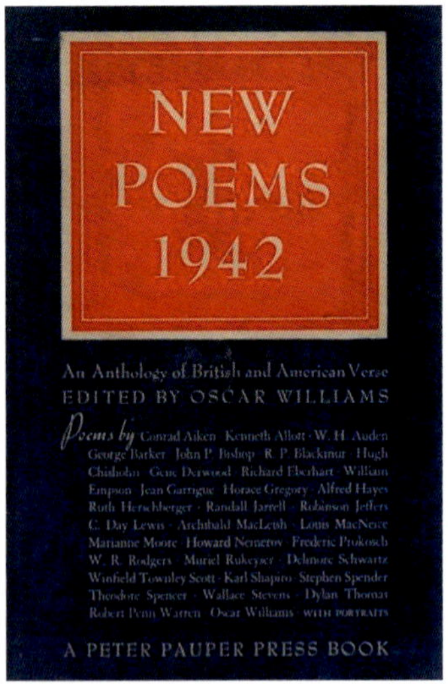

The special signed limited edition in a slipcase

knew nothing of quaint English folksongs. I would not give up; I really thought Dylan's flippant quip was a selling point. It was then that my very eccentric good friend and booth partner, Dr. Eric Korn, decided to step in to help and he broke into a rousing rendition of the rather tedious version of the repetitive song in a near impenetrable Devonian accent all the while urging me to join in.[11]

Maybe Maurie said 'I'll take it' just to end the cacophony, but he was nobody's fool and he knew a good book when he saw one. Maurie and I went on to become good friends and he visited me here in Swansea and I gave him the grand Dylan Thomas tour. He then became a colleague too, when he entered the book trade and opened his own stunning bookshop in Santa Barbara. I visited a couple of times and one time he took me back to his house and I marvelled at, and drooled over, his vast personal collection of rare modern literature.

Some thirty years later Maurie sold his magnificent collection over a few auctions in Sotheby's New York. I happened to be in Florida, vacationing with one of my best customers – a Lawyer and a Dylan Thomas Collector, when this copy was being offered in for sale at auction. I used my pal's law office in downtown Fort Pierce to bid on the telephone and I successfully got it for a few thousand dollars. I kept the book for longer this time but just recently sold it for a tad more than I paid.

Two Unrecorded Anthologies printed abroad.
POETRY OF OUR TIMES. Being a Compilation of | Modern Poetry together| with some of its Ancestors| THOTH BOOKSHOP CAIRO|1943. Not in Rolph or Maud.This small paperback in printed wrappers and seems to have been aimed at both literate soldiers and ex-patriots. It appears to be edited Eric de Nemes; the one page preface is signed E.N., and the book begins with a curious surrealist text 'Escape and Fall' described as 'A Ballad in seven drawings by Eric de Nemes. The anthology begins with Donne and ends with Vernon Watkins via Blake. the Romantics and most of the Moderns. It contains four poems by Dylan; *Light breaks Where No Sun Shines, On a Wedding Anniversary, Deaths and Entrances and The Force that Through the Green Fuse Drives The Flower.*

Twelve Modern Poets. An Anthology edited by Artur Lundkvist. Zephyr Books.[12]
The Continental Book Company. 1946 Printed in Stockholm. 12mo. pp. 222. Paper wrappers with d.j. Poets include Eliot, Pound, Sitwell, Auden, Day Lewis, Spender, Macneice, Empson, Bottrall, Dylan Thomas, George Baker and David Gascoyne. Contains 14 poems by Thomas including a few rarely

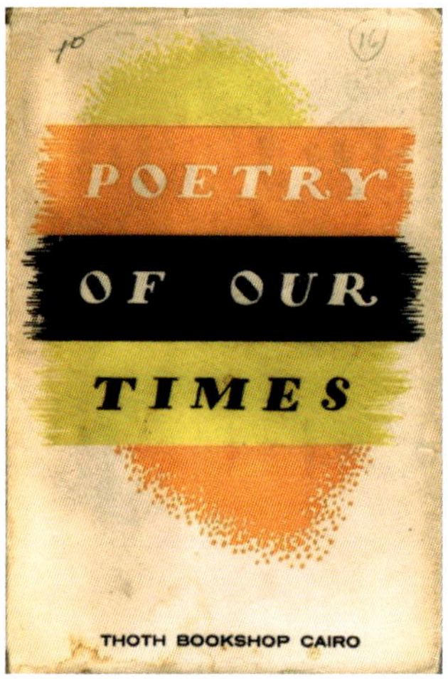

Neither in Rolph or Maud

anthologised. The editor Artur Lundkvist was an important Swedish intellectual, poet and critic. In his introduction he has this to say of Thomas:

Dylan Thomas represents another current in the English poetry of the thirties: the fantastic and myth-making. His Welsh provincialism is fused with a certain personal surrealism, a fertile imagination mixing biblical allusions and psychoanalytic ideas, folklore and modern neurasthenia, and so charging the blend with sexuality that the whole world becomes a sexual myth.

Neither in Rolph or Maud
AN UNRECORDED 'Book of the Film'
No Room at the Inn – A novel adapted from a film. No Room at the Inn/The Book of the Film/By Warwick Mannon/Adapted from Dylan Thomas and Ivan Foxwell's screenplay based on the play by Joan Temple. World Film Publications Limited/London/1948. A 'Double Feature Book of The Film'. Printed paper wrappers. This novelisation of a film which was co-scripted by Dylan Thomas is film profusely illustrated with stills from the film. Dylan does not make the cover but is acknowledged on the title page. Not in Rolph and although Maud lists three references to reviews of this film he does not record this book publication.

AN UNRECORDED Poetry Pamphlet of anti-war poetry
The Dove in Flames/An Anthology of Modern Verse/Edited by/Norman Kreitman/Published by/Housmans/London [1952]. An unrecorded, small yellow booklet in paper wrappers. An anthology of war poems which contains Dylan's two great second world war poems – The Hand that Signed the Paper Felled a City' and A Refusal to Mourn the Death, by Fire of a Child in London. Among other poets represented are Ruthven Todd, e.e. cummings, Alun Lewis and David Gascoyne. My copy has an inscription from the editor,

To Dylan Thomas in admiration and with warmest wishes
Norman Kreitman. Dec.1952.

Unrecorded in the bibliographies, Dylan did however, write a

Neither in Rolph or Ralph Maud

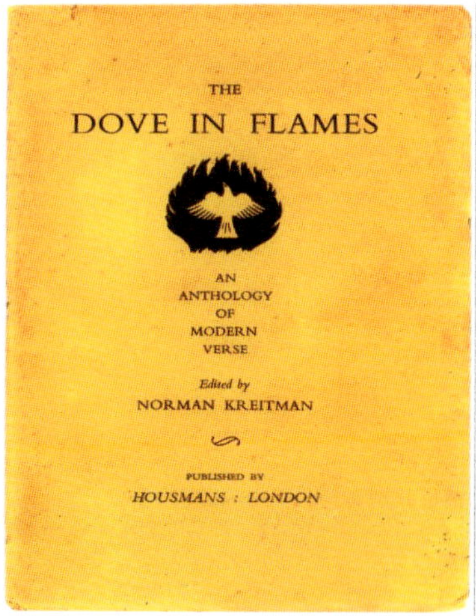

letter to a G. F.Hench (?) from Majoda in New Quay in 1945 in which he grants permission for the use of these two poems in an Anthology to be called Poems for Europe which in all probability was taken over by Kreitman and published here as *The Dove in Flames*.

Two unrecorded, American, fifties, pulp paperback anthologies, which include Dylan Thomas short stories.
Crazy Mixed-Up Kids. Jean-Paul Sartre Wm. Carlos Williams William Faulkner Dylan Thomas Charles Jackson Glenway Wescott And Others. Edited by William Hodapp Berkley Publishing Corps. 145 West 57th Street. New York N.Y. 1955.

This is a wonderful example of American Pulp paperback production. The back cover tells us that the contents are 'SHOCKINGLY DIFFERENT 'and that the stories all have; common theme – the "crazy mixed-up" behaviour of the young [containing,] startling examples of teen-age problems. Dylan's short story 'One Warm Saturday' from 'Portrait of the Artist as a Young Dog', apparently fits this billing. Dylan is one of five of the ten contributors to make the front cover, beside a bizarre image of a rather demure acrogenous person about to inject him/herself with a giant hypodermic syringe

LOVE Around the World.
A collection of stories about the strange byways of love by Vladimir Nabokov William Faulkner Alberto Moravia Dylan Thomas and Others. Berkley Book Published by Berkley Publishing Corp. 1959. This is another similar production to the previous book but from the West Coast. Another wonderful pulp paperback, which yet again republishes Dylan's short story *One Warm Saturday* from *Portrait of the Artist as a Young Dog*. Dylan is once more given front cover status, one of just four of the contributors, (along with Nabokov, Faulkner and Moravia) listed above a salaciously entwined couple, spread-eagled below a Mondrian-like coloured window. Inside on the first leaf we are told that the theme of these stories is of 'love's strangest hiding places'. Dylan's story is heralded as being about a;

'Boozy resort in England'.
But this story it is set in the heart of Swansea, which may be Boozy but is never, ever in England!

NOT IN ROLPH but Found in RALPH.
Two Epigrams of Fealty & Galsworthy and Gawsworth.
[London], Realm of Redonda, [1953]
Two single sheets folded to make eight pages. Both 'Privately Printed' for members of the Court of Redonda in an edition of 30 numbered copies. These copies are inscribed by Gawsworth to Wrey Gardiner, proprietor and publisher of the *Grey Walls Press*, but he uses his given Redonda name – *Rio di Oro, a souvenir of Gweno*. They are also marked as 'proof copies'. Redonda is the mythical kingdom created by the writer M. P. Shiel and continued at this time by his successor John Gawsworth (the pseudonym of Terence Ian Fytton Armstrong). Gawsworth had bestowed the title 'Duke of Gweno' on Dylan Thomas when he was admitted to the society in 1947. Rolph was unaware of these

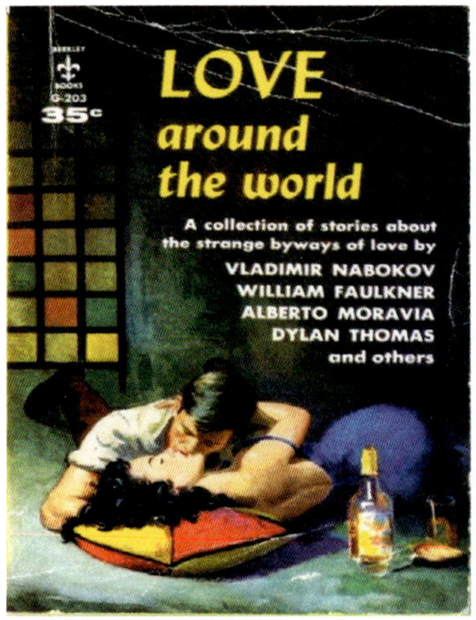

two ephemeral pamphlets but Maud does list these and reprints Gawsworth's account of how he came to publish these two very insignificant short poems, one about, and one for John Gawsworth. The back-story to these pamphlets is far better than the two slight poems they contain.

In 2003 to commemorate the fiftieth anniversary of Dylan's death, I compiled, with the bookseller and scholar Arthur Freeman, a booklet reprinting the two rare little pamphlets, together with Arthur's account of his dealings with the nefarious Galsworthy. It was Published by Ty Llên.

An UNRECORDED Single Sheet printed broadside announcement.
The King of *The Realm of Redonda* reveals his Court 1947.
A rare broadsheet Signed by John Gawsworth with his Regal

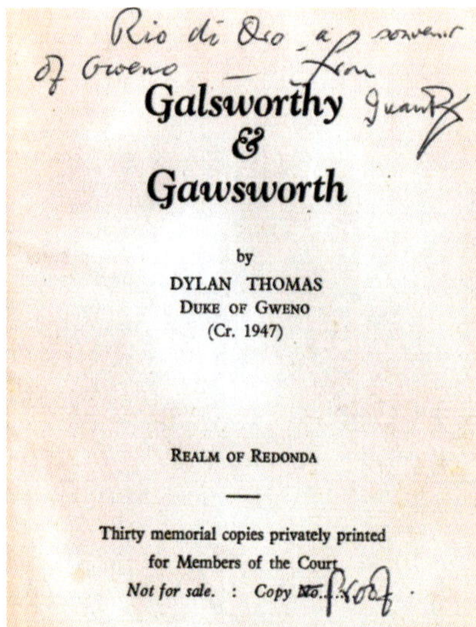

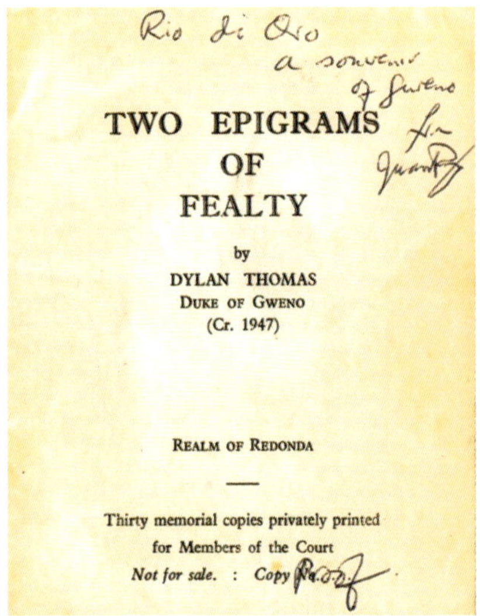

name King Juan, and by G.S. Fraser[13] who signed in his role as Chamberlain. Many of the Duchies are of a literary bent, including Arthur Machen, Henry Miller, Lawrence Durrell, Philip Lindsay, Oswald Blakeston and the Bookseller Bertram Rota. Dylan Thomas knew most of these writers and he himself is designated as a Duchy. In 1947 Gawsworth raised Dylan to Duke of Gweno.

By the time of his death in 1970, Gawsworth was a near destitute homeless alcoholic often sleeping on a bench in Hyde Park. He was succeeded as [one of] the notional monarchs of Redonda by the famous and prolific Spanish writer and translator, Javier Marias who died recently. As I was writing this I received some photocopies of a few pages from a paperback collection of Javier's short stories, one of which was set inside and outside Bertram Rota's Covent Garden Bookshop (now closed, but the firm continues). It involves a copy of the epigrams displayed in the window amongst other rare modern lit. The story was on these pages but it came with no covering letter. I enquired of another bookseller friend if it was her work – she denied any involvement with the photocopies but admitted that she had known Javier, who was more than a tad obsessed with Gawsworth and Redonda. Javier had died in 2022, but not before he had published a successful *Oxford novel, All Souls*,[14] which includes both an episode about Gawsworth and a description of my lady bookseller friend herself. The short story entitled *An Epigram of Fealty* is from his collection While the Women are Sleeping. I took great pleasure from this curious synchronistic journey.

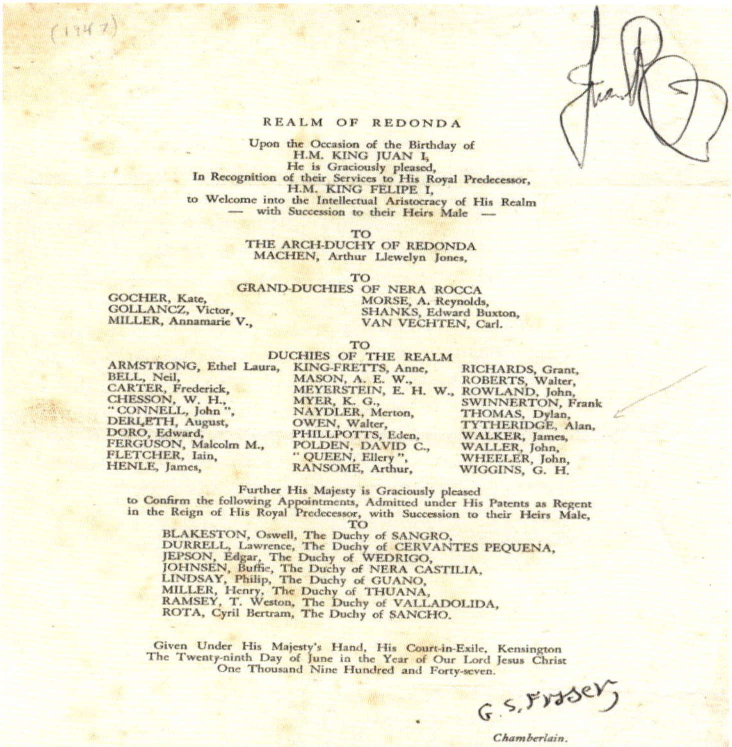

(1947)

REALM OF REDONDA

Upon the Occasion of the Birthday of
H.M. KING JUAN I,
He is Graciously pleased,
In Recognition of their Services to His Royal Predecessor,
H.M. KING FELIPE I,
to Welcome into the Intellectual Aristocracy of His Realm
— with Succession to their Heirs Male —

TO
THE ARCH-DUCHY OF REDONDA
MACHEN, Arthur Llewelyn Jones,

TO
GRAND-DUCHIES OF NERA ROCCA
GOCHER, Kate,
GOLLANCZ, Victor,
MILLER, Annamarie V.,
MORSE, A. Reynolds,
SHANKS, Edward Buxton,
VAN VECHTEN, Carl.

TO
DUCHIES OF THE REALM
ARMSTRONG, Ethel Laura,
BELL, Neil,
CARTER, Frederick,
CHESSON, W. H.,
"CONNELL, John",
DERLETH, August,
DORO, Edward,
FERGUSON, Malcolm M.,
FLETCHER, Iain,
HENLE, James,
KING-FRETTS, Anne,
MASON, A. E. W.,
MEYERSTEIN, E. H. W.,
MYER, K. G.,
NAYDLER, Merton,
OWEN, Walter,
PHILLPOTTS, Eden,
POLDEN, DAVID C.,
"QUEEN, Ellery",
RANSOME, Arthur,
RICHARDS, Grant,
ROBERTS, Walter,
ROWLAND, John,
SWINNERTON, Frank
THOMAS, Dylan,
TYTHERIDGE, Alan,
WALKER, James,
WALLER, John,
WHEELER, John,
WIGGINS, G. H.

Further His Majesty is Graciously pleased
to Confirm the following Appointments, Admitted under His Patents as Regent
in the Reign of His Royal Predecessor, with Succession to their Heirs Male,
TO
BLAKESTON, Oswell, The Duchy of SANGRO,
DURRELL, Lawrence, The Duchy of CERVANTES PEQUENA,
JEPSON, Edgar, The Duchy of WEDRIGO,
JOHNSEN, Buffie, The Duchy of NERA CASTILIA,
LINDSAY, Philip, The Duchy of GUANO,
MILLER, Henry, The Duchy of THUANA,
RAMSEY, T. Weston, The Duchy of VALLADOLIDA,
ROTA, Cyril Bertram, The Duchy of SANCHO.

Given Under His Majesty's Hand, His Court-in-Exile, Kensington
The Twenty-ninth Day of June in the Year of Our Lord Jesus Christ
One Thousand Nine Hundred and Forty-seven.

G. S. Fraser

Chamberlain.

It is interesting to note, from this letter that it was Gawsworth who began the process by which Rota's bought Dylan's four early poetic notebooks which are now in the Lockwood Memorial Library of The State University of New York at Buffalo.

March 29th, 1941

Dear Mr. Thomas,

In the course of conversation Mr. John Gawsworth mentioned to me that you might not be averse to selling the original manuscripts of some of your poems. I am interested in material of this sort and would be glad to have the offer of anything you cared to dispose of. Prices are not very high but I should hope to be able to send you an acceptable sum in return for a group of manuscripts.

Yours very truly, Bertram Rota.

Not in Rolph – Dylan Thomas' First Published poem in a National Publication

The Second Best is not recorded in Rolph but it is listed by Ralph Maud. What is of some interest is that there is also a poem in this volume written by Lillian Gard, a verse writer who had published a poem called "*His Requiem*" in the Boys Own Paper in 1923, which Dylan had plagiarised and sent it under his own name into the *Western Mail*, Wales' leading national daily paper, where it appeared in the "Wales Day by Day" column. Dylan was

Bound yearly Volume of the *Boy's Own Paper*. The poem appeared in the February 1927 issue (Vol. XL1X Pt.1)

"The Second Best."

YOU ask me for a toast to-night
In this familiar hall,
Where well-known objects greet the sight,
And boyhood's days recall.

"Some honoured name," I think you said,
But what have I to say ?
The King, the Services, the Head,
The heroes of the day—

To each with joyous shouts and pride
Has loud acclaim been paid ;
Forgive me, if I turn aside
From sunshine into shade.

For now a shadow-throng I see,
From seats long vacant rise,
A faint reproach there seems to be
In their world-weary eyes.

Their voices cross our song and jest
From camp and field and town—
The men who did their level best,
Yet never won renown.

Amongst the nameless dead they lie
In unrecorded graves ;
And o'er their memory roll high
The world's oblivious waves,

Yet though the school they loved so well
No more records their name,
Though on their brows there may not dwell
A crown of earthly fame,

Though on life's battlefield their part
Was not to gain the prize,
Still deep in some old comrade's heart
Enshrined their memory lies.

I give to-night no foremost name,
I give no honoured guest;
I think of those unknown to fame,
I give "The Second Best."

The rarest Dylan Thomas item

THIS long-awaited portfolio of original etchings was initiated at *Atelier 17* New York, in 1951, under Peter Grippe's direction. Each poem is in the poet's handwriting, in most instances engraved by the poet himself.

It will be published in October 1958 by Morris Weisenthal, himself one of the early contributors, and now director of the Morris Gallery. Mr. Grippe and he, over a period of years, enlarged the scope of the project to include many celebrated artists and poets.

Dylan Thomas, in life and in memory, was the spirit behind the task. James Johnson Sweeney, Director of The Solomon R. Guggenheim Museum, has written an Introduction.

The edition is limited to 50 numbered copies, printed on Rives paper.

Format of sheets, 16¾" x 20

Price in portfolio, $350.00

Orders received prior to July 15, $300.00

MORRIS GALLERY

174 Waverly Place, New York 14, N.Y. · WATKINS 9-5425

awarded a prize of Five Shillings. You can read the whole story of the eventual discovery of this literary theft in Chapter 6. in this book – *Dylan Thomas – Borrowed Plumes – Requiem for a Plagiarist.*

Two Items not in the Bibliographies, which I have never handled, but are known to exist.

THE RULERS by K.B. Koppel – with words by Dylan Thomas. The late great booksellers – Franny and Gary of Waiting For Godot Books in Easthampton Massachusetts (Beckett is to them, what Thomas is to me), sold it before I could get my hands on it. From my researches I think we are looking for a book of music by a socialist composer named Herman David Koppel (1908-1998), a Danish Jew who fled Denmark during the war and whilst here set some of Dylan's poems to music. I've hunted and hunted for it but can't find a copy anywhere.

Above is the original prospectus for a suite of etchings which includes, what I think, is the rarest of Dylan Thomas items – the etching made by Dylan and Peter Grippe for his poem *The Hand that Signed the Paper*. It is the closest I have ever got to this item. Below is a description of the only full set I have seen offered for sale by a great New York Bookselling firm, The House of El Dieff Inc at $3250 but this was back in 1964.

THOMAS, Dylan. THE RULERS. For Mixed Choir & Orchestra. (London): K. B. Koppel, [No Date; possibly 1940's]. 8vo, white printed wrappers, 22 pages, stapled. Music for "mixed choir and orchestra" with words by Dylan Thomas. Front cover had ink stamp: "K.B. Koppel/Musicians Union," and the last page of text had printed statement, "reproduced by the Workers' Music Association."

The edition of this suite of etchings comprised 50 numbered copies with 12 proof sets. It was conceived by the New York artist Peter Grippe in 1951 when he took over as director of Atelier 17 in its New York incarnation from S.W. Hayter the influential English artist [and sometime acquaintance of Dylan Thomas]. Grippe choose Dylan Thomas as his poet to work with. The project brought together in all twenty-one modern artists and poets.

The artists included many of the current New York school but most importantly the suite contains the only etching ever made by William de Kooning. The poets included many of Dylan's New York friends – William Carlos Williams, Theodore Roethke, Peter Viereck, David Lougee, George Reavey, Richard Wilbur, Frank O'Hara, Harold Norse and Herbert Read. Atelier 17 was disbanded in New York in 1954 but Grippe continued to work with the artists to bring the work to a conclusion. Eventually Morris

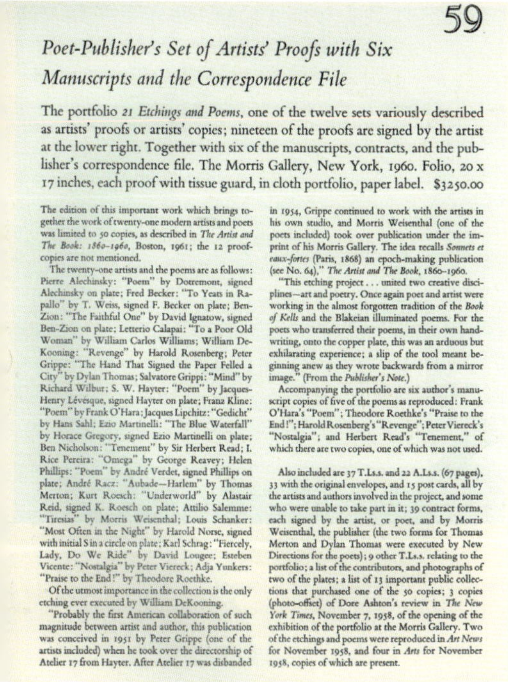

59

Poet-Publisher's Set of Artists' Proofs with Six Manuscripts and the Correspondence File

The portfolio *21 Etchings and Poems*, one of the twelve sets variously described as artists' proofs or artists' copies; nineteen of the proofs are signed by the artist at the lower right. Together with six of the manuscripts, contracts, and the publisher's correspondence file. The Morris Gallery, New York, 1960. Folio, 20 x 17 inches, each proof with tissue guard, in cloth portfolio, paper label. $3250.00

The edition of this important work which brings together the work of twenty-one modern artists and poets was limited to 50 copies, as described in *The Artist and The Book: 1860–1960*, Boston, 1961; the 12 proof-copies are not mentioned.

The twenty-one artists and the poems are as follows: Pierre Alechinsky: "Poem" by Dotremont, signed Alechinsky on plate; Fred Becker: "To Yeats in Rapallo" by T. Weiss, signed F. Becker on plate; Ben-Zion: "The Faithful One" by David Ignatow, signed Ben-Zion on plate; Letterio Calapai: "To a Poor Old Woman" by William Carlos Williams; William DeKooning: "Revenge" by Harold Rosenberg; Peter Grippe: "The Hand That Signed the Paper Felled a City" by Dylan Thomas; Salvatore Grippi: "Mind" by Richard Wilbur; S. W. Hayter: "Poem" by Jacques-Henry Lévesque, signed Hayter on plate; Franz Kline: "Poem" by Frank O'Hara; Jacques Lipchitz: "Gedicht" by Hans Sahl; Ezio Martinelli: "The Blue Waterfall" by Horace Gregory, signed Ezio Martinelli on plate; Ben Nicholson: "Tenement" by Sir Herbert Read; I. Rice Pereira: "Omega" by George Reavey; Helen Phillips: "Poem" by André Verdet, signed Phillips on plate; André Racz: "Aubade—Harlem" by Thomas Merton; Kurt Roesch: "Underworld" by Alastair Reid, signed K. Roesch on plate; Attilio Salemme: "Tiresias" by Morris Weisenthal; Louis Schanker: "Most Often in the Night" by Harold Norse, signed with initial S in a circle on plate; Karl Schrag: "Fiercely, Lady, Do We Ride" by David Lougee; Esteben Vicente: "Nostalgia" by Peter Viereck; Adja Yunkers: "Praise to the End!" by Theodore Roethke.

Of the utmost importance in the collection is the only etching ever executed by William DeKooning.

"Probably the first American collaboration of such magnitude between artist and author, this publication was conceived in 1951 by Peter Grippe (one of the artists included) when he took over the directorship of Atelier 17 from Hayter. After Atelier 17 was disbanded in 1954, Grippe continued to work with the artists in his own studio, and Morris Weisenthal (one of the poets included) took over publication under the imprint of his Morris Gallery. The idea recalls *Sonnets et eaux-fortes* (Paris, 1868) an epoch-making publication (see No. 64)," *The Artist and The Book*, 1860–1960.

"This etching project . . . united two creative disciplines—art and poetry. Once again poet and artist were working in the almost forgotten tradition of the *Book of Kells* and the Blakeian illuminated poems. For the poets who transferred their poems, in their own handwriting, onto the copper plate, this was an arduous but exhilarating experience; a slip of the tool meant beginning anew as they wrote backwards from a mirror image." (From the *Publisher's Note.*)

Accompanying the portfolio are six author's manuscript copies of five of the poems as reproduced: Frank O'Hara's "Poem"; Theodore Roethke's "Praise to the End!"; Harold Rosenberg's "Revenge"; Peter Viereck's "Nostalgia"; and Herbert Read's "Tenement," of which there are two copies, one of which was not used.

Also included are 37 T.Ls.s. and 22 A.Ls.s. (67 pages), 33 with the original envelopes, and 15 post cards, all by the artists and authors involved in the project, and some who were unable to take part in it; 39 contract forms, each signed by the artist, or poet, and by Morris Weisenthal, the publisher (the two forms for Thomas Merton and Dylan Thomas were executed by New Directions for the poets); 9 other T.Ls.s. relating to the portfolio; a list of the contributors, and photographs of two of the plates; a list of 13 important public collections that purchased one of the 50 copies; 3 copies (photo-offset) of Dore Ashton's review in *The New York Times*, November 7, 1958, of the opening of the exhibition of the portfolio at the Morris Gallery. Two of the etchings and poems were reproduced in *Art News* for November 1958, and four in *Arts* for November 1958, copies of which are present.

Weisenthal (one of the poets involved) opened a gallery, The Morris Gallery, and they finally produced the portfolio in 1960.

I am very happy to have a copy of the original prospectus. It reproduces just one of the etchings from the suite and I am truly thankful to them for choosing to illustrate Peter Grippe's lithograph for Dylan's great anti-war poem.

I also so drool over another ancient catalogue, this a very primitive production; duplicated and stapled. It dates from around the same time as the El Dieff catalogue but comes from a much smaller New York outfit. They were offering a proof of the Thomas etching at $200.They begin their description;

AN EXTRAORDINARY THOMAS ITEM

And end it;

Here is a unique opportunity to acquire a Thomas item of the first magnitude.

Where is a Time Machine when you most need it?

Some Unique and Rare Items That Have Passed Through My Hands

Dylan's Own Copy of His First Book with an intriguing trio of Presentation Inscriptions: given and retrieved from his first two girlfriends and then to be kept for himself!

18 Poems. Ist edition. First Issue. One of 250 copies published by the Sunday Referee and Parton Bookshop.1934. Inscribed three times on the front paste down.

First Inscription in ink, all but obliterated with pencil can be deciphered as reading:

To Pamela who knows [?] *well the things I'll suggest if she's going to write on the front of this Pawky book'.*

This presentation is to Pamela Hansford Johnson, Dylan's first serious girlfriend. In a long early letter to Pamela, Dylan heads a paragraph with the words;

'Pawky (Your Word) Remarks'.[15]

Below this, in pencil, is the next inscription;

'Given to Emily in 1937'.

This is Emily Holmes Coleman an interesting American novelist and poet best known for her novel about insanity *'The Shutter in the Snow'* [1930]. Dylan had a short, but intense affair with her between Johnson and Caitlin. There are four letters from Thomas to her in his *'Collected Letters'* and much about her and Dylan in David Gascoyne's memoirs and the memoirs of Peggy Guggenheim.

Finally, in a bold and quite possibly drunken scrawl, Dylan has written across the top;

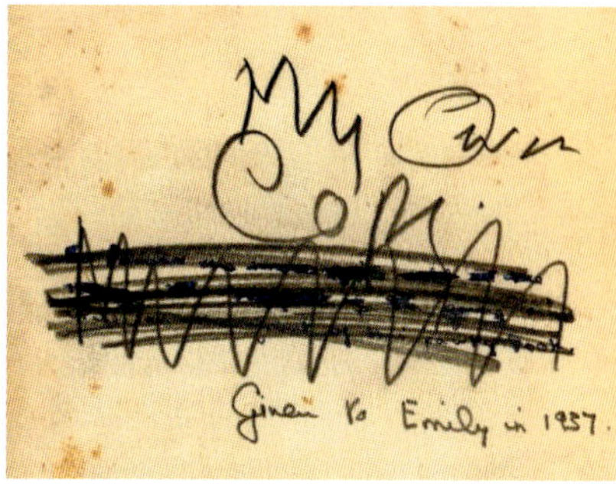

My own copy

This is a book with a remarkable history and provenance, which just got even more remarkable. While writing this essay, *Christies Auction House* in London announced it would be selling the extensive rare book collection left by Charlie Watts, the recently deceased, founder member and drummer of *The Rolling Stones* rock n' roll band. Their presale publicity highlighted some great books – Charlie had money and taste, two key attributes that made him an ideal book collector. One of the books chosen to be previewed was the copy of *18 Poems* described above. I had sold it at a book fair in Los Angeles a decade or so back to one of the pre-eminent London booksellers for a good price. They had sold it on to Charlie, who was a regular client of theirs. Now the book has a new layer of provenance and I wait with curiosity to see what the book sells for this time around.

And now the catalogue has become available and it transpires

that Charlie had another great inscribed Dylan Thomas book – Which also came from me! This is the Christies catalogue description.

Inscribed *The Map of Love*
THOMAS, Dylan (1914-1953). *The Map of Love. Verse and Prose.* London: J. M. Dent, 1939. Presentation copy of the first edition, first issue, inscribed by the author with a masturbatory poem: 'When I was old enough to learn / To kill the flesh and make it burn / I was stern to the skin and I hurt the bone: / I would not leave my shame alone'. Rolph B4a.

Octavo. Frontispiece after Augustus John (a few minor thumb-marks, light spotting to preliminaries and rear endpaper). Original mauve cloth (cloth a little rubbed and faded, particularly at spine, green paint marks to head of spine and top edge of upper board); original printed dust-jacket supplied from another copy (lightly rubbed, a few tears repaired with tape on reverse, a few spots, spine darkened and with small chip at head); housed in a custom green quarter Morocco box. *Provenance*: Virginia and David Tennant (1917-2003 and 1902-1968, respectively, founders of the Gargoyle Club, Soho; authorial presentation inscription in pencil front endpaper).

This is Dylan's somewhat onanistic short verse he inscribed to Virginia Tennant;

When I was old enough to learn
To kill the flesh
I was stern to the skin
And hurt the bone:
I would not leave my shame alone

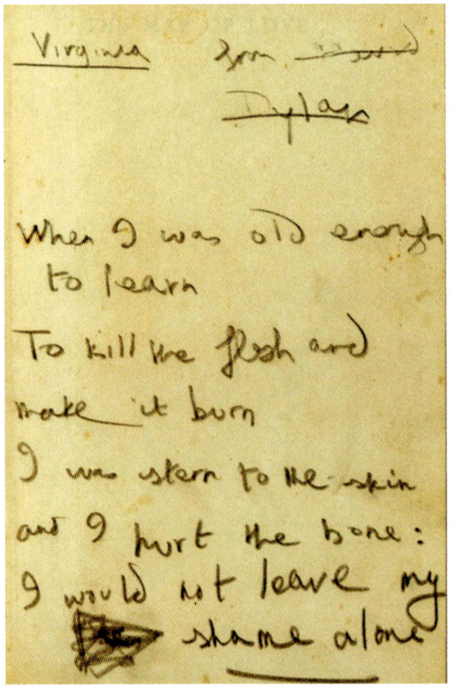

The back-story to this great copy is of interest. Some 15 years ago I received a telephone call out of the blue from a young woman. She began by telling me that her deceased mother had left her a book which she told her was inscribed to her and her husband by Dylan Thomas. However she was perturbed and upset because she had taken it into a leading London Book Auction house (not Christies) who had rejected it for auction, suggesting it was in some way improbable and lacked provenance. The woman was obviously disappointed but also upset that it cast some doubt on her mother's honesty. I responded first by asking the family name and was told 'Tennant'. My first reaction was that they were a local family – The Tennant family was well known around the Swansea and Neath area as late 19th and early 20th century industrialists, indeed there is still a Tennant Canal running through the local county. That would explain how she came to ring me – her local book dealer. However when I suggested this she straight away said this was not the case and on further inquiry she explained that her family were not Welsh and that her parents had run a late night drinking club in London – *The Gargoyle Club*. That's when bells really went off in my head, and my interest and excitement multiplied ten-fold!

The *Gargoyle* was a notorious infamous private members' club on the upper floors of 69 Dean Street, Soho, London, at the corner with Meard Street. It was founded in 1925 by an aristocratic socialite David Tennant, son of the Scottish 1st Baron Glenconner, and brother. David was the brother of Stephen Tennant who was called "the brightest" of the

"Bright Young People" and of Edward Tennant, the poet who was killed in action in World War I. It was also one of Dylan Thomas's favourite late-night haunts. I already had on my shelves Michael Luke's book about Tennant and his club[16] in which he writes;

> The charismatic Tennant was the self-appointed ringmaster to an arena where Bohemians could mingle comfortably with the upper crust… Mystery suffused with a tender eroticism…. On its dance floor Augustus John, Dylan Thomas and Tallulah Bankhead conducted a rite of hedonistic alcoholic abandon while Noël Coward and Francis Bacon looked on and Guy Burgess and Donald Maclean filled out membership applications…'

On the club's opening night its 300-strong list of members included more famous names in society and the arts than any other similar, including included: Somerset Maugham, Noël Coward, Gladys Cooper, Gordon Craig, George Grossmith, Virginia Woolf, Duncan Grant, and Nancy Cunard. Inside, its decadent, Moorish interior boasted the work of Henri Matisse, Augustus John and Edwin Lutyens. Just two anecdotes concerning Dylan Thomas will suffice; this first from a book[17] about the spy Kim Philby;

> The details are supplied by Mrs Marie-Jacqueline Lancaster, who was then working in the War Office. She found herself at a table in the Gargoyle with Burgess, Howard and Dylan Thomas. Mrs. Lancaster was wearing leg-paint, because stockings were in short supply. Thomas, gargantuanly drunk, insisted on licking the paint off 'in time to the music of the rather old-fashioned band the Gargoyle affected.' When the band ended the evening with a limping version of the National Anthem, Burgess refused to stand up (not, as it happened, out of ideology but because he had lumbago and was very drunk). In an unexpected fit of patriotism Thomas, applauded by Howard, leant across the table and knocked Guy out.

The second incident was related by Sacheverell Sitwell to his sister Edith. Apparently one night Dylan Thomas raced, like a

man possessed, into the main room of the Gargoyle;

> Once on the dancing floor (he was poetically dressed in tweeds, with curls of hair like Bacchus, shoes but no socks), he ripped off both shoes and danced barefoot for a while, in a sinister but distracted fashion. Then his purpose became evident. He moved up to the table where David Tennant was sitting, drinking a valuable bottle of claret, poured it into his shoe and drank it, finished the bottle and then with an extraordinary gliding movement traversed the entire length of the room and landed on a divan nestling his head against the thighs of Harold Nicholson, whom he hates…

Dylan also made numerous doodles while in the club and a tad inebriated. Most of them feature him with Ivan Moffat and they are all in the Harry Ransom Library in Texas. The example below shows Dylan and his friend from Strand films Ivan Moffat.

With all this stuff flying around my head, I set up a meeting with the owner of the book and we met in a café in London next to Camden Town Underground station. She brought in the book under consideration – I examined it, we talked more about her parents and the Gargoyle. I told her I had no doubts about the veracity of the book and offered her a suitable amount of money (a four figure sum with a low-ish first digit) She was happy and so was I, and I hope Charlie Watts was too!

Dylan Thomas Selected Writings – Inscribed to Charlie Chaplin.

A REMARKABLE PRESENTATION COPY; Thomas, Dylan; *Selected Writings*. 1946 New Directions. First edition first issue. A very good copy in d.j. which is a trifle worn. With a bold full-page inscription on the f.e.p. in what can only be described as a drunken scrawl from Dylan Thomas to his great hero Charlie Chaplin;

'L A
& love
homage
to & for
Charles Chaplin
From
Dylan Thomas
1950'

As you can read in Chapter 8. Dylan Thomas and Film, above, Dylan loved film and loved Charlie Chaplin. I bought this great book at a big London June Bookfair back at the tail end of the last century. I was setting my stand up before the fair opened when my closest book selling friend and colleague, Eric Korn,[18] wandered up to me proffering an uninspiring green cloth-bound book, saying in his louche, but delightfully posh received pronunciation.

I was a tad preoccupied, I barely gave the book a glance, and said disdainfully and dismissively, Eric; that's the rather common, American, Selected Writing of Dylan Thomas, and that copy lacks the dust jacket and it pretty well used to say the least ...

Undeterred and undaunted, he added nonchalantly,

You might care to look inside...

I somewhat reluctantly stopped shelving books and reached and took the book; I opened it; and gasped! I beheld a bold,

If you don't buy this I probably shall

inebriated, bur very warm inscription; from Dylan Thomas to his hero – Charley Chaplin! Sheepishly I asked Eric the whereabouts of the stand where he found the book, and I walked off as nonchalantly as my beating heart would let me. I bought the book for a very acceptable price and was also given a very good note of provenance.

My dear friend Eric succumbed to a horrible and vicious attack of Louy Bodies Alzheimer's and died back in 2014. It was a major loss to me and some 10 years on, not a day passes when I don't think of him at some point as I go about my work.[19]

Dylan Thomas was a life-long movie lover and was himself an accomplished actor and screenwriter. His great hero was always Charlie Chaplin – Dylan seemed to identify with Chaplin's film character and his friends sometimes likened Dylan to him. Dylan's last public appearance just before his death in New York in 1953 was at a 'Cinema 16' symposium on 'Film and Poetry' and here Dylan proclaimed that Charles Chaplin made the most 'poetic films'. When Dylan found himself in Hollywood old London film cohorts, Ivan Moffat[20] and Frank Taylor of Strand Films, along with Christopher Isherwood the writer they asked him what he most wanted to do and said he most wanted to meet Chaplin. (His second wish was to touch the breasts of a Hollywood Starlet. Even without a magical Genie around, both his wishes were granted! Before I sold the book I did a mass of background reading. I decided to collate the many accounts of this meeting from all the sources I could find. I ended up producing a twenty page document. It was fascinating, but puzzling, in that it seemed that some giant game of *Chinese Whispers* had taken place because no two accounts were the same; except that they all agreed that the meeting took place. Here is a small selection...

Dylan Thomas meets Charlie Chaplin.
Some various Accounts of the Encounter.

Dylan Thomas – Letter to Caitlin 18 April 1950

'Went to Hollywood, dined with Charlie Chaplin, saw Ivan Moffat, stayed with Christopher Isherwood, was ravingly miserable for you my true, my dear, my one, my precious love. I shall write to Llewelyn too tomorrow.

Dylan Thomas – Letter to Caitlin May 7 1950.

'I am glad Charlie Chaplin wired to you. He said he wanted to send his greetings. He's a very fine man. I was only 2 days in Hollywood, staying with Christopher Isherwood who took me along to Chaplin's to dinner. Chaplin danced & clowned all the time. I met also Ivan Moffat. Ivan says I could get a script to write almost any time. Once we are in San Francisco, we will

From Charles Chaplin's *My Autobiography*. 1964.

One day, our friend Frank Taylor telephoned to say that Dylan Thomas, the Welsh poet, would like to meet us. We said we would be delighted. ''Well,'' said Frank hesitantly, 'I'll bring him round if he's sober.' Later that evening when the bell rang I opened the door and Dylan Thomas fell in, if this was being sober, what would he be like when he was drunk? A day or so later he came to dinner and made better sense. He read to us one of his poems, endered in a deep resonant voice. I do not remember the imagery, but the word' 'cellophane' flashed like reflected sunshine from his magical verse.

I think it is worth sharing perhaps the most fanciful, outrageous but entertaining account of them all. It comes from the autobiography of Shelly Winters the American actress whose career spanned seven decades. She appeared in numerous films. She won Academy awards for *The Diary of Anne Frank* and *A Patch of Blue* and starred in many great films. She was quite a character as her account indicates but whether she was a fantasist or had a very bad memory is unclear, but her account does include Dylan driving Marylyn Monroe and Shelly to a party and Charlie's reaction. It is a wild and amusing read but maybe more fantasy than truth.

From the second volume of Shelly Winter's Autobiography [1990]

One night, when I showed up exhausted from filming Frenchie, complete with platinum hair and padded bra, Christopher Isherwood and Ivan Moffat were seated with an ugly, funny-handsome young Welshman. He had very black, curly, almost kinky hair, rather a stocky build (just a little taller than I), and very rumpled clothes. He was altogether charming, and I gathered it was his first night in Hollywood. His name was something Thomas—I didn't catch the first part but since we were retaking a scene the next day, and I didn't have to learn any new lines, I could enjoy the conversation with this cute Welshman. When I asked Mr. Thomas what he did, Ivan told me, "He draws accurate and biting images of people and events." So, I assumed he was a cartoonist, and they all let me assume this for a long time. The young man, of course, was Dylan Thomas, but he didn't look like any writer I had ever met in Hollywood. In those days writers wore suits and ties. My friends told me he was working for some London newspaper. In the course of dinner, I asked Mr. Thomas why he had come to Hollywood. He looked deep into my blue eyes and whispered sexily, "To touch the titties of a beautiful blonde starlet and to meet Charlie Chaplin." I gazed at the two literary figures beside us. They said nothing. "Okay," I said, "I can grant both your wishes." When we had finished the dessert and brandy, I

'Where is a time machine when you most need it'

AN EXTRAORDINARY THOMAS ITEM

242. **THOMAS.** The Hand That Signed the Paper Felled a City. New York, 1952. First separate appearance, in the form of an etching, the text of which actually etched onto the plate by Thomas shortly before his death. Then the artist Peter Grippe added a decorative border. Only 50 etchings were pulled to be sold in a complete series of 21. Also, 2 or 3 proofs were made for the artist and the poet. Separate etchings were not sold, and as all but one or two sets went into the collections of museums or libraries, there is little chance of these ever coming onto the market. We offer here one of the artist's proofs. Overall size $16\frac{1}{2}$x $19\frac{1}{2}$". Here is a unique opportunity to acquire a Thomas item of the first magnitude.

$200.00

announced, "You may touch each of my breasts with one finger, and the day after tomorrow will be Sunday, and Charlie Chaplin has open house, as Christopher and Ivan well know. I will take you up there." Ivan bought us a bottle of champagne and poured it. Then, with great ceremony, Mr. Thomas sterilized his index finger in the champagne and delicately brushed each breast with the finger, leaving a Streak in my pancake body makeup. A look of supreme ecstasy came over this Welsh elf's face. "Oh, God, Nirvana," he uttered. "I do not believe it's necessary for me to meet Charlie Chaplin now."

Christopher and Ivan were laughing uproariously. I knew I was being joshed, and I informed my dinner companions that the brakes on my car were not too good, and since Charlie was on top of Summit Ridge Drive, we could pass on that trip. "No, no," said Ivan. "I've loaned Dylan my green Hornet while he's in California, and if you keep him on the right side of the road, he can drive you up to the Chaplin house Sunday night. He really is longing to meet Charlie, and I'm sure Charlie is anxious to meet him." Why Chaplin would want to meet this obscure Welsh cartoonist was as a mystery to me. Also, he just sat there when the check came, so it was obvious he had very little money. So, I invited him to an early Sunday dinner the next night with me and my then-roommate, Marilyn Monroe. Then we would all drive up to Charlie's house after dinner. By the time I left the Players that night, I realized that Mr. Thomas had a serious drinking problem, and, if Ivan or Christopher couldn't drive us up to Charlie Chapin's house, I decided / would drive the green Hornet myself....

Christopher Isherwood and Ivan Moffat were pretending they didn't know Dylan and me, but suddenly everyone was looking at Dylan and wanted to talk to him. Since he was very drunk, I couldn't think why. He, on the other hand, obviously didn't want to talk to anybody but Charlie Chaplin. Charlie was sitting at the piano, playing a strange, beautiful tune. I quickly went over to Ivan and Christopher and asked them why they had asked me to take care of their difficult, drunken cartoonist friend. With a very straight face, as was his wont, Ivan asked me if I didn't like Mr. Thomas? 'When he's relatively sober, he's adorable," I replied. "But he has a terrible drinking problem, doesn't he? Perhaps I should make an appointment for him with a good Beverly Hills psychiatrist."... Dylan Thomas abruptly got up. and I slid to the floor. He suddenly seemed cold sober and took Charlie junior's hands and danced around the room with him, humming the tune in his melodious voice. Charlie junior kept right on la-la-la-ing off-key and sort of sarcastically Charlie senior crashed his hands on the keyboard, got up, and knocked Charlie junior's hands away from Dylan. Unable to distinguish who was doing what, Charlie senior hissed at Dylan, "Even great poetry cannot excuse such rude, drunken behaviour." Dylan turned on his heel and, in a very dignified manner, walked out into the solarium. Charlie junior sat on a hassock and began to weep bitterly. "Sydney is playing the lead in the film," he screamed. "I won't be an extra. I won't, I won't." As the guests left hurriedly, we heard a sound like running water. Dylan was peeing on a large plant on Charlie's porch. In this decade I seem to have known a lot of gentlemen who peed as an act of revenge.

* * * * *

Special Issue of Twenty-Six Poems – Inscribed to Caitlin

Perhaps the single greatest Dylan Thomas book I ever handled. Back towards the end of the last century I had been away at a book fair and on my return I asked my wife if there had been any interesting phone calls or enquiries – I always did this just in case... At first she said, no nothing... but a while later she said that down in my shop my part-timer had phoned about a book I was being offered and she handed me a scrap of paper with her notes from the call It seemed to involve Dylan Thomas book – of poems ... Caitlin Thomas ...bound in cat-gut... Little else but it also had a Dublin phone number. I needed to know more, I had a hunch. The next day I was down the shop early giving the poor lad an absolute grilling. It transpired the call was from Dublin, and a smooth talking Irish guy, maybe a general dealer, said he had a copy of *Twenty-Six Poems* by Dylan Thomas; that it was a special copy bound in 'cat-gut' and that it was inscribed by Dylan to his wife Caitlin. Part of me was incredulous – in fact a large part of me was disbelieving ...

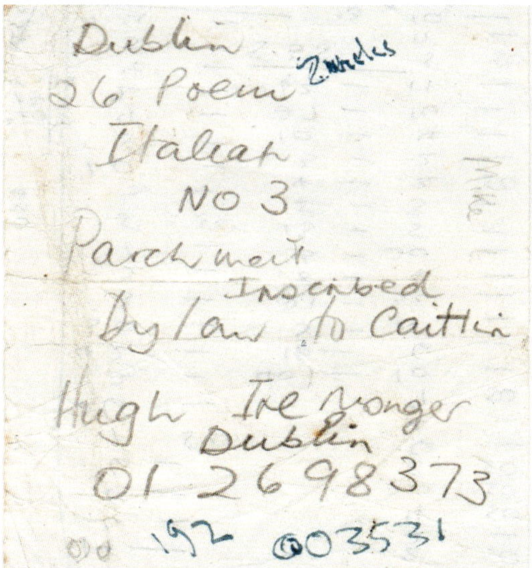

My wife's cryptic, but intriguing note

Twenty-Six Poems is the most elegant and finely produced Dylan Thomas book of all his publications and its existence. It was probably instigated by James Laughlin, who was himself a fine and elegant wealthy American book-lover and publisher. He founded and owned New Direction Press in New York and was Dylan's American publisher. The Colophon below is for the English copies (11-60). The colophon tells us it is a joint publication by him and Dylan's s English publishers J.M. Dent & Sons, Ltd. It is interesting to note that the American comes first and has no stated trade affiliation. The colophon also gives us the edition details, we are also told that the edition consists of ten copies on Japanese Vellum numbered I to X. and 140 copies on Fabriano hand-made paper, numbered 11 – 150 of which numbers 11 to 60 in Great Britain. It does not tell us that copies 60 – 140 are for America. The date given in Roman Numerals is 1949, but Rolph tells us that copies of the entire edition were received in January 1950 at the House of Dent in London. He goes on to say that the copies for New Directions were re-despatched from London to New York in March 1950. The English edition was published on 31st Aug. 1950, at £5 5s. (The whole of this issue being sold on publication day). The key sentence is the first: *This volume of poems by Dylan Thomas was printed in Griffo type by Hans Mardersteig on the hand –press of the Officina Bodoni in Verona...* Giovanni Mardersteig was born Hans Mardersteig in 1892. He was a German-born printer and typographer, making much of his career in Italy. He is particularly known for founding and running the Officina Bodoni, a small fine press producing high quality, small limited editions. He had developed an interest in the famed engraver Giambattista Bodoni and he was given permission from the Bodoni Museum in Parma to use his typefaces, known as Bodoni fonts, he relocated back to Switzerland, to in 1922, motivated by a decline in his health and there with help of friends he founded the Officina Bodoni named after his typographical hero. He is recognised as one of the great printers and typographers of the 20th century. He also printed in a similar format to Dylan's 26 Poems volumes of poems by T.S. Eliot and Ezra Pound. Dylan Thomas was in very fine company. Rolph also tells us that the American issue differ from the English edition by having no publisher's imprint on the title page. It also seems to have preceded publication of the English edition by about three months and the vellum copies came out a couple of days earlier than this.

But back to where I started with the enigmatic note. Rolph tells us that there were 10 copies printed on Japanese vellum – (the cat-gut on the note) and that copies 1. and 2. were designated author's free copies. (the other 8 vellum copies were all for New Directions). Dylan also got two of the regular paper copies, numbers 148 and 149 as free copies.

It was time now to make a call. I gathered myself together and dialled the number and was answered by a soft male Irish accent. I introduced myself and declared a serious interest in knowing more. He told me the book was copy number 2. And was inscribed – by Dylan –

For Caitlin with love – Dylan'

Now that made it for me a holy relic. I was a tad shell-shocked and asked if it had any history or provenance. He informed me that he has bought it in a bona-fide fashion from a noted male Irish poet but was not at liberty to give out his name. That was fair enough. I then asked how he had found me to offer the book too. He replied openly that he had looked in a few volumes of an annual publication – Book Auction Records, which did exactly that. Each year the publishers gathered up information from the best book auction houses around the world and published the sale details: hammer price, and buyer of every important book sold through the year. Remember, this was pre internet, and these books were all we had – they were a bookseller's bible! In his search he had found that the last few copies of the regular 140 copies to be sold at auction had been bought by – Dylans Bookstore Swansea!

I was still reeling and mentally scheming, but I asked if it was

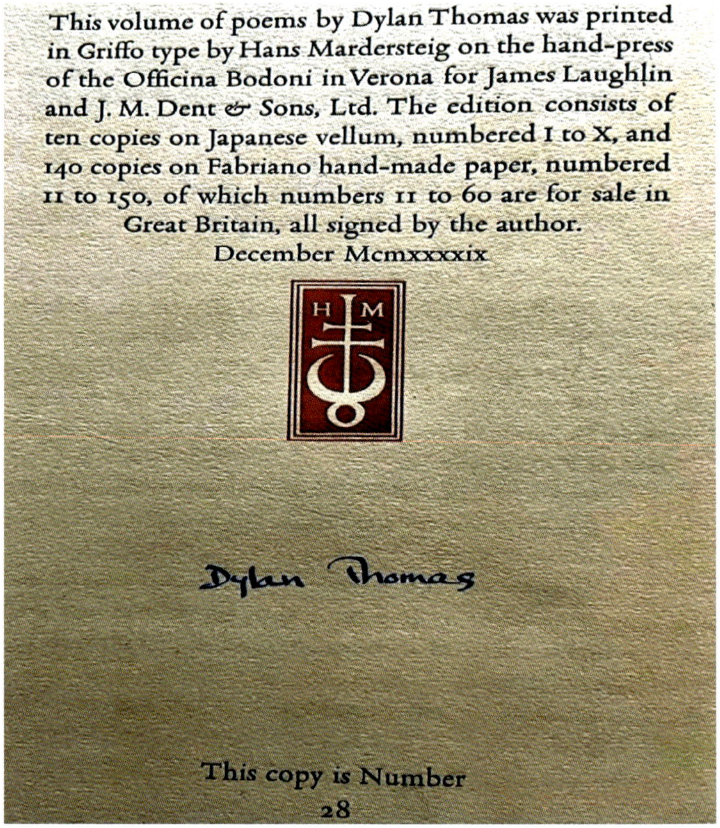
This volume of poems by Dylan Thomas was printed in Griffo type by Hans Mardersteig on the hand-press of the Officina Bodoni in Verona for James Laughlin and J. M. Dent & Sons, Ltd. The edition consists of ten copies on Japanese vellum, numbered I to X, and 140 copies on Fabriano hand-made paper, numbered 11 to 150, of which numbers 11 to 60 are for sale in Great Britain, all signed by the author.
December Mcmxxxxix

Dylan Thomas

This copy is Number
28

for sale, and could I buy it if I came up with an acceptable offer and he said yes, but gave no hint of what that amount might be. I said I would do some research and get back to him and the call ended most affably.

I could do no research apart from re-read Rolph. But I did find a reference by Dylan to the publication of the book ...

I could find no record of a vellum copy ever being sold. And this was an unmatchable inscribed presentation copy to his wife. And this was a famously tempestuous marriage, fraught with passion, occasional violence, occasional indiscretions on both parties, but they had just about stayed together. I thought and I thought, but got nowhere. It haunted me but I could not see where to go next – there was no yardstick; nothing to compare with. Days went by. I ponder on the book endlessly, but did not act. A day or so later I go off to exhibit at a bookfair in Bristol. I told the story to a bookseller pal. 'You have got to phone him now, and make an offer' he exclaimed. He galvanised me into action. I went to a pay phone and dialled. He answered and we exchanged pleasantries. All the time I was thinking – regular copies of the book I bought back cost me between £500 and £600 pounds, on which I could, and did make a small profit when I sold them on to collectors. But was this unique volume, worth double? or triple? Or ten times that?

I went quiet and then I said,

'I would really like to buy the book.'

I Paused, took a breath, and then I went on;

And I'd like to give you two thousand pounds for it.

I'm still not sure where I got that number from.

Silence...then he said; 'No I'd want Two and a half'

I said; (maybe a tad to swiftly...) 'Done! I said.

We exchanged addresses made a little more small talk, and I said I'd send a check and he said he'd send the book.

I came back from the fair and sent him a check for £2500. Meanwhile he had packed up the book and mailed it and the two items crossed in the post.

It was as moving and beautiful a book as I had hoped, more so even. I kept the book under wraps, at home for many years, but often I would take it off the shelf and my eyes would drool.

But eventually I did take it to a West Coast book fair where I sold it to a dealer friend for a little over ten times what I had paid for it. And then I saw it bounce around the trade each time for a tad more money until it stayed sold. It was a great, great book.

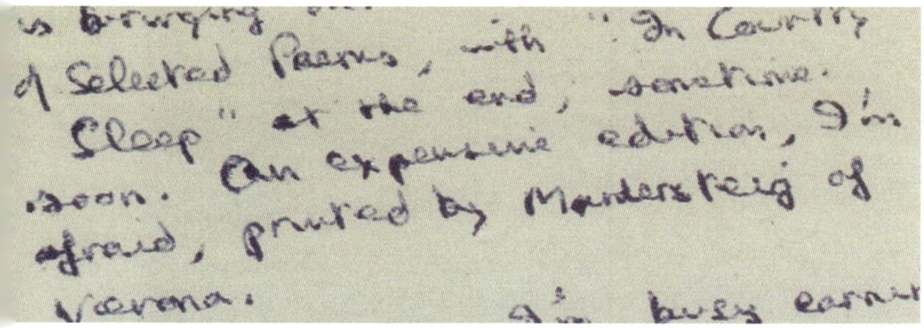

An expensive edition, I'm afraid, printed by Mardersteig of Verona

My Description of the Copy in Hand
TWENTY-SIX POEMS
Dylan Thomas
His greatest and rarest book inscribed to his wife Caitlin

In the late forties the great printer Hans Mardersteig printed a very fine, elegant edition of Dylan Thomas' poems on the hand-press of the Officina Bodoni in Verona. The colophon states that it was printed for 'James Laughlin and J.M. Dent & Sons, Ltd. but one suspects that this sumptuous edition was largely Laughlin's idea. The total edition was just 150 copies described thus on the colophon:

'The edition consists of ten copies on Japanese vellum, numbered 1 to X, and 140 copies on Fabriano hand-made paper, numbered 11 to 150 of which numbers 11 to 60 are for sale in Great Britain, all singed by the author.'

The actual distribution of the entire edition was [according to Rolph] as follows:

1-2 (Jap. vellum)	author's free copies
3-10 " "	to New Directions
11-60 (H/made paper):	to Dent
61-147 " "	to New Directions
148-149 " "	author's free copies
150 " "	Dent file copy.

Thus, we can see that Laughlin wanted all the available *'de-luxe' copies. As our copy would appear very much to be one of the author's copies, but it is copy number three, Rolph may not be entirely correct regarding these bibliographical nuances.*

Although the colophon is dated December 1949, Dent did not receive the entire edition until January of 1950 and sent the New Direction copies off in March. The UK edition was not published until the 31st. August 1950 [at £5 guineas], however the American edition **preceded** the English edition by about three months appearing towards the end of the second week of May,1950. Rolph further states;

"The vellum copies preceded the hand-made paper issue by about two days"

The copy on offer here is Copy number III of the Vellum issue and is inscribed;
"for my dear Caitlin from Dylan"

A very good copy in the 'de-luxe' binding not described by Rolph: Decorative boards covered in red and black hand printed paper with a vellum corner tips and spine lettered directly in gilt 'DYLAN THOMAS POEMS'.
[The hand-made paper edition has black and green paper and a canvas cloth spine and paper label].
In the grey cloth plain slip-case as issued. The vellum copies like all the American copies differ from the Uk copies by having no publisher imprint on the title page.
Rolph B.13 with two illustrations.

A few notes: In 35 years dealing in Thomas materials, we have only heard of or encountered a few of these vellum copies. A copy sold at an LA auction some 15 years ago for around $7000 and was in the trade for a while. Rumours that a few vellum copies existed as unbound copies circulated. We acquired this copy from Ireland around 1990. Maurice Neville had a vellum copy inscribed to the ubiquitous Norman Unger which sold at auction in 2004 for $16,800. Last year two American Dealers issued an amazingly rich catalogue which was offering vellum copy No 2 – one of Rolph's author copies, which the dealer describes as having 'remained in sheets until quite recently' and offered in a good modern French binding at $25,000.

Books inscribed by Dylan to Caitlin are also very uncommon, indeed the only other we know of is the famous copy of his first book '18 Poems' [the Eric Quale/House of El Dieff/Neville copy] which sold to Gekoski for $38,400 on 2004.

There are two other Signed Limited editions of Dylan Thomas poetry. They were all published in the last few years of his life and both are very scarce.

In Country Sleep and other Poems by Dylan Thomas
In February of 1952 Dylan Thomas' American publishers, James

The Limited Edition slip-case

The Title page

Laughlin's New Directions, issued a book which did not appear in the UK; In Country Sleep and Other Poems. The trade edition was of 5,000 cloth bound copies but they also issued a Limited Edition of just 100 copies, all signed, and in a different and better binding with a slip-case. The book consisted of just six late poems one of which was *Do not go gentle into that good night*, the first ever great poem.

Collected Poems 1934-1952, by Dylan Thomas.
Perhaps inspired by the New Directions signed Limited edition Dents published Dylan's *Collected Poems* in a cloth-bound trade edition with a paper dust jacket. The first edition was of just under 5000 copies. But they also issued what Rolph describes as the *limited issue*, and he describes it thus: *This differed from the ordinary issue only in the binding, paper and the Note on the verso of the title*. The book comes finely bound in full dark crushed Morocco leather, with a clear cellophane dust jacket. The spine is gilt blocked the same as the ordinary issue and the top edge is gilt instead of rust red. It also has headbands top and bottom of the

The special binding on the rare, signed Limited First Edition, of Dylan's *Collected Poems*

This is number 80 of one hundred copies
printed on Stoneridge paper and
signed by the author
Dylan Thomas

The *In Country Sleep*, signed colophon

spine. The note on the verso of the title reads;

This edition, printed
On mould-made paper
is limited to 65 copies.
Of which 60 are for sale.
This is copy No...

The number is in ink and below is the author's signature. Because of the very small size of the edition it is one of the hardest of all Dylan Thomas books to find, and one of the most expensive too.

Dylan's only gouache painting; A PETITION TO THE GOVERNMENT

Dylan wrote jokingly in a radio script;[21]

> Ectually... I was born in Cwmbwrla but Soho's better for my Gouaches.

However, he painted this rare gouache in his friend John Davenport's country mansion, *The Maltings*, in Marshfield Gloucestershire to entertain the Davenport daughters.

I bought this lively, somewhat surreal painting, at a Sotheby's book auction back in the eighties. Their catalogue description did not question the veracity of the attribution, but their provenance was pretty much non-existent – they just quoted an early letter from Dylan to Pamela Hansford Johnson when he tells her;

> [I] can't draw. I paint a good deal, but quite untechnically, and the startling effects I do sometimes do produce are owing to a diseased mentality and an entire lack of skill.

As a result the room did not seem to warm to it and kind of left it to me. Roy Davids, the head of the book department was on the rostrum and he looked somewhat incredulous when he was forced to bring his gavel down when nobody bid more than my bid of a couple of hundred pounds.

I was pleased, but I have to say I was not entirely convinced, but I had learned or read somewhere that the consigner of the painting had the surname Davenport. That rang a bell; John Davenport was a well-heeled, close friend and sometime-patron of Dylan's, who often stayed at his county house, *The Maltings*,

Dylan's only gouache painting; A PETITION TO THE GOVERNMENT

between Bath and Chippenham for periods of time in the mid forties. Davenport was Dylan's final collaborator on the spoof detective novel *The Death of the Kings Canary* (DENT 1978).

I rang Dylan's biographer and the editor of Dylans Collected Letters, Paul Ferris. Paul was a Swansea boy and a very good writer and over the course of the years we had become friends. I asked if he had any contacts for the Davenport family and he quickly found an address for one of Davenport's daughters. I wrote to her informing her that I had just bought the picture in Sotheby's and asked if she could give me any more background information. She responded quickly and it couldn't have been better. She began by saying that she was 'unaware that her sister had sold Dylan's charming painting; and then went on to recall how he had left a party at the house and joined her and her sister in their playroom and amused them by painting them the giraffe on the beach. I was very pleased with this outcome.

I found an old vintage frame and the picture looked fine in it. I kept it for a good while but now it hangs with pride of place in the permanent Exhibition in Swansea's Dylan Thomas Centre.

And finally!
DYLAN SWEAT!
This more recent piece of irreverent ephemera was definitely of Swansea origin – I know this for a fact because I bought the 200 tiny glass phials that held the precious liquid! That came taped to the card. It was the product of the fertile but somewhat twisted brain of a notorious Swansea character; Paul Durden, the co-scriptwriter of the scurrilous but hilarious dark comedy film TWIN TOWN. His business card described him as the head of the *Iconoclastic Foundation* He also promoted himself as a candidate for Mayor of Swansea; his home made mayoral Chain featured a huge medallion with a picture of a scantily clad Catherine Zeta Jones, a Swansea girl made good in Hollywood. Indeed! Paul was a good friend of mine and a regular visitor, if not a regular book buyer, to my Salubrious Passage bookstore.

Paul came by the shop one day towards the end of the last century and showed me the prototype card he had made with an

Now you can let his perspiration be your inspiration

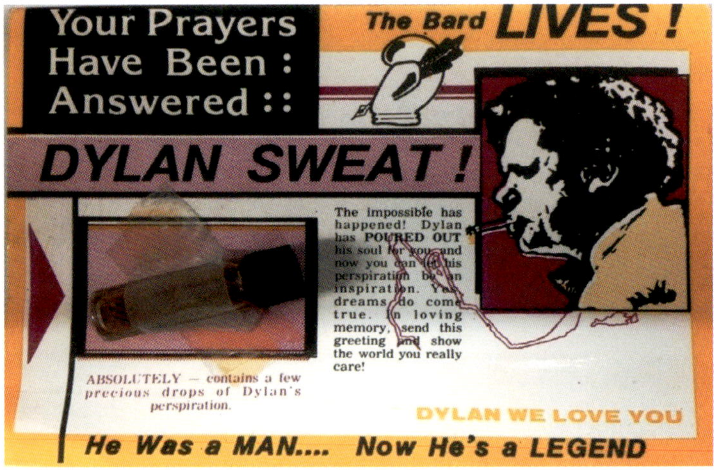

envelope printed with the slogan, *Yes, Dreams Do Come. True.* However Paul was as ever underfunded and the card was without the small phial of 'sweat' it needed to be complete. Paul had sourced a supply of the little glass sample bottles but wanted me to finance their purchase.

I was taken with the concept and thought it a pertinent comment on the burgeoning over-the-top media responses to Dylan Thomas. The bottles were procured; Paul got to work – cold tea was infused and the bottles were filled. Dylan Sweat was launched into the World.

A small media frenzy unfurled; some people took it all too seriously and complained; other reached for it with glee and Paul got much more of the kind of publicity that he fed off. I made a few open minded Dylan Thomas aficionados and completist collectors happy. The publicity was good for sales and pretty soon all the sweat had dried up and the Sweat passed into local folklore, almost as quickly as it arrived. I have just a few of them left.

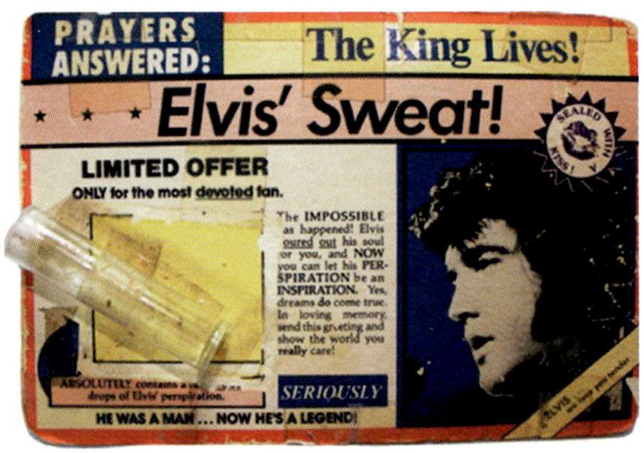

And that would have been that if, a good few years later, I was reading a Greil Marcus book about Elvis Presley and the constant media frenzy which still surrounded the long dead rock and roller. I was extremely amused to be confronted with this image. Once I had taken it in I realised I should not have been surprised when I turned a page and beheld this!

The demon plagiarist had struck again! The King of Rock'n Roll meets Swansea's Rock'n Roll poet...

* * * * *

I'll end this chapter with an article I wrote back in 2014 for book collecting magazine, The Antiquarian Book Monthly Review (A.B.M.R):

Why We Collect Dylan Thomas ...

The four page manuscript for Bob Dylan's "*Like a Rolling Stone*" recently sold for in excess of $2,000,000. Bob Dylan is a twentieth century icon. "*Like a Rolling Stone*" was a seismic moment in twentieth century song-writing, changing the landscape of popular culture forever. When something like that is written it finds a way into our collective psyche. It becomes iconic. We are drawn to the creative people who create these masterpieces in whatever form. And as collectors we dream of owning a part of them; something which gives us a glimpse of their genius. I remind you of this because Bob Dylan changed his name from Robert Zimmerman to Bob Dylan in homage to the Welsh poet Dylan Thomas, who's Centenary is being celebrated this year and this Auction is a part of that celebration.

Dylan Thomas is an ultimate 21st century icon. Born as the First World War began; he was prolific as a poet in the years before, and during the Second World War. His unique voice and style made him famous before he was 30. He then found further fame in America in the 1950s and many feel he was the catalyst for the counter culture movement that followed, a Godfather of the Beat Generation which gave us Ginsberg, Kerouac, Burroughs...and then Bob Dylan. He also "lived fast and died young" – just 39 years old when he passed away in a New York Hospital. Dylan Thomas's '*Do not go gentle into that good night* is considered one of the greatest, most loved, and most well-known poems in the English language. He was a favourite of US presidents, Carter and Clinton. To 'Rage against the dying of the light' has become one of Britain's most quoted lines.

In this centenary year, there have been global celebrations paying tribute to his work. At the heart of all these celebrations lies Dylan Thomas's 'play for voices' *Under Milk Wood*. Just as Like a Rolling Stone changed the face of popular music, Under Milk Wood" revolutionised the way we listened to drama on the radio. This year the play, based on the fictional Welsh village of Llareggub, has been given fresh life across all platforms. Living proof of the cultural power this work still holds. The Dylan Thomas Centenary Year opened with a rich and wonderful exhibition at the National Museum of Wales of Sir Peter Blake's fabulous illustrations of *Under Milk Wood*. The National Theatre of Wales adapted *Under Milk Wood* into a promenade performance through the streets of Laugharne, and it was also turned into a serious and wonderful Opera by John Metcalf to huge acclaim. Theatre Clwyd have toured the world with their stage version of the play. S4C and Kevin Allen are making an *Under Milk Wood* feature film starring Rhys Ifans. The BBC made their own Under Milk Wood starring Tom Jones, Michael Sheen and Charlotte Church. Two new bio-pics will soon reach the cinema, one starring Elijah Wood, another with John Malkovich. Cerys Matthews regularly plays a dub step remixed version of Richard Burton reading *Under Milk Wood* on her award winning radio show. Television documentaries have filled our screens, as celebrities and academics lined up to pay their respects to Wales' greatest writer...even I enjoyed a walk around New Quay's Dylan Thomas haunts with Derek Brockway for his ever popular *Weatherman Walking* series.

100 years after his birth, and just over 60 years after his death, Dylan Thomas and his work lives on. As does his iconic status amongst 21st century artists. And now as the year approaches its end Wales' première Auction House is offering a Welsh Art Sale with a rich a dazzling array of highly desirable and rare inscribed books, manuscripts, letters and works of art by, or inspired by

Dylan Thomas. A few highlights: On offer is the only 'from-the-life' sculpted bust of the poet by the sculptor Hugh Oloff de Wet, along with his original drawing for the piece and one of 10 miniature bronzes he cast; a fine oil painting of Dylan by Canadian/Welsh artist Gordon Stuart which was the last ever portrait made during Dylan's life. And other works of art by major Welsh artists Ceri Richards and John Wright inspired by the work of Dylan Thomas, together with a cluster of rare inscribed books manuscripts and letters...There still seems to be life in the old dog...

1. It was to be the third in a series – *Encounters with R.S.* [Thomas] and *Encounters with Nigel* [Jenkins] had preceded it.

2. Since writing this I am very pleased to say Jon has agreed to write a preface to this book.

3. A homage too, and a borrowing from the 17th century dramatist and lyric writer Ben Johnson who was buried on August 17, 1637, in Westminster Abbey. But it was no ordinary burial. For some reason – possibly the danger of overcrowding a hallowed space – the coffin holding his corpse was lowered into the ground vertically, not horizontally, and it went in head first. The diarist and gossip monger John Aubrey recorded that an attendee gave the workman eighteen pence to carve "a pavement square of blue marble about 14 inches square" with which to cover the opening. It bore a simple epitaph: *O RARE BEN JONSON.*

4. Among other books he also published an early critical introduction, *Entrances to Dylan Thomas* (Critical Essays in Modern Literature) in 1963, and later enlarged it with his *Where Have the Old Words Got Me?*: Explications of Dylan Thomas's Collected Poems, which came out in 2003. He edited an anthology of poems read by *Dylan Thomas The Colour of Saying* 19 and *Dylan Thomas The Broadcasts*, and working with Walford Davies of Aberystwyth he co-edited edited new editions of Thomas's Collected Poems and his radio drama *Under Milk Wood.*

5. Thomas was to appear alongside Kafka once more when he contributed to issue No. 6/7 March 1939 of Keidrych Rhys *WALES* magazine. Dylan Thomas had two poems and +Franz Kafka, two unpublished fragments.

6. He was paid a weekly salary when he joined Donald Taylor's *Strand Films* in 1941 – for more see Chapter 8.

7. I cannot resist mentioning that amongst the Dylan Thomas materials remains I acquired from Dr Daniel Jones was Dylan Thomas's ink-stained and scruffy School Physics Exercise Book, labelled on the upper cover 'D. M. Thomas 1V A'. It dated from 1926 and in amongst the rough notes from a lecture on Light, I was delighted to discover these prescient physics notes written in his schoolboy hand;

   Light
   Light is invisible.
   Light travels in straight lines.

   The exercise book is now part of the Jeff Towns /Dylan Thomas Collection at the National Library of Wales.

8. It was part of Desmond Hawkins archive and it is published in his book *When I Was.*

9. *Bar one; William R. Rodgers, the Belfast born Irish poet and broadcaster, who they failed to locate and who was unwell at the time the sheets were being sent around.

10. The unique Proof is now in the National Library of Wales as part of the *Jeff Towns Dylan Thomas Collection.*

11. *And Uncle Tom Cobly and all* – An allusion to the folk-song *Are you Going to Widdecombe Fair* where these words are at the end of the repeated refrain. The phrase Uncle Tom Cobley and all is used in an old English way of saying et al or everybody, often to express exasperation at the large number of people in a list. The phrase comes from a Devon Folk song collected around 1890 by folklorist Sabine Baring Gould. Each chorus

end with this long list of names people: "Bill Brewer, Jan Stewer, Peter Gurney, Peter Davy, Dan'l Whiddon, Harry Hawke, Old Uncle Tom Cobley and all."

12. Zephyr Books were published by The Continental Book Company, subsidiary of the Swedish Bonnier group. They issued books from 1942 to 1950, taking their name from the Greek god of the western wind to indicate their specialty. D World War 11 no books in English could be imported into Sweden. The Continental Book Company was established in 1942 with the object of publishing books in English in Stockholm. The intended market comprised Sweden and other parts of the European continent where it was possible to sell English books in spite of the war, namely Switzerland, Portugal and Turkey. Considerable quantities of Zephyr Books were also exported to Hungary, Italy, occupied Denmark and the non-occupied zone of France.

13. George Sutherland Fraser (1915-1980) was a Scottish poet, literary critic and academic. In 1957 he wrote the *Writers and Their Work* pamphlet on Dylan Thomas.

14. Javier Marias; *All Souls*. Harvill London 1992. His Oxford novel. *While the Women are Sleeping*. Chatto & Windus 2010. Short Stories.

15. Pawky; Old Scots word, adjective. Meaning: mocking, making fun of someone or something in a cruel way; derisive.

16. Michael Luke *David Tennant and the Gargoyle Years*. Weidenfeld & Nicolson..1991.

17. Ben Macintyre *A Spy among Friends*: Kim Philby and the Great Betrayal.

18. Micharl Eric Korn– but Eric to friends (1933-1014). I was blessed to have had him as my very friend, bookselling colleague, and fellow exotic travelling companion for some 40 years. The headline to his obituary in *The Independent* gives you a flavour of his remarkable and unique genius;
Eric Korn: Polymath whose work took in poetry, literary criticism, antiquarian Bookselling and the *Round Britain Quiz*. Korn, Jonathan Miller and Oliver Sacks attended St Paul's School in London, where they became the heart of a group of Jewish intellectuals.

19. I was of course immensely grateful for his selfless actions over the Chaplin book but he might have been remembering a Darwin item which I offered him shortly after we first met; the Murray early reprint of Darwin's *A Naturalist's Voyage* heavily and interestingly annotated by John Lort Stokes, Darwin's cabin mate. In awe of him I accepted his somewhat meagre offer...

20. Ivan Moffat, an American scriptwriter, worked alongside Thomas at *Strand Films* in London during the war. It may have been Moffat who arranged the visit to Chaplin's (others too have claimed the credit), when Thomas is said to have behaved badly. But no two versions agree.

21. *Swansea and the Arts*. BBC 1949.

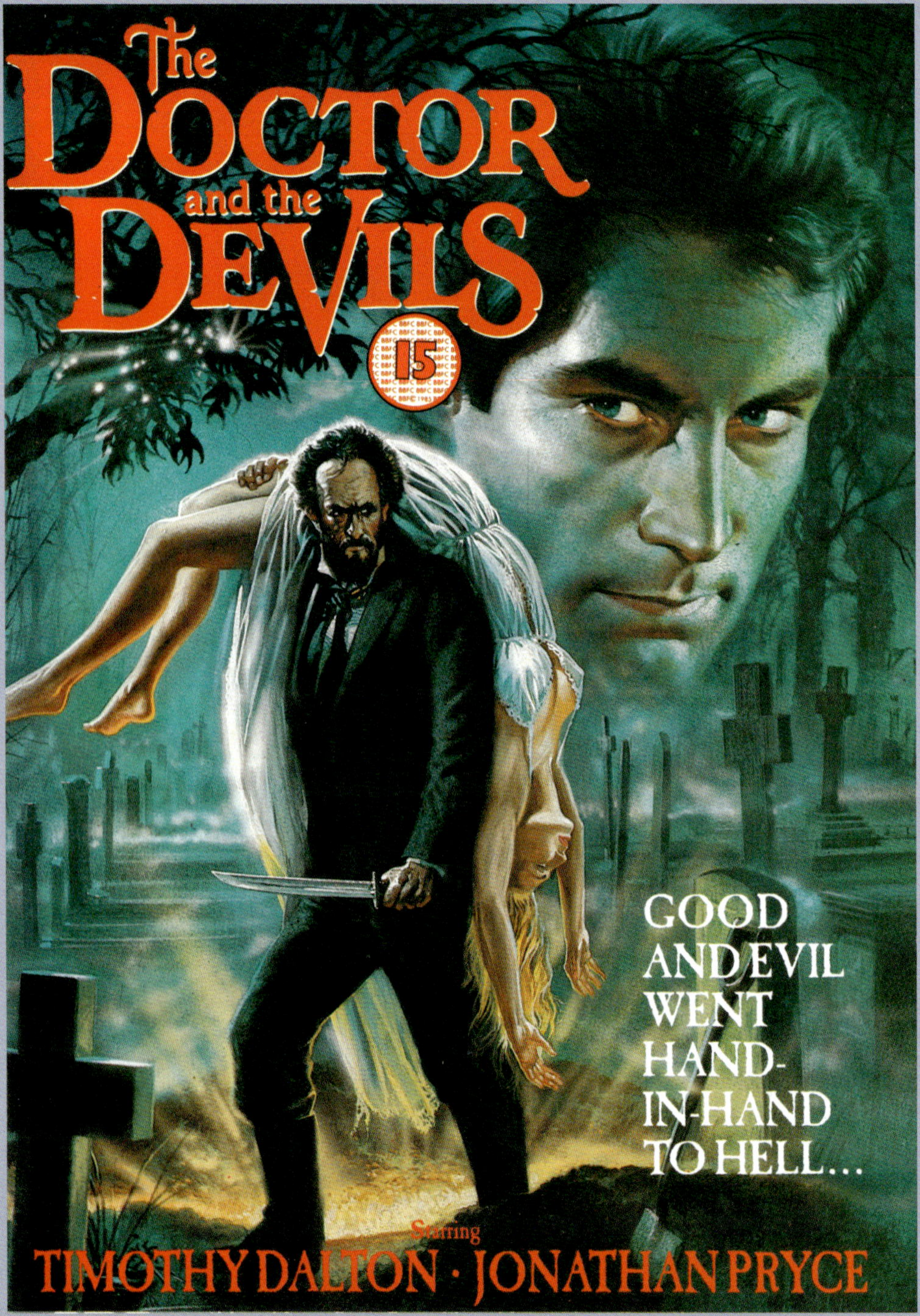

The 1985 film based on Dylan's script published in 1953 (his last life-time publication)

8.

Dylan Thomas: Film & The Search for Moving Images.

...the new Walt Disney film Dumbo. It's one of the very best I've seen.

Dylan Thomas to his uncle

Dylan Thomas had a life-long love of film. John Ackerman, who edited and compiled Dylan Thomas The Filmscripts,[1] begins his introduction;

'Dylan Thomas had a passion for the cinema'.

That this passion began early on in his life is evidenced by the precocious but informed essay, *The Films*, which Dylan contributed to the Swansea Grammar School Magazine in the July 1930 issue. He was aged just fifteen, yet his survey contains references to classic directors and films such as D.W. Griffith's *Birth of a Nation* and Adolph Zukor's *Queen Elizabeth*. Here are the opening and closing sections;

A few years later in 1934, the 20 year old poet was sending long letters to his first serious girlfriend, Pamela Hansford Johnson. In them, he tells her that *Film Pictorial* is part of his regular light reading, and later that month, in a long rambling letter, he includes a spoof play featuring this barely disguised imaginary exchange between his character, Salnady and Spajma (Dylan and Pam – Dylan loved an anagram) in which he harps on about his love of cinema;

> SALNADY: ...What have you been doing lately?
>
> SPAJMA: I've been to see John Barrymore in the films Don't you love his moustache?
>
> SALNADY: I'm afraid I rarely go to the pictures, the vast majority of films are atrociously bad, but that is not the reason which prevents me from going. My diurnal round...allows little time for me to sit...to wonder how much worse an actor John Barrymore, can possibly be in his next film ...Among the few films I have enjoyed are: *The Cabinet of Dr Caligari, Atlanta, Student of Prague, Edge of the World, Vaudeville, Waxworks, the Street, M, and Blue Angel (all German); Sur les Toits de Paris; Potemkin (Russian); The Gold Rush* and Marx Brothers Comedies (American).

That's quite a list, and as he grows older, this love of film is undiminished – a 1941 letter (as yet unpublished)[2] to his Uncle

THE FILMS.

The evolution of the motion-picture from the crude experimentalism of pre-war years to the polished artistry of to-day has taken place during a very short period. It was not until the beginning of the twentieth century that it was possible to present natural things in natural motion on a screen. To-day, less than thirty years later, every shade of physical emotion, however slight or subtle, can be shown among natural and often naturally coloured surroundings.

The first picture that *could* be taken seriously was produced by D. W. Griffith in 1907. He brought a greater sense of balance and artistic understanding to that film than had hitherto been thought of, and introduced the now familiar tricks of the " close-up," the " fade out " and the " cut back." He realised the importance of motion-pictures, not as freak exhibitions, but as works of art produced through an entirely new medium. The first film that *was* taken seriously was Adolph Zukar's " Queen Elizabeth," produced in 1912. Zukar had been for a long time contemplating the introduction of famous stage-stars on to the screen, and he made his first attempt at this by casting Sara Bernhardt as Elizabeth. The film met with instant appreciation, but, with a few notable exceptions, stage-stars have not been successful on the screen,

From his time has come a long line of actors and actresses who have made themselves universally admired for their brilliance and charm.

In the few points I have dealt with, I have made no mention of sound. The coming of the talkies has widened many fields and narrowed many others. There is no way of treating the motion-picture with sound and without sound : they are far too differentiated. Sound-technique is in the same state now as silent technique was when D. W. Griffith evolved his own methods of pictorial representation, adding inestimably to its progress. Whether there will be a Griffith for sound-films is a matter that is best left to time.

Synchronized films up to 1930 have been distinctly disappointing. Crudity was expected, but both American and English producers have taken sound for granted, and have been over-confident of themselves. The older and established producers, especially, have merely added it to their screen-properties, without realising that it is something new which cannot be tackled by any old methods but which requires a special way of approach. Even film-pioneers must start at the beginning of sound-film production, and learn what there is to be learnt.

D.M.T.

1930 Young Dylan (aged 15) as Film Critic in his School Mag

Arthur, a Port Talbot railway man, Dylan thanks him for Christmas gifts and concludes by urging him to go to the cinema and watch;

> ...the new Walt Disney film *Dumbo*.
> It's one of the very best I've seen.

Visits to the cinema with Dylan are recounted by many of his friends including Mervyn Levy and Theodora Fitzgibbon and in February of 1935, after his move to London, Dylan writes back to his Swansea left-leaning, socialist friend, Bert Trick with this positive list of must-see films;

> If these films come your way do see them: *Morgenrot*, the German Nazi propaganda film about submarine warfare, The Forbidden Territory, a sort of *Boys' Own Paper* version of an anti-Soviet message, *The Thin Man*...the best American film I think and any of the new Walt Disney's, especially '*The Orphans Benefit*'.

Once he became a writer and was writing scripts for the BBC, cinema is a constant point of reference. In his memoir *Reminiscences of Childhood*, written for, and broadcast by the BBC, in 1943, he describes his boyhood visits,

> ... to Saturday afternoon cinema matinees where we shouted and hissed our threepences away.

In his radio play *Return Journey* (1947) he describes the discussions he and his pals had in their favourite Swansea coffee house – The Kardomah, back when they were a bunch of late teenagers. These included writers, politicians, boxers, girls, free love and more girls, interspersed with Greta Garbo, Dracula and King Kong and later in his journey he arrives back in the Uplands where,

> ... was once the flea-pit picture-house where he whooped for the scalping Indians with Jack Bassett and banged for the rustler's guns.

His book of autobiographical short stories, *Portrait of the Artist as a Young Dog*, which was published in 1940, contains a story, *Old Garbo*, which is based on his first working experiences as a cub reporter on the local paper, after he had left school early, aged just 16. The story is a kind of right-of-passage tale about a Friday night pub crawl around some of the seamier Swansea drinking establishments, with a much older senior reporter and it has several nods to film and local cinema. The narrator, a thinly disguised young Thomas, has time to kill in the afternoon and calls in for a coffee with his friends;

> 'Sit by here' said Leslie Bird. He was in the boots at Dan Lewis's
> 'Been to the Flicks this week, Thomas?'
> 'Yes. The Regal. *White Lies*. Damned good show, too! Connie Bennett was great! Remember her in the foam-bath, Leslie?]
> 'Too much foam for me, old man.'

The narrator decides to kill more time before the pub by going to the cinema;

> I went to the Plaza. 'Press' I said to the girl with the Tyrolean hat and skirt.
> 'There's been two reporters this week.'
> 'Special Notice.'
> She showed me to a seat. During the educational film, with the rude seeds hugging and sprouting in front of my eyes and plants like arms and legs... The sinuous plants danced on the screen. If only Tawe were a larger sea-town, there would be curtained rooms underground with blue films. The potato's life came to an end. Then I entered an American college and danced with the president's daughter. The hero, called Lincoln, tall and dark with good teeth, I displaced quickly, and the girl spoke my name as she held his shadow, the singing college chorus in sailor's hats and bathing dresses called me big boy and king, Jack Oakie and I sped up the field, and on the shoulders of the crowd the president's daughter and I brought across the shifting-coloured curtain with a kiss that left me giddy and bright-eyed as I walked out of the cinema into the strong lamplight and the new rain.

Jack Oakie was a real regular American movie-star, but I can't pin-point the actual film described, but Thomas' account takes us right back to that magical time. One further anecdote; this from John Ormond, another Swansea boy, journalist, film maker and poet; younger than Dylan, but a good friend of Dylan's and most all of the Kardomah crew. Writing the *Introduction* to a 1964 American edition of Dylan's screenplay, *The Doctor and the Devils*, he gives an account of a typical afternoon for Dylan when he came back to Swansea;

> ...he'd consult the local newspaper to discover which cinema was showing the best cowboy picture...Once on a rainy Thursday afternoon, misled by some such title as *Desert Hotspot*, he sat, nearly alone in the *Carlton*, watching a film that turned out to be about an Eastern sheik in disguise bidding in the marketplace for a beautiful girl. The price went up and up. The bidding reached a crisis. The crackly silences on the sound track grew longer between the bids, "Will no one offer me more than five thousand pieces of gold? [*crackle, crackle.*] This exquisite wild creature [big close-up] – is she to be sold for so paltry a sum? Will nobody bid more on?" A loud cry from the auditorium – "I will!"
>
> It was Thomas, on his feet, as surprised as any by the sound of his voice.

Strand Films & The Doctor and the Devils

After the publication of the *Portrait of the Artist as a Young Dog* in 1940, Dylan began a stretch of time living and working in London, the only time that he held some kind of regular paid job; and that job was as a film scriptwriter. In the autumn of 1941 he joined the *Strand Film Co.* in that role.

Enter Donald Taylor, the founder and owner of Strand Films. Dylan already had a friend working there, the American film writer, Ivan Moffat, and he might have mentioned Dylan to Taylor who met Dylan in a pub, felt sorry for him and put him on the payroll at £10 a week; a living wage for Dylan, at last. In January 1942 Dylan wrote his first letter on *Strand Films* stationary. At the time Taylor was working almost exclusively for the M.O.I making war-time propaganda documentaries and Dylan got his first film credit in May for *This is Colour*

Dylan had already been engaging with broadcasting film-people while working for the BBC; now he joined a group of men involved in film-making, especially in the field of documentary and experimental films. Some he met through his literary and drinking friend John Davenport, but others came via the poet, (but also a well-connected advertising copy-writer) Norman Cameron.[3] Norman was a good friend and supporter of Dylan, but he knew his limitations and wrote a poem about him called *The Dirty Little Accuser*, which begins

> *Who invited him in? What is he doing here?*
> *That insolent little ruffian, crapulous little lout?*
> *When he quitted a sofa he left behind a smear*

Cyril Connolly mischievously published the poem in *Horizon*, opposite a poem by Dylan! It was through Cameron that Dylan would meet Len Lye, a lively New Zealander; an artist, a jazz aficionado as well as a respected maker of abstract, animated films; despite being a Kiwi he was nicknamed 'the English Disney'.

Len had perfected an innovative way of painting directly onto film. Despite their difference in age Dylan really warmed to Len and his wife and he would 'drop in, sit on the floor and talk.' One of the topics they discussed was Surrealism, which was just beginning to penetrate the UK's intelligentsia, and Len's ideas of combining poetry and film seemed somehow to fit in this new art movement's remit. Almost inevitably they were both involved in the seminal 1936 International Surrealism Exhibition. Lye contributed a recent painting 'Jam Session' and two early photograms to the exhibition. One of the main exhibition organisers, Herbert Read, was particularly taken with one of these and included it in his 1936 book *Surrealism*. Thomas made his presence felt at the opening and also contributed to a poetry reading alongside Paul Eluard.[4]

But very much like Dylan, Lye had reservations about all the rules and tenants of the movement but was intrigued by much of it, as was Dylan. They were both affected by the best-known Surrealist film, Dali and Bunuel's, *Un Chien Andalou*; one stanza of Dylan's 1935 poem; *I in my intricate image* is directly inspired by a harrowing scene in the film, it begins;

> (Death instrumental)

Splitting the long eye open, and the spiral turnkey,
Your corkscrew grave centred in navel and nipple,
The neck of the nostril
Under the mask and the ether, they making bloody
The tray of knives, the antiseptic funeral.

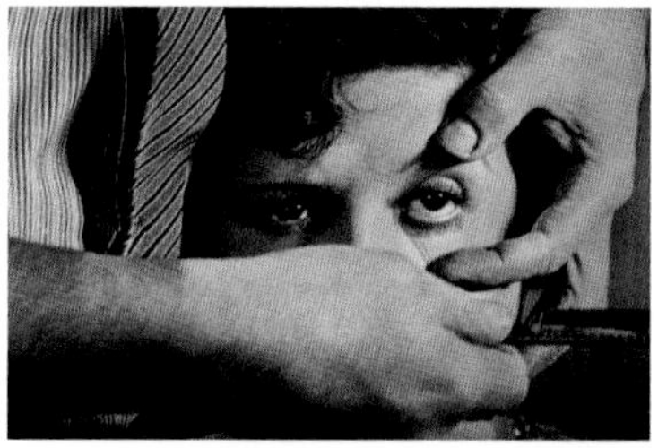

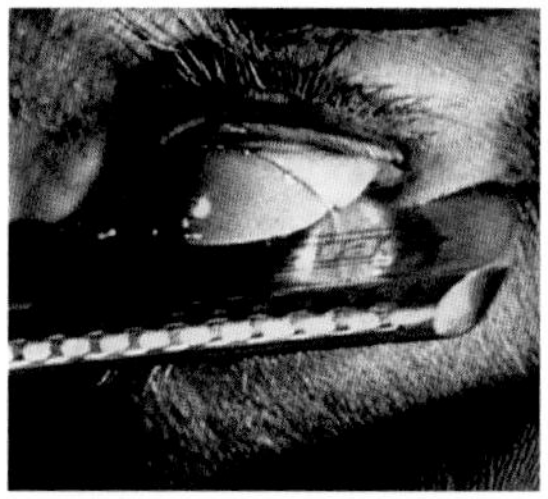

The eye-splitting scene from *Un Chien Andalou*

A little later, in 1936, Lye would write an essay for the literary magazine *Life and Letters Today*, appraising the Dali/Bunuel film from his own filmic standpoint of 'pure visual impulse and sensation stimuli'. Although nothing concrete came from this early friendship the two would meet up again in the 50's. The Lyes had moved to New York City in 1944, where they joined up with another of Dylan's London friends, the writer Ruthven Todd and also with Dave and Rose Slivka. Dave was a sculptor[5] and they were a typical arty Greenwich village couple who were also close New York friends of Dylan's. According to Rose Slivka;

> Dylan certainly knew that Len was an intellect,
> a very unique intellect.

When Dylan began his American reading tours in 1950 he re-encountered them both. On the first day of his first reading tour Dylan invited Len and Ruthven to join him for lunch in a Third Avenue bar. Brinnin was present and describes this raucous reunion;[6]

> ...the smoky air was soon loud with Rabelaisian reminiscence of prodigious drinking bouts that had laid everyone under the table, of literary parties that had not so much ended as disintegrated, of pub-room ribaldries that had shocked the fatuous and the famous, of escapades that had brought wives, mothers, and the London police running.

Once again Dylan and Len began talking about poetry and film and discussing various collaborations. Lye's biographer Roger Horrocks writes,

> Lye had always been enthusiastic about his friend's poetry, admiring its extreme individuality. He also had a personal respect for Thomas as someone who refused to compromise...

On his visits to New York in 1950 and 1952 Dylan once again spent time with Lye trying to come up with a new type of poetry film, Lye recalled;

> We ran all sorts of coloured abstract films in my studio accompanied by all sorts of poems (including Dylan's) on phonograph but Dylan agreed with me that none seemed to work. He offered to write something that he thought would work – such as something about a bicycle.[7]

A month before his third reading tour Dylan wrote to John Malcolm Brinnin, his American friend and agent;

> I am hoping that perhaps my old friend Len Lye, who lives in Greenwich Village, near Ruthven Todd, will put me up: I am only small after all, and alone, though loud.

However the Lye's apartment on Washington Street was hardly big enough for the two of them so Dylan returned to the infamous Chelsea Hotel. Although they talked some more about a film project, by now Dylan was spending more and more time in bars, drinking and socialising so that little or no progress was made. Lye went about making a few specimen films in his studio, including one based on *Full Fathom Five*, Shakespeare's Ariel's song from *The Tempest*, with the words spoken by John Gielgud. Sadly, if Lye did make any experimental films using Thomas's words and voice, none have survived.

On Dylan's final and fatal trip, Len was to have one last telephone conversation with Thomas. On the night of November 4, in the small hours of the morning, Len got a call from Dylan, who was at the *White Horse*. The call was ostensibly trying to arrange to borrow a dinner jacket to take on to California where he was to begin work on his opera project with Stravinsky, but it soon disintegrated as Len's wife Ann recalls;

> Dylan was obviously very high. He mentioned the tuxedo and Len said, "well I'm working in the cellar" and Dylan – said in

> a drunken voice because he was in a bad way – "Well I'm way down below the cellar!" "I'm lower" – a very goofy conversation... When Len talked with Dylan they were always in the clouds – or in the cellar.

And a few hours later Thomas was in St Vincent's Hospital in a coma from which he never recovered. Len sums up their friendship in his book *Zizz! The life and art of Len Lye in his own words*;

> Most important to me were Dylan Thomas and Norman Cameron, guys who were creating the real-essence stuff. I think it is far more difficult to discipline yourself *not* to discipline yourself than it is to discipline yourself. No matter how bad an artist's feelings or illnesses, no matter how lousy the times, it's marvellous when someone breaks new ground and lasting work comes out of it.

Dylan was kept busy at *Strand*, not just writing scripts, but occasionally directing, producing, and even calling on his BBC voice to be the narrator of the film's sound commentary. And he was soon to meet another interesting and eccentric character.

During *Strand's* busiest period in 1942, when they produced seventy-five films, staff came and went. Needing some extra creative input Donald Taylor, who had an uncanny knack of finding just such individuals, introduced Dylan Thomas to a new employee, Julian

Len Lye in New York. The film strips are examples of his scratched on patterns

Maclaren Ross, who was to be quite an influence on Dylan. Maclaren-Ross was a couple of years older than Dylan and in many ways he epitomised and was synonymous with the bohemian world of mid-twentieth-century Soho that Dylan had recently moved into. They already had many mutual friends and soon made more; John Minton, Nina Hamnett, Joan Wyndham, Aleister Crowley, John Deakin, Augustus John, Robert Colquhoun and Robert MacBryde. When it came to appearances, he could not have been more different; Julian went in for a theatrical dress sense; a sharp suit combined with his famous teddy-bear coat; aviator-style dark glasses and cigarette-holder; these accoutrements ensured that he stood out even in the most flamboyant company. Anthony Powell and Olivia Manning had used him as a model for characters in their fiction. A talented short story writer as well as screenwriter, Maclaren Ross left a wonderful and highly readable account of these years in his book, *Memoirs of the Forties*.[8]

The book has a very lively chapter on Dylan Thomas entitled, *The Polestar Neighbour*.[9] The first sentence sets the tone;

> Dylan Thomas in 1943 did not greatly resemble that much reproduced early photograph of him, known as the Fucking Cherub. Certainly I failed to recognise him from it, on the first morning we met.

A few pages on he relates Dylan's retaliation, which was not a long time coming. After a long nights drinking during which they progress through beer, (in the Café Royal), to Scotch, (in the Wheatsheaf) and on to gin, (in the Highlander). By then Dylan is drunk and hot, but still trussed up in his collar and tie. Ross was still in his elegant white jacket. He suggests that Dylan should remove his over-tight collar, to which he responds; Why don't you take that bloody jacket off?

ROSS: What's wrong with my jacket?

> DYLAN: Fucking Dandy. Flourishing that stick.
> Why don't you try and look more sordid.
> Sordidness boy, that's the thing.

Reading Ross' account of the next few months, the pair became good friends and good drinking partners, however they both liked to be the centre of attention and hold court so they began to inhabit different ends of the bar-room and then, as things got heated they would go separate ways to different low-life drinking gaffs. They did just about enough work to keep Donald Taylor just about satisfied. They worked on a documentary about the Home Guard, but it was never completed and they soon seemed to spend more time on a non-documentary project of their own – a bizarre, high-gothic horror film which sadly never reached the screen. In his biography of Dylan Thomas, Andrew Lycett sums it up;

> Apart from drinking they shared a passion for art-house cinema classics. They dreamt of producing a film called *The Whispering Gallery* or *The Distorting Mirror* in the style of *The Cabinet of Dr Caligari*. Dylan suggested a plot... involving fairgrounds and stately homes.

When they were unable to decide whether the villain should be male or female Dylan suggested the character should be both – or should have a sex change halfway through.[10]

Yet another film idea that never came to fruition involved Dylan trying to interest the novelist Graham Greene in *The Doctor and the Devils*. Greene was also on the payroll at Strand, but Dylan got one of his most loyal and longstanding lady patrons, Margaret Taylor (the wife of the historian A.J.P. Taylor) to make the first approach before Dylan wrote to him in January 1947, Dylan does not go in for the 'hard sell', he shoots himself in the foot!

> I looked the script over again – and it looks amateurish: the dialogue is over wordy, and the construction needs pulling together, Probably a good subplot is needed; probably nothing is needed but 'No'!

He either included a memo on the history of the script with this letter or included it in another longer letter – this it is not quite clear, but the memo certainly describes the long gestation of the project which he began with Donald Taylor when he was at *Strand* and continued when Taylor left and formed *Gryphon Films*, taking Dylan Thomas and the *Doctor And The Devils* project with him. Although Dylan was a tad more upbeat in this communication; suggesting that Michael Redgrave had read it and was 'extremely keen to play in it'. But it still sounded a very complicated business and nothing further seems to have come back from Greene.

Although *The Doctor And The Devils* was never made into a film during Dylan's lifetime,[11] it is the most lasting legacy of Dylan Thomas' time at the Strand. Donald Taylor was very keen to get away from propaganda documentaries, and get into making proper feature films and his favourite notion was to make a feature film about Burke and Hare the nineteenth century Edinburgh 'body-snatchers who he was deeply fascinated by. He commissioned Dylan Thomas to write a fully-fledged and researched script which Dylan did. The working title was *The Doctor and the Devils*. The plot revolves around a renowned Edinburgh Professor of Anatomy, Dr. Thomas Rock, who taught anatomy classes to tyro medical students at the university. His lectures feature actual post mortems on actual dead bodies of which he needs a continual supply. He uses his assistant Dr. Murray to buy corpses for his experiments from body snatchers paying a small fortune for each cadaver. When the despicable, hard drinking, petty criminals, Robert Fallon and Timothy Broom overhear a conversation of grave-robbers about Dr. Rock, they decide to go into business themselves with a much more sordid modus-operandi; they would supply fresher corpses, which were worth more to the doctor, by murdering some of the poor low-life they lived among. Taylor kept very close to the project and engaged with a playwright, James Bridie, whose play *The Anatomist*, was based around the same story. Dylan's *Doctor and The Devils* script is most important because it was published as a book. He wrote to one of his literary agents, Laurence

Pollinger at Higham's, in June 1944 about this possibility;

> I'm writing films now, and I have almost completed a feature film based on the lives of Burke and Hare. This film will be put into production ...sometime this year, but I do think it might be a good idea to publish the script separately, perhaps with an introductory essay...

But the project stalled, although in mid 1947 Dent produced 35 proof copies[12] of *The Doctor And The Devils*. But then another hiatus halted things, until another five years later, in April I953 a further 97 proofs were printed and the book ended up being Dylan's (unplanned), final life-time book, when it was published in on May 1953.

The book's title page reads;

'by/ Dylan Thomas/ from the story by/ Donald Taylor'

Taylor also provided a four page afterword – THE STORY OF THE FILM in which he includes some important observations about the book:

> In talking about this work as if it were a novel or a play, [we] forget the fact that ... a film script, even by a man of Thomas's genius, is only one contribution to the composite that is a film.

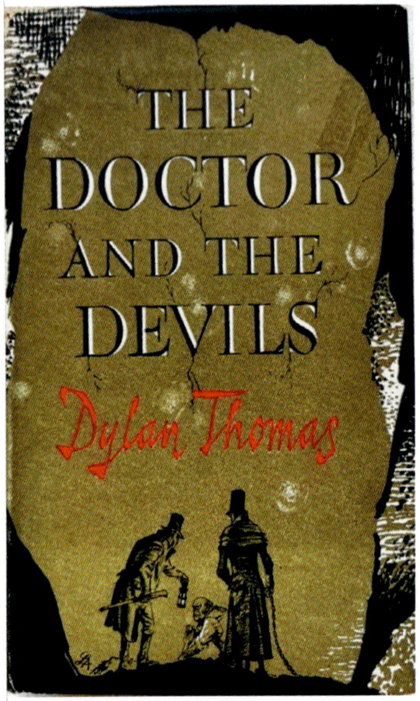

The First edition May 1953

The second proof copy, April 1953

Thomas was unhappy because his ambition had always been to write feature scripts. As he had said in a letter to Donald Taylor:

> You know that, above everything, I want to work with you, again, on Films, and exclusively, if possible, on feature films this time.

Thomas's ambitions went even further with his vision of creating an entirely new medium in which a film scenario could be read on the page and visualised exactly as it could and would be seen on celluloid. This involved writing without the direct use of camera directions or technical descriptions that might detract from the script as an artistic creation in its own right. It was not until Thomas met Julian Maclaren Ross at *Strand* along with his colleagues, Donald Taylor, and Philip Lindsay that Thomas found writers who shared his love of 'B' movies, but who all wanted to push the medium to new and more innovative heights. Thomas began to develop the theory of the complete script scenario. The concept was originally formulated by Thomas and Maclaren-Ross in a projected mystery film to be entitled either, *The Whispering Gallery* or *The Distorting Mirror*. The basic plot idea was to follow the exploits of some type of androgynous super-villain taking control of a stately home. Much of the film was to be presented within an atmosphere of mystery and suspense; it was to be set in a hall of mirrors, hence the title. In his *Memoirs* Maclaren-Ross described the basic theory;

> We... shared another ambition, which was to write a film-script, not a Treatment as the story-form is called, but a complete scenario ready for shooting which would give the ordinary reader an absolute visual impression of the film in words and could be published as a new form of literature. Carl Meyer ... is said to have written such' scripts; but neither Dylan or I could get hold of a script by Meyer, and the only ones we knew which almost succeeded in doing what we had in mind were those printed in *The Film Sense* by Sergei

> Eisenstein. The rules we laid down ourselves were that the script had to be an original specially written in this form and not any kind of adaptation and that actual film production must be possible. Our main obstacle consisted in the camera directions, which if given were apt to look too technical, and if omitted would lose the dramatic impact of, for instance, a sudden large close up, which Dylan hoped could be conveyed by one's actual choice of words.

This last line is at the centre of their writing philosophy. It was to be very thorough. The 'actual choice of words' that describe all visual film effects, down to the level of small camera movements, were to be conveyed. This 'intimate script' was to be *The Whispering Gallery*, but it was never (to my knowledge) even started, let alone completed. As Maclaren Ross goes on to say in his memoirs;

> Dylan Thomas in *The Doctor and The Devils* came as close as anyone to succeeding with this form of writing. This is probably the reason the scenario was printed before any production deal for the film was arranged, and thus became the first script ever to be published before its film counterpart. Even this completed version did not fully satisfy Thomas, who was sure he could improve on the style and structure, remarking in a letter to Graham Greene that "I should like it to be regarded as a sample of what I can write for the films."

Other scenarios followed in the same vein, with *Twenty Years A-Growing* based on the short story by Maurice O'Sullivan, an Irish writer born on the Great Blasket in 1904. '*Twenty Years A-Growing*' tells the story of his youth and of the way of life on the Blasket Islands unchanged for centuries. When Dylan Thomas left *Strand* he moved to *Gainsborough Films*, where he wrote a script for Robert Louis Stevenson's novella set on a South Sea Island, *The Beach at Falesa.*[13] Stevenson's story was first published in the Illustrated London News in 1892, and later published in book form in 1893, in his short-story collection Island Nights Entertainments. It was written in Samoa after Stevenson moved to the South Seas island of Samoa, just a few years before he died there. The script was eventually published posthumously in book form; first in New York in 1963 and then in the UK in 1964 by Jonathan Cape. It also came out in a somewhat sensational Ballantine pulp paperback in 1966.

One other *Gainsborough* script was published but never filmed; *Me and My Bike*. It was a kind of original film operetta about a crazed bicycle lover and this was the first instalment of a proposed five part series. It was published in the UK in 1965 by Triton Books. The book was put together by Sidney Box, the original proposed director/producer of the project and he writes a short introduction and also reproduces a 1948 letter by Dylan to another Gainsborough director, Ralph 'Bunny' Keene, in which Dylan is very enthusiastic about the project;

> But I'm extremely keen on the Bike. For me as a supposedly imaginative writer, it's got wonderful possibilities, and I feel very enthusiastic about it. Sidney's carte blanch as to freedom of fancy, non-naturalistic dialogue, song, music etc. is enormously encouraging.

It seems a great pity that the project did not have legs to sustain it.

In both of his earlier scripts, *The Doctor and The Devils* and *Twenty Years A-Growing*, Thomas succeeds partially in replacing camera directions with linguistic devices and in the creation of a tangible ambience through the text.

But neither film could claim success in fully achieving Dylan Thomas and Maclaren Ross' aims, as neither script was wholly as Ross had envisaged;

> '...original, specially written in this form and not any kind of adaptation, and that actual film production must be possible.

Perhaps the closest Dylan got to that was his script *Rebecca's Daughters*, which he wrote around 1948. The script was based on Dylan's own dramatization of an episode from nineteenth century Welsh history, when riots broke out in South Wales when local agricultural workers rose up against increasing levels of taxation. The rioters, often men dressed as women, took their actions against toll-gates as they were tangible representations of taxes and tolls. The rioters went by the name of 'Merched Beca' which translates directly from Welsh as Rebecca's Daughters. The script was published in 1965 and was eventually filmed by Karl Francis in 1992 with Peter O'Toole in the starring role. Sadly the film reduces Dylan's somewhat serious and political script to some kind of cross-dressing comedy farce.

Dylan Goes Wild at the Strand[14]

A mini-photo essay comprised of four, hitherto unpublished photographs, of Dylan Thomas

Scene: The offices of Strand Films in Golden Square London circa 1942. One of the secretaries sits at her desk. In walks an exceedingly dapper looking Dylan Thomas complete with jaunty trilby. He takes a seat at a desk and smiles benignly at the camera which is being wielded by Fred Brown, another Strand employee. However things took a turn for the worse when Dylan, after lighting a cigarette, discovered that an advance payment against his fee for a script was not available. Lack of money was always a problem for Thomas but on this day he must have been desperately impecunious and he flew into a furious rage and took it out on the office furniture; however the cigarette never left his mouth; as the following, hitherto unpublished, photographs illustrate:

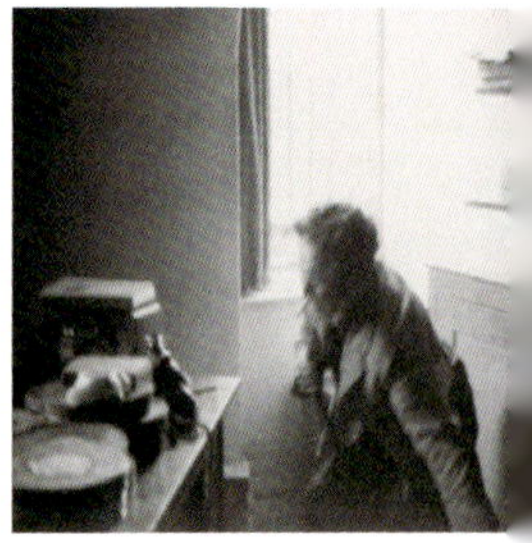

All images © Jeff Towns Dylans Bookstore Collection

Poetry and Film

Given Dylan's life-long love of films it is perhaps fitting that his second to last public appearance was to join the panel at a Symposium on *Poetry and Film*.[15] The event took place in NYC on October 28 1953 under the auspices of Cinema 16, at the Offices on Lexington Ave in New York City. It was organised by Amos Vogel, the executive Secretary, who joined Dylan Thomas, Arthur Miller, Maya Deren, Parker Tyler, on the panel chaired by Willard Maas. They did the event twice on the evening. Dylan Thomas was not in the best of health at this event and his drinking had been heavy on the day. In fact within two weeks he would be lying in a coma in St Vincent's Hospital.

But he was also not on his best behaviour particularly when responding to the only woman panellist, Maya Deren. Dylan had some history with this woman. Maya Deren was a Ukrainian-born (1917), American experimental filmmaker and important part of the avant-garde. Her family fled Ukraine because of the anti-

Amos Vogel's invitation letter to Liz Reitell [sic] with her note of the pick-up time for Dylan at the Chelsea

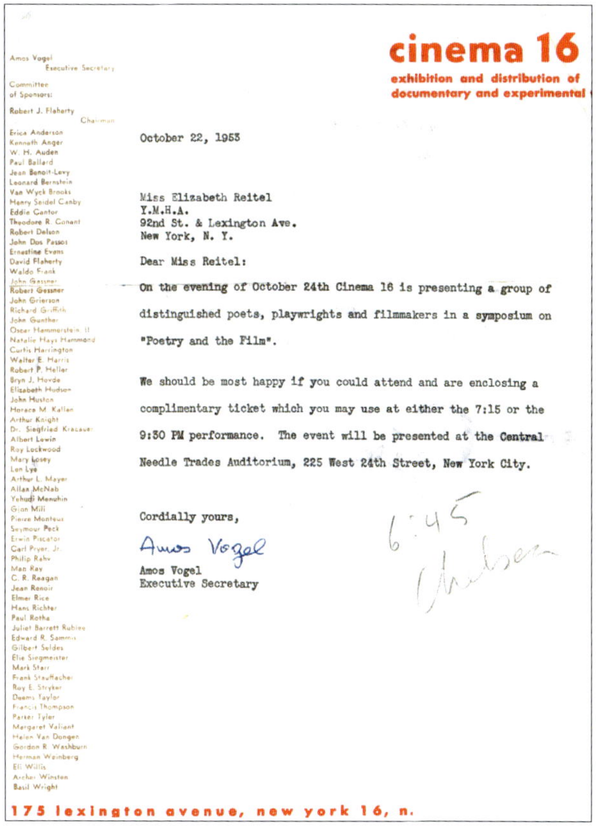
cinema 16
exhibition and distribution of documentary and experimental

Amos Vogel
Executive Secretary

Committee of Sponsors:

Robert J. Flaherty
Chairman

Erica Anderson
Kenneth Anger
W. H. Auden
Paul Ballard
Jean Benoit-Levy
Leonard Bernstein
Van Wyck Brooks
Henry Seidel Canby
Eddie Cantor
Theodore R. Conant
Robert Delson
John Dos Passos
Ernestine Evans
David Flaherty
Waldo Frank
John Gessner
Robert Gessner
John Grierson
Richard Griffith
John Gunther
Oscar Hammerstein II
Natalie Hays Hammond
Curtis Harrington
Walter E. Harris
Robert P. Heller
Bryn J. Hovde
Elizabeth Hudson
John Huston
Horace M. Kallen
Arthur Knight
Dr. Siegfried Kracauer
Albert Lewin
Roy Lockwood
Mary Losey
Len Lye
Arthur L. Mayer
Allan McNab
Yehudi Menuhin
Gjon Mili
Pierre Monteux
Seymour Peck
Erwin Piscator
Carl Pryer, Jr.
Philip Rahv
Man Ray
C. R. Reagan
Jean Renoir
Elmer Rice
Hans Richter
Paul Rotha
Juliet Barrett Rublee
Edward R. Sammis
Gilbert Seldes
Elie Siegmeister
Mark Starr
Frank Stauffacher
Roy E. Stryker
Deems Taylor
Francis Thompson
Parker Tyler
Margaret Valiant
Helen Van Dongen
Gordon R. Washburn
Herman Weinberg
Eli Willis
Archer Winston
Basil Wright

October 22, 1953

Miss Elizabeth Reitel
Y.M.H.A.
92nd St. & Lexington Ave.
New York, N. Y.

Dear Miss Reitel:

On the evening of October 24th Cinema 16 is presenting a group of distinguished poets, playwrights and filmmakers in a symposium on "Poetry and the Film".

We should be most happy if you could attend and are enclosing a complimentary ticket which you may use at either the 7:15 or the 9:30 PM performance. The event will be presented at the Central Needle Trades Auditorium, 225 West 24th Street, New York City.

Cordially yours,

Amos Vogel

Amos Vogel
Executive Secretary

6:45
Chelsea

175 lexington avenue, new york 16, n.

Semitic pogroms being perpetrated by the Russian White Volunteer Army. They settled in Syracuse in New York State. Her father shortened the family name from Derenkovskaya to "Deren" shortly after they arrived in New York. He became the staff psychiatrist at the state mental hospital and Deren's mother was a musician and dancer who had studied these arts in Kyiv.

Deren was very bright and intelligent and enjoyed a rich international education and went on to become a leading socially committed Avant Garde filmmaker, choreographer, dancer, writer and photographer. She was also very attractive in a savage way, and just back from her monumental expedition to Haiti, which became the impetus for her to write one of the classic texts.

All this was the background to one wild night in New York City. In January of 1952 Dylan Thomas arrived in New York for the start of his second monumental Reading Tour of America. This time he was not alone but was accompanied by his wife Caitlin. However she was not to be a helpful and calming influence, far from it. One evening they attended, a party at the apartment of Maya Deren. Deren was fresh from her monumental expedition to Haiti, and, once the drink was flowing, and to get the party going, Maya put on a recording of some frenetic Haitian Voodoo drumming music and she took to the floor and began to perform a fierce dance, showing off some Voodoo dance moves. Caitlin who had already been drinking saw this as a challenge and took to the floor as if it was some kind of dance competition. Another guest, a Greenwich Village based writer Anatole Broyard.[16] would later describe the evening in his published memoir;

She chose to liven proceedings up by playing (loudly) a recording of some frenetic Haitian Voodoo drumming music; to which she began to perform a fierce dance, showing off some spectacular Voodoo dance moves. Caitlin, who had been drinking, saw this as challenge and took to the floor as if it was some kind of Dance competition ... I only saw the bottom half of her, her legs, thighs and cotton underpants, because she was holding her dress up over her head as if she was pulling it off, or hiding behind it like a child. She was dancing, a sort of elementary hootchy-kootch that didn't have much to do with the

Cover photo shows Dylan, Arthur Miller, Willard Mass, Parker Tyler and Maya Deren

Maya Deren's seminal book on Haitian voodoo originally published in 1953

fast Haitian drum music that filled the room. It was like a war of the worlds out there on the floor: the child-bearing, cottage-keeping, pub-crawling wife of the Welsh bard against a rising star of Greenwich Village, Caitlin relied on the immemorial argument of bump and grind, while Maya Deren, who wore trousers, danced not exactly to the tapes, but the different drummer of the American Art establishment.

Then things got nasty; Broyard again:

> Deren and a young confederate tried to usher Caitlin off the dance floor. She punched the young man out, then proceeded to grab the small Voodoo statuettes that Deren had arranged on a shelf, flinging them against the far wall. Deren was horrified. Plunging her fingers into her curls, she cried like an Ibsen heroine, She's smashing my universe. Dylan takes control at this point by grabbing Caitlin's arm, spinning her around and flinging her with great accuracy from the living room into the bedroom. At one point, Broyard is given the job of restraining Caitlin Thomas on a bed. She stops struggling, then asks Broyard, "Are you queer?" The offended Broyard says No. Then She threw her arms around my neck and said, "Then for God's sake, man, love me! Love me!"

He takes her back to the Chelsea Hotel by cab and runs away when she invites him in for a drink.

An infamous incident, which only makes the pages of Andrew Lycett's 2003 biography of Thomas, although others do make reference to the Poetry and Film symposium. Lycett gives us a few more details: the party was on Friday February 22 1952 on the evening after he had made his famous first recording for Caedmon records which became his first L.P, featuring *A Child's Christmas in Wales and Five Poems*. Lycett writes of Caitlin as;

> Bumping and grinding for Britain with her skirt lifted above her head to reveal legs, thighs and cotton knickers...when Deren tried to get her off the floor Caitlin shot out a straight right that left a solicitous guest reeling.

After reading these accounts is it comes as no surprise that Caitlin would proudly describe herself as an *Irish fighting drunk*.

On the night of the *Poetry and Film* event, even in his sickly condition, Dylan must have recalled this earlier debacle at his co-panellist's party, but whatever the cause he did not give the film-maker the credit or respect she deserved. Maya Deren delivered a long, deep and quite abstract summation of her feelings about the titular topic, beginning;

> I'm going to do something I think is a bit risky, and that is to go a little bit into the question of what is poetry, and what distinguishes what we call poetry from anything else...

She then goes on for much more than her declared, 'little bit', during which she dwells on ideas juxtaposing horizontal and vertical movement in poetry and film and she eventually ends her theorising with;

> I think this is a way of handling poetry ***and*** poetry *in film*...
> I don't know how the other people feel about it.

At that the chairman for the evening, Willard Maas turns to Dylan Thomas and asks;

> Well. Mr Thomas what do you feel about it?

One can imagine a sick, tired, somewhat inebriated, anti-intellectual Welsh poet having nodded off through Deren's long speech so it's no wonder his responses are trite attempts at levity. He begins:

Thomas: Well I'm sure that all Maya Deren said was what I would have said, had I thought of it or understood it [*laughter and slight applause*]. I was asked, on the side, whether that meant that I thought that the audience didn't understand what Miss Deren was saying. I'm sure they did, and I wish I was down there. But it sounds different from that side, you know. Now I'm all for (I'm in the wrong place tonight)... I'm all for horizontal and vertical [*laughter*], and all for what we heard about in the avant-garde The only Avant Garde play I saw in York was in a cellar or a sewer, or somewhere [*laughter*]. I happened to be with Mr Miller over there ... We saw the play gong on ...I'm sure it was fine, and in the middle he said, "Good God this is Avant Garde." Then he said. "In a moment the hero's going to take his clothes off..."

Maas: Did He?

Thomas: He did, [laughter]

Maas then asked Arthur Miller to respond, which he did at length, but Dylan seems only to have heard and retained Deren's constant use of the words *Horizontal* and *Vertical* and with his unreconstructed schoolboy love of sexual innuendo as a description of copulation. He then kept returning to these words; in his next interjection he tries to be serious but resorts to;

...So as in a poem one image breeds another I think, in a film, it's really the visual that breeds another – breeds and breathes it...If it's possible to combine a verbal image to a visual image in this sort of horizontal way, I'd rather see horizontal films, myself. I like stories. You know, I like to see something going on. [*laughter and applause*]

After a long, and serious back-and-fore between Deren and Miller, Deren concludes;

Deren: I wish mainly to say that I'm a little bit flabbergasted at the fact that people who have handled words with such dexterity as Mr Thomas and Mr. Miller, should have difficulty with such a simple idea as the "vertical and the "horizontal" [*applause*].

Thomas: [*aside*] Here we go up and down again.

Deren: These seem to me the most elementary movements in the world and really quite fundamental.

Maas: I don't think you ought to get vulgar

This draws an exasperated response from the film-maker

Deren: That has really flabbergasted me to the extent that I am unable to develop the idea any further...I don't see anything so difficult in the notion that what I called a 'horizontal development .... And that of a 'vertical' development'...

Dylan Thomas seems not to have said another word and at

One of Liz Reitell's spontaneous drawings

the end of the evening he and Liz Reitell adjourned with some of the panel to the White Horse Tavern, where Dylan drank and she sketched and doodled.

The quest for moving footage of Dylan Thomas

Given Dylan Thomas' rich filmic background it has always been a source of constant amazement to me and many others that there was no surviving moving footage of Dylan Thomas. He made two television programmes for the BBC but neither has survived. In the first programme Dylan was taken to a studio in St Asaph where he delivered his wonderful humorous account of a Welsh, all-male, boozy pub crawl by charabanc, *A Story* (which has since become known as *The Outing*.) The other programme, variously known as *Hometown Swansea*, *Swansea-Hometown*, or *From a Painters Studio*, only survives in an envelope containing some 20 tiny thumbnail photographs of Dylan Thomas on

Thumb-nail images of Dylan on TV

screen and various other contributors. A portion of the script was published in *The Texas Quarterly*.[17]

In 40 years of looking and hunting I had never found any moving image of Dylan Thomas. Back in 2003 – the fiftieth anniversary of Dylan's Death, my good colleague Wyn Thomas, got a letter well featured on the letters page of the *New York Times* – we had convinced ourselves that moving footage had to exist as home movie cine film or local TV station footage in the States. Wyn explained our quest and requested folk hunt, search, enquire and were generally made aware of this glaring absence. We got a slurry of responses from people who had seen him read and never forgotten the experience; from fans, and a few cranks – but no footage.

But no longer is this the case – how fitting that in his centenary year, this Holy Grail of Dylan Thomas memorabilia has come to light, and even more fitting is that it has come to light as part of a quite remarkable Surrealist film – *Pandora and the Flying Dutchman*. This curious and largely overlooked film is a British drama released by Metro-Goldwyn-Meyer in 1951. The film was directed by Albert Lewin who co-produced it with Joe Kaufman.

Lewin also wrote the screenplay which is very loosely based on the classic legend of *The Flying Dutchman*. It was filmed mainly on the Spanish Costa Brava in Tossa de Mar but what is crucial to us is that the plot line includes a land speed record attempt, which was filmed, as if in Spain but in reality was shot at Pendine Sands in Wales – an amazing stretch of flat sands a very short way around the coast from Laugharne where Dylan was living at the time.

Albert Lewin has become something of a cult Surrealist film director. In 1997 a monograph by Susan Feldman was published. The book opens with a detailed chronology and this is the entry for 1950;

> 1950; Lewin films Pandora and the Flying Dutchman on location in and around Tossa, a town on the Costa Brava in Spain; in Wales; and in studios in London. Man Ray executes a painting for the film, which is not used, and a colour photograph of Ava Gardner, which is. While in London, Lewin

spends time with Roland Penrose and Lee Miller, from whom he borrows a Man Ray chess set to appear in the film; through the Penroses he met Dylan Thomas.

The first person to use Pendine Sands for a world land speed record attempt was Sir Malcolm Campbell. On September 25, 1924 he set a world land speed record of 146.16 mph (235.22 km/h) in his super-car *Blue Bird*. Campbell then battled it out with a Welsh driver J.G. Parry Thomas who in his car *Babs* decisively broke the 150 mph barrier. Campbell then raised the record to 174.22 mph in February. 1927 with his second *Blue Bird* but on March 3, 1927 Parry-Thomas in attempting to beat Campbell's record, suffered a horrendous fatal crash. Parry-Thomas was the first driver to be killed in a world land speed record attempt.

Dylan Thomas would have known all about this local motoring history, as did the director and producers of *Pandora The Flying Dutchman*. The film had a high profile cast – Ava Gardner and James Mason, supported by a group of worthy British character actors led by Marius Goring and a huge handsome Spanish hunk – Mario Cabre. The cinematographer was Jack Cardiff, who, despite his name, was from Norfolk. His career spanned the development of cinema, from early silent moves through the early experiments in Technicolor film-making in the 21st century and he is best known for his influential colour cinematography for directors such as Powell & Pressburger, Huston and Hitchcock.

But of even more interest is the Director/scriptwriter Albert Lewin. He was born in Brooklyn, New York and raised in New Jersey. He earned a Master's degree at Harvard and began a career teaching English at the University of Missouri. He did military serve in World War 1 and afterwards had a spell as assistant national director of the American Jewish Relief Committee before becoming the drama and film critic on the Jewish Tribune. But in the early 1920's Hollywood called and he travelled west and joined the great San Goldwyn's team as a script-reader and went on to work with King Vidor and Victor Sjostrom and by 1924 he was a fully-fledged screenwriter at MGM. His rise continued, and by 1937 he was producing for Paramount and his credits include *True Confession* (1937) and So Ends Our Night (1941). Lewin then began to direct as well. He made six films, writing all of them and producing several himself – *The Moon and Sixpence* (1942), *The Picture of Dorian Gray* (1945), *The Private Affairs of Bel Ami* (1947), *Pandora and the Flying Dutchman* (1951), *Saadia* (1954), and *The Living Idol* (1957). One can see by this list that Lewin harked back to his early English Literature grounding As a director and writer, he showed literary and cultural aspirations in the selection and treatment of his themes, and later in his life he would publish a novel, *The Unaltered Cat* (1966).

But there was much more to Albert Lewin. Recently the Harvard Film Archive held an Albert Lewin Retrospective – They called it *Beyond Good and Evil* and introduced it thus:

> While it might seem strange to name a retrospective of the films directed by an MGM screenwriter and producer after Nietzsche's classic, Albert Lewin (1894–1968) was anything but a typical Hollywood figure. Lewin's films are noteworthy for their fascination with the aesthetic, esoteric and perverse, as well as for their unusual protagonists – artists and decadents who's dark obsessions place them at odds with the conventional world...The consummate studio insider, Lewin was also a stalwart aesthete and passionate art collector who counted Man Ray and Max Ernst among his friends. When he began directing in the 1940's, Lewin attempted to fuse classical narrative film making with the baroque, the decadent and the surreal.

In fact Man Ray was the stills photographer on *Pandora* and Max Ernst at one point was going to paint the portrait of Pandora which features in the film. Albert later visited the UK; and here

he in the Garden at Farley farm, where he visited with Surrealists Roland Penrose and Lee Miller. In the image Albert is central and Roland is to his right and to the left is white haired Max Ernst. Lee Miller took the photo (Lee Miller also photographed Dylan Thomas for *Vogue* Magazine).

In her recent scholarly study of Lewin's oeuvre *Botticelli Hollywood*, Susan Felleman sums up *Pandora and the Flying Dutchman thus*;

> [A film] about a woman unable to love and a man unable to die – a baroque synthesis of classical myth and Germanic legend.

So all in all it was just the sort of film that would have interested Dylan Thomas. When the second unit arrived in Wales to film the Land Speed Record section of the film news obviously spread around the cluster of West Wales' coastal village including Dylan's Laugharne. So when an old actor friend asked him if he wanted to visit the set Dylan must have leapt at the chance. I had heard vaguely about this story at some point, but a year back I bought a good collection of Dylan Thomas letters, books and photographs and amongst these latter I found an original press style photograph of Dylan with his old actor friend and the big handsome Spanish hunk who played a bullfighter madly in love with Pandora in the film – on the verso it was described as being taken at Pendine sands. I recalled that Dylan's biographer Paul Ferris had sent me a photocopy of the image with some notes on the image – but I could find no reference to the film or Dylan in Paul's or any other biography. Then I remembered the 1953 issue of the literary monthly magazine *Adam* – A Memorial issue for Dylan Thomas. I dug out my copy and checked and among the many tributes and memories gathered together and found this

Garden Party, Farley Farm(sitting Dorothea Tanning, Roland Penrose Albert Lewin [standing) Max Ernst (sitting)

Dylan Thomas, Welsh actor Griffith Williams and Italian movie actor Mario Cabre on Pendine Beach

GRIFFITH WILLIAMS

On a hot July day in 1950 I went with Dylan from the bar of a country pub in a fast car along Pendine Sands, where the motor-racing location scenes for the film, 'Pandora and the Flying Dutchman', were being shot.

I was hoping to introduce him to the Spanish bull-fighter, actor and poet, Mario Cabre, who was starring in the picture with Ava Gardner. Dylan knew no Spanish; Mario no English beyond a few perfunctory sentences. The encounter was unique.

Suddenly Dylan asked: 'Who's producing this film?' Someone said: 'Henry Lewin.' Dylan's chubby face lit with the quiet delight that showed so rarely. 'Lewin, Good God. We met in America. We are old friends. Where is he?'

I shall never forget the meeting between the two, the careless shock-haired Dylan and the debonair little Hollywood director, maker of 'Henry the Eighth' and other film classics. Their mutual surprise at finding each other on a lonely stretch of Welsh beach, a few miles from the Boat House in Laugharne, where Dylan lived and worked and saw the 'Heron priested shores', had something of the archness of O. Henry's humour.

from an older Welsh character actor Griffith Williams, who gives us this insight, but he mis-remembers Albert Lewin as Henry Lewin.

I then turned to the edited transcripts of the Colin Edwards remarkable collection of Dylan Thomas related recorded interviews and there I found a reference – but more than just a reference it was the key to what happened next.

In *Dylan Remembered Volume Two 1935-1953* is the transcript of his interview with Jane Dark, a Laugharne friend of Dylan and Caitlin. She remembers them;

> I know they did do the other kind of life, too, because they dressed for dinner and I know they went to Tenby...*Pandora and the Flying Dutchman*, scenes were shot in Pendine, Dylan taking part in the crowd scenes, by the way. And when it was released he dined at Tenby with Mr Lewin, I know that.

Dylan taking part in the crowd scenes, by the way... Now this needed checking.

I bought a copy of the DVD, set it up to watch, and I a slowly freeze framed my way until I came to the land speed motor racing scenes which were filmed in Pendine. AND THERE HE WAS – on the edge of a crows walking across the sands – A REAL EUREAKA MOMENT if ever there was!

I quickly put a package together which I shared with the press and then with the help of Cerys Matthews we both went to a private screening Cinema in London and were filmed going through the whole recognition process which was then screened nationwide on the BBC nightly magazine programme, *The One Show*.

I know it's only a nano-second or two of moving pictures of Dylan Thomas, but, we had nothing; and now we have something. The media response to this discovery was strong and one still lives in hope of some more footage of Dylan Thomas being unearthed before too long.

The find comes as a series of events around Wales mark the centenary of Thomas's birth

The first moving footage of Welsh poet Dylan Thomas has been found, ending years of searching by fans.

1. *Dylan Thomas: The Complete Filmscripts*, edited by John Ackerman (1995). This is the most comprehensive book about Dylan Thomas and film with complete scripts or extracts from films that Thomas worked on. Eight of Dylan's propaganda films can be viewed on a DVD; *Dylan Thomas; The War Films Anthology* with notes by John Goodby, issued by *The Imperial War Museum*.

2. The Letter is now in the National Library of Wales, Aberystwyth as part of the *Jeff Towns/Dylans Bookstore Collection*.

3. Cameron worked on an advertising campaign for an oaty, milky, sleep-aid, beverage; *Horlicks*. The advertising campaign centred on Cameron's slogan which suggested the drink could ward off *Night Starvation*, a phrase that set Dylan off on creating his own panacea, dubbed *Night Custard*, a scatological concoction involving bizarre ingredients such as under bed fluff, hair cream and vaginal jelly'!

4. More on this in the last section of Chapter 4.

5. Dave Slivka was soon to be responsible for the creation of Dylan Thomas's death mask. This from his webpage

   > I decided to enlist the help of the sculptor, Ibram Lassaw, a friend,
   > who felt as I did about the importance of making the mask.
   > It was our successful collaboration that made this event possible

6. John Malcolm Brinnin; *Dylan Thomas in America*. Dent 1956

7. Perhaps Dylan was harking back to his screenplay *Me and My Bike*, which he wrote for Sidney Box at Gainsborough Films in 1948. It published in 1965 and eventually made into a short-animated fantasy puppet film in 1979 by BBC Cymru featuring Emlyn Williams.

8. J. Maclaren-Ross. *Memoirs of The Forties*. Alan Ross Limited. 1965. Published the year after his death.

9. The first chapters were previously published in Ross' *London Magazine* in 1964, to great acclaim.

10. For more on Dylan and Hermaphrodites see Chapter 5.

11. A modern rather inferior movie was made in 1985 as a British gothic horror film. It was directed by Freddie Francis (and produced by Mel Brooks). It starred Timothy Dalton as Rock and Jonathan Price and Stephen Rea as characters based upon Burke and Hare. Sir Ronald Harwood adapted Dylan's original screen play.

12. Rolph provides a note in his bibliography of Dylan Thomas. '... the Character of 'Rock' in the final version appears as 'Slater' In point of fact this character was originally 'Knox 'but was substituted at James Bridie's suggestion. The early proof copies are now extremely rare.

13. After Dylan Thomas died Richard Burton bought the film rights the film; he may have fancied the role of the island's Welsh minister who Dylan imbued with the obligatory Hywl. Burton and engaged Christopher Isherwood to work further on Dylan's script but his plans failed to come to fruition.

14. In 2015 I received a letter from a woman whose mother had been Donald Taylor's secretary at Strand Films in the forties.. Her mother had left her 4 remarkable unpublished photographs of an occasion when a very dapper Dylan Thomas visited the office to pick up a much-needed payment. When she told him the payment was not to be forthcoming he flew into a fit of rage which she had urged Fred Brown, a photographer who was in the office, to record. I acquired the original images from her and here they are, published for the first time.
    Images copyright: Jeff Towns/Dylans Bookstore Swansea.

15. A transcript of this symposium was first published in *Film Culture* magazine. Summer 1963, (No 29). Illustrated above is the *Gotham Book Mart*, 1972 booklet, which publishes an edited transcript. An edited audio recording of the event is available on YouTube.

16. *Kafka Was The Rage: A Greenwich Village Memoir*. Carol Southern Books. New York 1993. Broyard was on the edge of the Beat writers and a prolific reader and reviewer who also wrote short stories.

17. The Texas Quarterly. University of Texas. Austen. Winter 1961.

Philippa Jacobs' fine portraits of the two Welsh poetic Thomases

9.

Dylan Thomas: R. S. Thomas & Centenaries.

2014 was the Centenary Year of Dylan Thomas' birth on October 26th 1914. In the years running up to his centenary it began to cause ripples of interest, debate, enthusiasm, excitement, and in some quarters – distain. (As I write this the imminent Coronation of King Charles 111 seems to be having a similar effect around the country.) As the year approached The Welsh Assembly government established a quango to oversee the year-long celebrations and they produced the bold flyer pictured below.

In 2012 I was approached by the editor of the journal of The IWA, The Institute of Welsh Affairs, to write a piece about this phenomena – if that is what it could be termed.

This is the piece I wrote then:

As we approach 2014, which is the centenary of the birth, in Swansea, of Dylan Thomas, a hum, perhaps a buzz even, has begun to reverberate around some narrow corridors of power in South Wales and his name can be heard in theatres, in galleries, in arts centres, in and TV studios throughout the Principality. It can be heard whispered on the lips of current poets, artists, writers, musicians, dancers, publishers and booksellers. The Welsh Assembly Government has decided to back this event and promote a year-long Arts Festival already branded: DYLAN THOMAS 100. They are aiming to utilise Dylan's fame to promote Wales across the world, and major announcements about the shape, and style of the project are to be made at this year's forthcoming Hay Festival. But there will be some who question this whole project – doubting Thomases no less. However;

I was in London last week for the annual International Antiquarian Book Fairs. The night I arrived I got a call from the BBC in Cardiff asking me to contribute to a radio programme about the recent publication of the details of Dylan Thomas' last will and testament. My schedule prevented me from doing the broadcast but on the Underground early the next morning, I found myself, along with just about everybody else on the tube, reading the ubiquitous freebie *Metro* newspaper, and there on page 23. was a full-page article, the work of Ancestry.co.uk. The lead photo was of Florence Nightingale and the headline read '*The lady with the lump sum*' – (she left £36,127 in 1910). But below her, alongside George Bernard Shaw and Beatrix Potter was a picture of Dylan Thomas. I guess everybody on the train saw the photo and read the article ('*And alcoholic Welsh poet Dylan Thomas left just £100...*'). *Ancestry.co.uk* had just published over 6 million probate records on their website; but that of Dylan Thomas was one of just nine featured in the press. Reuters International began their report thus:

> *Welsh poet Dylan Thomas left a pittance when he died, Winston Churchill bequeathed a small fortune to his wife Clementine and "The Tale of Peter Rabbit" author Beatrix Potter gave almost all her land to the nation. Britain's wartime prime minister left nearly £4.8 million in today's money to his beloved "Cat", while the dipsomaniacal Dylan had just £23 to leave the long-suffering Caitlin when he died in New York.*

The previous Sunday, Cerys Matthews, on her BBC Radio Six programme, (not to be missed, highly recommended), had played a dazzling and haunting new track by a band called *The Dubwood Allstars* (put together by the clever outfit, *Caught by the River*). The track, named *Under Dubwood*, consisted of Richard Burton's performance of the opening soliloquy from *Under Milk Wood*, overlaid on a pulsing Dub/Reggae beat. It is described on the band's website thus:

On the A side, Under Dubwood takes a seemingly incongruous mix – the words of Dylan Thomas, the voice of Richard Burton and the studio sounds of King Tubby – and makes a psychedelic skank that places Llareggub somewhere just outside downtown Kingston, JA.

Cerys played the track un-introduced and three and a half minutes later when it ended she stayed silent for more seconds than usual, and then said something along the lines of, "I'm speechless – I just want to play it again".[1]

I immediately went to *Caught By The River's* website and bought the record.

And now, as I write this, far away down below me, on the other side of the world, the audience are probably taking their seats in the Sydney Opera House for the start of tonight's performance of the recently opened run of Dylan Thomas' classic *Under Milk Wood*. The glowing review in Murdoch's daily paper *THE AUSTRALIAN* begins;

'It is great to see this lovely, lyrical, bittersweet classic delivered so well by such a good cast.'

A couple of weeks back I took an American houseguest, who is a long-time Dylan Thomas aficionado, into Swansea's seafront's Patti Pavilion, the somewhat unlikely venue for a 'promenade' performance of the *Frantic Assembly/ National Theatre Wales* production *Little Dogs*, which we were led to believe, was based on, or inspired by, Dylan Thomas' dark short story, Just like *Little Dogs*, which, he wrote in 1938, for his forthcoming collection *Portrait of the Artist as a Young Dog*. The evening began with a relaxing curry (discounted for theatre-goers) in the Patti Raj, and then we followed the crowd into the dark, high-ceilinged space where we were galvanised, ravished and exhilarated by the whole experience. *The Guardian*'s theatre critic, Clare Brennan, had this to say in her very positive review (and great to see a piece of modern Welsh Theatre getting reviewed in a National newspaper:

What is Thomas-like about the production is its energy, visceral as blood beating through veins, sharp as starlight on a dark night. In the centre of the space a shabby sitting room is torn apart, separating the pair within: white-haired matriarch (riveting Sian Phillips) and edgy adolescent (palely interesting Darren Evans). Now he's surrounded by hoodies on a black rubbish-sack lined road. An ambush? No, a testosterone-fuelled dance that mutates into a sassy mating game which plays out its various moves with furious, fleshly intensity for the rest of the evening.

And the above occurrences are some of the many reasons for the growing noise I mentioned at the start of this piece. Put bluntly, it is quite simple – Dylan Thomas will just not lie down and go gentle into his good night. His life was pitifully short – he was just 39 when he died in a New York Hospital. His canon is by no means large – 100 plus poems, some 25 short stories, some 30 radio scripts, and a couple of dozen film scripts. Oh, and his final, just about completed master-work, *Under Milk Wood*. But these bare facts belie the continuing influence his life and work has on readers and artists around the world. So as we approach 60 years from his untimely death, and the centenary of his birth there are many reasons to think that the notion of a year-long pan-Wales (pan-UK, pan-World, if things go to plan), multi-discipline, multi-art, multi-cultural celebration of Dylan Thomas's life, work and legacy could well produce some great events across the artistic landscape of Wales and beyond. But we do have more than one poet to celebrate here in Wales.

Next year – 2013, is the centenary of the birth of another great Welsh poet surnamed Thomas; R.S. Thomas. However it looks like that his will pass with little of the same level of attention and celebration that is being accorded to Dylan. Why is this you may ask?

Some people might be unhappy, even enraged at this turn of events. Indeed a few years ago *The Western Mail* tried to stir up a heated debate on the matter, forcing people to side with one or the other for the title of Heavy-weight Champion Poet of Wales. My memory is that the majority of established Welsh academics and critics went for the Reverend. I was asked to step into the fray and my response then is still the same now – that poetry/literature is not a competition, we do not need league tables, and we should just celebrate and rejoice in the fact that Wales has produced two of the great poets of the twentieth century. However I do think there is something to be learned from comparing and contrasting these two writers, who would appear at first look to be as different as Swansea sand and *Y Fenni cheese*.

Dylan was the great Welsh poet of the first half of the century (His first book *18 Poems* appeared in 1934. His *Collected Poems* came out in 1952). R.S. is the poet of the second half (*The Stones of the Field* was published in 1946. His *Autobiographies* came out in 1997). Dylan was the poet of the town and the city, R.S. of the field and the farm. Dylan was at home in the industrial southlands of Wales, R.S. loved the hills and vales of the North. Dylan like to relax in the hub-bub of a traditional pub, R.S. sought the solitude of a twitcher's hide. But it is in their contrasting lives that the real differences lie. Dylan was a fun loving writer who 'lived fast and died young' and he died publicly, slowly and sensationally in New York City in the glare of the world's press. R.S. Thomas was a country vicar, poet and birdwatcher who died quietly and peacefully on September 25th 2000, aged 87, at his home at Pentrefelin, near Criccieth. As a result of these bare facts a great myth and celebrity glamour has been built up around Dylan Thomas. He has come to be seen as the archetypal romantic bohemian poet – a poet who inspired a young American Jewish folksinger to mutate from Robert Zimmerman into Bob Dylan, a poet who peeps over Tom Mix's Stetson on Sir Peter Blake's iconic 1966 LP cover for the Beatles' seminal '*Sgt Pepper*' Album. And a poet who has been the subject of three major biographies and countless other book length biographical investigations, critical works and theses by the shelf-full and the subject of numerous Film and TV documentaries culminating in the 2008 movie *The Edge of Love*, a John Mayberry film starring Keira Knightley, Sienna Miller Cillian Murphy, with the Welsh actor Matthew Rhys as Dylan. The screenplay is written by Sharman Macdonald who is Keira Knightley's mother, and it is based upon Dylan Thomas's wartime experiences in London and West Wales.

Meanwhile R.S. has inspired one interesting book by Byron Rogers *The Man Who Went Into the West*, but good though it is, it also seems to confirm that R.S.'s life is just not the stuff of exciting and riveting biography. And it is precisely these differences that mean that maybe it is OK that R.S. Thomas's centenary is celebrated with little more than a one-night reading in Bangor – this is not a negative reflection on his worth as a poet and his importance in Welsh culture and identity, but it is an acceptance of the fact that R.S. was a great poet who lived a quiet life in Wales, whereas Dylan Thomas, for reasons beyond the words he wrote, and beyond his control, has become an internationally famous "persona" that continues to resonate with the zeitgeist, and it is this that makes him quite capable of inspiring and motivating a year-long cultural circus. This state of affairs is neither of their own faults, they are both dead and blameless. What it does reinforce is just how our current culture and society, (not just in Wales), loves a renegade; loves an outsider; cherishes a '*no-good boyo*', and cannot seem to get enough of the legend and the myths that surround the Dylan phenomenon, to inspire new and exciting works of art in all areas and to subtly drive people back to the poems and words of Dylan Thomas, and to the country that inspired them.

He is a great Welsh writer, and a great writer, full stop. In 1935, the 21-year-old Dylan Thomas wrote a very Swansea based poem *Should lanterns shine*. It ends:

The ball I threw while playing in the park
Has not yet reached the ground.

77 years later that *ball* is still inviting us all to jump up, catch it... and run with it.

Jeff Towns 2012

Postscript

I remember I enjoyed writing the piece over a decade back but I also remember being disappointed that for some reasons I was never made aware of, it was not published. By chance, a little later, I did happen upon an issue of the magazine which had an article prompted by the centenary year written by a good friend of mine, the historian, cultural commentator and regular Welsh team-member on BBC radio' *Round Britain Quiz*, Peter Stead. Re-reading it has rekindled some further thoughts but, just as I was writing this, two stories broke concerning Dylan Thomas. Firstly Johnny Depp came to Swansea with his 'Older Rocker' band to play the new Arena. But all Johnny wanted to do was visit Dylan Thomas' Birthplace at 5 Cwmdonkin Drive in Swansea's Uplands. And visit he did and he was humble, emotional, almost to tears, concerned, generous and altogether the most approachable Caribbean pirate ever to visit the house. What's more, he left clutching a copy of my recent book about Bob Dylan and Dylan Thomas[2]. which the curator Geoff Haden gave him as a memento.

Geoff Haden of the Dylan Thomas Birthplace gives Johnny Depp a copy of *Two Dylans*

The posted photos and videos from the visit attracted over two million internet views.

And then a few weeks later it was announced in the media (with no small flourish) that the substantial private book collection of the late Charlie Watts, the legendary drummer for of the *Rolling Stones*, was shortly to be sold by *Christies* in their London saleroom. It transpired that Charlie, who died in 2021, wasn't just the drummer in one of the greatest Rock n' Roll bands in the world but he was also a refined and passionate book collector who diligently pursued his two main interests; great modern English Literature and books and ephemera pertaining to historic jazz and blues. Christie's press release highlighted just a few of the extraordinary items highlights to be on offer. They led with a killer copy of F. Scott Fitzgerald's masterpiece, *The Great Gatsby*. Charlie's copy was a 1925, first edition,, with a very significant author's presentation inscription,(estimate; a mind-boggling 200k – 300k). But the item that caught my eye was a first edition in d.j. of Dylan Thomas' rare first book, *18 Poems*, (only 250 copies printed back in 1934.), also signed but with more than one inscription. This was what caught the attention of Christie's, and then the press, just as it must also have done for Charlie. Dylan had inscribed and gifted the copy to his first serious girlfriend – Pamela Hansford Johnson (novelist and future wife of C.P. Snow the novelist). This was probably in early1935, just after the book's publication. The inscription was very warm and in it Dylan deliberately used one of Pamela's pet arcane words; 'Pawkey'. They almost got married, but by 1936 they were drifting apart and Dylan obviously decided to take the book back. He them met and had an intense short, passionate affair with an older American writer and art expert, Emily Holmes Coleman. So he gallantly scribbles out the inscription he had written to Pamela and inscribes it warmly again to 'Emily'. Then he meets Caitlin Macnamara and really does fall for her and they later marry. But once again he first retrieves the precious book and writes *MY OWN COPY*.

A great story which, like Depp a few weeks before, garnered huge media interest. However I was particularly interested because I once owned that very copy! I kept it for a long while trying to puzzle it out and it was a while before I came across Emily Coleman who was the key to the book's history. I eventually took it to a big L.A. Book Fair, maybe a decade or so back, where I had sold it to another London dealer; who evidently sold it to the Stones' drummer. I got a tidy price as, I'm sure, did my clever client. However I fear the price that the book may realise at the sale... such is the lure of provenance and celebrity.

And then I got the full Christie's Sale catalogue – and a very smart catalogue it was too, with great photographs and tributes to Charlie throughout its glossy pages.

Among those pages I discovered Charlie had not one, but two unusual inscribed Dylan Thomas books. Spread across a double page was the *18 Poems* and opposite a copy of *The Map of Love*, Dylan's 1939 book of stories and poems This copy was inscribed boldly to Virginia and Stephen Tennant who ran one of Dylan's favourite louche Soho drinking establishments, *The Gargoyle Club*. And he had scribbled a suitable masturbatory poem onto the blank endpaper. Both once been in my stock.[3]

All this seems to suggest that the interest in Dylan Thomas is still very strong. Whereas since his death in 2000, R.S. has rather disappeared from any news and as a bookseller, I can vouch that his early books have come down in price rather than appreciated. This is no comment on quality of his poetry, but a reflection of a fickle public. Here are my more recent thoughts ...

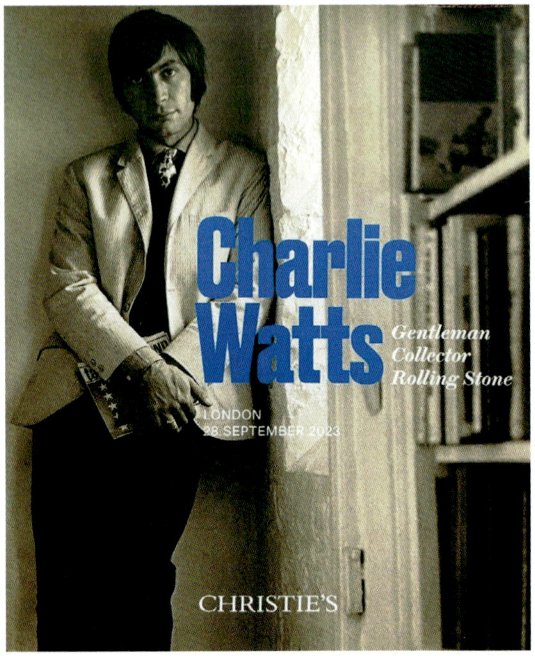

Charlie Watts Gentleman Collector Rolling Stone

R.S.Thomas in his neat shirt-tie in North Wales.

Dylan Thomas drunk in his bow-tie in N.Y.C. 1953.

A stiff, celluloid, dog-collar. Versus a tatty silk, polka-dot, bow-tie.

I recently came across an interesting piece written by Sam Adams, a great Welsh literary critic and sleuth (and a friend and old customer), in a book[4].of his collected articles that he had submitted over the years to the *PN Review*. It was a short essay from 2015; its title was *Dylan Thomas and Jan Morris*, which intrigued me as they were both writers I admire. Reading it, I discovered he was not comparing or contrasting the two, but writing about them separately.

He began with Dylan Thomas and it seemed to me to open with a very simple but wise summation of the relationship in Wales with our two Thomases. This is his opening paragraph;

> Dylan Thomas was born on 27 October 1914, and centenary celebrations in his name are winding down. It is not long since we celebrated the R.S. Thomas centenary. Predictably that was a low-key affair compared with the events of Dylan's year, for nothing vaguely controversial attaches to R.S. The life of Dylan Thomas on the other hand was full of the scrapes beloved of the media. As well as a truly wonderful poet, he turned out to be a posthumous celebrity.

It really does come as quite a surprise when one to realises that Dylan Thomas and R.S. Thomas were close contemporaries – R.S. was born in March 1913 and Dylan in the October of the next

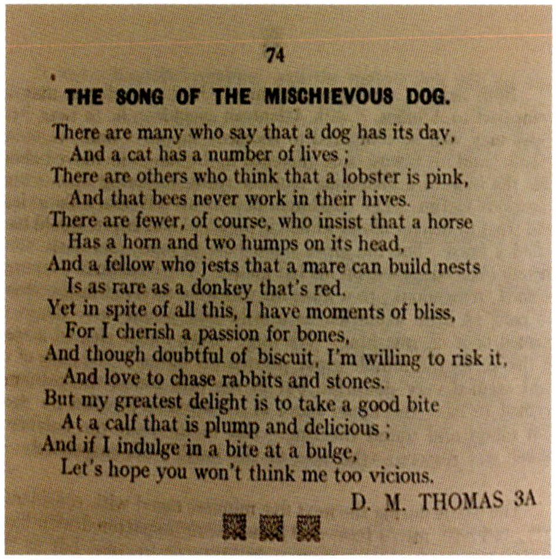

74

THE SONG OF THE MISCHIEVOUS DOG.

There are many who say that a dog has its day,
And a cat has a number of lives ;
There are others who think that a lobster is pink,
And that bees never work in their hives.
There are fewer, of course, who insist that a horse
Has a horn and two humps on its head,
And a fellow who jests that a mare can build nests
Is as rare as a donkey that's red.
Yet in spite of all this, I have moments of bliss,
For I cherish a passion for bones,
And though doubtful of biscuit, I'm willing to risk it,
And love to chase rabbits and stones.
But my greatest delight is to take a good bite
At a calf that is plump and delicious ;
And if I indulge in a bite at a bulge,
Let's hope you won't think me too vicious.

D. M. THOMAS 3A

Dylan's first poem in his School Magazine 1925

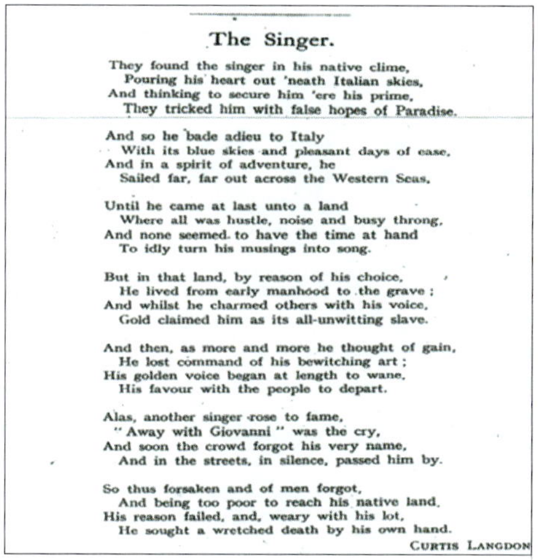

The Singer.

They found the singer in his native clime,
Pouring his heart out 'neath Italian skies,
And thinking to secure him 'ere his prime,
They tricked him with false hopes of Paradise.

And so he bade adieu to Italy
With its blue skies and pleasant days of ease,
And in a spirit of adventure, he
Sailed far, far out across the Western Seas,

Until he came at last unto a land
Where all was hustle, noise and busy throng,
And none seemed to have the time at hand
To idly turn his musings into song.

But in that land, by reason of his choice,
He lived from early manhood to the grave ;
And whilst he charmed others with his voice,
Gold claimed him as its all-unwitting slave.

And then, as more and more he thought of gain,
He lost command of his bewitching art ;
His golden voice began at length to wane,
His favour with the people to depart.

Alas, another singer rose to fame,
"Away with Giovanni" was the cry,
And soon the crowd forgot his very name,
And in the streets, in silence, passed him by.

So thus forsaken and of men forgot,
And being too poor to reach his native land,
His reason failed, and, weary with his lot,
He sought a wretched death by his own hand.

CURTIS LANGDON

R.S.Thomas poem in University Magazine 1933

year. They both took to poetry early; Dylan Thomas contributed poems to his school magazine in his early teens and went on to edit the magazine; R.S. Thomas, when he was studying Latin at Bangor University, also wrote and published poems in *Omnibus*, the University's magazine. Curiously R.S. chose to use a very American sounding, *nom de plume*; 'Curtis Langdon'[5]. Dylan has more youthful humour in his early poetry and is, perhaps thankfully; too young to have written this kind of stuff from another of late-teen *Curtis Langdon*'s effusions;

> But yester eve I found a maid at rest,
> Beside a half reaped field of corn reclined,
> Pale, listless violets drooping on her breast,
> And in her hair the memory of the wind.

Pretty appalling stuff, as was much of the other stuff Curtis Langdon, aka R.S. Thomas, contributed, including some prose; herewith a typical extract from a prose piece – *Those Who Gave* published in *Omnibus* in 1933:

> Up above a lark was singing its insistent hymn of praise to God. Ah! Yes, it was hard to leave. There was beauty everywhere. The large leaves of the trees formed a green canopy above him, the gaudy hawthorn was in full bloom, and large white clouds sailed up majestically before the gentle westerly breeze.

Reading Tony Brown's essay on R.S. and his wife Elsi, he credits her artistic and literary worldliness and the effects of the war, with turning Curtis into R.S. the serious poet. Dylan Thomas however seems to have realised this for himself. He seemed to understand that a certain type of poem suited the school magazine; humorous, light, but clever in tone and structure, while at the same time he had begun keeping his legendary poetry notebooks specifically for writing his serious 'poems'. He continued to patronise the school magazine to please his fellow pupils, and also to placate his father, D.J. Thomas, who was head of English in the school and had founded the school magazine in 1903. Dylan Thomas commenced his first serious notebook in 1930 and continued using them until the late 30's.

Both poets did send their poems off to the plethora of small literary magazines and periodicals for publication – with varying degrees of success. Dylan Thomas had a poem in *The Boy's Own Paper* in February 1927, but it was in May 1933 that his first 'serious' poem, an early version of *Death Shall Have No Dominio*n was published in A.R. Orage's, *The New English Weekly*. For Dylan, what began as a way to impress his father, as he got older it was pretty much his only source of income and he needed the money. Whether it was a conscious decision or happenstance, he was going to endeavour to make a living with his pen. So during this early hyper-productive decade or two, poems by Dylan Thomas were somewhat ubiquitous across in the current literary periodicals. He continued to have poems in, and to review for *The New English Weekly*. His poems graced pages of the B.B.C's *Listener*, Murray's *Adelphi*, Grigson's *New Verse*, Connolly's *Horizon*, T.S. Eliot's *Criterion*, Robert Herring's *Life and Letters Today*, Tanbimuttu's *POETRY* (*London*), *John O'London's Weekly* and many more. Although some magazines had little or no money to pay and others offered only a pittance. Dylan was grateful for, and needed every penny he could get; many of the letters in his *Collected Letter*s are gentle dunning letters in which he practically begs for payment. Cyril Connolly described his war-time transactions with Dylan Thomas in a BBC broadcast;[6]

> Dylan was now harassed by money worries...He really preferred to enclose all literary conversation in a kind of capsule of ridicule and parody. I used to buy his poems spot cash, from his wallet, as if they were packets of cocaine...

I doubt it was thus with R.S., who did not publish in a magazine until 1939, when he, almost reluctantly, sent poems off, and had some success, with *The New English Weekly* (which had published Dylan Thomas first magazine contribution back in 1933), and he also published in *The Dublin Magazine*. R.S. would continue to send poems to magazines and often this would be their only publication, he seemed unconcerned with gathering all his poems together. He was published in *The Times Literary Supplement*, *The Listener*, *Agenda*, *Encounter*, *Poetry Wales*, and *The Anglo-Welsh Review*, but also in curious domestic and foreign periodicals such as *Forethought* which came out of Eton College, *Helix* and *Overland* from Australia and *Ishmael*, based in Paris.

A little earlier in Wales, a curious but important Welsh literary figure, Keidrych Rhys[7]. launched a new literary magazine; from a farmhouse in rural west Wales. He names it WALES, with its striking minimalist red title. The first issue came out in the Summer of 1937 and the first series ran for eleven issues before the war forced its closure in 1940 (there was one further Wartime broadsheet in 1941). The first issue had a cover with an extract previewing a longer piece of prose by Dylan Thomas, who was to be a regular contributor and sometime assistant editor. He also encouraged other poets to send in contributions including his Swansea pals – Vernon Watkins, Charles Fisher and John Pritchard. However R.S. received no such encouragement and he did not appear in any of the first series of the magazine. In 1943 Rhys re-started the magazine as a six monthly publication, in a different format but still as **WALES**, (but not in red). Issue 4. 1944, R.S. has his first appearance in the magazine, which is a very supportive letter to the Editor.

In the same year Keidrych edited a seminal anthology for

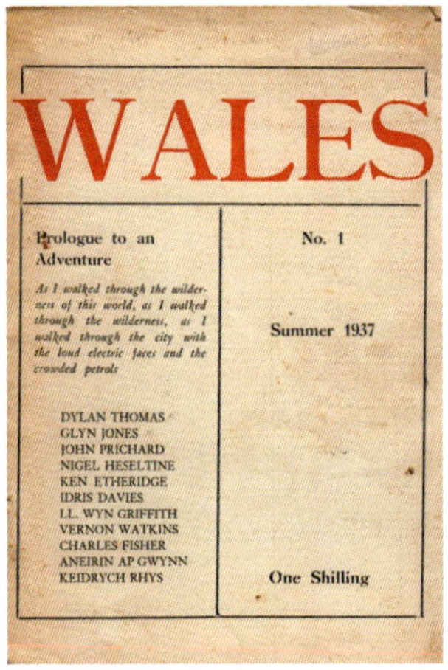

WALES first issue

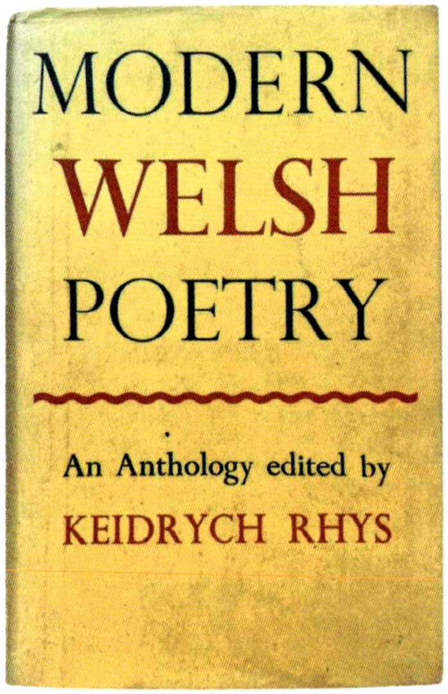

Keidrych important anthology

Faber and Faber – *Modern Welsh Poetry*. It contains work by 36 Welsh poets, all writing in English. It includes seven poems by Dylan Thomas – but it also has two by R.S.

So R.S. is now on Keidrych's radar and he would continue to contribute to WALES, with both prose and poems until it ceased this incarnation in 1949. In two issues he appeared alongside contributions by Dylan. December 1943, in issue No.2 of the new series, R.S. Thomas contributed *Five Poems*, while Dylan contributed an extract from the screenplay he wrote for the documentary film, *Our Country*, made by Strand films for the M. O. I. Dylan's contribution is the first part of this very poetic film, but however arty the film was, it was war-time; it was a propaganda film and it was considered one of his best. Curiously, and with an opposite synchronicity, one of R.S.' poems was titled *Propaganda*;

Nor shot, nor shell, but the fused word,
That rocks the world to its white root,
Has wrought a chaos in the mind,
Or drained the love from the split heart.

Nor shock, nor shower of the sharp blows,
That fall alike from life and death,
But some slow subsidence within,
That sinks a grave for the sapped faith

It seems that the raging war in Europe brought Dylan Thomas and R.S. closer together in their poetry, perhaps with them both singing off the same pacifist hymn sheet. R.S.' line;

'That rocks the world to its white root,'

echoes lines from Dylan's early poems *The force that through the green fuse drives the flower*.

R.S. did include *Propaganda* in his first book, *The Stones of the Field*, but it failed to make it into his curious Macmillan 1993, *Collected Poems 1945-1990*. R.S. was also a strong contributor to *WALES* Autumn 1946 issue, (Vol. V1, No. 3,). It includes two poems, *The Old Language and Man and Tree*, and then it prints R.S.'s responses to the WALES Questionnaire, for example;

1. *Do you consider yourself an Anglo-Welsh writer?*

No! A Welsh writer. An Indian journal recently described me as a young Welsh writer, and that pleased me as being essentially correct. The question of a writer's language is a mere matter of historical accident, and will be seen to have little ultimate significance.

One can sense his ire in his first response. And finally he contributes a prose essay, *Some Contemporary Scottish Writing*. Sandwiched somewhere between these pieces is Dylan Thomas' early precursor to *Under Milk Wood*, his New Quay based, *Quite Early one Morning*.

Dylan Thomas's first book, *18 Poems*, came out in 1934. He had just turned 20 and it was the result of winning a prize from a national Sunday paper for sending in the best poem for 1933. It was selected by the editor of the paper and Victor Neuberg who edited the paper's *Poet's Corner*. The book was published in a small edition of just 250 copies. The imprint was *The Sunday Referee and The Parton Bookshop Parton Street, London, W.C.I.* The book is decidedly Modernist in its design – from its stark title, to the title page printed in bold sans serif typeface, and *Printed on Glastonbury Antique Laid Paper*. The book is devoid of clutter; no notes, no author portrait, just the numeric title, no blurb whatsoever on the thin grey-paper dust-jacket and nothing on the inside flap bar the publishing details and the price of 3/6. Apparently this minimalism was at Dylan's behest.

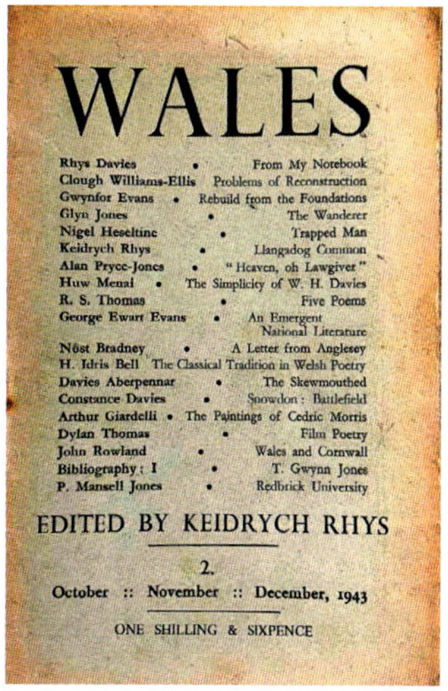

WALES

Rhys Davies • From My Notebook
Clough Williams-Ellis Problems of Reconstruction
Gwynfor Evans • Rebuild from the Foundations
Glyn Jones • The Wanderer
Nigel Heseltine • Trapped Man
Keidrych Rhys • Llangadog Common
Alan Pryce-Jones • "Heaven, oh Lawgiver"
Huw Menai • The Simplicity of W. H. Davies
R. S. Thomas • Five Poems
George Ewart Evans • An Emergent National Literature
Nöst Bradney • A Letter from Anglesey
H. Idris Bell The Classical Tradition in Welsh Poetry
Davies Aberpennar • The Skewmouthed
Constance Davies • Snowdon: Battlefield
Arthur Giardelli • The Paintings of Cedric Morris
Dylan Thomas • Film Poetry
John Rowland • Wales and Cornwall
Bibliography: I • T. Gwynn Jones
P. Mansell Jones • Redbrick University

EDITED BY KEIDRYCH RHYS

2.

October :: November :: December, 1943

ONE SHILLING & SIXPENCE

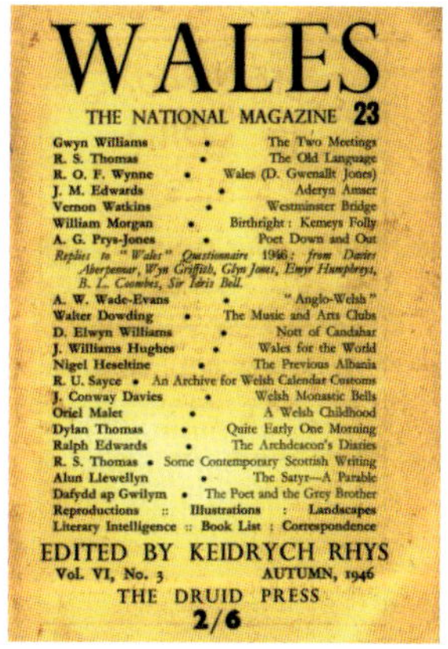

WALES

THE NATIONAL MAGAZINE 23

Gwyn Williams • The Two Meetings
R. S. Thomas • The Old Language
R. O. F. Wynne • Wales (D. Gwenallt Jones)
J. M. Edwards • Aderyn Amser
Vernon Watkins • Westminster Bridge
William Morgan • Birthright: Kemeys Folly
A. G. Prys-Jones • Poet Down and Out
Replies to "Wales" Questionnaire 1946: from Davies Aberpennar, Wyn Griffith, Glyn Jones, Emyr Humphreys, B. L. Coombes, Sir Idris Bell.
A. W. Wade-Evans • "Anglo-Welsh"
Walter Dowding • The Music and Arts Clubs
D. Elwyn Williams • Nott of Candahar
J. Williams Hughes • Wales for the World
Nigel Heseltine • The Previous Albania
R. U. Sayce • An Archive for Welsh Calendar Customs
J. Conway Davies • Welsh Monastic Bells
Oriel Malet • A Welsh Childhood
Dylan Thomas • Quite Early One Morning
Ralph Edwards • The Archdeacon's Diaries
R. S. Thomas • Some Contemporary Scottish Writing
Alun Llewellyn • The Satyr—A Parable
Dafydd ap Gwilym • The Poet and the Grey Brother
Reproductions :: Illustrations : Landscapes
Literary Intelligence :: Book List : Correspondence

EDITED BY KEIDRYCH RHYS

Vol. VI, No. 3 AUTUMN, 1946

THE DRUID PRESS

2/6

Dylan Thomas and R.S.Thomas both grace the pages of these two issues of *WALES* magazine

R.S. was later to the publishing party: He did not publish his first collection until 1946 when Dylan's good friend, Keidrych Rhys, published *The Stones of the Field* from his *Druid Press* Limited. 21a Lammas Street Carmarthen.[8]

These two 'first books' are noticeably different. R.S.' is published by a small Welsh publisher living on a farm in Carmarthenshire. His book, as an object, is smaller than Dylan's, but it contains 37 poems, just one more than double Dylan's 18. However, at 6s net, R.S' is almost twice the price of Dylan's. R.S.'s book has a pictorial dust jacket with a cover illustration by his wife, Mildred [Elsi] Eldridge. The back cover carries a list of other Druid Press publications and has a blurb on the inner flap, probably written by Keidrych, it begins;

R.S. Thomas needs no introduction to those discerning readers who delight in contemporary poetry and possess

Dylan's first book preceded R.S.'s by some dozen years and his next four books, *Twenty-Five Poems*, *The Map of Love*, and *Portrait of the Artist as a Young Dog* and *Deaths and Entrances* were all published by a major London publisher, J.M.Dent, and all precede R.S.'s first book to be published in London by a major publisher.

After graduating from Bangor in the late 30's with a degree in

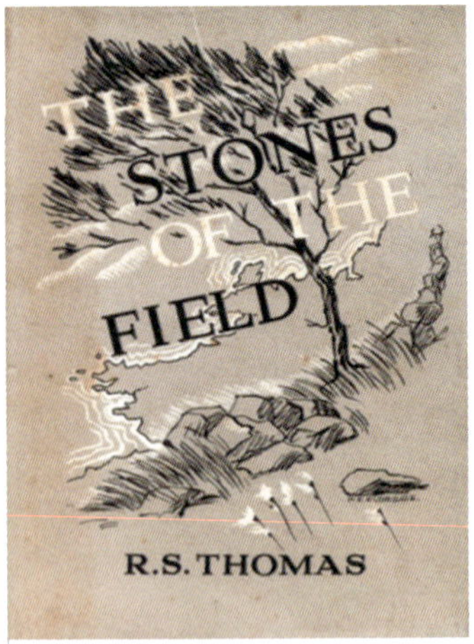

Elsi's design for the d.j. of R.S.' first book

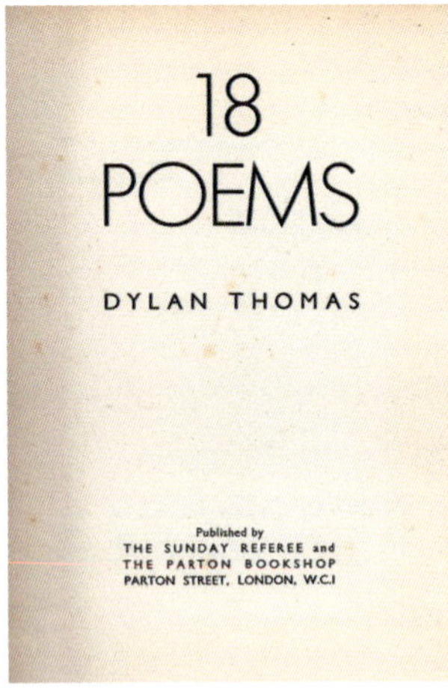

Dylan Thomas' first book – the title page

Classics, R.S. did compile a typescript collection of his poems and gave it a title, *Spindrift*, however it is not known if he ever sent it off to any publishers, but it has never been published. After *The Stones of the Field,* R.S. self-published two small slim pamphlets; *An Acre of Land* in 1952, and The Minister, in 1953, both printed by the *Montgomeryshire Printing Co.* located in Newtown. R.S. paid for the printing himself. In 1955, two years after Dylan Thomas's death, Rupert Hart Davies, the London publisher, brought out, in an elegant hardback, *Song at the Year's Turning*, R.S.' first ever London publication. He was 42. The book's genesis involves another Anglo-Welsh writer, James Hanley,[9] who R.S. became acquainted with when they were both living in North Wales. Hanley was part of a London literary coterie and he was impressed by R.S.'s poetry. He urged a London publishing friend, Rupert Hart Davies, to publish it. Hart Davies was also impressed enough, to do so, but felt that as R.S. was hardly known in London the book needed a lift, and he asked the popular poet, John Betjeman to write an introduction. In it Betjeman commented:

> This retiring poet [R.S. Thomas] had no wish for an introduction to be written to his poems, but his publisher believed that a "name" was needed to help sell the book. The "name" which has the honour to introduce this fine poet to a wider public will be forgotten long before that of R.S. Thomas.

R.S. T.' second publication 1952

Betjeman is right in many respects, R.S. is still remembered, but he does not elicit the popular following that Dylan Thomas attracts. There can be little doubt that the two poets were aware of each other; how could R.S. not have heard one of Dylan's many radio broadcasts. or not seen any of the reviews his publications garnered. This is backed up by a letter he sent to Cyril Connolly with some poems for his consideration. The letter[10] contained this sentence;

> *I wonder if any of the enclosed would suit 'Horizon'. The poem on the WILL seems precariously near Dylan Thomas, but believe me – it was quite unconsciously so...*

A little later Raymond Garlick persuaded R.S. to review Roland Mathias's third book of poems, *The Roses of Tretower,* R.S was a reluctant reviewer but his review did appear in Dock Leaves No.8. It begins inauspiciously – 'Mr. Mathias is one of the younger members of the, by this time, rather tatterdemalion[11]. school of Anglo-Welsh writers' but quickly goes on to censure the 'younger' poet (by two years), for being stylistically 'Protean', and for having fallen under the influence of Dylan Thomas.

R.S.' first London book. 1955

Dylan Thomas' death in 1953, provoked publication of many biographies, photo-books and critical books about him and posthumous collections of his writings were rushed into print. One of them, *The Craft and Art of Dylan Thomas* by W.T. Moynihan, was reviewed by R.S. Thomas in the Winter 1967 issue of *The Critical Quarterly*, a literary journal of some standing, edited by A.E. Dyson. It was fourteen years after Dylan's death and

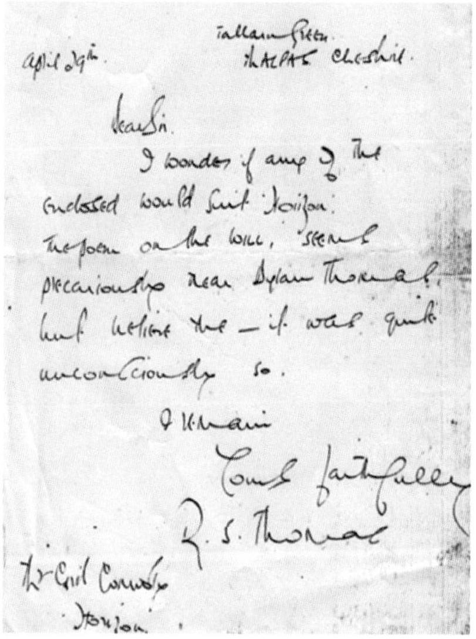
April 29th

Tallarn Green
Malpas Cheshire

Dear Sir.
I wonder if any of the enclosed would suit Horizon.
The poem on the wall, 'seems precariously near Dylan Thomas, but believe me – it was quite unconsciously so.
I remain
Yours faithfully
R.S. Thomas

To Cyril Connolly
Horizon

R.S.' to Connolly at *Horizon* 'precariously near Dylan'

R.S. was to make one of his very few references to Dylan Thomas in print. He is once again less than charitable towards his name-sake;

Dylan Thomas is of course a kind industry, and a good deal of enthusiasm is necessary to study and interpret the more chaotic and obscure outpouring of his imagination.

More recently Welsh poet and critic Tony Conran,[12] pointed out that the title poem of R.S.'s book, *Song at the Years Turning*, is based on the closing lines from one of Dylan Thomas' great birthday poems *Poem in October*:

> O may my heart's truth
> Still be sung
> On this high hill in a year's turning

Conran makes this reference in passing but Tony Brown pointed out to me that;

> Some years ago, I published a short note in *Review of English* Studies ....which argued that the poem 'Song at the Year's Turning' was in fact an elegy for Dylan.

Tony kindly sent me his article and he does make a good case for his supposition but it has not, so far, gained any further responses.

R.S. did make a few other oblique references to Dylan Thomas in his prose. In 1952 he wrote a short piece in the Welsh language journal *Y FLLAM*. The title *Llenyddiaeth Eingl-Gymreig* translates as Anglo-Welsh Literature.[13] In it he mentions Dylan Thomas twice. First in relation to Matthew Arnold's oft-reprinted classic 1867 *On the Study of Celtic Literature*, and suggests that some melancholic traits in English Literature derive from Celtic sources, and he mentions Edward Thomas, Gerard Manly Hopkins and Dylan Thomas. He reiterates this over the page by declaring that Dylan Thomas is one of the main influences on English literature and poetry alongside Edward Thomas, Manley Hopkins and James Joyce in prose.

In 1963 R.S. gave the W. D. Thomas Memorial Lecture at Swansea University and it was published as *Words and the Poet* in 1964. In his lecture R.S. mentions Dylan Thomas a few times, once somewhat negatively, as overpowering influence on W. S. Graham but when talking about the Imagists he is a tad more complimentary. He writes;

> The example that comes most readily to mind is Dylan Thomas. Some of his adjectives merely exemplify Pope's line 'What oft is thought, but ne'er so well expressed'. I am thinking of those such as the 'lunar silences' and 'golden weather'. But when we come to phrases such as 'sour humble hands,' 'dung-hills, white as wool,' and especially 'whinnying green stable' we have examples of that peculiar talent that helped to make Dylan Thomas, at his best, fascinating.

Praise, even if somewhat faint; just how complimentary is 'fascinating'? But his final comment is less equivocal,

> Expatriate Scots, Irish and Welsh, coming, as many of them did, from vernacular areas, were the very men to put new vigour into the worn out veins of English. As proof there were Yeats, Synge, and Joyce from Ireland and Dylan Thomas from Wales...

Various critics and reviewers comment on, and compare R.S.and Dylan Thomas. Cecil Price,[14] writing in 1952 in *The Welsh Anvil* on *The Poetry of R.S. Thomas*, which was prompted by the recent publication of *An Acre of Land*. Price begins it:

> Poetry in English and of the present century owes much to the tribe of Thomas. Edward's quiet voice remains alive in our minds when his louder and shriller contemporaries are long dead. Dylan's spells and incantations preserve us from evil in birth death and fire. Now, R.S. Thomas has given the world two volumes of verse that communicate both joy and keen perception.

Benedict Nightingale in a *Guardian* piece from 1964 is prompted by the publication of *The Bread of Truth* to make a telephone call to R.S. and his transcription includes this;

> He speaks warmly of his Welsh name-sake, though plainly Dylan's chaotic rampages of feeling contrast sharply with R.S.'s order and organization; he prefers Dylan's simpler poems, and says that whatever objections one likes to make he was 'every inch a poet'.

Critic and poet, John Ackerman, who has written on both poets, makes mention of the two of them in his *Dylan Thomas His Life and Work*. Oxford 1964. His second chapter is titled *The Intruders* by which he means post First World War, 'Welshmen writing in English' and he quotes Gwyn Jones, writing in the *Welsh Review* in 1939, describing them as;

> 'the most spectacular manifestation of the mental activity of their district'

Ackerman goes on to list some of these 'notable intruders';

> Caradoc Evans, Dylan Thomas, Gwyn Jones, Vernon Watkins, Alun Lewis, R.S.Thomas, Gwyn Thomas and Glyn Jones'

However, R.S. probably bristled at this if he read it because Gwyn Jones district was 'South Wales'! Ackerman later wrote in his *Dylan Thomas Companion*. [Macmillan 1991] about Dylan Thomas' poem *Incarnate Evil* he has this to say;

> ...in the final line of the poem on God's creation of the world ... 'A serpent fiddles in the shaping time' ...R.S.Thomas' more sardonic Old Testament vignettes are occasionally not dissimilar in tone and import.

And he continues, 'certainly R.S. Thomas' comment to me in 1980 that;

> 'There's nothing Welsh about Dylan Thomas except that he knew his Bible' is true in respect of his biblical knowledge and references.[15]

In 2005 another Welsh writer, Byron Rogers wrote an interesting attempt at a biography of R.S. *The Man Who Went Into the West*. At one point he is visiting R.S.'s only child – his son Gwydion and together they are sifting through four plastic supermarket bags stuffed with random R.S. ephemera;

> ...there were no diaries, no photo albums, nothing to remind one this had once been a family... a single photograph of the boy Gwydion... some crumpled manuscripts, some of Elsi's... paintings of small creatures and a copy of Dylan Thomas's poem *Do not go gentle into that good night*, written out in R.S.'s hand, even though he had so often and publicly decried his work.

And it is in this book that Rodgers reports a conversation R.S. has with his friend Peggy Mowat. who recorded the conversations between R.S. and she and her husband John. She recalled R.S. commenting:

> ...but *Fern Hill* he thought a great poem he would like to have written it himself.

R.S would later include the poem in two anthologies he edited. Firstly in his 1961 anthology *The Batsford Book of Country Verse* and then again, in 1963, when he compiled *The Penguin Book of Religious Verse*,[16] and he mentions the poem in his and he mentions the poem in his introduction;

> ...modern sensibility might wish to include more under the title' religious than traditionalists could accept. That is why I have included under the heading 'self' such a poem as Dylan Thomas's *Fern Hill*. Is there much essential difference between this and such a poem as Henry Vaughan's *The Retreat?*

A strong comparison which I'm sure Dylan would have been more than comfortable with.

When we come to examine the other side of this 'relationship: Dylan Thomas's references to, and acknowledgements of, R.S. Thomas, are conspicuous by their almost total absence in Dylan's writings. I have found just one reference to R.S. throughout all Dylan's writings and that is the briefest of references in a late letter to another Welsh friend, the valley's poet Idris Davies. It appears in long letter, written in February of 1953, which for the most part Dylan is writing, in detail, about working, with Aneirin Talfan Davies on a series of radio poetry anthologies. Dylan lists his preliminary choice of poems for the first programme, which was to be entirely Welsh poetry and be broadcast on the imminent St. David's Day;

It's made up of: Vernon's [Watkins] 'The Collier'; your Bell Poem from 'Gwalia Deserta'; Edward Thomas's 'Child on the Cliffs; Alun Lewis's 'Letter from Sacco to his Son'; my own 'Ceremony After A Fire Raid'; W.H. Davies's 'Child Lovers'; and Owen's Strange Meeting'.

He then goes on at length ruminating on the process of selection and one can see just how much thought he gives to this process, and he then admits that he gets some flack and negative feed-back, some of it concerning the Welshness or not of Edward Thomas and Wilfred Owen's but he then writes;

Another perfectly good criticism of the choice of poems by Welshmen is why didn't I put in more stuff by younger poets such as Glyn Jones, John Ormond Thomas and R.S.Thomas.

Notwithstanding that at the time of writing only John Ormond Thomas was 'younger' than Dylan (by nine years); R.S. was a year older and Glyn Jones nine years Dylan's senior. This is Dylan's only written reference to R.S Thomas throughout all his books and in the 1000 plus letters.

Dylan Thomas made his first radio broadcast, *Life and the Modern Poet* in 1937 and he went on to make over a hundred poetry programmes. As early as 1946 he compiled his first Welsh Poetry selection for John Arlott. The programme was a loose chronological journey, beginning with Henry Vaughan and on through Lewis Morris, Edward Thomas, Wilfred Owen, W.H.Davies, Glyn Jones, Idris Davies, Alun Lewis, concluding with his own *Poem in October*. But no R.S Thomas, despite the fact that *Stones of the Field*, R.S.' first book had recently been published by Dylan's good friend Keidrych Rhys. And nor would Dylan read any R.S in any of the future poetry programmes he recorded and they went on to number over a hundred! During the war years Dylan Thomas also worked for a while with a Swansea man of the theatre, Thomas Taig on putting together a theatre event that would consist of readings from Welsh poets and in a 1939 letter to Taig, Dylan sends;

... a selection – out of a great wad of material – of poems that might be suitable for some kind of dramatic presentation.

He mentions two new names, Alan Pryce Jones and George Woodcock, and declares;

I enjoy reading poems aloud so much & have got to understand most of the poems turned out nowadays by Our Young Welsh Poets.

But R.S. would appear not to be one of them.

It is the same when it comes to Dylan's 'live' poetry readings around the UK and then on his later, four monumental tours of America; there is no record of him ever reading an R.S. poem, nor do any appear on the numerous L.P. records which were released[17] towards the very end of his life and thereafter, and they are all still available today having survived all the subsequent audio technologies – reel-to-reel tapes, cassette tapes, C.D.'s and into the digital age with *MP3* downloads and *You Tube*. But Dylan never lived to see this nor to enjoy the substantial revenues.

So how do we explain this apparent stand-off between these two great Welsh poets of the Twentieth Century? Well chronology is a starting point – Dylan died very young and R.S lived much longer; so he does have the time to acknowledge Dylan more fulsomely. But Dylan must have been aware of R.S. and his work; his close friend Keidrych Rhys published R.S' first book and accepted contributions from him for his *Wales* magazine which Dylan must have seen, read even? And that goes for R.S. too; he could not have been able to ignore Dylan and his literary successes. Geography plays a part – Dylan was Swansea, Laugharne, South West Wales and London; R.S. was far West Wales, remote North Wales and Bangor.

Their radically different lifestyle and character would have made it hard for them to ever really become friends; Dylan was a 'Townie', an urban creature and a renowned '*Pubber of Genius*.[18] He was unkempt and scruffy; turned out 'like and unmade bed'.[19] Dylan Thomas was also at the opening of the 1936 Surrealist exhibition in London where he crawled around on the floor offering attendees a cup of string, while enquiring if they would like it 'weak or strong'; R.S. was no Surrealist but a contemplative lover of ancient Spanish art and he would never, ever make a spectacle of himself.

R.S was almost the complete opposite; a countryman, a birdwatcher, conservative in dress and demeanour, a quiet minister of religion. This last is tricky; Dylan Thomas was not irreligious like his atheist father, as R.S. admitted 'he knew his bible'. Dylan wasn't anti religion; one of his best Swansea friends was the Rev Leon Atkin, but I have to admit that he and R.S only had one thing in common; the dog collar!

Dylan had his own pantheistic faith; in the preliminary note to his 1952 *Collected Poems*, he states;

> These poems with all their crudities, doubts, and confusions, are written for the love of Man and in praise of God, and I'd be a damn' fool if they weren't.

Aneurin Talfan Davies wrote a whole book, *Druid of the Broken Body*, subtitled *An Assessment of Dylan Thomas as a Religious Poet* (Dent. 1964) and most critics spend some time discussing 'religion' as it manifests itself Thomas's poetry.

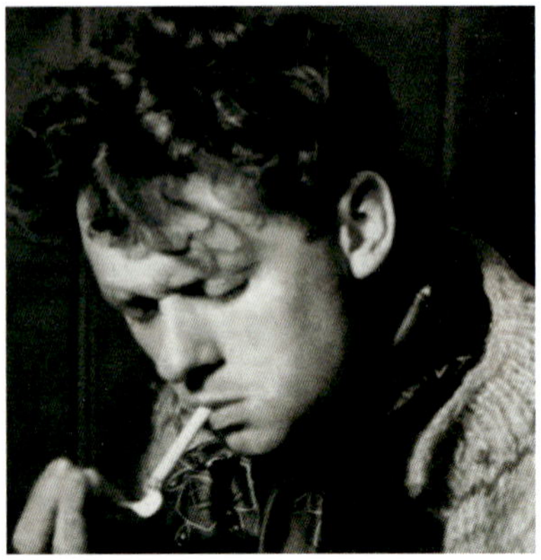

These two images could not be more disparate – so herewith …

Dylan Thomas & R.S.Thomas
Some Random Similarities, Synchronicities and Coincidences.

Initials

Dylan was named Dylan Marlais Thomas. When growing up Dylan often signed himself Dylan M. Thomas, but in the School Magazine his contributions were attributed to D.M.T. R.S, Thomas was named Ronald Stuart Thomas – not wanting to be Ron Thomas he chose to use R.S. Thomas to differentiate himself from the masses of Thomases in Wales. He became widely known as just R.S.

Mothers

Byron Rodgers, in his attempt at a biography of R.S. Thomas, *The Man Who Went Into The West*[19] devotes a few pages to Welsh Mothers and mentions both Thomases. He quotes R.S. talking with Raymond Garlick about his mother, Peggy who he described as being;

> … a strong woman, a very dominant mother, a bourgeois figure who kept herself to herself… and pushed him, her only boy, on.

Rodgers then writes more generally about the received perceptions on the maternal in Wales;

> Welsh Mothers are notorious for 'spoiling' their male children, especially if there is only one of them, and he is a pretty boy. There is even a [Welsh] word for the result, *spoilyn*.

In his autobiographical book *Neb*,[20] R.S. when aged 19, describes the night before he was due to leave home to study at Bangor University. He was awakened by his weeping mother who entered his bedroom and began kissing him over and over.

Dylan Thomas' mother, Florence; but known as Florrie, was a typical rural *Welsh Mam* born and bred in rural Carmarthenshire and was both a tad too fastidious and overbearing. A *Welsh Mam* is pretty much like the overbearing stereotypical, *Jewish Mother*; but with Cawl instead of Chicken Soup. Florrie doted on, and mollycoddled her second born-child and only son. Allegedly she took the tops off his boiled eggs throughout his life. Poor Florence lost her husband, daughter and son in the space of one a year. It would appear that the loss of her son was the most significant to her and she began to sign her letters as 'Mam Dylan'.

The Naming of Son's

Dylan Thomas's name was from The Mabinogion. Dylan called his first son another name from Welsh history; Llewellyn, a boy's name of Welsh origin, It translates as 'like a lion'. R.S. named his boy Gwydion – also a name from the Fourth Branch of the Mabinogion. Gwydion was the son of Don and the nephew and heir of Math, King of Gwynedd.

The Education of Son's

With the help of A.J.P. Taylor's wife, Margaret, who was a generous patron to Dylan with whom she was besotted, Dylan's eldest child Llewelyn was sent away to Magdalen College School in Oxford, where he was none too happy.

R.S. Thomas sent his only son away to school, who also was none too happy and wrote about it thus;

> When I was eight years old my parents sent me to boarding school in England... Mine was a magical childhood. And they sent me away...Imagine it, being told to piss off for twelve weeks at a time.

Later he would shout at his father

> Why did you send me to that fucking school...

He was none too happy at his school either.

> worth watching. The Form Relays were quite a success. The event of the afternoon was the winning of the Mile (under 15 years) by D. M. Thomas. Because of his age and size he had a long start ; he ran so well however that he was further ahead at the finish than he was at the start. Other boys who distinguished themselves

The Grammar School Magazine account

Grammar School Mile Winner.

D. M. Thomas (Mansel), who won the mile race for boys under 15 years of age, at the Swansea Grammar School sports. He is only 12 years of age.

The local paper reports on young Dylan's athletic prowess

Sport

It comes as quite a surprise to some reader when they learn that Dylan Thomas was a plucky and successful long-distance runner in his youth. For two years running he won the Mile race at the school Sports day. The first year, 1926 when he was 12, his victory made the School magazine.

It was also written up the local paper with a picture!

Dylan would carry a copy of this cutting in his wallet throughout his life as revealed by John Malcolm Brinnin in his *Book Dylan Thomas in America*. He and Dylan were in Washington and on the way to the Library of Congress where Dylan was to record some poems. He writes;

> On the way to the library we stopped for a mid-morning glass of beer. As we sat in a dark booth, Dylan took his wallet our from his vest pocket and began to finger through its somewhat flimsy contents. He did not seem to be looking for anything in particular, but then he unfolded a yellowed newspaper clipping. It was a photograph, very dim and hazy, a thin little boy dressed in a droopy sort of gymkhana costume. His curly hair hung unevenly on his forehead, his face was serious, his eyes upturned, no hint of a smile on his lips. The caption beneath read: 'Dylan Marlais Thomas, aged 12, son of Mr and Mr D. J.Thomas of Swansea,' and went on to report that he had been victor in the 220 yard dash [sic] at the annual games of some grammar school competition...Dylan had carried this grimy scrap of paper with him for more than twenty years...

It was found still in his wallet when he died in the Chelsea Hotel in 1st November of 1953

R.S. Thomas was also a good sporting schoolboy and student. He enjoyed played competitive rugby and his team made the local paper mainly because the entire team consisted of trainee vicars. Like Dylan Thomas, R.S. also kept this newspaper cutting

Horse Racing – some of the camels we have mounted

While on a sporting theme let's turn our attention to the turf. In his thirties while living in Laugharne, Dylan Thomas enjoyed a

R.S. is on the extreme left in his rugby team made up entirely of trainee clerics!

little flutter on the gee-gees. On more than one of his innumerable poetry worksheets the names of horses he fancies are scribbled in the margins. I also had a postcard which a visiting American friend was sending back to the states, on which Dylan wrote an impromptu nonsense poem made up from the names of the day's nags, runners and jumpers which he had backed that day.

Running Water &Nuts
French Bounty & Knuckles
D'angelo & Chammie
Balby Balby Balby
Jackmil and Ambiguity
Are some of the camels we have mounted

R.S. also loved horse racing – I find this as astonishing as young Dylan being a long-distance runner. The Welsh poet and critic John Idris Jones[21] of Ruthin wrote this in a magazine

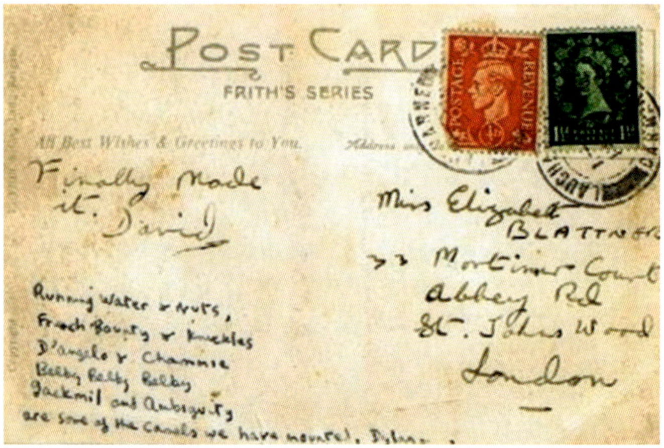
POST CARD
FRITH'S SERIES
Finally made it. David
Miss Elizabeth Blattner
33 Mortimer Court
Abbey Rd
St. Johns Wood
London
Running Water & Nuts,
French Bounty & Knuckles
D'angelo & Chammie
Balby Balby Balby
Jackmil and Ambiguity
are some of the camels we have mounted. Dylan.

Dylan's poem inspired by the horses he had backed and lost money on

about an impromptu visit to see R.S;

My wife and I called there recently. The front door was open. We knocked and a voice called us in. 'Left the door open for the delivery man,' his widow explained. He was watching horse racing on TV. 'R.S. loved horse racing,' she said. 'He followed the horses; he could name them...' She smoked and joked and we could see why R.S. found her very good company.

I wonder how R.S. would have felt if he had lived a few years more when the racing pages in the newspapers and horse racing media were dominated by stories of a thorough-bred horse named, Dylan Thomas which enjoyed a very successful racing career which lasted from June 2005 until December 2007, during which time it was the horses' story, not the Welsh poet he was named after, that dominated the press and internet. He ran twenty times and won ten races. After winning two minor races in 2005 he improved to become one of the leading European three-year-olds of 2006, winning the *Irish Derby* and finishing a close third in *The Derby*. In 2007 the horse won three of Europe's most important weight-for-age races. His performances led to his being named European Horse of the Year 2007. Would R.S. have risked a cheeky fiver on him one Saturday afternoon?

Christmas

Dylan Thomas contributed an early version of what was to become his famous broadcast *A Child's Christmas in Wales*, to issue 24. Winter 1946, of Keidrych Rhys's WALES magazine. It was then called *Memories of Christmas*. It was full of his regular, humorous and nostalgic childhood memories. It was the first article in that issue.

Some years later in 1958 R.S. Thomas was to contribute an article about Christmas to the same editor for the same magazine in its final incarnation. His essay was also the opening article and it was entitled *The Qualities of Christmas*. Keidrych provided a short introduction, describing R.S. as a 'Welsh country parson' and his essay could hardly be further than Dylan Thomas' whimsical tale. It also was illustrated by reproductions of two Renaissance religious old master paintings.

R.S. began his article with quotes from T.S. Eliot and John Milton and ended with a quote from Hardy. It is quite revealing to compare these two Welsh Thomas's, whose Christmas spirit is a world apart and totally different tone and content. First, here is an extract Dylan Thomas' article who starts as he means to go on; a stream of rich, whimsical, typical linguistic inventions:

> *All the Christmases roll down the hill towards the Welsh-speaking sea, like a snowball growing whiter and bigger and rounder, like a cold and headlong moon bundling down the sky that was our street; and they stop at the rim of the ice-edged, fish-freezing waves, and I plunge my hands in the snow and bring out whatever I can find; holly or robins or pudding, squabbles and carols and oranges and tin whistles, and the fire in the front room, and bang go the crackers, and holy, holy, holy, ring the bells, and the glass bells shaking on the tree, and Mother Goose, and Struwelpeter – oh! the baby-burning flames and the clacking scissorman! – Billy Bunter and Black Beauty, Little Women and boys who have three helpings, Alice and Mrs. Potter's badgers, penknives, teddy-bears – named after a Mr. Theodore Bear, their inventor, or father, who died recently in the United States – mouth-organs, tin-soldiers, and blancmange, and Auntie Bessie playing "Pop Goes the Weasel" and "Nuts in May" and "Oranges and Lemons" on the un-tuned piano in the parlour all through the thimble-hiding musical-chairing blind-man's-buffing party at the end of the-never-to-be-forgotten day at the end of the unremembered year. In goes my hand into that wool-white bell-tongued ball of holidays resting at the margin of the carol-singing sea.*

And this from R.S.'s article:

> *I remember one Christmas Eve; I think it was in 1941.There were rumours that the Germans would attempt an airborne landing that night. The countryside where I lived was wrapped in a thick, damp fog. The lanes were empty. No lights shone from the scattered farmsteads.The tress loomed up, windless and eerie, in the darkness. The silence was terrifying, the suspense intolerable. But it was suspense for the wrong thing. On other Christmas eves I have walked up hill lanes to take a present of home-made cakes to a bedridden farmer. But how different the atmosphere! The air cold and clear, the ash trees bone-white against the sky...*

The Welsh Language

These two poets offer quite different responses towards the Welsh language. Dylan Thomas was born into a Welsh speaking household – both his parents had been raised in rural Carmarthenshire, a very Welsh speaking county, and Welsh would have been their first language. However Dylan's father, D. J.Thomas, by dint of his dedication to education and study, climbed out of this farming working class environment, earned an outstanding first class honours degree in English from Aberystwyth University and joined the middle classes of Swansea when he took up his post as the Head of English at Swansea Grammar School. In making this jump D.J. (as he was familiarly known) seems to have left his native tongue behind and, like many of his peers, he saw the Welsh language as the language of the proletariat and not the language for social advancement. This, not uncommon viewpoint, was shared by the parents of most of Dylan's friends and, having met many of them; Alfred Janes, Dr. Daniel Jones, Mervyn Levy and Charles Fisher – I can vouch that they all spoke quite naturally in perfect English in near perfect received pronunciation, with just a soft hint of a Welsh accent. To this end their parents, including Dylan's, sent their boys to elocution classes. It is curious to note that in spite of his stance on the language D. J. added to his income by teaching Welsh at evening classes; in his biography of Dylan Paul Ferris sums this up;

> [this]must have gone against the grain for a man whose daytime colleagues never heard him speak the language

So although Dylan was not a Welsh speaker, he undoubtedly knew a smattering of Welsh, most learned out of necessity when he spent his childhood holidays with his Welsh speaking aunts, uncles and cousins. He uses a few Welsh words in his prose – *twp* [an idiot or fool]; twll [hole] – a pub in his short story *The Outing* is named *Twll in the Wall*, and *Ach a Fi* [An explanative Welsh dialect expression of disgust or abhorrence], echoes around *Milk Wood's* Llareggub.

I also believe that Dylan Thomas puns on the Welsh word *Parch* [a minister of religion] and the English word *Parched* meaning a dry arid landscape. In his poem *After the Funeral*, he writes:

> I stand, for this memorial's sake, alone
> In the snivelling hours with dead, humped Ann
> Whose hooded, fountain heart once fell in puddles
> Round the parched worlds of Wales.

Dylan is using the same word to suggest an overbearing presence of ministers of religion at the same time alluding to the dry mental atmosphere that prevailed across rural Wales.

R.S. Thomas had a hugely different relationship with the Welsh language. To start with neither of his parents were Welsh speakers. R.S. Thomas was born in Cardiff the only child of Margaret (née Davies) and Thomas Hubert Thomas. The family moved to Holyhead in 1918 because of his father's work in the Merchant Navy. His father's occupation took him away for long periods and R.S. was raised mainly by his mother. His education was through the medium of English and it was only after he was ordained and was appointed to a parish in a Welsh speaking area of Wales that he decided he needed to speak the language of his congregation and he set about learning Welsh. He eventually became relatively fluent but he acknowledged that it was his second language and he believed he could only write the poetry he wanted to in his native tongue. However he often preached in Welsh and wrote most all his prose in Welsh. R.S. would spend the rest of his life amongst Welsh speaking folk, moving farther and farther into North Wales. There is no doubt that this dichotomy was a constant worry to R.S. The American critic Jeffery Alan Triggs sums it up;[22]

> Thomas himself looks on Anglo-Welsh literature not as a means of magnifying Welsh influence through English culture, nor as a charitable contribution to English culture, but "as a means of rekindling interest in the Welsh language culture, and of leading people back to the mother-tongue" (*Selected Prose 53*[23]).

This somewhat paradoxical hope that the Anglo-Welsh movement might "simply be a phase in the re-cymrification of Wales"' (*Selected Prose 33*) has been an important part of Thomas's thinking all through his career.

To this day he maintains that Anglo-Welsh poets are writing in a foreign language. R.S. never really came to terms with this gnarly conundrum and describes it himself in a later article;

> I remember the evening: the chapel with its oil lamps, the wind blowing outside, and about twenty local farmers and their wives, come to listen to this freak – an Englishman who had learnt Welsh. Then off I went for about three quarters of an hour, like a ship being blown this way and that by the wind.

WALES

Dylan Thomas is often lambasted as being anti-Welsh when his accuser's trot out this line of his;

> Land of my Fathers, My Fathers can keep it!

However, this is wrong, It is not Dylan speaking; it is a line Dylan wrote in the screenplay for a 1948 melodramatic film, *Three Weird Sisters*, directed by Daniel Birt, it was based on a novel, *The Case of The Three Weird Sisters*, by Charlotte Armstrong. The film is set in a Welsh mining valley where three sisters live, one blind, one deaf and the one badly arthritic.

Their family own the mine. After an accident underground they implore their wealthy but greedy brother, Owen Morgan Vaughan, a nasty piece of work, who lives a rich anglicised life in London, who refuses to finance the rescue and reparation work and it is Owen who declares;

> Land of my Fathers, My Fathers can keep it!

That is not to say that Dylan did not tire of the pettiness of Swansea and Wales on occasions; a pettiness summed up in the constant refrain of the fish-wives in *Under Milk Wood*;

> *What will the neighbours say! What will he neighbours say*

In one very early letter (1933) to Pamela Hansford Johnson, his first serious girlfriend, he tries to impress her by being aloof, sophisticated and superior to his town and its inhabitants, he writes;

It's impossible for me to tell you how much I want to get out of it all. Out of the narrowness and dirtiness, out of the eternal ugliness of the Welsh people....

But five years later in 1938 after being in London and Hampshire he writes to Keidrych Rhys;

I want to be in Wales... I'd take any job in Wales, because I like living there the best.

R.S.Thomas is considered the more patriotic Welsh poet yet he too could write negatively about his homeland, lines such as these from the beginning of his poem, *A Priest to His People*;

Men of the hills, wantoners, men of Wales
With your sheep and your pigs and your ponies, your sweaty females
How I have hated you for your irreverence, your scorn even
Of the refinements of art and the mysteries of the church.

So like Dylan R.S. had a complicated ambivalence towards Wales. Professor M. Wynn Thomas,[24] R.S.'s friend, editor, and also his pre-eminent critic, sees R.S.'s two slim volumes *What is a Welshman*? (1974) and *Welsh Airs* (1987) as being R.S.'s strongest pronouncements on Welsh Nationalism, which he attributes to 'Margaret Thatcher's 'a rampant English Nationalism' with which;

[she] had managed to accomplish what the Welsh nationalists had failed to achieve...

Byron Roberts has this to say on the subject;

Curiously, [R.S.] is a Welsh nationalist to the lengths of not supporting the Welsh Nationalist party because it recognises Westminster.

And he then quotes R.S. in conversation;

Britain does not exist for me, it's an abstraction forced on the Welsh people.

When it comes to Dylan Thomas and Welsh Nationalism it can be dealt with very quickly. Kingsley Amis takes great pleasure in sharing a few words from the *Adam Dylan Thomas Memorial Issue* from 1954;

Thomas was asked his opinion of Welsh nationalism...
for which the interviewer fell back on reported speech:
Mr Thomas answered the question in three words,
of which the second and third were
'Welsh nationalism'.

Unlike R.S. Thomas, Dylan Thomas had a predilection for strong Anglo-Saxon bad language...

Kingsley Amis (let's stick with him)

Kingsley Amis used to visit my bookshop, often he'd come twice in one day, before lunch, sober and sneery, and then after lunch, drunk and obnoxious. He had lived in Swansea when he was an English lecturer at the University in the late forties early fifties, and often returned to stay with friends,; the main one being Stuart Thomas, a local solicitor who acted for Dylan Thomas's family and then for Dylan and Caitlin. Stuart was the main trustee of the Dylan Thomas Estate, and, in an act of profound nepotism, he made his drinking pal, Kingsley a trustee too. Kingsley loathed Dylan Thomas and made no secret of it. They met once, when Dylan was invited to speak to Swansea University English Society; it did not go well. After Dylan's death Amis seemed to revel in discrediting, describing him as;

...a pernicious figure who has helped to get Wales and Welsh poetry a bad name and generally has done lasting harm to them both...

And he's not finished yet, he goes on describing his fellow poet as;

an outstandingly unpleasant man who cheated and stole from his friends and peed on their carpets...

It comes then as another surprise to discover that Kingsley Amis was a huge fan of R.S. Thomas. The title of his review in The *Guardian* in 1964 of R.S.'s *Song At The Year's Turning*, was simply. 'A True Poet', and throughout the review he heaped praise upon R.S.;

...what I take to be an obvious fact; That R.S. Thomas
is one of the half-dozen best poets now writing in English.

And he closes with this observation;

To describe the effect of his work it is enough to say that he often moves to tears, and that creation lines of his impress themselves ineradicably, upon the mind. His example reduces most modern verse to footling whimsy.

This is from 1964 but as Amis advanced his schoolboy wit and cynicism especially when in cahoots with Philip Larkin he could not controlled and they would refer to R.S. as 'Arse Thomas' and occasionally even more coarsely as 'Arsewipe Thomas'.

RICHARD HUGHES

R. S. Thomas

He has gone now
to join his ship, too late
to board her. I remember
his beard, tangled
as his right mind
was not. I never got
to the bottom of him, but stuck
half-way down, clinging
to my preconceptions. Bald
brow, blue eye, watery
as a rainbow—his words
were dry spice seasoning
our nonsense. It was his trade,
sitting by the Welsh sea
forgetful of Branwen,
to use his pen for the incision
into the festering body
of Europe. There came out
the discharge of history
running gradually
clear for us in his precise prose.

Richard Hughes

Richard Hughes was a novelist and a playwright who had made his name with his novel *A High Wind in Jamaica* (1929. He was not Welsh by birth, but in 1934 he had bought Castle House, in Laugharne which adjoined the ruins of the quite spectacular castle and overlooked the estuary. He moved in with his wife, Frances Bazley, an artist.

Paul Ferris says of him 'he was already an established author. He lived in some style'. This would have appealed to Dylan who wrote to him in 1935 to arrange a meeting. That meeting never took place but, in 1936, he wrote again to invite himself and his Swansea artist friend Alfred Janes, to visit that weekend. This time Dylan had a cunning ulterior motive – he had met and been immediately smitten, by Caitlin Macnamara, when they were introduced in the Wheatsheaf, a louche pub in Soho, by Augustus John. At that time Caitlin was the old goat's young arm-candy. Dylan had learned that Augustus and Caitlin were also going to be visiting Hughes. Dylan wanted to continue their romance. And he was successful, but only after he and the old painter had had a brief physical altercation. Dylan and Caitlin were married in Penzance in July 1937. The newly-weds were taken with Laugharne and in April 1938 he wrote a cheeky letter to Hughes seeking accommodation in Laugharne which had the result he wanted – the couple moved in to a spare room with the Hughes family and they became good friends. Hughes was very generous to them. He also let Dylan use his writing room – a simple gazebo perched in the high ramparts of the Castle, where Dylan wrote and assembled his book of autobiographical short stories *Portrait of the Artist as a Young Dog* (1940). I was fortunate to buy a first edition of the book with a warm inscription from Dylan to Hughes thanking him for his kindness and help. It began, 'To my dear Diccon...' as this was how Hughes was addressed.

Not surprisingly I have no such stories about R.S. and Richard Hughes, however R.S. did write a poem to him which I happened upon by chance when sorting a huge collection of back issues of *Planet* magazine in my bookstore. In issue 33, August 1976, a lone poem by R.S. is printed with no further information than the text, but Hughes had died four months before.

Edward Thomas

This wonderful writer who died in the First World War in 1918, was London born from Welsh parents and a great lover of Wales. He was a great favourite writer of both Dylan and R.S.

Dylan Thomas made a radio programme just about Edward Thomas 1949, for the Welsh Home Service in which he read eight poems and said this of him;

> I said I did not know how Welsh he was, but we know from his poem that he loved the country of Wales. Walter de la Mare says of him, 'his voice low and gentle, but musical,with a curious sweetness and hollowness when he sang his old Welsh songs to his children.

Dylan would constantly badger radio producers to reprise, and re-commission programmes involving Edward's writings and he mentions him eight time in his Collected Letters; the last time in

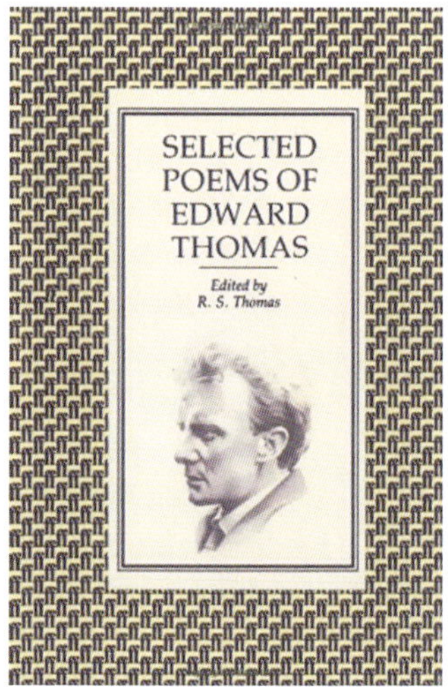

The cover of recent edition of R.S.'s selection

February1953, when writing to Idris Davies about another prospective Welsh poetry programme, he writes;

> Edward Thomas is only somewhat of a Welshman, even though *Child On The Cliffs* is experienced in Wales.

R.S. Thomas was given the task of editing a small *Selected Poems of Edward Thomas* for Faber and Faber in 1964 and it has been reprinted many times. He had read Edward's poems early in his life and admired them, but this task took him back to the poems and they had an even more profound impact on his own later poetry. R.S. dedicated the book to his wife Helen and his short, three and half page introduction is an amazing summation of Edward Thomas's life and work but it strikes me that some of what R.S. writes could equally apply to himself.

Here is the final paragraph;

> Those who are mindful of the vanishing features of the English country-side and anxious to preserve them, will find in Edward Thomas one who loved them as they do. But there are more lasting aspects of country living, the ever-changing moods of nature and weather, which can say deep things to the human spirit. Thomas knew those as well, and told of them in lines which make their impact, even in this industrial-technological era; perhaps more so because of it...

Change 'English' to 'Welsh' and 'Edward' to 'R.S.' and this passage still holds true.

Vernon Watkins

The Poet of Gower, as folk in Swansea refer to Vernon Watkins, was one of Dylan's closest Swansea friend 's especially in his twenties (they did not meet until 1935). Dylan Thomas was close to Dan Jones, Fred Janes, Mervyn Levy and Charles Fisher but it was only Vernon who he trusted to share his early poems in draft versions and the two of them had a wonderfully symbiotic relationship. Vernon relates the story of how shocked and a tad appalled he was when, in 1934 on a lunchtime browse in Swansea's main bookshop, Morgan & Higgs, he was confronted with a window display of a slim volume of poems, with a large sign **'Local Author – Dylan Thomas – 18 Poems'**. Vernon was under the impression he was the only poet in town. But he had to go in and give the book a judgmental browse. However, he was drawn back to the shop each following lunch break, reading deeper and deeper into the book, until he succumbed, overcome by the power of poems he was reading, and bought a copy. He then enquired around town and discovered Dylan lived in the Uplands and they soon met up and began a long and fruitful friendship.

This is very much in evidence in the book Vernon published in 1957, just a few years after his friend had died. *Dylan Thomas Letters To Vernon Watkins*[25] is that, but is so much more than just that due to wonderful commentary and background information that Vernon writes between each letter. Sadly the book is out of print at present, although it's not too hard to find. The letters are gathered together in *The Collected Letters of Dylan Thomas* but although they are great letters, without Vernon's notes so much is lost. Vernon was quite in awe of Dylan and this love and respect lasted well after Dylan died[26] and provoked a succession of poems inspired and in memorial too Dylan – some twenty in all.[27]

Dylan did not write any poems for Vernon, but he was always warm and grateful to him in his writings and letters In his radio play *Return Journey* he predicts their future;

> Vernon Watkins and Young Thomas write the most boiling poems, How they ring the bells of London and paint it like a tart.

In 1949 Dylan 'chaired' and introduced a radio program, *Swansea and the Arts*, in which four of his *Kardomah Café* mates; Dan Jones, Fred Janes. John Prichard and Vernon, all gave their accounts of living and working in the town. Vernon spoke first and Dylan introduced him thus;

> First of all then, Vernon Watkins, poet and present. I think him to be the most profound and greatly accomplished Welshman writing poems in English, and he is one of the few poets I know, intensely occupied with his craft ...

Dylan may not have given Vernon a poem but he did give him a warmly inscribed photograph of himself which prompted Vernon's first poem for him. Writing to him in 1938 from Ringwood Hants, where he and his new wife Caitlin, were staying with her mother. He enclosed a large recent photograph of himself. He expounds on it in his letter.

> Here's a photograph, taken by a woman[28]. near us. It's one of many: this is the toughest. Why I want you to think of me, – photographically, when I'm not about – as a tough, I don't know. Anyway its very big; you can write a poem on the back, draw whiskers on it, or advertise Kensitas[29]. in the front Window...

In his notes to the letter accompanying the photograph, Vernon wrote;

> The next letter suggested to me my poem *Portrait of a Friend*[30]. based on Dylan's own photograph which forms the frontispiece to this book and which was sent to me imperfectly packed, with the letter. This is the poem which was later printed in *Ballad of the Mari Lwyd*.[31] here is the first Stanza;
>
> He has sent me this
> Late and early page
> Caught in the emphasis
> Of last night's cartonnage
> Crumpled in the post
> Bringing to the lamplight
> Breath's abatement
> Over-and under-statement
> Mute as a mummy's pamphlet
> Long cherished by a ghost.

In 1983, Gwen Watkins wrote a fine and very honest book[32]

Nora Summers extraordinary portrait of young Dylan

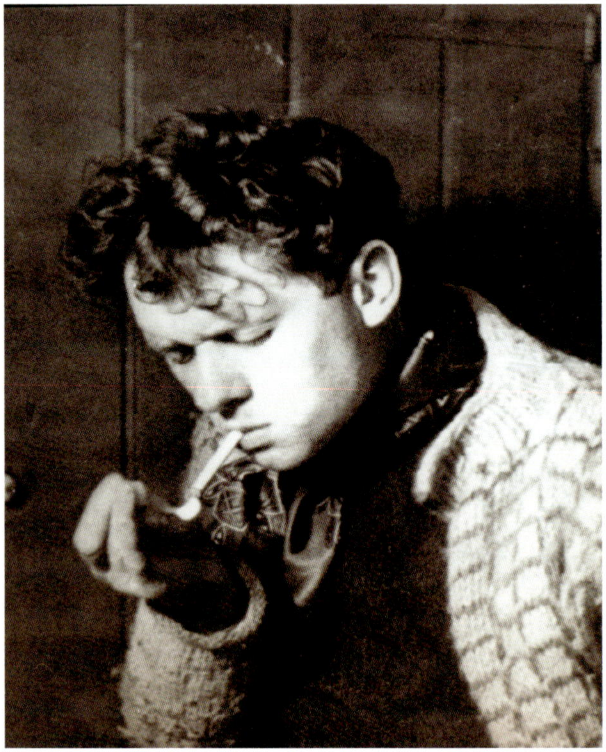

about the complicated, but deep friendship between the two poets. Vernon's friend, the poet and critic Leslie Norris, writes in his forward;

> One of the great literary friendships, and one of the most productive, was that of Dylan Thomas and Vernon Watkins, two of the finest poets of our time...

It would appear that R.S.Thomas never met Vernon Watkins but then R.S. never travelled south much and Vernon died in America 1967, (but not by staying in the pub too long – he stayed on the tennis court too long). But R.S. did come to Vernon's memorial service in Swansea[33]. and did write a poem for Vernon. It was called *The Bank Clerk*:[34]

> It was not the shillings he heard,
> But the clinking of the waves
> In the gullies and the rocks of
> Pwll Du. Turning them over
> To the customers at the counter

He offered them the rich change
Of his mind, the real coinage
Of language for their dry cheques
Punctually in the evenings
At Pennard he returned to
The poem's sun, wrestling with it
For delight, but with the sea's
Care, that on the blank sand
Tots itself.
Clerks, businessmen,
Grousers about the cost
Of a poet, he has balanced honourably
His accounts, but – what about you?

Pacifism and Propaganda

The second issue of the post war re-continued publication of Keidrych Rhys *WALES* magazine (December 1943), is one of the rare instances when R.S. and Dylan are literary bedfellows. Even more of a coincidence is that they both writers engage with anti-war propaganda.

R.S. Thomas contributes Five Poems, the forth of which is a short poem – *Propaganda*;

POEMS 49

Propaganda

NOR shot, nor shell, but the fused word,
That rocks the world to its white root,
Has wrought a chaos in the mind
And drained the love from the split heart;

Nor shock, nor shower of the sharp blows,
That fall alike from life and death,
But some slow subsidence within
That sinks a grave for the sapped faith.

R. S. THOMAS.

Dylan Thomas' contribution to this issue of Wales is listed on the cover and the contents as, *Film Poetry*, but it is actually an excerpt from the script/commentary that he wrote for his most respected wartime, *Ministry of Information*, propaganda film, OUR COUNTRY. We are told in the heading that:

> These are the words for the first two reels of a five-reeler M.O.I. Documentary Film, "Our Country" made by John Elridge and J. Jago (Strand Film Company).

John Ackerman, who edited, Dylan Thomas The Filmscripts,[35] describes *Our Country* as Dylan's 'most celebrated documentary' and he quotes a contemporary review in the *Spectator*[36] which describes the film; 'Our Country represents the most exciting and provocative film ... for many a long day. The film was originally made to be shown in the USSR with a commentary by Stanley Holloway, a very popular humourous monologist, but his attempt was rejected and Dylan Thomas was called upon to deliver the script. During the war, instead of joining the forces, which he was determined to avoid, (he was eventually exempted on medical grounds)he was employed by *Strand Films*[37] to write documentary and propaganda film scripts for the *Ministry of Information*. In all he worked on fourteen propaganda films. Ackerman also writes of how this documentary and his others relate to the poems which he wrote during the war; poems such as: "Among Those Killed in a Dawn Raid was a Man Aged a Hundred", "A Refusal to Mourn the Death, by Fire, of a Child in London", and "Ceremony after a Fire Raid". Indeed, the latter written around the same time as *Out Country* was in development contains similar recollections of Thomas' London's war experiences.

R.S. Thomas too, wrote some anti-war poems as he too had lived through the war, but he was in the countryside not the city. In his first collection, *Stones of the Field* is this poem *Homo Sapiens* 1941:

> What is interesting is that it was first published three years before his first book, in Cyril Connelly's *Horizon* Magazine, in an issue which was a dedicated to war writing.

And from R.S.'s *Uncollected Poems* is this short poem.

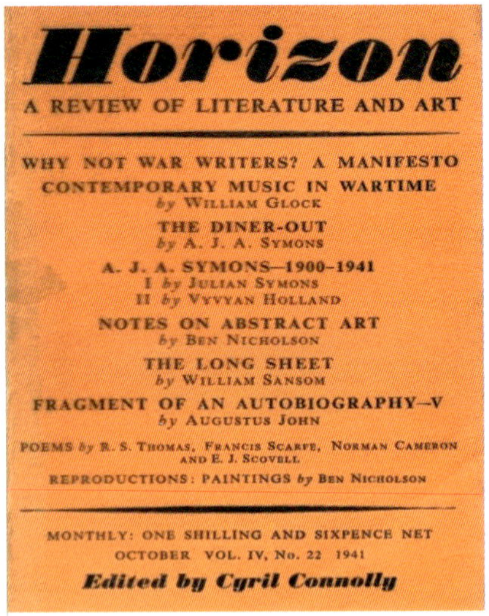
Horizon
A REVIEW OF LITERATURE AND ART
WHY NOT WAR WRITERS? A MANIFESTO
CONTEMPORARY MUSIC IN WARTIME by WILLIAM GLOCK
THE DINER-OUT by A. J. A. SYMONS
A. J. A. SYMONS—1900–1941 I by JULIAN SYMONS II by VYVYAN HOLLAND
NOTES ON ABSTRACT ART by BEN NICHOLSON
THE LONG SHEET by WILLIAM SANSOM
FRAGMENT OF AN AUTOBIOGRAPHY—V by AUGUSTUS JOHN
POEMS by R. S. THOMAS, FRANCIS SCARFE, NORMAN CAMERON AND E. J. SCOVELL
REPRODUCTIONS: PAINTINGS by BEN NICHOLSON
MONTHLY: ONE SHILLING AND SIXPENCE NET
OCTOBER VOL. IV, No. 22 1941
Edited by Cyril Connolly

HOMO SAPIENS 1941

Murmuration of engines in the cold caves of air,
And, daring the starlight above the stiff sea of cloud,
Deadly as a falcon brooding over its prey
In a tower of spirit-dazzling and splendid light,
Pedestrian man holds grimly on his way.
Legions of winds, ambushed in crystal corries,
Conspiring to destroy him, and hosts of ice,
Thronging him close, weigh down his delicate wings;
But loud as a drum in his ear the hot blood sings,
And a frenzy of solitude mantles him like a god.

"Dylan hated passionately the whole idea of war, and would have been quite incapable of lifting, let alone using, any weapon of war. But, since he did not want to belong to a soft set of conscientious objectors, whom he considered on the same pathetic level as vegetarians and teetotalers, he had to fabricate a state of collapse. Not difficult for him with his chicken bone body and advanced state of drinking habits. So he simply presented himself, on medical examination morning, shaking and quaking from head to foot with a selfmade monumental hangover. When, stripped and shivering, they prodded him in the belly, he promptly coughed up all his guts and the accumulated acid and bile of weeks past, thus managing to get himself registered as an acute asthmatic sufferer; fatal in the army; and put abysmally low on the fighting list."

Caitlin's account of Dylan's attitude to warfare and it's horrors

PACT

This is my child;
that is yours. Let
peace be between them
when they grow up.
They are far off
now; let it not
be through war they are brought
near. Their languages
are different. Let them both
learn it is peace-in the hand is the translation
of peace in the mind.

As early as 1934, when he was just twenty, Dylan Thomas wrote a letter, co-signed by his socialist friend Bert Trick, to a local solicitor(later a barrister), Ithel Davies, who was a life-long pacifist who had been imprisoned for his principles in the First World War:

Dear Mr Ethel Davies

We are informed that you are an official of the No More War Movement. If that is so, we would like to have details of membership – how to join, because we believe the present militarist trend of national politics makes it imperative that those who object to war in any shape or form should actively identify themselves with the Movement ... we wish to enrol ourselves, not merely as nominal members but as active propagandists ... We would wish to propagate, through the columns of all the journals at our disposal, the urgency of bringing together in a common front those who hold similar views to ourselves.

While I was writing this I happened across an original letter by Bill Read, the American academic and partner of John Malcolm Brinnin. Read is writing to thank Vernon and Gwen Watkins for their generous help when he was writing his book on Dylan Thomas – *The Days of Dylan Thomas*. In the letter he shares a quote from a statement Caitlin about Dylan and his feelings about war which she sent to him in a letter;

I think we can take these as the last words on the subject ...

For his part R.S. Thomas was a long-time, ardent member and active supporter of CND, speaking at rallies and going on protests, which included the occasion when R.S. Thomas and others sat down in the road in front of the council offices in Carmarthen town where a nuclear bunker was said to have been built. He would also contribute poems to anti-nuclear and anti-war collections.

Birds

Imagery of birds and the names of birds are ubiquitous in the work of both poets.

For Dylan they populate many of his poems and prose pieces, His description of the view from his Laugharne Boathouse window, from one of his famous 'birthday poems,' is often quoted by poetry buffs (and the writers of West Wales tourist brochures!) Here is the first verse:

Poem In October
It was my thirtieth year to heaven
Woke to my hearing from harbour and neighbour wood
And the mussel pooled and the heron
Priested shore

The morning beckon
With water praying and call of seagull and rook
And the knock of sailing boats on the net webbed wall
Myself to set foot
That second

The second verse has 'water-birds', 'birds of the winged tree' and another 'heron'; the third verse begins with 'A springful of larks, and continues with 'whistling Blackbirds' and 'sweet singers'; the forth verse has 'brown as owls' and 'lark full cloud'; and then the penultimate verse gives us,

And the mystery
Sang alive
Still in the water and singingbirds

A quick glance through a concordance of Dylan's Collected Poems tells us he uses the word bird [s] more than 80 times/ Looking for specific species we find 'heron[s] fourteen times; a dozen 'owls' often compounded; six 'wrens'; 'lark'[s] and 'curlews, five; and a solitary 'robin', and even a lone 'pelican' ...

R.S. Thomas did not only fill his poems with avian images but he filled much of his life engaged in serious and dedicated bird-watching, (I'd bet he hated the word 'twitcher'), and was more of an amateur ornithologist. Birds figured large in his life and in his poems herewith just a few titles:

Thirteen Blackbirds Look at a Man
They yearn for the tongues of curlews
Let me tell you of the raven's sins
Those craning birds are chicer for you

And an example:

A Bird's Prayer'
A bird's prayer is its song,
addressed to nobody
but the unknown listener
to its feathered vernacular.

Man's prayer is a trickle
of language gathering to a reservoir
to be drawn on by the thirsting
mind in its need for meaning.

The Sea

The only sea I saw was the seesaw sea with you riding on it.
Lie down, lie easy. Let me shipwreck in your thighs.
Captain Cat in Under Milk Wood.

The sea features in the original Welsh meaning of the name Dylan. His father, D. J. Thomas, took the name from the text of the forth branch of The Mabinogi, in which a boy-child is named Dylan. He was the son of Arianrhod and the twin brother of Lieu Llaw Gyffes. Immediately after he was baptized he took to the sea, where he could swim as well as a fish. He was slain accidentally by his uncle Gofannon. According to some theories the character might be rooted in an earlier and otherwise unattested Celtic god of the sea. Other translations have arisen such as, 'Sea-Son of Wave'. How aware of this derivation the young Dylan was is hard to ascertain, but from his bedroom window in the Uplands he could look out at the, then thriving Swansea Docks, and in his later life he spent some of the most productive times were when he was living close to the sea – at Majoda the shanty bungalow on the cliffs at New Quay and later in Laugharne in The Boathouse which was built on stilts overlooking the estuary.

In his poetry he uses the word **sea** some 110 times but he also uses a plethora of compound words – *sea-blown, sea-faiths, sea-ghost, sea-girls, sea gut, sea-halved, sea-hatched*, and in his *I make this in a warring absence,*[38] we get *sea-hymen*;

Is corner-cast, breath's rag, scrawled weed, a vain
Or like the tide-looped breastknot reefed again
Or rent ancestrally the roped sea-hymen,
And, pride is last, is like a child alone
By magnet winds to her blind mother drawn,
Bread and milk mansion in a toothless town

In the same year as he wrote this poem he also wrote the short prose story, *A Prospect of the Sea*. It became the first story and gave the title to the posthumous collection of prose that Daniel Jones edited in 1955.

R.S.Thomas was born within the sound of the sea and it was the backdrop to his childhood. He was brought up in the port town of Holyhead on Anglesey. He wrote about this in the third poem of *The Echoes Return Slow*, when he recalls gazing down onto the harbour: 'a forest of masts, where ships of sail sought shelter from the storm.' Through these sights, he writes, 'dreams were laid at the roots of a boy's curls.' He wrote in a letter to his friend the poet and critic Raymond Garlick, that: 'It was Holyhead itself that made me what little of a poet I am. A little town, with a glorious expanse of cliff and coastal scenery. I shall never outgrow my *hiraeth* for it.'

R.S.'s father Thomas Herbert Thomas was became an apprentice seaman under sail at age 15 and went on to become a sea-captain. As a Merchant Seaman he served in the Merchant Navy in the First World War and subsequently plied the ferry route between Holyhead and Ireland. It was this work that took the young, five-year-old R.S. from Cardiff to Holyhead where he began to find solace from the sea. The sea features in many of his poems here is just one;

Sea Watching.

Grey waters, vast
as an area of prayer
that one enters. Daily
over a period of years
I have let my eye rest on them.
Nothing
but that continuous waving
that is without meaning
occurred.
Ah, but a rare bird is
rare. It is when one is not looking
at times one is not there
that it comes.
You must wear your eyes out
as others their knees.
I became the hermit
of the rocks, habited with the wind
and the mist. There were days,
so beautiful the emptiness
it might have filled,
its absence
was as its presence; not to be told
any more, so single my mind
after its long fast,
my watching from praying.

Hell

As Dylan Thomas was embarking on his journey towards his death in New York in November 1953, his assistant (and lover) Liz Reitell reported that on one night in the Chelsea Hotel he collapsed and gave out a frightening cry: '*I have seen the gates of Hell tonight.*'

Shortly after he went into a coma from which he never recovered and a few nights later he died in St Vincent's Hospital.

On his retirement R.S Thomas moved to a 13th century cottage set deep into the side of the hill at *Sarn-y-Rhiwn*, which overlooked a sweeping wild bay, *Porth Neigwl,* which translates into English as:

Hell's Mouth

After all this I am still left wondering and more than a little curious about just what R.S. Thomas made of Dylan Thomas's creation of the Rev. Eli Jenkins' *Evening Prayer* from in Under Milk Wood:

Every morning when I wake
Dear Lord – a little prayer I make
Oh please do keep thy loving eye
On all poor creatures born to die

And every evening at sundown
I ask a blessing on the town
For whether we last the night or no
I'm sure as always – touch and go...

We are not wholly bad or good
Who live our lives under Milk Wood
And Thou, I know, wilt be the first
o see our good side not our worst

I'd like to think that even if R.S. didn't wholeheartedly approve, he could at least tolerate its mawkish charm because, by and large, in my experience most audiences do.

And Professor Walford Davies tells us in a 'personal correspondence' in 1987, R.S. informed him that he had;

' ... nothing at all against Dylan

I think Harri Webb[39] sums things up pretty well at the end of his letter to *Poetry Wales*, published in their 1972 *Special R.S. Thomas Number*;

> We have been fortunate in Wales to have two great and dissimilar poets to extend the frontiers of our land in different directions. Dylan gave us a country, in which it was lovely to be a child, his successor as Prifardd[40] of English-speaking Wales has given us a county in which it is necessary to be a man.

I don't think we could ask for more

1. The track can still be found and heard on *YouTube*.

2. *Bob Dylan and Dylan Thomas The Two Dylans*. McNidder & Grace 2022.

4. Sam Adams: *Letters From Wales. Memories and Encounters in Literature and Life*. Parthian. 2023.

5. R.S. revealed this in his autobiography *Neb* (Translated from the Welsh by Jason Walford Davies), published as *Autobiographies*, Dent 1997. The strange and unlikely Yankee tone to this pseudonym is thought to have come from the names of the romantic novelists his mother loved to read. R.S. also admits that is a 'laughably literary pseudonym' and describes the poems as 'limp sentimental poems'. Dylan Thomas also composed verse using pseudonyms. He and his polymath friend Dan Jones would write poems with each contributing alternate lines: producing weird and wonderful surrealist nonsense. They wrote under the joint pseudonym WALTER BRAM, which could not be further from R.S.'s – Bram is Welsh slang for Fart. When Dylan left school he continued to contribute to the magazine and used the pseudonym 'Old Boy'.

6. Quoted by Fitzgibbon in his 1965 *Life of Dylan Thomas*.

7. Keidrych Rhys was born William Ronald Rhys Jones in 1915. He grew up on his father's Penybont Farm near Carmarthen. He changed his me to Keidrych Rhys to sound more authentic and founded the literary magazine *Wales* in 1937, and served as its editor for all three of its future incarnations. The journal was published initially by his *The Druid Press*, Carmarthen.

8. Harri Webb somewhat deflates this when he writes in a letter to *Poetry Wales* published in their 1972 *Special R.S. Thomas number*, that the *Druid Press* office was "in the upper room above Mr. Baughli's chip shop in Lammas Street opposite the Crimean War memorial".

9. James (Joseph) Hanley born in 1897 was a Liverpool born, British novelist, short story writer, and playwright of Irish decent. He was a seaman before taking up full time writing. He moved from Liverpool to near Corwen, North Wales in 1931. In 1939, he moved to London, to write documentaries and plays for the BBC but moved back to Wales, to Llanfechain, the other side of the Mountains from Corwen. He wrote several works with a Welsh setting and subject matter and began to be considered as an Anglo-Welsh writer. He became friends with John Cowper Powys who lived in Corwen. J. C. wrote the "Preface" to James Hanley's *Men in Darkness* (1931).

10. A copy of this letter was given me by a fine old customer Mr. Boone from Oxford, who had a wonderful R.S. Thomas collection which is now very much at home in the *R.S. Thomas Research Centre* Bangor.

11. *tatterdemalion*; a very Dylanesque word. I had to look it up, it means tatty, shoddy or dilapidated.

12. Anthony Conran: *Frontiers in Anglo-Welsh Poetry*. Cardiff 1997.

13. *R.S. Thomas Selected Prose*. Edited by Sandra Anstey. Poetry Wales. 1982.

14. Cecil Price was Professor of English at Swansea University. He edited the Oxford Sheridan.

15. Dylan's Father was a staunch, self-confessed atheist so he was anything but the source of Dylans Bible knowledge. That came from the regular boyhood visits he made with his mother Florrie, to spend weekends visiting his favourite aunt, Theodosia [aunt Dosie] his mother's sister. Dosie had married a minister, the Rev David Rees of Paraclete Chapel in Newton, a village above Mumbles, on the edge of Gower. The church had a schoolroom and Dylan regularly attended Sunday school and a service or two where he absorbed the stories of the Old and New Testaments which so enriched his future poems. But Dylan disliked his uncle and his hell-fire preaching (which may have influenced his later declamatory style). In one of his early note-books he wrote a poem beginning 'Mathias spat upon the lord ' the second stanza begins, 'The reverend Crap, a holy pimp/ Reads the bible and loves children,/.

16. This anthology includes one other poem by Thomas; *There was a Saviour* is included in the book's first section GOD.

17. This is very much due to the remarkable accomplishments of Barbara (Cohen) Holdridge and Marianne (Roney) Mantell, founders of Caedmon Records. Both were graduates from Hunter College degrees in Greek and began working in publishing. However, on seeing Dylan Thomas read on his first tour of America they were smitten and wanted the world to be able to hear his performances. Failing to interest their current employers they cobbled together around $1,500, managed to meet and convince Dylan that it would be a money-spinner for him and started Caedmon Records, a label that would pave the way for the huge growth of the audio book industry. Their first release in 1953 and L.P. of Dylan reading Five Poems on one side and *A Child's Christmas in Wales* on the other. The record was so successful that it sold over 250000 copies in the first five years it was available. The two founders eventually sold out to Harper Collins Audio Books.

18. Mervyn Levy describing Dylan in an article *John O London's Weekly*.

19. Charles Fisher in a Talk at The Dylan Centre Swansea 2003.

20. R.S. Thomas; *Neb*. Gwasg Gwynedd.1985. Edited by Gwenno Hywyn. Neb translates into English as Nobody.

21. John Idris Jones was a Welsh Academic, poet, writer and publisher from Ruthin. He was my lecturer in English when I was at college in Cardiff in the late 60"s. We became friends and when he opened a bookshop in Cardiff we did business together and stayed good friends until he died in 2020.

22. Jeffrey Allan Triggs; *R.S. Thomas and the Problem of Welsh Identity* (long version). http://triggs.djvu.org/global- language.com/triggs/Nationalist.htm

23. Sandra Anstey[edits]; *The Selected Prose of R.S. Thomas* 1983

24. M. Wyn Thomas; *R.S. Thomas Serial Obsessive*. University of Wales Press. 2013.

25. Vernon Watkins: *Dylan Thomas Letters to Vernon Watkins*. J.M. Dent and Faber and Faber. 1957.

26. Gwen writes in her book; Not a day passed, till his own death that he did not think of Dylan.

27. Vernon Watkins: *Poems for Dylan*. Gomer. 2003. I worked on this with Gwen Watkins

and provided the cover image and Vernon's *Times Obituary* for Dylan and his own account of their first meeting.

28. The woman was Nora Summers, a fine artist and photographer who was at Art school with Augustus John who also lived nearby. In 2014 I collaborated with her grandson Gabriel Summer and his wife Leonie of a book about Nora and her photographs; *Dylan Thomas and the Bohemians The Photographs of Nora Summers*. Parthian. 2014. I have owned this photograph for near 50 years – it is the only known original print and there is no negative. In Dylan's centenary year 2024 I loaned it to the National Museum of Wales where it took pride of place in their memorial exhibit.

29. *Kensitas* were a popular brand of cigarettes in the thirties. An early advertising slogan was *Our Belief, the Finest Leaf,* but in 1932 they used deceptive copy in newspaper advertisements, claiming their cigarettes "*protect the throat*" and promising that *1004 British Doctors have stated KENSITAS to be less irritating*. They are apparently still available!

30. Gwen Watkins would use this as the title of her book about Dylan and Vernon; *Portrait of a Friend*. Gomer. 1983.

31. *The Mari Lywd* is a popular figure in South Wales folk-lore which began in the 19th century. The tradition features a real horse's skull, usually decorated with coloured ribbons and rosettes and with glass bottle eyes. The lower jaw is fixed on a spring which shuts the mouth with a loud snap. It is carried from door to door by a wassail-singing group during the Christmas season. It was used as the title of Vernon's first book of poems, overseen by T.S. Eliot

32. Gwen Watkins; Portrait of a Friend. Gomer. 1983.

33. Gwen Watkins told me that a friend who was sitting near R.S. overheard him refer to Vernon as a 'good second division poet.'

34. The poem can be found in; *Vernon Watkins 1906-1967. Faber & Faber*. 1970. Edited by Leslie Norris.

35. *Dylan Thomas The Filmscripts*. Edited by John Ackerman. Dent 1995.

36. Edgar Anstey a member of the Documentary Film Movement writing in the June 1945 *Spectator*.

37. For more on this see Chapter 8. Dylan Thomas and Film.

38. Written in July-November 1937, first published: *Twentieth Century Verse,* January-February 938 with the title 'Poem' (For Caitlin), and then in *The Map of Love* (1939).

39. Harri Webb writing in the R.S. number of *Poetry Wales* (Spring 1972).

40. Prifardd; Translates literally as *The Chief Bard*, or maybe just the leading poet of English-speaking Wales.

Dylan Thomas, Mad Girls and Hawks

10.

Dylan Thomas:
Sylvia Plath & Ted Hughes.

'Sylvia loved Dylan more than life itself'
Gordon Lameyer, Sylvia Plath's boyfriend in the early fifties[1]

Sylvia Plath shared the same birthday as Dylan Thomas.[2] Furthermore, both Sylvia and Ted Hughes saw and heard Dylan Thomas read very close to the same time in 1953, shortly before he died, but on different sides of the Atlantic Ocean; and before they had met each other.

Sylvia attended Dylan's reading at Amherst College, Massachusetts and Ted was at his reading in Cambridge University. They were both passionately smitten with him as an inspiring poet and an intriguing and powerful character. When they eventually met they continued to share this enthusiasm for Dylan Thomas and his poetry.

Sylvia Plath and Dylan Thomas.

Plath began her university life as a freshman at Smith College[3] in 1950, the same year that Dylan made his first of four reading tours of America. So her formative college years coincided with Thomas's conquest of America and the growth there of 1950's 'Dylanolatry', which would have a profound effect on her. Sylvia Plath considered Dylan Thomas her favourite contemporary poet.

A few years later and Dylan Thomas was coming to the end of his third reading tour of America and on May 20th 1953, Sylvia went to Amherst College in Massachusetts, (very near to Northampton where she was attending Smith College) to see her favourite poet in action.[4] Little is known or written about this event, but it came a week after the New York *Kaufman Auditorium* premiere performance of *Under Milk Wood*. According to Plath, Thomas seems to have reprised at least some of the play as a solo performance. Sylvia Plath was soon to be very close to being much more involved in Thomas's great play.

So far success had come easily to Sylvia. She had published many short stories and won two poetry prizes from Smith, the *Ethel Olin Corbin* prize and the *Elizabeth Babcock* award and, in 1952, she had won the *Mademoiselle*[5] Magazine's Fiction Contest, which led to her receiving this telegram in April 1952;

> HAPPY TO ANNOUNCE THAT YOU HAVE WON A
> MADEMOISELLE GUEST EDITORSHIP.
> YOU MUST BE AVAILABLE FROM JUNE 1 TO JUNE 26.

Around this time Sylvia was experimenting with writing villanelles.[6] She wrote three, the best of which was the *Mad Girl's Love Song*. This poem made a deep impression on the up-and-coming poetry critic Helen Vendler, who wrote to Sylvia's mother, Aurelia about the poem describing it as;

> 'The only decent villanelle in the English language besides Dylan Thomas's 'Do Not Go Gentle Into That Good Night'

High praise indeed.

Sylvia was elated that she had secured one of these month-long *Mademoiselle* intern placements which was to start in June 1953. It was an important step towards fulfilling her literary aspirations. She would write about her achievement in a letter.[7]

> Being one of the 20 winners in the U.S. of this month in New York was a dream of an opportunity for invaluable job experience, and I feel like a collegiate Cinderella whose Fairy Godmother suddenly hopped on the mailbox and said "What is your first woosh?" and I, Cinderella said "New York" and she winked, waved her pikestaff. And said "Woosh granted".

Sadly this 'Fairy Godmother' was not always going to be around. Her first minor disappointment came when her initial task was to conduct a 'celebrity interview' with a writer of note. Sylvia would have dreamed of interviewing J.D. Salinger, as she loved *Catcher in the Rye,* or the gothic writer Shirley Jackson, or Irwin Shaw. But she ended up with the Irish novelist Elizabeth Bowen. Although not her writer of choice, Sylvia went to Cambridge, Massachusetts, on May 26th to conduct the interview and she acquitted herself well. Bowen chain-smoked *Chesterfields* and a photograph of them together shows them both wearing three-strand pearl necklaces and looking quite at ease with each other.

But most of all Sylvia wanted to meet Dylan Thomas; she knew he was still on tour in America, and he was her current, passionate, literary love. However, this dream had a set-back on her first day in the *Mademoiselle* office in New York City when assignments were announced. Sylvia was not designated *Fiction Editor*. That job went to Candy Bolster, who remembers Sylvia being quite jealous, as Candy would get to meet all the famous writers who came into the office, such as Tennessee Williams and Truman Capote. But what galled Sylvia the most was that Candy would get to deal with Dylan Thomas.[8]

Bolster even interviewed Thomas in his room at the infamous *Chelsea Hotel*, which she recalls was 'a little shabby'. She describes him as being;

> ...generous and approachable, albeit a little bleary-eyed. She asked the poet about his name – Dylan means water in Welsh. She asked him to read his favourite poem – one he had never read in public. Thomas obliged and read *In Memory of Ann Jones* dedicated to his nanny-nurse.[9]

Sylvia did adore Dylan Thomas – even his rumpled look and chunky pullovers that looked like they belonged to Breton fisherman. Sylvia would have been even more upset had she known that Dylan would write to Cyrilly Abels in June '53, warmly remembering the meeting.

> 'I did enjoy meeting you and Miss Bolster... for that very short time in the hotel and I only wish I could have been more helpful to your guest editor. I got the little interview and there was of course nothing wrong.[10]

But far worse was still to come. From Elizabeth Winder again:

> 'When Thomas popped into *Mademoiselle*'s pink and green lobby Sylvia happened to be out ...'

Devastation ensued and Sylvia decided that the only course of action left to her was to seriously stalk her Welsh poet/prey. As Elizabeth Winder tells it, Sylvie enlisted the help of three of the other girls, Carol LeVarn, Neva Nelson and Janet Wagner. Between them they devised a plan; They would hang around outside Dylan's legendary favourite drinking spot, *The White Horse Tavern*, on the chance they could accost him in some way. They gamely hung about outside for around six hours; pacing up and down the pavements and watching the drinkers come and go, but to no avail: there was no sign of Dylan Thomas:

> 'Sylvia was determined to meet her hero... she grabbed Carol; and marched straight right into the Chelsea Hotel, passed its deep, wrought iron balconies, the high ceilings, the loopy staircase with its iron balustrades... Sylvia and Carol plopped themselves in the hallway a few feet from Thomas's room. They lounged on the floor all night and kept watch. Sylvia thrilled to the hotel's ratty flash. Slumped against the wall in the Chelsea with bloodshot eyes... carving out her gleamy little chop of New York. Twelve hours later both girls were delirious and Dylan-less – yet somehow victorious... The whole mad frolic became known as 'the *Dylan Thomas episode* ...[11]

In fact it was a doomed effort from the start as Dylan had flown home on June 3.[12] What makes this all the more ironic is that the position Sylvia had been assigned on that first day; to be Cyrilly Abels' assistant, did draw her deep into Dylan's engagement with *Mademoiselle*. She had been proud to write back to her mother on June 4:

> 'Assignments announced... I'm Managing Ed and moved my typewriter into Cyrilly Abels' office today.'

At that moment in time Cyrilly Abels was deep into discussions with Dylan Thomas, with a view to securing the serial rights for the first ever publication of *Under Milk Wood*. She had already made him an opening offer of $750, and, after attending the premiere on May 14, she had commissioned John Malcolm Brinnin, Dylan's American friend and agent, and the photographer, Rollie Mckenna, to visit Wales and prepare an illustrated article on Laugharne and west Wales to accompany the eventual first publication of Dylan's play.

But everything changed when Dylan Thomas died on November 9 1953, in St. Vincent's Hospital in New York City after being in a coma for several days.

There was a memorial service was held for Dylan at St Luke's Episcopal Chapel, the third oldest church in New York, on Friday 13th November 1953, four days after he died. Caitlin was there, as were most of his New York friends including poet, e e. cummings and his wife, the sculptor Dave Sliva, who had already taken a death mask of Dylan; and there is a photograph of playwright Tennessee Williams entering the church, but no record of Sylvia being in attendance.

Sylvia slowly began coming to terms with the reality of Thomas' tragic death. In a letter from early 1954, a few months after his death, she wrote;

> 'the lyrical Welshman I've been in mourning for these past months, Dylan Thomas. I just got a copy of the tear sheets from Cyrilly Abels at *Mademoiselle* containing his verse play *Under Milk Wood* which I heard him read at Amherst last spring ... I could get drunk just on the sound of the words ... or on the boisterous Welshness of his humour.'

A note attached to these proofs of *Under Milk Wood*, written by Cyrilly Abels, read:

> 'I hope you will find *Under Milk Wood* as exciting as I do each time I read it – and I've read it five times to date!

Sylvia flew back to New York for a few days in March 1954 and met up with Cyrilly Abels again for lunch in the Ivy room at the Drake Hotel. Clark writes;

> They spoke mainly of Dylan Thomas, and Abels confirmed that Dylan 'had been drinking to excess on an empty stomach' in the days before he died.

Under Milk Wood in *Mademoiselle* magazine

In Early August in 1955 Sylvia was staying on Martha's vineyard with her current boyfriend, Peter Davidson, who worked at the Harvard Press. He recalls seeing Sylvia;[12]

> Lying on his apartment floor with her 'listening with rapture' to Dylan Thomas reading *Fern Hill*.

But her time in New York, as well as not facilitating a meeting with her beloved poet Dylan Thomas, had also drained her; her mother described her as looking "tired" and "unsmiling" and, as a result, she dreaded telling Sylvia that she had not been accepted on to Frank O'Connor's short-story class at Harvard summer school, which she really aspired too. Sylvia had tried to take her mind off her immediate anxieties by spending more time with her boyfriend, Gordon Lameyer, who was living with his mother in Wellesley while he waited to enrol in the navy's Officer Candidate School in Newport. Sylvia and Gordon saw each other almost every day for the next two weeks, often at his aunt's house in Jaffrey Centre, New Hampshire, listening to the symphonies of Beethoven and Brahms and recordings of Frost, e e cummings and Dylan Thomas. The month of 'pain, parties and work' had taken its toll, and her mental health began to deteriorate leading to periods of hospitalization and psychiatric treatments. These she eventually incorporated with other memories of her time in New York and subsequent events into her only novel, *The Bell Jar*. It was originally published under the synonym Victoria Lucas, in 1963. It is a semi-autobiographical *roman a clef*, but with personal and place names altered, however, she chose to make no fictional reference to *The Dylan Thomas Episode*.

It was a few years before Dylan Thomas re-entered her life. In early 1956 Sylvia, having re-entered academia, was awarded a Fullbright Scholarship which allowed her to travel to the UK to continue her studies. She arrived at Newnham College, Cambridge, where she continued studying and writing. Dylan Thomas would re-enter her world when, in March, she first met Ted Hughes at a literary party in a Cambridge pub, where students and post grads were celebrating the launch a new poetry magazine, *The St. Botolph's Review*. Although Ted had already finished his studies and was working in London he regularly visited his Cambridge writer friends and was both deeply involved in the inception of St Botolph's but also was a major contributor of poems.

It was after this first meeting with Ted that Plath used Dylan Thomas as a measure against which to judge his qualities: she wrote to her mother, Aurelia;

> [Ted Hughes'] voice is richer and rarer than Dylan Thomas, booming through all the walls and doors... He reads his own poems which are better than Thomas and Hopkins...

This very well documented first meeting would eventually see them getting married a few months later on June 16 1956. When they moved to London where their first temporary accommodation was in a flat[13] that Dylan Thomas used to visit when a Welshman lived there. They also enjoyed the Soho pub-crawl that took them to the famous French House with its tricolours waving proudly in the street outside. Originally called *The York Minster*, the French House also became a gathering place for writers. Brendan Behan and Dylan Thomas visited the pub and it is one of the places that claim to be where Thomas left the manuscript of *Under Milk Wood*.

More recent academic critics, particularly Professor John Goodby late of Swansea University and now Professor of Arts and Culture at Sheffield Hallam University, have been trying to re-invigorate Thomas studies and place Thomas as a key Modernist writer. Goodby has pointed out various new links between Plath and Thomas. He writes[14] of them;

> Despite their many differences, then, it may be no coincidence that the title which Plath used for both a poem and a short story, *All the Dead Dears*, echoes Captain Cat's valediction at the end of his opening colloquy:
> *Oh my dead dears!* in *Under Milk Wood*.

The depth of Sylvia's passion for the poetry of Dylan Thomas is best evidenced by this bibliographic treasure:

Sylvia Plath's copy of Dylan Thomas' Collected Poems 1924-1952

This was one of the greatest books I have ever had the pleasure to handle. In 2018 I got a call or from an acquaintance who worked in the book department of a major London Auction house. He knew of my 'interest' in Dylan Thomas and had kindly called to let me know that in an upcoming sale they were to be offering up for sale Sylvia Plath's annotated copy of Dylan *Thomas' Collected Poems 1934-1952*.

This was astounding news. I responded by thanking him, confirming my interest and he replied saying he would e-mail an advance copy of their catalogue description. Shortly this arrived in my in-box.

> LOT. 238: THOMAS (DYLAN) The Collected Poems, SYLVIA PLATH'S COPY, ANNOTATED IN FIVE PLACES AND EXTENSIVELY UNDERLINED, with upwards of seventy sentences or passages underscored, marked or bracketed in the margins, in two places with Plath's distinctive "star" symbol in black ink, 13

poems in the Contents marked, photographic frontispiece, publisher's blue cloth, worn, spine soiled and split, 8vo, New York, A New Directions Book [by James Laughlin],[1953].
Footnotes
SYLVIA PLATH'S COPY OF DYLAN THOMAS'S COLLECTED POEMS. Writing to Ramona Maher, guest editor of Mademoiselle, on 16 March 1954, Plath stated categorically "Dylan Thomas is my favourite modern poet", and in her formative years he undoubtedly exerted an enormous influence on both her own poetry, and her sense of what a poet could be. On May 20 1953 Plath went on "a literary pilgrimage" to hear Thomas give a poetry reading at Amherst, and early the following year reported to her friend Gordon Lamayer that she had been listening to recordings of Thomas ("the lyric Welshman I've been mourning for these past months" following his death the previous October) reading his own poems, "making me shiver and sometimes even to cry to hear ['Do Not Go Gentle into That Good Night']" (The Letters of Sylvia Plath... 1940-1956, edited by Peter K. Steinberg & Karen V. Kukil, Faber, 2017); this a poem Plath has marked with a star symbol in this copy of the Collected Poems.
Her copy of Thomas's Poems is extensively underlined throughout, with passages marked up in the margins. Beside 'The Hunchback in the Park' she notes "hunchback's vision-", "That hunchback makes out of his vision", and "fantasy games of boys-"; alongside the text of 'Twenty-Four Years' she notes "Shroud of flesh – journey to the grave-", and, intriguingly, beneath the final stanza of 'Fern Hill', she states "Freedom with necessity".
Provenance: Sylvia Plath, ex-libris on front free endpaper and annotations in her hand; Elizabeth Sigmund (1928-2017, co-author of *Sylvia Plath in Devon: A Year's Turning*, 2014, and under her former married name of Elizabeth Compton the co-dedicatee of The Bell Jar). Beneath Plath's bookplate Elizabeth has written in the quotation ("Even amidst fierce flames...") used for Plath's headstone; by descent to the present owner.

What a holy relic of a book! I had to respond, but being somewhat retired from front-line bookselling, I felt I needed some help, so rather cheekily, I phoned a colleague who worked as the Literature Specialist at a top London booksellers. I calmly gave him the benefit of my early *head's up* and described the book as best I could. I then suggested that we get together and bid on the book together. He was as excited as I was and readily agreed to partner up on the book. We decided that we should both do some research and consider the sale-room estimate (£6000-10,000 as I recall,) in relation to what our maximum bid should be. We accomplished this with ease and waited for the sale. The auction day arrived, I sat anxiously at home in Swansea while my colleague attended the sale; I couldn't even face following the sale online. Late in the afternoon he called and gleefully said we had been successful with a bid just inside our upper limit!

Now we had to sell it on. We both began to work on maximizing the books significance, I began to send my research notes to London and eventually my colleague came up with a strong catalogue description. We also had a smart leather-backed clamshell box made for the book as Sylvia's copy was so wretched, and its covers were worn and stained. However they were telling visual proof of just how much Sylvia had read and used her copy, and they were an integral part of the story. In a short time my colleague had placed the book in a great American library, and it now resides in the American Poetry Collection at the Beinecke Library, at Yale University. Part of me wanted the book to stay in private hands, and in the UK, and I did have a go at placing it, but to no avail. The Beinecke has a mandate for significant items in the history of American poetry, and when looked at through a transatlantic lens this is actually a much more American book than it is British. So now I am proud to have been a temporary custodian and I am pleased to see it well placed in a great library.

Right, are some images of this remarkable literary survival.

Sylvia's copy – the exterior – almost read to death!

Sylvia Plath's annotated copy of the *Collected Poems of Dylan Thomas*

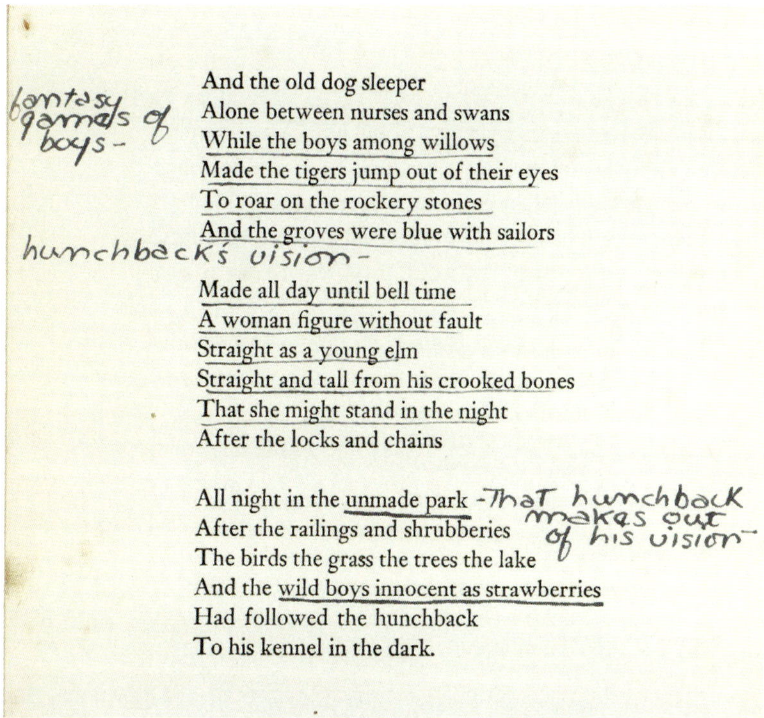

And the old dog sleeper
Alone between nurses and swans
While the boys among willows
Made the tigers jump out of their eyes
To roar on the rockery stones
And the groves were blue with sailors

Made all day until bell time
A woman figure without fault
Straight as a young elm
Straight and tall from his crooked bones
That she might stand in the night
After the locks and chains

All night in the unmade park
After the railings and shrubberies
The birds the grass the trees the lake
And the wild boys innocent as strawberries
Had followed the hunchback
To his kennel in the dark.

Sylvia's annotations to *Hunchback in the Park*

Ted Hughes and Dylan Thomas

> 'I read no contemporary poetry whatever apart from Eliot, Thomas and some Auden.'
> Hughes to Ekbert Faas.1971.

As early as 1951, during his first term at Cambridge, Ted Hughes was writing a long and very bookish letter to his sister Olwyn. After mentioning C. Day Lewis and then Auden, he writes;

> I went into a bookshop the other day and began to look for Dylan Thomas' new book of poems before I realised he hadn't produced any, or one rather.[15]

And he signs off the letter with:

> I'll send you a Dylan Thomas too.

Hughes had left Cambridge in 1954 and took a series of jobs in London; at London Zoo and in a rose nursery before he finally he got a job in the script department of J. Arthur Rank. However, he made regular trips back to Cambridge and kept up with his fellow poets and friends who remained at the University. Ted had set up home at 18 Rugby Street, a borrowed somewhat primitive flat. He was often joined by a band of artistic friends; his neighbour, Jim Downer,[16] an artist, French filmmaker Jacques Tati, Lucie Rie a ceramicist and Peter O'Toole, who was on his way to becoming a great actor. Jim recalls then all chipping in to buy batteries for their tiny radio so that they could tune in and listen to the BBC broadcast of Dylan's *Under Milk Wood* starring Richard Burton and a host a Welsh actors.

In early 1956 Ted wrote to his Cambridge Irish friend, Terence McCaughey informing him that;

> 'Danny Huws and Luke Myers and I produced a magazine. We called it *St Botolph's Review* ...the best thing about it was the party we had on the night of its first day out...more women than men'

One of those women was Sylvia Plath and it was to be her first meeting with Ted. Hughes.[17] However, when I first read this, I was more interested in Ted's mention of 'Danny Huws'.

When I first drove from Swansea to Aberystwyth in the early

1970's to offer books and manuscripts to the *National Library of Wales*, I encountered the then keeper of Manuscripts, Daniel Huws. He was a soft spoken, fine, upright and imposing Welshman. Welsh was his first language but he spoke beautiful English and it was very quickly evident that he was obviously an expert in manuscripts from the medieval period right up to and including the twentieth century and a world class librarian. One got the feeling he did not suffer fools gladly. On my first visit I was offering the library a large collection of original manuscripts, typescript poetry and correspondence by the Swansea poet and close friend of Dylan Thomas, Vernon Watkins. I was in awe of Daniel, but I think I held my own and the library bought what I offered.

That was to be the first of many visits to the library and over the course of time I think Daniel and I built up a good relationship. It might have faltered when he not only turned down some important Dylan Thomas material I offered to the library, but asked, maybe demanded, that I extricate the Vernon Watkins material included therein and offer that alone. When I had the temerity to ask why he did not want to take the Dylan Thomas materials, Daniel explained that, as he saw it, most all of the significant Dylan Thomas materials were already catalogued and filed in academic libraries across American universities and cultural institutions, so much so that the National Library of Wales could not build a significant and meaningful holding.[18] I accepted this as fact although I thought it a tad negative, but we did not fall out and I continued to visit Daniel a few times a year and encounter him at Welsh book fairs and at the Eisteddfod.

At some point on one of my visits, I mentioned Ted Hughes, and Daniel revealed that he was a good friend of Ted and Sylvia when they were all students at Cambridge University; and that he had let Ted and Sylvia stay in a London flat his family owned (and that same said flat was visited by Dylan Thomas in earlier times). He also let on that he too was a poet.[19]

Daniel would eventually write a short but wonderful account of his friendship with Ted and Sylvia. He had carefully waited

Cover Photograph © Carol Hughes

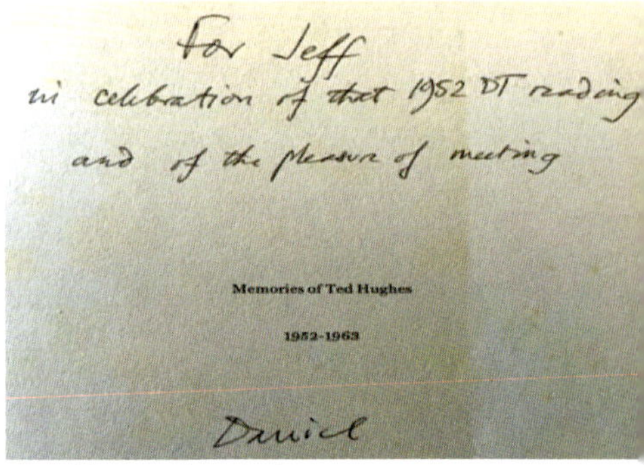

Daniels's warm inscription

until all the, sometimes hysterical comments and toxic stuff about Ted and his life with Sylvia, and his life after her death, had largely died down before in 2010, he published his own book.[20]

The book opens thus:

In the autumn term of 1952, my first term at Cambridge, Dylan Thomas came to give a reading. The reading was in the Union. He read work of his own, but my clearest memory – remembered probably because the choice was to me unexpected, is of his reading of Auden's poem *At Dirty Dick's and Sloppy Joe's*. Since that evening that poem, which I half knew, has remained in my head. That was the only time I remember seeing Dylan Thomas. Later, after I had come to know Ted, I would boast that Dylan used to sometimes, as my mother told me, come home with my father from the pub and sleep at my parent's flat in Anghalt Road Battersea. That was 1926-7, and after the war he was an occasional visitor to my father's flat in 18 Rugby Street, the flat Ted and Sylvia later lived in.'

And he continues:

'After the reading that night in Cambridge I called at the room of a friend in Pembroke College...Francis Holmes a Court who had been at the same school as me...When I was about sixteen I began to read a lot of poetry, running quickly from Keats and Shelley to Eliot and Auden and Dylan Thomas. Francis was the

> only boy at school with whom I talked about literature. At Pembroke College on that night in 1952 we were sitting in Francis's room. Late, with much commotion, three or four students burst in and joined us. One of them was Ted [Hughes]. These had also been at the Dylan Thomas reading... Ted was animated. After the reading Dylan had been taken by officials of the English Society ...to the *Eagle* in Bene't Street... Ted and his friends had followed, in the hope of being able to eavesdrop on Dylan's conversation, and had succeeded. Ted was full of the fantastical nature of what they had overheard. All I now recall is a fantasy of filling Swansea Bay with beer. I sat in the corner of the room and listened. When I got to know Ted, sometime later, Dylan Thomas was still high in the pantheon, lower only than Shakespeare, Beethoven and Yeats.

Daniel also states:

> 'When I got to know Ted the poets he talked about frequently were Yeats, Blake, Dylan Thomas, Hopkins.'

In October 1956, shortly after Ted and Sylvia had married, Ted writes to her from London and reminds her:

> 'Don't forget to send me that book with the Dylan Thomas letters in it. I would like to read what else is in it.'

By 1959 Sylvia Plath had been married to Ted Hughes for three years, having first met in Cambridge in 1956. In 1959 they were both included together in an article in Mademoiselle, a feature, entitled *Four Young Poets*.[21] The article begins with a quote that cites the importance of the influence of Dylan Thomas on the poets who came after him;

> 'Two events shook the concept of the poet as the impractical, unimportant figure of our time – the holocaust of T.S. Eliot's *The Waste Land* in the twenties and the drama and death of Dylan Thomas that rated a *Times* editorial in the fifties.'

As someone who has spent most of my life in the world of books and libraries, so indeed had Daniel Huws, who has spent his working life surrounded by the magnificent collection of rare books and manuscripts housed in The National Library of Wales high above Aberystwyth. In his brief memoir of Ted, Daniel writes of Ted's love of curious books and Ted's relationship with printed books and their profound influence on him. Dan explains that the fact that at Cambridge students were allowed to browse in the vast stacks of the University's magnificent Library, areas which are usually reserved for Library staff only. This freedom of access allowed Ted to wander in to this warren of shelves with that special scent, an aroma of old vellum, paper, and leather. This liberty was a major influence, when in his third year, Ted decided to change his degree from English to Anthropology and Archaeology as he found the shelves of books of Folklore, Myths, Mysticism, Magic and Ethnographica so much more interesting than the literature canon. What he discovered in these arcane works would later inform his poetry.

I was to witness something of this the first time I met Ted at Leonard Baskin's Devon home. The meeting took place in the incredible library in their ancient Devon manor-house home that Lenny and his wife Lisa, had amassed from the book trade in both America and Europe. Lisa and Lenny both suffered from *bibliomania* – as indeed do I. They were both fanatical book collectors and had become very good customers. I was a bookseller first. but this also served to facilitate my own passion to collect. However, although Ted loved books with a passion, he loved them for what was inside them, he did not need to possess them; he read and studied them, enjoyed them, but he was not a collector. That day, before Ted arrived, I had shown Leonard a handsome, rare Victorian, leather-bound, quarto; it was a detailed history of the bagpipes, in all their manifestations in various nations. It intrigued Leonard, he loved any bibliographic curiosity, but it wasn't for him, but he thought Ted might be interested in the book. When Ted arrived we were introduced and I was instructed by Lenny to show Ted the bagpipe book. Ted did like. He was intrigued by it; he relaxed on the Settee and immersed himself in it, but he didn't need to own it. The power of books was different for him; it did not need possession...

Daniel Huws was to remain a life-long friend of Ted's and he and his wife Helga often spent time with Ted and Sylvia. Surprisingly, Daniel reveals that it was Ted, the Englishman, who introduced Daniel, the Welshman, to the poetry of two other great 20th Century Anglo-Welsh poets; Edward Thomas and R.S. Thomas. These two poets were also part of Dylan Thomas' background.

Dylan Thomas was also a lover of Edward Thomas' poetry and he made radio programmes about him and would also read his poems on his American tours. On 11 November 1985, in Poet's Corner in Westminster Abbey, a Memorial Stone commemorating sixteen First World War Poets was unveiled by Ted Hughes, who, as poet Laureate delivered the address in which he described Edward Thomas as '*the father of us all*', such was his admiration for the poet.

R.S. Thomas, although older than Dylan was a contemporary of his, but he and Dylan seemed to mutually agree to stay distances apart, both geographically and intellectually. R.S. in his later life was also a contemporary of Ted's, and R.S. did write a poem for Ted, *In Memory of Ted Hughes*

> I think looking askance
> into nature's mirror he saw,
> even as I do, a god
> hiding his face.'

At the funeral service for Ted, held in Devon, his great friend and fellow poet, Seamus Heaney, read Dylan Thomas's *Do not go gentle into that good night*.

Dylan Thomas and Ted Hughes had other commonalities; they both had mixed feelings about Robert Graves. Dylan praises Graves among other First World War poets, in his precocious essay, *Modern Poetry*, which he wrote for the Swansea Grammar School magazine in 1929, when he had just turned 15;

> What changed the course of English poetry completely was the Great War, the brutality of which...caused some of the bitterest and loveliest poetry in the English language to be written...Out of the darkness came the clear light of genius: Siegfried Sassoon...Rupert Brooke...Robert Nichols...Wilfred Owen, Robert Graves, Julian Grenfell and other heroes who built towers of beauty upon the ashes of their lives.'

A year later, the now sixteen-year-old schoolboy sent some of his earliest poems to Robert Graves for comment; Graves blandly deemed them 'unexceptional'. Much later Dylan would include Graves' poem *Welsh Incident* in his American poetry readings. Thankfully he was dead before Graves attacked his writing in his infamous series of Oxford Clark lectures.[22]

Ted Hughes was very much affected and inspired by Graves' *The White Goddess*,[23] which fitted into his other readings into folklore and the occult and he was pleased that he introduced the book and it's meanings to Sylvia Plath. Replying to his critic and friend and correspondent Keith Sagar[24]. through his sister Olwyn, Ted states;

> The real immediate influence he [Ted] had on her, apart from increasing her concentration on poetry was that he supplied a fully worked out belief in the poetic mythology expounded by Robert Graves in his book *The White Goddess*.

In her recent and monumental study of Sylvia Plath, Heather Clark[25]. writes in her *Prologue* about Ted and Sylvia;

> Their relationship was soldered on the work of Lawrence, Yeats, and Thomas.

Dylan Thomas and Ted Hughes were both ornithophiles and birds of many species fly throughout their poems and prose. If we take just one species – the Curlew – as an example, Dylan Thomas' poem, *In The White Giant's Thig*h, opens with the bird's distinctive call;

> 'Through throats where many rivers meet, the curlews cry,
> Under the conceiving moon, on the high chalk hill,
> And there this night I walk in the white giant's thigh
> Where barren as boulders women lie longing still
> To labour and love though they lay down long ago.'

In the poem Dylan Thomas's brings to life a superstition that infertile women could conceive if they made love in the thigh of the white giant on the chalk hill at Cerne Abbas.

'They yearn with tongues of curlews for the unconceived'

Ted Hughes also cherished the curlew. He grew up later and in a different landscape to Dylan's Wales. For him it was the rugged Calder Valley and Pennine Moors where he responded to the Curlew's call. Hughes wrote an entire poem dedicated to the curlew. In the poem *Curlews*,[26]. the first stanza describes the birds as they take off;

Curlews Lift
1.
Out of the maternal watery blue lines

Stripped of all but their cry
Some twists of near-inedible sinew

They slough off
The robes of bilberry blue
The cloud-stained bogland

They veer up and eddy away over
The stone horns

They trail a long, dangling, falling aim
Across water

Lancing their voices
Through the skin of thin light

Drinking the nameless and naked
Through trembling bills

In November 1966, Ted Hughes reviewed Constantine Fitzgibbon's book, *The Selected Letters of Dylan Thomas*[27] for the New Statesman. I have just managed to get a copy[28] of an extract from the review and I think it's worth quoting here:

> Everything we associate with a poem in its shadowy tenant and part of its meaning, no matter how new critical purist we try to be...Thomas's life, letters and legends belong to his poetry, in that they make it mean more... Poetry he said, was to drag into "the clean nakedness of the light even more of the hidden causes that Freud could realize."
> He made a half-conscious attempt to take on all the underground life that the uppercrustish, militant, colonial-suppressive cast of the English intelligentsia exudes. It is apt that he seemed physically such a representative of the old Moorish strain of blood in South Wales.'

Ted ends his review with this;

> All life was one and he was open to it
> and "he'd be a damn fool" if he weren't[29].

Elsewhere in this collection of Ted's prose writings, Ekbert Faas includes transcripts of interviews he conducted with Ted. This quote is from a 1971 interview; *Ted Hughes and Crow* published in the London Magazine, in which Ted declares:

> As for Thomas, *Deaths and Entrances* was a Holy Book for me for quite a time when it came out.

In August 1970, Ted Hughes married Carol Orchard, a nurse who he had met in his main place of residence, North Tawton in Devon, and they settled into his house, Court Green. I like to think that this marriage brought Ted even closer to Dylan Thomas as Carol, although born in Crediton, had strong connections with Swansea. Her grandfather was a Welsh coal miner, her father, Jack Orchard,[30] was a Devonshire farmer but her mother, Minnie (nee Evans) was from Fforestfach, Swansea, a bustling, very 'Swansea' urban suburb to the east of the town. Minnie went to school in Glanmor Girls School in the Uplands, a more middle-class area near where Dylan Thomas grew up. She told her children that when she was a schoolgirl in the 1930's she recalled seeing the real *Hunchback in the Park*, of Dylan's famous poem. Minnie left Swansea in 1937 aged 17 to train as a nurse in Devon. She met her husband Jack, a farmer's son, at a dance and they married in 1944. Carol and her elder sister Jean used to go over on the ferry from Ilfracombe in north Devon across to Mumbles Pier every summer to stay with their grandmother in Carmarthen Road, Fforestfach. Mumbles is an ex-fishing village just a short distance westwards towards the Gower peninsula. The village is now an affluent middle-class area popular with tourists, visitors and holiday-makers. It was once famous for the *Mumbles Mile*,[31] a seafront stretch of road that hosted 20 public houses and was a regular local stag-night or birthday celebration destination, where mainly young males tried to down a pint in every bar, a very demanding pub-crawl with the emphasis on crawl. As a lover of pubs it was a regular haunt for young Dylan Thomas, who as a member and actor with Swansea Little Theatre, used to rehearse there regularly in their nearby headquarters.

In 1977 a Dylan Thomas Society was founded in Swansea, the prime movers were one of Dylan's oldest friends, the composer Daniel Jones,[32] and senior members of Swansea Little Theatre. A memorial monument to Dylan was suggested. Two other of Dylan's oldest friends, and the sculptor Ronald Cour, and the poet, Vernon Watkins and it was they who went to a local quarry and selected a huge piece of granite to feature as a for a memorial to Dylan. Ron carved a line from *Fern Hill* onto it and the stone was installed in Cwmdonkin Park on 9 November 1963 – the tenth anniversary of his death.

Ted Hughes was also one of several influential writers who joined with American President Jimmy Carter and luminaries such as Richard Burton, in lobbying the Dean of Westminster Abbey to install a memorial to Dylan Thomas. Arguing the case for Dylan Thomas to be honoured, Hughes wrote to the Dean;

> I regard him as a true genius with the holiest and most absolute dedication to his calling that it is possible for a poet to have. His work was a profoundly illuminated event in our literature. It is recognized by the poets of all other nations as A poetic human testimony of the most important kind.

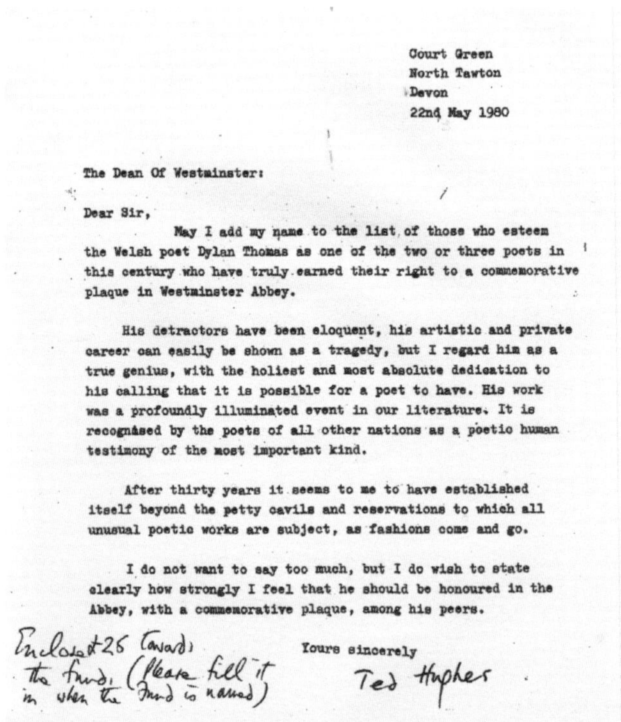

Court Green
North Tawton
Devon
22nd May 1980

The Dean Of Westminster:

Dear Sir,

May I add my name to the list of those who esteem the Welsh poet Dylan Thomas as one of the two or three poets in this century who have truly earned their right to a commemorative plaque in Westminster Abbey.

His detractors have been eloquent, his artistic and private career can easily be shown as a tragedy, but I regard him as a true genius, with the holiest and most absolute dedication to his calling that it is possible for a poet to have. His work was a profoundly illuminated event in our literature. It is recognised by the poets of all other nations as a poetic human testimony of the most important kind.

After thirty years it seems to me to have established itself beyond the petty cavils and reservations to which all unusual poetic works are subject, as fashions come and go.

I do not want to say too much, but I do wish to state clearly how strongly I feel that he should be honoured in the Abbey, with a commemorative plaque, among his peers.

Enclosed £25 towards the fund. (Please fill it in when the fund is named)

Yours sincerely

Ted Hughes

Ted Hughes' letter to the Dean of Westminster Abbey

November 9 1963: The Fern Hill memorial for Dylan Thomas is dedicated in Cwmdonkin Park, Swansea, by fellow poet Vernon Watkins and sculptor Ronald Cour, who lettered the piece of Granite. Its unveiling marked the 10th anniversary of Dylan's death[33]

Dylan's stone in POET'S CORNER was finally unveiled on St. David's Day 1982. Ted's joined him in 2011

Ted & Carol at Dylan's birthplace[34]

Photo © @Robert Orchard

Carol did bring Ted to Swansea. In 1983 they came to Wales to see her brother, Robert, in Cardiff and they all made a visit to Swansea, where they visited Dylan's Birthplace. It was not yet open as a museum attraction but they were photographed in the front garden. They also visited Laugharne and went to Dylan's Boathouse and had a drink in his favourite Laugharne pub, Browns Hotel. (known by locals as *The Browns*) The above photograph may well have been taken when Ted and Carol attended at least one Annual Dinner of the Dylan Thomas Society. They were accompanied by Carol's brother Robert Orchard and his wife, Ainslie. It was around 1979-1983, when, John Rhys Thomas, the Swansea headmaster and stalwart of the Swansea's Little Theatre and later the touring Swansea Players, was heavily involved. The actor, Gareth Armstrong, was the guest speaker and Robert Orchard recalls that Ted met and spoke to Daniel Jones that evening. Ted was then made an Honorary President of the DT Society and remained so for some years.

And Ted Hughes still reaches out to help Dylan Thomas posthumously; this was a recent headline and article from the Wales Online News website;

> **Surprise twist in the battle to keep Dylan Thomas' childhood home in Cwmdonkin Drive open thanks to late poet Ted Hughes.**
> **The fight to save legendary writer Dylan Thomas' family home has given a massive boost - thanks to a former Poet Laureate.**

Surprise twist in the battle to keep Dylan Thomas' childhood home in Cwmdonkin Drive open thanks to late poet Ted Hughes.

The fight to save legendary writer Dylan Thomas' family home has given a massive boost – thanks to a former Poet Laureate.

In 2020. the privately run and self – supporting curator and manager of Dylan's Birthplace, Geoff Haden, started an online crowd-funding campaign to raise money for the continuing necessary and urgent repairs that the near 120-year-old semi-detached house, at number 5 Cwmdonkin Drive, Swansea,[35]. is in need of. More by luck that judgment many of the original features of the house have survived, and those that had been removed, Geoff and his team of volunteers have lovingly replaced, but, but like the painting the Seven Bridge, it is an ongoing, costly, never-ending business. Geoff had set his crowd-funding target at £15,000 and was amazed and overjoyed when Ted's widow Carol Hughes donated a generous £3,500 on behalf of the Ted Hughes Estate towards the cost of repainting the dilapidated outside of the house.

Carol Hughes commented;

> "The significance of Dylan Thomas's birthplace as a literary landmark, and as part of the cultural heritage of Wales and beyond, cannot be overestimated."

Not only that, her friend Clare Reihill, a trustee of the T.S. Eliot Foundation then stepped in and matched the Hughes' contribution to ensure urgent repairs and redecoration could go ahead. Geoff was now already almost half-way towards his target and the appeal went on to achieve its ambitious aim. Clare Reihill made this generous comment on behalf of the T.S. Eliot Foundation.

> "T.S. Eliot admired Dylan Thomas[36] and actually personally helped him out financially so we're delighted to match the Hughes estate by pledging £3,500 as well... It's the least we could do and I'm delighted to contribute on behalf of the Eliot estate."

What great, worthy and positive gestures by all parties concerned.

The refurbished Blue plaque and the recently added Welsh version, at 5 Cwmdonkin

1. 'Young, with movie-star looks, he was a senior studying English at Amherst College and she was at Smith when they met. From the first moment, there was a strong rapport between them: they lived only a mile apart in Wellesley; their mothers had married Germans and, perhaps most important, they shared a love of literature. In 1954, they became unofficially engaged, or 'pinned' as the slang had it, before their mutual ardour faded.' From a review in the *Daily Mail*.

2. Given that both Sylvia and Ted were deeply interested in serious astrology and horoscopes, it is surprising that this co-incidence of Sylvia sharing the same day/month of birth, albeit 18 years apart, as Dylan Thomas, does not seem to have been noticed by either of them.

3. While at Smith, Sylvia was taught by, and got know, the American artist Leonard Baskin. He made no small impression on Sylvia and in her first poetry collection the poem, *Sculptor* is dedicated '*For Leonard Baskin*'. Leonard would also become great friends with Ted, collaborating with him on numerous books and providing many powerful images for Ted's poems. It was through my long friendship with Lenny and his wife Lisa that I got to meet Ted and Carol.

4. Sylvia cherished this memory; writing in her Journal in March 1958, she describes a long conversation with Miss Mill an elderly lady ('fat dowdy... ugly') about Dylan Thomas's reading at Mount Holyoke; 'the Dylan Thomas story lasted till dinnertime'

5. In 1953, Mademoiselle's circulation was over 500,000 and it was well known for publishing established writers such as Truman Capote, Alice Munro, Tennessee Williams and William Faulkner, as well as searching out and launching new young writers. It was one of the three main up-market fashion and arts magazines based in New York – the others two being *Vogue* and *Harper's Bazaar*. Dylan Thomas would contribute to, and be featured in all three.

6. A villanelle is a somewhat difficult fixed verse form with, with a set of fixed rules governing verse form and a repeated rhyme scheme.

7. For this, and much of this section I have used *Pain, Parties, Work Sylvia Plath in New York, Summer 1953*. by Elizabeth Winder. (Harper 2013). It is a detailed and well researched and very readable account but not always strong on facts and sources.

8. *Sylvia Plath Letters Home. Faber and Faber 1976. Edited by Aurelia Schober Plath (Sylvia's mother)*

9. Ann Jones was not Dylan's 'nanny-nurse' but a favourite aunt. When he was a young boy, Dylan he would spend holidays with her on her farm in rural Carmarthenshire named Fern Hill. Her death inspired this poem and his holidays at her home inspired perhaps his greatest poem *Fern Hill*.

10. And to add to the irony on the reverse of the letter are original drafts for some of Captain Cat's lines from *Under Milk Wood*.

11. In her book, Elizabeth Winder has a chapter with this title and the quotes here are taken from this chapter.

12. It is worth remembering what happened when, on his first trip to New York, Dylan Thomas went into the offices of *Harper's Bazaar* magazine (a rival to *Mademoiselle*), to offer them, for publication, his prose piece, *A Child's Christmas in Wales*. He was seen by a new young employee, Pearl Kazin – and this meeting led to Dylan and Pearl having intense love affair. Some years ago, I bought and later published Dylan's love letters to Pearl (*A Pearl of Great Price*. Parthian 2014) and I could not help ruminating if this outcome would have been similar if Dylan had met the already infatuated Sylvia?. Later in her life Sylvia would be taught by Alfred Kazin – Pearl's brother. A synchronicity. As I was writing this I visited a Swansea writer and old friend, Jo Mazelis, we got talking about Plath and mentioned that I had been thinking on what might have happened if Sylvia had met Dylan Thomas and she cooly announced that she had just written and published a short story based on that notion, it's called *Atlantic Exchange* and it's in her 2022 book, *BLISTER and Other Stories*.

13. The flat was located at 18 Rugby Street. It was being lent to Ted by his Welsh Cambridge friend Daniel Huws, whose father Richard Huws had lived there in the forties and had met Dylan Thomas in local pubs they both frequented and Dylan sometimes crashed on the floor there. Sylvia must have lapped up this story.

14. Dylan Thomas *A New Casebook*. Edited by Goodby & Wigginton. Palgrave.2001. Chapter 10. *Later Poems* and *Under Milk Wood*.

15. The book Ted wanted to buy was Dylan's forthcoming *Collected Poems 1934-1952*. Dent.1952. for which he was awarded the Foyles poetry prize for the book.

16. Jim Downer would later illustrate Ted's a children's rhyme and describes this event in his afterword to the book; *Timothy The Tug* by Jim Downer and Ted Hughes Thames & Hudson. 2010.

17. It was at the party for the launch of their new Poetry Magazine St. Botolph's Review and that evening it was Daniel Huws who Sylvia first approached; to challenge him on a scathing review of he had recently written of one of her a poem. Later she met Ted.

18. Although I saw Daniel's point at the time, things did change. Over the ensuing decades the Library was gifted some good Dylan Thomas materials. Daniel retired in 1992 and a new regime made some judicious purchases at auction and I acted for them at in the London Salerooms on one or two occasions and bought several groups of Thomas letters. They eventually reached for my extensive personal collection of Dylans Thomas materials build up over 40 years and they now do have a, 'significant collection' of Dylan Thomas.

19. His first collection was *Noth*. Martin Secker & Warburg.1972; followed by a small pamphlet, *From an Old Book of Riddles*. Sceptre Press 1974. And then his best collection, *Quarry*, which Ted's publishers, Faber & Faber, published in 1999.

20. Daniel Huws: *Memories of Ted Hughes*. 1952-1963. Hollis

21. This review of 4 poets, was published in *Mademoiselle Magazine* in January, 1959.

22. The infamous, *Clark Lectures* delivered in Cambridge in 1954 and 1955 and Oxford between 1961 and 1965.

23. Robert Graves; *The White Goddess* a Historical Grammar of Poetic Myth. Faber & Faber. 1948.

24. Poet and Critic *The Letters of Ted Hughes & Keith Sagar*. British Library Edited by Keith Sagar.

25. Heather Clark: *RED COMET* The Short and Blazing Art of Sylvia Plath. Jonathan Cape. 2020.

26. From Ted Hughes: *The Remains of Elmet*. Faber. London 1979.

27. Constantine Fitzgibbon: *The Selected Letters of Dylan Thomas*. Dent 1966.

28. Ekbert Faas: Ted Hughes: *The Unaccommodated Universe*. Black Sparrow Press Santa Barbara. 1980. An uncommon book especially in the UK.

29. Hughes is quoting from Dylans' *Note* to his *Collected Poems 1934 1952*. I wrote these poems ... for the love of Man and in praise of God, and I'd be a damn fool, if they weren't.

30. The opening poems in Ted's 1979 poetry collection *Moortown* are inspired by Jack Orchard, who managed the farm of that name owned by Ted and Carol. The book is dedicated to his memory.

31. In 1934 Dylan wrote to a Swansea drinking pal lamenting the strength of local ale; *Oh, woe, woe, woe unto Mumbles and the oystered beer.*

32. Immediately after Dylan's death Daniel Jones wrote a symphony in homage to Dylan; *Symphony No 4 In Memory of Dylan Thomas*. He also wrote the music for the songs Dylan wrote for Under Milk Wood and he edited the posthumous collection of Dylan's prose *A Prospect of the Sea* Dent 1955. In 1971 he edited an edition of Dylan's poetry; *The Poems of Dylan Thomas*. Also for Dent. He also wrote a memoir *My Friend Dylan Thomas*. Dent.1977. More on this in Chapter 6.

33. Although this memorial was the first and for a very long time, the only such tribute in the city, it was not a council project but a private one, supported by a group of Dylan's oldest friends. It was eventually funded by the two young American women; Barbara Holdridge and Marianne Mantell, who had founded *Caedmon Records* in America, in order to release vinyl L P recordings of Dylan reading his own and other writers' poems and stories. They heard of the memorial stone project and sent a telegram to Vernon just saying; "WE WILL COVER ALL COSTS".

34. The faint appearance of the blue plaque is no fault of the photographer, Carol's brother Robert. That plaque was the original that had been funded and installed by TWW (Television Wales & West.) It was the idea of Dylan's Swansea friend, Wynford Vaughan Thomas, who worked for TWW. The day of its unveiling, Nov 10th 1963, the 10th anniversary of Dylan's death. On the same day the BBC screened Jack Howells' Oscar winning documentary on Dylan Thomas, voiced by Richard Burton. This tired-looking plaque was replaced in 2008 by Geoff Haden and, in 2022 he added a Welsh language plaque beside it.

35. Dylan Thomas was often disparaging about his birthplace describing it as '*A mortgaged villa in an upper-class professional row. A small not very well painted, gateless house...very nice, very respectable.*

36. In the 1930's T. S. Eliot was at the helm of Faber & Faber. Dylan visited him and showed him his early poems. Eliot was encouraging, gave him some money but did not offer to publish him. 1934 Dylan did offer him the chance to publish his first collection but got no immediate response so the book went into as a joint publication between *The Sunday Referee* newspaper and the Bookseller, David Archer of the *Parton Bookshop* as joint publishers. However, Eliot did change his mind and contacted Dylan but by then it was too late so Dylan's *18 Poems* was not a Faber book. Eliot did then go on to publish other Anglo-Welsh writers; Vernon Watkins, Idris Davies and Lynette Roberts – all three good friends of Dylan Thomas.

Charles was totally accepted into the Gypsy clan and was taught to play Flamenco Guitar

11.

Dylan Thomas: Charles Fisher & the Kardomah.

The Kardomah, – 'My Home Sweet Homah.'
Dylan Thomas in a letter to Charlie Fisher

September 1953. I had just enjoyed a very low-key fifth birthday in the East End of London as Dylan Thomas was dying in a New York City hospital. At that point he was totally beyond my ken. It would be decade before I had any kind of notion who Dylan Thomas was. The only Welsh thing I then had in London was my mother, Lavinia May Parry. She was from a small Monmouthshire mining village – YNYSDDU, a place-name which I could not fathom nor pronounce but it was my introduction to the mystery of the Welsh language. She was not a Welsh speaker but she would regularly scold me with Welsh phrases such as; *Ach Y fi, you dirty mochyn!*[1] In the early sixties I heard of this Welsh poet through Bob Dylan, who changed his surname from Zimmerman to Dylan in homage to Thomas; and the Beatles' *Sgt. Pepper* album cover, which features both Bob and Dylan. In another decade, in the early 70's and by a strange run of pleasing coincidences I was in Swansea, married to a Swansea girl and running *DYLANS BOOKSTORE* – primarily a second-hand bookstore, but with a proud display of gleaming new J.M.Dent, paperback copies of all Dylan Thomas' works then in print.

The Kardomah, my 'home sweet Homah'
Dylan Thomas in a letter to Charlie Fisher

In those early years selling books in Swansea I came to realise that although Dylan Thomas died tragically young, his local friends from school, coffee bar and then the pub, seemed not to have lived such bibulous and unhealthy lives as Dylan and most of them were still enjoying healthy lives in Swansea and London and elsewhere. Over the course of my 50 years selling books I've been lucky enough to have met and become friends with many of those men-friends who, in popular parlance, have become known as the Kardomah *Gang*. I'm not sure such a gang ever really existed and I believe, as do many others, that it is just another piece of gimmicky journalise, (I abhor *gang*; and can just about manage *Kardomah Boys*). Central member Alfred Janes will put it straight a few pages below. The notion is that this group of intelligent, arty, local young men used to meet up for intellectual conversations and masculine banter in Swansea's *Kardomah Café; Kardomah* being the name of a nationwide chain of coffee shop/restaurants.

The group loosely comprised: Dylan Thomas, poet, Alfred Janes, artist, Mervyn Levy, artist, Daniel Jones, classical musician and polymath, Vernon Watkins, poet, Charles Fisher, poet, journalist and adventurer, Bert Trick, communist grocer, Tom Warner, musician, John Prichard occasional writer, and less frequently, Wynford Vaughan Thomas, journalist, broadcaster and bon viveur and Mabley Owen. Over the years I encountered all of them apart from Tom Warner[2] and John Prichard who I never met. I also did not meet Bert Trick but became very good friends with his son Kerith Trick. I never met, nor know much, if anything about Mabley Owen, except that Dylan named a family dog Mabley. Dylan Thomas wrote them into Welsh literary history in his brilliant first radio play, *Return Journey*.[3] In the play Dylan revisits the Swansea of his youth searching for his former self. He eavesdrops on a conversation as his pals envisage their futures as they sit talking in the *Kardomah*;

> 'Here, he and his friends would talk of how 'Dan Jones was going to compose the most prodigious symphony, Fred Janes paint the most miraculously meticulous picture, Charlie Fisher catch the poshest trout, Vernon Watkins and Young Thomas write the most boiling poems...'

He then encounters a local 'passer-by' and asks if he knew 'young Thomas'. And he answers,

> 'Oh him! He owes me half a crown. I haven't seen him since the old Kardomah days He wasn't a reporter then, he'd just left school. Him and Charlie Fisher – Charlie's got whiskers now...'

Later, five of the group added to the myth when they made a

Charles Fisher, in uniform holding an Abacus. But with splendid whiskers!

The facsimile of the Vernon Watkin's original *Swansea and the Arts* script which I put together for the Dylan Thomas Centre

radio broadcast – *Swansea and the Arts*,[4] with Dylan as the compere and presenter. They all spoke, extolling the virtues of the town for artists of all kinds.

The posthumous media hype surrounding the group would portray and promote them as the vanguard of Swansea's 1930's literary and artistic renaissance although the more grounded and honest artist Fred Janes doubted that they all, or even half of them ever sat in the same room together. However, Gwen Watkins wrote a play about them and there was a BBC televised drama documentary made and broadcast which has made them '*world famous*' but just in Wales. But not only did I eventually get to know many of them, more importantly I bought many of their personal libraries, papers, letters, portraits and ephemera, concerning the focal point of the 'group' – Dylan Thomas.

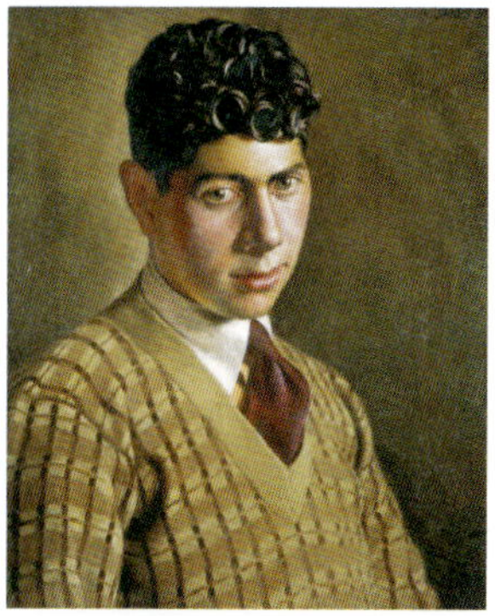

The first of them I encountered was Mervyn Levy, a Jewish artist, he was a very small man, but he made up for his lack of height by his smart, artistic appearance in both his dress and his coiffeur. He was well into his 70's and still somewhat priapic and almost always has a somewhat younger lady-friend in tow. When I first met him he sported a fine head of silver, quaffed-back, wavy-hair and a well-trimmed, matching, silver goatee-beard. Fred Janes always joked that he painted three portraits of Mervyn but Mervyn never painted him once. The third portrait (below) is the Mervyn I knew.

Mervyn had somehow made his way from Swansea art school to art school in London and then became a broadcasting artist, making early, black-and-white art programmes. He presented a long running series *Painting*

for Housewives on the BBC, which made him a 'Housewife's Favourite' in the fifties, before he went on became a serious writer on art and a hustling art dealer with plenty of guile and cheek.

Mervyn boasted to me that he and he alone took care of Dylan's sex education; maybe by loaning him a copy of his book; *The Moons of Paradise Reflections of the Breast in Art*. In the late 70's Mervyn swanned into my shop in Salubrious Passage for the first time and proceeded to badger and bully me into selling him a recent acquisition: a copy of an *Anthology of English Poetry* which bore Dylan's signature on the front endpaper. It was the first signed Dylan Thomas I had ever bought and I was very reluctant to sell it, but he begged and pleaded with me, almost tearing up as he told me how, during an acrimonious divorce, his first wife had burnt all his precious original letters and manuscripts and signed books that Dylan had given him. I succumbed, he beat me down on the modest price I suggested and left smug and smiling. Less than a month later, the very same copy turned up on a catalogue from the leading London dealers in rare modern literature but now it was gently improved by Mervyn who had added some judicious pencil underlining to a number of poems had given a detailed new provenance, declaring that it was the very book that Dylan used on all his U. S. reading tours! In spite of this we remained friends because he was such a lively character and a crucial part of Dylan's early life. Mervyn and Alfred Janes had both gone off to art school in London and they took young Dylan into their hovel of a flat when Dylan decided to move to London in November of 1934, just after his 20th birthday. Dylan immediately typed an over-excited postcard back to back to Dan Jones in Swansea, in which he describes himself and his flatmates as 'mannered pigs'.

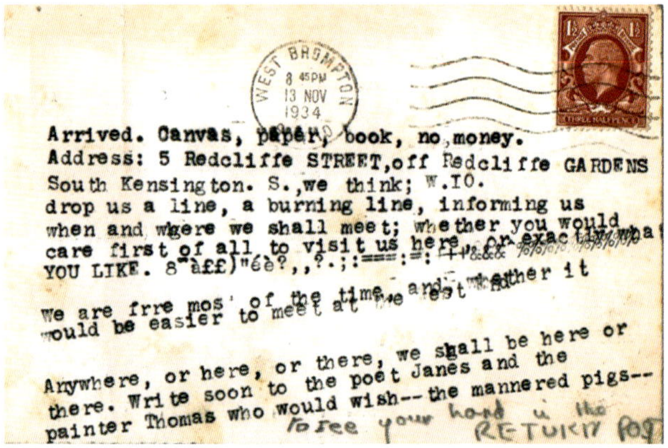

Arrived. Canvas, paper, book, no money.
Address: 5 Redcliffe STREET, off Redcliffe GARDENS
South Kensington. S., we think; W.10.
drop us a line, a burning line, informing us
when and where we shall meet; whether you would
care first of all to visit us here, or exactly wha
YOU LIKE.
We are frre mos' of the time and whether it
would be easier to meet at the
Anywhere, or here, or there, we shall be here or
there. Write soon to the poet Janes and the
painter Thomas who would wish-- the mannered pigs--
to see your hand in the RETURN POST

The 'mannered pigs' write home from London to Dan Jones in Swansea

I did not know Dan Jones well enough to offer him more than just a cursory nod when I encountered him, a gesture which often went unrequited. In his last years Dan lived just 500 yards away from me in Newton village, up above Mumbles. I would see him most days slowly shuffling up and down the lane for his twice daily visits to his local pub, *The Newton Inn*, at first with his wife but after she passed away he would cut a sad solitary figure. But Dan was nothing short of a polymath genius; a serious classical musician and composer; but also with a real flare with languages; he spoke over a dozen, including Chinese and Russian which made him a shoe-in for the Bletchley Park code-breaking hub during World War II.[5] I think Dan viewed me as an arriviste who had come to Swansea and jumped on the Dylan Thomas bandwagon (which I think is a tad harsh). Luckily for me, after he died in his eighties, his daughter and her husband were happy to offer me, perhaps,

MERVYN LEVY leads a very full life in his roles of writer, broadcaster, lecturer, journalist and art critic, as well as being Features Editor of *The Studio*.
He has written several books on painting as well as a monograph on L. S. Lowry, A.R.A., and a dictionary of art terminology.

The dust jacket and the inner blurb of Mervyn's *Moons of Paradise*

Fred Janes painting of the bombed Kardomah after the Blitz

the single greatest haul of Dylan Thomas materials I have ever acquired.

In 1967, just a few years before I got to Swansea, Vernon Watkins had died, aged 61, playing tennis in Seattle, where he had gone to teach a course on modern poetry at the University of Washington. However, I became very good friends with his widow Gwen, who, as I write, is approaching 100. I met her in Swansea's other used book shop – *Ralph The Books*, which was owned and run by Ralph Wishart, himself a good friend of Dylan Thomas. I began buying good academic books from Gwen and the few remaining Dylan related items she had left and eventually I handled the remaining huge manuscript archive that Vernon left behind (now in The National Library of Wales). I think I learned more about Dylan Thomas from Gwen than I did from any other person or book – every time I called to see her I'd ask her a different question and she always had an answer. She never told me the same story twice unless I asked her to. In 1983 she published a book about Dylan and Vernon. *Portrait of a Friend*.[6] is a fine book, which Paul Ferris, Dylan and Caitlin's biographer and the editor of Dylan's *Collected Letters*, declared his opinion that it was the best, most balanced and truthful book on Dylan Thomas.

As I write this just after Christmas 2023, Gwen celebrated her 100th birthday! And we are still good friends and I still call to see her in the Nursing home back at Pennard, Gower, nearby where she lived in the cliff-top bungalow with Vernon after their marriage.

Fred Janes was perhaps the nicest man of them all; quiet and dignified, with a soft voice and gentle manner and also a quite amazing artist. He and Charles Fisher were the two dapper gentlemen of the group. They both loved to scrub-up on a Saturday night, don their glad-rags and go out dancing and socialising, as this picture of them at a dinner-dance in Swansea's Brangwyn Hall, so wonderfully captures. The two girls at the back of the picture are the Phillips sisters Vera and Evelyn Killick. They were close both friends to many of the Kardomah habitues. Vera was a good friend to Dylan and later with Caitlin too. When Vera married a serviceman William Killick, during the war, Dylan was their Best Man. But Vera and Dylan were also embroiled in what has become known as the Majoda Incident, perhaps the one truly sensational event in Dylan's colourful short life. Dylan and Caitlin lived as neighbours in with Vera in two adjoining cliff-top primitive bungalows in New Quay during the wars. When Vera's husband, William, a serviceman who was fighting behind enemy lines in Greece, came home on leave he was a bad way. Today he

Fred is on the left and Charles on the right – probably circa 1935 – in Swansea's, new Guildhall. The girl next to Fred is Mary Ross, who Fred would later marry

would immediately be diagnosed as suffering from PTSD, but Killick received no such help. He argued with Dylan in a pub and a scuffle ensued. He left the pub, went back to his bungalow and collected his weapons and went and fired his machine gun into and through the walls of the wooden bungalow named *Majoda*, inside which were with Dylan, Caitlin some friends and babies huddled behind the sofa! Killick then entered with a grenade in his hand which he threatened to detonate. Dylan showed no small amount of courage in talking the distressed soldier around and calming things down. This whole nasty debacle was the basis for the glossy and glitzy 2014 film, *The Edge of Love* which centred on the sensational *Majoda Incident*.

I first met Fred Janes at an exhibition at Swansea's *Glynn Vivian Art Gallery*, but I would later visit him in his delightful home in Dulwich, very close to the splendid *Dulwich Picture Gallery*, the world's first, purpose-built public art gallery, founded in 1811 when Sir Francis Bourgeois RA, bequeathed his collection of old masters "for the inspection of the public". Fred made great use of it and also taught in the local Art School. He continued to paint in a variety of styles but each work was executed with meticulous care and craft. We never did much business together but he was a joy to sit and talk with, as was his sweet wife Mary, who fetched us tea and cake. I love his paintings, especially his early still-life paintings and his exquisite portraits. His paintings are hard to come by and I cherish the few I have acquired over the years.

One day towards the end of the last century a local solicitor came into my Salubrious Passage bookstore. Stuart Thomas of *D.O.Thomas & Co.* was no ordinary solicitor. He had been at Swansea Grammar School with Dylan Thomas and, on joining his father's law firm, he became solicitor to Dylan's parents and then later to act as solicitor for Dylan Thomas and his family. On Dylan's death, Stuart became one of the three founding members of the *Dylan Thomas Trust*.[7] I have had various run-ins with him over the years, mostly a tad uncomfortable and negative[8] but this day was different. In his usual grumpy growl he asked if I would be interested in a large collection of books in a house in Pembrokeshire. I declared an interest so we arranged a day when I would follow him down west above Haverfordwest.

And that is how I got to acquire the library of the recently deceased, Wynford Vaughan Thomas who I had met once or twice in his role as a professional Welshman. Wynford had known Dylan quite well and in their cups they had loved to sit around inventing limericks and co-authoring obscene limericks, which they would recite with gusto. Wynford was a Welsh speaker and he excelled at coming up with Limericks using Welsh place-names with complicated orthography, which he neatly inscribed in his copy of a scarce, very obscene and famous collection of limericks published by *The Olympia Press* in Paris in 1956. *Count Palmiro Vicarion* was the Nome-de-plume of Christopher Logue.

It is a treasured possession and memento of mine, reminding me of a great Library and a very funny Welshman. Wynford even came up with a Limerick for;

Llanfairpwllgwyngyllgogerychwyrndrobwllllantysiliogogogoch

However it does not scan too well

So here (below) is an example; one of the least offensive! Written in by Wynford.

On my arrival I was introduced to Lottie, Wynford's widow, and his young son David. After brief formalities I was shown into a fine room full of books, which reflected the many facets of Wynford's rich, very Welsh, bon-viveur's life. There were antiquarian books on Welsh literature, topography and folklore, shelved alongside books on gastronomy, wine, mountaineering and with a smidgen of rare erotica. However I was surprised and

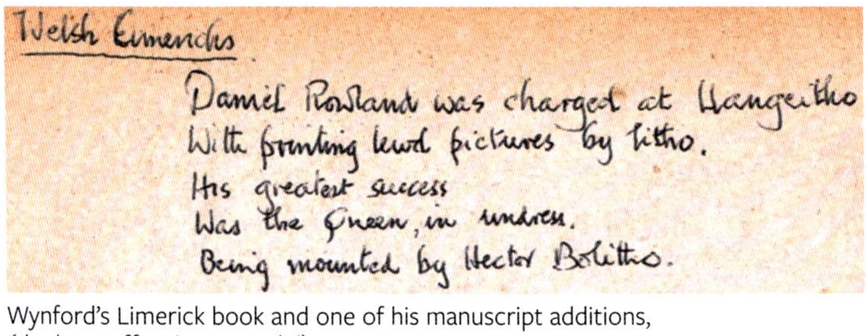

Wynford's Limerick book and one of his manuscript additions, (the least offensive example!)

disappointed that Dylan Thomas material was conspicuous by its almost total absence. While I went about my appraisal, in another room Stuart Thomas with some his Swansea cronies who had travelled down with him, had joined Lotte and David in indulging in yet another loud and boozy wake for their much-loved friend, Wynford. Every so often David would pop in with a glass of something alcoholic for me and to check on my progress. I'd wait for him to leave and then pour each glass of wine and dram of Scotch into a nearby potted plant. I'm not averse to a drink, but I needed to keep my wits about me for the task at hand and I would be driving back to Swansea later. As I was getting to the end of my task his son David came to see me again and I gently enquired after any Dylan Thomas manuscripts or letters. He reached down and opened a drawer of a nearby filing cabinet and came up brandishing a sizable quire of original Dylan Thomas manuscript poetry worksheets and wordlists! Somehow I kept my cool – I had never encountered such materials and I thought all that had survived were in one or another of numerous American University or City libraries'.

I did not acquire them on that visit but six months later I returned and did come away with them but with sizable dent in my bank account. They all now reside in Academic intuitions in Wales and a few in Japan.

But where was Charles Fisher in all of this?

For a long while, all we had to go on was Constantine Fitzgibbon's 'Official' biography of Thomas.[9] Overleaf is Fitzgibbon's previously unpublished letter to Charles, asking for his help in writing the biography.

Charles did take the time to write a 'long letter' to Fitzgibbon but being Charles he did not keep strictly to the proposed brief but wrote a racy one, which Fitzgibbon includes verbatim over two pages in his published biography. Charles appears regularly throughout the book; we learn that when, in 1932, Charles joined Dylan as another cub-reporter on the Swansea local newspaper, Charles advised him to take shorthand lessons which Dylan started but could not cope with, whereas Charles mastered the

This remarkable manuscript word-list was among the Dylan Thomas poetry worksheets I acquired from Wynford's Library

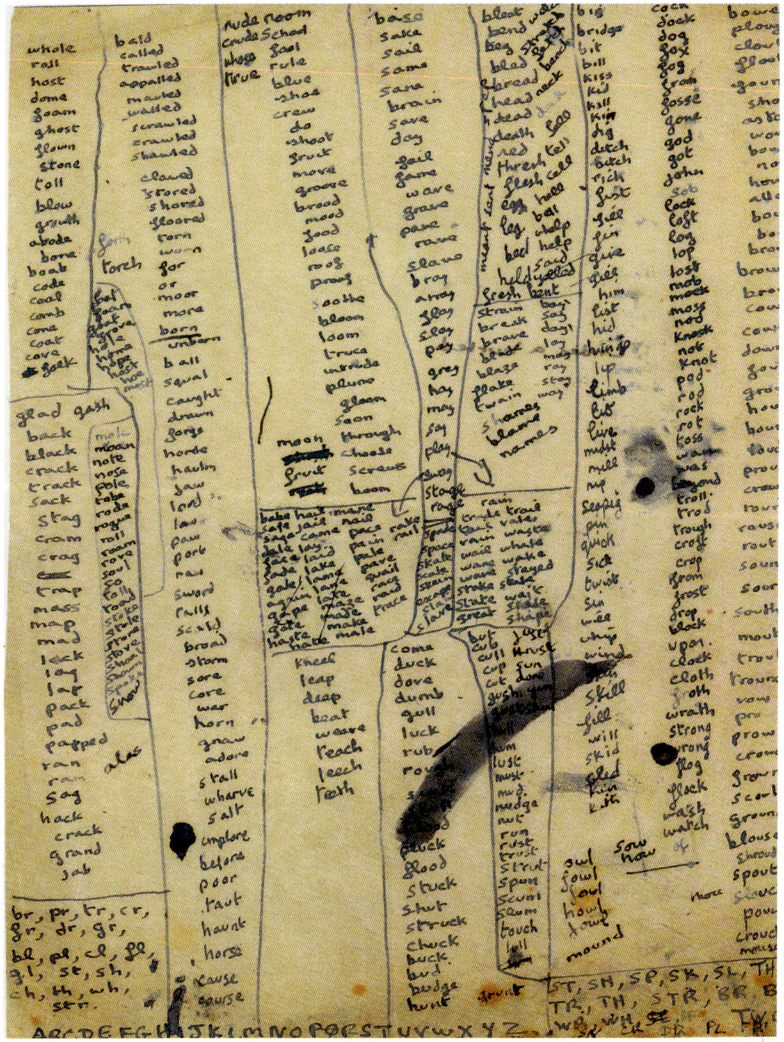

technique. Fitzgibbon also quotes at length from Charles's letters to Dylan[10] which Charles must have made available to him. He also names Charles as Dylan's first collaborator on the projected spoof detective novel, *The Death of the Kings Canary.*[11] He also quotes Fisher's comparison of the Kardomah to:

'...our Dôme and our Rotonde, in one.'

A sophisticated allusion[12] that sets Charles apart from the Dylan's other provincial pals and contributed to Fitzgibbon's remarkable judgement that:

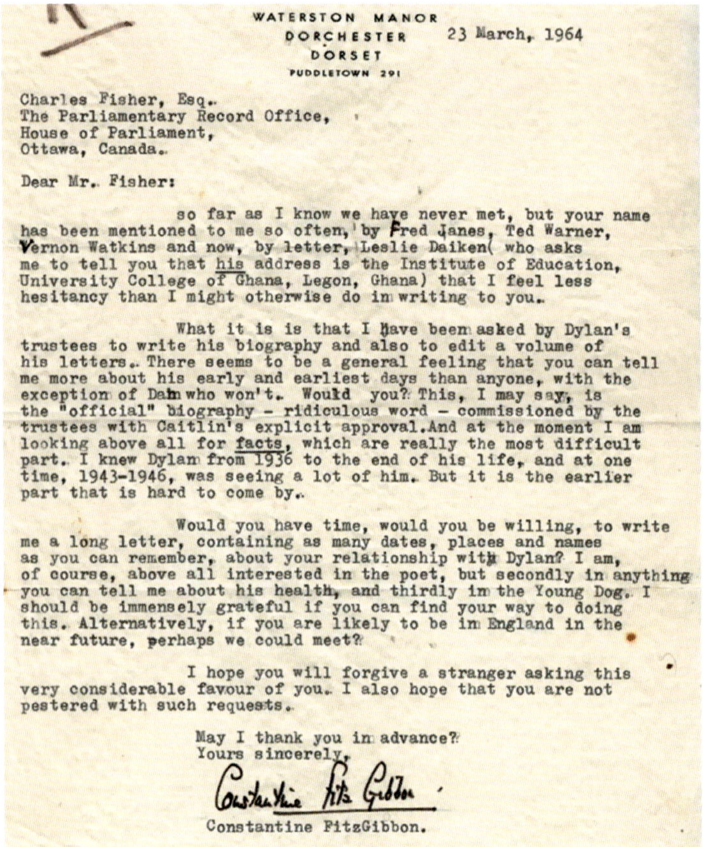

WATERSTON MANOR
DORCHESTER
DORSET
PUDDLETOWN 291

23 March, 1964

Charles Fisher, Esq.
The Parliamentary Record Office,
House of Parliament,
Ottawa, Canada.

Dear Mr. Fisher:

so far as I know we have never met, but your name has been mentioned to me so often, by Fred Janes, Ted Warner, Vernon Watkins and now, by letter, Leslie Daiken(who asks me to tell you that his address is the Institute of Education, University College of Ghana, Legon, Ghana) that I feel less hesitancy than I might otherwise do in writing to you.

What it is is that I have been asked by Dylan's trustees to write his biography and also to edit a volume of his letters. There seems to be a general feeling that you can tell me more about his early and earliest days than anyone, with the exception of Dan who won't. Would you? This, I may say, is the "official" biography - ridiculous word - commissioned by the trustees with Caitlin's explicit approval. And at the moment I am looking above all for facts, which are really the most difficult part. I knew Dylan from 1936 to the end of his life, and at one time, 1943-1946, was seeing a lot of him. But it is the earlier part that is hard to come by.

Would you have time, would you be willing, to write me a long letter, containing as many dates, places and names as you can remember, about your relationship with Dylan? I am, of course, above all interested in the poet, but secondly in anything you can tell me about his health, and thirdly in the Young Dog. I should be immensely grateful if you can find your way to doing this. Alternatively, if you are likely to be in England in the near future, perhaps we could meet?

I hope you will forgive a stranger asking this very considerable favour of you. I also hope that you are not pestered with such requests.

May I thank you in advance?
Yours sincerely,

Constantine FitzGibbon

Constantine FitzGibbon.

> 'Charles Fisher was more than just a journalist and was thought by many at that time to show greater promise as a writer than did Dylan Thomas.'

We learn a little more about Charles, but not much, from Paul Ferris' Biography.[13] He does include a story from Charles, who remembered Dylan in his last year at school;

> '... the prefects room where [DYLAN] would sit before a coal fire, boring a hole in the floor with a hot poker to spy on the Staff-room below...'

In 2003 the established biographer Andrew Lycett, wrote the last full-length biography to appear, and in it he reveals that Charles was a contemporary of Dylan's at Swansea Grammar School and that he acted with Dylan in school plays. In fact Charles was Dylans first 'wife'! As the Grammar School was an all-boys school some lads had to cross-dress and take the female roles.

In December 1930 Dylan took the lead role as the strike leader, Roberts, in *Strife*, a play was written in 1909 by John Galsworthy. Charles looked splendid as Roberts' wife as a surviving photo illustrates – it was annotated by another school-friend of both Dylan and Charles's, Bill Rees.

Lycett also tells us that along with some of his other pals, Charles went off to join the army and he quotes the clerihew the he wrote to Dylan announcing the news:

'The poet Charles Fisher
Will be compelled to join the militia
With a lot of other pricks
On June sixth'

After the war Charles seems to disappear. After serving and seeing some action and some distinguished service in France and other parts of Europe when he was attached to the S.O.E and British Intelligence, he returned to London, married a Spanish opera singer (they had a daughter but they later split up.) He went back into journalism and began work with Reuters. He attended Dylan's Funeral in Laugharne in 1953 and then flew to Canada to begin a new life working in the Canadian Parliament in Ottawa as that government's one man Hansard – sitting in the government chamber with a stenography machine, recording the daily transactions. He became very well connected – even persona-grata with the Canadian President Pierre Trudeau from 1968 to 1979.

Charles remained in this job until his retirement; the job suited him as the long parliamentary recesses gave him the time to indulge his passion for exotic travel. First he conquered Spain – particularly Andalusia and more specifically Grenada's Gypsy community. So much so that in 1964, the Canadian

Charles at work on the Swansea Daily Post circa 1933

Dylan and his 'wife' Charles onstage

Charles with Pierre Trudeau Canada's then Prime Minister

version of our *Picture Post: WEEKEND MAGAZINE*, ran a piece in which the picture above and the two below illustrated a long article on Charles and his life with Grenada's Gypsy community;

But I heard nor learned nothing more of Charles Fisher until around 1995, when the late Gilbert Bennet, the long-time President of the *Dylan Thomas Society*, spotted a letter in the local Swansea newspaper complaining of how the local council was exploiting Dylan Thomas. Interesting content for sure, but even more interesting was that it was sent from Canada by a 'Charles Fisher'.

Gilbert got in contact via the paper and, after nearly half a century, Charles Fisher was re-discovered alive and well and living in Ontario.

Then fate took a hand ... At that time I still had my small bookstore in *Salubrious Passage*, but also ran a very large used Bookshop Café in Swansea's *Dylan Thomas Centre*, located in the revamped *Marina Quarter* of the city. My longtime friend and assistant, Tim Batcup was running it and another local lady, Ann Hughes, ran the coffee shop and helped with the books. I called in the few times a week. One morning I was there in the shop when I overheard a white-haired, pleasant older lady ask at the counter for a book on Vernon Watkins and Dylan Thomas. I went over to assist, because I knew the book in question. I told the lady I had a copy of the book in my storerooms and could bring a copy of the book into the shop for her. She was very pleased and added

"No rush, but I want to send it to my brother in Canada"

A bell went off in my head and I blurted out

"Is your brother Charles Fisher?"

And he was!

That became the start of another wonderful friendship. I began to correspond with Charles who, although in his eighties, was well teched-up and used e-mail. He was a very, lively correspondent. I had also learned from Paul Ferris, who had also been in contact with Charles when writing his Dylan Thomas biography, that Charles still had in his possession the dozen letters that Dylan Thomas had sent him preserved and cherished the biggest single selling force in Canada

WEEKEND MAGAZINE

VOL. 14, No. 19 MAY 9, 1964

Ottawa's Busy/Lazy Gipsy

By Robert McKeown
Weekend Magazine Staff Writer

CANADA'S House of Commons and the gipsy caves at Sacre Monte in Spain have just one thing in common — Charles Fisher.

During Parliamentary sessions Fisher sits at a desk on the floor of the Commons recording the debates in shorthand. When Parliament is not in session he lives with gipsies in Spanish caves and plays flamenco guitar for their singing and dancing.

"In Sacre Monte I am as unreliable and lazy as all the rest," Fisher says. "I think I am respected because I have the same failings as all the gipsies.

"Sacre Monte is a great place for a person with imperfections. It is the one thing **Continued on next page**

Best man at gipsy wedding, Fisher stands next to bride, right, during big party after ceremony. Gipsies regard him as one of their happy-go-lucky cla

Pausing in plaza in Granada, Fisher chats with Josefa Heredias, matriarch of Heredias clan, of which he is member. He was accepted after he and gipsy friend mingled blood to become "brothers."

Studying report of House of Commons proceedings, Charles Fisher carries out his duties as an employee of the federal government. During sessions he helps record debates in shorthand. When the House is not sittin goes to Spain and lives with gipsies in the caves on Granada's outs

Charles Fisher at work

throughout his busy life for well over fifty years. This information had a definite effect on my avaricious inclinations. After a year or so Charles said he was coming to Swansea to catch up with his sister and he very much wanted to meet me. I told him to keep in touch and that I was very happy to meet up.

One fine day thereafter, there was a knock at my back door. I went out opened it; and there was Charles! He looked like a cross between Geronimo and Dr Timothy Leary.

Geronimo

Charles

Leary

His arrival was unannounced and a complete and joyful surprise. Charles was looking splendid, with a winning and open smile. He explained that he had arrived in Swansea late the previous night and checked into the 'HOTEL' opposite the station. At that point in time it was dangerous dump of a place full of low-life, drugs and prostitutes and although Charles was well travelled and not squeamish, it was no place for him; so did I have a bed for the night? Of course I said yes.

He stayed for a week and a glorious week it was too, full of fun and incident. Each night we would have dinner and after sit together with a small Dutch cigar and a bottle of red wine and happily 'chew the fat' with Charles telling me all sorts of stories from his eventful life. After a few such evenings he looked at me and said;

'I don't smoke and I don't drink but I do enjoy a cigar and a glass of wine'.

Charles and me, in my back garden

Charles made a splash in the local papers and we kept busy. We met up with his sister; he came swimming with me and was very impressed by my front crawl and demanded I coach him to swim as fast and challenged me to an arm wrestle that saw me thrown across the kitchen into a small table that broke, luckily I was not injured. And all this seemed to seal our firm friendship.

Charles went back home to Canada and we kept in touch. 2003 was approaching, which was 50th anniversary of Dylan Thomas's death in America. I was already deeply involved with programming an extra-special *Annual Dylan Thomas Festival* in the *Dylan Thomas Centre*, where I had worked since 1995 when Swansea hosted the year-long Literary festival *THE UK YEAR OF LITERATURE*, which had been backed by the national and local government Arts bodies. I suggested to David Wooley, who I had worked closely with on a series of Dylan Thomas events, that we bring Charles back to Swansea, to deliver the main key-note address for the 2003 Commemoration events. David agreed and took the idea to Swansea Council and thankfully they also agreed.

Charles came back for a memorable second visit. He came accompanied by his daughter Caitlin, an academic and creative writer publishing mainly on the Internet. Charles was rightfully fêted and welcomed and the event was a sell-out huge success. A transcription of his lecture is printed below.

There was still one important, last piece of unfinished business; Charles had agreed to sell me his Dylan Thomas letters and some other bits and pieces of Dylan Thomas memorabilia which he had cherished for 50 years. We made a plan. In the

The Evening Post, Charles' old employer, loved his return journey

Kardomah boy back home

THE last surviving member of Swansea's Kardomah Boys has been rekindling memories of his fascinating times in the city with its most famous son, Dylan Thomas.

Now 87, Charles Fisher, one of the talented contemporaries of the celebrated poet who regularly gathered at the Kardomah Cafe in pre-war Castle Street emigrated to Canada to work in 1953.

Since then he has lived for part of the time with cave-dwelling Spanish gypsies and travelled extensively in the Far East.

He returned to Swansea this week to visit his sister Doreen in Morriston and take a 21st Century look at the city.

MEMORY LANE: Charles Fisher friend of Dylan Thomas (inset) when he was a Kardomah Boy. Main picture: Gayle Marsh 00-06-01/8295/GM/P3

"Swansea has changed enormously. The buildings, the people, even the dialect. The whole atmosphere is different," he said. "I am not sure Dylan would approve. It's much different to the Swansea he loved."

He has been staying as a guest of Dylan's bookstore owner and passionate Dylan expert Jeff Towns.

Mr Fisher said he was vexed by the Dylan industry that has sprung up. "They make money out of Dylan when what they should realise is that it is the poems that matter," he said.

Brought up in Sandfields and Brynmill Mr Fisher rarely gets the chance to return to Swansea, but is in regular contact with his sister.

"She keeps me in touch with all that happens," he said.

Like Dylan Thomas, He was a reporter at the Post.

Together they spent time with a host of Swansea's rising artistic stars including composer Daniel Jones, artist Fred Janes, broadcaster Wynford Vaughan-Thomas, composer Thomas Warner and poet Vernon Watkins. History tagged them the Kardomah Boys.

Mr Fisher is fascinated with modern Swansea.

"Dylan would be hard-pressed to locate any of his favourite pubs now," he said. "They have all vanished. But an amazing array of new ones has sprung up in Wind Street.

"Having been in one or two I think he would have written some magnificent prose about them and the people there too."

● More on Charles Fisher's life and times in next week's Evening Post.

coming November I was exhibiting, as I had done for 20 years, at the annual Boston International Antiquarian Bookfair. I looked at a map of North America. Charles had retired from his job in Ottawa and was living in a small town, Almonte, in the middle of Ontario. To me, it looked a straight run due North from Boston into Canada and on to Almonte. So after a successful book fair, I rented a red flat-bed truck and headed North. After a good days drive I pulled into the small town where I found Charles, good to his word, on the sidewalk outside his apartment, waiting to greet me with a tall glass of champagne, as he had promised...

When I got inside his apartment, I handed back my empty glass and commented on its beauty, an exquisite glass, finely engraved and with a silver rim. Charles modestly informed me that I was drinking from a glass that had belonged to Federico Garcia Lorca and it had been presented to him by the Gipsies of Grenada! This was one of many great stories that Charles shared with me. I stayed a week.

And what a week we had. Charles drove a very rare, bright red, vintage Jaguar[14] in which we sped through country roads, visiting bookshops, his friends and bars and restaurants. And I even got behind the wheel for a few miles.

Charles also remembered I was a keen basketball player. He had been especially impressed when I let him know I had been capped by the Wales Men's Basketball team. He proudly took me to a funky local museum which celebrated the life of a local man, James Naismith, who is the acknowledged inventor of game of basketball, which he did by cutting off the bottoms of peach picking baskets and nailing them up for the ball to thrown through.

James Naismith of Almonte; the originator of Basketball with his ball and his cropped peach basket

At the end of my week, on my last day with him, we sat down at his table and conducted a some very amiable and mutually satisfying business. I acquired his clutch of great Dylan Thomas letters and some other wonderful Dylan-related materials and Charles's retirement travel-fund received a very substantial boost. Among the 'other materials' was one item that I knew I was going to keep. Before I left Wales for this trip Charles had sent me this note;

I knew this painting well – It hangs in the small gallery in Cyfatha Castle in Merthyr Tydfill; I have visited it many, many times; I have bought many postcard reproductions of it, and sent them to friends; and it appeared that Charles had an original pencil preliminary drawing for the central figures.

When I finally saw the amazing little original pencil study of the two female heads, hung on Charles' wall, I coveted it so much. My lust for it overwhelmed my shallow belief in the Tenth

Here is Xerox of a snap I took while 'Salome' was in progress. Incidentally Fred gave me the cartoon (in pencil) used for the faces — it's hung up here, framed & very lovely but faded somewhat

G

Alfred Janes original pencil cartoon tor his painting Salome which hangs in Cyfatha Castle Museum Merthyr

Commandment. Perhaps I wanted that drawing even more that the Letters, but in the end I got them both; Charles sensed my desire and was gracious and kind, happy it was coming back to Swansea where it was first created some 75 years earlier. I have kept this wonderful small Alfred Janes pencil study for his amazing painting, *Salome*. It hangs in my kitchen and every day I look at it and it reminds me of Charles and my visit.

Dylan's letters to Charles were none too shabby either, full of humour warmth and hiraeth, but also containing some serious reflections on his poetry practice and theory, something he rarely opened up about.

I gave Charles a cheque drawn in sterling on my Swansea Bank account, which he was to hold until I got back home and could transfer Canadian dollars directly into his account. I did it immediately and a few days later I received an air-mail letter from Charles, full of news and memories but also with my original cheque neatly sliced diagonally in half. He used the input of $$$ to once more go travelling eastwards again to his beloved Bangkok, where a few years later he died peacefully in his hotel bed with a benign beatific smile on

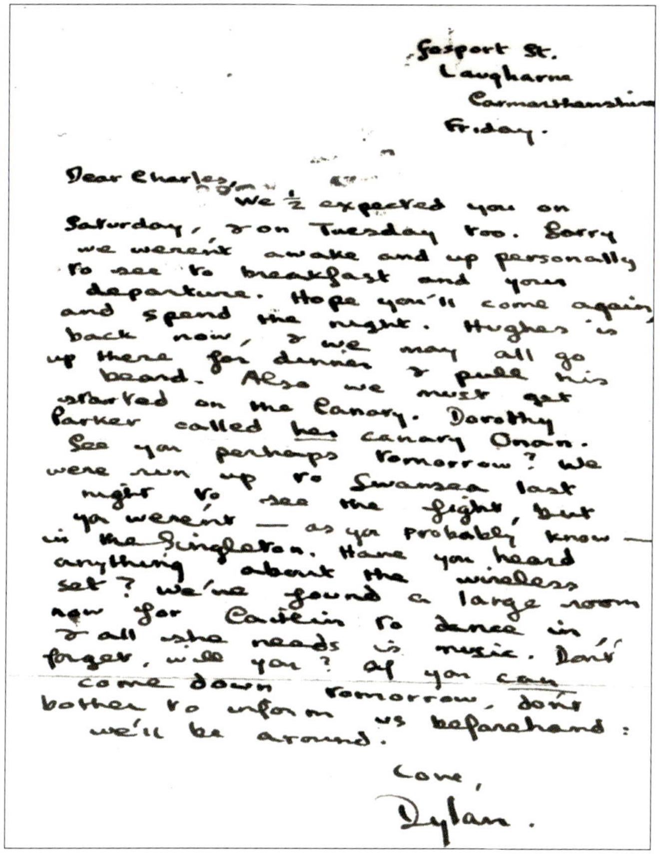

Gosport St.
Laugharne
Carmarthenshire
Friday.

Dear Charles,
We ½ expected you on Saturday, & on Tuesday too. Sorry we weren't awake and up personally to see to breakfast and your departure. Hope you'll come again and spend the night. Hughes is back now, & we may all go up there for dinner & pull his beard. Also we must get started on the Canary. Dorothy Parker called her canary Onan. See you perhaps tomorrow? We were run up to Swansea last night to see the fight, but you weren't — as you probably know — in the Singleton. Have you heard anything about the wireless set? We've found a large room now for Caitlin to dance in & all she needs is music. Don't forget, will you? If you can come down tomorrow, don't bother to inform us beforehand: we'll be around.

Love,

Dylan.

One of Dylan's Letters to Charles

his face (I like to think) and his ashes were scattered in his favourite Bangkok Buddhist Temple

Charles Fisher as a poet

Dylan Thomas famously did not like to talk or be questioned about his poetry, its meanings, origins and influences but he did occasionally when, if provoked, he would respond quite petulantly in writing and to a few select fellow writers he would send new poems for comment. His early trusted sounding board was Vernon Watkins, but he also sent poems and wrote explanations to another fellow poet Charles Fisher. He wrote this to him in a much quoted early letter, sent in 1935 from his London Redcliff Street flat:

> 'You asked me about to tell you about my theory of poetry. Really I haven't got one...
> Poetry, heavy in tare[15] though nimble should be as orgiastic and orgasmic as copulation, dividing and unifying, personal but not private, propagating the individual in the mass and the mass in the individual. I think it should work from words, from the substance of words and the rhythm of substantial words set together, not towards words. Poetry is a medium, not a stigmata on paper. Man should be two-tooled, and a poet's middle leg is his pencil. If his phallic pencil turns into a pneumatic drill, breaking the tar and the concrete of language worn thin by tricycle tyres of nature poets and the heavy six wheels of the academic sirs, so much the better...'

In his early Swansea days Charles wrote and published poems. Like his pal Dylan, he was involved with the *Swansea Grammar School Magazine* and he took over as editor after Dylan left school. Later he also contributed to Kiedrych Rhys' exciting new Welsh literary magazine WALES, in which Dylan was very much involved. An unpublished piece of prose by Dylan is announced on the front cover of the first Issue and Charles is listed below. Remarkably, four Kardomah lads contributed to this issue – Dylan, Charles, Vernon and John Prichard – of this important new magazine.

Charles appeared in another few issues of the first series of the magazine, which closed down at the start of the war. Charles, again like Dylan, published poems in many of the varied literary magazines coming out of London in the thirties and forties such as *Seven*, *Caravel*, and Tambimuttu's *Poetry London*. He went on to write a few programmes for the BBC; a couple of his plays were

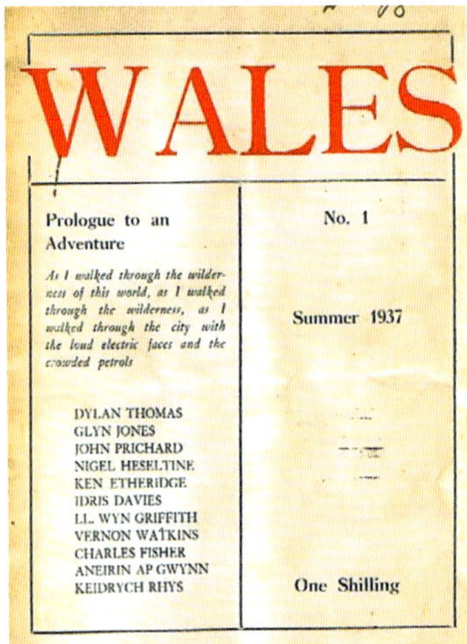
WALES

Prologue to an Adventure

As I walked through the wilderness of this world, as I walked through the wilderness, as I walked through the city with the loud electric faces and the crowded petrols

DYLAN THOMAS
GLYN JONES
JOHN PRICHARD
NIGEL HESELTINE
KEN ETHERIDGE
IDRIS DAVIES
LL. WYN GRIFFITH
VERNON WATKINS
CHARLES FISHER
ANEIRIN AP GWYNN
KEIDRYCH RHYS

No. 1

Summer 1937

One Shilling

Issue 1. Dylan leads but Charles has a poem too

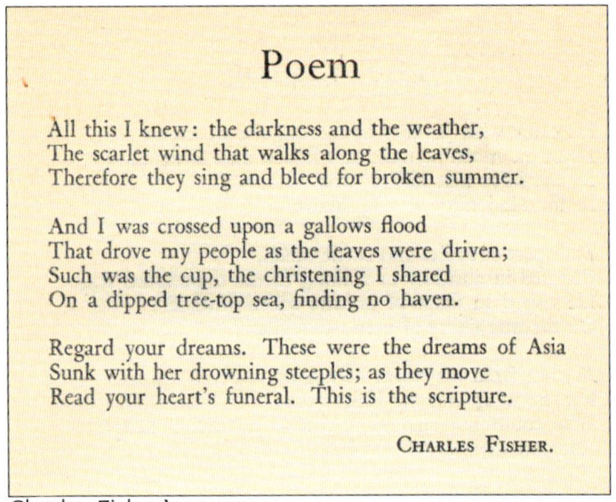
Poem

All this I knew: the darkness and the weather,
The scarlet wind that walks along the leaves,
Therefore they sing and bleed for broken summer.

And I was crossed upon a gallows flood
That drove my people as the leaves were driven;
Such was the cup, the christening I shared
On a dipped tree-top sea, finding no haven.

Regard your dreams. These were the dreams of Asia
Sunk with her drowning steeples; as they move
Read your heart's funeral. This is the scripture.

CHARLES FISHER.

Charles Fisher's poem

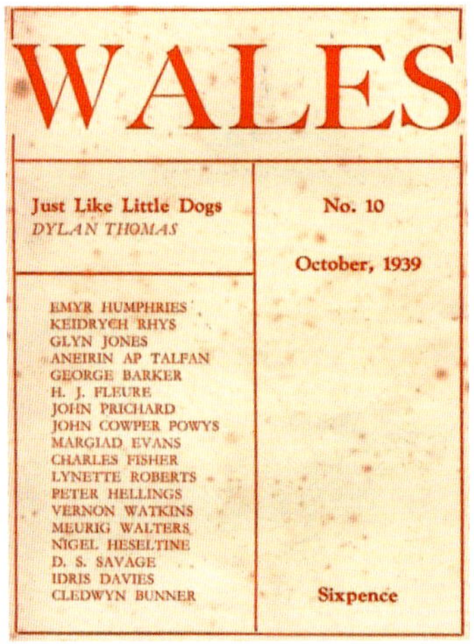
WALES

Just Like Little Dogs
DYLAN THOMAS

EMYR HUMPHRIES
KEIDRYCH RHYS
GLYN JONES
ANEIRIN AP TALFAN
GEORGE BARKER
H. J. FLEURE
JOHN PRICHARD
JOHN COWPER POWYS
MARGIAD EVANS
CHARLES FISHER
LYNETTE ROBERTS
PETER HELLINGS
VERNON WATKINS
MEURIG WALTERS
NIGEL HESELTINE
D. S. SAVAGE
IDRIS DAVIES
CLEDWYN BUNNER

No. 10

October, 1939

Sixpence

Issue 12 A new short story from Dylan

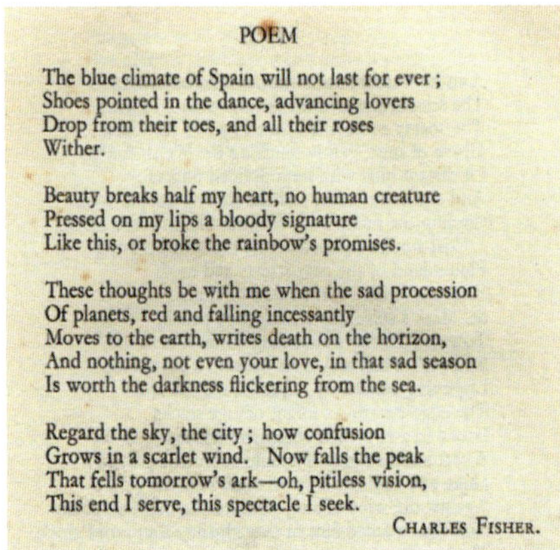
POEM

The blue climate of Spain will not last for ever;
Shoes pointed in the dance, advancing lovers
Drop from their toes, and all their roses
Wither.

Beauty breaks half my heart, no human creature
Pressed on my lips a bloody signature
Like this, or broke the rainbow's promises.

These thoughts be with me when the sad procession
Of planets, red and falling incessantly
Moves to the earth, writes death on the horizon,
And nothing, not even your love, in that sad season
Is worth the darkness flickering from the sea.

Regard the sky, the city; how confusion
Grows in a scarlet wind. Now falls the peak
That fells tomorrow's ark—oh, pitiless vision,
This end I serve, this spectacle I seek.

CHARLES FISHER.

And Charles' poem inspired by his love of Spain

broadcast too, but he seemed to stop writing during his war years. Later, once settled in Canada, having to spend all his days at a desk transcribing speeches, he seemed to stop writing altogether, and instead, he begun to travel widely in Spain and the East. However during his more relaxed retirement he began to write again and revisit earlier works. In 1998, Athos Books published his well received collection of poems The Locust Years.

Here is a much later poem, which he read and then inscribed for me just before he left Swansea after his visit in 2000

The Christmas Fly
Tonight I have a Visitor
A Christmas fly
It buzzes on my pudding plate
Then drifts on by
It's up there on the Christmas tree
Serene above the greenery
Come straight from Hell for company

Charles Fisher
The Locust Years

Charles Fisher came to Canada in 1953 from Swansea, a town in South Wales remarkable, or so it seems in retrospect, for the quality of its social and intellectual life in the 'thirties. As a schoolboy at Swansea Grammar School he shared a form-room with the redoubtable Dylan Thomas and both worked together for a time as reporters on the S.W. Evening Post (see *Return Journey* for the best account of that episode.) Dylan went on to London and fame and Fisher continued to write for the Post until the outbreak of war. Poems and other writings of his in those early years appeared in a number of current literary magazines, *Seven*, *Caravel*, *Wales* and *Poetry London* among them, but the major part of his non-journalistic work was done for the B.B.C., then at the peak of its stuffy, snobbish brilliance. Two radio plays — *Tristram* and *Theme for Audience*, come to mind.

Back from war service (Int. Corps, France and Germany) he joined Reuters and was for some six years parliamentary correspondent at Westminster. A domestic crisis provoked his departure for Canada (in the character of Childe Roland — Toronto was to have been the Dark Tower but turned out to be nothing of the kind.) Tri-lingual, a compulsive traveller with a yen for the Far East, veteran talking head, subject of two embarassing movies, he is presently writing a tormented account of life with gypsies in various parts of Spain.

The Locust Years Back cover blurb

ON LEAVING ENGLAND, 1953

Not much by way of luggage or farewell
Here at Southampton harbour. Be it so.
Whatever might be said is said by now
As one by one along a warehouse wall
Pathetic ribbons break apart and fall.

Music. A cheerful bell, an organ blast
To clear the deck and blow away the past.
A time for celebration? Time will tell.
The great ship moves to meet the Atlantic swell.

Vast emptiness. I pitch the locust years
Like rubbish to the gulls for they were full
Of broken promises. Some good may come
From parting, inasmuch as common cares
Make all directions equal and the whole
Dark-spinning, crowded globe to be my home.

Beyond the coast in oriental skies
Venus is rising. Mirrored in the foam,
Her path is radiant.
Circles.

The opening poem in *The Locust Years*

The Christmas Fly
For Jeff Towns.
Tonight I have a visitor
A Christmas fly
It buzzes on my pudding plate
Then drifts on by
It's up there on the Christmas tree
Serene amid the greenery
Come straight from hell for company
- My Christmas fly
It flies about content to share
A sausage or a stale éclaire,
In short, the usual Christmas fare
It flies about on coloured wings
A thing of air – inspecting things
And often it alights upon
A page of the Satyricon.
I call it Shem. Together we
Revolve around our Christmas tree
Rehearsing seasons long ago
Talking of Michel Angelo –

And did this fly whose name is Shem
Once buzz about in Bethlehem?

Charles Fisher Newton May 2000

The Christmas Fly

207

My Christmas Fly
It flies about content to share
A sausage or a chocolate éclair
In short the usual Christmas faire
It lies about on coloured wings
A thing of air – inspecting things
And often it pulls up on
A page of the Satiricon
I call it Shem. Together we
Revolve around our Christmas tree
Rehearsing seasons long ago
Talking of Michaelangelo
And did this fly whose name is Shem
Once buzz about in Bethlehem

A transcription from a tape recording of Charles Fisher's Lecture at the Dylan Thomas Centre 2003 to commemorate the 50th Anniversary of his Dylan Thomas' Death.

Well, who could easily follow that introduction, who could easily stand aside Jeff and expect to find an instant rapport with his audience, but I shall do my best.

The week before last I was in Vancouver, speaking to the Dylan circle there, his muse is with ourselves tonight; but you see how far flung his influence is, expanded to this include the circle in Vancouver with whom I made many friends, so I can say that I feel that immediately since I'm in my own town now, no question about that, changed though it is. I feel that I am among friends and I need to be if I am to talk about Dylan. What was it like knowing him, spending time in his company, as a boy, as a young man, as a London journalist and about town in the years of his celebrity? How can words of mine reflect his wit, his eloquence, the charm and the power of his presence – drunk or sober – I shall need his help and your indulgence for this is the first time I have tried to talk about those days at any length. Though my daughter Caitlin came with me from Canada and is here tonight, Caitlin reminds me that long ago I did indeed write a short sketch for a Canadian magazine, not so much about Dylan, but as about the London scene in the early 50's and his part in it. I thought I might begin by reading part of this note, since I must begin somewhere and something anywhere written down just now will help. So here we are.

Looking for Dylan and not finding him[16]

In the days of his early celebrity, not long after the war had ended innocent friends of mine at a loss for an occupation, were anxious to meet the man who had become a legend in his own lifetime. Often someone would say to me, just as the pubs were about to close in shabby Soho, 'Let's look for Dylan'. Ugh. I was reluctant to do this but someone would say 'why not? Go on', so we'd move briskly about, scanning the faces of late drinkers. It would be all of ten o' clock. In the Intrepid Fox, the Wheatsheaf, the Prince of Wales, the Bell, the French pub, the Marquis of Granby and, at each and every one, a wish the proprietor would say 'He was here but he'd gone'.

Undismayed we would continue to look in the bars of the Gargoyle, the Colonnade, Club Eleven, Caves de France, and other such places as had leave to sell drinks until midnight..

Ah, here is the green man at the height of his acclaim. He sits in the corner of the Gargoyle club, propped up by two walls, a smouldering, soggy, firework sending up stars of singular lucidity. His admirers surround him. 'What will he do next?' they wonder. 'Will he burst? Will he explode?' A long silence. Dylan moves his head, a dozen necks crane forward alert to gather the crumbs of irreverence or perhaps to learn how to write a poem.

'A pint, I say' he rumbles in the deep belly voice that makes audiences shiver. A pint is quickly fetched. 'Oh Mr Thomas' says it's his provider 'what do you think of the new Italian poets?' In a voice fatally like that of the enquirer but [mincing] effeminate Dylan repeats the question as an expression of disgust with the whole business. 'Oh Mr Thomas what do you think of the new Italian poets?' The subject is dropped. More silence followed by more questions. It is obvious from twenty feet away that Dylan is feeling sick but as long as he can speak he never gives up: 'Tell that doorkeeper dressed like a huntsman to keep those goldfish quiet.' He talks in a variety of accents, changing voices like a stage spy; changing beards by turns for Kensington or BBC or a curious establishment voice as affected by Nina Hamnett who probably wore it. He has a target and the target is pretentiousness; wherever he can find it, but especially in the Mandrake after twelve o' clock. His favourite weapon is a Welsh accent, or rather a Swansea accent, thin as a worn kitchen knife: Who are 'eiw, I preesoome'? It would be wrong to say that his presence makes anyone uncomfortable but it encourages them to be cautious. He's so much drunker and more sure of himself than the others, besides being more articulate, if only sporadically. In addition, he is ruder, or potentially ruder, at a time when in leading circles in London it is the fashion to be rude in public. All in all it is a formidable presence, as expected. Dylan is wearing nondescript clothes of home-spun appearance, flannel or corduroy trousers, bagged at the knee, a stained tweed jacket and a dark shirt with a loosely knotted tie. He looks – I forget who thought up the phrase but it's a good one – like an unmade bed.

He smokes continually and once he has put a cigarette in his mouth he doesn't touch it until it's finished. He wears his cigarette. His curly hair is uncombed, his stomach bloated, his face flushed, his eyes luminous, especially when he speaks.

I'll leave that sketch there, thank you ladies and gentleman. This type of writing seems old fashioned today. Dylan would not have approved; too la-de-da. His own style, even when he was stretching things a bit, was never as pretentious.

I don't remember when I first met him, he was one schoolboy along with three hundred others at the Swansea Grammar School, thirty-three of them in our form which was 4[A]. He was good looking then and fourteen though no-one minded, this sullen cherub with curly hair, not interested in playing fives or prisoner's base. His tastes were literary, one which I shared but along with fives and prisoner's base and making gunpowder from saltpetre. He used to play in his Cwmdonkin Park, not far from where he lived. I played in Brynmill Park, not far from where I lived. Brynmill Park is where the hunchback used to sit in a chair beside the pond, remember? *'Like the water, he came early, like the water he sat down'*[17]

Dylan was the same age as me but he grew up earlier as I realised one morning when a half insane school master was screaming abuse at us. Dylan directly confronted [Brooms] and addressed him with dignity:

'Sir, I do not wish to learn mathematics in your class, then picked up his books and left the room. All boys silent, amazed, such an act of courage was inconceivable to them. I've never forgotten that incident. I feel bound to add that all the masters who taught, or pretended to teach mathematics at the Swansea Grammar School then appeared to be lunatic and still do in retrospect.

Of course, the fact that Dylan's father, D.J., taught English, might have had something to do with his composure. D.J., as all of us knew well, had a manner which combined a considerable hauteur with an acid turn of speech. I do not think he liked boys very much. He was, for all that, by far the best teacher in the place. Of all influences on Dylan, his was the most profound as to taste. The rest too, but in a negative form, springing from dissent.

Dylan never returned to maths classes and indeed his attendance of classes from form five on, was, shall I say, fitful. But he was already writing. I recall his showing me these lines:

'You collect such strange shapes in the cool palm of your hand.

Who with the long sinewy arms and muscles breaking through the skins Such cool sponges and water flies'

Something like that. The sureness of the spun rhythms, the deftness of the pun 'mussels'. The half secret amusement; it was a time for collecting words, for testing the rhythm of substantial words set together. We collected words like entomologists collecting moths or butterflies. Words like 'palanquin'. Dan Jones would invent phrases; 'metrical biscuitry' was one.

'Metrical biscuitry'

Dylan would mutter, tasting the sound. No meaning, no meaning looked for, just the sound. We made and read poems. 'Why didn't you write "foam" in line two instead of "froth"? then Dylan fiercely 'If God Almighty were to ask me to write "foam" when I'd written "froth" I wouldn't alter it.' Not to be taken seriously.

Later, he spent long hours in a room set aside as the study for senior boys, a retreat to dream of because it had the grate and the coal fire. I can see Dylan there now. He is holding not a book, but a red hot poker, and he is using it to bore a hole through the floor into the master's room below. A pity it was destroyed by fire and neglect, that hole would probably be roped off now, a tourist attraction.

But something else is going on, something less evident, a mysterious process of education. The acquisition, as if by magic, of that close encyclopaedic knowledge of Eng Lit., which was at that period possible, and indeed taken for granted among literary people of my Tchaikovsky Dvorak generation. 'Who's your favourite, favourite composer?' I ask.

'Stravinsky'

'And your favourite writer?'

'Henry James'

We would cut school to sit in the Kardomah to talk about surrealism and about girls, as though they were an altogether separate species from ourselves, Welsh culture being founded on this proposition. I have succeeded Dylan as editor of the school magazine. He was about to sign on with the Evening Post as a reporter and I would join him in the news room six months later. His main activity there was writing articles on various topics for the Herald of Wales, a weekly companion paper which paid ten shillings for each one. The articles he wrote were far more sophisticated, wittier than mine. The fee was the same though and proved an equal inspiration to both of us. But Dylan was not interested in writing about traffic accidents and village rugby matches. He had his eyes on stories of another sort; the doings and eccentricities of his colleagues, the latter were many. 'I'll put you all into a story one day' he vowed. And so he did, as we all know.

The institution which became known as '*The Kardomah Group*' or, in today's gutter English, '*The Kardomah Gang*', took shape at this point. Let me explain. The Kardomah café, I don't need to tell you people, on the first floor of an elegant crescent, Castle Street, in the very centre of Swansea, was dear to Dylan as indeed it was for us all. It was a place where he could count on seeing his friends, and seeing them all together. These meetings became something of a ceremony. And in that spirit, I prepared some notes a year ago in memory of the old *Kardomah* and the circle of friends who met there. They could never be complete, of course, so much having passed beyond my recollections, since we were there upstairs in that spacious, sweet-smelling room, because the man who wrote them, who is now addressing you, is eighty-nine years old, the last then of that circle to be alive. It is unlikely that any remaining gaps will ever be filled. I wish that this were not the case for merely to outlive one's contemporaries is a melancholy distinction, sounds a bit like Sir Thomas Brown, eh? Mably and I would spend evenings talking in sentences like that, Mably Owen another undisputed member of that group. I still miss these people. Dylan, Fred, Tom and Mably, especially, and Vernon and Frederick Trott. It was my good fortune to be able to sit upstairs in that café corner, not only on popular days, Saturdays, but on most other days as well. It couldn't have been more convenient, since my own office was just across the street, a few steps away. Also, I was officially supposed to be out making morning calls, something which involved, or rather should have involved, a leisurely walk between the hospital, the police station and the ships in port. Dylan did that before me, or was supposed to have done it. As things were, I found myself able to drop into a place where I could be sure of finding good conversation as well as good coffee, no, correction, fairly ordinary coffee. From very early on, perhaps as early as 1934, I always sat in one particular corner on the first floor, joined there most mornings by Dylan, who also found the place to his liking. Around that time he was preparing to leave the paper, if he had not just done so, to seek wider fame in London. Looking back, I can understand that the arrangement I've just described, so long lasting and so agreeable to me, was made possible by the kindness of Edward Jones, chief reporter of the *Evening Post*, in turning a blind eye to my long absences. Let him, in future be thought of as supporting us in absentia. In any case, before I leave the subject, let me declare that there never was such a thing as a Kardomah Group, in the sense usually applied to people who meet to reinforce commonly held artistic or social aims. I can say at once that we never thought of ourselves as a group in this sense. We were far too individualistic for that. We had no manifesto to publish, no theory of art to propose. Janes and I, quite certainly Dan and Dylan, would be uneasy about ever using the word 'group'. We never did. We never thought of ourselves as being a group. Our purpose in meeting was simply to exchange news and pleasant conversation, which we did at great length and to some effect for the best part of a decade. Talking, you see, was something we were all good at, whereas more material pleasures were largely beyond our means.

But getting back to Dylan. How was he regarded by those who knew him best? Well, first of all, whilst how shall I put it, very well regarded, very much liked, I could easily say loved, this was the general response plus an inclination I suppose to be protective. I daresay we all recognised, quite early on, that there was an outstanding lyric poet among us. We realised, too, just what that meant, what it ought to mean, but deference there was none. No one had time for that, we were all too busy being ourselves and trying to live our own lives. This didn't prevent us listening with rapt attention to Dylan's stories of affairs in the great city, his first meetings with the famous, his talk of: Surrealism, of the *Botteghe Oscure*,[18] of the Sitwells. But our relations are always intimate, and I speak for the whole of that circle. Anyone reading my absurd diary of 1938 might well be surprised at the tone of some of the entries. This, for example: 'Drove Dylan and Caitlin to Laugharne, stayed the night, very dull, was shown a collection of shells.'

New thoughts, new Dylan stories. I was staying at Laugharne and so was Augustus John, who had come by motorcar. We were drinking heavily; Dylan was drinking treble whiskeys which was fatal for him, he could not drink treble whiskeys, neither could I. Augustus, however, could. And when the pub closed, we returned to the house – not the Boathouse – and continued to drink around the kitchen table. A spirited conversation, as far as I can recall, I can recall it was about the Balkans. It was about gypsies, about the Balkans, Augustus wanted all three of us to go there. Caitlin went to bed. Anyway, it occurred to me that, during the end of this conversation, that Dylan hadn't said a word since several minutes. So, I turned to him and said, confronted him: 'Why aren't you saying things Dylan?' He looked at me wide-eyed:

'I want to, I want to say things, it's just that I'm unable to speak'

And those were his last words for the night.

On another night, as we were heading for Laugharne, the car was stopped by police for some technical reason. The constable finished his examination of documents then abruptly turned his flashlight on Dylan, who was sitting in the back. 'And what have you to say for yourself?' he demanded.

'Nothing to say' replied the great Bard

Perhaps I should have tried harder to remember what Dylan said or did but the idea never occurred to me. Perhaps occasionally a flash but I quickly forgot even my own bon mots. But one or two things have come through. Dylan saying, 'The world will break any man if he is strong enough'. And as to alcohol: 'Nothing is stronger than mild.' What he meant, of course, when taken in sufficient quantities.

A few years ago, the Welsh arm of the BBC had a notion to reunite survivors of the Kardomah days, a collection of old crumblies of whom I am presently one, to reminisce about times we spent together so long ago. I have no idea what they said, though no doubt a tape exists somewhere. Fred told me later, when I saw him and Mary Ross in London that he, Fred, had denied the very existence of a Kardomah group, but if there was one I had started it. I don't know whether others shared this view. I was in America. I don't know even if the notes I sent to the BBC were helpful. I do know, however, that in our Kardomah circle the BBC was never an unseen presence, it was a force in our lives never to be taken lightly, albeit shifty, unpredictable and treacherous.

(There was a problem at this point with the microphone)

I do know, however, that in our Kardomah circle was ever an unseen presence, a force in our lives not to be taken lightly, albeit shifty, predictable, unpredictable, and treacherous. For young composers especially, the organisation was a nightmare. For Dylan, it was an opportunity which at last could not be denied him. Thomas Warner had bad luck with it. The manuscripts he sent to the music department were kept for endless months, for years it seemed and may well have been. In accordance to the corporation's policy of encouraging young Welsh composers. He changed the name of his comedy overture from 'Seascape' to Mor Olwg in an attempt to please, but even this didn't work. We were all happy for him when the overture was accepted at last and scheduled for performance. Dylan, Fred, the composer and myself were gathered in a back room to listen. Radio, of course. We soon realised that things were going wrong. Entries kept coming in bars too late; the whole performance was a disaster. Tom summed it up philosophically in a letter to me from Windrush: 'Well, it was a comedy overture and they treated it as such.' The corporation was kinder to me. My contributions, talks for children, pieces about fly fishing and the like, sneaked in under the radar. The plays came later when I was better known, at least in Swansea. *Tristan* first of all then '*Theme for Audience*' which was precisely about the BBCs neglect of young composers.

What was it like to be living in Swansea in those days? Well, it was a very indulgent town. There was a kindness about it, a comprehension of the circumstances people were facing in a time of no money. It was a town that loved social life and dressing up, a town of celebratory dinners and commemorative balls at which everyone wore evening dress and no one felt in the least superior if men turned up, as they did, wearing street shoes and carrying their patent dance shoes in a paper bag. The highlights of our winter were the two hospital balls along with the Caledonian ball and the hunt ball, plus a dozen others. Even the fishing club, under the grand name of Piscatorial Society held a dance entrance fee five shillings. It was a town at which there was latitude for eccentricity, a place where – can you imagine this? I was able to go to work in riding costume and on horseback. And this, where my wage amounted to all of three pounds fifteen a week, less than twenty US dollars. This was a local secret. Of course, prices were low and the young people I knew, having as yet few obligations in the way of rent, food, lighting or laundry, were able to sport themselves in a certain style, not their fault that the economy laid in ruins about them. As a reporter I was able to get free tickets for everything. As an anchor, writing articles under the name 'Blue Nun, I was offered miles of free fishing on the Tawe and on the Wye. Think of that now. Free fishing on the golden mile below Dinefwr Castle. To get to it I used to borrow my father's car, an ancient Singer, with negligible horsepower but a high roof made to accommodate a top hat. Registration 'CY' the town's first letters. One set of traffic lights to contend with. Gosh, how marvellous the town must have been in those days. Nowadays it's protected by embankments and railings everywhere I go.

There is one picture of Swansea which has always stayed in my mind. I'm standing near the doors at the entrance to the Brangwyn Hall and three hundred couples, carefully and beautifully dressed, are waltzing to music played by two bands: *The Manhatton's* and the *Qu'est-ce que c'est's*. The floor, cleverly sprung and designed to be danced on, ripples beneath them like the sea. It is a sight more typical of Vienna than one might think of a South Wales coal port. I was there today and I saw how mouldy the doors were, the bronze unclean, and the steps crumbling in less than a life time.

More snap shots. We are at a party given by myself and an agreeable young man who's thrown open his apartment above the bars and steam laundry down by the slip. A notable affair with sixty guests and a large supply of over-proofed naval rum on board. Dylan was there but ran away when he saw a man in policeman's uniform. He was half way down the stairs before the Philips girls caught him: 'Come back' they called, 'it's only Walter Flower'. Mollified, Dylan returned. He liked Walter Flower, we all did. Many glasses of rum later, I noticed Dylan leaning over a machine called, at that time, a radiogram. He was trying to read the title on a moving record. Round and round went his eyes. Suddenly the music stopped. 'What had happened?' they asked. Just that Dylan had been sick into the machine.

Item. Dylan's soberly perfect in a darkened upstairs bedroom at the Philips house on Philips Parade. We are playing party games, seven or eight of us. 'Knock knock'- it is Dylan's turn.

'Who's there?'

Sacheverell.

Sacheveral who?

No one answers

Dylan answers in an imitation of his rumbling, tipsy London voice.

Sacheveral people. [editor SEVERAL PEOPLE]

Then we tried to guess the names of film stars from various cryptic clues. It is my turn. 'July the fourteenth.' Silence. 'no-one guesses, does anybody?'

'We give up.'

"It's Frances Day of course." Zilch applause.

Vera and Evelyn Philips are without doubt the muses of this circle. We all seem to live at their house, as we do at Tom Warner's house, not far away in the same street. Their parents don't mind at all, at least we think so. Mr and Mrs Philips tell me they have bought a mansion in Carmarthenshire, possibly to get away from us. 'Fancy a mansion' says Mrs Philips brightly, 'we are peasants really.' Tom Warner's house is where I meet Dan and Dylan together on musical evenings. They play trios, totally improvised on whatever instruments are at hand, pressing forward on the principle that Dylan is always right. The music sounds, well, ahead of its time.

Music is important to us. Dylan, Fred, Dan and I hire a taxi to Cardiff to hear the Vienna Philharmonic; a memorable evening for us. Back, much later, in Warner's house, we tried to play the whole programme through again on the piano. Pianissimo, with plausible imitations of French horn and banging on the drums on the woodwork of the piano. And, strange enough, it sounded a good imitation of what we heard... to us. Well, this is the room where I found Dan Jones resplendent in white tie in tails, conducting a Brahms symphony from the whole score. No orchestra, just a gramophone and drum kit. In quiet moments you can hear the sound of a flute coming from a room upstairs. 'It is my flute playing brother' says Tom'. In all the years I was close to Tom and familiar with that house, I never saw this brother, never met him on the stairs, never set eyes on him. Curious.

Dylan in Castle Street, outside the Kardomah:

'What do you know about the British council?'

'Not much.'

'You think they might make me a grant?'

'It's possible, for future work.'

'I want a grant of money now, for work I've already done, that work not having been profitable.'

'Forget it Dylan, they will all be glad to help you one day, when you no longer need it.'

Attempts have been made to portray Dylan as some sort of martyr, doomed and neglected and persecuted by a cruel society. But it's nothing at all like the truth. As far as possible, Dylan was exactly where he wanted to be, doing just what he wanted to do, that is to say drinking in famous pubs around Chelsea and Soho, at the centre of artistic and bohemian life, moving on equal terms with people of talent and passion and ability. Where else would he have wanted to be? You can say what you like about grungy Soho in the late forties, a lot could happen there, Dylan with Nina Hamnett in the French pub, with Augustus in the Wheatsheaf, in the Mandrake club in Meard Street, in company with half literary London, though not always at the same time. We had many adventures together. I recall ending one evening asleep on top of a grand piano in a flat presumably belonging to Anastasia Eagle Anrap. Dylan was asleep below, but persecuted. Ever heard of a persecuted man taking a taxi to Oxford after a nights drinking? What persecuted man belongs to the Savage club? That, mes chers, is pure, pure establishment. Like the evening I spent with Casper John when we ended up staying at both the Cumberland and Mayfair hotels. But in general I found the Soho scene promised far more than it ever delivered; a boring scene on the whole, with men elbow to elbow, shouting in bars. Confirmed that the other day when I passed the French pub with half the people out on the pavements, still doing the same, still looking the same as if nothing had changed. As I say, I knew it well. Now, I read '*Soho Days*'. Thank you.

I have known Finch's I have known the Wheatsheaf,
Black Horse and French Pub in my long Fitzrovings.
All, all forgone, the old familiar places.

I have spent seasons captive in the Mandrake,
Greek street and Charlotte Street, alleyways of Soho,
Trace and retrace my old, familiar places.

I have sat silent, waiting for some signal
Poured from a big beermug in the sad York Minster,
Move, move away from old, familiar stasis.

I have felt suddenly queasy in the Granby,
Chained to a wine glass, girls would never go there,
(Piss-poor arrangement; not my kind of evening.

I have been heavily Plastered in the Fitzroy
Good friends around me; painters, men of letters;
All, all are glossed in book, in bevelled mirror.

Famed alcoholics, prisoners of tap rooms,
five star eccentrics, idols of Fitzrovia.
These were my fellows, I shall not forget them.
Raise, raise a glass to old, familiar faces.

Item. How was Dylan regarded by those who knew him best? Easy to answer. He was looked on with something close to affection, coloured by an obscure protective wish. We all liked Dylan, looked forward to his company. We did of course have a good idea how special his writing was. Our relations continued on to be intimate and personal. Dylan, to me, early on outside the Kardomah: 'Do you really like beer?'

'Not really, I don't like it much.'

Dylan: 'I like beer, I like the taste of it.'

Ummm. Anyone with a taste for beer would find that the Swansea custom of drinking in schools confirmed it. A man entering a favourite bar at lunchtime was presumed to know everyone there, and probably did. 'Hello Charlie, what will you have?' The time to escape was then or never.

'Half a mild.' The trap was sprung. Ten glasses of mild beer later, it would be your turn to pay a round and the circle had grown bigger. 'Hello Keidrych, what will you have?' So, as one would expect with such encouragement, Dylan's drinking habit developed and began to concern his parents. His uncle was especially vexed.

'Do you know what he said?' Dylan reported. 'He said "put the boy in a mad house".* Instead of a mad house, Dylan was sent to a monastery in Ireland where, according to his account to me, the monks poured beer over his food, into his tea, over his sleeves. The object being, to make him sick of beer. If that was their object, I'm afraid they never succeeded. Besides drinking, Dylan had a vice which was shared by myself and most men who grew up in South Wales, habitual smoking. You see, he'd stick a cigarette in the corner of his mouth and puff, puff away until it was gone. I did this too. No stains of nicotine ever on our hands. I believe we thought cigarettes were good for us. It would not surprise me. Lots of things that happened in South Wales in that period were idiotic, clueless; no-one knew how to cook or anything, salads, fresh food, minimal diet needs, hygiene, keeping clothes clean, another kind of poverty. All this has no doubt been put to right long since. A couple of years ago I met a lady by chance in a teashop in Saigon. She came from Swansea she said. 'What do you think of Swansea now?' she asked me. I said:

'It has greatly changed.'

'I think it has lapsed into barbarism' she commented sadly.

Two main centres of influence during the Kardomah period: The BBC Third Programme and the columns of the views and criticisms that appeared in the two Sunday papers, the Sunday Times and the Observer. It was a time of few luxuries but one I did enjoy, courtesy of my mother, was reading those two papers in bed with my breakfast on a Sunday morning. Thus during the afternoon I would not find that everyone had read Newman on music or Harold Nicolson on current affairs while I had not. The Third Programme at that time was a marvel, cos really our education, made up for the deficiency of the grammar school. The foremost thinkers and literary men of the period, the finest chamber music, the proms, the world's great orchestras all there and live and not recorded. This was all ours. And the sound qualities of our radios, certainly better than is found generally in our houses today. The vampiric days of radio, as a disgraced medium run by D.Js according to a formula, had yet to begin. I'm thinking now of as a disgraced medium.

Nearly, so much has been left unsaid. I pause now to remember a man who's never received the recognition he had earned. If any man deserved the applause of his friends, it was Daniel Jones. Never have I heard his music played in Canada, I possess but one symphony of his by courtesy of Jeff Towns. But as I listen to it I am convinced that he is a composer of the highest order, equal in stature to the leading masters of the century. Yet where are his shrines, where is his picture gallery? He and I were never really close but we understood each other well and saw each other often. He was closest of all to Dylan. He was ahead of me in years, in sophistication and then, from early on, there were all his academic achievements and his witty minor verse. 'I will not be Dylan's friend' he would say. Nine symphonies of great beauty and complexity. What else did he have to do? Translate from the Chinese? Well, he did that too. But still.

Turning to a lighter side, Dylan, he and I at his home high up on Town Hill. 'Let us weep and wail' he would urge, and all three of us would break out into a lugubrious lament, punctuated by heavy sobs, cries of despair, fragments of forgotten sermons, tears choked back: a most theatrical performance.

I have not given due time to talk about Vernon Watkins. Shy Vernon, honoured in our circle. How well he could write in his quiet manner. Remember this which might serve as his own epitaph:

Now the soul knows the fire that first composed it
Sinks not with time but is renewed hereafter.
Death cannot steal the light which love has kindled
Nor the years change it.[19]

And I've not given Fred his due either but I know he won't mind. Let me quote this from what Vernon said about him. By the way his studio was high above a flower shop in Orchard Street and those flowers had a sweet smell:

'And this the painter of fish on top of the fragrant stairs, extravagant hearer of night, his iconoclastic frown.'

Great lines, they don't sound like Vernon at all. And I wanted to write, even in this scruffy way, about Keidrych Rhys, about Mably Owen, about the Little Theatre but by now the last words should probably belong to Dylan. Now, it was a rare thing for me to put a direct question to him but I did once and then only because it flowed from our conversation.

'Under what poetic rack do you place yourself?' I asked. Then immediately, Dylan in his best voice:

'I know what I am. I am first class or seventh class.'

This is the fiftieth anniversary of his death this year, we've marked the occasion, but we celebrate the life. The work remains. Death shall have no dominion.

The events of his funeral run in my head like a movie, I think they'd make a great story if only Dylan could write it. At the wake we were in tears but we were dancing.

I was dancing with Caitlin. Someone touched her sleeve, the hand held a full mug of ale. Caitlin took the mug and flung the contents to the ceiling shouting: 'Here's to you Dylan, wherever you are.'

Here's to you Dylan, wherever you are, I take up her cry.

CHARLES FISHER

Last of the 'Kardomah Boys'

In his 1965 *Life of Dylan Thomas*, Constantine Fitzgibbon, the official biographer of the Welsh poet, writes, "Charles Fisher was one of Dylan's closest Swansea 'friends of my youth' ". He also claims that "Charles Fisher was more than just a journalist and was thought by many to show more promise as a writer than did Dylan".

Born in Swansea in 1914, Charles Fisher was an almost exact contemporary of Dylan Thomas. They both attended Swansea Grammar School, where they met and became friends – indeed, Fisher could claim to be Thomas's first "wife" inasmuch as he played that role in the school's all-boy production of John Galsworthy's *Strife*, with Thomas taking the lead role of Roberts the strike leader.

After school they both became reporters on the local newspaper, *The South Wales Evening Post*, where Fisher's father was head printer. Fisher was by far the better journalist and wrote general news, music criticism and a well respected angling column under the by-line "Blue Dun". He loved the outdoors and country pursuits and was known to arrive at the urban newspaper offices dressed in riding breeches, having hitched his horse to a lamppost outside. Even in 1930s Swansea this was eccentric behaviour. Fisher once described Thomas as "looking like an unmade bed". But Fisher was the complete opposite, a well-groomed dandy, who, every Saturday, would don top-hat and tails and head for the local dinner-dance, where he cut a swathe through the Swansea girls.

Fisher and Thomas were both part of a group of bright young men who have come to be known as the "Kardomah Boys", after the Swansea café where they would meet up on an *ad hoc* basis. All were talented artists in one field or another – the poet Vernon Watkins, the painter Alfred Janes and the musician and polymath Daniel Jones, together with other talented writers and musicians like John Prichard and Tom Warner. Dylan Thomas would describe these meetings at length in his 1947 radio broadcast *Return Journey*, writing "Charlie's got whiskers now" and saying that he will become famous for "catching the poshest trout".

After their work on the local paper, they both moved up to London – Thomas to pursue his literary career and Fisher to continue his journalism, working for Reuters. But Fisher continued to write poetry and plays – his poems were published in the early issues of Kiedrych Rhys's seminal literary magazine *Wales* alongside Dylan Thomas and other key Anglo-Welsh writers.

Fisher and Thomas stayed in touch and they began to collaborate on a spoof murder mystery, *The Death of the King's Canary*. But with the advent of the Second World War, Fisher volunteered and joined the Army Intelligence Corps. His place as co-writer on *The Death of the King's Canary* was taken up by John Davenport and the book was eventually published in 1976, with an introduction by Fitzgibbon, who wrote warmly of Fisher's early involvement.

Fisher had married a Spanish singer some years older than himself but by the time of Dylan Thomas's death in 1953, this marriage had broken up. Fisher was shocked and saddened by his friend's untimely death and he attended Thomas's infamous funeral in Laugharne before striking out for a new life in Canada.

He ended up in Ottawa, where he worked at the Canadian parliament, transcribing the proceedings for their version of Hansard. It was an ideal job for Fisher as it brought him into contact with a rich and colourful social scene which he thrived on. But it also gave him long holidays where he could indulge his passion for travel. To begin with, he was captivated by Spain – in particular Granada and its gypsy population. Remarkably he won their affection and respect as a flamenco guitarist, dancer, drinker and bon viveur, and was eventually accepted into a gypsy family, even giving away the bride at a huge gypsy wedding.

Fisher: a well-groomed dandy who cut a swathe through the Swansea girls

On his retirement, Charles Fisher continued to travel, but now he explored the Far East and Pacific islands. He came to love Thailand, which became a favourite destination. He also began to write poetry and prose again and in 1988, his volume of poems *The Locust Years* was published to critical acclaim. His account of his time with the Spanish gypsies, *Adios Granada*, is to be published shortly.

In 2003, Fisher returned to Swansea and gave a mesmerising talk to a packed auditorium at the Dylan Thomas Centre on the last night of the festival commemorating the 50th anniversary of the poet's death. Nearing 90 himself, Fisher cut a fine figure in a midnight-blue Armani jacket, upright and chiselled, his steel-grey hair tied back in a neat pony-tail – he looked like a cross between Geronimo and Timothy Leary.

He was on another of his long solo journeys across the globe when he died peacefully in his sleep in a hotel in Bangkok.

Jeff Towns

Charles James Fisher, writer and journalist: born Swansea 21 November 1914; twice married (one daughter); died Bangkok 24 January 2006.

And this is the Obituary I wrote for Charles for the *Independent* Newspaper

Charles reading in Salubrious Passage Swansea

In his 1965 *Life of Dylan Thomas*, Constantine Fitzgibbon, the official biographer of the Welsh poet, writes, "Charles Fisher was one of Dylan's closest Swansea 'friends of my youth." He also claims that

> 'Charles Fisher was more than just a journalist and was thought by many to show more promise as a writer than did Dylan.'

Born in Swansea in 1914, Charles Fisher was an almost exact contemporary of Dylan Thomas. They both attended Swansea Grammar School, where they met and became friends – indeed, Fisher could claim to be Thomas's first "wife" inasmuch as he played that role in the school's all-boy production of John Galsworthy's Strife, with Thomas taking the lead role of Roberts the strike leader. After school they both became reporters on the local newspaper, *The South Wales Evening Post*, where Fisher's father was head printer. Fisher was by far the better journalist and wrote general news, music criticism and a well-respected angling column under the by-line *Blue Dun*.[20] He loved the outdoors and country pursuits and was known to arrive at the urban newspaper offices dressed in riding breeches, having hitched his horse to a lamppost outside. Even in 1930s Swansea this was eccentric behaviour.

Fisher once described Thomas as "looking like an unmade bed". But Fisher was the complete opposite, a well-groomed dandy, who, every Saturday, would don top-hat and tails and head for the local dinner-dance, where he cut a swath through the Swansea girls. Fisher and Thomas were both part of a group of bright young men who have come to be known as the "Kardomah Boys", after the Swansea café where they would meet up on an ad hoc basis. All were talented artists in one field or another – the poet Vernon Watkins, the painter Alfred Janes and the musician and polymath Daniel Jones, together with other talented writers and musicians like John Prichard and Tom Warner. Dylan Thomas would describe these meetings at length in his 1947 radio broadcast *Return Journey*, writing "Charlie's got whiskers now" and predicting that he would become famous for "catching the poshest trout".

After their work on the local paper, they both moved up to London – Thomas to pursue his literary career and Fisher to continue his journalism, working for Reuters. But Fisher continued to write poetry and plays – his poems were published in the early issues of Kiedrych Rhys's seminal literary magazine, *Wales*, alongside Dylan Thomas and other key Anglo-Welsh writers. Fisher and Thomas stayed in touch and they began to collaborate on a spoof murder mystery, *The Death of the King's Canary*. But with the advent of the Second World War, Fisher volunteered and joined the Army Intelligence Corps. His place as co-writer on *The Death of the King's Canary* was taken up by John Davenport and the book was eventually published in 1976, with an introduction by Fitzgibbon, who wrote warmly of Fisher's early involvement.

Fisher had married a Spanish opera singer some years older than himself but by the time of Dylan Thomas's death in 1953, this marriage had broken up. Fisher was shocked and saddened by his friend's untimely death and he attended Thomas's infamous funeral in Laugharne before striking out for a new life in Canada. He ended up in Ottawa, where he worked at the Canadian parliament, transcribing the proceedings for their version of Hansard. It was an ideal job for Fisher as it brought him into contact with a rich and colourful social scene which he thrived on. But it also gave him long holidays where he could indulge his passion for travel. To begin with, he was captivated by Spain – in particular Granada and its gypsy population. Remarkably he won their affection and respect as a flamenco guitarist, dancer, drinker and bon viveur, and was eventually accepted into a gypsy family, even giving away the bride at a huge gypsy wedding.

On his retirement, Charles Fisher continued to travel, but now he explored the Far East and Pacific islands. He came to love Thailand, which became a favourite destination. He also began to write poetry and prose again and in 1988, his volume of poems The Locust Years was published to critical acclaim. His account of his time with the Spanish gypsies, *Adios Granada*, is to be published shortly.

In 2003, Fisher returned to Swansea and gave a mesmerising talk to a packed auditorium at the Dylan Thomas Centre on the last night of the festival commemorating the 50th anniversary of the poet's death. Nearing 90 himself, Fisher cut a fine figure in a midnight-blue Armani jacket, upright and chiselled, his steel-grey hair tied back in a neat pony-tail – he looked like a cross between Geronimo and Timothy Leary.

He was on another of his long solo journeys across the globe when he died peacefully in his sleep in a hotel in Bangkok.

Charles James Fisher, writer and journalist: born Swansea 21 November 1914; twice married (one daughter); died Bangkok 24 January 2006.

Here's to you, Charles, wherever you are ...

1. Loosely translated as *You disgusting dirty little pig!*

2. I had heard nothing of Tom Warner until on a recent episode of BBC Antiques Road trip coming from Cardiff a splendid portrait of Tom's wife painted by Alfred Janes was brought onto the programme for valuation – and a splendid picture it was and Tom got a brief mention too.

3. *Return Journey* was first broadcast June 15th 1947. It was repeated 6 times over the next 7 years. This radio programme was a carefully pre-scripted discussion. It was recorded in *The Grove* studio in Uplands, Swansea on 6 October and broadcast on the 24th.

4. First Broadcast on October 29 on the Welsh Home Service. Later published in full in John Ackerman's Dylan Thomas The Broadcasts Dent 1991.

5. Vernon Watkins and his soon to be wife Gwen were also stationed at Bletchley Park throughout the war.

6. Gwen Watkins: *Portrait of a Friend*. Gomer. 1983.

7. The Dylan Thomas Trust (or the Trustees for the Copyrights of Dylan Thomas) was created after Dylan Thomas's death in 1953 in order to administer the income from Thomas' estate for the benefit of the beneficiaries, namely Caitlin and the three children Llewelyn (1939-2000), Aeronwy (1943-2009) and Colm (b. 1949). The original trustees were Thomas' friend Dr Daniel Jones (1912-1993), his literary agent David Higham (1895-1978) of Pearn, Pollinger & Higham (and later David Higham Associates) and his solicitor Stuart Thomas (1914-1995) of D.O. Thomas & Co., Swansea. Daniel Jones resigned as a Trustee in January 1955 and was replaced by Wynford Vaughan-Thomas (1908-1987).

8. See the end of Chapter 2. *Letter to Loren* for an account of one such interaction.

9. The Life of Dylan Thomas Constantine Fitzgibbon.aq J M Dent & Sons Ltd, London, 1965.
Charles also included a long extract from it when he spoke at the Dylan Thomas Centre in 2003. A transcript of the talk is included below.

10. Letters which I eventually acquired – They are now in the National Library of Wales and form part of the *Jeff Towns Dylan Thomas Collection* in the National Library of Wales Aberystwyth. There is an online catalogue of the collection which informs you that the collection is stored in a space of 0.452 cubic metres and comprises 49 boxes of varying sizes.

11. In fact, Charles was Dylan's second partner in prose; he had first approached Desmond Hawkins to work with him and he eventually wrote the book in 1941 with John Davenport. 1941. It was not published by Dent until 1976, due to fear of litigation if it was to be published while those lampooned were still alive. When I later visited Charles, I acquired the original Ms. of his first chapter, which is now in the National Library of Wales.

12. The Dôme and the Rotonde were two legendary swish Parisian Coffee shops in the early half of the last century.

13. Dylan Thomas A Biography. 1977 with a new enlarged edition coming out in 2000.

14. For any petrol heads reading this – it was one hell of a car: A very rare 1953 Jaguar XK 120 OTS. It left the factory with a special power boosting Westlake cylinder head. In 1949, the same model set a new record, running the measured mile at 132 mph.

15. *Tare*. I had to look this word up it. It means a certain weight and is sometimes called unladen weight. It is the weight of an empty vehicle or container. By subtracting tare weight from gross weight (laden weight) one can determine the weight of the goods carried or contained (the net weight).The word originates from Middle French word *tare* meaning 'wastage in goods, but also deficiency, imperfection' (15th c.).

16. This is a revamped and edited version of the material Charles wrote for Constantine Fitzgibbon on his request, when he was about to start work on the Official Biography of Dylan Thomas. Fitzgibbon included it in his biography which came out in 1965.

17. A line from Dylan's poem, *Hunchback in the Park*.

18. *Botteghe Oscure* was an International Literary magazine published in Rome by a very wealthy American, Marguerite Caetani (Princess di Bassiano) It ran from 1948 to 1960. And Dylan was a regular contributor – Marguerite paid well and became one of Dylan's main patrons – in return she got to publish *Do Not Go Gentle* and the first half on *Under Milk Wood.*

19. These lines are on the memorial plaque to Vernon inside Pennard church. They are from his poem *Great Nights Returning*, initially published in *Cypress and Acacia*. Faber & Faber 1959.

20. A term from the Angling lexicon. Blue Dun (sometimes Dunn) is the name given to a classic trout dry fly pattern that was originated to imitate the early mayfly hatches. Charles Fisher used this term as his by-line when he wrote the weekly angling column for the *South Wales Post* newspaper in the early thirties when he was working alongside Dylan Thomas.

Dylans' manic self-portrait doodle

12.

Dylan Thomas:
Depicted in Prose-Fiction & Poetry.

Take your place, like Dylan; in the deepening sense of truth.
Stand where the gods are idle, smiling, By the secret streams of youth.
Stephen Tennants' unrecorded poem, ***Homage to Dylan Thomas Christmas 1960***

Dylan Thomas was an habitual doodler and was not shy of depicting himself, often as a rather grotesque self-caricature; the example above was scribbled down in the Wheatsheaf[1]. pub in Fitzrovia London. He also wrote a few descriptions of himself in his prose writings in which he again went mainly for comic effect. Writing letters to Pamela Hansford Johnson in the 1930's, (she was his first serious girlfriend) before they had actually met, he offers her various somewhat unappealing vignettes of what she should expect:

> A thin, curly little person, smoking too many cigarettes, with a crocked lung ...

And again;

> I am not a particular nuisance, and I smell quite nice. I look about fourteen, And I have a large, round nose; nature gave it to me, but fate and a weak banister, broke it; in cold weather it is sufficiently glossy to light up any room...

And in his only attempt at a novel *Adventures in the Skin Trade*, (which he left unfinished) the character of Samuel Bennett, his hero; or maybe he is more anti-hero, is in many ways based on his own younger self;

> Call him Sam Bennet. He wore a felt trilby hat that been lying by his bedside ... In striped pyjamas tight under the arms and torn between the legs ...his eyes were still heavy from a dream of untouchable city women ...

His other prose work was the collaborative attempt at a country house detective story – a genre which he loved to read. He was considering it early, in 1935 and he tries to get his London pal Desmond Hawkins involved. He seemed they seemed already to have a title – *The Murder of the King's Canary*; and an outline; a satirical, spoof, detective *roman a clef*, poking fun at thinly disguised literary figures of the day. But nothing transpired, so a few years later, he tried to get his old Swansea newspaper colleague, Charles Fisher on board. He wrote to him in 1938;

> Murder of the King's Canary: I'd very much like to do it with you ... Make it the detective story to end all stories ...

Although Charles wrote a first chapter, he went off to war and in 1940 Dylan finally worked on it with his well-heeled literary pal, John Davenport. Even at this third attempt they never really completed the book and amidst fears of libel and law suits, what did get written was finally published in 1976 as *The Death of the King's Canary*. It garnered scant praise from reviewers. Dylan appears in the novel as *Owen Tudur* and Davenport is *Tom Agard*. The best scene is of the two of them drifting in a boat off the Cardigan coast, drinking copiously from a bobbing keg of Irish Whiskey. The plot centres on the Prime Minister having to select a new and suitable Poet Laureate – the *King's Canary* of the title. There are some fine satiric poetic parodies of T.S. Eliot, W.H. Auden, George Barker, William Epson and the Sitwells, but the poem attributed to Albert Ponting seems to be an extreme parody of Dylan's own most difficult and obscure poems; it begins;

> I, I, my own gauze phantom am,
> My head frothing under my arm,
> The buttocks of Venus for my huge davenport,
> I orgillous turn, burn, churn,
> As his rubbery bosom curds my perspiring arm.

In his own poetry Dylan is a tad more serious, but his late poem *Lament* is also a somewhat poetic autobiographical ramble through his past life; beginning

> When I was a windy boy and a bit
> And the black spit of the chapel fold
> (sighed the old ram rod, dying of women)
> I tiptoed shy in the gooseberry wood

In his radio broadcasts he often lampooned himself and his contemporaries. In his 1947 radio play *Return Journey*, he describes his older self returning to search out his lost youth in Swansea. It opens with him asking a barmaid if she recalls his former self;

NARRATOR:

I wonder whether you remember a friend of mine....
He'd be about seventeen or eighteen, and about medium height. above medium height for Wales I mean, he's five foot six and a half. Thick blubber lips; snub nose; curly brown hair; one front tooth broken... speaks rather fancy; truculent; plausible...a bombastic adolescent provincial bohemian...a gabbing, ambitious, mock-tough, pretentious young man; and mole-y too.

He is still at it in 1953 in his radio broadcast, *A Visit to America*, his pen-ultimate piece for radio. It was recorded late in October 1953; a little over a month before his death. It his humourous account of his experiences on the lecture/poetry reading circuit of America, based on his own three mammoth tours. It is replete with self-mocking descriptions but many have the real ring of truth;

There they go... from New York to Los Angeles; exhibitionists, polemicists. histrionic publicists ...ulterior decorators, windbags, and bigwigs and humbugs...men with elephantiasis of the reputation...men from the BBC who speak as though they have the Elgin Marbles in their mouths. Potboiling philosophers, professional Irishmen (very lepri-corny) and, I'm afraid, fat poets with slim volumes.

So this is Dylan depicting himself in sketches and doodles and words but, before we get on to how other writers have used him in their fictions and poems, herewith a delightful designer hand-tooled leather binding depicting our poet. It was commissioned by the late Sir Roderick Brinkman Bart,[2] but to me he was Roddy, a bookselling colleague who traded as Monk Breton Books, dealing mainly in fine private press books and antiquarian and illustrated Children's books from his fine Toronto home. He also was a serious collector of Dylan Thomas, bringing both taste and money to the game – always a winning combination. I eventually, in a very roundabout way, acquired most of the better items from his collection but sadly he kept this book in the family.

Roddy commissioned a great British-born but Canada based, world-class master bookbinder, Michael Wilcox, to design and execute a full black straight-grained Morocco leather with gilt and inlaid leather decorations on a copy of Dylan's first book, the 'slim volume' of the 1934, first edition of *18 Poems* [only 250 copies of the first edition were printed].

And what a delightful binding it is Dylan, but his spotted bow-tie has transformed into a spotted jacket, and he is fully loaded, holding a book in one hand, a pint in the other and a lit cigarette is hanging from his lips. It is a stunning binding. Roddy kindly sent me a photograph of the finished binding.

I covet this book so much that I have just commissioned a Ruthin-based North Wales designer bookbinder, Adam Jurkojc to come up with his version of this splendid design on a set of unbound sheets of my book *Letter to Loren*.

Dylan Thomas depicted in Books

A good few contemporary novelists and short story writers, some world famous; others not so, have also chosen to use Dylan Thomas as the model for characters in their fictions, often also incorporating incidents from his short but busy life. Herewith a loosely chronological survey of the examples I have encountered, but it is subjective, rather than exhaustive survey.

***Social Climbers in Bloomsbury*. Count Potoki. 1939.**

Perhaps the earliest example of Dylan depicted comes from a curious and eccentric writer, Count Potoki of Montalk. The publishers of the recent biography[3] described him as;

> Poet, polemicist, pagan and pretender to the throne of Poland and one of the great eccentrics of the 20th century.

He was born in New Zealand in 1903 and from an early age he believed he was destined to become a great poet. He decided that England would offer him his best chance at literary success and so he came here in 1928. He declared that l left 'the republic' of New Zealand because;

> Poets are badly treated in this land of savages and All Blacks

However things quickly went pear-shaped when he wrote some immodestly ribald poems, one of which was inspired by the sexual frustrations of a friend. Having no means to print them himself, in searching for a publisher he fell foul of the law. In a notorious court case he was convicted at the Old Bailey for publishing an "an obscene libel" and sentenced to serve six months in Wormwood Scrubs Prison. On his release he decided to set up his own printing press and print his own writings. By 1936, with the help of a few well heeled friends, he had set up his own private press in London. Potoki told his biographer that he was present in the Fitzroy Tavern when Dylan Thomas met Augustus John and it is this meeting that he satirises in his, now rare, 1939 publication *Social Climbers in Bloomsbury Done from Life*. He used as an imprint *The Right Review*. This was the name of his scarce hand-printed right wing periodical where this satire was first published over a few issues.

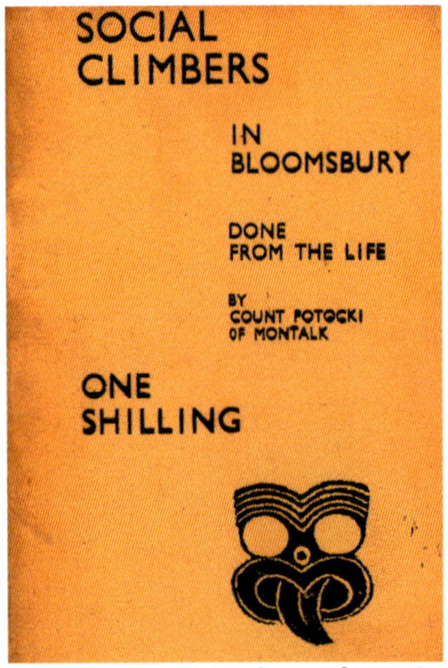

The rare, 1939, First edition of *Social Climbers in Bloomsbury*. The cover bears a Māori motif as homage to Potocki's birthplace

The recent biography of Potoki

The Cover of Potoki's *Right Review* in which he vents his spleen at Thomas

This bitter social satire is aimed at Leonard and Virginia Woolf, who had at one time supported him, but he also lampoons Dylan Thomas who he portrays as a young drunken poet, *Andyl Motsah* and Augustus John is *Divine Thomas*. They both frequent;

> *THE FATBOY TAVERN – THE PLACE WHERE YOU MEET THE REAL BOHEMIANS!*

And Potoki also provides a lurid 24 line pastiche poem which Andyl recites with much ceremony;

> Suddenly...he lost the accents but not the mannerisms of drunkenness
> And sets to disclaim...

He begins;

> About the senile tops of level mountains
> in the fifth house of whoredom lies my loved one
> when, lost in lore, the swilling ocean hollows
> the cup-crowned Hebe-heaven of her backbone

This from the 2nd stanza in all its gory detail;

> This is the drift of danegeld; dylanned damask
> I make a verse, a version and a veering
> tickling technique, tongue-twist, in Tartar tantrums-
> a hale, a whore, a hound, a hyleg-heron:

And it ends;

> With tantric octopus and cousined creatures

in the gulf stream deepsea currents waving:
this sex-act fantasy with filthy features.

Potoki had a very low opinion of Dylan Thomas as a poet but this may be attributed to envy and jealousy when confronted with Dylan's early successes. He would not give Dylan Thomas any credit as a writer and referred to him a;

Sedulous manufacturer of Poetry

Dylan for his part seems to have been unaffected by Potoki's attack and make no reference whatsoever to Potoki in and of his writing including his voluminous correspondence, and nor does he get mentioned anywhere in the many major or minor biographical works that have been published about Thomas.

With the synchronicity that I always enjoy; as I was writing this chapter I re-discovered quite by accident, a modern reprint of Potoki's filth which my good bookseller friend, the late Len Kelly,[4] self-published at his Frijon Press in Toronto in 1968 in an edition of just 50 copies and he gave me one.

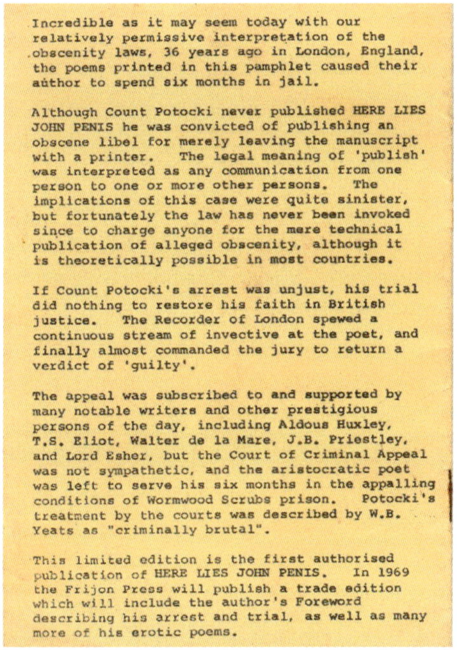

Incredible as it may seem today with our relatively permissive interpretation of the obscenity laws, 36 years ago in London, England, the poems printed in this pamphlet caused their author to spend six months in jail.

Although Count Potocki never published HERE LIES JOHN PENIS he was convicted of publishing an obscene libel for merely leaving the manuscript with a printer. The legal meaning of 'publish' was interpreted as any communication from one person to one or more other persons. The implications of this case were quite sinister, but fortunately the law has never been invoked since to charge anyone for the mere technical publication of alleged obscenity, although it is theoretically possible in most countries.

If Count Potocki's arrest was unjust, his trial did nothing to restore his faith in British justice. The Recorder of London spewed a continuous stream of invective at the poet, and finally almost commanded the jury to return a verdict of 'guilty'.

The appeal was subscribed to and supported by many notable writers and other prestigious persons of the day, including Aldous Huxley, T.S. Eliot, Walter de la Mare, J.B. Priestley, and Lord Esher, but the Court of Criminal Appeal was not sympathetic, and the aristocratic poet was left to serve his six months in the appalling conditions of Wormwood Scrubs prison. Potocki's treatment by the courts was described by W.B. Yeats as "criminally brutal".

This limited edition is the first authorised publication of HERE LIES JOHN PENIS. In 1969 the Frijon Press will publish a trade edition which will include the author's Foreword describing his arrest and trial, as well as many more of his erotic poems.

The cover of Len's John Penis and his account of it's history on the back cover

I have reproduced the above's titular poem in the footnotes[5]... be warned – it really is quite obscene ...

* * * * *

Kingsley Amis: *That Uncertain Feeling*, Gollancz 1955 and *The Old Devils*. Hutchinson. 1986.

Kingsley Amis once scathingly wrote that Dylan Thomas;

> ...was an outstandingly unpleasant man who cheated and stole from his friends and peed on their carpets.

They encountered each other just once, in Swansea in the early fifties, when Kingsley was an English lecturer at the University here. It did not go well. This, in Kingsley's words[6] is how it began;

> I met Dylan Thomas on a single evening in the spring of 1951, when he had accepted an invitation to give a talk to the English Society of the [University] College [of Swansea]. The secretary of the society, a pupil of mine, asked me if I would like to come along to the pub and meet Thomas before the official proceedings opened. I said I would like to very much, for although I had lost all my earlier enthusiasm for his writing, I had heard a great deal, not only in Swansea, of his abilities as a talker and entertainer of his friends.

But, during the 'official proceedings' Amis and Dylan began to clash and bicker; each trying to outsmart the other. Amis never changed his opinions of Dylan, and in at least two novels he used Dylan as the model for unpleasant characters.

That Uncertain Feeling is a satire on life and culture set in Aberdarcy,[7] a fictional Welsh seaside town, which is quite obviously Swansea. The story concerns a married librarian who begins an affair with the bored wife of a local bigwig. Amis mocks Wales's devotion to culture and learning as false and pretentious. It features a character Gareth Probert; a poet and writer who is clearly based on Thomas. The key scene in the novel is when hero accompanies an upper class lady he fancies to a performance of Probert's appalling verse play, *The Martyr* based on medieval Welsh History which is both bogus and amateurish way the same time. It is so bad that the couple sneak

The first edition

A vintage pulp-paperback edition

out and their illicit affair begins.

In 1961, the book was made into a very successful film starring Peter Sellers and Mai Zeterling. The title was changed to *Only Two Can Play*, to avoid confusion with another big Hollywood film with a very similar title. Much of the film was made in and around Swansea and made use of the Swansea Reference Library and the near-by Glynn Vivian Art Gallery. Richard Attenborough played Probert with Peter Sellers and Mai Zetterling took the lead roles.

Kingsley Amis' penultimate novel is set back in Swansea. It was an absolute return to the form of his first novel, *Lucky Jim*,

The re-titled Film spin-off edition

The Old Devils 1986

(which he wrote while living in Swansea; *The Old Devil*s was written in Laugharne). The novel was a commercial and critical success, winning the Booker Prize before being successfully adapted for Television. The plot involves Alun Weaver, a writer of modest celebrity, returning to his native Wales with his wife, Rhiannon, sometime girlfriend of Weaver's old acquaintance Peter Thomas. Alun begins associating with a group of former friends, including Peter, all of whom have continued to live locally while he was away spending their days daily in the local pub and the nights having affairs with each other's partners. The book is a real local *roman a clef* and when it was published working out the real identities of the characters became a regular amusement to locals of a certain age. The central character, Alun Weaver, is portrayed as a "stage-Taffy" and is most likely inspired by the broadcaster, writer and professional Welshman, Wynford Vaughan Thomas – a friend of both Dylan Thomas and Kingsley Amis, One of his roles is that of the main memoirist of a fictional Welsh poet Brydan, a thinly disguised parody of Dylan Thomas and very similar to the Probert character in *That Uncertain Feeling*. Amiss's overall depiction of Swansea, wider Wales, and Dylan Thomas is unremittingly negative: Amis makes most of his characters in turns, devious, false, sentimental, melodramatic, and shallow. In 1992 the BBC made it into a three part mini-series which was as well received as the original novel.

However Amis's opinion of Thomas never improved and he penned this short poetic squib that plainly referred to Thomas. The three-line *A Poet's Epitaph* was considered too offensive to be included in his *Collected Poems*:

They call you "drunk with words"; but when we drink
And fetch it up, we sluice it down the sink.
You should have stuck to spewing beer, not ink.

It was later published in *A Case of Samples* in 1956. Considering that Amis had such a low opinion of Dylan Thomas both as a man and as a poet, it was quite a surprise when, on the death of Wynford Vaughan Thomas, Amis was appointed as his replacement on the Dylan Thomas. Such a curious appointment was never explained but perhaps his long and close drinking and

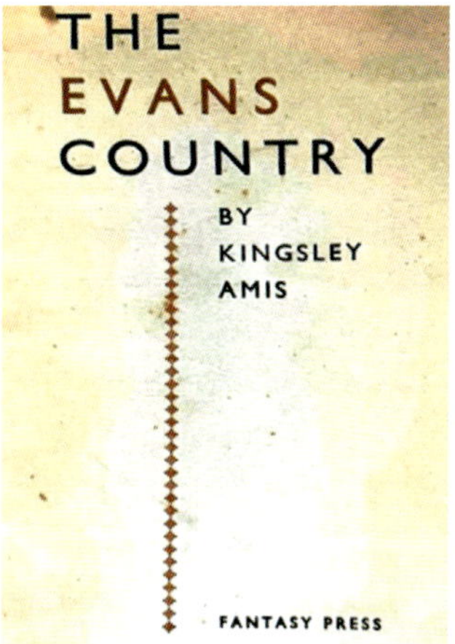

eating friendship with Stuart Thomas, the Swansea solicitor who administered the Trust had something to do with it. Although he enjoyed visiting Stuart in Swansea for regular 'Trust Meetings', mostly conducted over long bibulous lunches in Swansea's best restaurants, he ridiculed the town once again in his slim 1962 poetry pamphlet *The Evans Country* in which, the six short poems follows the sordid love-life around the town of a native, Dai Evans.

The opening stanza of the first poem, Aberdarcy, the Main Square, sets the tone;

> By the New Boot's, a tool box with flag-poles
> Glued on, and flanges, and a dirty great
> Baronial doorway and things like port holes,
> Evans met Mrs Rhys on their first date.

* * * * *

The First Edition dust jacket 1957

The Perishable Quality
by Rhys Davies. 1957.

Rhys Davies, was born Vivian Rees Davies in 1901. He went on to become one of the most prolific and successful Welsh prose writers of the 20th century, writing upwards of a hundred short stories, as well as twenty novels, three novellas, two books about Wales and an autobiography. He mostly lived his adult life in London, Davies' work is often set in the Wales he grew up in Blaenclydach, a side-valley of the Rhondda. Davies died in 1978 so *The Perishable Quality* is a relatively late novel. Davies hung out in the same Soho/Fitzrovia areas of London that attracted Dylan Thomas but Davies was not a drinker so he and Dylan did not become real friends but Rhys Davies did praise him in his book My Wales,[8] which came out in 1937...

> The young poet, Dylan Thomas, another dark horse, whose furious wealth of imagers is as wild and fearsome as a Welsh preacher involved in transports of *Hwyl*...

In *The Perishable Quality*, a central character Iolo Hancock,[9] is clearly based on the younger Dylan Thomas, as he was in his first few years in London. Like Dylan Iolo has a fine speaking voice which is often heard on the radio but more often heard in Soho/Fitzroivian type public houses. He is often pitifully and helplessly drunk, lives in squalor, sponges off people, whenever he can. These sentences echo many found in the serious biographies of Dylan Thomas. This is Eva's account of their first meeting:

> She had known Iolo Hancock one of the Goat' more celebrated habitués, for a few years. Iolo seemed ever looking for a stray bed...He was a compatriot, good poet and ornamental talker. Once she had accommodated him for the night, but he was too drunk to be anything but a childish nuisance.

Davies, for the most part, treats his *Iolo/Dylan* character with a fond good humour, but he goes over the top when he describes a night when Eva and a young friend join forces to get an extremely intoxicated Iolo home to his squalid Covent Garden bedsit. On the journey Iolo begins to feel queasy and is obviously about to be sick – an eventuality which is described in sickening detail:

> "Put your finger down your throat," Val advised...
> Iolo began to vomit. First came gurgling-out of easy
> Liquid, followed by more concentrated deposits. He
> Put up his left hand to catch these last, and the fingers
> of his right hand turned over the palmful of gleaming
> matter, scrabbling like a priest seeking in the entrails of
> a sacrificed beast the forecast of momentous events.
> "Melted green of stars," he gurgled, "oils of silver, water blues
> ... dissolved pearls...fluid eyes. A man bears within him the

fabulous liquids of death. I'm going to die."

This is unrestrained, grotesque and distasteful to say the least.

Things get more slapstick and amusing once the trio make it inside the shabby rooms; Iolo has insisted on dragging home a damaged tailor's dummy found in an alleyway which he proceeds to introduce to a nude wooden carving of his sometime girlfriend Ann, which has 'the aspect of a Minoan snake goddess' as Iolo has draped an eel he had bought to cook as he was eating a diet loaded with seafood to help him write a commissioned new poem about the sea.

* * * * *

Peter de Vries: *Reuben, Reuben* 1964

Writing in the Los Angeles Times, Charles Champlin begins his review of *The Collected Letters of Dylan Thomas*, with this:

> During a certain span of literary time, the foolish popular image of the poet was the chap in long hair and velvet cape, strolling through dew and buttercups, desperately appreciative of all about him. The later image, hardly less pervasive, is of the poet as a chain-smoking, alcoholic womanizer lurching down the road to hell with a song on his lips and a rip in his tweeds. By any name, the poet is always Dylan Thomas, most recently fictionalized by Peter De Vries

An early paperback edition

Tom Conti on the cover The Penguin Film spin-off

and portrayed by Tom Conti in the film "Reuben Reuben".

Peter de Vries was an American novelist and writer known for his satiric wit. In 1944, on James Thurber's recommendation De Vries joined the staff of The New Yorker where, apart from Thurber he was surrounded by the cream of American humourous writers, including Robert Benchley, S J Perelman and Dorothy Parker. He worked until 1987 during which time he published a large body of work; short stories, reviews, poetry, essays, a play, novellas, and some twenty-five novels. He settled in Connecticut where he found this middle class post-war suburbia a rich tapestry for his mild and funny novels described in his obituary as *Cheever country without the grimness*. De Vries was, according to Kingsley Amis, *The funniest serious writer to be found on either side of the Atlantic.*[10]

One of his most successful novels was his 1954 book *Reuben Reuben*, in which the central character is based on Dylan Thomas but re-cast as a visiting Scotch/Welsh blocked poet named Govan McGland (the clue is in the name), whose insatiable amorous thirst is as once both sad and funny.

Although we are led to believe that he was once a talented poet, he has become chronic drunk, serial philanderer and indifferent to the wounds he can casually inflict with his drunken wit, such as his quip when one of middle-aged conquests undresses for him, he mutters, to himself but loud enough for her to hear;

> *Released from their support, her breasts dropped like hanged men,*

It reduces her to tears.

This is from the New York Times review of the book;

> The intricacies of the plot of "Reuben, Reuben" would make the maze of the Minotaur look like a child's puzzle. Enough to say that the poet McGland appears quite early in the narrative and then takes over when the going gets too rough for the chicken-farmer. The troubling thing about McGland is that he is obviously a smudged carbon copy of Dylan Thomas, strongly endowed with the appetites for which Thomas became so famous on his celebrated tours. This latest expropriation of the Dylan myth is curious and disturbing – as

it leads to a kind of double exposure of fiction over fact. On the other hand, the characterization enables Mr. De Vries to display his great talent for parody and to record some Dionysian capers alien to the normal life of Woodsmoke.

The book had a strong afterlife; In 1967 it was adapted for the stage by Herman Shumlin, who also directed its successful run on Broadway. This play then inspired the very successful film adaptation in 1983 by Julius J. Epstein which was based both on the original book and the stage play It returned to the original title *Reuben Reuben*, and was directed by directed by Robert Ellis Miller. The British actor Tom Conti, then at the height of his fame, gave a strong performance as McGland. The film is not exactly true to the book in as much as in the book McGland commits suicide whereas the film has him pull back at the last minute in order to save a dog.

*　*　*　*　*

Pamela Hansford Johnson: *The Survival of the Fittest*. Macmillan. 1968.

Pamela Hansford Johnson met Dylan Thomas in the early thirties through the *Poetry Corner* of the *Sunday Referee* newspaper, where they both submitted poems and had their earliest work published. She wrote to him in after his poem, *That sanity be kept*, was published in the paper on 3 September 1933. The first surviving letter from Dylan to her was sent on 17 September. They did not meet up until February, 1934, when Dylan travelled up to London, but before then, Dylan had conducted a determined epistolary courtship which comprised of some dozen letters some of them over a dozen pages long. After his first visit they began their intense love affair with a few more visits and Dylan them moving up to London himself. The relationship lasted a few years and almost ended in marriage, before it petered out in August 1937. Approaching thirty letters from Dylan to Pamela are now held in the *Library at the New York State University Buffalo*. Many are several pages long and they give us a very complete picture of Dylan in his late teens and early twenties. Pamela's side of the correspondence sadly does not exist. She went on to marry an Australian Journalist in 1936. They had two children and then in 1949 they divorced and she married the novelist C.P. Snow in 1950. She published her first novel *This Bed Thy Centre* in 1935; the title was supplied by Dylan. She went on to publish 26 more novels in all as well as plays and a few critical works. Her memoir *Important To Me* (1974) contains a chapter on Dylan.

The 1968 First Edition

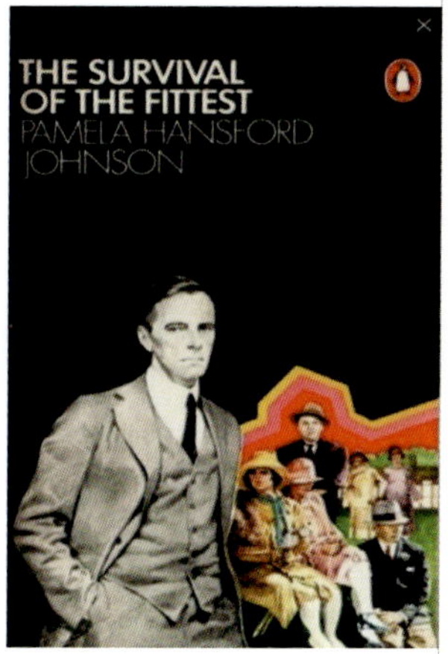

The Penguin paperback edition

The Survival of the Fittest is a novel which follows a group of friends from their youth in the 1930's, through into middle age in the 1960's. It weaves together threads of politics, history, love and literature which bind the group together. They come of age in the shadow of second World War which sets them apart, but their mutual love of literature keeps them together as a group. The unassuming, sympathetic and grounded Alison and the hard-drinking Kit rise from anonymity to become successful novelists. The other members of the group are; Clem, a well-known political journalist; Bobby who writes communist novels; and Jo who has published just a single short story. Each, both writers and non-writers, attempts to help the aspiring writer Jo, who cannot escape his childhood home because he and his sister must care for their domineering, crippled mother.

Wendy Pollard, who wrote a very detailed biography Johnson[11] refers to this book as her 'principal novel' and she suggests that the original idea had included versions of Pamela's younger self and of Dylan Thomas, was instigated by the media response to the publication of Dylan Thomas' *Selected Letters*[12] Although she was distressed by some of the press,[13] it made her cast her mind back to those heady days and she recalled how, after she and Dylan broke up, she was relentlessly pursued by one of Dylan's Swansea friend's, Trevor Hughes.[14] He was deeply obsessed with her and constantly told her how much he loved her; feelings which were completely un-reciprocated. Hughes was a close friend of Dylan's and it is he who accompanies Dylan on long trek to the far end of Worms Head, the westernmost tip of Gower Peninsular, which Dylan uses as the basis for his later, poignant, autobiographical short story, written in 1939, *Who Do You Wish Was With Us*. It was published in *Portrait of the Artist As Young Dog*. Hughes is named Raymond Price in the story. Hughes moved up to London before Dylan, but Dylan wrote to him a series of long and intense letters about his life and poetical development during the exact same time he was writing similar letters to Pamela.

Pamela began a draft which she referred to as being 'based on the Trevor Hughes story' and already had a title in her head – *The Survival of the Fittest*. The group of young men and women in the book contains three characters; Kit Mallings loosely based on Dylan, Jo based on Trevor Hughes. Pamela always distanced herself from these suggestions and in the case of Jo she categorically denied them, however her character Jo has an invalid mother who cramps his life and is eventually diagnosed with TB and Trevor's whole family – father and brother all suffered with TB and his brother, had died of the disease. It is this dead brother that Ray wishes was with them in the story. She also locates this group of young fledgling bohemian writers in the louche area of Fitzrovia and does not change the names of the famous local pubs; The Fitzroy Tavern and the Six Bells that the group regularly patronise and which she and Dylan Thomas both frequented during the time they were together.

When the novel was published Pamela was pleased with the general positive reviews the book received in the London press but she was both amazed and hurt by a review in the Welsh newspaper, the *Western Mail* which suggests that the character, Kit and his treatment in the book, amount to Pamela's revenge on Dylan's rejection of her some 30 years in the past.

* * * * *

John Summers 1928-2008: *Dylan: A Novel*. New English Library. 1970. John Summers lived out the last quarter of his life in Swansea, in Eaton Crescent in the Uplands, Dylan Thomas's boyhood and adolescent stamping ground. After a self-imposed education through travels – he left as a young man on a world tour with £20 in his pocket, he had become a writer – a prolific journalist, travel writer and novelist. Towards the end of the last century he began to come to my Bookshop in Salubrious Passage and later to the Dylan Thomas Centre where I had another bookshop. We became friends and I called on him a few times. He was charmingly eccentric and very intelligent. He entrusted me with the manuscripts and typescripts of some of his early works and of the stage play which inspired his novel based on Dylan Thomas's life, and these are now in the National Library of Wales. However I still have in my garden a rare surviving seat from a Mumbles railway carriage which adjusts to travel both backwards and forwards, which he gifted to me.

John had met Dylan Thomas a couple of times and knew the area around Laugharne, Llanstephan, Llanybri areas well. He was around Laugharne when the fine American photographer, Rollie McKenna was on an assignment from the New York up-market glossy *Mademoiselle* magazine to take photographs of Laugharne and the surrounding areas to accompany the first printing of *Under Milk Wood* in the February 1954 issue of the magazine and John got to know her and took splendid photographs of her which he gave to me. In 1966, he was working for the *Sunday Telegraph* and they sent him to Aberfan to cover the horrendous, deadly and disastrous landslide that buried the small mining village. His experience of the tragedy itself, and his relentless campaign to uncover the shabby treatment meted out by officialdom to the survivors and bereaved, formed the basis of his first novel, *Edge of Violence*.

Despite attempts from some official sources to suppress its publication, the book has emerged as a journalistic classic, and it sold in large numbers. It attracted a great deal of media coverage, including a famous interview by Joan Bakewell on *Late Night Line-Up*, and widespread praise from critics and fellow writers. John wrote his novel Dylan in his 39th year – the tragically young age that Dylan Thomas was when he died in New York in 1953. Summers novel is about the perils a fame and the precariousness of a writer's life. This from the *Sunday Telegraph*, 4 June 1970

> And the Dylan novel? What Summers says he has done is to make it a Dylan. 'I have had to fictionalise. I have tried to get at the truth by skirting the fact. Some Dylanophiles will bleat because it is not exactly the life of Dylan Thomas. Well, of course it isn't. It can't be. Maybe a hundred years from now somebody will have a go at that, but I wanted to get the story of all the Dylans across now, today, in our own times, under the theme of that famous Hemmingway quote: "We kill all our best writers because we are afraid of them...I want to tell the story of Dylan Thomas and all the other Dylan Thomases that have been before him. And will come after him. The Scott Fitzgeralds and the Jack Londons and the Behans and all the others still to come.

* * * * *

Chris Hood: *Banana Cat*. Secker & Warburg 1985.

Christopher Hood was born in Lancashire but arrived in Swansea in the 1970's, an untamed itinerant bohemian, front man to Blues bands,[15] writer, poet, and performer. Chris took the local arty set by storm. He eventually worked on the first few Swansea Fringe Festivals which sucked him into the world of crass desecration and exploitation of the city's famous literary son Dylan Thomas, by locals, arrivistes but mainly by members of city council. All this gave him ample material, inspiration and motivation to produce this comic novel, set very obviously in Swansea and so named in the book, which revolves around the fate and fortunes of a fake Dylan Thomas poetry manuscript the title of which is the novel's title as well. Here are the first stanzas that give a flavour of the spoof;

The narrator of the novel, George, is a kind hearted probation officer bemused with life and with coping with his "partly ex-wife" Alice. He also has to battle and contend with Dugdale, a con-man who is one of his charges and has made fraud an art form. Dugdale convinces Holloway, a caricature of a visiting American professor of English, that their awful pastiche

How should my wellspring cat

How should my wellspring cat,
Electric lard within a mottled tomb of cancer
And the shouts of praise,
Forsake the succour of oblivion's womb
And copper bindweed on the husks of time, to ride
Out on a shriek of stars
Athwart the foghorn bark of bailiffs
And the iron tit pip whistle of the priested air,
Streak on the streaming tiles
And, pistil hammered in the heart of night,
Conjour the treacle dark into a nest of spells,
The giddy winds of heaven and the kiss
Of polyp rotten daisies in the darling
Reek of creation's plundered well?

How should he hypnotise
The squalling female in her frozen rage,
Unpetrify the channels of the blood
In speaking capsules of his bony gaze,
Rant of his mummer's tale in delving throngs
Of wailing, and the reach of want
To spin, on ashtip summits of the skullwise loins
A clawtooth minuet of hair raise mawk,
Neckbreak and headlong southsea making
Cant of the slanted tongue,
Kick, trigger and conjoin the maw
And muscles in a wrack of rain
And warm spreadeagle down in spurts of ooze;
Split of his sprung banana to her inward glades?

of a Dylan Thomas poem that he, George and an artist friend composed during a drunken evening is a previously undiscovered, and genuine, thus very valuable. The plot unfolds in a very Tom Sharpe kind of way. It even includes a production of *Under Milk Wood* but adapted and performed nude, by a local Avant Garde theatre group Company named Theatre of Conflict. In fact back then and still going strong, Swansea still has a long-established Avant-Garde theatre company named VOLCANO, and they did once adapt *Under Milk Wood* into a rich explicit sexual romp which the Dylan Thomas Trustees chose to ban! all in all, having lived here in Swansea for over 50 years, this whimsical farce is maybe a tad too close to what actually goes on here for me to find it funny and it's a tad too close to how the place does react to their famous poet.

Some Welsh Responses:
Marcel Williams: *Diawl y Wenallt*. Y Lolfa, 1990.

Diawl y Wenallt is the only Welsh language novel in response to Dylan Thomas I have come across. The title, I believe, translates as *The Devil of Milk Wood*. The book caused a minor controversy in the Welsh press when it was first published mainly due to its sexual content and for its rather hostile treatment of the most famous Welsh writer of the Century. The novel is set in the fictional village of Cwmsylen,[16] wherein the local inhabitants have not yet forgiven the great poet Dylan Thomas, for what happened the night of his visit to the area. At last they seek a dreadful revenge. I was aware of the mild furore which accompanied the book's publication but as it has never been translated into English so I have not been able to read it. However, I was struck by the cover illustration which featured a strong image of a rather distraught looking Dylan Thomas being very publically crucified!

I was in fact so struck with the cover image that I quickly approached the publishers, *Y Lolfa*, a very Welsh nationalistic publishers based in the village of Talybont, just north of Aberystwyth. They were very generous and were happy to share contact details of the artist, a local girl, Ruth Jen Ifans. I tracked her down to Aberystwyth where she was still at the art school. We met in a local pub, she had brought along a large folder of all her preparatory and finished work towards the book's cover jacket. I bought her a pint and then went through her folder, which I was even more taken with. Some gentle negotiation ensued and she got a bundle of much needed cash and I had a splendid group of strong images of a much tortured Dylan Thomas.[17]

More recently I was reading a of essays on Welsh Literature by M.Wynn Thomas.[18] I am very glad to be able to call M.Wynn a friend. He is a Professor in the English Department at Swansea and when we first got to know each other he was head of CREW.[19] To my mind Wynn is the foremost commentator and critic on Welsh literary writing across all genres and in both languages writing today. One essay in the book entitled *Hidden attachments* deals with the complex relationships and symbiosis between the two literatures of Wales and he uses Marcel Williams's novel to

The wonderful cover by Ruth Jen Ifans for Y Lolfa's edition of the novel

make an interesting point. In the course of which he gives us a neat summary of the book's farcical plot, so I am now thankful to Wyn for giving me a much better idea of what the novel is all about. And very intriguing it is. Wynn begins by describing the book as 'a recent highly entertaining... pot-boiler of a novel' and he goes on to describe it;

> 'as a slightly raunchier version of the *Carry On Films* ... *Carry On Dylan Thomas* ...enthusiastically carrying on (in every sense of the phrase) the Dylan Thomas tradition of lust and lechery).

Wynn has whetted my appetite and now I wish someone would translate the book into English.

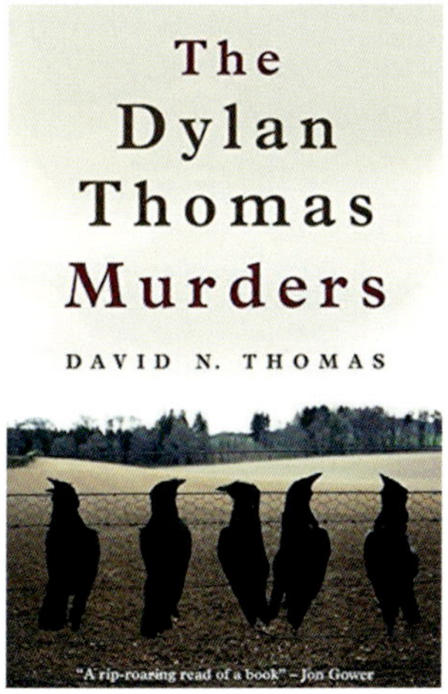

David N. Thomas; *The Dylan Thomas Murders*. Seren, 2002.

I must start by saying I'm not a fan of this book; I read it on publication and found it somewhat distasteful. I know the author and his work; he has done some amazing, in-depth research into Dylan Thomas's time around about in New Quay and Cardigan and produced a string of factual books on the subject.

This novel is a very sinister story in which 'real' people are depicted in very curious situations. Early on Dylan and T.S. Eliot share a Welsh mistress who has a child and the two great poets have a physical fist fight over paternity rights. My friend Jon Gower (who has written the foreword to this book) gave it a punchy and largely positive review,[20] but he does offer this warning about the content;

> Nothing can prepare you for the biliously black tale of serial Murder and unbridled nastiness which follows.

The love-child of either T.S. Eliot or Dylan Thomas is named Waldo and Jon has this to say about him:

> Waldo makes Hannibal Lecter seem like a custodian of morality, a real pussycat. He's a sociopath and old fashioned nut-case and what he gets up to is the true stuff of nightmares.

And he singles out this incident;

> Our first glimpse of Waldo himself finds him bending down into the bath with 'something wriggling in his mouth. He turned away and spat into the lavatory bowl. He went back to the bath and leaned over, stretching down inside. He came back up. There was a large brown spider between his lips.'
>
> This is just a hint of the unspeakable cruelty to follow...

I had a quick re-read before writing this, and again I was not impressed with the sub-Dylan Thomas linguistic excesses which begin on the first page:

> And Les still dreaming of topless gypsy dancer, and wondering if he'd caught anything from a tasselled Andalucian nipple dunked in his wine glass

But it was when I was about 40 pages in I came across the passage that had irked me the first time I read the book. It is a completely invented account of why Dylan Thomas failed to turn at the London church to act as Best Man at the wedding of his close friend Vernon Watkins – Swansea's other great modern poet. Dylan's failure to turn up deeply hurt Vernon, almost to the extent of ending their deep friendship and his new bride, Gwen was very embarrassed by the debacle.

Gwen Watkins was and, amazingly still is, a remarkable woman. She celebrated her 100th birthday just after Christmas 2024. We have been good friends since the late 70's and as a sprightly octogenarian and inveterate reader she read the novel and told me how much this fictional account had upset her.

Jon also describes the novel as 'a filmic book – cinematically structured' I for one am glad it has not been filmed.

THREE QUITE DIFFERENT PUBLICATIONS FROM 2014 – THE DYLAN THOMAS CENTENARY YEAR.

Rob Gittins: *The Poet & The Private Eye*. Y Lolfa. 2014

I first came across Rob Gittins back in 1986 when I acquired a copy of an intriguingly named book *The Last Days of Dylan*

Thomas, the author was unknown to me I read it with interest but it puzzled me; although I knew it was based on the real biographical accounts of Dylan's life as published in the major biographies of Constantine FitzGibbon, Paul Ferris and Andrew Sinclair, this book read like a novel and had no final bibliography of any list of sources. I did not know how to view it especially because it contained such detail about Thomas's devastating last few days in New York city in late October/early November 1953 leading up to Dylan's death on November 9. The author also seemed to know what was going on inside the heads of the main Characters – Dylan, His assistant and lover Liz Reitell and his long-suffering 'agent' John Malcolm Brinnin.

I could find out little more about the author until I happened upon a HTV documentary about Dylan' last days in New York called *A Far Ago Land* and it transpired that this film had been instigated by Rob Gittins however he left the film project but turned his research into a kind of biographical novel. The documentary, which was produced by Geraint Talfan Davies,[21] featured Liz Reitell, John Malcolm Brinnin and two of the actors who took part with Dylan Thomas in the premiere performances of *Under Milk Wood* in New York late 1953.

The Film went on to win prizes at the Celtic and San Francisco Film Festivals. Not long after Rob Gittins came by my bookshop and we quickly bonded over our mutual interest in Dylan Thomas. I learned that he was Rob was a leading TV scriptwriter and dramatist and this was the main focus of his work.

I was amazed to discover that Rob is longest serving script-writer on East-Enders and has completed well over 200 episodes of the programme, as well as contributing to almost every top-rated network UK TV show from the past thirty years, including *Casualty*, *The Bill*, *Emmerdale*, *Heartbeat*, *Soldier Soldier* and *The Story of Tracy Beaker*. Rob co-created and wrote all eight episodes of the BBC1 prime time drama series *TIGER BAY* as well as a three-part political thriller for ITV, *IN THE COMPANY OF STRANGERS* and for S4C, Rob has story-lined over two thousand episodes of the popular daily Welsh language drama serial Pobol y Cwm as well as co-creating the drama series *HALEN YN Y GWAED* (SALT IN THE BLOOD) which ran for four series. Dylan Thomas was Rob's self-indulgent, pleasurable, side interest and it led him back to write his novel *The Poet & The Private Eye*.

This book too, is closely based on a true incident in Dylan's life. On April 6 1953, the hugely prestigious American weekly magazine *Time*, carried a full page review of Dylan's recently publishes American *New Directions* edition of his is *Collected Poems*. This was approaching six months after the English edition but just a week after the book first appeared in the States. The contents were identical to the UK edition apart from the title, which dropped the from/until dates and the frontispiece was changed to a photograph by Marion Morehouse[22] in place of the reproduction of Augustus John's portrait of Dylan. The review itself was favourable and also featured a side box printing extracts from two poems – *Vision and Prayer* and *Fern Hill* – with a cute, flattering caricature. However Dylan Thomas was not at all happy with the introductory comments. What irked Dylan was the sentence at the beginning of the article;

> When he settled down to guzzle beer, which is most of the time, his irresistible yarns tumble over each other in wild Welsh dithyramb in which truth and fact become hopelessly smothered in boozy invention.

He borrows with no thought of returning what is lent, seldom shows up on time, is a trial to friends and a worry to his

The Cover of the April 6 1953 *Time Weekly*

family...Thomas only intermittently sits down to the work he can do best...

Although I'm sure that Dylan knew this to be a pretty accurate summation of his character and behaviour but it bothered him because at the time he was desperately trying to prolong his lucrative American lecturing work and he did succeed in signing a new contract with a proper American literary agent which guaranteed him a weekly average of $1000 per four to six week tour; but sadly he put his signature on the contract just a few days before he lapsed into a fatal coma. Dylan may also have thought that he could squeeze *Time Weekly* for some a serious defamation settlement and with this in mind he instructed his Swansea solicitor, Stuart Thomas to instigate proceeding against *Time*. A foolhardy gesture – David and Goliath spring to mind. Time immediately hired a *gumshoe* private-eye to tail Dylan around New York and beyond and to report incidents and compile a dossier that supported the claims made in the review; a review that when it comes to his poetry was very complimentary; he is described as; ...the finest lyrical talent of any poet under the age of 40... what he has written for himself is the envy of most other contemporary poets, a pleasure to anyone who can savour rich language.

It is this passive-aggressive response from *Time* magazine to the letter from a Swansea Solicitor that informs shapes, and is driving force for this very readable Rob Gittins novel. I had the

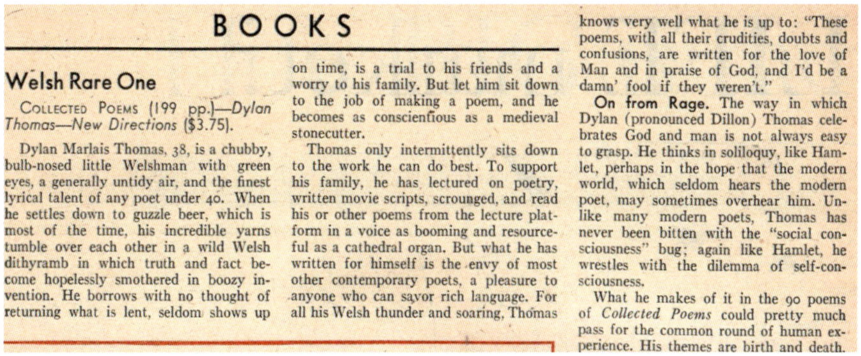

BOOKS

Welsh Rare One

COLLECTED POEMS (199 pp.)—*Dylan Thomas—New Directions* ($3.75).

Dylan Marlais Thomas, 38, is a chubby, bulb-nosed little Welshman with green eyes, a generally untidy air, and the finest lyrical talent of any poet under 40. When he settles down to guzzle beer, which is most of the time, his incredible yarns tumble over each other in a wild Welsh dithyramb in which truth and fact become hopelessly smothered in boozy invention. He borrows with no thought of returning what is lent, seldom shows up on time, is a trial to his friends and a worry to his family. But let him sit down to the job of making a poem, and he becomes as conscientious as a medieval stonecutter.

Thomas only intermittently sits down to the work he can do best. To support his family, he has lectured on poetry, written movie scripts, scrounged, and read his or other poems from the lecture platform in a voice as booming and resourceful as a cathedral organ. But what he has written for himself is the envy of most other contemporary poets, a pleasure to anyone who can savor rich language. For all his Welsh thunder and soaring, Thomas knows very well what he is up to: "These poems, with all their crudities, doubts and confusions, are written for the love of Man and in praise of God, and I'd be a damn' fool if they weren't."

On from Rage. The way in which Dylan (pronounced Dillon) Thomas celebrates God and man is not always easy to grasp. He thinks in soliloquy, like Hamlet, perhaps in the hope that the modern world, which seldom hears the modern poet, may sometimes overhear him. Unlike many modern poets, Thomas has never been bitten with the "social consciousness" bug; again like Hamlet, he wrestles with the dilemma of self-consciousness.

What he makes of it in the 90 poems of *Collected Poems* could pretty much pass for the common round of human experience. His themes are birth and death.

The article that Dylan Thomas found offensive – especially the opening sentences that upset

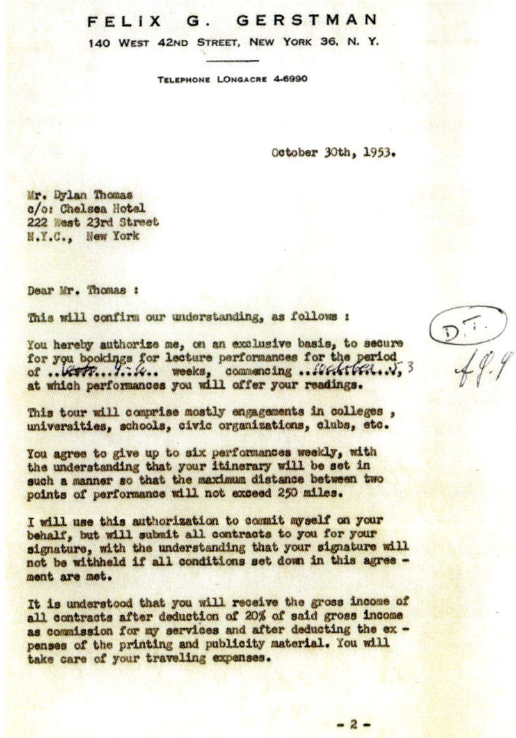

FELIX G. GERSTMAN
140 WEST 42ND STREET, NEW YORK 36, N. Y.

TELEPHONE LONGACRE 4-6990

October 30th, 1953.

Mr. Dylan Thomas
c/o: Chelsea Hotel
222 West 23rd Street
N.Y.C., New York

Dear Mr. Thomas :

This will confirm our understanding, as follows :

You hereby authorize me, on an exclusive basis, to secure for you bookings for lecture performances for the period of .... weeks, commencing ...., at which performances you will offer your readings.

This tour will comprise mostly engagements in colleges , universities, schools, civic organizations, clubs, etc.

You agree to give up to six performances weekly, with the understanding that your itinerary will be set in such a manner so that the maximum distance between two points of performance will not exceed 250 miles.

I will use this authorization to commit myself on your behalf, but will submit all contracts to you for your signature, with the understanding that your signature will not be withheld if all conditions set down in this agreement are met.

It is understood that you will receive the gross income of all contracts after deduction of 20% of said gross income as commission for my services and after deducting the expenses of the printing and publicity material. You will take care of your traveling expenses.

- 2 -

Dylan's final signed contact – sadly he never lived to enjoy the earnings it guaranteed

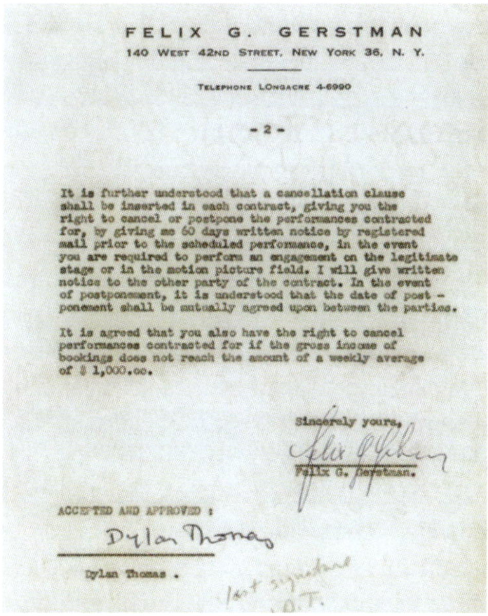

FELIX G. GERSTMAN
140 WEST 42ND STREET, NEW YORK 36, N. Y.

TELEPHONE LONGACRE 4-6990

- 2 -

It is further understood that a cancellation clause shall be inserted in each contract, giving you the right to cancel or postpone the performances contracted for, by giving me 60 days written notice by registered mail prior to the scheduled performance, in the event you are required to perform an engagement on the legitimate stage or in the motion picture field. I will give written notice to the other party of the contract. In the event of postponement, it is understood that the date of postponement shall be mutually agreed upon between the parties.

It is agreed that you also have the right to cancel performances contracted for if the gross income of bookings does not reach the amount of a weekly average of $ 1,000.00.

Sincerely yours,

Felix G. Gerstman.

ACCEPTED AND APPROVED :

Dylan Thomas

Dylan Thomas .

last signature D.T.

pleasure of being at the launch of the book at the Dinefwr Literary Festival and Rob was a very engaging and knowledgeable speaker. Rob later turned the book into a full-cast radio play for BBC Radio 4

* * * * *

Gwyneth Lewis: *Advantages of the Older Man*. Seren. Wales. 2014

A few years ago I went to Cardiff and helped the poet Gwyneth Lewis dispose of the bulk of her parent's vast library; they were both bibliophile teachers and readers and had raised their two daughters in the same traditions, so the house was overrun with books everywhere. I had met Gwyneth a few times at literary events; I knew her poetry and I was in awe of her because, as the incumbent *National Poet of Wales*, she came up with giant words that embellish the great facade of *The Millennium Theatre*, a modern architectural gem which dominates Cardiff recent Cardiff Bay redevelopment.

The words are;

Creu Gwir fel Gwydr o Ffwrnais Awen

Which poetically translates as;

Creating truth like glass from inspiration's furnace

Each letter is six-foot tall and formed of stained glass, set in glass-reinforced gypsum and mounted on the structure's giant copper snail-like dome. It is both magnificent and timeless.

I am not sure I can enthuse in quite the same way about this *fluent and entertaining ...light-hearted novella*[23] The small book (it's only 100 pages – one page for every year since Dylan's tragic death) came out in paperback only in 2014 – The Dylan Thomas Centenary Year, which can be held responsible for the appearance during that year of a vast array of Dylan Thomas 'stuff'. Not just books of all kinds but also a plethora of, pamphlets and brochures, music (both 'pop and classical and opera), feature films, documentary films, T.V. Programmes, Blogs, Websites; no platform escaped being 'Dylanized'. This book is one such example. The first sentence of the book is;

I know exactly the moment the spirit of Dylan Thomas possessed me.

The book opens with a fairly accurate account of an actual event that occurred in Swansea. when a well-respected Swansea photographer attempted to animate and make a short film of a 3D image *Dylan Thomas; A Virtual Dylan*, using the Death Mask which New York based American sculptor and friend of Dylan, Dave Slivka[24] had painstakingly cast in the New York mortuary back in 1953. I went to the premiere of the film in Swansea's Dylan Thomas Centre. I sat in the front row with Gwen Watkins, the widow of the Gower poet Vernon Watkins. Both Vernon and Gwen had known Dylan Thomas well. As short film played, she leant into my ear and whispered that she thought Dylan 'looked like he had been drowned and then fished out of the sea.' It was a bizarre afternoon.

Gwyneth Lewis' short tale unfolds in the voice of a young woman named Jennifer who has returned to Swansea from London, is in love with a local poet, but her passion is unreciprocated. Naturally all is not as it seems. Jennifer works in the Dylan Thomas Centre and is apparently possessed by the spirit of Dylan Thomas. Naturally all is not as it seems. Her

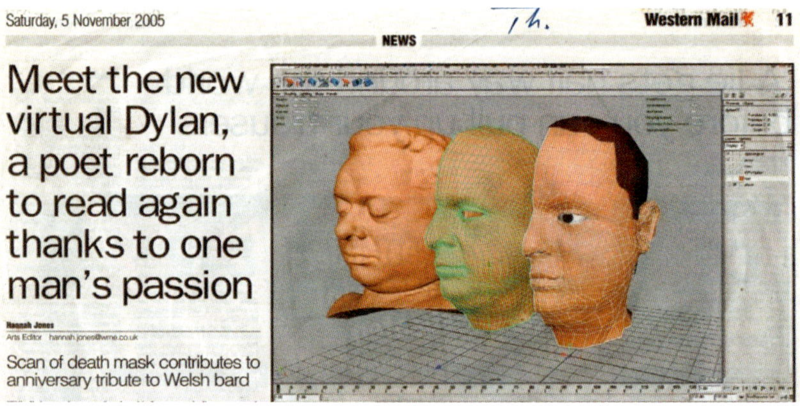

David Slivka in Swansea with the Dylan Thomas Death mask

Photograph by Bernard Mitchell

possessor is rather different Dylan from the one she knows by repute, one who doesn't t really fit in with the ghosts of other poets in heaven and is desperate to train himself to join the fitter shades of the long distance runners instead. Jennifer's own life, which has been lonely and sad, is completely transformed by the encounter. I'm not entirely sure I got the rest of the plot but somehow she goes to America with Dylan and just before the end she shouts at him 'get away from me you fucking pervert'. I'll leave it there.

* * * * *

Laura Sheldon: *Mr Mahli's Shed and a ghost named Dylan.* Firefly Press Cardiff. 2014

This is in some ways a children's version of Gwyneth Lewis's book. It's sweet and saccharine and has cartoon-like illustrations. But, if it introduced a clutch or two of young children in a light-hearted way, to the poet Dylan Thomas, then that is all well and good. I'm sure that the fact that 2014 was the Dylan Thomas Centenary Year had something to do with its publication... but it garnered some positive reviews:

> Fluent and entertaining, the story is written with all the confidence and panache you would expect from the former national poet, also a playwright and award-winning author of fiction and non-fiction.

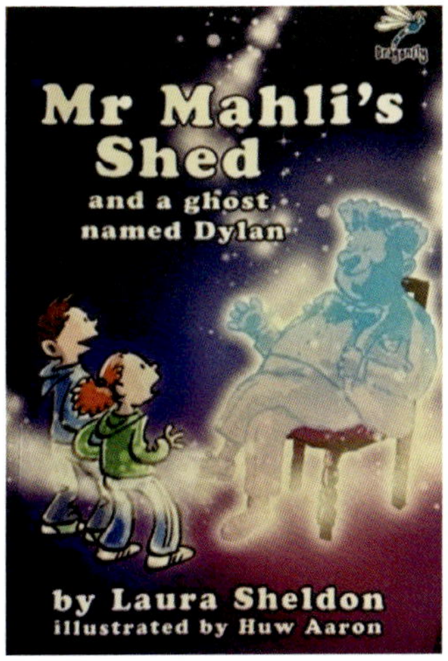

Alongside the humour there is warmth and pathos, and some pithy observations on poets and poetry and the nature of fame.

* * * * *

DYLAN THOMAS IN THE MODERN SHORT STORY

Dylan Thomas appears in a number of short stories in a variety of different ways.

Rhys Hughes: Stories from a Lost Anthology. Tantarus Press. 2002.

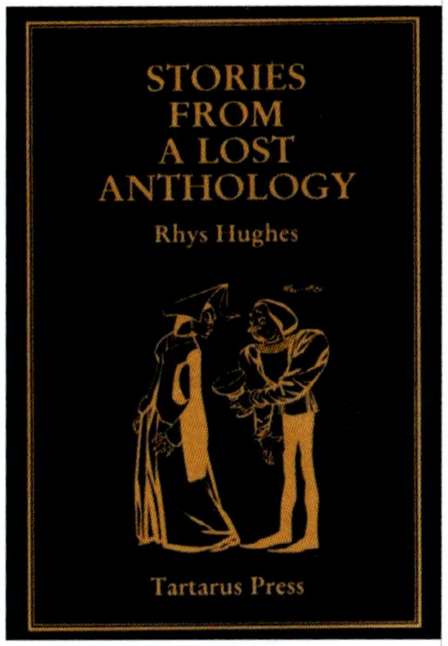

This elegant and well produced hardback came as a signed limited edition of just 100 copies. It has a laudatory foreword entitled *A Welsh Raree* by no lesser writer than Michael Moorcock. Hughes is from Cardiff and is well known and respected in Fantasy writing circles. However his is a somewhat surreal form of fantasy that embraces Science Fiction, Absurdism; and he is not afraid to make use of lipograms[25] palindromes, coded plots and techniques taken from the *Oulipo*[26] work-book. The opening story, *Portrait of the Artist as a Rusty Bus*, involves a strange couple living in a real urban suburb of Swansea, who wish to rid their beloved city of its obsequious worship of, and cultural domination by Dylan Thomas. They would like to kidnap him and hide him away or even end his life – but he is dead already. Instead they kidnap a local transport authority double-decker bus which is named *The Dylan Thomas Bus* in honour of the great local poet. They hide the bus in their unlikely, but suitably tall garage, whereupon the bus begins to recite and broadcast Dylan Thomas style poems but they are replete with commercial vehicle jargon. An example:

> And timetables shall have no dominion

Passengers in a hurry shall be one
With the snail in the shell and the glacier
When their tickets are punched and the punches are late
They shall have no refund in pocket or purse...

* * * * *

OTHER THOMAS RELATED SHORT STORIES BY FAMOUS WRITERS

Richard Farina 1937-1966: Most famous for being married to Joan Baez's sister, Mimi and for writing his cult-classic, post-Beat novel, *Been Down So Long It Looks Up to Me* and for dying in a motor cycle accident on his way to a book-signing session few days after the publication of his novel. He was just 29.

In 1958 he had contributed the winning undergraduate short story his University's magazine entitled, *With a Copy of Dylan Under My Arm*. Cornell Writer, Vol. V. No. 2. Ithaca, Cornell University.

It is worth noting that "Tom Pynchon" is listed as being on the editorial board. This is the Thomas Pynchon who went on to write three great modern American novels – *V*, *The Crying of Lot 49* and *Gravity's Rainbow.* As undergraduates he and Farina were good friends and they worked together on a production of *Under Milk Wood.*

Charles Bukowski: The popular cult-hero and post-Beat poet and short story writer includes a short story, *This is what killed Dylan Thomas* in his 1973 book, *South of no North*. The protagonist is based on Bukowski himself. In the story describes a pretty exhausting reading trip a louche poet undertakes involving planes and trains and cars and drink. Quite a lot happens and a lot goes wrong; he ends up an exhausted poet and declares;

This is what killed Dylan Thomas.

Margaret Atwood: Booker Prize winner and celebrated novelist, Margaret Atwood included a story, *The Grave Of The Famous Poet*, about a young couple visiting Dylan's grave at Laugharne, in her short-story collection *Dancing Girls & Other Stories*. *McClelland & Stewart*. Toronto 1977. And again in the revised *Simon & Shuster* 1982 edition. The Laugharne setting is easily recognisable to anyone who has visited the small town as Atwood must have done before writing this story. However Dylan is never actually named but he is referred to by pronouns and suggestions throughout the story of the couple's visit and their worsening troubled relationship.

Terry Pratchett: In his monumental huge body of books, over thirty now, that make up his *Discworld* series there is a country named *Llamedos*. Like Dylan Thomas *Under Milk Wood* setting in Llareggub which is Bugger All backwards Pratchett's LLamedos spells Sod 'em all. The country is hilly and permanently rainy country on the main continent. It is the home of druidism and druidical music. It is also home to some dwarf clans, who mine coal in its hills. Famous inhabitants include Rhys Rhysson a King and Imp Y Celyn the lead singer of a rock band/. Other inhabitants are *Sgt. Dai Dickins* and the explorer, Llamedos Jones. The main town is Pant-y-Girdl. As we can see Llamedos and its inhabitants closely resemble Wales and the Welsh, so Dylan Thomas and *Milk Wood* live on in Discworld.

* * * * *

THE WILDER SHORES OF DYLAN THOMAS DEPICTIONS

Apart from the variety of books described above, there is a somewhat bizarre and lunatic fringe of curious publications out there for thrill-seekers of all kinds. After Pratchett these comic books and graphic novels are a short step away ...

Dylan Dog

Dylan Dog is a long-running Italian horror comic series created by Tiziania Sclavi published by Sergio Bonelli Editore. It first appeared in 1986 and I believe it is still going. The series features the eponymous character, a paranormal investigator who takes on cases involving supernatural elements such as ghosts, demons, vampires, undeads, werewolves and other creatures, but

also horrifying sociopathic criminals and serial killers. It defies the whole preceding horror tradition with a vein of surrealism and an anti-bourgeois rhetoric. Dylan is supported mainly by his trusty sidekick Groucho, (a Groucho Marx lookalike) who adds humour to an otherwise very grisly genre and counterbalances Dylan Dog's's sombre temperament. The series is mainly set in London, where the protagonist lives, though he does occasionally travel elsewhere.

I first encountered him when a good bookselling friend, who dealt mainly in Italian material spotted a rack of them outside a news-agents in Venice and bought a copy back for me. It was a curio for sure and I shelved it with other similar Dylan odds-an-ends. It ended up leaning against a soft-toy of *Dylan*, the laid-back and a sleepy hippie rabbit, a regular character on a popular and long running childrens TV stop action animation progtamme, *The Magic Roundabout*.

I never discovered any Dylan Thomas link to the TV rabbit but it transpired that Dylan Dog was named for poet Dylan Thomas (his surname derives from "*Dog figlio di...*", the Italian title of the 1972 pulp thriller by Mickey Spillane; "*Erection Set*". The main character himself admits this nomenclature homage in Dylan Dog No. 8, *Il ritorno del mostro*, Sergio Bonelli Editore, March 1986 but I have not managed to source a copy. However his creator Tiziania Sclavi is quoted as saying;

> His name, Dylan, is inspired instead by the Welsh poet Dylan Thomas. I read his poems as a boy, and I liked them enormously. And then there was his life as an alcoholic, like mine and Dylan.

However unlike Dylan, aside from a slight relapse in the early 2000s, Sclavi has been sober since 1987.

Two further coincidences – Dylan Dog's appearance is based on the actor Rupert Everett and he was once in the running to play Dylan Thomas in the movie *The Edge of Love* (the emerging Welsh actor Matthew Rhys eventually got the role). And Dylan Dog's side-kick Groucho is closely modelled on Groucho Marx, who Dylan Thomas revered. He cherished all the Marx Brother's movies[27] and Gwen Watkins told me his favourite all time song was *Lydia the Tattooed Lady*, which was written by Yip Harburg and Harold Arlen and it was first sung by Groucho in the *Marx Brothers* film *At the Circus* (1939). [You can read all the lyrics in Chapter 15]

The Preacher

The Preacher is a more modern, and a notable example in the genre described as *graphic novels* – a kind of more serious comic book, aimed mainly at a demographic of mid-to-later teens and beyond.

The Preacher was published in America from 1995 until to 2000 by *Vertigo*, an imprint of the huge DC Comics empire. The series was created by writer was Garth Ennis; the artist was Steve Dillon, and it feature graphic painted covers by Glenn Fabry. The series consisted of 75 issues in total; 66 regular, monthly issues; five one off specials and a four-issue *Preacher: Saint of Killers*, limited series. The final monthly issue, number 66, was published in October 2000.

In PREACHER Book 2: by Garth Ennis and Steve Dillon. The character *Cassidy has a flashback and during it*, Dylan Thomas is shown suddenly and unexpectedly collapsing on the sidewalk outside of a bar. Thomas is depicted as a previous acquaintance of the character Cassidy, who is with Dylan Thomas when he collapses outside the White Horse Tavern – Dylan's favourite New York City watering hole. Thomas's last words are:

> ***The trouble with you fuckin' Irish is, you don't know how to drink...***

The cover of the volume of the *Preacher* containing a brief cameo about Dylan Thomas

DYLAN THOMAS GETS RAUNCHY!
Evelyn Lau: Fresh Girls & Other Stories. Harper Collins Toronto 1993.

This is an intriguing collection of short prose fictions. The dust jacket blurbs will give you an idea of what we are dealing with:

> What Ann Rice does for Vampires Evelyn Lau does for sex:
> Fills us with a kind of longing for perverse pleasure and pain.
> Lau explores realms of sexuality which might seem foreign and bizarre Lau explores the forbidden

We learn more by delving into a little of Lau's biography. Born in Vancouver 1971. At 17, after living on the streets of Vancouver for two years, she writes the bestselling *Runaway: The Diary of a Street Kid* [blurb; An unforgettable and true story of a young girl's life on the street', and this is made into CBC TV film. Evelyn Lau is now a successful writer and poet but *Fresh Girls* proper published book. There are ten stories in the book and it is the eighth story which intrigues me most. It is entitled;

> **MERCY** and it opens:
> "It is your wife's fortieth birthday, and I am torturing you to the sounds of a tape of Dylan Thomas giving a poetry recital. His voice is theatrical, and at times it hovers at the edges of breaking into song. *Do not go gentle into that good night... Rage, rage against the dying of the light*...His words, charged with command, seem to pulse through my own body. Obediently I slip the spiked heel of my shoe into your mouth"

And it goes on thus for nine pages, S&M to the tune of Dylan's great elegy for his blind and dying father:

> I will not go gentle into you. The high heel of my shoe is your mouth....
> Old age should burn and rave at close of day,' Thomas instructs sternly.
> Perhaps only in the clutches of pain, when your eyes are closed and your lips are forced apart, does the day seem long.

And the last paragraph begins:

> It is your wife's fortieth birthday and Dylan Thomas's voice slows to a stop on the tape. You edge out the door with the sun bouncing off your glasses and your briefcase tucked under your arm."

I like the story but I wonder how will I feel at the next Welsh funeral I attend, when this poem is sombrely intoned – what images will leap into my mind. I fear it will never be the same again.

First Hardback edition

* * * * *

The saucy paperback cover

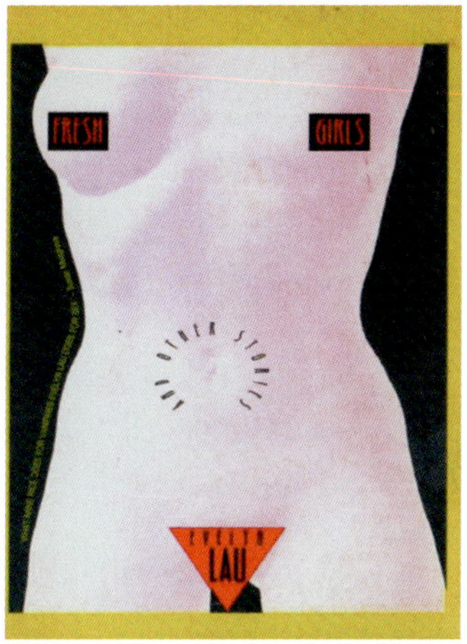

Two Novels which feature Dylan Thomas, Surrealism, The Great Beast and Sex. Robert Irwin; *Exquisite Corpse*. Dedalus. 1995

The title of the book comes from the dada/Surrealist serious pastime; Cadavre exquis (exquisite corpse)[28] a collaborative drawing approach first used by artists to create bizarre and intuitive drawings; a kind of visual version of the writing game *Consequences*.

The novel is set in London Paris and Munich and follows to life of an aspiring artist Caspar and his pursuit of Caroline an enigmatic young typist. When Caroline suddenly vanishes, Caspar embarks on a terrifying and sometimes comic journey to find her, which takes him through a somewhat seedy, surrealist, and war-ravaged London, Paris, and Munich. In the course of this obsessive quest, Caspar enters into a world of drink, drugs, orgies, and eventually, the madhouse,. And he encounters along the way the likes of Orson Welles, Larry (sic) Durrell, Salvador Dali, Andre Breton, Aleister Crowley and Dylan Thomaso

Reviewing it in the times A.S. Byatt wrote:

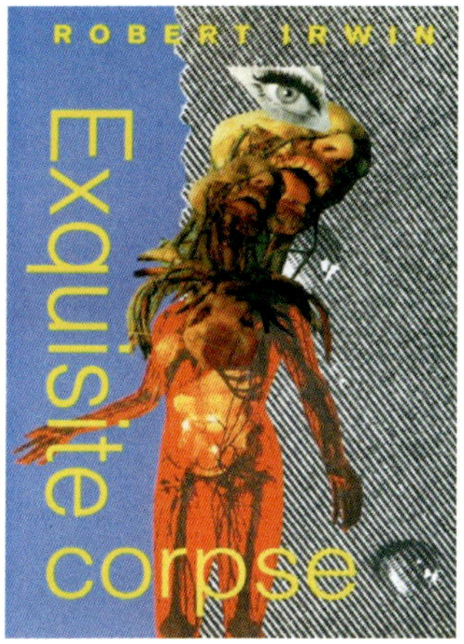

The 1995 Dedalus First Edition

Proof copy of the American reprint

> Irwin's novel about English surrealism is funny, profound and hugely satisfying.

She was very taken with the novel campaigned for the novel to win the 1995 Booker prize. The book however faded but has recently been republished by the Overlook Press in New York, America.

Richard McNeff: *Sybarite among The Shadows*. Mandrake Oxford 2004.

This novel started out first as a short story back in 1977 in the pages of the in the infamous counter-culture newspaper, *The International Times*. Strangely it involves some of the same material used in the previous novel but this one has seems to be much more reliant on the Fitzgibbon biography for good Dylan Thomas stories which it lifts verbatim. It is much more concerned with Victor Neuberg – acknowledged as Dylan's literary god-father manly because that allows the author to dwell on Aleistair Crowley who used Neuberg as his magical assistant in earlier times. In 1934 Dylan wrote this to his Swansea pal Bert Trick;

> The creature himself – I must tell you one day if I haven't told you before how Aleister Crowley turned Vicky into a camel – is a nineteenth century crank with mental gangrene, lousier than ever before, a product of a Jewish nuts factory, an Oscar tamed.

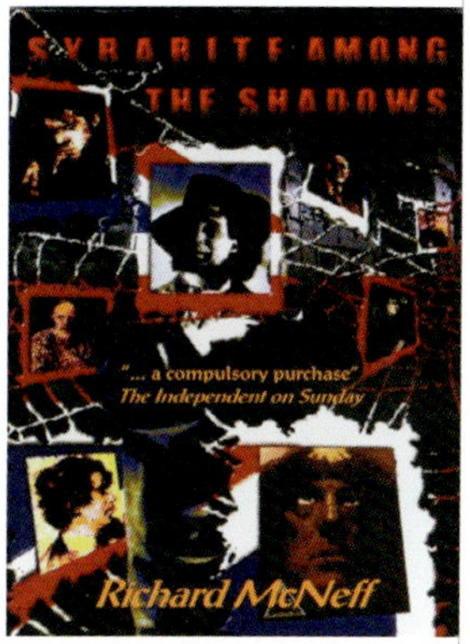

This is cover blurb to the book:

> It is June 1936, and Dylan Thomas surprises Victor Neuburg, his former editor, with a visit. Dylan has had a sinister encounter in a West End pub with The Great Beast 666, Aleistair Crowley. [Dylan did have a scary encounter with Aleistair Crowley in his real life It is described by all three of Thomas major biographers FitzGibbon, Ferris and Lycett] This launches an adventure whose backdrops are the

Surrealist Exhibition, the pubs of Fitzrovia and clubs of Soho, and whose characters, some of the most celebrated of the period. The foreground is a fatal reunion. In walking again in the shadow of the Beast, however, Neuburg not only has to confront the actual demons of his past, but also Aleister Crowley's current links with MI5 and the plot that would change history.

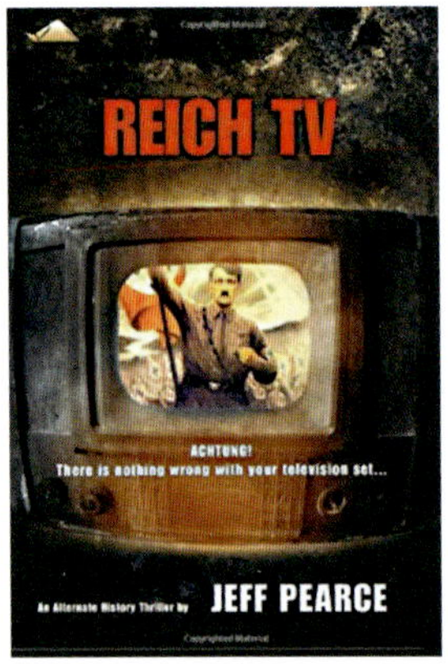

Jeff Pearce: *Reich TV*

This book is billed on the cover as an *Alternative History Thriller*, not a genre I am familiar with and I have to say the same about this book. I stumbled upon a reference to it and to Dylan Thomas' personification in it online but cannot source a copy in a pleasing format or price, but I have not given up hope yet. It seems to be only published in America or as an e-book – a format I am loathe to engage with.

This is the *Amazon* synopsis of the book;

> The Germans had television in the early years of the Hitler regime. Now see what happens when TV changes the history of Nazi Germany and World War Two! The BBC has lured the Marx Brothers away from America to London so they can perform a variety show each week that's transmitted all the way into Berlin. Their producer is the young, hard-drinking, womanizing Dylan Thomas, who goes from hating foreign politics to being obsessed with stopping the Nazis. Meanwhile, on the night of the Reichstag Fire, young English correspondent George Orwell manages to explore the ruins and makes a startling discovery: the burned bodies of five men handcuffed together, one of them a Brown Shirt and another a high-ranking army officer. Orwell has to team up with a roving band of pirate signal broadcasters to expose the truth about the fire – and the secret of a terrifying new weapon in Nazi hands. Espionage, murder, sabotage and betrayal. They'll all be exposed on Reich TV, culminating in the most sensational trial of the century.

I have absolutely no interest in reading this.

And finally in this group – Dylan Thomas as Porn Star!

MAN to MAN magazine circa 1960

DYLAN THOMAS ...HIS SEARCH FOR NAKED LADIES IN MACKINTOSHES

This is an example of Dylan Thomas gracing the covers and inside pages of American Men's soft porn mags in the years after his death. I must admit that this top-shelf magazine and the following pulp paperback are both in my current collection. This next is the story of how I recently discovered this hard-porn depiction of the poet...

Steve Savage: Barefoot Among the Virgins. Greenleaf Classic. San Diego. 1968.

With 'cutesy-cutesy fuck scenes' and 'even Dylanistic poetry'

A porno pulp paperback which Dylan depicted as a porno sex god

One of the most remarkable and unusual booksellers I have ever encountered is David Sachs. He is based in Oakland, California. I was introduced to him by the late Peter Howard, another legendary Bookseller and the proprietor of *Serendipity Books* in Berkeley California. Peter ran a giant bookstore, the size of big warehouse (it had previously been a winery). It was a rabbit warren of passageways, cubby holes and stairs to different levels, holding a vast stock of used books and with at different times four of five staff.

David Sachs, on the other hand, was a lone operator, working out of a small apartment where you could hardly move amongst piles and piles of books. Peter was a 'full service' retail bookseller; David was what is known in the trade as a 'runner'. Most days David would go out into the surrounding areas, or sometimes further afield and search out (in America they say

'scout out') books from small used bookstores and 'Thrift shops' (we say 'Charity shops'), in his chosen subjects for his coterie of loyal customers. If you were lucky enough to be taken on by David he would produce all sorts of books that you did not know existed. Peter loved and supported David and he recommended him and introduced me to him. He told David that I was the world's leading dealer in the works of Dylan Thomas, and that I was a 'completist', which meant that I desired to collect anything and everything ever printed or otherwise connected with this Welsh poet. David did not disappoint. Each visit to San Francisco I would meet David, usually in *Serendipity* and he would hand over a small clutch of esoteric little poetry magazines or self-published vanity press poetry collections or anthologies, or piece of ephemera, and each one would bear his small faint pencil note on the first blank page with a page number and the words 'Dylan Thomas'. Turning to the page indicated and I would find a sentence, or a poem or an illustration with a mention of said Welsh poet. Most example were pretty bad but I can guarantee I had never seen or heard of them before and would never see them again if I didn't buy them. They were cheap; a couple of dollars each – I always took everything sometime it was a small regional poetry magazine that just took its name from a word or phrase in a Thomas poem. Oftentimes sometimes it would be something more ethnic – an aspiring Chicano street poet or an American Indian writer. In himself David, was a pretty humourless and taciturn solitary character but I liked him and what got to me and amazed me the most was when I realised that beyond his hawk-eyed dedication, he must have taken the time and effort to read, or at least flick through, every single item he choose to buy, to discover these extreme minutiae of tiny references to a long dead poet. And I had no doubt that he did the same for how many other obsessive collectors who he serviced in the same way. I did learn that he had one bibliographic obsession of his own. David had a young deaf young son who he cared for. This led him to amass a huge collection of printed materials on Deafness and a silent world deaf people inhabited, I was pleased to be able to pass on a few items to him and he was in turn very grateful.

In 2013 I stopped visiting America for various reasons but mainly due to the deaths of many of my American bookselling friends including Peter Howard and my long term travelling friend Eric Korn. I never saw nor heard anything of David Sachs again. But then in November 2023, out of the blue, I received the first and only e-mail I had ever had for David Sacks; a total but very pleasant surprise. It read:

To Jeff Towns
https://efanzines.com/EK/eI21/
section: Into the Abyss

10th page:
One of my favorite Greenleaf Classics titles was Barefoot Among the Virgins [by Steve Savage, GC346, 1968] that was actually based on one of Dylan Thomas's besotted reading tours in the U.S. If Peter De Vries got away with it in Reuben, Reuben, why couldn't I? I went nuts with this magnum opus, writing the archest of exposition, sentences that went around the block, pedantic conversation, and cutesy-cutesy fuck scenes. I even wrote Dylanistic poetry. (Great cover by Harry Bremner!) I thought it came off rather well. But, other than a check, nary a peep from the far west."
Mexican-American author
1 copy online, cheap enough
(& many copies of the De Vries).
With kind regards,
David Sachs
Oakland, Calif. U.S.

I puzzled over the message for a while before I realised that David was giving me a *heads up* about a book he had somehow stumbled across in a very obscure online bibliography, (here described as an *efanzine*) of American pulp paperback fiction. I checked out the references, found the copy for sale online; it was located in America and indeed it was *cheap enough* by any standards bought it and awaited its arrival. It did not disappoint and I am happy to share it with you. dear readers. The faint at heart should perhaps skip to the next chapter now.

Barefoot Among The Virgins is a pseudonymous work by a mega-prolific jobbing writer of Pulp-Fiction across most all of the genres that this category of writing embraces. The author of this pornographic tour-de-force is a remarkable Mexican American, Thomas Ramirez, who settled in Wisconsin with his family. Tom began life playing in his father's Mexican band, but got an education and became a teacher. However he began to write which led to him receiving an offer he couldn't refuse; this from his obituary:

> Ramirez attended Oshkosh State Teachers College, and went on to teach middle school in Campbellsport and at Franklin School for eight years. In 1961 he left the teaching profession to pursue his writing passion. "At the time, I was making $6,000 a year working as a teacher, and my agent found me an opportunity to write a book a month where I would make $18,000," he said. "I had to leave mid-semester to take advantage of it....
>
> As a freelance journalist, Ramirez wrote dozens of short stories and was published in magazines such as American Heritage and Boy's Life. He authored more than 150 paperbacks, spanning such genres as mystery, military and erotica, and worked as a stringer for the National Enquirer for over 20years.e was on the staff of National Features Syndicate in Chicago for four years...Ramirez was a founding member of the Allied Authors of Wisconsin, one of the state's oldest writing collectives.

Steve Savage's (a.k.a. Tom Ramirez's) novel tells the tale of a half-English, half-Welsh poet; Galen Dangerfield, who is obviously based on Dylan Thomas and very much inspired by John Malcolm Brinnin's account of Thomas' reading tours to the states; *Dylan Thomas in America*. First published in 1955, Brinnin's book was one of the first *kiss and tell* biographies to appear. Because of this it garnered huge press interest. Even the bohemian Caitlin, no shrinking violet herself, insisted that every copy contain a one page statement in which she questioned the veracity of the book and its depiction of her husband.

We first encounter Galan when he is on a busy and successful reading tour of American colleges, although in this version the poet's success is less literary and much more libidinous. His success comes more, (pardon the pun), in the form of numerous, extreme, regular, energetic, sexual encounters with a succession of willing women all of which is described in a very enthusiastic, rich and explicit prose. On the third page of the paperback we get the first of his *Dylanistic Poems*;

> Stalwart trunk, dark and brooding
> One-eyed Cyclops staring blindly at the sky.
> Pulsing lianas twining, blood-force of Eternity
> Noble crown of roseate texture
> Mottled in finite tapestry, mystery of a universe.
> I glorify thee.
> And in miserly comprehension I ...
> Once more the words drifted off, he was outraged by their *pawkiness*, at there laboured meter their over-obvious imagery.

The use of the word Pawkiness is very intriguing, and I think it suggests that Mr Savage/ Ramirez, had actually done some research, and read up in Dylan's published correspondence, where he could have read Dylan commenting on the use of this arcane word of old Scottish origin; meaning; arch, shrewd, subtle, cynical or mockable. It appears as a paragraph heading in one of Dylan's long letters to Pamela Hansford Johnson and he suggests that it was one of her favourite words. Dylan must have been taken by the word because he used it himself when he inscribed a copy of his first book, *18 Poems* to Pamela in 1934;[29] *To Pamela who knows* [?] *well the things I'll suggest if she's going to write on the front of this Pawky book'.*

The poem is quite obviously a flowery hymn to his penis, and it leads him into explicitly recounting his sexual fantasy that inspires and sustains his resulting masturbation (which is also graphically described). He is interrupted by a faculty wife who has come to be sexually serviced and is delighted to find him partially undressed and ready for action of which we are treated to yet another graphic explicit description. All this in the first 25 pages! And it goes on for another dozen chapters and 200 similar pages of graphic and salacious descriptions of Galen's prowess in the bedroom or wherever else he can perform. And this turns out to be the authors favourite novel and he even acknowledges Peter De Vries's!

One of my favourite *Greenleaf Classics* titles was *Barefoot Among The Virgins* [by Steve Savage, GC346, 1968] that was actually based on one of Dylan Thomas's besotted reading tours in the U.S. If Peter De Vries got away with it in *Reuben, Reuben*, why couldn't I?

So it comes as quite a shock to read the author's Memoir printed in the online fanzine which begins thus;

Into the Abyss

A Memoir By Thomas P. Ramirez

I should have known the minute I got home late on that snowy December afternoon that something was up. My wife Fern's expression – rapt and excited – was warning enough. The year was 1960, and I was in the sixth year of my schoolmaster shtick, teaching grade 6 at Franklin School, Fond du Lac, Wisconsin. I was returning to the little cubbyhole we called home, a house Fern and I had built with our own four little paddies.

"What's up, kiddo?" I asked when she began jumping around, waving this letter at me.

"Wonderful news, honey," she chirped, "the most wonderful news in the world."

His agent was offering a substantial new contract and the prospect of relatively rich rewards.

His memoir is long and very readable and in his regular life he comes across a well-respected and decent member of local community, although he does describe his involvement in an obscenity trial that did make the local press:

A year later, on July 5, 1966, the other shoe fell. I received two phone calls, one from Scott Meredith telling me that I would be receiving a call from a Los Angeles lawyer named Stanley Fleishman, who would be ringing me. More than that he would not say. That afternoon Fleishman was on the phone. The gist of it: he wanted me to fly to Houston, Texas for a conference in regard to an obscenity trial involving some of my novels. Involved, hell! There were seven books cited, and four of them – *Passion Carousel* [SR543, 1965], *Orgy Club* [PB833, 1964], *Swap Sect* [NB1738, 1965 (don't those titles just kill you?), and *Shame Hunger* [PB850, 1964] were mine. All expenses would be paid and I would be away three days. What would the conference entail?

Just minor point – we'd like you to appear as a witness for the defence... Fleishman would load me up with books, articles, and tracts, all dealing with dread pornography. I would read these at my leisure at home and get myself steeped in how contemporary writers were handling sex scenes. And how were my books that much different from these hardcover books that were acceptable to present day mores?

Another box of books would be shipped to me when I arrived home. I would spend the rest of July doing nothing but reading these, formulating corollaries between modern day fiction and my own dreck. I was getting paid to read books? I had died and gone to heaven! ...Some of the books I can still remember, most I can't. Things like William Burroughs, *Last Exit From Brooklyn*, Pauline Reage's *Story of O*, *The Velvet Underground*, by Michael Leigh, *Pretty Leslie*, by R.V. Cassill, *A Cold Wind in August*, by Burt Wohl. There were many, many more – even some Genet and some Marquis de Sade delicacies – the sort of sex lit deemed acceptable back in the '60s. Also I read a lot of Stanley Fleishman's articles defending pornography and other tracts, all the reading intended to raise my mettle and turn me into an invincible witness... So, back to Wisconsin the following day, and almost a month straight of reading books, fiction and non-fiction – until semen was coming out my ears.

I can't help feeling that if Dylan had known about Steve Savage's portrayal of him in a porn paperback he would have carried copies around and distributed them from the bar of every pub he drank in return for beer or whisky ...

Dylan Thomas depicted in poetry

Back to something a tad more uplifting. There exists a substantial anthology of poems inspired and written for Dylan Thomas.

A Garland For Dylan Thomas gathered and with a preface by George Firmage. Advisory Editor Oscar Williams. Clarke and Wat. New York 1963. It contains eighty-four poems by poets, including five by Vernon Watkins and three by George Barker. It also includes *Thou Shalt Not Kill* by Kenneth Rexroth [see below] and a few others mentioned throughout this chapter and book.

It also have some interesting photographs and the first printing of Dylan's Poetic Manifesto.

Norman Cameron – The Dirty Little Accuser.

Norman Cameron (1905–1953) was a Scottish poet, who between the two world wars was associated on the Island of Majorca with Robert Graves and Laura riding. Back in the UK after the war he mingled with the bohemians in Fitzrovia and became a friend and some-time generous patron of Dylan Thomas. However as this famous poem suggests Dylan's excesses sometimes tried his patience – this poem may have been a kind of safety valve. Cameron was a successful advertising copy-writer and famously came up with the phrase *Night Starvation* the lynch pin of a famous Horlicks advertising campaign. Interestingly Dylan Thomas in one of his drink fuelled surreal fantasies came up with his own invention – *night custard*. In his twisted mind it may have been linked to seminal fluid in wet-dreams but I happened upon an article by Jeanette Winterson[30] – *Making Christmas Custard with Kathy Acker. On Sharing Traditions with a Very Nontraditional Friend* – I discovered this passage;

> Kathy Acker liked Horlicks, and I used to make it for her. Kathy, drinking Horlicks and laughing about the impossibility of custard (she could not cook—she could not even stir), and obsessive about everything, found out for me that Dylan Thomas had invented a fantasy product called Night Custard. In the 1930s while Dylan was dozing on the sofa of a well-paid friend in advertising, who happened to have a contract with Horlicks, Dylan thought he might make his fortune with Night Custard, and speculated that it might also be used as hair crème or a vaginal lubricant. This rather put me off custard for a while. But Christmas is Christmas and Christmas is custard. In fact Acker, with her bluestocking fascinations and zero culinary skills, had now blended together forever custard and New York City.

Cameron's poem was first published in Cyril Connolly's Horizon magazine; Vol. 6, No.31 July 1942. Although Dylan is not named in the poem Connolly mischievously printed Dylan's short parody

(WOOLF, Virginia) TURNELL, Martin. "Virginia Woolf". An article in Horizon,Vol. 6, No. 31, July 1942, pp. 44-56. London : Horizon, 1942. Pp. (1)-73, + 4 p. of plates, including verso rear cover. 8vo, printed grey card covers. Contents: Lord Berners's "The Performing Mushroom" and "Surrealist Landscape", Dylan Thomas's "Request to Leda", Norman Cameron's "The Dirty Little Accuser", Gavin Ewart's "Officers' Mess", Beryl de Zoete's "Frederick Ashton", Archimedes's "The Freedom of Necessity--I", T. D. Kendrick's "The Art of the Anglo Saxons", Eudora Welty's "The Petrified Man", George Orwell's "Selected Notice", and George Rostrevor Hamilton's "Letter 'On Interpreting the War'".

The contents of Conolly's *Horizon* and Cameron's gently vindictive but honest poem

The Dirty Little Accuser

Who invited him in? What was he doing here,
That insolent little ruffian, that crapulous lout?
When he quitted a sofa, he left behind him a smear.
My wife says he even tried to paw her about.

What was worse, if, as often happened, we caught
him out
Stealing or pinching the maid's backside, he would
leer,
With a cigarette on his lip and a shiny snout,
With a hint: 'You and I are all in the same galère.'

Yesterday we ejected him, nearly by force,
To go on the parish, perhaps, or die of starvation;
As to that, we agreed, we felt no kind of remorse.

Yet there's this check on our righteous jubilation:
Now that the little accuser is gone, of course,
We shall never be able to answer his accusation.

of William Epsom, *Request to Leda* on the opposite page to Cameron's squib. In this booksellers description of the Horizon issue Leda hovers above the dirty little accuser

Cameron included it in his Collected Poems [1957] and Dylan Thomas included his parody in the spoof detective novel he wrote with John Davenport – *The Death of the King's Canary*, which was not published until 1976 (23 years after his death).

Stephen Tennant – Homage to Dylan Thomas.

Stephen James Napier Tennant (1906–1987) was an upper class British socialite known for his decadent and eccentric lifestyle. He was a central member of the group of posh mainly young men referred to as the *Bright Young Things* by the tabloid press of the time. Tennant was noted for his affected demeanour and appearance. He is widely considered to be the model for Cedric Hampton in Nancy Mitford's novel, *Love in a Cold Climate*, and the major one of the inspirations for Lord Sebastian Flyte in Evelyn Waugh's *Brideshead Revisited*. His friendship with Dylan Thomas goes unrecorded but Dylan Thomas was good friends (when he was behaving well) with Stephen Tennant who, with his wife Virginia established and ran the infamous *Gargoyle Club* in Soho, which was a favourite haunt of Dylan's when he was in London. This small, inscribed, folded ephemeral one-sheet pamphlet, privately printed publication, seems to be wholly unrecorded.

HOMAGE TO DYLAN THOMAS

Take your place, like Dylan Thomas;
In the deepening sun of truth.
Stand where the gods are idle, smiling,
By the secret streams of youth.
Make the night your dear enchanter,
your confidant and slave:
Make the splendid songs and banter,
Of a glorious poet yours.
A poet who stands in the sunrise,
And laughs at daily chores;
Laughs in the face of destiny,
And greets him like a friend.
Take your place, like Dylan Thomas,
On the road without an end.

Christmas, 1960 STEPHEN TENNANT *Wilsford Manor*

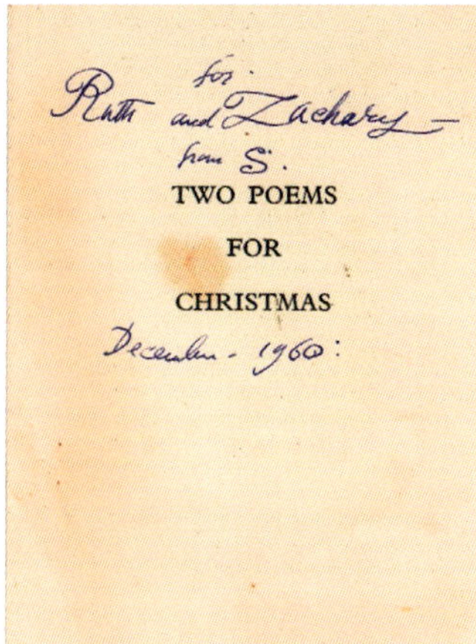

The Inscription on the front cover of the folded sheet. I have been unable to identify the Ruth and Zachary the recipients of this little Christmas gift

Kenneth Rexroth Thou Shalt Not Kill – A Memorial for Dylan Thomas[31] Sunnyvale, CA: **Horace Schwartz, 1955.** 12 pp, pamphlet in red, printed card wrappers. Rexroth went on; 247

> This poem was written in one sitting, a few hours after a phone call came from New York with the news that Dylan had died.

Kenneth Rexroth was an American poet, translator, and critical essayist. He is regarded as a central figure in the 1950's *San Francisco Renaissance*. This movement was followed closely by the *Beat Movement* and although Rexroth did not consider himself a Beat poet he was dubbed the "Father of the Beats" by *TIME* magazine. He became friends with Dylan Thomas when Dylan visited San Francisco and they became good hard drinking buddies. He wrote this long passionate poetic rant shortly after hearing of Dylan's death. A little later in 1955 he organized and emceed the Six Gallery reading in 1955 where Allen Ginsberg read *Howl* which

Many critics think was influenced by Rexroth's *Thou Shalt Not*, especially in his preoccupation with Moloch which Ginsberg also uses in *Howl*.

Herewith the opening lines;

1.
They are murdering all the young men.
For half a century now, every day,
They have hunted them down and killed them.
They are killing them now.
At this minute, all over the world,
They are killing the young men.
They know ten thousand ways to kill them.
Every year they invent new ones.
In the jungles of Africa.
In the marshes of Asia,
In the deserts of Asia,
In the slave pens of Siberia,
In the slums of Europe,
In the nightclubs of America,
The murderers are at work.

From a global opening in the first three sections Rexroth gets on to Dylan Thomas in particular...

IV
He is dead.
The bird of Rhiannon.
He is dead.
In the winter of the heart.
He is Dead.
In the canyons of death,
They found him dumb at last,
In the blizzard of lies.
He never spoke again.
He died.
He is dead.
In their antiseptic hands,
He is dead.
The little spellbinder of Cader Idris.
He is dead.
The sparrow of Cardiff.
He is dead.
The canary of Swansea.
Who killed him?
Who killed the bright-headed bird?
You did, you son of a bitch.
You drowned him in your cocktail brain.
He fell down and died in your synthetic
heart.
You killed him...
There he lies sandbagged,
At the foot of the Statue of Liberty.
The Gulf Stream smells of blood
As it breaks on the sand of Iona
And the blue rocks of Canarvon.
And all the birds of the deep sea rise up
Over the luxury liners and scream,
"You killed him! You killed him.
In your God damned Brooks Brothers suit,
You son of a bitch."

248

A Hut at the Edge of the Village by John Moriarty

I had finished this chapter of the book and it was fast approaching being sent off to my publisher to be made into a new book when a bookseller[32] friend alerted me to this book, by this writer; John Moriarty, and to the Dylan Thomas inclusion, from near the end of the book. I had never heard of this writer but I very quickly got hold of a copy of his book and was very taken by it, especially by his use of, to my mind, Dylan Thomas' greatest poem; Fern Hill, and I think this excerpt is well worth including in this chapter as it is written in a very poetic prose. Here is an extract from his last book.[33]

And where do you come from? asks the young woman sitting beside me in the bus. From a place inside me I say. From a farm inside me. From a farm far away inside me called Fern Hill I say. Your name, please? the man in the passport office

asked me. Honoured among wagons, I replied. That's my name on Monday.
On Tuesday the blackbirds call me Prince of the apple towns.
On Wednesday the geese call me Famous among the barns.
On Thursday the owls who are carrying me away call me Nightly under the simple stars.
On Friday morning coming home I am The Wanderer white with the dew, the cock on my shoulder.
On Saturday alone on the hills I am The Farm forever fled.
On Sunday, there it is, summer again, Fern Hill again, horses again, the spellbound horses walking warm out of the whinnying green stables on to the fields of praise. Horses walking spellbound, constellations walking spellbound. Ursa, Aries, Capricorn, Cancer, Leo, Virgo walking spellbound, Taurus walking spellbound on to the fields of praise. Dylan came singing summer. He came bringing a new first page for our Holy Book. Like Horses we have all walked spellbound out of a whinnyinggreen stable on to the fields of praise.

And a few paragraphs on he includes the whole of Thomas's poem *And Death Shall Have no Dominion.*

I was very intrigued by this unknown writer and mystic so I read his obituary.[34] It's well worth a read as John Moriarty lived a quite extraordinary life, This is how the obit ends;

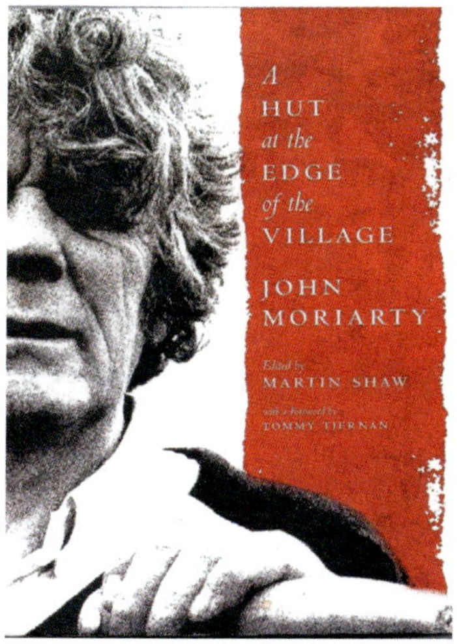

John Moriarty. (*2 February 1938 – 1 June 2007*) *was an Irish writer and philosopher A native of County Kerry. He was educated in Listowel and at University College Dublin. In 1974, he moved to England from Canada where he had taught English literature at the University of Manitoba, and subsequently became a live-in gardener in the Carmelite monastery at Boars Hill, Oxford. Moriarty subsequently lived at the foot of Mangerton Mountain in County Kerry in until his death.* [*I can recommend a film "inspired by the works" of Moriarty, Dreamtime Revisited, which was directed by Dónal Ó Céilleachair and Julius Ziz and released in October 2012.*

And Now, and to my mind, a worthless and despicable book, which not so much as *depicts* Dylan Thomas, as *decapitates* him!

* * * * *

The Beautiful Poetry of Donald Trump [?]

This terrible worthless book came out in 2017, at the height of Trump' crazed antics on the world stage. Some less-than-sensitive, bright-spark, in a publishers office thought a book of naff, spoof poetry, allegedly written by Donald Trump was worth publishing. They were actually written by Rob Sears.[35]

The Beautiful Poetry of Donald Trump t was published by Cannon Gate. My feelings are that, easy as it is to ridicule and satirise Donald Trump, he is in reality, a far too serious threat to us all so that nothing about him can really be in any way funny. Above is the cover of this worthless waste of paper. As soon as I saw it, the pose and the garb rang a bell in my brain. The face was hideous; perhaps it was supposed to depict a thoughtful creative Trump trying to connect with his poetic muse. But the image distressed me and I turned to the end of the book looking for explanations. I found this...
May they all, apart from (Dylan Thomas), get stuck in a lift together for many hours without food or drink

Eureka! I knew it, but how could Canon Gate and Getty come up with this foul example of *cultural approbation*? The publishers, graphic artists and publicists had taken it upon themselves to colour the vintage black and white image of a young Dylan Thomas; for once not looking like a proverbial 'unmade bed,' but a healthy, sober and well turned out poet – cravat and all. And then they butcher it and Dylan's head is excised from this fine original image and replacing it; by grafting on the head of the monster Trump.

The original cover

The reprint cover

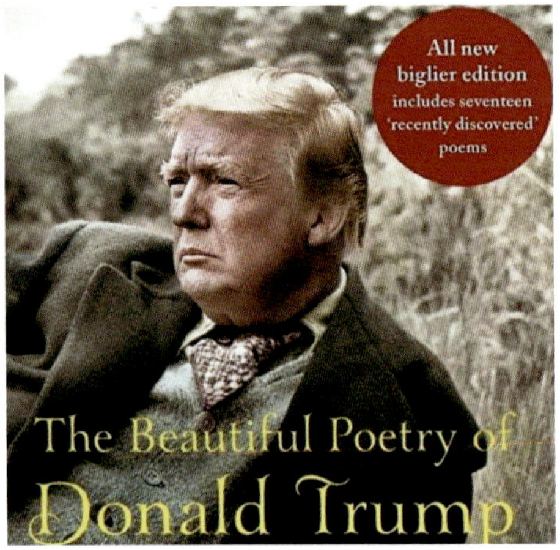

The original photograph of Dylan

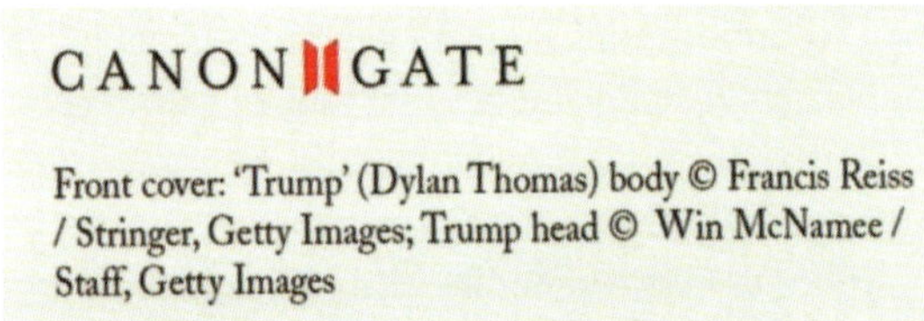
CANONGATE

Front cover: 'Trump' (Dylan Thomas) body © Francis Reiss / Stringer, Getty Images; Trump head © Win McNamee / Staff, Getty Images

Sadly, I've just seen that this dreadful book has been enlarged and reissued with the same cover!

* * * * *

I cannot end this somewhat bizarre chapter on such a sour trump card so I'm going to lift us up, and restore our faith in poetry with Seamus...

Seamus Heaney & Dylan Thomas.

I was lucky to engage with Seamus Heaney three times, twice in Swansea and once in Massachusetts, U S A. On his first visit to Swansea in 1993, I never got to meet him but I went to the lecture he gave which I remember to this day. But I heard on my bookstore grapevine most of the story. He was invited to Swansea by an Irish prof, in the English Department at the University, who knew Seamus and persuaded him to visit and deliver a lecture in the University's Taliesin Arts Centre.

Apparently the Professor met Seamus off the train at Swansea station on a cold January morning and when he asked Seamus how he wanted to spend the day, Seamus immediately said he wanted to visit Dylan Thomas' birthplace at 5 Cwmdonkin Drive, up in the middle-class suburb of Uplands. At that time the house was in private ownership and was being let as student accommodation. It transpired that the current tenants were a group of girls, some of whom were English undergraduates. How very surprised they were to open the door, some still in dressing gowns and curlers, to behold their Prof and a soon to be, Nobel-Prize-Winning-poet, and a handsome, charming man to boot. I sure they made their visitors welcome and no doubt they came to the evening lecture which was entitled, *Joy Or Night: Last Things in the Poetry of W. B. Yeats and Philip Larkin*. One of my customers, who was in the English Department at the University got me a precious ticket to the lecture so there was no way I was going to miss it.

Throughout the evening I sat transfixed as Seamus strode back of forth across the stage. Seamus began his lecture by reading a translation of *The Dead*, by Czech poet and immunologist, Miroslav Holub.[36]

THE DEAD
After his third operation, his heart
riddled like an old fairground target,
he woke upon his bed
and said: Now I'll be fine,
fit as a fiddle. And have you ever seen
horses coupling?
He died that night.
And another dragged on through eight insipid years
like a river weed in an acid stream,
as if pushing up his pallid
skewered face over the cemetery wall.
Until that face eventually vanished.
Both here and there the angel of death
quite simply stamped his hobnailed boot
on their medulla oblongata.
I know they died the same way.

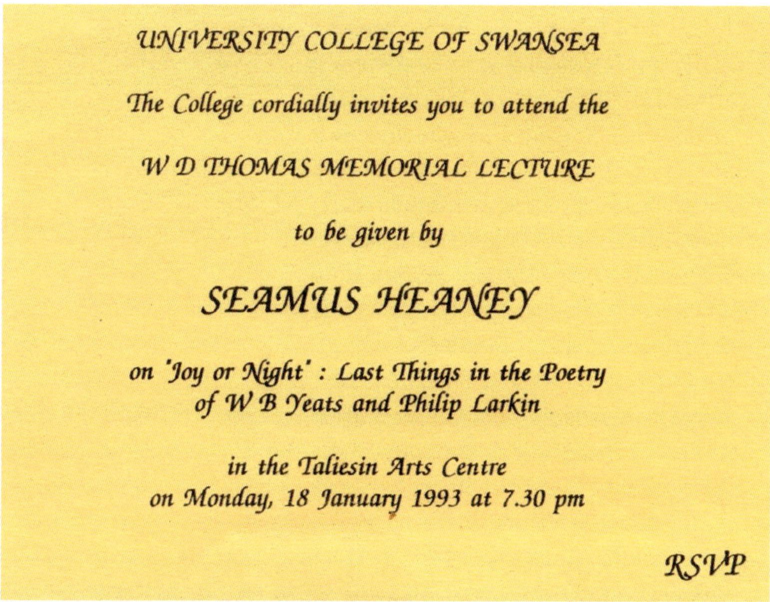
UNIVERSITY COLLEGE OF SWANSEA

The College cordially invites you to attend the

W D THOMAS MEMORIAL LECTURE

to be given by

SEAMUS HEANEY

on 'Joy or Night' : Last Things in the Poetry
of W B Yeats and Philip Larkin

in the Taliesin Arts Centre
on Monday, 18 January 1993 at 7.30 pm

RSVP

But I don't believe that they are
dead the same way.

Seamus gave an amazing passionate, but controlled rendition of this a powerful poem and this level of warm intensity never dipped throughout the whole lecture. I also recall that after reading other poems by both Larkin and Yeats, he would sometimes pause, and then say;

I'm going to read it this poem again ...

Because he knew how his audiences minds could wander off. It was a remarkable evening and I went home knowing I had been in the presence of a great poet. Sometime later the University published the text of the lecture in a very mean, poorly produced little pamphlet; the text xeroxed and the pages stapled into limp card covers; it deserved so much better.

It was however, later included in a volume of Heaney's critical writings *The Redress of Poetry*.[37] It is worth noting that Vernon Watkins and Dylan Thomas both admired Yeats tremendously. Vernon eventually made a trip to Dublin in 1938 and spent an afternoon with Yeats, just months before Yeats died. Vernon on the train back to Wales wrote down as much of the conversation he could recall and turned it into a one of his finest poems – Yeats in Dublin. And Vernon was also an early inspiration to a young Philp Larkin and they became good friends.

Seamus was back in Wales and Swansea in 1995, when Swansea was hosting the year-long festival – The UK Year of Literature,[38] And this time I got to meet him in the most desirable of environments. I had curated and installed a huge exhibition; Dylan Thomas Word and Image, in the newly restored Old Swansea Guild Hall which was now opening as *Ty Llên – House of Literature* aka *The Dylan Thomas Centre*. All of the exhibits – books, manuscripts, prints, photographs and ephemera telling the story of Dylan Thomas' life and works came from my own collections. And I was asked to give the visiting Irish poet a guided tour to the exhibition.

I met Seamus Heaney one mid-morning at the Centre before the exhibition opened to the public. I was excited, but nervously

The lecture as published as a small pamphlet by Swansea University

trepidatious, but Seamus was so warm and enthusiastic from our very first handshake, helped so much by his soft Irish brogue that the hour or so we spent going from cabinet to cabinet, with me explaining significance and back-stories of certain artefacts and images, and answering Seamus's many questions and observations. It was a delight and by the time he left we were on very warm and friendly terms. I asked him to sign the visitor book and he wrote;

After the first truth there is no other

Little did I know that I was destined to meet Seamus one more time. Every year, from around 1980 into the early years of this century, each November I would take as stand at the Boston International Antiquarian Book Fair. At a certain point, Leonard and Lisa Baskin[39] my good friends and indefatigable book buyers, had moved from Tiverton in Devon back to Massachusetts and settled just outside the town of Northampton, The location of Smith University which counted Sylvia Plath among their Alumni. It then became my habit to fly into Boston a few days before the start of the bookfair, rent a car and drive to Northampton and spend a few days with the Baskins. I did this in November of 1996 and no sooner had I walked into their large New England homestead when Lisa and Leonard informed me that Seamus Heaney was in town; that he was giving a reading at Smith, that was already underway, but that we were invited to the after-party at the Chancellor's residence! How lucky was I? I got myself showered and smartened up and off we three went. The way I recall it; we arrived on the campus and approached a rather grand mansion where we were greeted by the Chancellor. I was introduced as a visiting Welsh antiquarian bookseller. After some pleasant small-talk we were ushered into a large and crowded room. I immediately saw Seamus slightly elevated and surrounded by a throng of excited young female sophomores. What happened next happened fast. Seamus saw me, recognised me from our Swansea encounter a year back and began to make his excuses and extricate himself from the crush of excited students and make his way towards me. Without stopping he gently took my arm, whispered 'follow me' and led me down an adjoining passageway and then we ducked into a kind of anti-room, come cloak-room with a washroom off. Seamus took a deep breath, then shook my hand warmly whilst suggesting I join him in a Guinness from the dozen bottles lined up on a nearby shelf. And there we stayed for an hour or so before we both felt we should rejoin the throng. Seamus was indeed surprised and pleased to see me again but he also saw me as his liberator, his decoy to get him away from his fans and acolytes. We talked of books, poets, poems and Dylan Thomas. Time passed. Lisa Baskin, ever-thoughtful had been into Northampton before I arrived and bought me the only new Seamus Heaney book[40] they had in stock, which he warmly inscribed for me.

With us both refreshed by a few Guinness we went back to the main room where we found Lisa and Leonard in conversation Seamus's wife, Marie. They were pleased to see us and I was thanked again for giving Seamus some respite. I assured them the pleasure was all mine.[41]

Before I met Seamus he had delivered a Ben Bellit lecture at Bennington College, entitled *Dylan The Durable* and in 1992, they had published the text in an elegant card covered chap-book.[42] I can't remember when I first found a copy but I kept it and read it with great pleasure. I've quoted from it on the Dedication page and in Chapter 17 on Peter Blake and *Under Milk Wood*. Here is one final pithy quote;

> The records of Dylan Thomas reading his own poems, records which were lined on the shelves of undergraduate flats all over the world, were important cultural events. They opened a thrilling line between the centre and the edges of the Anglophone world. For all us young provincials, from Belfast to Brisbane, the impact of Thomas's performance meant that we had a gratifying sense of access to something

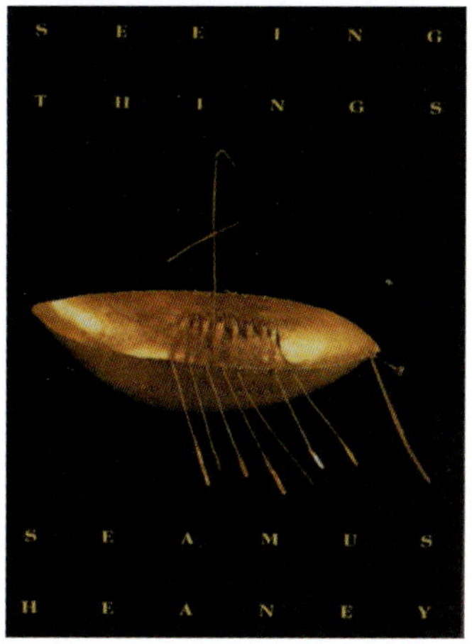

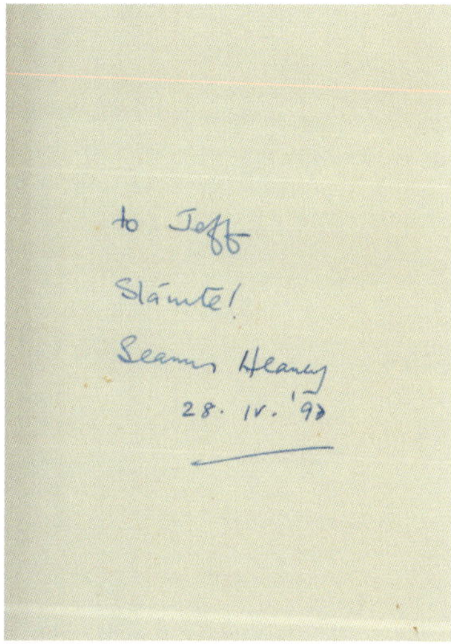

> that was acknowledged to be altogether modern, difficult and poetry.

I had *finished* this chapter and in fact I thought I had *finished* the book. I was reading for pleasure a book about another favourite writer, the recently deceased Jan Morris. The book was *ARIEL A Literary Life of JAN MORRIS* by Derek Johns.[43] I was surprised and delighted to read this comment by Jan on Dylan Thomas which comes from her book, *Wales; Epic Views of a Small Country*, and it comes after she has lauded Owain Glyndwr, but she sees Dylan Thomas as a more recent personification of Wales ...

> In his life and in his art, he represented the quandaries of Anglo-Welshism, a traumatic split of the emotions which can leave a sensitive man divided not only in his loyalties, but in his personality. The figure of Dylan Thomas, the world's idea of the Welshman, growing more volubly Welsh with every whisky, wandering the West End bars or the cocktail parties of Manhattan, is a figure to tug the Welsh heart, so poignantly does it suggest old betrayals and injustices.

1. It was in this pub that Dylan first met Caitlin Macnamara – who he would later marry. You can read about this and many other of Dylan's favourite drinking dens in my book – *Dylan Thomas The Pubs*. Y Lolfa. 2013. It is well illustrated with some splendid pictures by my friend Wyn Thomas.

2. Monk Bretton Books, Toronto. I met Roderick when I first exhibited at the Toronto International Antiquarian Book Fair in the late 70's. He always threw a wonderful and very generous pre book fair party for exhibiting booksellers. He also employed a fine assistant – Glynis Barnes, who hailed from Llanelli! She was a lively and accomplished cataloguer and bookseller but sadly she succumbed too early to cancer.

3. Stephanie de Montalk: *Unquiet World The Life of Geoffrey Potoki de Montalk*. Victoria University Press N.Z. 2001. The author is a cousin to Potoki.

4. Len Kelly worked in the London book trade in his youth but them emigrated with his wife to Canada and established a successful used and rare Bookshop on Spadina Avenue in Toronto. He returned to the Uk and had a bookshop in Tiverton Devon where he began a very imaginative, and innovative specialization in books on the history, both technical and sociological, on Broadcasting, which became very successful.

5. The Potoki dirty poem:

HERE LIES JOHN PENIS
by
The Hon. Geoffrey de Brooke

Here lies John Penis

buried in the Mount of Venus.

He died in tranquil faith

that having vanquished death

he shall rise up again,

and in joy's Kingdom reign

HERE LIES A POET

Here lies a poet who never had a fuck—

let's hope in Heaven he'll have much better luck.

6. Amis on Dylan was first published in the *Spectator Magazine* in 1957 and reprinted in his 1970 collection *What Became of Jane Austen* and later again it is included in his 1991 memoirs

7. Amis being cruel as ever – There was once an eye-sore on the coast just as you were entering Swansea – It was the first oil refinery in the UK. It was known as BP LLandarcy, which inspired Amis' nom-de-plume for Swansea

8. Rhys Davies: My Wales (My Country Series). Jerrold's. London, 1937.

9. A name inspired by the 18th century bardic antiquarian Iolo Morganwg, and Hancock was the name of a famous Welsh brewers.

10. Peter De Vries is also responsible for contributing to the cultural vernacular such

witticisms as *Nostalgia ain't what it used to be* and *Deep down, he's shallow*. Another ubiquitous writers mantra;write drunk, edit sober, which is often attributed to Papa Hemmingway is actually also one of in McGland's pronouncements in *Reuben Reuben*, when he declares, *Sometimes I write drunk and revise sober, and sometimes I write sober and revise drunk.*

11. Wendy Pollard: *Pamela Hansford Johnson Her Life, Works and Times*. Shepheard Walwyn. London. 2014.

12. Constantine Fitzgibbon: *Selected Letters of Dylan Thomas*. J.M.Dent 1966.

13. The *Daily Mail* suggested that the book miss-represented the relationship between Dylan, describing him as *19-year-old chain smoking beer swilling ...provincial* and Pamela as the *'nice' 21-year-old London girl*, The *Daily Mail* described it as, *'one of the most unlikely love affairs of our time...* 'And they added, 'It was always platonic'.

14. Trevor Tregaskis Hughes was also an ex Grammar school pupil but he was ten years older than Dylan and was a clerk but he had literary ambitions. Hughe's paper are all in Buffalo (as are Pamela's) and in his memoir he writes of meeting Dylan and his family on a rare holiday to Llandrindod Wells. He later responded to Dylan's request in a local Swansea paper for help and contributions for a projected new literary magazine Prose and Verse, which never materialised.

15. The Swansea band Chris fronted was called *GUTBUCKET*. I saw them play once and they were above average, and Chris looked most at home behind the microphone.

16. Cwmsylen is not a real place, but there is a peak named Craig Cwm Silyn in Snowdonia.

17. I kept one version of the cover image which I have framed and hung in my office. Ruth's originals are now in the National Library of Wales in Aberystwyth in the iconography section of *the Jeff Towns /Dylans Bookstore /Dylan Thomas Collection*. Ruth and I became friends and I followed her career and saw her every year for a decade at the National Eisteddfod where we both took stalls.

18. M. Wynn Evans: *Corresponding Cultures the two literatures of Wales*. University of Wales Press. Cardiff 1999.

19. CENTRE FOR RESEARCH INTO THE ENGLISH LITERATURE AND LANGUAGE OF WALES. Swansea University

20. Jon's Review can be found online at gwales.com

21. Geraint is the son of Aneurin Talfan Davies who was a close friend and supporter of Dylan Thomas, giving him support and work on BBC radio, editing in 1954 the posthumous collection of Thomas's scripts; *Quite Early One Morning* and writing his own views on Dylan Thomas in 1964 in his book *Druid of the Broken Body*, an assessment of Dylan Thomas as a religious poet.

22. Marion Morehouse was one of the first super models, before switching and getting behind the camera, and becoming a well-respected photographer. She was the third wife of e e cummings, who Dylan had met on his earlier tours to America.

23. The publishers back cover *blurb* to Gwyneth's book.

24. In 2001 I approached David Slivka who I had previously corresponded with and he agreed to cast one final bronze copy of his Death Mask of Dylan Thomas from the original molds, for Swansea. I then liaised with Swansea Council who agreed to foot the bill to make the cast and bring David Slivka to Swansea when the bust would be unveiled and I would interview Dave during that year's Dylan Thomas Festival. Dave died in 2010 aged 95.

25. *A lipograms,* is a piece of constrained writing – from just a paragraph or to a whole poem or novel in which the writer chooses to omit any words with a certain letter or writes a poem using only one of a few rhyming sounds and letters. One of the most remarkable examples of a lipograms is Ernest V. Wright's 1939 novel Gads, which has over 50,000 words but not a single letter E!

26. Oulipo is the name of a French literary movement the word comes from the French descriptive name and acronym: Ouvroir de littérature potentielle; roughly translated: "workshop of potential literature" it was founded in 1960 by Raymond Queneau and François Le Lionais.

27. In 1934 Dylan writes to his first girlfriend with a list of films she should see, he includes amoung serious european classics *'the Marx Brothers comedies* (American)'. And late in his life, in 1950, when he secretly met up with his American lover, Pearl Kazin, in London, he took her to see a Marx Brothers movie. More on this song in Chaper 15. Dylan and Music.

28. The name is derived from a phrase that resulted when Surrealists first played the game, "*Le cadavre exquis boira le vin nouveau.*" ("The exquisite corpse shall drink the new wine.") André Breton writes that the game developed at the residence of friends at an old house in Montparnasse. Besides himself he mentions Marcel Duhamel, Jaques Prevert, Yves Tanguy and Benjamin Peret as original participants.

29. I once owned this copy! See Chapter 7.

30. On the Literary Hub website; https://lithub.com

31. I also write about this poem in Chapter 14 Dylan Thomas and the Beat Poets.

32. Ed Maggs of Maggs Bros. Ed is semi-retired and lives most of the time nowadays in Southern Ireland.

33. John Moriarty: *What the curlew said. Nostos continued*. The Lilliput Press, 2007.

34. The Guardian Obituary by Peter Clare can be found here https://amp.theguardian.com

35. Rob Sears has got form he has also spewed out *Vladimir Putin: Life Coach and Choose Your Own Apocalypse with Kim Jung-un and Friends. Kim Yong Un*. I feel he should stick with Kid's books. How does he sleep at night?

36. Miroslav Holub (1923 – 1998) was a Czech poet but also a serious Immunologist. His poetry is heavily influenced by his experiences as an immunologist, writing many poems using his scientific knowledge to poetic effect.

37. The Redress of Poetry. Faber and Faber. 1995.

38. I revisit this year-long literary jamboree in Chapter 9. Above.

39. I write more on Leonard and Lisa in my opening Introduction and in Chapter 10. on Sylvia and Ted.

40. The book \Lisa got for me was a recent collection of new poems, *Seeing Things*. Farrah Giroux; New York. 1991

41. over the course of my 50 years bookselling I have come to realise I was lucky enough to meet most of the best poets of my generation, In the Chapters of this book I have written about Allen Ginsberg, Ted Hughes, R.S.Thomas and Heathcote Willimas is none too shabby a poet. So why should I leave out Seamus Heaney?

42. Bennington: Bennington College, 1992. First Edition. Illustrated wrappers; 8vo. 33 pp. edition of 1000 hand-numbered copies; Heaney's printed signature on the bibliographic page. Intro. by Stephen Sandy. Printing a lecture given at the college by Seamus Heaney. Brandes & Durkan A53. A Bennington College Chap-Book.

Dylan Thomasa, Leon Atkin and the Landlord of The Bush Hotel Swansea. 1953.

13.

Dylan Thomas:
Leon Atkin & Heathcote Williams..

He never came to church, not to my church. The only time I saw Dylan in a church was when his coffin was taken in for the funeral service.

Leon Atkin talking to Colin Edwards...

Leon Atkin was born on 26 July 1902 in Spalding, Lincolnshire. His father was a gas manager and Leon was raised as a regular Anglican. He had six siblings, and as a boy he began to participate in various activities at the Methodist chapel that was next door to the family home. In 1914, the family moved to Biddulph in Staffordshire. In his mid-teens Leon made two choices that would govern the rest of his life; he became a Methodist and began preaching. He became famous as a boy-preacher and at 16, he joined the Labour Party. He was to be a life-long Methodist and very left-leaning Socialist from then on. Following an engineering apprenticeship, he decided on a 'religious' life and began to train in Birmingham for the Methodist ministry. Even here he began to have difficult confrontations with the college authorities and they were glad to pack him off to the Welsh mining valleys and he was appointed Probationer-Minister at St John's Church, Risca, Gwent, in 1930.

Leon Atkin C.F. The frontispiece to his 1947 poetry book, *If Men Should Ask...Poems of War and Peace*

At this point he adopted the Social Gospel.[1] and challenged the militant Communists and the secularist movement in the mining valleys. He began to hold a weekly open-air meeting inspired by the work of his contemporary Donald Soper in London. For a whole year he debated every Friday night in a working men's club in Risca, and with members of the Communist Party as well as with unbelievers who attended the Sunday evening services. His congregation regularly comprised of a remarkable 800 to 900 people. In 1932 he moved to the Methodist Central Hall in Bargoed and quickly went about transforming the place; to assist the poor and unemployed the large chapel and its schoolroom was opened daily. He installed a free shoe repairing workshop, a barber shop, and a kitchen which provided free meals. Next he converted part of the building as a hostel for 28 young unemployed people who were denied dole because their fathers earned a few shillings too much under the Means Test. These actions served to anger the authorities and Atkin was threatened with prosecution for 'obstructing the administration of his Majesty's Government'. His response was a typically feisty one; he criticised the local Labour Party and churches in Wales for being so ineffective. The Synod were disturbed by him and arranged for him to be moved to Cornwall.

Leon was by now very much at home in South Wales and he accepted the challenge of taking on a very run down church in Swansea; St Paul's, a large church near the hospital. The church at that time, only had 12 members and a debt of £2,000. As ever he immediately began in Swansea as he had done elsewhere before; holding weekly open-air meetings in a place called the Forum. Such was his charisma that his congregation grew at St Paul's from twelve to two hundred on Sunday nights in the winter, and to five hundred in the summer, the majority of these being holiday visitors. With his usual resourcefulness he adapted the crypt of the chapel as accommodation for his family, his wife May and their two children (later, when they had found a house, this Crypt was also opened to down-and-outs and men of the road.) His bold anti-establishment stance and strong socialist and anti-fascist views kept him at odds with the authorities.

Leon soon became become a well-known figure in Swansea with his beret and clerical collar, but always extremely unpopular with Labour Party activists and Free-Church leaders who ostracised him from all their committees. He was a natural born maverick: public disapproval never deterred him, and unlike most ministers he would christen the babies of single mothers. He was an extreme individualist who missed few opportunities to taunt the Nonconformists and the Labourites.

However, he had also developed a penchant for a drink; his love of alcohol and the conviviality of pubs, was yet another failing in the eyes of most ministers and churchgoers in West Glamorganshire. But he wanted to take his ministry into the pubs and clubs of the town. He made regular Friday night visits to the public houses of Swansea to collect money to enable poor children from Swansea to enjoy Guy Fawkes night and to be taken by him to the circus. Atkin developed his ministry among needy people, and his care for the disadvantaged and the 'down-and-outs' became known through his articles in the press, in particular through the *News of the World*. In many a bitter winter his chapel became a refuge for dozens of men who would otherwise have perished.

Leon outside St. Paul's with a young acolyte

So it should come as no surprise that he should become a good friend of young local poet, Dylan Thomas, who would always refer to Leon as 'my Padre' or 'my Priest'. They were first introduced by Bert Trick, another very left wing friend of Dylan's. Dylan and Leon would often join each other for a pint in one of the local pubs of which there were many.

Leon eventually went into local politics to further his efforts on behalf of the disadvantaged. From November 1935 he served as a Labour councillor for Brynmelyn Ward; changing to an independent in 1947, and remaining on the Council until 1964.

Rev. Leon Atkin *THE PEOPLE'S CANDIDATE*

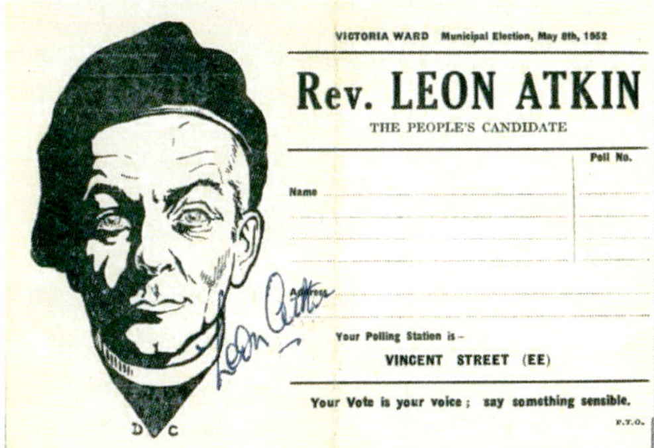

In July 1934, Leon Atkin made the news when he cheekily, but also courageously challenged Oswald Mosley's anti-Semitism at a huge British Union of Fascists rally at the *Plaza Cinema*[2] in July 1934. It was an event that Dylan Thomas also attended with his friend Bert Trick whom Dylan referred to as his 'Communist Grocer'.

Leon gave his account of the event in his interview[3] with Colin Edwards, a journalist from Wales who worked mainly in Wales.

> And then there appeared all over Swansea large posters thirty feet tall by fifteen with the slogan
> **'Mosley speaks Plaza Cinema – Sunday'.**
> ...as a minister of religion and as one interested in local politics I was given a complimentary ticket to sit with the elite in the first three rows.
> ...on this particular Sunday night it was filled to capacity...I wore a frock tailcoat with my clerical attire. And there I sat. The hall lined, downstairs and in the galleries, with hundreds of Black-shirts...then Mosley came to the platform.., he began to speak. For an hour and a half he spoke; from beginning to end, his speech consisted of a tirade against international Jewry. The Jews, he argued were responsible for everything bad on the planet...
> When he had finished, he announced ...he would take a few questions – not oral ones...I could not resist writing on the back of my special invite, my question.
> "I have been working for a Jew for quite a number of years. Ought I to change my employer?"

And by a miraculous coincidence it was the first question to come out of the hat. Drawing himself to his full six foot plus, the would-be dictator read the question

"I have been working for a Jew for quite a number of years. Ought I to change my employer?"

"Certainly," he said. "I am sure if you looked around you would find a far more reliable Gentile.

Rising to my feet in the front row in full clerical attire, I said Mr. Mosley could you give me his name and address?"

Mosley turned the colours of the rainbow.

"Is this man a *bona fide* parson?" he cried

"Of course he bloody is!" shouted someone

It soon became a chorus within a few seconds pandemonium reigned. Fist fights were breaking out everywhere.

The event prompted the 19-year-old Dylan Thomas to describe the event in a letter to his then girlfriend, Pamela Hansford Johnson describing the proceedings with no small measure hyperbole;

If you read the newspapers you'll see that Swansea is at the centre of all revolutionary activity this week ... I have just left the socialist party, and offered my services to the communists. I was in time for Mosley's meeting, and was thrown down the stairs[4] No harm done, however. I have just completed a seditious article attacking the shirted gentleman, having discovered, quite by accident, that he is the biggest owner of slum property in Birmingham.

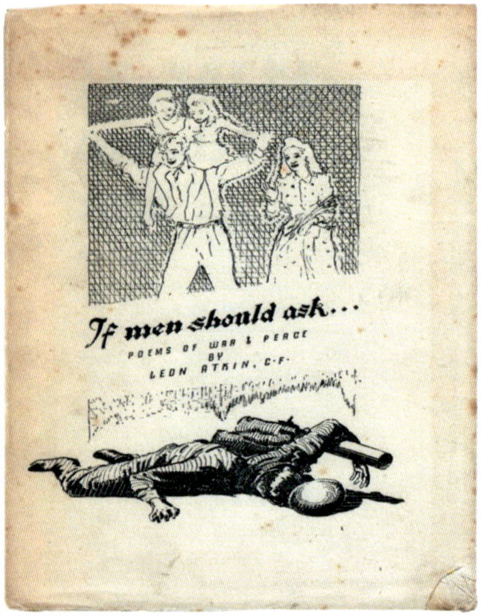

Leon also wrote poetry, prose and plays and he published a volume of his work, *If Men Should Ask Poems of War & Peace.*[5] Many of his poems are based on his real experiences during the war. Though formerly a pacifist, during the war he joined the Royal Artillery, before being invited to become an Army Chaplain, in which capacity he served in the Netherlands. Ironically the outbreak of war curtailed performances of his play at the Llewelyn Hall *Until the Day Break*, with its exposure of injustice. The volume also includes some aphorisms from his prose works. This example from a work called *Uriah's Widow*, no doubt raised the eyebrows of some more straight-laced puritanical readers and goes some way towards explaining why Dylan found him such an attractive a friend;

TO FIND the man – the undraped man within the man – give him wine, good wine in plenty; until the sparkling cup o'erflows ...In wine, a man is what he would be.

MUSIC AND WINE were wedded in the scheme of God: They enlarge the heart; adding strange charm to all things...

GIVE WINE to the man who is ready to die – and you'll find him anon more ready to live.

Leon would figure one last time in Dylan's life but in an altogether more poignant occasion. In Early October of 1953 Dylan had committed himself to a forth reading tour to America. He was persuaded to go by John Malcolm Brinnin, who had visited Dylan in Laugharne in September to prepare an article about the background to *Under Milk Wood* for the American magazine *Mademoiselle.* Caitlin was not in favour of the trip which was put back a few times before Dylan sent Brinnin a telegram informing him that he was finally flying on October 19th. In the week previously he had travelled into Swansea from Carmarthen to record a radio piece about the quirkiness of small-town Laugharne[6] for the BBC, produced by another good Swansea friend Aneirin Talfan Davies. He seemed to have decided to take this chance to say his goodbyes to his Swansea pals. He met with

Vernon Watkins and talked of his forthcoming collaboration with Stravinsky and also sent a telegram to Dan Jones to meet him for a final drink in a *The Bush*, a High Street pub, just down from the station.

Daniel Jones describes this final meeting in his book *My Friend Dylan Thomas*[7] but does not mention that Leon Atkin joined the session. However, a local photographer Tal. E. Jones, had been hired by *Time* Magazine to get photographs of the poet at play and this meeting was recorded for posterity and later featured in the Swansea Evening Post.

It was to be Dylan's last drink in Swansea and the last ever photograph taken of him in his hometown. Within a few weeks he would be lying comatose in St Vincent's hospital in NYC, never to awake.

Leon would never see Dylan alive again but whenever asked about him he was always warm and respectful, when interviewed by the journalist Colin Edwards, he told him;

> He never came to church, not to my church. The only time I saw Dylan in a church was when his coffin was taken in for the funeral service. As to him being fundamentally religious, I'd say no; you could never fit Dylan into a creed or to a

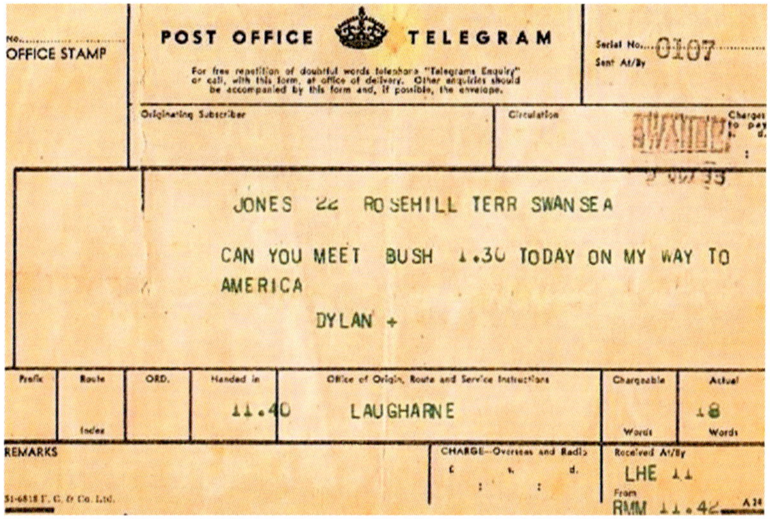

No.
OFFICE STAMP

POST OFFICE TELEGRAM

For free repetition of doubtful words telephone "Telegrams Enquiry" or call, with this form, at office of delivery. Other enquiries should be accompanied by this form and, if possible, the envelope.

Serial No. 0107
Sent At/By

Originating Subscriber
Circulation
Charges to pay s. d.

JONES 22 ROSEHILL TERR SWANSEA

CAN YOU MEET BUSH 1.30 TODAY ON MY WAY TO AMERICA

DYLAN +

Prefix	Route / Index	ORD.	Handed in	Office of Origin, Route and Service Instructions	Chargeable Words	Actual Words
			11.40	LAUGHARNE		18

REMARKS
CHARGE—Overseas and Radio £ s. d.
Received At/By LHE 11
From RMM 11.42

Dylan's last telegram to Dan Jones

Dylan at home in *The Bush*

261

DYLAN'S LAST EVENING IN SWANSEA

THE POET Dylan Thomas captured here in a previously unpublished photograph taken in the Bush Hotel, High Street, Swansea, the evening before he left for his last American tour.

With Dylan in the picture is another well-known Swansea figure, the late Rev. Leon Atkin, the Non - conformist minister of St. Paul's Church, St. Helen's Road.

Photographer Tal Jones tells how he searched for Dylan for Time magazine, who had phoned from Luxembourg asking for a photograph of the poet.

He eventually tracked him down to the Rosehill Terrace home of composer Daniel Jones. From there he was driven to the Bush where this after-hours shot was taken as one of a session.

"Dylan insisted that the photos should be informal," says Tal Jones.

One of the shots taken that evening was used as a cover picture for Time in that late summer of 1953. Dylan, who died in New York of alcohol and morphia, never returned to his native Swansea.

More on Dylan Thomas — Page 17.

8

denominational conception of religion. That was to the good, because he was far too big Leon Atkin died in Swansea on 27 November 1976, having served the town for 42 years in his unique but often controversial style.[9]

Heathcote Williams, Leon Atkin and Dylan (both)
Around 2012, the writer and biographer, Andrew Lycett[10].contacted me because he was about to write a new biography of Dylan Thomas. Through the course of this project we became good friends and I think his Thomas biography adds much to what Fitzgibbon and Ferris, among others, have written on the poet. Sometime later he got in touch to say a writer friend of his wanted help, in particular with the picture research for a book he was writings on Dylan Thomas and Bob Dylan[11] His friend was Heathcote Williams, who I knew of as a political activist, counter-culture hero and poet. I was intrigued by him but we had never met. I told Andrew I would try and assist and that he could give Heathcote my contacts.

I went to my shelves and found I had a couple of books by Heathcote – first editions of *Whale Nation* (a presentation copy to Edward Lucie Smith) and *Autogeddon*, and then I read up a bit about him on the internet. He had quite a CV; poet, actor, political activist and dramatist and also a vibrant member of the 1960's counter- culture and a leading activist in the London squatting scene in the 1970's who had run a squatters "estate agency" called the *Ruff Tuff Cream Puff*; and for a time was associate editor of the literary journal *Transatlantic Review*, as well as being one of those responsible for the controversial alternative sex newspaper, *Suck*. He was also frequent contributor to the foremost influential London underground newspaper paper *International Times* (IT).

This was all music to my ears and I very much looked forward to hearing from him. In a few days a parcel containing a copy of his manuscript arrived. I settled down to read it and contemplate doing the picture research. It turned out to be quite a roller-coaster, I knew it would be unusual but I was unprepared for its powerful and unexpected iconoclasm. The book's title was, *Of Dylan and his Deaths.*[12]

13

I have to begin by explaining why that that title in itself was very provocative for me. It was a literary red rag to a bull. I've been at this game for a long time and the dissections, prevarications and conspiracy theories and sordid details surrounding Dylan Thomas' tragic and untimely death in NYC in 1953, has for me, already been absolutely done to death (if you pardon the distasteful pun).

For me it's really like literally flogging a dead horse! (another bad pun). All three of Thomas's major biographers; Fitzgibbon in 1967, Ferris in 1978 (revised 2000) and Lycett in 2014, covered the end of Thomas' life in detail and each one, in turn, offered some extra information. Despite their efforts, a certain amount of conspiracy theory and sensational rumours have always been around and, by the 1990's, this unfortunately had begun to spawn a mini-industry.

1986 a Welsh based writer, Rob Gittins published a book; *The Last Days of Dylan Thomas*. I read the book with interest but it was hard to discern the genre I was reading, in as much as it purported to be fact, but read like a novel and came without any indication of any sources for the text. It did deal with the

circumstances surrounding Thomas's death almost as if the writer were an eye witness.

A few years later, in 1991 a Laugharne-based bookseller and journalist George Tremlett brought out a biography of Dylan Thomas,[14] followed very closely by a book he co-wrote a book with an American doctor, James Nashold. This book was called *The Death of Dylan Thomas*.[15] George had also already written a book with Dylan's widow Caitlin,[16] and both Tremlett's biographies contained detailed accounts of Thomas's final days in New York and of his death. But he could still produce another dark volume, sheathed in a black dust jacket!

The Death of Dylan Thomas was a hefty book, running to some

260 pages. It focused in great (and quite tedious) detail, on the last months of Thomas' life in Wales and America. The pre-publicity claimed new sensational information suggesting medical malpractice. It caused a bit of a stir but Paul Ferris dammed it in a review in *The Western Mail*, in which he declared that it contained nothing that was not in his biography and he directed the author's to the specific page numbers where they could check!

Then in 1995 the poet Adrian Mitchell came to Swansea, which was hosting a year-long Literary Festival, un-imaginatively named, The UK Year of Literature[17] Adrian was the selected to be Poet in Residence for a month-long celebration of Dylan Thomas and part of his remit was to deliver an academic lecture on the poet. However that was not Adrian's way. He is an unreconstructed, 60's hippy, peacenik; Adrian wrote a long piece of performance poetry *Who Killed Dylan Thomas*. I was at his performance, which was passionate, funny and unforgettable. Then Adrian sent a copy of his text to his pal, the great artist /illustrator, Ralph Steadman. Apparently for a week, each night, before bed, Ralph would sit at his kitchen table with a very large whiskey and proceed to drink and draw. He illustrated the text manically and magnificently as only Ralph Steadman can. In the space of a week Ralph had produced *Fear and Loathing* in Llareggub!

A reviewer[18] of the book ended his review with this;

> Mitchell's tribute to Dylan Thomas reclaims the writer for all of us. He argued that 'his sympathies were always with the underdog...Dylan Thomas was the exact opposite of Margaret Thatcher?' It wasn't the alcohol alone that killed him. Mitchell, aided by Ralph Steadman's unsettling graphics,[19] reveals some of the humiliation and pain that lies in the attempt of a creative artist to bare his souls while failing to make a living...

263

The reviewer got it spot on. As far as I was and am concerned this wonderful book should have been the very last word (and pictures) on the subject, but it was not to be – it seemed that there was a literally morbid fatal fascination with this sad story and a new writer appeared and took up the coffin.

But not everyone gets it like Adrian and Ralph. David N. Thomas is a Welsh man from just outside Swansea who worked in London in high level Social Work Theory and Practice until, in the early 1990's, he retired back to Wales, to Ceredigion, and began to write books about the life (and sadly, the death) of Dylan Thomas.

He began by writing about Thomas's time around New Quay. His first book on Dylan Thomas; *A Farm, Two Mansions and a Bungalow*, was published in 2000. It included the one truly sensational incident in Thomas' when a disgruntled neighbour,

Ralph Steadman's cover for Adrian Mitchell's rant

Ralphs inebriated embellishments on the title-page of my copy

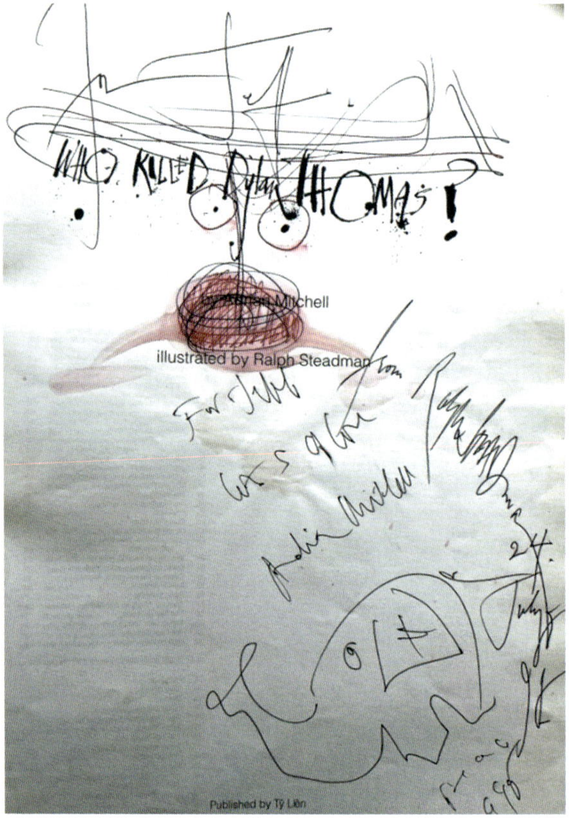

William Killick a member of the SOE attacked the asbestos bungalow that Dylan was living in with a grenade and machine gun! The film rights were sold to make a big budget movie *The Edge of Love*.[20]

D. N. Thomas then wrote, in swift succession, a few more books and magazine articles about Dylan Thomas in West Wales, mainly guide books, but also a curious, and what I found somewhat distasteful, novel; *The Dylan Thomas Murders*.[21]

He was then asked by the National Library of Wales to edit the transcriptions of a remarkable archive of audio archive, reel to reel tape recordings of interviews conducted by Colin Edwards in the late fifties onwards with just about everybody he could track down who knew and engaged with Dylan Thomas – from the cradle to the grave. David did a good job of the editing and they were issued in two chronological volumes. Each volume was comprised of half edited interviews and half new essays by D. N. Thomas, inspired or provoked by the interviews.

The second volume contained an essay; *Death by Neglect*; two appendices, *Chronology of Death*, and *Post Mortem Report* with some 40 plus pages of dense medical ruminations.

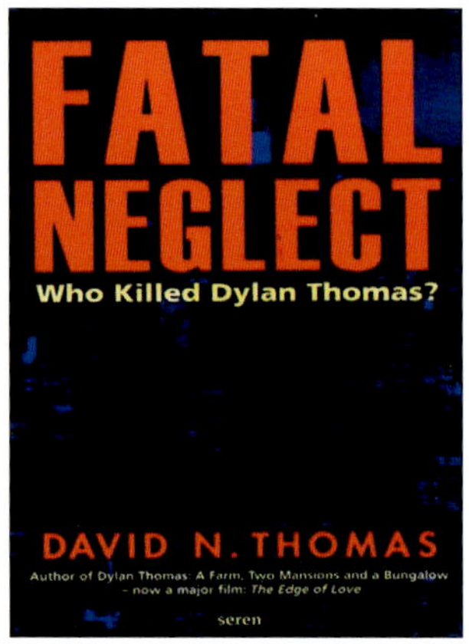

Enough already? I'm afraid not: in 2008 D. N. Thomas published *FATAL NEGLECT Who Killed Dylan Thomas*[22] Another 232 dense pages.

No small part of the book is a rather vicious character assignation of John Malcolm Brinnin and all I can say is that his depiction in this book could not be further away from the John Malcolm Brinnin with whom I spent a very wonderful and rewarding day with in his Key West, Florida home in 2000.

Photo by Vincent Llyod

J. M. T. with J. M. B. in John's Florida home

And then in 2014, a poet and essayist I admire; Robert Minhinick, published an elegant little pamphlet *The Mythic Death of Dylan Thomas*,[23] in which he rather tastelessly explores what he sees as the advantages for a Poet of dying young; quite pointedly and more particularly of being Welsh, and dying young in New York; suggesting that if this had not been Dylan's sad fate he would not enjoy the positive acclaim in which his writings are held throughout the world today. Not an opinion to which subscribe. The publisher informs us (in parenthesis) that; (This mischievous overview was delivered as a short talk in the Stanza Poetry Festival 'Past and Present' series, 2013.)

Maybe It came over better live....

And then there are the feature films and T. V, documentaries; so many since Dylan died in 1953. There have been some very good informative documentaries on his life and work perhaps the best was Jack Howells' early short documentary, *A Tribute to Dylan Thomas* which won the Oscar the 35th Academy Awards in 1963 Documentary Short Subject. The Academy's Film Archive preserved the film in 2000. It features a fine narration by a young Richard Burton.

But many of the succession of TV documentaries can't help in dwelling on those last few weeks in NYC. Even the BBC's flagship arts programme, Arena. made a documentary in 2003 for the fiftieth anniversary of Dylan's death, in which they decided to be clever and tell the poets life in reverse; so *Dylan Thomas: From Grave to Cradle*, began with the poet's death.

Enough already; perhaps this sad, small, scrappy official document says it all...

With all this in mind I approached Heathcoat's typescript with no small measure of trepidation. And it all began so well;

As a reward for my having learnt William Blake's poem 'Tyger,

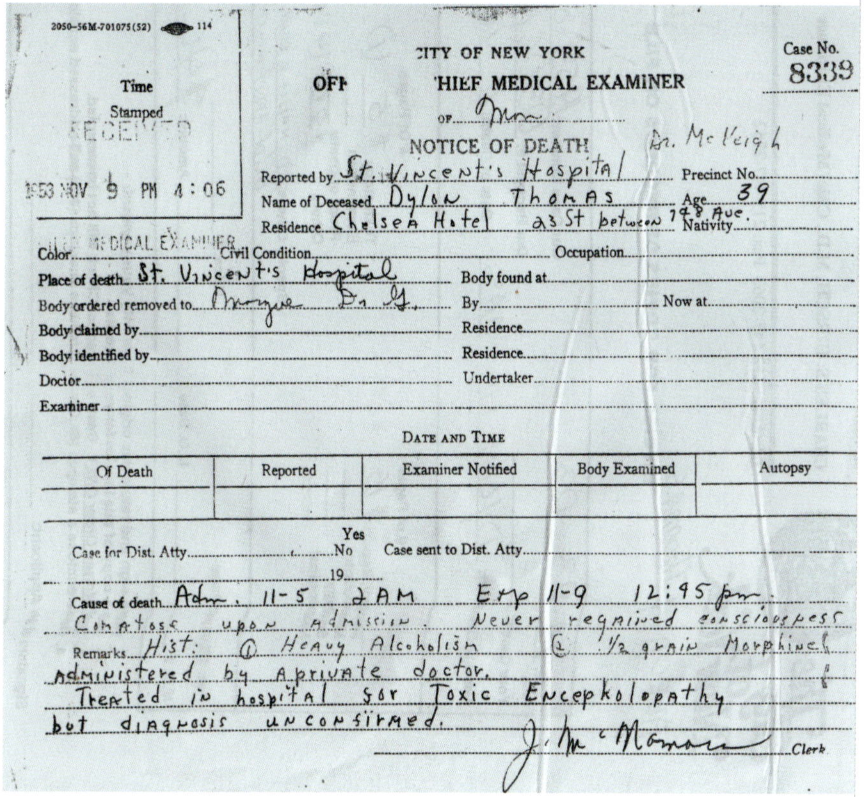

2050-56M-701075(52) 114

Time Stamped

RECEIVED 1953 NOV 9 PM 4:06 MEDICAL EXAMINER

CITY OF NEW YORK
OFF[illegible] CHIEF MEDICAL EXAMINER
OF Man

Case No. 8339

NOTICE OF DEATH Dr. McVeigh

Reported by St. Vincent's Hospital Precinct No.
Name of Deceased Dylon Thomas Age 39
Residence Chelsea Hotel 23 St between 7 & 8 Ave. Nativity
Color Civil Condition Occupation
Place of death St. Vincent's Hospital Body found at
Body ordered removed to Morgue Dr. G. By Now at
Body claimed by Residence
Body identified by Residence
Doctor Undertaker
Examiner

DATE AND TIME

Of Death	Reported	Examiner Notified	Body Examined	Autopsy

Case for Dist. Atty Yes No Case sent to Dist. Atty
19

Cause of death Adm. 11-5 2 AM Exp 11-9 12:45 pm.
Comatose upon admission. Never regained consciousness
Remarks Hist: ① Heavy Alcoholism ② ½ grain Morphine administered by a private doctor.
Treated in hospital for Toxic Encephalopathy but diagnosis unconfirmed.

J. McManara Clerk

Hist: ① heavy alcoholism ② ½ grain Morphine

Tyger' and for having precociously recited it to him without stumbling, my father promised to take me to hear Dylan Thomas reading at the Victoria and Albert Museum.

I was nine. "Your treat," he said. "He's a poet. He's Welsh."

Heathcote writes that, "the promised outing" took place on a Saturday, August 11, 1951, in the Victoria and Albert Museum's Lecture Hall.[24] Heathcote had actually seen and heard Dylan Thomas read! Not only that, he goes on to describe the whole afternoon and the effect it had on him in great detail and in beautiful prose;

> My father and I found our way to the front of the audience and we sat down directly beneath a small, plump man with curly auburn hair, a raffish bow-tie, loud chequered tweeds and a shining face that stood patiently behind a wooden lectern a few feet above us...I was almost immediately below him. From my perspective, he was spasmodically hidden behind a large pint glass of amber-coloured liquid from where he would tantalizingly slide in and out of view. This human metronome, seemingly set to some slow internal beat, shuffled his slightly soggy handwritten papers and then... Dylan Thomas sprang to life... His eyes bulged and his voice resonated, boomingly and rhythmically with a series of florid arias spilling out of his diminutive frame.
> (A phenomenon which was accompanied by misty sprays of saliva that I remember my father found hard to forgive.)
> Dylan was so possessed that I thought he might go off like a bomb with his fizzing and surging. I'd not seen anyone drunk before and he was clearly drunk but he was also a phenomenon, as drunk on language as on alcohol... I can only recall one line from the reading with any certainty,
> 'I see the boys of summer in their ruin ...'
> I particularly remembered it because my father would repeat it over the years. Whenever it looked to him as if I was going off the rails, he'd trot out this line, to my chagrin as he'd quite spoil it by giving it a stern, judgmental almost taunting edge.

And he concludes;

> After Thomas' reading was over my father and I filed out of the auditorium and my father brought me home, announcing to my mother in a matter-of-fact fashion, "The boy was hypnotized," which was true. I still cherish a vivid, dreamy sense of having been entranced. Rhapsodically entranced.

After this ravishing opening section Heathcote carries on with his brisk autobiography and we learn that after a comfortable childhood and adolescence, involving Eton, Heathcote did as his father predicted and went 'off the rails'. He began this journey towards becoming a major player in the counter-culture happenings of the 1960's and 70's. But first he decided to go on the road in a kind of retro W.H. Davies fashion. He decided to hitchhike to Wales to engage with his Celtic ancestry and search for the ghost of Dylan Thomas. Heathcote was in his late teens. He writes of his motivation;

> For no reason other than the germinative Victoria and Albert reading, I'd set my sights on Swansea, thinking and hoping that this might be somewhere to find a different kind of spiritual sustenance, given the poet whom Swansea had spawned.

Heathcote made it to Swansea and had the good fortune to land up meeting with none other than the; Rev. Leon Atkins;

> ...after a tip from an elderly vagrant in the centre of town, I made my way to the Crypt below St Paul's Church in St Helen's Rd.[25] Swansea, where just as this providential gentleman of the road had indicated,
> 'the Reverend Leon Atkin will see you right.'

Very quickly Heathcote and Leon became firm friends and compatriots; they sang out of the identical secular socialist hymn-book and song sheets. When Heathcote told Leon that he loved Dylan Thomas' poetry and stories and that as a young boy he had seen and heard Dylan Thomas reading; Leon revealed that he had been a good friend and a drinking pal of Dylan's and regaled Heathcote with his story of the Swansea anti-Moseley, Black-shirts-episode.

This leads Heathcote into a laudatory few pages extolling Dylan's credentials as a hero of the left-wing counter-culture (as Heathcote himself became). He quotes from one of Dylan's early letters to Pamela Hansford Johnson, sent in 1933 when he was just 19, in which Dylan declares that they are both living in 'an outgrown and decaying system' in which;

> 'light is being turned into darkness by the capitalist and industrialists'

And Dylan climbs on his soap box and proclaims;

> There is only one thing you and I, who are of this generation, must look forward to, must work for and pray for and, because, as we fondly hope, we are poets and voicers not only of our personal selves but of our social selves, we must pray for it all the more vehemently.
>
> It is the Revolution.

This is very close indeed to Leon Atkin's beliefs in the *Social Gospel* and also deeply appealing to young Heathcote, who goes on to compare Dylan's poem, *My world is Pyramid* which Dylan published in New Verse in December 1934,[26] to Picasso' *Guernica*; quoting lines from this stanza;

> My world is cypress, and an English valley.
> I piece my flesh that rattled on the yards
> Red in an Austrian volley.
> I hear, through dead men's drums, the riddled lads,
> Screwing their bowels from a hill of bones,
> Cry Eloi to the guns.

Leon had one more treat in store for Heathcote. Across the road from his church was a branch of Lloyds Bank. The senior counter clerk was Swansea's other great poet Vernon Watkins. Leon and Vernon were good old friends; but Vernon was also Dylan Thomas's closest ever friend in poetry.[27] They had met in 1935, when Vernon was astonished and ravished by Dylan's *18 Poems* when he discovered it filling the window of his local new bookshop, and bought a copy He thought he was the only poet in town and he determined to meet this remarkable young upstart poet. They did meet almost immediately and became close, firm friends both in a literary and social fashion.

Leon arranged for Heathcote to have lunch with Vernon at a small Italian Restaurant near to the bank. The meeting was another epiphany for Heathcote and he describes the lunch at length in his book. He was very taken my Vernon and at times very moved:

> It had only been seven years, in fact, since Dylan had died and while Vernon was obviously pleased to talk enthusiastically about Dylan's work, Dylan being snatched away so dramatically and so many thousands of miles away at the age of just 39 obviously still grieved him dreadfully. At what I imagined to be a welter of unspoken memories pumping through his head he'd suddenly look transfixed, hollow eyed and shattered. Then he'd press his napkin to his eyes, dab his face and recover. He went on quietly:

Dead poets can be your contemporaries you know, that's if the whole of the past is a simultaneous experience, and it is. In which case... He studied me closely,

> Dylan's right here now you see. He's sat at this table. Not dead – And then he repeated it quite insistently, as if it were a phenomena he often experienced – Not dead.

After this, Heathcote gives his attention, in great detail, to Dylan's death. He recounts most all known facts and concludes; 267

> "The received wisdom is that Dylan died as a result of a drinking bout at the White Horse Tavern in New York, but the story's authenticity has lately been undermined. For a start, the post-mortem revealed no signs of alcoholic damage to the brain and nor was there any cirrhosis of the liver. It now seems likely that the real cause of Dylan's death was medical negligence. Four days prior to his death a New York doctor, a Dr. Feltenstein, gave Dylan an unusually high dose of morphine as a sedative."

Although, while he was staying at the Chelsea Hotel in New York, Dylan had boasted "I've had eighteen straight whiskies. I think that's a record," it turned out that Dylan had, in fact, drunk nothing like that amount and that, rather than his suffering from a colossal alcoholic assault on the brain as the legend favours, he was actually suffering from a severe chest infection, probably bronchial pneumonia, possibly undiagnosed diabetes, and he was experiencing extreme breathing difficulties as a result of one or other of these two conditions rather than from an alcoholic stroke, the received wisdom.

Dylan had suffered from bronchitis and asthma since childhood and his Chelsea Hotel crisis required to be treated with antibiotics rather than with the paralysing high doses of morphine that Feltenstein would give him on three visits. Feltenstein injected 30mg of morphine, three times the normal dose for pain relief... It's now thought that Dylan's mistreatment with morphine by an incompetent and flamboyant doctor accentuated his respiratory problems and brought on the coma from which he would never recover.

Heathcote then adds his own hazy conspiracy theory about Dylan's left wing views making him a target for the Americans government;

> ...it was 1953; it was the height of the Cold War and here was a crowd-puller. Not averse to broaching revolutionary ides in a US that was then staid, so stultifying, and so paranoid about Communisms. Mightn't it be better if he were disposed of?

He even brings the death of Paul Robeson into his argument. but even Heathcote concludes:

> Momentarily intriguing as the notion is, there is no evidence for it...

And then we get to the crux of the book; the point where I begin to get uncomfortable.

Heathcote begins quietly;

> In the case of Dylan Thomas, it can be said that he was to suffer no less than two deaths at American hands. Less than a decade after his death, his identity was eerily pilfered so that the Dylan Thomas that everyone had come to know and love pre 1953 would be eclipsed by his name being borrowed or more properly stolen.

But then he launches into a full-on attack and character assignation of **Bob Dylan**, because he had the audacity to change his birth name, given him in 1941; Robert Allen Zimmerman; and adopt as his stage name and eventual everyday moniker; **Bob Dylan.**

Now screeds have already been written about this nomenclature issue; not least because Robert Zimmerman himself, at various times agreed that he chose DYLAN as homage to a famous Welsh poet. But at other times has denied this vehemently and offered no end of other fatuous inspirations; the name of a road in his home town, the name of an uncle, the name of a TV show. It seemed he was suddenly trying to distance himself from his earlier homage to Dylan Thomas. And I too had been involved in this ongoing debate in a minor way. 2011 was Bob Dylan's 70th birthday year and a very keen local *Bobcat*,[28] David Boucher decided to celebrate this. When he is not writing[29] about Bob Dylan, or listening to Bob Dylan L.P's, or watching Films and Documentaries about Bob Dylan, David is Professor of Political Philosophy and International Relations at the School of Law and Politics at Cardiff University, but he found time in 2011 to stage some events in celebration of Bob Dylan's birthday. Because he is Welsh and the events took place around Wales he focused on and called the events *THE TWO DYLANS; Bob Dylan and Dylan Thomas*. I was enlisted to talk on Dylan Thomas and David lured Michael Gray[30] a world leading Bob Dylan authority to leave his French hideaway and join us three days in November 2011 – for a two day symposium in Cardiff University followed by a one off at the Taliesin Arts Centre at Swansea University. We reprised it at Aberystwyth Arts Centre when a senior Professor in the English Department. Daniel Williams joined us. These events celebrated both *Dylans* equally and were in no way hostile to either the singer or the poet. I returned to this kind of approach in 2021 when I met another very serious Bobcat, K.G.Miles[31]. We were introduced by a mutual friend in a Tenby pub and over a few pints and a lot of Dylan talk (both of them), Keith suggested we collaborate on a book which would celebrate the coincidences, synchronicities and shared enthusiasms that existed around Dylan Thomas and Bob Dylan. A year later to the day *Bob Dylan and Dylan Thomas The Two Dylans*, was published. The cover features a ravishing Peter Blake[32] collage of his *Tattooed Tina.*

Our book was a benign and somewhat frivolous celebration of

two widely different cultural icons, but it was well received by fans of both singer and poet. In the light of this, Heathcoat's fierce attack on Bob Dylan was a difficult pill to swallow. Heathcote also tells the complicated story around the name-change saga, stressing how carefully Dylan's father, D. J. Thomas named him;

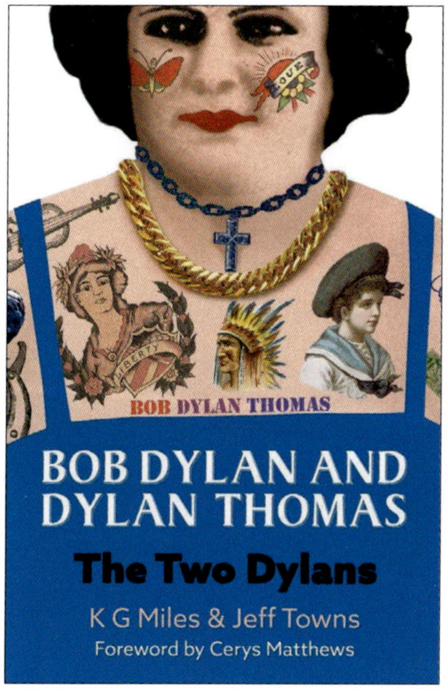

> ...with a scholarly care. D.J. had noted his new-born son's likeness to the Dylan ail Don, the "curly-haired boy" mentioned in the epic poem, 'Mabinogion'. The mother of the Dylan ail Don, Arianrhod, gives birth to Dylan through magical means – through a wand that bestows life.

But Heathcoat's account is also charged with a furious disappointment. Heathcote's reasons for despising Bob Dylan – and that in not too harsh a word to use, is that, for Heathcote, Bob Dylan *sold out*, and he brands him a modern day *Mammon*.

And this goes on for many pages, with undiminished ferocity. Heathcote quotes Joni Mitchell who said;

> Bob [Dylan] is not authentic at all. He's a plagiarist, and his name and voice are fake. Everything about Bob is a deception

And then this:

> But Bob Dylan's unrestrained kleptomania would prompt the folk singer Tim Hardin to say of him: "He's a cold motherfucker, man. He was thinking, he was listening to what everybody said all the time and going, "*Uh-hummm, yup,*" and writing it down in his little photo-fuckin-graphic memory, you know what I mean? Taking pictures of everything and reproducing the whole lick for himself.
>
> Then he learned to give somebody else a little credit, by having their picture on the album or something. Fuck him."
>
> Heathcote then turns to Joan Baez and writes:
>
> [She] however was cut from a different cloth. When her debut at the Newport Folk Festival in 1959 made her an overnight star, she would have the moral integrity to turn down a $50,000 offer to advertise Coca-Cola. Bob Dylan by contrast was eager to embrace every opportunity to sell out, to court American capital and to have the troubadour bow to Mammon.
>
> Unlike Dylan Thomas who never once sold out – who never 'shilled' for anyone – his deadly doppelganger would prove as keen as mustard to have his voice serve any and every American corporation.
>
> Sidney Carter once said, "The word poet means different things to different people. Strange, you can talk about a commercial artist, but you can't talk about a commercial poet. A poet has to have something holy as well to have genius."
>
> "So let Germany brew your beer," Dylan tells the world. "Let Switzerland make your watch. Let Asia assemble your phone," he pauses, "*We* will build your car."
>
> With stunningly meaningless gravitas he concludes, "Is there anything more American than America?"
>
> Bob Dylan's seemingly insatiable material appetite prompted Joan Baez, along with Pete Seeger and Country Joe McDonald the musical bedrock of the US peace movement – to enquire of him,
>
> "Have you forgotten what it's like to be poor, Bobby?"

Reading this ten page rant for the first time in the typescript Heathcote had sent to me was very tough. My immediate reaction was to toss it aside and have nothing more to do with it, but Heathcote was, up to this point, a hero of mine too, and I puzzled over why we were so far apart over this issue. Then I noticed that I had been forewarned; the book had a subtitle;

An Essay on Poetry and Fakery

Maybe I should have borne that in mind. I thought on, and had another moment of enlightenment.

Heathcote had actually seen and heard Dylan Thomas read. He had made a pilgrimage to Swansea and met two of Dylan's closest friends from his youth – Leon Atkins and Vernon Watkins. For Heathcote he saw a saintly Dylan Thomas. I believe when he first encountered the early Bob Dylan of the first few albums full of passionate protest songs he saw a saintly Bob Dylan. But Heathcote's political stance made him turn on the naive folksinger/songwriter when he became a very wealthy and successful global superstar.

I, on the other hand, had come to Bob Dylan first. The first long-playing record that I ever bought was Bob Dylan's first ever L.P. It was released in March 1962, and I bought it shortly afterwards. I was a young impressionable teenager and already, as child of the sixties, I was a precocious nascent hippie flower child, and Bob Dylan ticked all the boxes for me and became my go-to guru in most matters. I bought the next six of his L.P.s and played them all on a *Dancette*, mono, record player in my bedroom, until they were so worn that they played both sides at once. It was around then that I saw somewhere that Bob had been christened as young Jewish boy as Robert Allen Zimmerman and that he had changed his name by deed-poll to Bob Dylan; as an homage to a Welsh poet; Dylan Thomas. This name was new to me and, intrigued, I asked my Welsh and bookish mother what she knew about this Welsh poet. By now it was around 1966/67 and the first official biography of this Welsh poet had just been published; Constantine Fitzgibbon's *The Life of Dylan Thomas*. My mum duly brought a copy back from our local library for me. I read it with great pleasure, but I now know it is a pretty romantic version of Dylan Thomas's chaotic and tragically short life, but back then I was smitten by the man and his poems and stories; there were now two Dylan's in my life and I admired them both – and now, some 55 years on, I still do.

I then looked back through and noticed this paragraph;

In September 1977 the Soviet Literature Gazette dismissed Bob as "nothing more than a money-hungry capitalist" and when Bob Dylan displays his contempt for a poet whom he says he's outgrown, and when he happily does what Dylan Thomas never did, and that is to sell out to any and every commercial outfit and does so on an industrial scale, then perhaps it's tempting to recall Norman Mailer's harsh verdict on him: "If [Bob] Dylan's a poet, I'm a basketball player."

The clue, for me, was in the name of the source of the quote; the *Soviet Literature Gazette*. I realised that I was a soft, romantic, old lefty, but Heathcote was a full-on unreformed, unreconstructed, old-school Marxist, and as such took grave offence at Bob Dylans' pursuit of wealth. I'd like to think that Bob Dylan engages in some generous philanthropy, but he never seems to seek publicity for any such endeavours short of playing in a few mega charity concerts and events around the globe. I had resolved my angst, and went about sorting out the relevant images for Heathcote. I sent them off and eventually a copy of the book came in the post with a bold thank-you card slipped

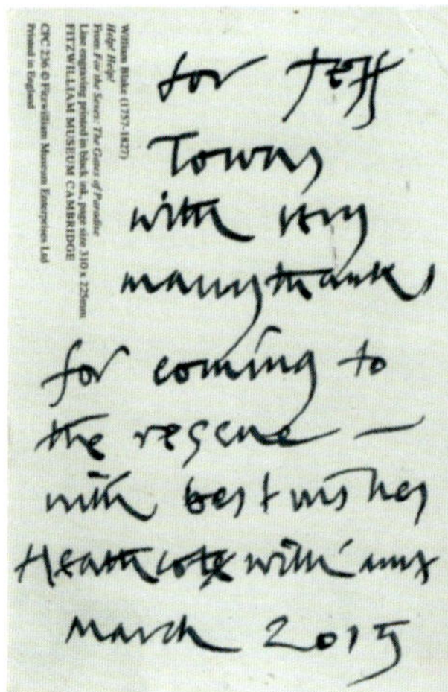

Heathcote's thank-you card

inside;

And the book contained a warm printed acknowledgement;

to Jeff Towns for his generosity in making his archive available.

I was grateful for the book, especially as it was from a very small edition, but more than just the book, Heathcote and I became friends, exchanging regular letters, cards and books, new and old. But sadly it was to be a wholly epistolatory friendship; Heathcote died in 2017, before I had a chance to visit him in Oxford. However Heathcote had not done with Bob Dylan and he published this broadside poem as his final word on the singer/songwriter. He sent me a copy and despite my misgivings I treasure it – the cover gives you the gist of what's inside...

1. The Social Gospel was a Protestant religious and social movement which originated in the U.S. A. and Canada in the early part of the last century. It sought to blend Christian ethics and theology with left wing politics particularly aimed at, economic levelling up, racial hatred, poor housing and, unclean environments, child labour coupled with poor schooling, supporting unionisation and pacifism – all things that Leon Atkin embraced ....

2. The Plaza Cinema was a grand imposing building on Swansea's Kingsway. It was the largest cinema to be erected in Wales and it opened on 14th February 1931 with Paul Whiteman in "King of Jazz". The cinema was equipped the very latest high tech sound system and a massive Rank cinema organ and provided seating for 3000.

3. Colin Edwards (1924–1994) was a Welsh born radio journalist and documentary film maker, who lived most of his life in Canada and the U.S.A. Through a family connection he became involved with Dylan Thomas' life and work. Edited extracts from the transcriptions of Colin Edwards Tapes can be found in two books: *Dylan Remembered. Vol. One 1914-1934. Vol. Two 1935-1953.* Seren 2003/4. For more on Colin Edwards see Chapter 16.

4. In his Biography Ferris writes that, 'according to Trick, he and Thomas scuttled out like a brace frightened rabbits'.

5. *If Men Should Ask Poems of War & Peace.* Cardiff: Western Mail and Echo Limited. 1947.

6. *Laugharne*: This was Dylan's last and shortest broadcast. When it was broadcast on November 5th the townsfolk of Laugharne gathered in the Town Hall to enjoy a communal listening. Caitlin Thomas attended but during the broadcast a policemen entered the hall and delivered her a cable. The producer, Aneirin Talfan Davies presented the film and gave a short speech at the end. In his notes the Dylan Thomas' posthumous Dylan Thomas collection *Quite Early One Morning*, he writes; "After I sat Mrs. Thomas turned to me to say that she had received a cable that her husband was lying unconscious in an American Hospital."

7. Daniel Jones: *My Friend Dylan Thomas.* J.M.Dent & Sons Ltd.1977.

8. *TIME magazine who had phoned*; At this moment in time Dylan had instructed his Swansea Solicitor, Stuart Thomas, to issue a writ against *Time Life International* for libel. Dylan objected to some phrase they had used about him in a recent review of his *Collected Poems*, such as 'When he settles down to guzzle beer, which is most of the time ...his incredible yarns become hopelessly smothered in boozy invention. He borrows with no thought of returning what is lent, seldom shows up on time, is a trial to his friends and a worry to his family...' *Time* intended to settle out of court, but to defend the case they had a detective to tail Dylan in NYC and were getting photographers, including Tal Jones, to collect images of him especially of him drinking, to build their case.

9. In 1971 opened a shop on St Helen's Road very close to Leon's church and I regularly saw him in his signature black berry and drab olive-green raincoat. He always greeted me with a wry, benign smile on his face.

10. Andrew's books include; *Qaddafi and the Libyan Revolution, 1987*, Ian Fleming, 1995); *From Diamond Sculls to Golden Handcuffs: A history of Rowe & Pitman* 1999. *Rudyard Kipling* 1999); Kipling 2001; *Dylan Thomas: A new life*, 2003; Conan Doyle: *The man who created Sherlock Holmes*, 2007; and Wilkie Collins: *A life of sensation*, 2013. We became

good friends during his writing of his Dylan Thomas biography

11. In 2020 I would publish my own book on the subject *The Two Dylans – Bob Dylan and Dylan Thomas,* with my co-author K.G.Miles.

12. *Of Dylan and his Deaths.* Cold Turkey Press. 2015 first edition limited to 35 copies. The publisher Jan Herman had this to say about it; *A writer as prolific as Heathcote Williams runs the risk of having his poems and prose taken for granted. But this essay – a memoir so rich in personal history, so evocative of his first inspiration, Dylan Thomas, and so indignant about the cultural theft of Thomas's identity by a famous imposter – merits attention as a masterpiece of literary investigation. It stands out for high purpose even among his most provocative and polemical works. Yet it is infused with a private tenderness that defies and surpasses moral abstraction. It has a genuineness of feeling that makes it unforgettable.*

13. I provided this splendid cover image by Nora Summers and four more images in the text.

14. George Tremlett: *Dylan Thomas In the Mercy of his Means.*

15. George Tremlett and James Nashold: *Death of Dylan Thomas*; M.D. MAINSTREAM. 1997.

16. Caitlin Thomas (Author), George Tremlett (Adapter): Caitlin: Life with Dylan Thomas – A Warring Absence. Secker & Warburg, London, 1986.

17. I later heard that this idea for a succession of Arts Festivals leading up to the Millennium, came to the then Tory Arts minister, Michael Portillo as he lay in his bath sipping red wine – not an image I needed. But at the time we got involved. In 1995 I opened a large bookshop offering new and used books in the newly refurbished Dylan Thomas Centre, a.k.a. Ty Llên The National Centre for Literature. In the building's large exhibition space, I curated and installed my personal extensive Dylan Thomas Collection as Dylan Thomas Word and Image, which was the major Festival Exhibition and worked as a consultant on the festival programme and events.

18. Huw Pudner in the *Socialist Review.*

19. In 1993 Ralph made a series of large lithographs of famous writers. He included an extreme caricature of Dylan Thomas. The edition was small – just 20 copies but I could resist it and I acquired a copy, which I still have. We used my copy to generate the cover on which Ralph scrawled the title in blood red ink.

20. *The Edge of Love* 2008. A British biographical, romantic drama. Directed by John Mayberry. Starring Keira Knightly, Sienna Miller Cillian Murphy and Matthew Rhys.

21 D. N. Thomas: *The Dylan Thomas Murders.* Seren 2002.

22 D. N. Thomas: *FATAL NEGLECT Who Killed Dylan Thomas.* Seren 2008.

23. Robert Minhinick *The Mythic Death of Dylan Thomas.* HappenStance 2014. An independent poetry press originated and run by Helena Nelson and based in Fife, Scotland.

24 I had never heard of this Reading at the V&A, and was sceptical but I went online and found it recorded in the Museums website.

25 In recent years the Church has been deconsecrated and became for a while a cinema and bizarrely the crypt was opened as a small screen venue for showing X-rated sex films!

26 Dylan had just turned 20; just moved to London and just seen his first poetry collection, *18 Poems.* published. 1934 was quite a time for Dylan Thomas.

27. A testament to this friendship is Vernon's annotated edition of Dylan's letters to him; *Dylan Thomas Letters to Vernon Watkins*, Dent & Faber. London.1956.

28. Bobcats is the name that is fondly applied to obsessive Bob Dylan fans. You can Listen to *The Bobcats, A Bob Dylan Fan Podcast* on various online platforms.

29. David published *Bob Dylan and Leonard Cohen* in 2004 and an enlarged new edition: *Bob Dylan and Leonard Cohen Deaths and Entrances* came out in 2021. He also edited: *The Political Art of Bob Dylan* in 2005.

30. Michael Gray published one of the first studies of Dylan; *Bob Dylan, Song & Dance Man: The Art Of Bob Dylan* in 1972, and continued to publish on Dylan: *All Across The Telegraph: A Bob Dylan Handbook* (1987, 1988) – co-editor; *The Art Of Bob Dylan: Song & Dance Man* (1981, 1982). *Song & Dance Man III: The Art of Bob Dylan* (1999, 2000); *The Bob Dylan Encyclopedia* (2006, revised & expanded 2008); *Outtakes on Bob Dylan* (2021).

31. Keith had Published; *Bob Dylan in London: Troubadour Tales; Bob Dylan in the Big Apple: Troubadour Tales of New York* and finally, *Bob Dylan in Minnesota: Troubadour Tales from Duluth, Hibbing and Dinkytown.* All were published by McNidder and Grace who also published our Two Dylans.

32. Peter is a fine and generous friend. I had bought the life-sized print of Tattooed Tina. I rang him to tell him how much I loved it and he told me that he had collaged BOB DYLAN THOMAS above Tina's bikini top as a nod to me ! When we were promoting the book I would quote Willie Dixon, via Bo Diddley (who also features on Tina's tummy), saying in this instance,
You Can Judge a Book by Lookin' at the Cover.

Image: Karl Morgan (Facing West Prints)

Welsh Ginsberg

14.

Dylan Thomas: Allen Ginsberg & The Beats.

Ah, Dylan Thomas, I would have liked to know you that night, wish I could have communicated who I was, my true feeling, and its importance to you...
Allen Ginsberg, N.Y.C. 1952 after an uncomfortable first meeting ...

As a youngster, growing up in the East End of London, I managed to pass the 11+ exam, and went on to attend an historic, once venerable, small, traditional Grammar School. But I was not a good student. I was a tad rebellious and spent more time in the gym playing basketball than in lessons; I was a more of a *jock* than a scholar. However I was lucky to have very good English Teachers[1] who encouraged me to read widely and eccentrically. I just about kept up with the written work. I never won any prizes at the traditional annual Speech Day, until one year around 1964/5 (I was 16), I was declared *Victor Ludorum* at the annual School Sports Day. It was a surprise to me, but I was a good all-round athlete and had competed successfully in a few track and field events. And that meant I would get a prize at the next Speech-Day.

Then lady luck stepped in again; Mr. Burness, our Headmaster, who was always decked out in a gown and mortar-board, decided to 'get modern', and he did away with the usual prize books of dull, gold embossed half-leather-bound classics; this year winners would be allowed to choose their own book from a designated local bookstore; I think you could have any book up to five shillings (25p. those were the days). As I mentioned, I was somewhat precocious in my reading and had already decided that the best current writing was coming from America. I had discovered the holy trinity of the *Beat Movement* – Kerouac, Burroughs and Ginsberg, whose great poem *Howl* had been first published around a decade back. And that was the book I chose for my prize.

On the big day, I turned up, as smart as I could manage in a cobbled together semblance of the school uniform. I sat and waited, a tad bored with the whole business. I almost failed to recognise my own name when *JEFFREY TOWNS* was called up; I was always *Jeff* or *Townsy*. Up I went and out across the stage; 'Old Bunny' congratulated me and handed over the small square *City Lights*, black and white, paperback edition of Ginsberg's incendiary *Howl*.

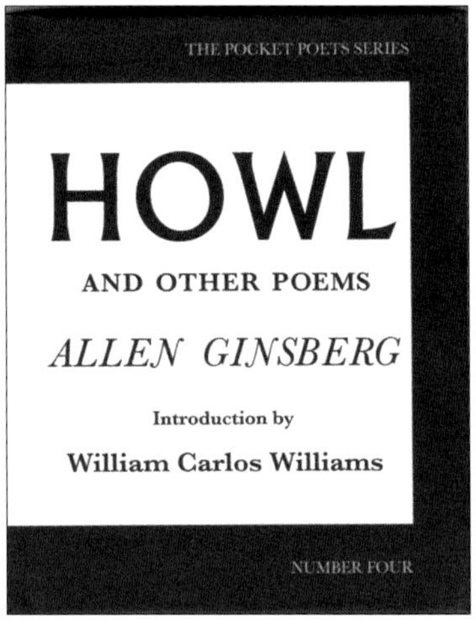

I was inwardly extremely smug and very pleased; I had a great book, and I had pulled off my own act of sedition. I'm sure 'Old Bunny' the ancient headmaster, had no idea of the passionate anarchy that filled those small pages of my prize and prized book; and I had no idea that some 30 years later, I would be a bookseller in Swansea and Allen Ginsberg would come into my Swansea Bookstore and I would sell him a copy of Lady Charlotte Guest's *Mabinogion*. But more of that later...

Allen Ginsberg And Dylan Thomas.

February 20th 1950: Dylan Thomas lands at Idlewild Airport, New York for the first of his four lecture tours to America. It is his first visit to America. Allen Ginsberg had recently been discharged from New York State Psychiatric Hospital in New Jersey and is holed up in the Bowery, in a seedy apartment being visited by various other participants of the Beat movement.

January 20th 1952: Dylan Thomas arrives back in New York for his second tour. This time he is accompanied by his wife Caitlin. Allen Ginsberg is living in Apartment 16 on the third floor of yellow brick building at 206 East 7th Street and William Burroughs is often staying there too. While in New York, Caitlin and Dylan stayed at the famous (now notorious) *Chelsea Hotel*. Shortly before the end of their trip, in early May, they were back in New York from a trip to the West Coast, and one evening they were going out with their friends Dave Slivka – a sculptor(inside a year he would be casting Dylan's Death Mask), and his wife Rose, with whom Caitlin had become close friends. Dylan and Caitlin were curious and keen to be taken to a lesbian club having failed to find one in Chicago. On this night they failed again and the party broke up. Caitlin went home with Rose and Dylan and a friend ended up at *The San Remo*, a bar popular with the East Village arty and literary crowd. Already in there was Allen Ginsberg.

They had never met, but Ginsberg approached Dylan at the bar. It was not a hugely successful encounter and Ginsberg, as was his habit, went straight home and scrawled his account of their meeting in his journal

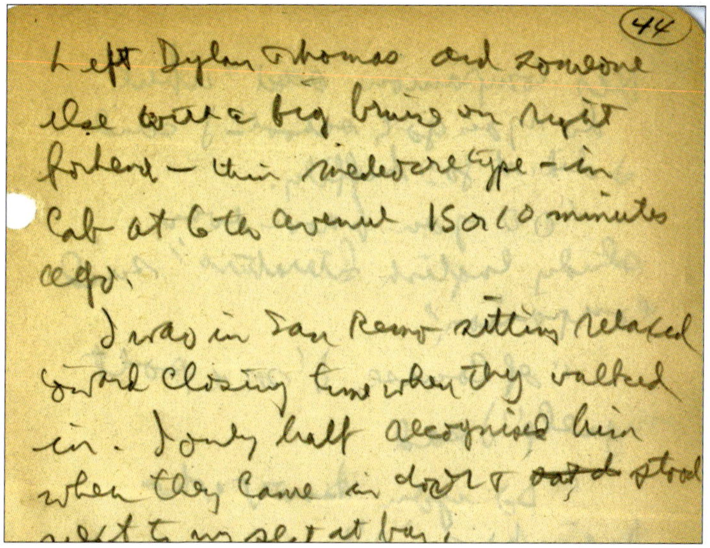

44

Left Dylan Thomas and someone else with a big bruise on right forhead – thin mediocre type – in Cab at 6th avenue 15 or 10 minutes ago.

I was in San Remo sitting relaxed toward closing time when they walked in. I only half recognized him when they came in door & ~~out~~ stood next to my seat at bar.

Dylan sketched in the San Remo by Peter Evershed

He Wrote:

Left Dylan Thomas and someone else with a big bruise on right forehead – thin mediocre type – in cab on 6th Avenue, 15 minutes ago.

I was in San Remo sitting relaxed towards closing time when they walked in. I only half-recognized him when they came in door & stood next to my seat at bar.

Thomas said, "Congratulations" and "Imagine that", when bartender spoke his name overloud & said he'd read his poem over the bar.

"Don't believe everything you hear", Thomas said to me.

"Only if it's spoken loud enough, I answered.

His companion said, "Where do you go to school?" – I said I didn't go, huffily.

"Do you know – ever study English literature", said companion.

"Of course, I'm a poet myself", I said.

"Do you know who this is?" he said

"Of course, man, it's obvious"

"Oh, another", said Thomas.

"Well don't look at me", I said, stiffening up.

Thomas, "I was just in another pub – drinking place – whatever you call them – and a girl said to me – would you like somewhere to go to see a girl and me do a trick?"

"Is it a question of interpretation of "trick", I said

"No, I'm a professional", Thomas said, "I'm a professional".

"Well I just thought it was a question of language", I said
"But she wanted $50 which I didn't have"
"Oh well".
"Do you know any amateurs?" he asked.
"I think the best I can do is knock on a door and it will be opened by a pretty girl who'll offer us a bottle of beer".
"Will she do a trick?"
"I can only supply one pretty girl who'll open her door", I said
"Well, that's a lot, that's half of it".
"That's the way the world is", we agreed.
"But that's a lot", he said. "What can you do?" I said.
I then said that Lucien and Cessa would be newspaper people at home. "But they have 'likker, but they aren't "intelligent"."
"Well I insist they'll have to be intelligent" – he.
"No, I didn't want to mention that – they, of course, of course, have feelings, heart, mind, suffering – and nobility".
He nodded understanding.

I was very eager to see him off and go along. But everything was very chancy and superficial and no action took place. I called Lucien. There was no answer. Alas!

I came back and said they weren't home – and on and on. Mary Jo was there [at bar]. "Who's she?" they wanted to know.
He could have had her but she was silly & he a fool about reputation.
Said, "I've got the shortest legs in the world. My belly hangs down to my groin".
She chatted and camped but no action.
I tried to get him to go to Dusty's – the bartender took him aside and asked me to leave. I said to Thomas, "Shall I wait outside? He nodded very gently & graciously, perfect gentleman tho' he didn't know me.
Later outside I remembered my attic and he said, "but not an attic… Just you and me?" "That's all", I replied. He had said he had a bottle along too. "I want to go to drink the bottle where there are other people around".
Outside Victor and several other heavy-handed hipsters – 3 of them stood by the door while I sat on gutter & waited – They were conversing, wondering why narcissistic girls went for weak-chinned people like him – talking about him in manly cultural underground terms, but spitefully, asserting their own virility and new generation removal from dependence or sympathy with him – said, "Byron had strength", and complemented each other too.
I yelled "Hey" when he came out and got up and joined them too – wasn't sure he'd even remember. He said, "I never was so bored" by the action inside Remo with proprietors –
I had difficulty raising subject of continuing on with him as I asked inside by saying, "I don't know what will happen but if I may I wish to continue and go on with you wherever you are going tonight if you have anywhere to go". He said, "Yes, I'd be glad, of course" – but with eye wandering, alas but, so dissolute he was he meant it too, just as well.
On way he stopped in middle of street. "I don't know what to do" –
I took up the initiative and said,
"OK, I'm telling you, then come with me!
Meanwhile companion said, "I'm awfully tired, should go home", and "Caitlin is waiting".
Finally Thomas decided to go and I closed a cab door on them, ran to other side & stuck my tongue in window at him which I immediately regretted tho' I meant it as a friendly gesture. He stared out at me, drunkenly, without response.
We had been followed down corner and West 4th Street by 3 Subterraneans. I ran off, leaping.
Friend companion earlier had said about bruise – "In fight" – on account of Thomas saying things – an hour ago, wound up in hospital.
Ah, Dylan Thomas, I would have liked to know you that night, wish I could have communicated who I was, my true feeling, and its importance to you. For I too am a lover of the soul.
How disappointing to come away empty-handed with no recognition from this Chance meeting – I felt sick and unhappy because I could not make a great sweet union of the moment of life – now this is 45 minutes after, it will pass but it is sad & true.

When I first read this account in the published volume of Allen Ginsberg's *Journal*[2] and learned he and Dylan had met I was surprised, astounded and elated. It made so many things fall into place. All the time Dylan Thomas was in New York city in the early 50's, Ginsberg, Burroughs, Kerouac and Corso were holed up down in a succession of seedy apartments mostly is the sleazy East Village, conjuring the words and mind-set that defined the next great literary movement – *The Beats*. And at least one of them – another great and favourite poet of mine – Allen Ginsberg – had met Dylan Thomas.

Some years later I happened upon some more tangible evidence. I was in San Francisco to exhibit and hopefully sell books, at the annual International Antiquarian Book fair. My regular base each year was over the bridge in Berkeley, with Peter Howard who ran one of the world's great bookstores – *Serendipity Books*. – an enormous store on many levels in an old Winery on University Ave. It contained at least half a million books with the emphasis on good literature. I always arrived a few days before the Book Fair began, in order to scour, hunt and scout out books and ephemera from vast quantities of printed materials which crossed subject borders, centuries and genres, filling the shelves and much of the floor space. Recent acquisitions were usually stacked in random piles on the floor. I was working through them in a relaxed but diligent way when I recognised the black and white dust jacket of the American edition of *Dylan's Collected Poems. 1934-1952.*

I picked it up to check if it was a first edition; the true first edition has a misprint on the last page on the last line of the final poem, where the word daughters, has an uncorrected typo and is misspelled daughers. The misprint was there, so I turned to the front to see the price, but on opening the book I noticed a scrawled, but legible, dated ownership signature, on the front end-paper;

Allen Ginsberg N.Y 1953

It was a first edition but it was also Allen Ginsberg's copy! What a find! The book was un-priced. Nervously I sauntered over to Peter's cave-like cubbyhole and handed the book to him and mumbled that I would quite like to own it, trying to sound nonchalant. He knew. His ludicrous bargain price made it possible; $100. I still have it – a treasured book among many and, when I later got to examine it, I found that the presumptuous young 27 year old Beat poet had scrawled an extra line at the end of one of Dylan's great early poems – *Light breaks where no sun shines.*

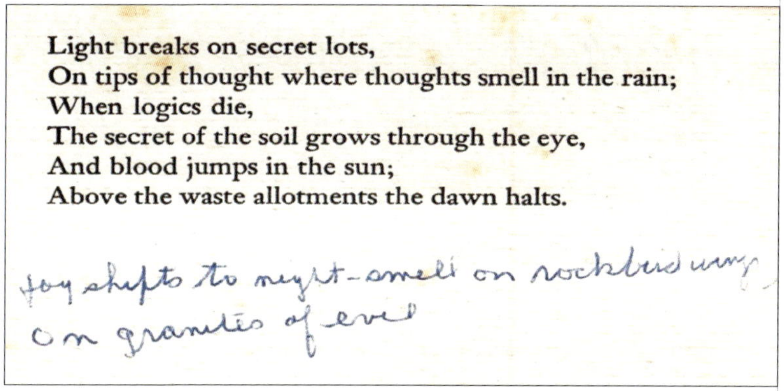

Light breaks on secret lots,
On tips of thought where thoughts smell in the rain;
When logics die,
The secret of the soil grows through the eye,
And blood jumps in the sun;
Above the waste allotments the dawn halts.

joy shifts to night-smell on rockbird wing
on granites of eve

But Ginsberg was not done with Wales and Dylan Thomas... In 1967 Ginsberg made his first visit to Wales with his friend, the publisher Tom Maschler. They stayed at Maschler's cottage on the Welsh borders near Llanthony Abbey and Capel-y-ffin. Ginsberg had been having a wild time in London joining in with big legalise pot rallies and preparing for the countercultural milestone the *Congress on the Dialectics of Liberation and the Demystification of Violence*. The event was the brainchild of anti-psychiatrist R.D. Laing and his acolytes, and it had brought together a heterogeneous collection of vaguely defined international "Leftists", anarchists, and well-stoned hippies who kept Allen very busy. Tom thought a break in Wales would do Allen some good and on the way they stopped at Tintern Abbey, which had an understandably profound and mystical effect on

Ginsberg. When they had settled into Tom's cottage, Allen produced two doses of L.S.D. which they consumed together and then went out into the hills, where Tom dreamed acid dreams and Allen wrote his great L.S.D. Poem – *Wales Visitation*. I have several copies of the published editions of the poem, one has a very informative autograph inscription.

Allen was back in Wales again in 1995 and this time he came to Swansea. which was hosting a year-long Literary Festival. He was to read in the main hall of Swansea University and it was to be a highlight in a year full of wonderful events. I'll never forget him coming out from the wings crossing the stage, sitting down cross-legged, and then vamping his little hand pumped organ

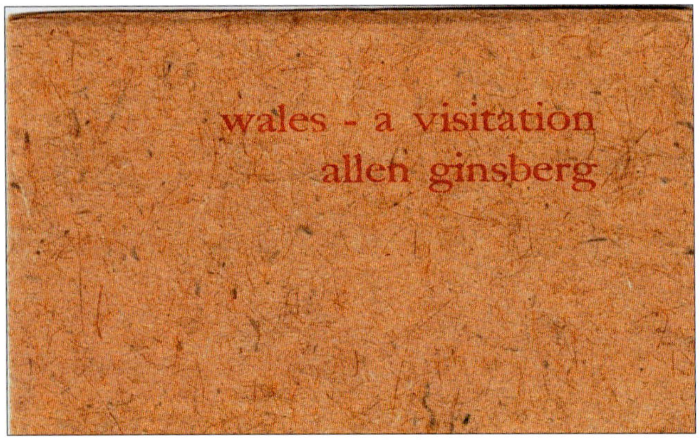

Wales a Visitation. First Edition Cape Goliard 1968

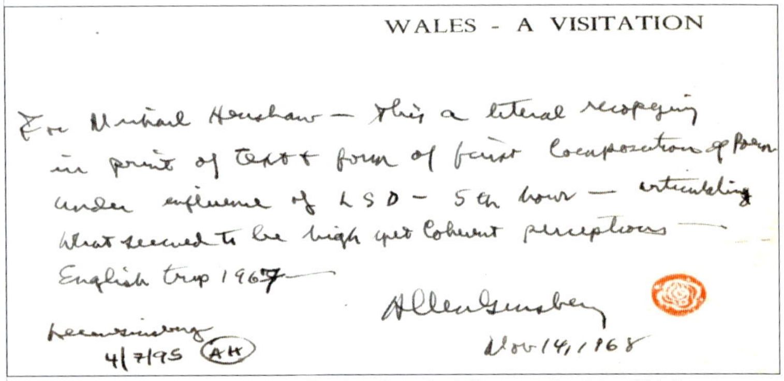
WALES - A VISITATION

For Michael Henshaw — this a literal recopying in print of text & form of first composition of poem under influence of L S D — 5th hour — articulating what seemed to be high yet coherent perceptions — English trip 1967

Allen Ginsberg
Nov 14, 1968

Remembering 4/7/95 AH

Allen's inscription; ... *Poem [written] under influence of L S D – fifth hour-articulating what seemed to be high yet coherent perceptions ...*

My copy of the Limited Edition with flexi-disc of Allen reading the poem

whist chanting William Blake's *Tyger Tyger*. The hairs on the back of my neck stood up stiff and tingling and they hardly went down... A couple of poems later he introduced his next poem by explaining that it was written after he had told his father, a rabbi, that he was a homosexual;

His father responded:

Allen, does that mean you take another man's penis into your mouth ?

Allen responded: No father. I lied.

His reading was sublime and unforgettable however perhaps the real highlight was his visit to my bookstore in Salubrious Passage the next day. He was quiet and charming and browsed my poetry and folk-lore shelves purposefully. He bought a copy of the Charlotte Guest translation of the *Mabinogion*, the great collection of Welsh chivalric tales and legends and a few small British, ephemeral, 60's small-press poetry magazines, that had contributions in by himself. And he signed a couple of things for me, including the flexi-disc of him reading his poem *Plutonium Ode* which came with the 1979 first issue of Tanbimuttu's *Poetry London/Apple*, and he also signed my copy of Cape Goliard, *Wales Visitation*, for the second time!

But I was too awe-struck to ask him any questions; so I had the same feeling Allen had after he met Dylan Thomas;

I felt sick and unhappy because I could not make a great sweet union of the moment of life.

Before leaving Wales Allen made a pilgrimage to Laugharne with

My copy of the Ginsberg flexidisc, signed for me in my Salubrious Passage bookstore

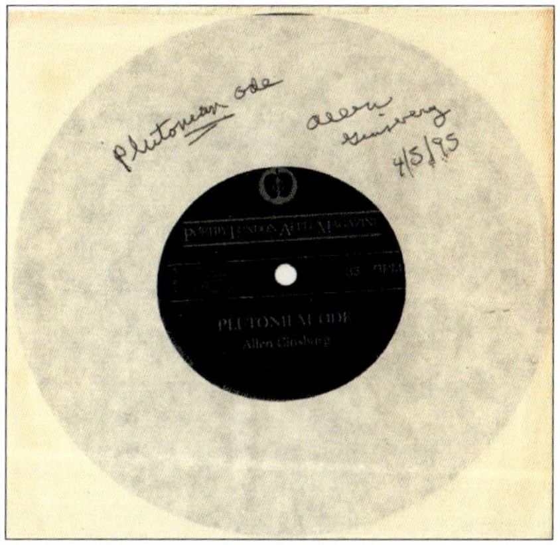

a fine Welsh language poet, Dafydd Rowlands, who took him to Dylan's grave where Allen fell to his knees and chanted a Buddhist mantra.

Lawrence Ferlinghetti, Allen Ginsberg's friend and the publisher of his great Poem *HOWL* from his San Francisco *City Lights Bookstore*, had this to say about Allen;

> *I have heard the Gettysburg Address and the Ginsberg address, and Allen's voice has grown deeper and lusher over the years turning ever closer to Blakean celestial harmonies...The only voice with such timbre to compare with it in 20th century poetry is Dylan Thoma.*

Praise indeed, and Ferlinghetti should know because he was in the audience for Dylan Thomas' reading in San Francisco and had reviewed it for the *San Francisco Chronicle.*

* * * * *

Allen Ginsberg: *Welsh Poet Dafydd Rowlands above Laugharne Bay & Dylan Thomas Boathouse, he'd driven us back from Aberystwyth Eisteddfod englynion competition where we'd met ex-Bardic Chair-holder former Dic Jones, thence we returned to Swansea Poetry Festival where I'd stayed six days, April 5, 1995*

Dylan Thomas and The Beats

Kenneth Rexroth.

Kenneth Rexroth (1905-1982) was an American poet, translator, and critical essayist. He is regarded as a key figure in San Francisco's vibrant poetry scene in the late fifties, early sixties which gave rise to the *Beat Movement*. Rexroth did not consider himself to be a Beat Poet, but *TIME* magazine dubbed him the "*Father of the Beats*".

Dylan Thomas met Kenneth Rexroth in San Francisco in April 1950 when he was on the West Coast leg of his first reading tour to America. Rexroth invited Dylan to stay with him but Dylan was already settled with the doyen of the San Francisco poetry scene, Ruth Witt-Diamant. Rexroth was impressed and amused by Dylan's performance at the Wheeler Auditorium and to begin with they were on very good terms but Rexroth was irascible and vacillated over his opinions of the poet and his behaviour.

Before he had met Dylan Thomas, Rexroth had included him in an anthology of British poetry he had compiled for publisher James Laughlin's New Directions (Laughlin also published Dylan Thomas). *New British Poets* came out in 1949 and in his introduction to the book Rexroth devotes four pages to Dylan, which is mainly an over-the top laudatory panegyric;

> *If Auden dominated the recent past Dylan Thomas dominates the present. There can be no question but that he is the most influential young poet writing in England today ... He doesn't wear his heart on his sleeve. He takes you by the neck and rubs your nose in it. He hits you across the face with a reeking bloody heart, a heart full of worms and needles and black blood and thorns, a werewolf heart... Thomas smote the Philistine as hard a blow with one small book, Eighteen Poems... Thomas' impact was not just literary, it was in a special sense social, a cultural coup d'état... After Thomas literature was wide open to others than the sons of gentlemen*

After Rexroth met Dylan and heard him read his regard for Thomas grew and it rose even higher when he learned that Thomas had shunned a posh academics party, held in his honour at a Berkeley Professor's home, to take a trip to Big Sur with Ruth Witt-Diamant, where he met Henry Miller instead. But later Rexroth wrote about Dylan Thomas to his friend Charles Wrey Gardiner;

> At first I thought he was only a pest, the son of a bitch gets up at 8:00 to start drinking... I gather that he is not in full possession of his marbles ...

But a few years after Dylan's death Rexroth published an important essay; *Disengagement. The Art of the Beat Generation*, in which he powerfully singled out Dylan Thomas and the great jazz saxophonist, Charlie 'Bird' Parker as the two strongest influencers, inspirations and precursors of the Beat Generation;

> Like the Pillars of Hercules, like two ruined Titans guarding the entrance to one of Dante's Circles, stand two great dead juvenile delinquents – the heroes of the post-war generation: The saxophonist, Charlie Parker, and Dylan Thomas.
> If the word "deliberate" means anything, both of them certainly deliberately destroyed themselves.

In 1955 Rexroth also wrote and published a powerful, long poetic eulogy for Dylan Thomas; *THOU SHALT NOT KILL A Memorial for Dylan Thomas.*[3] This poem is now regarded as a major influence on the form and content Allen Ginsberg's *HOWL* and Rexroth was the MC at the monumental first ever, epic, public reading Ginsberg gave of *Howl*. The reading took place at San Francisco's famous *Six Gallery*, in October of 1955. Along with Ginsberg, the evening included readings by Gary Snyder, Philip Whalen, Philip Lamantia, and Michael McClure, Jack Kerouac and Lawrence Ferlinghetti were in the audience.

Rexroth, quite possibly the oldest man in the room, was on the microphone holding things together. He was dressed in a bow-tie and cutaway dinner jacket, bought in a thrift store. When he took to the stage instead of a lectern there was a small old wooded grape crate from a winery; Rexroth began;

> *This is a lectern for a midget who is going to recite the Iliad in haiku form.*

That set the tone for the evening.

Rexroth recorded his *THOU SHALT NOT* on one side of an album, with his friend and fellow poet Lawrence Ferlinghetti

filling the other. *Poetry Readings from the Cellar* was released on dazzling pink vinyl...

Rexroth's last words on Dylan are dark, but also very perceptive;

> The last time I saw Dylan, his self-destruction had not just passed the limits of rationality. It had assumed the terrifying inertia of inanimate matter.
> Being with him was like being swept away by a torrent of falling stones.

Dylan Thomas and Lawrence Ferlinghetti.

Lawrence Monsanto Ferlinghetti (1919-2021) was an American poet, painter, social activist, and famously the co-founder of City Lights Booksellers & Publishers He wrote poetry, translations, fiction, theatre, art criticism, and film narration. His best known work is his second collection of poems, *A Coney Island of the Mind*, which has been translated into nine languages and sold over a million copies. When Ferlinghetti turned 100 in 2019, the city of San Francisco turned his birthday, March 24, into *Lawrence Ferlinghetti Day*.

Lawrence Ferlinghetti never really considered himself a Beat writer or wanted to be closely identified with them; he had finished his education at university in Paris and saw himself more as part of a European Modernist literary tradition. But no history of the Beat Generation could be written without including him and his Bookshop, *City Lights* and its associated publishing imprint. Ferlinghetti was born in New York and his early education was there. He then served in the Navy throughout the war and then returned to New York and began

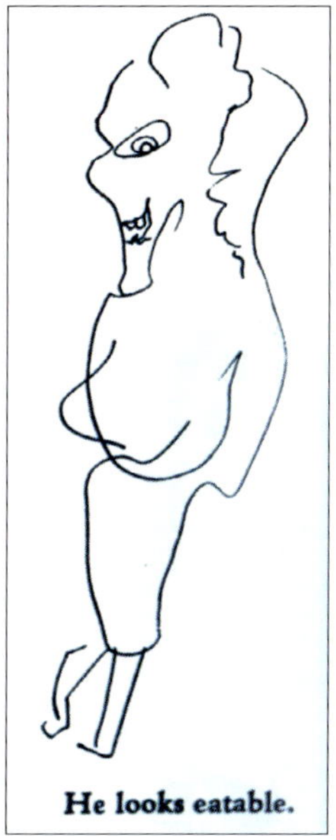

When Dylan Thomas visited the United States
His laughter hardly tinkled among the teacups.
I thought of Fragilion, that shy figure among the birch-trees,
And of Priapus in the shrubbery
Gaping at the ladies in the hall.
In the foyer of the Museum, at Professo Witt-Diamant's
I looked for the head of Mr. Thomas rolling under a chair
Or grinning over a screen
With seaweed in its hair . . .

studying at Columbia, where he tried his hand at sports journalism.

Around 1946 he began to read Dylan Thomas and was intrigued by the musicality of the Welsh diction in his poems. He had already decided that he wanted to pursue some kind of literary career. He moved to San Francisco in 1951, a year after Dylan Thomas had made his mark there on his first American Reading tour. Ferlinghetti was trying to get established as a writer and was sending unsolicited and unpaid features and reviews in to local papers and journals. When Dylan Thomas returned in 1952 Ferlinghetti was sent in a review of Dylan's reading to *Counterpoint* a local Arts and literacy magazine;

> The Poetry he read at the San Francisco Museum of Art constituted, on the whole one long meditation on dying... [including] his own *Ceremony After a Fire Raid* and his poem beginning *Do not go gentle into that good night...*
> His reading voice was strange and wild.

And the following year Ferlinghetti submitted a review to the *Chronicle* newspaper of Thomas' *In Country Sleep* which was only published in America, and comprised just six late poems, including the first book appearance of *Do not go gentle...* His review was one of unqualified praise;

> There is nothing like Dylan Thomas in Poetry today.
> There is wholeness, a harmony, a radiance, about everything he has written which sets him apart

In a fine book Ferlinghetti co-wrote with Nancy Peters, *Literary San Francisco* he draws attention to another *Counterpoint* article by a San Francisco artist Knute Stiles; *Side View of a Poet*, in which they reproduced a series of curious and surreal doodles/drawings Thomas 'tossed off in a bar on night'.

The images prompted Ferlinghetti to 'toss off' a poem for Dylan in the form of a parody of T. S. Eliot;

Ferlinghetti would later borrow from Dylan's most well-known poem, *Fern Hill,* for his 1968 poem, *Assassination Raga*. The poem is a vivid and haunting exploration of death, violence, and the cultural undercurrents of the assassination of President John F. Kennedy and its aftermath, blending cultural references, religious imagery, and musical motifs to create a tapestry that is both mournful and enraged. One line references Dylan Thomas' *The Force That Through the Green Fuse Drives the Flower.*

> Outside the plums are growing in a tree
> The force that through the green fuse
> drives the flower' drives Death TV.

And later again Ferlinghetti would write a fine poem for Dylan Thomas, which confirms he never lost his high opinion and deep reverence for him. It was first published in *The Cool Eye:* Lawrence Ferlinghetti Talks to Alexis Lykiard(Exeter Stride 1993). Here are the first and last verses;

> BELATED PALINODE FOR DYLAN THOMAS
> In Wales at Laugharne at last I stand beside

his cliff-perched writing shed
above the coursing waters
where the hawk hangs still
above the cockle-strewn shingle

Where he walked in a glory of all his days
(before the weather turned around)
And *aie! aie!* a waterbird far away
cries and cries again
over St. Johns Hill...
(*Aie! aie!* it calls and calls again)
As in his listing boathouse now
his great recorded voice runs out
(grave as a gravedigger in his grave)
leaving a sounding void of light
for poets and herons to fill

(Drowned down in New York's White Horse Tavern
he went not gentle into his good night)
And Far West poets calling still
over St. Johns Hill
to the loveliest poet of all our days
sweet singer of Swansea
lushed singer of Laugharne
Dylan of all our days

Dylan Thomas and William Burroughs

This tale, sadly begins and ends with the death of Dylan Thomas. The foyer of the infamous *Chelsea Hotel* in New York City has plaques in homage to its many famous guests amongst whom Dylan Thomas and William Burroughs loom large. This is what they tell us;

> **Death of Dylan Thomas**
>
> The entrance to the hotel bears several plaques to former residents, but perhaps the most famous is the one dedicated to Welsh poet Thomas. It reads: "Dylan Thomas lived and wrote at the Chelsea hotel and from here he sailed out to die." Thomas worked on the final version of Under Milk Wood while at the Chelsea and died there in 1953, shortly before its premiere, aged 39. He fell into a coma that was induced, so the legend goes, by drinking 18 whiskies in a row. The truth may be more prosaic: Thomas suffered from diabetes and had contracted bronchitis and pneumonia.
>
> **William Burroughs writes Naked Lunch**
>
> Burroughs was one of a band of beat poets – Allen Ginsberg and Jack Kerouac among them – who took up residence in the hotel in the late 50s and much of Burroughs's seminal 1959 novel, Naked Lunch, was written there. The beats' enthusiasm for narcotics was met with extraordinary tolerance on the part of Stanley Bard, the now-ousted manager. "I knew Timothy Leary, Allen [Ginsberg] and that whole beat generation," Bard has said. "I thought that each person had their own right to do what they wanted as long as it wasn't destructive to the hotel".

William Burroughs and Dylan Thomas never crossed paths although Burroughs was in New York in the early 50's when Dylan made his four visits to America, so they might have had a chance meeting. That never happened but I did chance upon one rather macabre coincidence.

In 1945 Burroughs was in New York, hanging out most of the time with Herbert Huncke, a street hustler, heroin-addict and a fringe member of the *Beat Generation* (he is reputed to have coined the term). Burroughs was getting deeper and deeper into heavy drug use. Burroughs monthly allowance from his comfortable family was no longer sufficient to fund his habit so he resorted to sourcing his drugs using forged medical doctors prescription pads which they stole whenever they got the opportunity. But, before long they were rumbled; Burroughs carelessly misspelled *Dilaudid* (he used two l's) attracting the attention of a suspicious pharmacist who then noticed that the doctor purporting to be the prescriber was long dead.

Two detectives called on Burroughs arrested him (Burroughs would later model the detectives in *Naked Lunch* on them). He was busted in April of 1946. He was mug-shot, finger-printed and banged-up with bail set at a prohibitive $1000. His parents were notified and horrified – they had not seen him for six months and had no idea that he was using drugs. It transpired that the only way to secure his release was to get a medical doctor to say he was under treatment for his 'affliction'. The family and Bill's psychiatrist secured the services of an obliging **Dr. Milton Feltenstein** – [*Remember that name*].

This nefarious and cavalier doctor secured Burroughs release from jail.

Just four years later, on February 21 1950, Dylan Thomas landed at Idlewild airport for the first of what were to be four reading tours of America. He was not in great shape, he was overweight, stressed and drinking too much; this last encouraged by his new hosts and 'friends', worsened by his swiftly acquired taste for *Old Grand Dad* bourbon whiskey. These problems increased during the course of his visits. Andrew Lycett, Dylan's most recent biographer, describes his second tour in January 1952, when his wife Caitlin (she too was a fine toper) accompanied him, as the *Battle against American Hospitality*. On his third tour in April 1953, his 'agent' and 'friend', John Malcolm Brinnin could not take the strain of looking after Thomas anymore and assigned his assistant, Elizabeth Reitell to the task. Very quickly she and Thomas began an affair and when he fell down stairs when drunk and broke his arm, she arranged for her fashionable New York a doctor to treat him. This doctor also began to give him injections of cortisone – then a new 'wonder drug' which could ease the discomfort caused by gout, gastritis and excessive drinking. On his return to Wales Dylan writes to Liz and gives her a health update;

'My arm is still in plaster: new Welsh plaster.'

And he also asked her to send his thanks to her New York physician;

> All my best wishes to him; he picked me out of the sick pit
> with his winking needle and his witty wild way.

When Dylan Thomas arrived in New York on October 19 1953, he was not a well man. As his drinking increased so did his need for 'the winking needle. Liz called her doctor on several occasions. Finally as October 27th approached which was his 39th birthday, he began to go into a tailspin; he had always boasted that he would not make forty and would die young like many of his literary heroes. His drinking continued to increase and his health and behaviour got more and more erratic. By early November his *primary carer*, Liz Reitell was at her wit's end; Dylan was constantly taking sleeping pills, and often took to his bed in the daytime.

On November 3rd Dylan was again confined to bed for the day but he did rouse himself to venture out that night. On his return to The Chelsea he announced to Liz with some pride;

I've had eighteen straight whiskeys; I think that's the record.

Although that phrase has entered into history as his famous last words, it is highly unlikely that he consumed anything close to this quantity of alcohol. If Dylan had drunk eighteen straight whiskeys, and American measures are much larger than those served in British pubs, it would probably have killed him then and there. And this hyperbolic and boastful declaration was almost immediately shown for what it was when his friend, Ruthven Todd visited the White Horse Tavern and the barman remembered him drinking no more than six measures of *Old Grandad*, his favourite Bourbon whiskey; but why spoil a good story with the truth…?

Dylan managed to get up the next day, went back to the *White Horse* and had a couple of beers before returning to the *Hotel Chelsea*. It was there that he started having severe breathing problems and Liz called her doctor who would visit three more times that day, administering the steroid ACTH by injection and on his third visit, half a grain (32.4 milligrams) of morphine sulphate. This suppressed Dylan's breathing and he went into a coma. From the hotel he went to St. Vincent's Hospital. He never recovered from the coma and died on November 9th.

Although you cannot take drink away from being part of Dylan's untimely death, that large dose of morphine is most likely what put him into a coma. And the name of the doctor with the winking needle was one,

Dr. Milton Feltenstein!

So the doctor who sprung Bill Burroughs from jail was the self-same doctor who helped Dylan *sail out to die*, as they so poetically phrased it back in the Chelsea.

This is how the Nobel prize winning, Irish poet Seamus Heaney saw Dylan's death;

> ...it was very much Thomas the poet that my generation of readers and listeners encountered in our teens. He died in New York, immediately because of a wrongly prescribed dose of morphine, but inevitably because of years of spectacular drinking, and he does it at the height of his fame, at the moment when print culture and the electric media were perfecting their alliance in the promotion of culture heroes.

* * * * *

Dylan Thomas and Jack Kerouac

Jack Kerouac's first novel, *The Town and the City*, was published in the UK by the English publishers Eyre and Spottiswoode who had bought the UK rights of the book and prepared their own edition for 1950. Kerouac decided for some reason to use the name "John Kerouac" not Jack. Dylan Thomas could have reviewed it. Back in the 30's Dylan made most of his living as a

writer by a contributing a large number of reviews to many of the leading literary magazine and journals, but he stopped when his first books begin to be noticed and his work broadcasting at the BBC developed. He did very little book reviewing after 1940, but he did write a very positive and perceptive review Amos Tutuola's *The Palm Wine Drinkard* in the *Observer* newspaper in July 1952. It was Tutuola's groundbreaking first novel. How I would have loved to have read Dylan Thomas' take on Kerouac's first book; but it didn't happen and Thomas and Kerouac never engaged.

In May 1955 Kerouac writes a drunken, almost incoherent, letter to William Burroughs about his planned book on Buddhism, *Buddha Tells Us*, in which he disparages Dylan Thomas and other writers;

> My new full-length book Buddha Tells Us is, a direct quote from scriptures, some mixed, some my own words ("my") (who owns words?) designed for to be clear to westerners – Buddhism is not for the West only means Buddhism is not for ...Bill Burroughs and Jack Kerouac but let it go at that. I'd still rather see Buddhism than D. H. Lawrence and his Dylan Thomas and Reich and allied it iditos. Idiots.
>
> Now i'm drunk, cant type

In 1956 in a letter to John Montgomery, Kerouac enquires;

> Did Rexroth ever publish that article about Dylan Thomas & Charlie Parker in New World Writing?

The answer was that yes; Rexroth would, and his important essay [mentioned above] appeared first in *New World Writing* 11. in 1957.

Which leads us to a final, and for me, very pleasing coincidence. Kerouac and Dylan Thomas appeared together in another volume of *New World Writing*. This is a killer book for me in three ways; the *Jean Louis* who contributes the first essay is none other than Jack Kerouac writing blissfully about Jazz of the Beat Generation; then further on we get a bunch of great Dylan Thomas letters to Oscar Williams, together with a colour plate of Gene Derwood's curious, but not uninteresting portrait of Dylan Thomas; and finally, a little off-piste, but a treasure for me – the first-publication of taster of Joseph Heller's work in progress, *Catch 18* which is an early excerpt from one of my all-time favourite novels,[4] and just how much better is its eventual title – Catch 22.

Gene Derwood portrait of Dylan Thomas

Dylan Thomas and Gregory Corso

Gregory Nunzio Corso (1930-2001) was an American poet and a key member of the Beat Movement and also the youngest of the inner circle of Beat writers – Kerouac, Ginsberg and Burroughs. He was born Nunzio Corso at New York City's St Vincent's Hospital. He later selected the name "Gregory" as a confirmation name but around his Little Italy neighbourhood he was always known as "Nunzio," while he dealt with others as "Gregory." And that is the name he used when he became a writer. His troubled adolescence included a stint of several months in the Tombs, the New York City jail, for a case involving a stolen radio, and three months of observation in Bellevue. At seventeen, he was convicted of theft and sentenced to Clinton State Prison for three years. Corso used his time in prison to good advantage, reading the better part of the prison library and studying a 1905 English dictionary inherited from a fellow prisoner. It was in the prison library that he discovered P.B. Shelley and developed a life-long enthusiasm for the poet. It was during these years in prison that he began to write. After his release in 1950, he met Allen Ginsberg, through whom he also became acquainted with William Burroughs and Jack Kerouac, as well as other New York writers and artists. As with Kerouac, strong connections between Corso and Dylan Thomas are not to be found, but there are a few sweet synchronicities; they did both appear in the same literary periodical *Two Cities* containing a posthumous publication of Dylan Thomas' letters to Lawrence Durrell alongside Six Poems by Corso.

A Publishers blurb for Corso's 1960 collection of poems The Happy Birthday of Death, compares these poems to the work of Dylan Thomas;

> *It is true that he has been one of the inner circle of the 'Beats' from the first, but many admirers of his poetry feel that it belongs quite as much to other and older traditions in world literature. One of these is the revival of pure poetry whenever an "original"... has broken with current verse conventions to give free rein to the magic of language. Another is that ancient pre-occupation of poets – the sense of the immediacy of death. Like Villon or Dylan Thomas, Corso lives close to the mystery of death. It is, perhaps, his central theme, on which variations ranging from the terrible to the comic are sounded.*

And 33 years after newborn Nunzio Corso took his first breaths in New York City's St Vincent's Hospital; in early November of 1953; Gregory Corso would make a return visit to his birthplace; but this time he was one of many who called at the hospital to pay homage and respect to Dylan Thomas, as he lay comatose and breathing his final breaths...

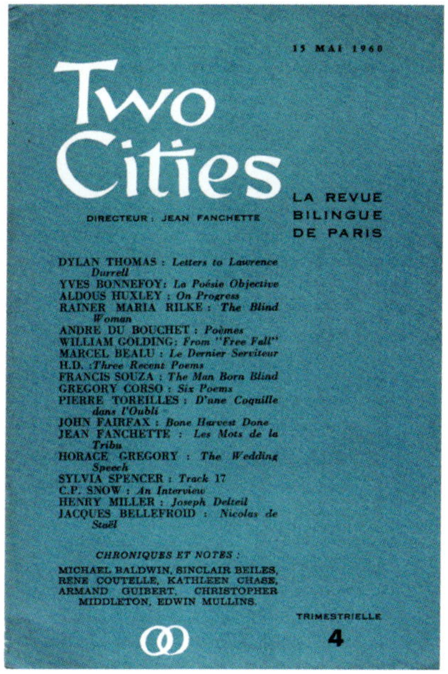

1. The staff at the school were mostly young and diverse the English Department was very good. My most influential teacher was Nial Devitt, who taught me English at O and A level. He wore a black needle cord suit with a ban-the-bomb CND badge on the lapel. As I was leaving his class one day he slipped me a piece of paper and murmured 'read a book by each of those' – it was a select list of Nobel Prize winners for literature. Some dozen years later I was exhibiting at a Book Fair in Chichester, browsing the stalls before opening and saw a stall with a signboard with two names – one of which was *Devitt* – It was Nial! I was amazed and elated – Nial had a vague memory of me but he and I both began to exhibit at the Monthly London book fairs in Bloomsbury's fine Russell Hotel and we became good friends – and he had married my history teacher who joined him on his stand. He was as fine bookseller as he was a teacher and interview with him can be found here: https://www.sheila-markham.com/interviews/nial-and-margaret-devitt.html. He starts by saying:

   > I first met Margaret when we were teaching at Stratford Grammar School in Bow... Teaching can be very boring. I'll never forget 4B on a wet Friday afternoon in West Ham. However on a brighter note one of my pupils was Jeff Towns, now such an excellent international bookseller.

2. Journals: Early Fifties, Early Sixties. Allen Ginsberg, Allen, and Gordon Ball, (Editor).Grove Press.

3. This poem is discussed in Chapter 12.

4. One of my favourite personal collections is my small bijou collection of various different editions of Catch 22; including a signed screenplay for the movie and a signed large-print edition so as I can read it in my dotage. The collection currently contains 22 items and I am loathe to add to it.

A fine vintage publicity image of Stravinsky I found in a Prague flea-market

15.

Dylan Thomas: Stravinsky, & Music – Old & New.

As soon as I met him, I knew the only thing to do was to love him.
Stravinsky speaking after Dylan's death...

Daniel Jones

Dylan Thomas learned what he knew of classical music from his lifelong Swansea friend, Dr Daniel Jones – a polymath, musician and composer. In his book *My Friend Dylan Thomas*,[1] Daniel Jones gives a funny and detailed description of a bizarre orchestra they formed as young schoolboys with other eventual Swansea coffee-shop and bar-room friends. They would all meet in Dan's family home, Warmley, a grand house on Eversley Rd. in West Swansea.

Dan begins with this preface:

> Music, or, to use a broader term, sound, played a very important part in our Warmley life.

And he continues...

> The fact that Dylan had no knowledge of music, and no musical skill was much more of an advantage than a disadvantage, because it ensured that anything we produced in concert would be unconventional....

Between them they wrote programmes, with each musical piece given surreal titles, such as Buzzards at Dinner, and Badgers Beneath My Vest. Dan also made-up palindromic, backward spelled names for their imaginary composers; Zoileb and Ffeifokorp from Berlioz and Prokofiev.[2] Dan states quite categorically that Dylan was 'musically illiterate', and he relates this story as evidence.

> Dylan did have one favourite classical favourite; Verdi's great opera *Il Trovatore*. However, once when they met up in London, Dylan was thrilled and excited to demonstrate a recent enrichment of his life: he had been lent an old gramophone and an old 78 r.p.m. record of the opera. But when Dylan dragged Dan away from the pub to share his favourite music with him, Dan was shocked and horrified to see that Dylan was playing it at maximum speed; everything was delivered in a high-pitched screech! Dan described it as if it was being sung by a choir of castrati singers. When Dylan praised the music by declaring 'those Italian tenors wear their testicles in their throats' Dan added 'So that was where they had gone.'[3]

Dylan and Daniel

In his own writings Dylan suggests that he knew of Stravinsky in his teens. Dylan name-checks him in his autobiographical BBC radio script, *Return Journey*, in which he describes the wide-ranging conversation he has had with his school pals where they discussed:

> Music and poetry and painting and politics.
> Einstein and Epstein, Stravinsky and Greta Garbo,
> Picasso and girls...

Daniel Jones went on to become became a professional musician and composer and would eventually write the music for most of the songs in *Under Milk Wood*, though this may have been after Dylan's death. He also composed a symphony, his fourth, which he dedicated to the memory of his friend; Symphony No. 4, *In Memoriam Dylan Thomas* (1954).

In 1961 Daniel Jones was asked to give the prestigious *Annual Lecture* for of the *BBC in Wales*. Dan spoke on Music In Wales and his subtitle was *An Aspect of the Relationship between Art and The People*. It

was published as an elegant, small booklet and it really is an interesting read, especially if you read it and imagine you have Daniel's fruity, posh, Anglo-Welsh accent.

* * * * *

Stravinsky

Although Dylan name-checked Stravinsky in his 1947 radio script *Return Journey*, I'm sure he never dreamt that five years later he would be asked to collaborate with the great composer on an opera. It wasn't until Dylan's last years in 1952/53 that there was any mention of Dylan Thomas actually working with Stravinsky. The film director Michael Powell (*Black Narcissus, Peeping Tom*) approached Dylan with the idea of him writing a treatment for an arthouse film version of the *Odyssey*, Stravinsky providing the music.

The composer had already been alerted to Dylan Thomas by W. H. Auden, who had recently collaborated with Stravinsky on the opera, *The Rake's Progress*. *The Odyssey* project never materialised due to lack of finance, but Stravinsky remained keen to work with Thomas. Just a few months later in May, Stravinsky was in Boston conducting performances of *The Rake's Progress*, and the Boston University opera workshop expressed interest in sponsoring a collaboration between Stravinsky and another poet. Dylan Thomas' name was suggested. Dylan received an official telegram from the workshop's director on May 20th enlisting his services. At this time Dylan was on his third trip to America and staying with John Malcolm Brinnin near Boston, so he was able to visit the composer in his suite at the Copley Plaza. Stravinsky writes about their only meeting:

Elsewhere he wrote:

> I met Dylan Thomas only once, and unfortunately much too briefly, in Boston last May, when he came to my hotel room to visit me. Immediately I was as much fascinated by his intelligence, personality, genuine charm, as I had been left impressed by the reading of his powerful and highly poetical writings.

As soon as I met him, I knew the only thing to do was to love him. Stravinsky goes on to discuss their very first notions of this collaboration. He writes that although he and Thomas never reached the stage of a fully-fledged subject; Dylan Thomas had *a very beautiful idea*. Thomas's notion was for the piece to be about;

> The rediscovery of our planet following an atomic mis-adventure.
> There would be a recreation of language, only the new one would have no abstractions; there would be only people, objects and words.
> He promised to avoid poetic indulgences: No conceits, I'll knock them all on the head.

Tragically that's as far as the idea ever got. Stravinsky invited Dylan to come with his wife and live with him in a specially built garden extension to his Lilliputian house in Hollywood, in expectation of a lengthy collaboration, and he wrote his address on a scrap of hotel notepaper.

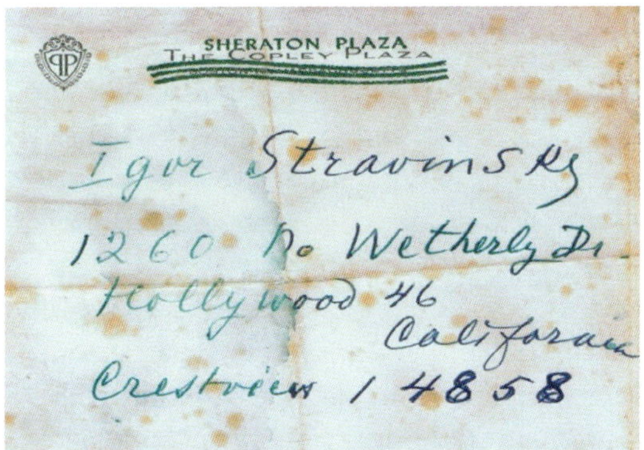

I found this autograph note in the papers of Daniel Jones, which I acquired after his death. Dylan had obviously gifted it to his musical friend.

On his return to Wales Dylan wrote to Stravinsky, expressing his excitement about the project:

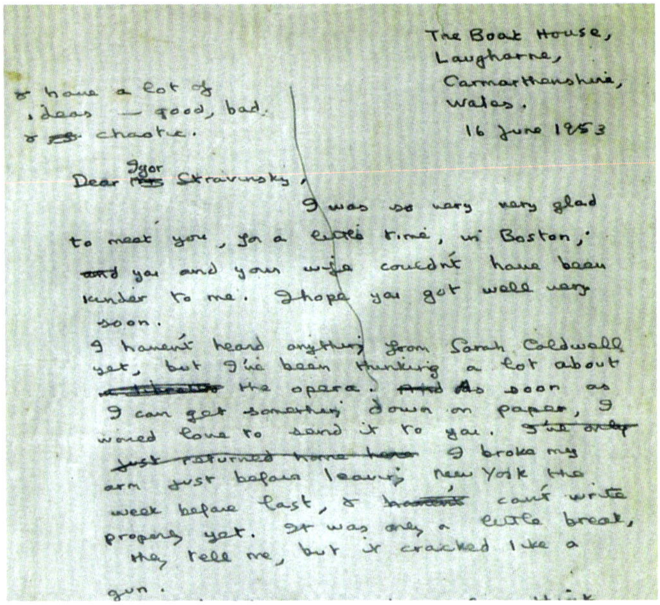

The Boat House,
Laugharne,
Carmarthenshire,
Wales.
16 June 1953

I have a lot of ideas — good, bad, & chaotic.

Dear ~~Mr~~ Igor Stravinsky,

I was so very very glad to meet you, for a little time, in Boston; ~~and~~ you and your wife couldn't have been kinder to me. I hope you got well very soon.

I haven't heard anything from Sarah Caldwell yet, but I've been thinking a lot about the opera. ~~And~~ As soon as I can get something down on paper, I would love to send it to you. ~~I've only just returned home here~~ I broke my arm just before leaving New York the week before last, & can't write properly yet. It was only a little break, they tell me, but it cracked like a gun.

I have a lot of ideas – good, bad & chaotic

The above is a noble fragment of draft letter which I once owned – it was found in Dylan's writing shed and it is almost identical to the finished letter that is in the *Collected Letters*.

Stravinsky later typed a letter to Dylan in October ending it:

> ...everyone is anxious to see and hear you here and we should be able to arrange some private affair from which enough money could be drawn to pay your fare to and from California...you know you will be my guest here...Do come, the weather is beautiful, too much maybe...we live in short sleeves...Ah Bien tot.

Stravinsky wired Thomas on October 25th, asking when he was likely to arrive, but the reply that came on November 9th was the telegram informing Stravinsky that Thomas had died in New York City. The musician's response, a forlorn:

All I could do was cry.

All we do have from this tragic affair is the piece of music Stravinsky was moved to write and record. *In Memoriam Dylan Thomas* is poignant, melancholic but dynamic setting for tenor and string quartet of the villanelle, *Do not go gentle into that good night*, Dylan's poem for his own dying father. In true Stravinsky mode he sets its powerful refrain, *Rage, rage against the dying of the light*, into two 'dirge-canons' for string quartet and a quartet of trombones!

It's hard to imagine that a collaboration between the hard-drinking, dishevelled Welshman and the neat, elderly, discreetly scented and vastly urbane Stravinsky would have been entirely untroubled, but they had some definite affinities – both were incorrigible womanisers with a heroic capacity for Scotch, and Stravinsky would have loved the idea of a language with no abstractions. Plus there was that shared passion for tight formalism, which they both needed to harness their fantastic imaginations. Sadly we will never know.

A fine, long running literary magazine, *Adam* (*An International Revue*), published, in 1953, *Our Dylan Thomas Memorial Number*. It was full of fine tributes and warm memories, but none more so than the letter they received from Stravinsky, which they reproduced in full in facsimile:

* * * * *

John Cage

It is worth mentioning that on his first reading tour of America Dylan spent a day with another giant of American music – John Cage. Dylan's friend and quasi 'tour manager' John Malcolm Brinnin, in his book *Dylan Thomas in America*, recounts a day-long drive from Washington back to New York with Dylan and two other passengers. One was John Cage – the American composer and music theorist, who pioneered all manner of modern

Mr Miron Grindea
Editor
ADAM
28 Emperor's Gate
London S.W. 7 (England)

Dear Sir,

Your letter of December 15, 1953, reached me with some delay, and I am also answering it with delay, due to the fact that I am currently on a concert tour and travelling all over the country.

Dylan Thomas' sudden passing away has left me deeply shocked and painfully wounded. As you know, he was in New York on the first leg of his journey to my home in California, and we were both eagerly looking forward to getting better acquainted personally and working on the idea of an opera.

I met Dylan Thomas only once, and unfortunately much too briefly, in Boston last May, when he came to my hotel room to visit me. Immediately I was as much fascinated by his intelligence, personality, genuine charm, as I had been left impressed by the reading of his powerful and highly poetical writings.

Dylan Thomas' hopes and enthusiasm were certainly the same than mine when he embarked on his ill-fated voyage. He did not live to let them take shape materially and artistically, but he left to me, with the strong imprint of his personality, the great sadness of a beautiful dream which could not be born to life.

I wish your memorial number of ADAM on Dylan Thomas will be a so well deserved tribute to him. Among all those who are better qualified than I am to make the eulogy of this very great poet -- because they have been privileged to know him better and longer -- my own tribute must necessarily be short but it is a most sincere and enthusiastic one, even it has to be limited to this letter to the Editor of ADAM.

Sincerely,

Igor Stravinsky

experimental music and the imaginative, non-standard use of musical instruments. The other traveller was Merce Cunningham, Cage's partner, who was equally instrumental in the field of modern dance and choreography. Although very different from Dylan in so many ways, Brinnin is at pains to indicate how well-behaved and friendly Dylan conducted himself throughout the journey; he writes:

> We stopped for a single beer and [Dylan] and John Cage began to weave a zany, pointless and disconnected conversation that lasted all day. It was as if Dylan found Cage's contrary views on anything conventional or, for that matter on anything remotely human, as irresistible goads to flights of his own. Merce and I were far more audience than they needed in this mood, and the trip was entertained by hilariously insane discourses on life in America at this time.

* * * * *

Do Not Go Gentle. An Opera by Robert Mano

Dylan Thomas sadly never got to write his libretto for Stravinsky, but he has inspired a few recent operas. An accomplished American musician and composer Robert Manno[4] has been working on an opera based on the life of Dylan Thomas for many years. He and his wife, former Metropolitan Opera Orchestra violinist Magdalena Golczewski, reside in the Northern Catskills where they established the long-running *Windham Chamber Music Festival,* a concert series now in its thirteenth season. He is Music Director and Conductor of the *Windham Festival Chamber Orchestra* and *Catskill Mountain Chamber Orchestra*. He teamed up with Welsh writer Gwynne Edwards who wrote the libretto for his opera *Do Not Go Gentle* which is based on the life of Dylan Thomas and his wife Caitlin. Excerpts from it were performed by the New York City Opera at the Skirball Centre in NYC in 2008.

Under Milk Wood. An Opera by John Metcalf

In 2014 a Swansea-born, Welsh composer, John Metcalf completed a new opera inspired by Dylan Thomas's *Under Milk Wood* which used the original words of the radio play as its libretto. It is Metcalf's seventh opera, which he began working on in 2007. It was performed as part of the 2014 DT 100 Centenary celebrations, and I attended the world premiere which was produced by Swansea University's Taliesin Arts Centre as a joint production with Le Chien Qui Chants from Quebec, Companion Star from New York, and the Welsh National Opera in April 2014. The production was directed by Keith Turnbull with musical direction by Wyn Davies who also gave a virtuoso performance playing piano and synthesiser plus singing the role of Organ Morgan. I am far from being an opera buff, but I enjoyed it and agreed with the review by Rian Evans in the Guardian:

> What comes through is a deep affection for the populace of Under Milk Wood and an understanding of their quirkiness, bitchiness, humanity and crucially their black humour.

I was also very pleased when the boxed double CD came out

with a dazzling cover, which featured one of Sir Peter Blake's most surreal illustrations from his illustrated *Under Milk Wood*.[5]

Dylan Song Cycle by Michael Stimpson

Michael Stimpson is a remarkable musician, composer, and music writer. To mark the 70th anniversary of Dylan's death in New York City, Michael's song cycle, Dylan, was performed by the Royal Harpist, Alis Huws and leading baritone, Gareth Brynmor John. The first performance was from the very house where Thomas was born, 5 Cwmdonkin Drive, Swansea, on 4th November 2023. Two subsequent performances from New York

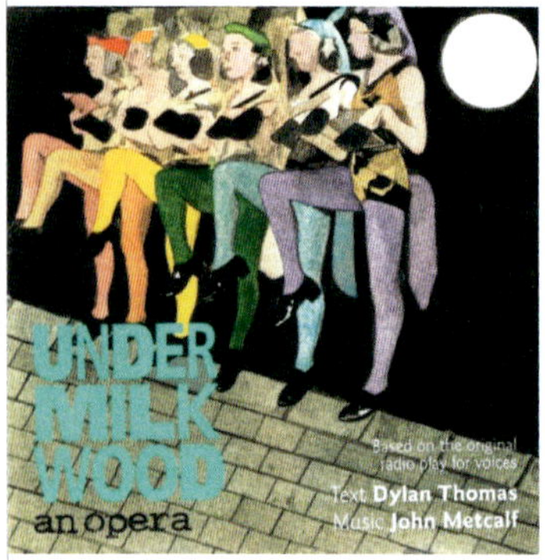

took place at Rutgers Presbyterian Church on 11th November and St John's in the Village on 12th November. The Swansea performance was also live-streamed.

On the CD, which Michael kindly sent to me, the soloists are Roderick Morgan and Sioned Williams. Michael writes of the development of the project in the sleeve notes;

> It is intriguing how the subject matter for a new work initiates, develops, and takes its final form. The work of Dylan Thomas was introduced to me during college days both by a Welsh girlfriend and a music teacher of the time. I dipped into Dylan Thomas's poems and stories on occasion until in 2001, at the final rehearsal for a new piece for harpist Sioned Williams, a throwaway remark about setting some Dylan Thomas for voice and harp was left in the air. As the 50th anniversary of Dylan Thomas's death approached we began to discuss a work more seriously. During further reading I was taken by a whole series of little coincidences, not least that I had lived in Delancey Street in London, where Dylan Thomas lived for a time as well.

Dylan Thomas & Modern Popular Music

I was very lucky to be a long-time friend of Gwen Watkins, the widow of Vernon Watkins, Dylan's close friend in poetry. Like Dylan, Vernon died in America; but Vernon was relatively healthy and in his early sixties when, in 1967, he died on the north-west coast of America due to an excess of tennis, not whiskey!

I met Gwen for the first time in Ralph Wishart's bookshop – known by all as *Ralph the Books*, who owned and ran Dylan's favourite Swansea used bookstore. That was back in the late 70's; we are still friends and Gwen has just celebrated her 100th birthday! For all these years I called on Gwen regularly, especially when she moved back from Oxford to live in Mumbles here in Swansea. Over the course of these many visits I learned so much from Gwen about Dylan and Vernon, but she also knew, and was close with, most all of the 'Kardomah habitués' so I learned about them too. She was incredibly well read and intellectually bright, but also very generous with her time and knowledge. I was very lucky to be able to call and talk with her, sometimes for hours on end. I often visited with a specific question or odd query in mind. Before one such visit, I had realised that I knew little or nothing about Dylan Thomas and music, apart from the Stravinsky story above, so on this occasion I asked Gwen about this; was he musical? was he keen on classical music or the popular music of the day? Gwen became pensive but after some deep thoughts she brightened up and began to speak. As ever with Gwen, her detailed answer was both informative and amazing. She recalled and declared that Dylan loved most of all humorous, maybe slightly smutty, music hall songs.[6] But she delighted in revealing that his most favourite song of all, which he would often sing ad infinitum, featured in one of his favourite films; his beloved Marx Brothers comedy, *At The Circus*. The song was sung, with his trademark gusto, by Groucho Marx. It was called, wait for it:

Lydia The Tattooed Lady

Gwen, forever a font of knowledge, recounted the gist of the film, and even sang the chorus for me from memory! When I got home I found the film and the song on YouTube and enjoyed it for myself. Here are the lyrics, and it's not hard to see why Dylan was so taken with it…

Oh Lydia, oh, Lydia, say have you met Lydia
Oh, Lydia, the tattooed lady
She has eyes that folks adore so
And a torso even more so
Lydia, oh, Lydia, that encyclopaedia

Oh, Lydia, the queen of them all
On her back is the Battle of Waterloo
Beside it the Wreck of the Hesperus too
And proudly above the waves
The Red, White and Blue
You can learn a lot from Lydia
La la la la la la La la la la la la
She can give you a view of the world
In tattoo if you step up and tell her where
For a dime you can see Kankakee or Paree
Or Washington crossing the Delaware.
La la la la la la,

Lydia, oh, Lydia, say have you met Lydia
Oh, Lydia, the tattooed lady
When her muscles start relaxin'
Up the hill comes Andrew Jackson
Lydia, oh, Lydia, that encyclopaedia
Oh, Lydia, the champ of them all
For two bits she will do a Mazurka in Jazz
With a view of Niagara that no artist has
And on a clear day you can see Alcatraz
You can learn a lot from Lydia
La la la la la la
Come along and see Buffalo Bill with his lasso
Just a little classic by Mendel Picasso
Here is Captain Spaulding exploring the Amazon
And Godiva, but with her pyjamas on
La la la la la la
La la la la la la
Oh Lydia, oh, Lydia, say have you met Lydia
Oh, Lydia, the tattooed lady
When she stands, her laps go littler
When she sits, she sits on Hitler
Lydia, oh, Lydia, that encyclopaedia
Oh, Lydia, the queen of them all
She once swept an Admiral clear off his feet
The ships on her hips made his heart skip a beat
And now the old boy's in command of the fleet
For he went and married Lydia
I said Lydia (he said Lydia)
I say Lydia (we said Lydia)

How Dylan must have loved *She has eyes that folks adore so/ And a torso even more so*; how he would have relished (and coveted) the rhyming of *Lydia* with *Encyclopaedia*; and how he would have roared at: *When she stands, her laps go littler/ When she sits, she sits on Hitler!*

Johnnie Ray

It is interesting that perhaps the only contemporary music Dylan actually alluded to is found in John Malcolm Brinnin's *Dylan Thomas in America*. Brinnin writes of how he picked Dylan up after he had his only meeting with Stravinsky at the Copley Plaza hotel in Boston. Brinnin thought they would be heading home but Dylan left the meeting in a very buoyant and excited mood and wanted to celebrate this new project. Dylan had seen that the very popular crooner, Johnnie Ray was playing at a fancy supper club and that as a homage to his wife Caitlin, who was languishing and unhappy back in Laugharne, and who, like many women was enamoured with the singer, Dylan insisted that they drink the bottle Stravinsky had given him and he demanded they go and see Johnnie Ray and celebrate. John Malcolm Brinnin in his memoir of the event in his book *Dylan Thomas in America* relates how contagious the event was, especially after they had made short work of the bottle. Brinnin writes;

> Dinner over, we could do nothing but allow excitement to carry us out on the town. Johnnie Ray, then at the height of his career as a sobbing, floor pounding minstrel, was the big attraction at an enormous night club in South Boston. By all means, we must go to hear him said Dylan – if only for Caitlin's sake: she had a crush on Johnnie Ray and listened to his recordings endlessly. It was apparent that Dylan himself was somehow fascinated by the singer. We drove to the jam-packed establishment, got a front row table among some fifteen hundred other devotees, and drank double Scotches awaiting the entrance of the jukebox idol. At the carefully prepared moment, catapulted onto the stage in an ear-splitting fanfare of songs, he came at us roaring, moaning, beating his hands on the floor and clubbing the piano, holding the microphone in his hands as if it were a bride about to be ravished. As the cavernous room echoed the din of shrill creams and orgiastic sighs, Dylan shouted in my ear:
> *"He's terrific! Fantastic!"*

Other Popular Crooners: Shirley Bassey & Eartha Kitt

Apart from the great Johnnie Ray, Dylan Thomas would engage with two other popular singers – in this case chanteuses. Dylan had become very good friends with the BBC's 'Voice of Cricket', John Arlott, who also shared Dylan's love of reading and writing poetry, of watching cricket and of having a good drink in lively pubs. They worked together on radio programmes and played together, often at cricket matches. At one time, the two met in Cardiff and watched the cricket until close of play when Arlott informed Dylan that he had been tipped off that a new and quite dynamic young girl singer, who was being talked about as the 'next big thing' down in the pubs and clubs of Cardiff's colourful suburb, Splott. The two found the young singer performing in a rough club. She turned out to be the young Shirley Bassey.

Another of his good-time friends was his Swansea pal, Charles Fisher,[7] who had been a schoolfriend and work colleague on the local Swansea paper where they both worked as cub reporters. Later they would both be in London and would meet up. Charles was quite a dashing and handsome ladies' man about town, and he got to know the feline singer, Eartha Kitt. He would meet her at her hotel for drinks, and on one occasion at least he took Dylan and introduced him to the purring diva.

* * * * *

Dylan Thomas and Jazz

Considering Dylan Thomas spent time in London and New York when jazz was in its vibrant infancy, he never makes any reference to visiting any jazz bars. The closest I've got is a painted sketch by an English artist, Peter Evershed, who I became friends with back in the 80's. He specialized in making quick portrait sketches of famous writers artists and musicians who he encountered on his travels. One of whom was Dylan Thomas. Peter had spent the fifties in New York City where he made many drawings of Dylan, a few of which I bought from him directly. The reason I'm writing this is that I was excited to find, in a small oblong sketch book,[8] which I bought from Peter, a page with a spirited portrait of Dylan paired with an equally spirited portrait of the great Jazzman, Charlie 'Bird' Parker! This is the only image I know of that links Dylan with Jazz.

However, Dylan has been linked to Charlie Parker in some serious critical writings. The 'father of the Beats', poet and critic Kenneth Rexroth, wrote an important essay on the origins of the Beat movement in his essay *Disengagement*,[9] in which he writes:

> *Like the Pillars of Hercules, like two ruined Titans guarding the entrance to one of Dante's Circles, stand two great dead juvenile delinquents – the heroes of the post-war generation: The saxophonist, Charlie Parker, and Dylan Thomas. If the word "deliberate" means anything, both of them certainly deliberately destroyed themselves.*

More recently the Welsh academic Daniel G Williams wrote a

long essay; *'Wales Bird' – Dylan Thomas and Charlie Parker*[10] in which he quotes Rexroth but then expands his thesis by including a number of other American poets and writers including African American poets such as LeRoi Jones, who in his autobiography[11] declares:

I was heavily into Dylan Thomas.

Daniel also included a great quote from a letter from Jack Kerouac to Allen Ginsberg[12] in which Kerouac boasts that his poetry and jazz albums, which he made with a variety of esteemed jazzmen such as Steve Allen, Zoot Sims and Al Cohn, were the:

Dylan at play in the *White Horse Tavern*

greatest poetry records since Dylan Thomas.

What makes Daniel's essay different is that he himself, apart from being a Professor of English at Swansea University is also a fine saxophonist with his own jazz quintet – Burum.

So, even if Dylan Thomas was not into jazz he did spend a lot of down time in the *White Horse Tavern*, and he really mixed in with the locals as this rare contact sheet depicts.

Stan Tracy. *Under Milk Wood. Jazz Suite*

It was up to the grand-father of British Jazz, Stan Tracy, to produce some serious Jazz inspired by Dylan Thomas, and once more it was Thomas's most popular work that he hit upon, *Under Milk Wood.*

Stan Tracy was born in 1926 and he was one of the greatest British jazz pianists and composers. His most important influences were Duke Ellington and Thelonius Monk. But Tracy's best-known work was his jazz suite *Under Milk Wood*, which he composed in the early sixties. It was released on Columbia records in 1965 to great critical acclaim and it is acknowledged as one of the best UK jazz recordings. Tracy toured it live and would often return to it with different line-ups and various celebratory readers. Donald Houston who played First-Voice in the early stage productions of the play, performed the spoken-word on the first LP, and various other actors took the part in later performances and recordings.

Two Album Covers

Stan came to Swansea on a few occasions and his performances were always sold out. In a series of articles in *The Guardian – 50 Great Moments In Jazz*, the critic John

Fordham wrote this about the album:

> *Under Milk Wood* was an evocative collection of sparky themes inspired by the Dylan Thomas radio play (it's sometimes performed with a narrator reading the parts). And thanks to Tracey's sparing piano and Wellins's softly hooting sax, the rippling tone-poem 'Starless and Bible Black' is widely acclaimed as one of the great jazz performances.

Jen Wilson. The Dylan Thomas Jazz Suite. 'Twelve Poems' set for Quintet and Voice

Jen Wilson did more to document and promote Jazz in Swansea than anyone else. She was a gifted pianist and a fine teacher, researcher and writer – all skills she used to their full extent when she first established *The Welsh Women in Jazz Archive* which grew and mutated into *Jazz Heritage Wales*. She was at the forefront all along the way, linking up with the Swansea University of Wales Trinity Saint David (UWTSD). She was indefatigable and pioneered it through to its current established and highly respected status. It was just in November that she curated the brilliant 'Documenting Jazz' event – an international conference in 2022. Sadly she passed away in May of 2023. She was always a close friend of the Dylan Thomas Centre and the archive is now located there. Back in 2010 the Centre commissioned her to write and record a Dylan Thomas-inspired CD of her own musical interpretations of some of her favourite Thomas poems.

* * * * *

Dylan Thomas in Modern Rock & Pop Music

This story broke on all media platforms, all around the world as I was writing the final chapters of this book. I inserted it as a STOP PRESS in Introduction. Briefly, the title track of Taylor Swift's new 2024 album, The Tortured Poets Department references Dylan Thomas in these lines:

> *I laughed in your face and said, 'You're not Dylan Thomas. I'm not Patti Smith. This ain't the Chelsea Hotel. We're modern idiots.*

It is the latest of many such usages of Dylan Thomas in popular song in the years after his death. However, the many instances whereby Dylan Thomas is referenced in pop and rock lyrics or inspires instrumental music across these genres, does not, in my opinion make him a Rock 'n' Roll poet. I will explain ...

Dylan Thomas is NOT a *Rock 'n' Roll Poet*

I was not happy, nor impressed in 2014 when it became commonplace to describe Dylan Thomas as the first *Rock 'n' Roll Poet* – this is from the BBC's website in October 2014; and it was echoed by lazy journalists on a variety of news platforms in Wales and beyond.

As it happens, the song usually credited as the birth-cry of the Rock 'n' Roll genre (*Rock Around the Clock*) was written in 1953, by Max Freedman and James Myers. It is a 12-bar-blues song written while Dylan Thomas was still alive and visiting America, but I doubt very much that he heard the tune anywhere. It was some months after his death in 1954 that *Bill Haley & His Comets* took America, and then the world, by storm with their seminal recording of the song which topped the charts in America and the UK for a few months and is regarded as the birth of Rock 'n' Roll.

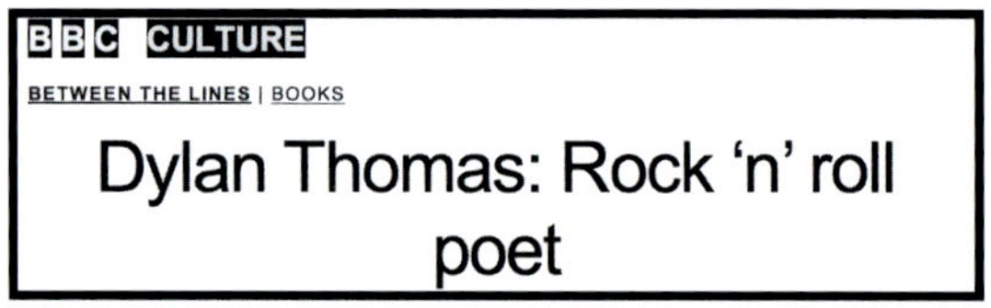

The only thing vaguely *Rock 'n' Roll* about Thomas' later life was the extent of his touring in America. His three reading tours were long and arduous affairs during which he criss-crossed the continent using various ad hoc means of transport. These tours left him seriously exhausted and vulnerable. This map shows the real extent of Dylan's first reading tour which surely matches the tours of the first wave of UK rock bands, and Dylan did not have roadies or an air-conditioned luxury tour bus at his disposal. It was produced by an American academic, Martin E. Gingerich who visited Swansea University on a sabbatical in 1978. He wrote an essay, *Dylan Thomas and America* which was published by the Swansea Dylan Thomas Society.[13] In his detailed examination of Dylan's visits to the US, he tells us that he did thirty-five performances in ninety-seven days; so he took to the stage and read every two-and-a-half days, travelling some 12,000 miles.

But Dylan was a poet and not a guitar-toting rock and roller. However, Dylan Thomas was a prolific recording artist; but he was not a singer or a musician. He entertained with his rich voice and declamatory readings and recitations of his own and other great poets' work; and it was these performances, which gave rise to the vast number of recordings, which began to appear before he died, and have continued to be released and are still available. He featured on many spoken word LPs – some recorded live and others compiled from events and his radio broadcasts. Dame Edith Sitwell had this to say of his vocal talent:

> [Dylan] had a speaking voice of the utmost magnificence, range and beauty, and his speaking of poetry was as sublime as his writing of poetry. 'The Lions and fires of his flaming breath' to use a phrase of his own were such that all pride, all light, walked in the lines that, speaking he made his own. To hear him read his own poetry was a revelation. It was a great pride to me to hear him read my own poetry.

The New York Times made a point of this after his 1950 tour of the states:

> Dylan Thomas's voice has added a new dimension to literary history... He will surely be remembered as the first in modern literature to be both a maker and speaker of poetry... the typical reader will become entranced after hearing him recite.

Two young New York girls, working in book publishing were so impressed after hearing an early Thomas reading that they founded a spoken word record label and issued Dylan's first LPs so swiftly that on his later tours Dylan would be photographed signing records.

It was in January 1952, these two bright and determined women, Barbara Cohen[14] and Marianne Roney [Mantell], recent graduates of Hunter College, attended a reading by Thomas at New York City's 92nd Street Young Men's Youth Centre. Cohen and Roney were so taken by his performance, they wrote him a letter and eventually got to meet him in the bar of the Chelsea Hotel, where they persuaded him to make a record of him reading poems and stories.

The first record they produced consisted of Dylan Thomas reading five of his best poems on one side of the LP and then the whole of his recently published final version of *A Child's Christmas in Wales* on side two. The first spoken word LP on their new record label, Caedmon Records (named for the first poet to write in the native language of Old English) was launched into the world. The two founders kept busy, and their small label grew. In the years that followed, Caedmon went on to establish itself as the preeminent publisher of spoken-word

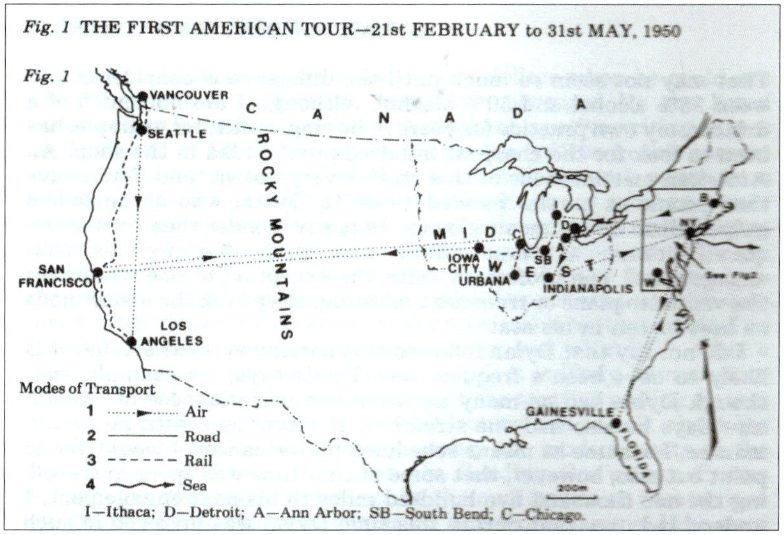

Fig. 1 THE FIRST AMERICAN TOUR—21st FEBRUARY to 31st MAY, 1950

Two Frasconi Caedmon cover designs

audio in the English language in the categories of literary fiction, poetry, plays, and children's titles, publishing such distinguished authors as T. S. Eliot, James Joyce, Ernest Hemingway, Zora Neale Hurston, Sylvia Plath, and William Faulkner, among many others. But Dylan Thomas was a constant bestseller, and his recordings were offered on vinyl, then cassette, then on CD, and now they are on *YouTube* and *Spotify*.

The first album was a rather lacklustre and rushed production with a very dull cover, but they quickly realised the selling potential of an eye-catching cover and they began to use good artists, photographers and designers. The most popular were those designed by a now famous American artist – Antonio Frasconi who created many album covers and also a life-size woodcut portrait of Dylan Thomas.

Eventually Caedmon was taken over by Harper Collins who, with the help of Barbara and the staff at New Directions, issued an 11-CD unabridged collection of all the Caedmon records with notes by the then American poet Laureate Billy Collins. And in 2003 the box-set of Dylan Thomas CDs were up for a prestigious Grammy award.[15]

But not even a mega corporation like Harper Collins could resurrect a long-dead poet as this advert suggests, reproduced here thanks to my friend Andrew Lycett:

At a coming Author Event Friday, November 01. 2002
DYLAN THOMAS WILL BE PROMOTING (?!)

Before we leave the topic of Dylan Thomas on record, one further curiosity. Many years ago, a local car boot fair enthusiast brought a jet-black, vintage Shellac, 78 record into my shop. I, of course, bought it but I have no memory of what I paid. I had no

The two founders of Caedmon Records, Barbara Holdridge and Marianne Mantell

Dylan Thomas recording in battle for a Grammy

11/01/03

ROBIN TURNER
robin.turner@wme.co.uk

ALMOST 50 years after his death, hard drinking poet Dylan Thomas will by vying with the likes of Kylie Minogue, Bruce Springsteen and Eminem for the 2003 US Grammy Awards.

An album of the Welshman reading his famous works in his trademark "educated Welsh" lilt has been nominated for a Grammy.

The awards will be given out at a glittering ceremony in New York's Madison Square Garden on February 23. Televised throughout the world by CBS, it will be watched by an estimated audience of two billion in 180 countries.

Eminem, arguably the most successful recording artist of 2002 has been nominated for five awards including Best Rap Album, Best Male Rap Solo Performance, Best Video, Record of the Year and Album of the Year.

Pop newcomers Norah Jones and Avril Lavigne have kicked off a successful 2003 by collecting five nominations each for this year's Grammy awards.

And Kylie Minogue, whose family hails from Maesteg originally, is nominated in a new dance category for her work *Love at First Sight* while Bruce Springsteen's *The Rising* is nominated for Song of the Year.

The Dylan Thomas CD box compilation entitled *Dylan Thomas : The Caedmon Collection* is the brainchild of American Leslie Mona-Mathus working with producers Rick Harris and David Nolan.

They compiled the CD of Dylan's readings of poems such as *Fern Hill, Do Not Go Gentle Into That Good Night* and the "play for voices", *Under Milk Wood.*

The CD has been nominated in the Best Historical Album category, one of 104 categories in the awards which reward country, latin, rap, R&B, dance, rock and other music genres.

Competing for the best historical album prize will be *Artie Shaw : A Self Portrait* (Bluebird Records), *The Complete Okeh and Brunswick, Bix Beiderbecke, Frank Tumbauer and Jack Teagarden Sessions 1924 - 1936* (Mosaic), *The Genius of the Electric Guitar* (Columbia) and *Screamin' and Hollerin' the Blues* (Revenant).

The Dylan Thomas CD is being sold at Dylan memorabilia collector Jeff Towns's Swansea bookstore, in the Dylan Thomas Centre. He said, "This really does show the lasting appeal of Dylan Thomas and his work. The recordings are classic and have a good chance of winning that category."

Caedmon Records has been in business for 50 years and specialises in spoken word recordings and has produced a number of records, tapes and latterly CDs of Thomas's broadcasts and readings. A spokeswoman for the company, now owned by Harper Collins, said, "It is a great honour to be nominated for the awards but given the unique, timeless nature of the Dylan Thomas collection it is not surprising."

Artistic achievement

THE Grammy Awards have been running for 45 years and celebrate the best in recording arts honouring fields as varied as rap, pop, rock, blues, jazz, classical and polka to new age, alternative and the spoken word.

The awards are presented on technical or artistic achievement, not chart positions or sales.

Established in 1957 National Academy of Recording Arts and Sciences based in California started the awards, regarded as the "grandaddy" of music awards. It is to music what the Oscars are to movies.

The awards are known as Grammys (short for gramophone) since the awards themselves are shaped like old-fashioned gramophone records.

Over the years, Los Angeles and New York have played tug-of-war with the Grammy Awards show with the ceremony having been held 33 times in Los Angeles, 10 times in New York and once in Nashville.

The 45th annual awards will take place on February 23 at Madison Square Garden, New York. Tickets to the shows are not available to the public, being by "invitation only".

MAJOR CONTENDER: *Eminem*
'TIMELESS NATURE': *Dylan Thomas*

"The recordings are classic and have a good chance of winning that category"

idea what was on the record, all the label told me was that it was a '*Private Recording*' and hand-written title was '*19th century Ballad.*' I eventually sourced the technology to play it and discovered it was a recording of Dylan Thomas sonorously reciting, but in no way singing, a classic music hall song, *Pretty Polly Perkins of Paddington Green*. I have written about Dylan's love of music hall songs and this one was composed by a London-based music hall songwriter and performer, Harry Clifton, and first published in 1864. The song was hugely popular at the time, and it was eventually included in the *Oxford Book of Comic Verse* with the original manuscript now in the Bodleian Library!

But for me, the real question was, when, why and where, did Dylan Thomas go into a self-recording booth and record himself? The label on the recorded side to the disc, caried the legend

From: Andrew Lycett
Sent: 11 October 2002 13:09
To: JEFF TOWNS
Subject: thought this evidence of a second coming would amuse you

HarperCollins.com

Authors Browse Bestsellers Channels Reading Guides About Us

Title

Search

1 to 2 of 2 matches for coming Author Events

Friday, November 01, 2002
Dylan Thomas, will be promoting *Dylan Thomas CD (Unabridged)*
Appears on/at: POETS & WRITERS/Caedmon Feature

Friday, November 01, 2002
Dylan Thomas, will be promoting *Dylan Thomas CD (Unabridged)*
Appears on/at: BOOK MAGAZINE/Caedmon Feature

University Recording Co. Cambridge.

So far, my investigations have got me nowhere, but I live in hope – however the mystery does not quite end there. In 1971Caedmon records issued an LP of the BBC recording of Dylan's *Return Journey* but the play was not long enough to fill it, so they added an ad-hoc group of recordings of Dylan reading a curious miscellany of other poets – and lo and behold; 303

Track 1. Side 2. is:

Anonymous, *Polly Perkins* 2:07

Polly Perkins Side 2 Track I. Anonymous

The sleeve notes to the track are somewhat pathetic and tell us next to nothing:

The proceedings open in high spirits with the ballad of Polly Perkins, who was as beautiful as a butterfly,

but nothing at all about when, why and where it was recorded. The recording was also included in the 2004 boxed set of 11 CDs, *Dylan Thomas The Caedmon Collection*[15]. but with no further expaination as to this track's origination.

And the mystery does not end their either. In May of 1982 Roy Plomley's guest castaway on *Desert Island Discs* was the writer, broadcaster and founder of the BBC's Natural History Unit, Desmond Hawkins.[16] Dylan and Desmond were good drinking pals in London in the mid-thirties, and Hawkins published a few

The front and back of the record

of Dylans' early poems in *Purpose*, a new magazine that Hawkins was associated with, for which Dylan received a very welcome *guinea* for each one. Hawkins later published an interesting memoir of his literary life in London; *When I Was – a Memoir of the Years between the Wars.*[17]

You can still access and listen to the Hawkins episode of Desert Island discs on BBC Sounds which has this to say on the programme's website:

> *One of the more unexpected selections was made by the writer and editor Desmond Hawkins who'd published some of Dylan's poems in the New English Weekly, and who told interviewer Roy Plomley that he used to meet Dylan in the Yorkshire Grey public house in London. He chose a recording of Dylan reciting the music hall song Pretty Polly Perkins of Paddington Green.*

* * * * *

Dylan Thomas in Rock & Pop Music

Making records does not make you a Rock n' Roll poet. I have already written about my first experience of Dylan Thomas being dragged into the realm of *Popular Music* in Chapter 13.[18] when I write about Heathcote Williams. In that essay I say:

> Some seven or eight years after his death this Welsh poet was annexed into the world of rock music when a 19-year-old, budding folk singer, born in 1941 in Duluth Minnesota to Jewish parents, changed his name from Robert **Zimmerman** to Bob **Dylan**. At the time this was reported as being some sort of homage to the Welsh poet.

After the huge success and influence of the Beatles' Sgt Pepper LP[19] back in 1967, on the cover of which both Dylan Thomas and Bob Dylan are featured, it would appear that Dylan Thomas began to inhabit the imaginations of many musicians across rock, pop and jazz. What follows here is not in any way an exhaustive listing of all the references to Dylan Thomas in modern song-lyrics and music, but a largely subjective account of a few of my favourites, in no particular order, but perhaps vaguely chronological if possible.

Simon & Garfunkel

Even before *Sgt Pepper* the great American duo Simon & Garfunkel used Dylan Thomas to gently mock Bob Dylan in their 1966 song, *A Simple Desultory Philippic* (*or How I was Robert McNamara'd into Submission*) includes the lines:

> *He's so unhip, that when you say Dylan, he thinks you're talking about Dylan Thomas, whoever he was.*

And the full title also references Dylan Thomas' wife Caitlin Macnamara. The track featured on their 1966 Album *Parsley, Sage Rosemary and Thyme.*

Mason Williams

In 1968, the year the LP with this track on came out, I was spending the summer enjoying my first trip to America. For a month I worked as a counsellor on a Jewish Summer camp in upstate New Jersey – Camp Glenwood; and the tune that came through loudly and most often through the radio was an instrumental called Classical Gas, composed and played by a remarkable multi-instrumentalist, Mason Williams. The infectious instrumental tune features Williams playing each and every instrument on the track which he recorded separately and then edited together. When I got back to the UK a year later, I saw a copy of his first LP named aptly, *Mason Williams Phonograph*

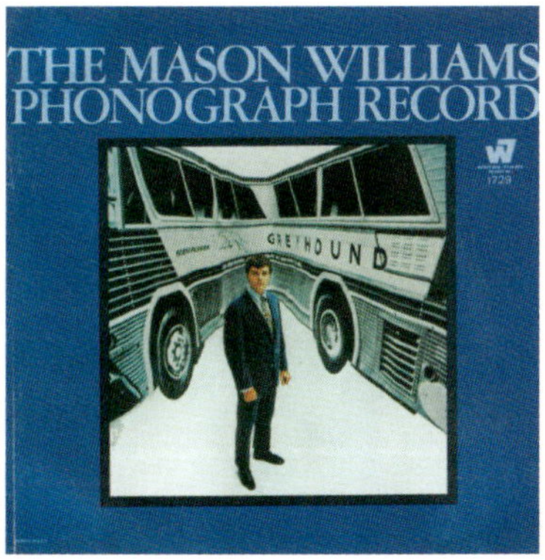

Record which contained Classical Gas, and I bought it as a strong aide-memoir to a great summer. I was very surprised when I got the record home to see that it also included a track titled *Dylan Thomas* – a curious, jaunty, banjo-ditty based on the melody of London Bridge Is Falling Down, but this time with a much darker rhyme...

Dylan Thomas has come and gone, come and gone
Dylan Thomas has come and gone
His blood has turned to words...

King Crimson

In the early summer of 1969, I hitchhiked across Europe to Turkey, and then across Turkey to the Persian border where I was refused entry. So I returned home. It was a lively trip and when I got back to London it got livelier. I learned that my favourite ex-Rolling Stone, Brian Jones, had recently died of drugs and drowning, aged just 27. The remaining members of the band including his replacement, Mick Taylor, were holding an impromptu farewell memorial, all-day, free festival concert in Hyde Park.

I got up early and joined the other quarter to half a-million nascent hippies and rockers for the entertainment. I found myself a comfy little branch halfway up a big tree that overlooked the stage and settled in for the day. The Stones were already becoming a pastiche of themselves, and I was not impressed with Mick Jagger's white-silk, frock-like doubloons, nor his faux estuary *Lundun* accent when he recited a Shelley poem for dead Brian. And

most of the white butterflies he released seemed drugged or dying...

But it was a great and memorable day, if not a tad uncomfortable. Apart from the Stones there was a great line up of current British contemporary rock bands, but the band that attracted me most were *King Crimson*. I began to listen to them and buy their records, especially their debut studio album *In the Court of the Crimson King* (subtitled *An Observation by King Crimson*). I bought the album and played it endlessly, and then in 1974 they delivered a real gem, *Starless and Bible Black*, which used a Dylan Thomas phrase, from the opening of *Under Milk Wood*, as its title. Not only that, but the album artwork was also by a favourite artist – Tom Phillips (of Humument fame). The track itself is a long, live, prog-rock improvisation. Their next album, *Red*, had a track which contains a song called "*Starless*", which does contain the phrase "*Starless and bible black*"

John Cale

Perhaps, of all modern musicians, John Cale is the one you would most expect to respond to Dylan Thomas. It should come as no surprise that Dylan Thomas has been a major influence on this fellow Welshman. Cale was born in the small Welsh village of Garnant, just a dozen miles west of Dylan Thomas's hometown Swansea. Unlike Dylan Thomas, growing up Cale only spoke his native Welsh at home and only learned English at primary school, aged 7. His natural gift for music revealed itself early on; he played the organ in a local church and at 13 took up the viola and joined the National Youth Orchestra of Wales. This led him to study music at Goldsmiths College, London, where he began to veer towards more experimental and avant-garde music, becoming associated with *Fluxus*. Then this classically trained violinist turned to rock music and left Wales for America, where in 1964, he co-founded *The Velvet Underground* with Lou Reed, the hugely influential band that Andy Warhol conjured up in his notorious New York City atelier, *The Factory*.

This is the quote to be found on the title page of Cale's wonderfully titled and brilliant memoir, What's Welsh for Zen;[20]

No man, however highly civilized
can listen for very long to African
drumming or Welsh hymn singing and retain his critical and self-conscious personality. Aldous Huxley

In the book, Cale reveals how, beyond African drumming and Welsh choral singing, a major influence, and the writer who shaped his appreciation for the written word, was Dylan Thomas.

Cale writes:

> I wanted to write an opera on Dylan Thomas's life. When you grow up in Wales, you can't skip Dylan Thomas. At school we were taught that he used his English the way other poets used their Welsh. In Welsh you can express a lot with only a few words. He was someone to identify with, a contrast with the strict Presbyterian community in Wales, with his sense of humour – God knows he needed it... I had imitated the Thomas style in grammar school and was a little afraid of it. The poems seemed to carry so much baggage with them and the language made was daunting enough. I worked very freely, chose a poem and started to play...

Cale played with the Velvets for about a decade before the band slowly broke up and he began to pursue solo projects, and it was then that his interest in Dylan Thomas began to emerge in his work. Cale's first attempt to "borrow" from Dylan Thomas appeared on his stunning album, *Paris 1919* (1973), on which he was backed by two members of Little Feat, Lowell George and Richie Hayward. The album included a track entitled *A Child's Christmas in Wales*, taking its title and borrowing words from Dylan Thomas's original broadcast. After a long gap, Cale returned to Dylan Thomas, when, in 1989, he released *Words for the Dying*, his eleventh studio album. Though it contains a few short orchestral and piano pieces, it has more to do with words than music, much of which was written by Cale seven years earlier, during and in response to the Falklands War. The centrepiece of the album is a cycle of four songs called *The Falklands Suite*, the words for which were taken from four different Dylan Thomas poems, with his famous villanelle *Do not go gentle into that good night* at the centre (produced and arranged by Brian Eno). The idea was to memorialize those aboard the British ship *Sheffield*. The only addition to Thomas's words was a reference, at the end of *Lie Still, Sleep Becalmed*, to the 'drowned of

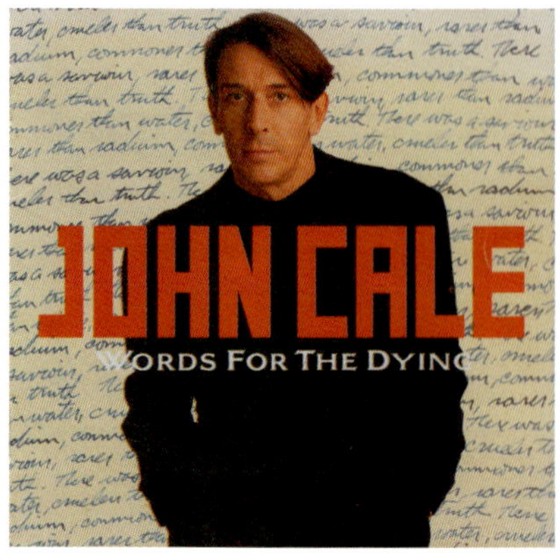

Falklands.' The sombre funereal tone of the words and slow emotional crescendos of Cale's music enhanced by an orchestra and children's choir, are offered as a stark and poignant response to Margaret Thatcher, the sabre-rattling PM, who'd provoked the stupendously stupid and pointless conflict fought over a faraway group of mostly desolate windswept islands off of the coast of Argentina.

Ralph McTell

This blues and country, virtuoso guitar-player and singer-songwriter is known mainly for his one, timeless, classic hit, *Streets of London*; a modern-day folk song, written by, and first recorded by Ralph on his1969 album *Spiral Staircase*. It was not released in the United Kingdom as a single until 1974. (Ralph himself has noted that there were 212 known recorded versions of the song). The song was McTell's greatest commercial success, reaching No. 2 in the UK charts, at one point selling 90,000 copies a day and winning him the 1974 Ivor Novello Award for Best Song. But there is much more to Ralph than this, not least that he is still touring as a solo artist as he enters his young eighties! But more to the point; he is scholar of Blues and Country Music; an avid reader and collector of books; and one of his most favourite authors is – Dylan Thomas.

This deep interest led him to read the biographies of Dylan Thomas and many of the books by him. This interest in linking his love of Dylan's life and poetry to his music eventually led, in 1992, to a BBC commission to write and make a radio broadcast of a richly poetic song cycle, *The Boy with A Note*, that dramatised in songs and short narrative sections the poet's short but very full life. Ralph's subtitle was *An Evocation of the Life of Dylan Thomas in Words and Music*. The broadcast went ahead with the help of actors Michael Elphick, Nerys Hughes and Bob Kingdom, and with musical arrangements by Graham Preskett.

The piece was very well received and Ralph wanted to release the recording as a CD, but contractual problems meant this couldn't happen so Ralph re-recorded the whole piece, and he took Michael Elphick's part. It was released on McTell's Leola label as an album, sold well, and still does.

Ralph is very proud of this ambitious piece:

"Two or three years went into that," he said. " It's grown-up work'

It was only a few years before he arrived in Swansea to perform it in the Dylan Thomas Centre.

Once again it was a big success. I got to meet Ralph and we struck up an immediate friendship which developed with his frequent return visits. He became a gentle but keen customer and I am proud to have developed his Dylan Thomas collection.

In return, when I was chair of the Dylan Thomas Society in 2014, Ralph was our main guest at the Society's annual birthday dinner, and after the special centenary wreath-laying event at Poet's Corner in Westminster Abbey, Ralph played a special gig for us all at the after-celebration in the crypt of St Martins in the Field: both were very memorable occasions.

Robin Williamson

Well-known as a founder member of the avant-garde folk-rock group, *The Incredible String Band*, Robin Williamson engaged with Dylan Thomas on two occasions. In 1981 he wrote and recorded an album, *Songs of Love and Parting*, which included a track in tribute to Dylan Thomas, *For Mr. Thomas*. This song got much more notice when soulful Irish blues singer/jazz superstar Van 'the Man' Morrison covered the song on his double-album *The Philosophers Stone*, which came out in 1998. Here are Robin's Lyrics:

From faded newsprint used to wrap a fish
Inscrutably the muse selects your face
As I sit drinking namelessly in a nameless bar
Five thousand miles and thirty years away

With all the usual ceremonial you were crowned one night
King of the field where doctors nail the cows
To make of the cock's quill the rights of language
And the pricking heart a sword against the hours
Let smirking scholars writhe in their favoured bondage
To hold you plaintiff to the charge of art
Exhibit A: He falls on legendary lines
Singing mother I want a bullet in the heart

The judge in me sucks eggs and jerks the sacred meat
For the boy in me still dreams in Milk Wood town
Like two provincial bastards playing the galleries
I hold your photo to the mirror upside down
Ah, Mr. Thomas, let us ramble through the midnight fair
Let us throw old bottles at the ferris wheel
Let us paint library on the library, let us raid the moonlight
Let us steal away whatever we are supposed to steal

In 2000 Robin Williamson returned to Dylan Thomas with his first solo album on ECM records *The Seed-At-Zero* which sets poetry by Dylan Thomas to music, but it also examines Thomas's relationship to the Bardic tradition of visionary Welsh poets including Henry Vaughan, Llywarch Hen and Taliesin. Williamson who was then living in Cardiff was very interested in what he refers to as wrought language, and he too came to the Dylan Thomas Centre and performed these settings of poetry to music.

The Coral

In 1996, a bunch of six musical, Scouse scallywags got together on the Wirral on Merseyside and formed a band – *The Coral*. They became the front-runners in a second wave of the *Liverpool Sound*. Their first LP, eponymously titled *The Coral* was well received, but they really broke through in 2003, with the release of their hugely successful second album, *Magic and Medicine*.

This album alone produced four UK Top 20 hit singles. The main songwriter was the guitarist and singer James Skelly, and he was responsible for the song that I was happy to discover – track 6, *Milkwood Blues*. The lyrics are not genius, but it's a catchy tune and there is no doubt as to its inspiration:

Saw myself through another's eyes
What did I see to my surprise?
Nuts and bolts, rows of shops
Black Crow nights and chimney tops
And one too many sad songs

Bible black and captain cat
Keeps the world inside his hat
With deep dry wells and cockled shells
He holds his wife beneath his paws.

Katy Moffatt

A touch of American country and western now. When I was a regular exhibitor at the big antiquarian book fairs across America, one of my favourite and loyal ever-returning customers

was the acknowledged greatest card-manipulator and magician/entertainer and later movie-actor – author and bibliographer – Ricky Jay. Moreover, Ricky was also the greatest collector of books, manuscripts, ephemera and printed broadsides concerning stage magic, card-sharping, swindlers, confidence-tricksters, mountebanks and freak-shows (genuine and fake) around at the time. We became friends and I enjoyed good business with him. When he did a run at the Old Vic in 1999, he invited me to the show – *Ricky Jay & His 52 Assistants* (aka his deck of cards) – a spellbinding night and I was invited backstage to meet with Ricky – with another member of the very small audience – John Cleese...

Ricky was well aware of, and empathised with, my obsession with collecting the be-all and end-all of Dylan Thomas memorabilia, and so one time, in the late nineties, at the Los Angeles Book Fair, Ricky was keen to tell me of a good friend of his who he wanted me to meet – a Texan country singer-songwriter named Katy Moffatt, who also had a thing about Dylan Thomas. She had co-written a song inspired by the American Poet Kenneth Rexroth's tribute poem *Thou Shalt Not Kill*[21]. Rexroth described Dylan in his poem as 'the sparrow of Cardiff, the canary of Swansea'. Katy Moffatt went with *Sparrow Of Swansea (For Dylan Thomas)*, which she recorded on her 1996 album *Midnight Radio*. Ricky gave me a copy of Katy's CD which I still have ...

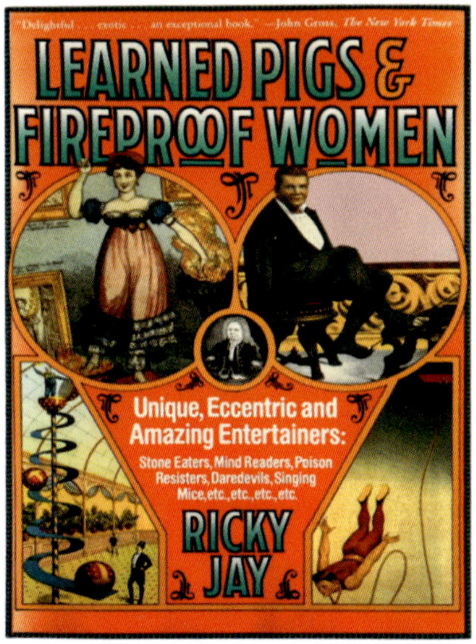

One of Ricky's many wonderful publications, all based on his own collection

A decade back, Katy Moffat toured the UK and had a gig in a small coffee shop in the Uplands, Swansea, not far from Dylan Thomas' birthplace. We did manage a long phone-call but I was away chasing book sales when she passed through town. Here are the last verses of her song...

In the White Horse Tavern
On a bleak New York Evening
The Sparrow Of Swansea
Was wounded in flight
He took eighteen straight shots
From a barrel of whiskey
His Caitlin lies weeping
In the Southwest of Wales

Oh, see how he flies, the Sparrow of Swansea
The Sparrow of Swansea, see how he sails
O'er the snail-horned churches
O'er the three-legged horses
Through the grey misty mornin's
In the Southwest of Wales
Through the grey misty mornin's
In the Southwest of Wales

Nick Cave &The Bad Seeds

Born on September 22, 1957, in Warracknabeal, a small town in Victoria, Australia, Nicholas Edward Cave embarked on a path that would lead him to become an emblematic figure in music. Cave's early exposure to literature and music, especially the works of Dylan Thomas and Leonard Cohen, deeply influenced his artistic development. In *Nick Cave and the Bad Seeds*'2002 song *There She Goes, My Beautiful World*, Cave sings:

Dylan Thomas/he died drunk/in St. Vincent's Hospital
Karl Marx squeezed his carbuncles

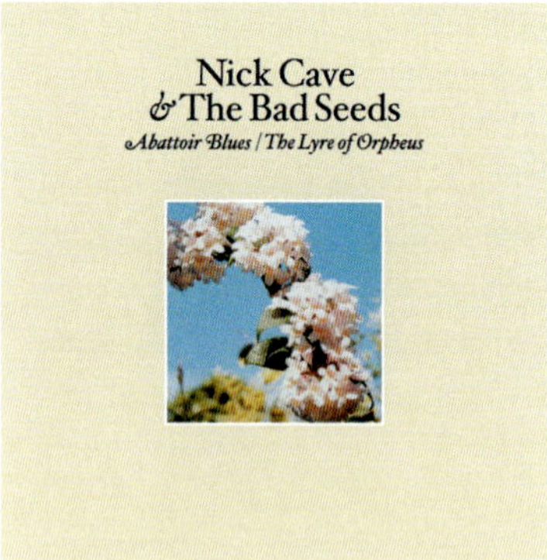

While writing Das Kapital
And Gauguin, he buggered off, man
And went all tropical

While Philip Larkin stuck it out
In a library in Hull
And Dylan Thomas died drunk in
St. Vincent's hospital.

I will kneel at your feet, I will lie at your door
I will rock you to sleep, I will roll on the floor
And I'll ask for nothing, nothing in this life
I'll ask for nothing, give me everlasting life

I just want to move the world
I just want to move the world
I just want to move the world
I just want to move

Hansonis

I am not sure now how I came across this German musician – Michael Hansonis, who obviously had a thing for Dylan Thomas. I was immediately intrigued by the mischievous, catchy, and alliterative title, of his 2003 CD – *Drink and Drive with Dylan Thomas*. I was well aware that although he had many faults; Dylan Thomas did not drive sober or drunk.

Once I had obtained a copy of *Drink and Drive with Dylan Thomas*, I discovered that it was more than just a catchy title. No-less than six tracks set Dylan Thomas poems to music – including some lesser known poems such as *Last night I dived my beggar arm, Paper and Sticks*, which Dylan himself took out of his *Collected Poems* at the second proof stage. All I could discover about him was this translated German wiki page:

> **Michael Hansonis**, earliest musical influences include Marc Bolan, John Lee Hooker and Bob Dylan. He first gained experience as a street musician, and in the early 80s as a session musician in the occupied Stollwerck chocolate factory in Cologne. In 1985 he became the singer of the pop formation Les Immer Essen. The band released just one album, "Tally Ho", and reached a top 40 position with the single Hand-Take. In 1988 Hansonis founded the independent rock band King Candy and released four albums by 1994. The band has toured several times with the Australian indie band Go-Betweens, whose member Robert Forster covered Hansonis' song Bird on his 1992 solo album "I Had a New York Girlfriend". Hansonis also writes German lyrics and songs, including the music for the title song of the album "Sohn aus dem Volk" for Gunter Gabriel. In the 1990s, after studying acting privately, he turned to theatre. Until 2002, he was a permanent ensemble member at the Horizont Theatre in Cologne. In 2004, he released his highly acclaimed album "Drink And Drive With Dylan Thomas" with texts by the Welsh poet Dylan Thomas set to music. Michael Hansonis also works as an audio book narrator.

LSD March

LSD March are a Japanese psychedelic rock group, hailing from the city of Himeji, led by singer and guitarist Shinsuke Michishita. The group is named after a track by Krautrock group GURU GURU. Michishita has also played with Magura Mozart and Doodles.

I have no idea why this Japanese outfit chose to use a Dylan Thomas title for their 2007 album of psychedelic rock music – *heavy riffage* – no less.

The new LSD March album Under Milk Wood is their first full-length since 2007's Constellation of Tragedy for Important Records. With grace (in the rock sense), style, humour & the perfect touch of heavy riffage, this tremendously unique and original recording is a classic of the new Japanese underground.

Under Milk Wood is a fascinating ghostly rock album replete with clean, untreated restraint and the grounded calm compliments of Takahashi Ikuro's drumming. Not until midway through the record does the heavy riffage begin – though it is slowly buried beneath the white blizzard blanket that is the remainder of the album. Much critical praise awaits this fine album and it's likely to become your favourite snowstorm record, too. Let the electric snow fall. Recorded by Richard Horner at Black Snowflake Sound in Japan. Photographs by Abe Maki & layout by Darryl Norsen.

Eggs Laid By Tigers

This highly original and eccentric Danish band are my go-to favourites for setting Dylan Thomas words to music. They got together in 2009 and were made up of Jonas Westergaard, bass, piano and vocals, Peter Bruun, drums, guitar and vocals, and Martin Ullits Dahl, guitar, vocals. This is the main trio but when the full band perform, they are joined by four extra musicians: Simon Toldam (piano), Jimmy Nyborg (trumpet), Anders Banke (saxophones)and Jacob Munck (trombone). The band bases most of their music on the words of Dylan Thomas. They took their surreal band name from a phrase that Dylan Thomas used when he was writing about his early attempts at writing poems:

Their second album, *This Red-Eyed Earth*

> I wrote endless imitations, though I never thought them to be imitations but, rather, wonderfully original things, like eggs laid by tigers.[22]

The band has played here in Swansea, and on both occasions it was it was during the annual *Do Not Go Gentle Festivals*. For the first festival they stayed in Dylan Thomas' birthplace and played nearby in *The Garage*, an old-school venue in the Uplands. They returned in 2014 to be part of the DT100 celebrations. They played again in the Garage, Uplands but they also joined the vast throng of artists, celebrities, school-kids and ordinary folk who participated on the stage at the Grand Theatre Swansea, as part of Michael Bogdanov's remarkable, DYLATHON – A 36-hour, non-stop performance of Dylan's entire major canon.[23] The band have made two albums of Dylan Thomas material often opting to set some of Dylan's most difficult and surreal poems to voices and instruments, (on the second album I was only familiar with three of the 11 poems included!) Both albums come with magnificent sleeve art, which feature clever and elaborate Arcimboldo-esque collage portraits of Dylan.

Recordings of *Do Not Go Gentle Into That Good Night*

This magnificent, but nowadays, somewhat ubiquitous, oft-recited poem has spawned many versions. Little did Dylan know when he wrote this villanelle in 1951, for his father who was losing his sight and would soon die, how it would enter into our national consciousness to such a degree. Dylan sent the poem to his last great generous patron – Princess Marguerite Caetani, the owner and editor of the European literary journal, *Botteghe Oscure*, for her to publish. In his covering letter he wrote:

I have just finished the short poem I enclose…
The only person I can't show the little poem to is,
of course, my father, who does not know he's dying.

Although it is a great *poem* and not a *song*, it seems to have become a thing for famous musicians and actors to record their own spoken word versions of it. The holy trinity of Port Talbot-born, Welsh actors Richard Burton, Anthony Hopkins and Michael Sheen, have all recorded it, and recently another fine Cardiff born Welsh actor has joined their ranks. The poem itself features in the science fiction movie *Interstellar* read line by line by various great movie thespians. Various rock and pop musicians have also felt the need to have a stab at it, although a few used a very blunt knife…

In 1986 **Holly Johnson** the songwriter and singer with his band *Frankie Goes to Hollywood* released their second album *Liverpool*. The first single from the album was a pacy powerful song – Rage Hard which was inspired by Dylan's famous villanelle, the chorus refrain repeats this phrase:

Into the light
(Rage Hard) Doing it right, doing it right
(Rage hard) Against the dark

Donovan Track 11, *Do not go gentle*

When asked to explain the song by a journalist, Holly Johnson replied:

Have you read the poem *Do Not Go Gently Into That Good Night* by Dylan Thomas? It was kind of inspired by that. It's an incantation against death and lethargy and it's supposed to encourage lots of creative idealism in the listener.

I don't think you could say it better than that – I always had a soft spot for Holly Jonson…

As we entered the new century a global figure came to Wales. **President Bill Clinton**[24] came to the Hay Literary Festival and delivered the keynote BBC Wales World Lecture in which he gently misquotes Dylan's Do Not Go Gentle… And before him *President Jimmy Carter* had named it as his favourite all time poem.

Back to Music and in 2004, the sixties folkie Donovan recorded a version on his album *Beat Café*. In 2019 the gravel voiced aging wild punk rocker – Iggy Pop recorded his version on his ambient album *Free*.

And a final offering; in the last years of his eventful life, notorious cannabis drug-baron Howard Marks was down on his luck, a tad skint and dealing with serious health problems. Various friends rallied round to help and various projects were mooted to help him through tough times. One such scheme was to release, on vinyl, an LP of Howard reading Dylan Thomas. It was not a totally crazy idea; Howard was a well-educated Welsh boy from Kenfig Hill, just east of Swansea, and on his release from jail he was a popular regular at the annual Laugharne Weekend Festival. This green transparent disc duly appeared in

2016. Sadly it did little to help Howard who succumbed to a nasty cancer that year.

Finally, Although not an actual recording, I feel I must mention that Bob Dylan gave a plain and straight forward reading of *Do not go Gentle*...on one of his *Theme Time Radio Shows*. It comes at the very end of the programme themed *Death and Taxes* (episode 49. First Broadcast April II, 2007). Earlier in the programme he reads two other poems: an e e cummings poem, *dying is fine) but death*. He introduces it by declaring Cummings is;

...for my money the most profound poet of the 20th Century.

Then after reading Dorothy Parker's poem Resume, he comments;

Wise words from Dorothy Parker.

Dylan reads it after playing Richard and Linda Thompson's song *Withered and Died*. This was his very curt introduction to his reading of the poem has no praise or comment;

***Poet Dylan Thomas wrote the following for his Father who was dying*;**

If you are prepared to invest in a diligent search on the internet you can hear Bob's gravely rendition...

*　　*　　*　　*　　*

Manic Street Preachers

Let us close this non-exhaustive round-up back here in Wales with Blackwood's finest, *The Manics*. Their 2018 album, *Resistance is Futile*, a very *Manics* – sounding title, like a *Situationist* slogan, but it appears to be attributed to some evil aliens in *Star Trek*. The album features a track about the marriage of *Dylan & Caitlin* Thomas, written by Nicky Wire from a first-person perspective, titled Dylan & Caitlin. The first person would appear to be Caitlin Thomas. The track was to be the third single and was released as download in March 2018. It is a duet between singer James Dean Bradfield and the band The Anchoress[25]. It stands out as one of a few times Nicky Wire wrote a lyric about some

> I wanted to write something a bit character-based, which isn't really me. The extreme love and extreme hate that can take part in a relationship from both sides. You know us as a band, we've always felt a duty to pass on things that we think are more interesting than we are...

1. Daniel Jones: *My Friend Dylan Thomas*. Dent.1977. There is more on Daniel Jones in Chapter 11.

2. Dan suggests this might have inspired Dylan's later *Under Milk Wood* invention – *Llareggub – Bugger All*, backwards!

3. Dan also adds that when Dylan later met Stravinsky, the great composer asked Dylan 'What is your favourite music' to which Dylan replied innocently *Il Trovatore*.

4. Robert Manno and his wife came to Swansea in 1995, and I met them in my bookstore in the Dylan Thomas Centre. We stayed in touch, and he sent me a copy of his finished opera which is now in the Dylan Thomas collection at National Library of Wales, Aberystwyth.

5. See Chapter 17. Peter Blake and *Under Milk Wood*.

6. Dylan Thomas would eventually write his own saucy song for the climax of *Under Milk Wood*, when Mr. Waldo sings with gusto the *Chimbly Sweeps Song*. In the rousing chorus the kind young women entreat the poor sweep to:
   Come and sweep my chimbley
   Bring along your chimbley brush!
   The exclamation mark is a hint towards the song's sexual double-entendre.

7. For more on Charles see Chapter 11.

8. This sketch book is now part of the Dylan Thomas Exhibition in the Swansea's Dylan Thomas Centre, which is based largely on my *Word and Image* Exhibition – See Chapter 3.

9. The Art of the Beat Generation (1959) in *The Alternative Society*. New York. Herder. 1970.

10. This essay can be found in Dylan Thomas *A Centenary Celebration*. Bloomsbury 2014.

11. LeRoi Jones later changed this, his slave name, to the African name, Amitri Baraka This quote is from his play, *Dutchman*.

12. Jack Kerouac *Letters to Allen Ginsberg*. Edited by Bil Morgan and David Stanford. Penguin 2011.

13. Dylan Thomas Remembered. Dylan Thomas Society. 1978.

14. In 2002 I invited Babara Cohen to Swansea and interviewed her in front of a packed auditorium in The Dylan Thomas Centre. On Dylan's death in 1953 the two founders of the label heard of the plan by Dylan's friends led by Vernon Watkins and Sculptor Ron Cour to erect a memorial to him in Cwmdonkin Park. They decided that as a token of thanks they would foot the bill. I once owned the telegram they sent to Vernon; "Re. Memorial Stone. stop. Will cover all costs. Stop. Caedmon Records. Stop."

15. In the interest of full disclosure, I must confess to being named as CONSULTANT on this release – albeit on the bottom of the box.

16. I acted for the National Library of Wales at a Sotheby's auction a few decades back and bought on their behalf 33 letters From Dylan Thomas to Desmond Hawkins – and a very interesting correspondence it is too.

17. The rest of Hawkins' literary archive recently surfaced with a London Bookseller, and I acquired a missing letter and the original collaged portrait that Dylan sent with it, and which Hawkins includes in his book.

18. Chapter 13. Dylan Thomas, Leon Atkin & Heathcote Williams.

19. More on this in Chapter 17. On Sir Peter Blake.

20. *What's Welsh for Zen: Autobiography of John Cale* edited by Victor Bockris. Bloomsbury.

21. For more on Rexroth's poem see Chapter 12.

22. This quote is from Dylan's essay known as his *Poetic Manifesto*, which consisted to his responses to nine questions set to him by a young American student in Laugharne in neat nine-page holograph manuscript, which was first published in facsimile in *A Garland for Dylan Thomas*, edited by George Firmage and published in 1963.

23. I worked with Michael on this stupendous event. Michael was a very good customers who became a very good friend He asked me to compile/write the dramaturge for the whole weekend of performances so I was in the theatre the whole time often having to add-in extra materials and often having to go on stage and perform them. I loved every minute of it.

24. I can forgive Clinton but I was horrified just a week or so back when heard Israel's President Netanyahu on live TV news utilise this magnificent poem in a hideous justify stance towards all his neighbouring countries.

25. The Anchoress is the stage name of Welsh-born multi-instrumentalist, songwriter and author Catherine Anne Davies. Davies was born in Glynneath, Wales but at 10 weeks old was taken to Australia with her parents before returning to the UK at the age of Anchoress as her stage persona in 2013. She has joined the *Manics* live onstage a few times now.

Cerys' Dylan Thomas CD with a coloured up image from my collection as the cover.

16.

Dylan Thomas: Cerys Matthews & Colin Edwards.

It sometimes feels like Dylan Thomas was always present in my life we shared the same view of the crescent-shaped Swansea bay.
Cerys writing in Her Dylan Thomas CD in 2014

Cool Cymru** (Welsh: **Cŵl Cymru**) was a Welsh cultural movement in music and independent film in the 1990s and 2000s, led by the popularity of bands such as **Stereophonics, Gorky's Zygotic Mynci, Manic Street Preachers, **Catatonia** ***and Super Furry Animals.***

That's from Wiki, and that is a cracking line up of Welsh bands. If you were living in Wales back in the last decades of the last century and you were interested in popular culture, then you would know something about Cerys Matthews. She was born in Cardiff but grew up in Swansea where she went to Bryn Y Mor Welsh language school until 11 years of age. She then attended St Michaels School Llanelli until her family moved west to the village of Trefin in Pembrokeshire and there she attended Ysgol Bro Gwaun comprehensive school. Then she spent some time at school back here in Swansea. This varied education left her liberal, well versed and speaking fluent English, Welsh, Spanish, and French. She says that her childhood heroes were Pippi Long Stocking and the writers Yeats, and who else but Dylan Thomas! She also had a musical bent and learned guitar and had begun to sing Welsh folk songs.

This last led her into the world of rock and pop and she ended up fronting, playing guitar and co-writing songs for the hugely successful Welsh band – *Catatonia*. She was described as the Welsh equivalent of New York's Debbie Harry, who fronted the band *Blondie*: and that is no mean comparison. Catatonia formed in 1990 and was a major part of the popular music soundtrack of the ensuing decade, having numerous chart hits and albums; the standout being *International Velvet*. That album alone sold more than 900,000 copies in 22 months, being certified triple platinum by the *British Phonographic Industry*.

What set them apart from many other bands was the cheeky wordplay that infused their songs, mainly co-written by Cerys and Mark Roberts, who was the guitarist and co-founder. Here are just two examples from *International Velvet*. The song *Mulder and Scully* makes direct reference to FBI special agents Fox Mulder and Dana Scully (played by actors David Duchovny and Gillian Anderson) the two main characters of the hugely popular sci-fi TV series *The X-Files* who work on cases linked to the paranormal. Although the title and refrain reference this hugely popular show, the song has little to do with the two characters. Instead, the reference to Mulder and Scully is a metaphor for a relationship being so "strange" that it could be "a case for Mulder and Scully", This is the chorus:

Things are getting strange, I'm starting to worry
This could be a case for Mulder and Scully
Things are getting strange, now I can't sleep alone

And the song *Road Rage* makes use of a phrase[1] that had only recently entered our speech as the lyrical hook for the song:

Cause you and I know it's all over the front page
You give me road rage racing through the best days
It's up to you boy you're driving me crazy
Thinking you may be losing your mind.

Catatonia songs use verbal and media terms in their songwriting in a similar way that Pop artists, such as Peter Blake, use rich visual images from popular culture to create their *Pop Art* collages.

Such was the attention and popularity of the band and particularly their charismatic singer that a book[2] appeared just focusing on her and the surrounding phenomena.

It's a lively read and leaves not a pebble unturned, documenting every step in the band's rise in 1990 and eventual break up in late 2001.

Although I was familiar with a lot of this, I did not meet Cerys until around 2008. By then she had left the excesses and stresses of being in a rock band behind and had transformed herself into a solo artist. She released her first album, *Cockahoop*, in 2003.

Her second album, *Never Said Goodbye* followed in 2006. She had also begun presenting on the radio and TV and around the time of our meeting she had begun to programme and host her own shows on BBC Radio 6 Music.

By this time I had been involved in numerous books, TV and radio documentaries about Dylan Thomas' life and work, sometimes as a consultant, sometimes as a contributor or sometimes sourcing images and artefacts from my holdings. Thus I was not surprised when in 2008 BBC2 got in touch and said they were going to be making a programme about Celtic Poetry and they wanted to visit my bookshop here in Swansea. It sounded interesting so I agreed. It then got more interesting when they explained it was to be an hour-long documentary from a four-part series called *My Life in Verse* and the episode they wanted to make would start in Swansea and would feature Cerys Matthews beginning her search to explore Celtic Verse. Now that sounded right up my street.

Telephone calls were made, and arrangements sorted, dates and times were agreed and presently, early one morning, a cameraman, a sound guy, a young director and the former Queen of Welsh popular music finally arrived at my bookstore. I had hastily tried to clear, order, cleanse and tidy the many book rooms, but the store was still a shambles. As it turned out, Cerys loved it, and the director decided he could work with it too. Lights and cameras were set up and the crew proceeded to film location shots while Cerys and I got acquainted.

She couldn't have been easier to get on with. She loved being in Wales and Swansea; she loved the shop; she loved the books, and we discovered we had many mutual favourite poets and writers.[3] Most importantly she loved Dylan Thomas. She had known of him in her Welsh schooldays but many years later when she was living near Nashville, she told me how she had found an American miniature edition of Dylan Thomas's classic *A Child's Christmas in Wales* with wonderful woodcut illustrations by Fritz Eichenberg.[4] The tiny book was fashioned to be used as a Christmas Tree decoration. Sadly she mourned its loss during her move back to Wales. However, I knew the book and when I was doing book fairs in the states I would buy it whenever I saw a copy. So I had a couple of copies, and I gave Cerys a new copy. I had been somewhat in awe of her, when she dived into my store but she was so enthusiastic and unpretentious and so thrilled to have the book again that I soon relaxed.

The American miniature Christmas Tree Decoration edition of *Child's Christmas*... the coin is to give a sense of scale

Eventually we sat at my book-strewn desk, and I began to go back and for to the shelves and bookcases, bringing over book after book of Welsh poetry, from the earliest; The Mabinogion and Dafydd ap Gwilym, not too many Victorians, but as she spoke Welsh, I found examples of nineteenth century Eisteddfodau Bards. Then on into the Twentieth Century, we went through all the Thomases – Edward, R.S. and of course Dylan. I talked and enthused, and she lapped it up and was ravished by the older leather-bound volumes and the signed and inscribed copies I pulled out. For me it was a very rewarding and memorable experience. And it was all caught on film. We talked at length about Dylan Thomas' place in Celtic poetry and I mentioned his close friend, Swansea's other major poet, Vernon Watkins. Vernon had lived longer than Dylan's tragic 39 years, but he died in 1967 in his early sixties. I had never met Vernon, but I was good friends with his widow Gwen, herself a great reader, critic and a writer too. We arranged that on the following day I would take Cerys and the crew down to Gwen's home in

Mumbles and Cerys could talk, interview and film her for the programme.

This was another memorable day as Gwen was soon captivated with Cery's openness and hungry enthusiasm. I sat quietly in the corner hanging on their every word. And then they left – for Cardiff, for York – they decided Ted Hughes and his love of Elmet[5] brought him into their Celtic remit; then Ireland and finally a Burns Night in Scotland, filming all the way. I had had a great couple of days and was looking forward to watching the finished documentary.

A month or so passed and then one day I got a call from Cerys. She was a tad hesitant and sounded somewhat discombobulated. I asked how the rest of the filming had gone and how the edit had gone. At that point she paused and then gently told me that all that had transpired in my bookshop had ended up 'on the cutting room floor' but that Gwen did get a few minutes. She was very apologetic, and quite beside herself. I was of course disappointed, but I've got broad shoulders, and I had enjoyed her visit to my bookshop immensely. Little did I know then that it was to be the start of a long and rich friendship.

I waited patiently for the programme to be broadcast and finally it was flagged up with this blurb:

In a personal journey across the British Isles, Cerys Matthews traces the evolving role of the poet in society from the earliest Welsh bards to the writers of Northern Ireland's Troubles, exploring the ways that poets have shaped Celtic identity. Starting in her native Swansea, Cerys immerses herself in the surreal vision of Dylan Thomas, retracing his steps and analysing his musical use of language. She moves on to Cardiff to explore the subversive, sensual poetry of 14th-century bard Dafydd ap Gwilym and the rich heritage of Welsh-language poetry. From there it is on to Yorkshire and Ted Hughes's vision of the ancient Celtic kingdom of Elmet[5]

Cerys has been collecting folk songs for decades, and many of her favourite songs come from Ireland. She travels to County Sligo on the wild west coast to explore the beautiful landscapes that inspired Ireland's great poet William Butler Yeats. In Belfast, she looks at the rich outpouring of poetry from Northern Ireland during the Troubles. Cerys ends her journey in Scotland with the joyous, exuberant work of Robert Burns, and discovers why Burns connects with readers all around the world. During her travels, Cerys reflects on the emotional impact of poetry on her own life and work, and on the power of words to change the course of history.

I watched the programme and I enjoyed it. I was a tad peeved not to have made the cut, but I did get a credit and Cerys and I stayed in touch and our friendship grew. We met in London a few times and I met her partner (and her new manager) Steve Abbott. A year or so later she very kindly and unexpectedly invited my wife and I to her and Steve's wedding. It was an amazing day in Cardiff; a quite splendid, quite gothic affair, with everything a good wedding needs; a great and moving bilingual ceremony, in a stunning Cardiff Baptist chapel, great singing as one would expect, a great reception, great company, great food and drink and of course wonderful music. This was how the front page of the local paper described the event:

CERYS MATTHEWS dodged the downpours yesterday as she dashed to church to marry her long-time boyfriend. The singer, who wore an elegant medieval-style black and ivory gown, tied the knot with her manager Steve Abbott during a bilingual ceremony in Cardiff. But while the service at the Tabernacle Welsh Baptist Chapel in the city centre may have been traditional, the newly-weds showed their quirky side by holding their wedding reception at the Glee Club in nearby Cardiff Bay. The rain showers, which had struck intermittently throughout the day, stopped before Cerys, 41, arrived at the church in a horse-drawn carriage, 15 minutes after the 4.15pm service was due to begin. She was accompanied by her young attendants, who included her children – Glenys Pearl Y Felin, seven, and five-year-old Johnny Tupelo Jones – also wearing medieval-style black and white outfits.

After that great day we were often in touch. Cerys had begun to do more TV work and was making regular short films for the *BBC's nightly, The One Show*. Whenever it was to do with Dylan Thomas, she would get me involved and we made a Dylan

Thomas Christmas film in *The Queens* – our favourite Swansea pub. But the most significant was the film we made in 2014, when we announced my discovery of a nano-second or two of moving footage[6] of Dylan Thomas – still the only moving footage of Dylan Thomas ever to be found. This film was very special for Cerys because it pretty much stemmed from the work of a favourite uncle of hers, Colin Edwards, but more about this remarkable man later.

In 2009 Cerys had joined BBC Radio 6[7] and before long had a regular three-hour show on Sunday mornings. It is still running, has regular huge listening figures and has won many accolades and awards. The program is an astonishing eclectic mix of music from all genres, originating from all parts of the globe, combined with live music sessions, great poetry readings, and curious and interesting guests who talk about anything and everything – from seaweed to global ethnic cookery, from church bells to discovering lost women writers and artists. She has invited me onto the programme a few times and we have talked about Beat Literature and Music, Allen Ginsberg and Wales, the history of the song *The Bells of Rhymney*, the First World War poet Edward Thomas. Oh, and that Dylan Thomas chap too.

After this, my chronological memory gets a tad hazy, but we remained good friends and began to see each other at various events. In 2013 Cerys and Steve had joined up with Charles Gladstone and his wife and the four of them created a new festival – *The Good Life Festival* – on the Gladstone Estate in north Wakles. Coincidentally this coincided with me acquiring an old decommissioned local Council Mobile Library vehicle and rebranding it *Dylans Mobile Bookstore*. Although Cerys invited me to bring my bus, I could not make it to their first festival in 2014 as we were too caught up in the Dylan Thomas Centenary celebrations, but we rocked up in 2015 and had wonderful fun at every festival and in all the succeeding years until my beloved Book Bus fell victim to Covid in 2023.

Steve Abbott, Cerys' partner, was always interested in all manner of cultural schemes. He's a Luton boy and very passionate about his hometown. He likes to think outside the box, so I was not too surprised when in 2016 he asked me to celebrate and curate a Beat Literature Exhibition in *The Hat Factory* arts centre in the middle of town, with an opening daylong celebration of all things *Beat*. I asked my good Swansea friend Simon Dark, an ace skateboarder and graffiti artist, to work with me and we did put on a pretty remarkable exhibition of Beat books, ephemera and posters based on my collection and Simon's original art. I worked hard on Ginsberg in London. Swansea academic and saxophonist professor Daniel Williams gave a lecture – *Black Breton: White Negro – Ideas of Race in Jack Kerouac's Writings* and then he played cool jazz late into the night. David Shulman, a London-based New York filmmaker talked with me and screened his film Allen Ginsberg and Guerilla TV; my friend Mike Garry, a dynamic performance poet, gave a great reading including a passionate rendition of *Saint Anthony*, his Mancunian celebration of his hero Tony Wilson, St. Anthony. The finale was quite wonderful; my Welsh actor friend, Ceri Murphy, gave a dazzling performance in recreating Ginsberg's first ever reading of *Howl*, with projected images from the graphic novel version of the poem screened large behind him. The whole event was a grand success for all who came, and Cerys was very supportive of the whole project.

Along the way Cerys has been constantly drawn back to Wales and more especially to the Wales of Dylan Thomas. So it did not surprise me when she told me she was working on a CD of spoken word poetry of Dylan Thomas with gentle musical settings. Fine words with music; what a wonderful combination. I was honoured when she asked me to provide some liner notes to go with the CD. Furthermore, many years prior I had bought a tiny picture of the schoolboy Dylan Thomas photographed with Nancy, his elder sister, down on Swansea bay. I remember buying it from Dylan's friend, Mervyn Levy, at the Café Royal in London where I was exhibiting books – Mervyn was acting on behalf of Aeronwy, Dylan's daughter. Mervyn and I became good friends and did all sorts of business together. It was a dazzling and incredibly rare little image. The original was black and white… This is how it came to me:

And this was the image that Cerys wanted for her CD cover; but first she got her tech genius to colour it up. The finished version is the opening illustration to this chapter. The CD was released to coincide with the Dylan Thomas Centenary in 2014.In the accompanying booklet Cerys writes:

It sometimes feels like Dylan Thomas was always present in my life – we shared the same view of the crescent-shaped Swansea bay, and my uncle Colin Edwards amassed the largest amount of interviews on him, starting in the years following Dylan's tragic death in New York City. Colin would talk to us about him for hours, and it wasn't long before I too fell for his magical, maverick voice. 'The world is never the same place once a good poem has been added to it'. Said Dylan, who never prefaced his readings with explanations, but rather with a simple 'I am going to read aloud now'. Reading his work aloud, feeling those syllables roll around your mouth with the rhythms finding their own ebb and flow is one of life's greatest pleasures. In Welsh (and similarly in Somali) there is only one word to cover both music and poetry – the powerful, transformative qualities of each have always led me to treat them both with a similar approach. I often hear music when I read great writing, especially Dylan's, which is so infused with melody and rhythm, and so the idea for this project was born. Jeff Towns, chairman of the Dylan Thomas Society, and owner of the one and only Dylan Thomas Mobile Book Bus has written the notes on the poems, excerpts and short story released in this double album and also generously shares with us some of his wonderful collection of Dylan Thomas photographs and illustrations. Choosing the works presented here seemed to come naturally, some are familiar, some more obscure. As for 'A Child's Christmas in Wales? Well, I've always loved the matrimony of music and narration in Prokofiev's Peter and the Wolf and dreamed, many years ago, that A Childs Christmas should also dance with music. Together with composer and arranger Mason Neely from Chattanooga, I began working toward this goal. With the help of some of the country's leading players and soloists – Catrin Finch on harp, Alice Neary on cello, and David Adams on violin, we made this a reality. Tiger eggs[8] *indeed.*

Cerys had chosen her favourites, and I then provided these brief background sleeve notes, as well as a finding more interesting and unusual illustrations from my collection to enrich the sleeve notes.

A Childs Christmas. Side 1

Dylan Thomas first introduced us to his vision of the ideal Christmas on BBC radio's *Children's Hour* in December 1945, but even by then his reputation had 'Uncle' Derek McCulloch somewhat nervous about just what his unsuspecting youthful listeners might expect; 'There is a tremendous risk... he is notoriously tricky' he wrote before the broadcast. But his fears were unfounded, and the program was well received. Dylan too realised he was on to a winner and over the next few years revisited, revamped and most importantly – re-sold various versions of the text.

This first radio version was called '*Memories of Christmas*' and was first published as that in the '*Listener*' in 1945. A year later it was republished in Keidrych Rhys's *Wales* magazine. A couple of years later he extracted the middle section of the piece, re-titled it 'Conversation about Christmas' and sold it to Picture Post for their 1947 Christmas issue. Next, he thought to try it in America, which was to prove the most receptive audience. Upon his arrival in America, he amalgamated both earlier versions, added a bit more and sold the piece yet again to *Harper's Bazaar,* with the new title – *A Child's Memories of Christmas in Wales* for their 1950 Christmas issue. He was paid a handsome, and much needed $300! And it was this magazine that was procured when he was making his first and groundbreaking recording for Caedmon Records in New York in February 1952. The poems he had chosen to read only filled one side of the proposed LP, but Dylan recalled the magazine piece, and a copy was hastily and luckily obtained. Dylan gave a particularly animated and lively rendition of his story which established this new spoken word recording phenomena and, in selling millions of copies, spread Dylan's name around America and the world.

Under Milk Wood. Side 2

Under Milk Wood had a long and sometimes tortured gestation stretched over some thirty years. Dylan first mentioned his idea about a play set in a small Welsh village which poetically described the vagaries of the curious inhabitants to his early Swansea friend and mentor, the 'communist grocer' Bert Trick. Bert recalls in an interview with the Canadian broadcaster Colin Edwards, Dylan visiting them at their holiday chalet at Swansea's Caswell Bay in 1932 and outlining his plans for the play set in a Welsh seaside village and reading them early drafts of an embryonic *Milk Wood*:

He read it to Nell and me in our bungalow at Caswell around the old Dover stove, with the paraffin lamps lit at night ... the story was then called Llareggub, which was a mythical village in South Wales, a typical village, with terraced houses with one ty bach to about five cottages, and the various characters coming out and emptying the slops and exchanging greetings and so on; that was the germ of the idea which ... developed into Under Milk Wood.

A decade later and Dylan was explaining to his Laugharne friend, the author Richard Hughes, that what he thought Laugharne folk needed was a play about themselves. For a while this play was to be about a village that stayed sane when the rest of the war-mongering world went mad except that the bigger world sealed off the village and declared all the inhabitants to be mad. But Dylan struggled with plot, and he resorted to taking his inspiration from his literary hero James Joyce and like his *Ulysses*, he shaped his play to depict just one day in the life of his eccentric Welsh village which he had called Llareggub (spell it backwards to get his cheeky joke). Another decade on and The Mad Town's idea had morphed into a radio play; *Under Milk Wood – A Play For Voices*, and it was hastily rushed to some kind of cobbled together completion minutes before its first full live performance at The Poetry Centre at 92nd Street Y, in New York city on May 14th 1953 by Dylan and a cast of five American actors, who together played the parts of some fifty-odd characters. And what a cast of wonderful characters they unleashed on the world that momentous night; thwarted lovers, vile perverts, simple cowgirls, blinkered ministers of religion, a gorgeous slutty gypsy,[9] a cannibal butcher, an incontinent policeman, ghostly sailors and their unseeing captain all lusting after a whore with a heart, Nogood Boyo and an over-inquisitive postman; and not forgetting sweet Mrs Cherry Owen who is so delighted with her habitual beer-swilling husband, who boasts,

I always say she's got two husbands. One drunk and one sober

and then she joyously declares,

And aren't I a lucky woman? Because I love them both.

In My Craft Or Sullen Art

Written in 1945, this poem is one of a group of shorter, more direct poems that moved away from the obscurity of the earlier poems. One of his editors, and critics, Ralph Maud, describes it as one of his 'most perfect poems' and wrote of it:

> I am sure that many lovers abed have read it to each other as Thomas knew they would. Beauty is Truth; romantics will see here portrayed the truest that a poet can be.

Should Lanterns Shine

Another poem from the early thirties, Dylan sent it to Geoffrey Grigson who included it in his magazine *New Verse* in 1935. It was poem No.2 of 'Three Poems' published in 1935. It was then included in his second book *25 Poems* (1936). In its original form as published in *New Verse* it had two extra lines as a last verse:

> *Regard the moon, it hangs above the lawn;*
> *Regard the lawn, it lies beneath the moon*

I for one am very glad he listened to his great friend in life and poetry, Vernon Watkins, who advised and persuaded him to drop them. Vernon writes,[10]

> *These two lines seemed to me to echo Eliot, and indirectly Lafforgue, and not belong to the poem, whereas the two previous lines, with their hidden nuances, made a fine autobiographical ending*
> *The Ball I threw while playing in the Park*
> *Has not yet reached the ground.*

These two lines are perhaps my favourite lines from all his poems.

Laugharne

BBC First Broadcast Nov 5th, 1953. On his first visit to Laugharne in 1934, Dylan wrote to Pamela Hansford Johnson describing the place as,

> *the strangest town in Wales... the nearest approach under the sun to a Stygian borough.*

His biographer Constantine Fitzgibbon wrote that Laugharne:

> *fitted Dylan like a single, eccentric, tattered glove.*

Laugharne was the title and subject of Dylan's last radio feature. It was recorded in Swansea in late October of 1953, when he stopped off in the town on his way to London on the first part of his ill-fated journey to America. With a cruel, ironic poignancy it was first broadcast live on November 5th from Laugharne school hall to a radio audience and the hall full of Laugharne locals, among whom was Caitlin Thomas. It was during the broadcast that the local policeman shuffled along the rows in the packed hall and delivered a telegram to Caitlin informing her that her husband was lying unconscious in a New York hospital.

Dylan Thomas never regained consciousness and was to die on November 9th.

But in his broadcast, Dylan is still celebrating his beloved Laugharne in all its eccentric glory, describing it as:

> *his timeless, beautiful, barmy (both spellings) town ...*
> *a legendary lazy little black-magical bedlam by the sea.*

Do not go gentle into that good night.

In 1949 Dylan moved his family into the Boat House at Laugharne. At the same time, he moved his aging parents, D.J. and Florrie into a house named The Pelican opposite his favourite pub, *Browns Hotel*, on the main street. His first and official Biographer Constantine Fitzgibbon, writes of this time,

> *When Dylan was home there was never a day when he did not go to see his father; to chat; to do the crossroad together and, so long as D.J. could cross the street; to drink a pint together in Browns.*

Thus, it was that Dylan was at hand to observe his father's slow decline, his gradual loss of sight and the general deterioration in his health. And this diurnal filial closeness prompted the great poem that is now used at so many funerals throughout the English-speaking world... In May 1951 when Dylan sent the poem to be published in the magazine, Botteghe Oscure, he included a note saying:

> *The only person I can't show the little poem enclosed to is,*
> *Of course, my father, who doesn't know he's dying.*

The hand that signed the paper.
This poem appeared in the same issue as *Should Lanterns Shine* as Poem No.1. It was also included in 25 *Poems*, but Dylan changes the first line of the last verse from *The hand counts* to *The five kings count* and he makes another change before it is printed in his Collected Poems (1952) where he changes another phrase in the last verse – pat the brow becomes *stroke the brow.*

Being but Men.
Dylan wrote this poem into one of his early notebooks on May 7th, 1932 (he was just 17) and there it would have stayed – unpublished anywhere in his own lifetime, had his close friend and sometime collaborator Daniel Jones not included it into his 1971 edition *The Poems of Dylan Thomas*. And a good choice it was too. It is another beautiful poem of longing for, and wonder at the innocence and joy of childhood – the word wonder is used three times in the short poem:

Children in wonder watching the stars,
And the wonder that man knows
Children in wonder watching the stars
Is the aim and the end.
This last line is quite wonderful.

Fern Hill.
First published in Cyril Connolly's *Horizon* magazine in 1945, *Fern Hill* was included in *Deaths and Entrances* (1946) before taking on a life of its own, being translated across the world and endlessly anthologised, read and enjoyed. Some folk even have lines from it tattooed on their bodies.[11] It is, along with *Do not go gentle into that good night*, Dylan's greatest poetic achievement.

It is a poem that Dylan was born to write, a poem celebrating the love and innocence of childhood, and it is interesting to note that Dylan wrote it soon after V-J day (15th August 1945) when the horrors of war were beginning to subside, and he could rekindle hope.

That Sanity be Kept.
One of Dylan's earliest published poems, it was his first poem to appear in the 'Poet's Corner' feature in *The Sunday Referee* in September 1933. It was not reprinted in any of Dylan's lifetime books, but it was reprinted in the memorial edition of *Adam* in 1953. It was the poem that prompted Pamela Hansford Johnson, another 'Poet's Corner' contributor, to write to Dylan and begin their courtship by mail, which developed into a serious relationship which almost resulted in marriage. Dylan wrote back to her a fuming but witty and impressive letter including some self-deprecation:

The more I think of my Referee Poem the less I like it. The idea of myself, sitting in the open window, in my shirt, and imagining myself as some Jehovah of the West, is really odd. If I were some Apollo, it would be different. As a matter of fact, I am a small person with much untidy hair.

And while flattering Ms Johnson he reveals his thoughts on contemporary poetry:

What I like about your poems is that they state, not contradict, that they create not destroy. Poem after poem, recording in sickening detail, the wrinkles on the author's naval, fill the contemporary journals, poem after poem recording none too clearly, the chaos of today. Out of chaos they make nothing, but them-selves part of the post-war carnage, fade away like dead soldiers.

The Hunchback in the Park.
One of Dylan's few poems rooted in a specific place and time. Dylan's close life-long friend, Daniel Jones tells us:

Cwmdonkin Park was a favourite haunt of truants from Swansea Grammar school because it was bordered on one side by a road that led directly to the school but sometimes didn't

The poem became a key closing section of his 1943 radio broadcast *Reminiscences of Childhood*. He had written the first draft of the poem in his second notebook in 1932 but revisited this draft and developed it in 1941. In effect he was 18 when he first wrote it but revised it almost a decade later. This was the last revision he made to his early notebooks – he would sell his four poetry notebooks to a London bookseller later in 1941 – they are now held in New York State University at Buffalo but in this Centenary Year (2014)[12] they were graciously loaned back to Wales where they were displayed in Swansea and Aberystwyth. The park-keeper was real enough. Dylan describes him in *Reminiscences* as:

> *an ancient keeper...was a tyrannous and whiskered snake in the grass one must keep off of.*

* * * * *

On the release of the CD Cerys invited me to join her at *Rough Trade East*, in the heart of my old stamping grounds in London's East End for the live launch. On the day, my car travelled up to London full of a fine bunch of Swansea no-good boyos, for a splendid and memorable evening of spoken words and fine music, followed by a fine Indian curry with Steve and Cerys!

Towards the end of a busy year, 2014, Cerys made a radio documentary for the BBC, *Cerys goes Under Milk Wood*. I was lucky enough to go with her some of the way and she put together a very informative programme. This is how the BBC flagged it up:

Onstage with Cerys at Rough trade East – nearest I've ever been to being in a band!

I can assure you I am speaking and NOT singing

Released On: 25 Oct 2014

Cerys Matthews unlocks an archive of rare interviews, made by her uncle Colin Edwards, with Dylan Thomas's closest friends and family. The recordings date from the early 1960s, a decade after the poet's death, when his reputation was becoming clouded by scandal. Cerys believed the recordings lost or destroyed. In fact, over a hundred hours of interviews were bequeathed to the National Library of Wales by her uncle's widow and some of them are broadcast here for the first time. This personal journey into the archive is both a celebration of the life of Dylan Thomas and a glimpse into the life of her uncle – 'an eccentric, radical journalist and filmmaker'. Here Cerys goes Under Milk Wood – into the communities in which Dylan Thomas lived. We hear Dylan's mother, Florence, describe how the eight-year-old Dylan would write poems about the kitchen sink. Dylan's school friend Charles Fisher recalls how he 'collected words like rare butterflies'. Dylan's daughter, Aeronwy, reflects on his daily rituals and drinking habits. One of his closest friends Bert Trick, a Marxist grocer from Swansea, describes Dylan's profane sense of humour. And we hear from theatre director Philip Burton and poet Robert Lowell about meetings with Dylan towards the end of his life. 'Listening to these tapes I started to understand the strange contradictions at the heart of Dylan Thomas. The boozer with the self-discipline to write verse, the child with a visionary voice, the buffoon who took life so seriously,' says Cerys. Some of Cerys's favourite Dylan Thomas poems and writings are set to music in the programme. Jeff Towns, Terry Jones, Andrew Lycett, Gwen Watkins and David Thomas also contribute.

This was the first time that Cerys really spoke about the remarkable coincidence that her equally remarkable and favourite uncle, Colin Edwards, had recently come to real prominence as a would-be Dylan Thomas biographer which would have been based on the vast archive of tape-recorded interviews with so many ordinary and extraordinary folk who all knew Dylan Thomas; but more about Colin below.

Cerys kept on coming up with new Dylan Thomas projects; A

ballet based on *A Child's Christmas in Wales* set to her and Mason Neely's music which she narrated when it was performed by Ballet Cymru which featured choreography by Darius James and Amy Douglas. The pre-publicity described it thus:

> **Ballet Cymru presents a timeless interpretation of the Dylan Thomas classic...step into the imagination of a genius and follow us on a journey through snow, cats and melancholy... evocative, eloquent costume, Ballet Cymru bring to life this timeless story...**

Cerys kept one recent Dylan Thomas project a secret from me for a good while, in fact it was in a first draft before she mentioned it to me. This was around 2020 and I guess she thought I might disapprove of it, or think it presumptuous or unnecessary and although, when she told me about it for the first-time, I have to admit that thoughts along *those* lines flashed through my head, but her infectious, almost evangelic enthusiasm, for the project got to me. When I first saw the drafts of the finished book, I was in awe and admiration. I was sold *hook, line and sinker*[13] on it. What was the project?

> **Cerys was editing Under Milk Wood with younger readers in mind.**[14]

Cerys had scoured the country for a suitable book illustrator, and she tried and experimented with a good few, but she had a vision in her head she needed to satisfy. She eventually chose Kate Evans[15] who did a really wonderful job with her splendid very modern and stylish collage like illustrations.

Cerys kept me informed of the final push to get the book ready for publication, but it was her book completely. I was not asked for, nor did I offer any input whatsoever. But we did arrange for a big Swansea launch; I would interview her onstage in front of a large audience, packed into Swansea's Waterfront Museum. The book was coming out just before Christmas 2022, and its final design made it look like a Victorian gift book – a rich deep blue with raised gilt lettering – an ideal Christmas gift for young readers from parents or grandparents. It was a great night, and many copies were sold by my old running mate, Tim Batcup, who does a great job running the best local Independent Bookshop – *Cover to Cover* in Mumbles.

The original first edition of the book was subtitled *A retelling by Cerys Matthews*, but she had her publishers Weidenfeld & Nicolson changed it for the first reprint where it became; A Children's Edition created by Cerys Matthew, which I like much better too...

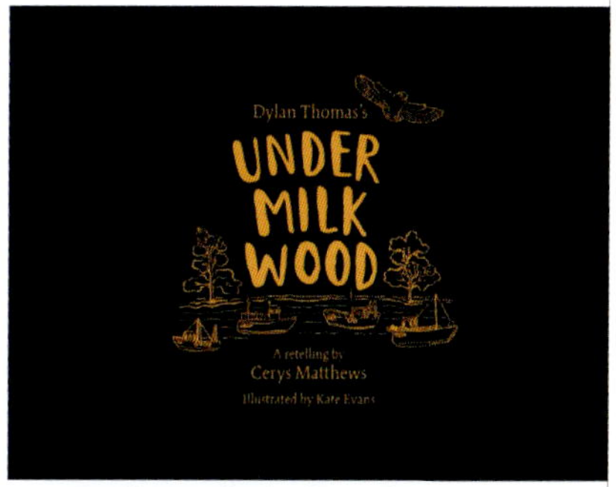

Cerys' Milk Wood. The first edition.

Kate Evans' delightful cover Illustration for Cerys' *Milk Wood*

Although I said above that I had no input in the book, Cerys mischievously managed to put *Me*[16] into the book by getting her illustrator to base certain characters in the play on people Cerys knew. So in the book I was surprised to see my younger self as *dead Mr Ogmore* in bed with *Mrs Ogmore Pitchard* and with actor Adil Ray as Mr Pritchard.

OUT OF CHAOS COMES BLISS

In this year, 2024, Dylan Thomas's published writing went out of copyright in the UK, which has led to a plethora of reprints and many fatuous new themed anthologies and sadly, I'm sure there are more to follow. But one really worthwhile new edition is *Out of Chaos Comes Bliss,* a new selection of Dylan Thomas poems published in an elegant paperback by a serious publisher the Pushkin Press.

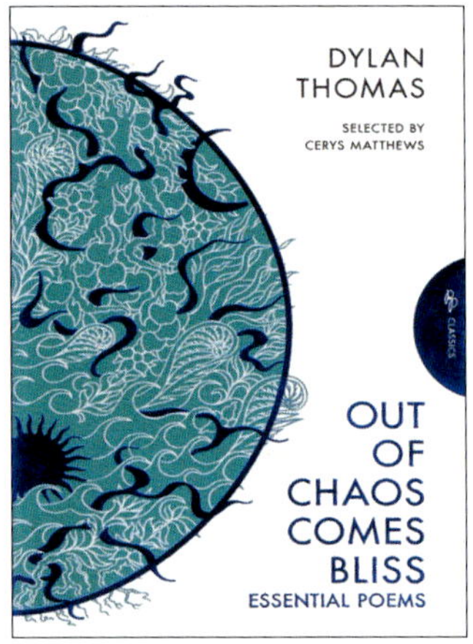

As you will discern from the cover, in a rather diminutive typeface, the editor of the selection was Cerys Matthews. And what a great job she has done too. Her title alone is worth the price of admission which she discovered in an almost lost poem, *Being but men, we walked into the trees*, a poem from 1932 found in his second notebook. It's a fine simple poem that gets scant attention anywhere, although Ralph Maud includes it in his two editions of Dylan's Notebook Poems where it is first printed and it is included in Goodby's new edition of *The Collected Poems* which came out in 2014, but again

Me on the left as dead Mr Ogmore and Adil Ray as dead Mr Pritchard

Photo: Emyr Young

Jeff and Cerys after a great event at the *Laugharne Weekend Festival* in 2023 the poem receives little attention. Cerys told me about the book when she first got the commission from *Pushkin Press,* and we did keep in touch via e-mail and the odd phone call. Cerys worked long and hard on this book and her pithy but non-academic short notes to the poems are a bonus not a hinderance. She also gave me a very warm acknowledgement which I really appreciate.

COLIN EDWARDS

I first came across the name Colin Edwards back in the late 1970's when Gwen Watkins gave me the original reel-to-reel tape recording of an interview of her husband, Dylan's close friend and a fine poet, Vernon Watkins. She recalled that the interviewer was one Colin Edwards, a Welsh-born radio and TV journalist based in Canada. He had visited Vernon at his Gower home in the late fifties and conducted the interview which Gwen recalled was part of a much larger project, but she knew no more than that. The tape had Vernon talking at length about his great friend Dylan Thomas on one side of the tape, with very short questions put to him by Colin in a light Welsh accent and answered at length by Vernon in an extremely 'posh' very English cut-glass, received pronunciation. On the other side the same voice reluctantly answered questions about his own poetry and life.

I heard no more about Colin Edwards until Glyn Jones, one of the finest of the first wave, passed away in 1995. His friend and another writer who wrote in English and Welsh, Meic Stephens, offered me most of Glyn's Dylan Thomas collection which I gladly acquired. It had all sorts of interesting secondary materials but a few better items including a copy of Colin's first ever interview, which was with Dylan's mother Florrie. It transpired that this interview began and strengthened his vision to track down, seek out and interview anyone and everyone who had known or encountered Dylan Thomas. In July 1958, Florrie Thomas invited the Canada-based Welsh radio journalist, Colin Edwards, to travel to Laugharne to take tea with her. This was five years after Dylan's death in New York City and Florrie was still grieving, but she was also upset and unhappy with the way in which Dylan Thomas was being written about in the popular press, which was obsessed with and often-exaggerated stories of Dylan's excesses in drinking and womanising. Colin was contemplating writing a biography of her son and Florrie encouraged Edwards to go out and talk to people who would feature in his book; people who knew:

> The real Dylan, the Dylan of the years of growing up and maturing...before what happened towards the end.

I was lucky to have a decent tape machine and could listen to the tapes; both were very informative, and the interviewer had a very easy way with his subjects and a soft accent-less voice with a slight lisp.

Colin's name began to be bandied around in Dylan Thomas circles, but he passed away in Oakland California where he had been living with his wife for some thirty years. On July 1994 his ashes were brought to Swansea, and are interred at Oystermouth cemetery. This began the full repatriation of Colin Edwards' life and work, as a few years later, his wife Mary, donated his archive of tapes and papers to the National Library of Wales. They worked slowly and diligently sifting and cataloguing his papers and digitising and transcribing the tapes. It was a mammoth task – back in 1968 Colin had stated that:

> *I have interviewed one hundred and twenty-two other relations, close friends and literary colleagues of Dylan during five extended visits home.*

By the mid-seventies, he had interviewed one hundred and fifty-one people, adding France, Switzerland and Iran to the list of countries visited. Based on these interviews Edwards wrote an unpublished biography of Dylan, the first chapters of which – on Thomas's boyhood, school and time with the Little Theatre – are in the National Library of Wales. Edwards also made three documentaries for the Canadian Broadcasting Company, called

The Real Dylan, Dylan as a Youth and My Son Dylan. Finally, at the beginning of this century the National Library commissioned a diligent researcher, scholar and Dylan Thomas writer – David N. Thomas – to edit and publish two volumes[17] of extracts from the wealth of materials available. Both these books are invaluable and informative and well worth having, but they are very much just tips of the iceberg; so they are tempting and appetite-whetting; one wants to take off to Aberystwyth for a week or two and immerse ones-self amongst Colin's tapes and papers.

Perhaps, when this book is finished and published, that's just what I'll do!

1. NEBRASKA LAW REVIEW INTRODUCTION. Although most of us may be unaware of the phenomenon, the English language gains hundreds of new words and phrases every year driven by a host of cultural variables such as new technologies, emerging social concerns, and ethnic interaction. This "new word" creation is more precisely referred to as "lexical creation. The phrase "road rage" entered the American-English language lexicon sometime in the late 1980s and early 1990s. It was initially bantered about and amplified in the general media – which sought to describe a hodgepodge of intentional, vengeful, irrational, stress-induced, mean-spirited actions involving motorists and, sometimes, automobile passengers, cyclists, or pedestrians – was gradually picked up and used by the legal press and, eventually, by legal scholars in journal articles and in judges in written opinions, plus legislators in legislative materials.

2. David Owens. *Cerys, Catatonia and the Rise of Welsh Pop*. Embury Press 2000.

3. And Musicians – we discovered that we both listened regularly to Snooks Eaglin, a blind American blues guitarist and singer based in New Orleans. In his early years he was sometimes credited under other names, including Blind Snooks Eaglin or, "Lil" Snook. He died in his early 70's in 2009.

4. Fritz Eichenberg (1901 – 1990) was a German-American illustrator and arts educator and book illustrator, who worked primarily in fine wood cut engravings. He illustrated many classic books. His *Child's Christmas in Wales* came out in many formats and became a firm American favourite. He also illustrated and American edition of Rebecca's Daughters and designed the sleeves for LPs on Caedmon Records.

5. Elmet or in Old English the more Welsh *Elfed*, was an independent Brittonic kingdom. It occupied the area of what became the West Riding of Yorkshire. Elmet appears in records during the Early Middle Ages between the 5th Century and the early 7th century; it was the last surviving British kingdom in the early Anglo-Saxon period.

6. See Chapter 8 for more on Dylan Thomas and moving images.

7. Cerys' Radio career has grown, and she now curates and presents The Blues Show on Radio 2 and Add to Playlist on Radio 4.

8. *Eggs laid by Tigers* – the surreal term Dylan Thomas used to describe his early poems. More on the *Eggs* in Chapter 15

9. More on this in the final part of Chapter 17.

10. For this and more like it get yourself a copy on *Dylan Thomas Letters to Vernon Watkins*. It is a great book first published in 1957 by Dent/Faber and was often reprinted in hardback and paperback.

11. See the Front cover of this book. The arm in view in mine, the pointing finger my grandson Ted's.

12. See Chapter 18. where I describe capturing a newly discovered FIFTH Notebook for Swansea University.

13. Cerys altered this fishing saying for the title of her first book – a sing-along-book *Hook, Line and Singer*

14. Cerys has done the complete opposite to what Sir Peter Blake asked me to do when he was illustrating *Under Milk Wood*. See the end section of Chapter 17.

15. Kate Evans graduated from Falmouth college of Arts in 2006, with a degree in Illustration. She works as a freelance illustrator and fine artist. As a mixed media artist, Kate works in collage, ink, and watercolour to produce illustrations that reflect the richness of their subject matter, capturing subtle emotions and complexities of particular places and situations. This definitely works in her *Milk Wood* images. Her work can be seen online at: studio.@jamaicastreetartists.co.uk.

16. See Chapter 17. to find out how Sir Peter Blake made it into Cerys book

17. Dylan Remembered Volume One 1914-1934. Dylan Remembered Volume Two 1935-1953. Seren 2003/2004.

My favourite of all Peter's paintings; *Self-Portrait with Badges*, embellished with Peter's *Under Milk Wood* badges

17.

Dylan Thomas: Sir Peter Blake & Under Milk Wood.

Thomas is one of the great eccentric poets, and ***Under Milk Wood*** *is his masterpiece.*
Peter Blake speaking of Dylan Thomas in 2014.

This is the WIKIPEDIA entry for Sir Peter Blake – a Pop Culture intro to a Pop Culture icon.

Sir Peter Thomas Blake CBE, RDI, RA (born 25 June 1932) is an English pop artist. He co-created the sleeve design for the Beatles' 1967 album *Sgt. Pepper's Lonely Hearts Club Band*. His other works include the covers for two of The Who's albums, the cover of the Band Aid single *Do They Know It's Christmas?*, and the Live Aid concert poster. Blake also designed the 2012 *Brit Award* statuette. Blake is a prominent figure in the pop art movement. Central to his paintings are his interest in images from popular culture which have infused his collages. In 2002 he was Knighted at Buckingham Palace for his services to art.

But there is so much more to Peter Blake than this. I first encountered his work back in 1967, with the release of the Beatles seminal LP *Sgt. Pepper's Lonely Hearts Club Band*, which I bought on the day of its release and was thrilled to see both my Dylan heroes depicted on its pop-art album cover.

Dylan Thomas looking like the early rocker, Gene Vincent[2]

Dylan Thomas and *Sgt. Pepper's Lonely Hearts Club Band*[1]

Dylan Thomas died a rather premature, public and slow death in New York City on November 9th 1953. He was aged just 39. His death was one of the first of a succession of '*live fast-die young*' fatalities which have since punctuated popular culture – James Dean, Brian Jones, Keith Moon, Janis Joplin, Jimi Hendrix, Lenny Bruce, Kurt Cobain – you can add in the rest. The photo above – taken by a bisexual bohemian artist and photographer, Nora Summers, casts Dylan exactly in the early, louche, rocker Gene Vincent, come-teddy-boy, sultry, no-good-boyo, mode. It dates from 1937, when Dylan was in his early twenties.

Some nine years after his untimely death this Welsh poet was suddenly annexed into the crazy world of rock music, when, on August 2 1962, a 21-year-old, budding folk singer, born in 1941 in Duluth Minnesota to Jewish parents, entered the Supreme Court Building in Downtown Manhattan and officially changed his name from Robert **Zimmerman** to Robert **Dylan**. From then on he was forever known globally as **Bob Dylan**. At the time this was reported as being some sort of homage to the Welsh poet Dylan Thomas.

The Beatles were well aware of all of this when they began to work on the cover of Sgt. Pepper. At the end of August 1966, the Beatles had permanently retired from touring and pursued individual interests for the next three months. During a return flight to London in November, Paul McCartney had an idea for a song involving a vintage Edwardian military band that formed the impetus of the *Sgt. Pepper* concept... Speaking in 1987 McCartney said;

> For the cover we came up with a list of our heroes, like Oscar Wilde, Marlon Brando, Dylan Thomas, Aldous Huxley. Lenny Bruce. Everyone had their choice.

The artist who they commissioned to design the album cover was a celebrated British 'POP' Artist – Peter Blake, who was already well-versed in the "magic crowd" idea...Blake commented;

> The appeal of a crowd goes back to being a young kid as a football fan. I'd worked in crowds, with a series of circus collages, made up of bits of engraving or photos. I'd painted a scene of a battle, where there was a balcony at the top and famous people looking over it, such as W.C. Fields. These were *Sgt. Pepper's* antecedents.

Working with his then wife Jann Haworth and taking suggestions and ideas from the band, the concept began to develop. Peter Blake has confirmed to me that Dylan Thomas was in fact John Lennon's choice. McCartney has also gone on record saying:

> I'm sure the main influence on both [Bob] Dylan and John was Dylan Thomas. We all used to like Dylan Thomas. I read him a lot. I think that John started writing because of him, and the fact that Bob Dylan wrote poetry added to his appeal.

The Album's producer, George Martin, also commented on this lineage:

> Dylan Thomas...was a great influence on Bob Dylan, and I think that the kind of words that Dylan Thomas would construct came down through Bob Dylan into John Lennon.

In 1988 George Martin paid his own tribute to Dylan Thomas by producing a new version of his radio play *Under Milk Wood*, starring Anthony Hopkins and a wealth of Welsh acting talent – along with musical contributions by Elton John, Mark Knoffler, Mary Hopkins Tom Jones and Bonnie Tyler. And it is also worth noting that Peter Blake, the artist who produced the album cover [together with his then wife Jann Haworth and the photographer Michael Cooper] was also a Dylan Thomas aficionado. He had been smitten by the radio production of *Under Milk Wood* which was broadcast by the BBC in 1954.

McCartney writes of how the Beatles empathised with Dylan Thomas early on in their development. Writing of their time in the early sixties in Hamburg he describes it thus;

> I had been reading Shakespeare, Dylan Thomas and Steinbeck, so that when we came to this Hamburg experience it was as students, a little bit as artists...we saw it differently from the other groups. I think we saw it as if we were Dylan Thomas and this was his time in Germany.

John Lennon himself referenced Dylan Thomas when he made comments about his use of soft drugs:

> *Rubber Soul* was the pot album, and *Revolver* was the acid. It was like pills or pot. I mean we weren't all stoned making Rubber Soul, because in those days we couldn't work on acid. It's like saying 'Did Dylan Thomas write *Under Milk Wood* on beer? The beer is to prevent the rest of the world from crowding in on you. The drugs are to prevent the rest of the world from getting in. They don't make you write any better.

This was one of many traits that John Lennon and Dylan Thomas had in common. They were both romantic left-wing liberals – always on the side of the underdog. Theirs was a social conscience as gut-reaction, not based on any specific political theory or party allegiance. They both had an aversion to academia and the intellectual examination and dissection of their work. And they shared a similar surreal, immediate and spontaneous sense of humour which they enjoyed in verbal flights of the imagination – sometimes written and sometimes expressed in spirited doodles, cartoons and drawings.

So there you have it – John Lennon shared many of Dylan Thomas's attitudes, his love of words and his sense of humour[3]. And John chose Dylan to be in the crowd for the cover of *Sgt. Pepper*. Dylan Thomas can be seen peeping out over Tom Mix's Stetson and Marlon Brando's biker cap and sandwiched between two other writers – Aldous Huxley and Terry Southern. Sadly the

Dylan Thomas on the cover of *Sgt. Pepper* looking out over the biker-hat and Stetson of Marlon Brando and Tom Mix, flanked by two other writers – Aldous Huxley and Terry Southern

life-size cardboard cut-out head of Dylan Thomas has been lost, but Peter Blake has promised it to me – should it ever come to light again.

Peter Blake and Under Milk Wood

> *"Thomas is one of the great eccentric poets, and Under Milk Wood is his masterpiece."*
> *"As soon as I decided to illustrate Under Milk Wood, I researched it, read it and listened to it again and again. I still play it a couple of times a week and read it once a month. I've always treated it as a separate piece of work. I work on Under Milk Wood at home in the evening. It's almost like 'a separate me' doing it."*
> Sir Peter Blake speaking to a journalist in 2014

Peter Blake's portrait of Dylan Thomas inspired by a famous Rollie McKenna photograph of Dylan directing *Under Milk Wood* in New York 1953

In 1986 I bought a long, eleven page verse letter[4] sent from Laugharne by Dylan Thomas to a New York couple who had looked after him on his first few days in America, in February 1950. I held onto it for a few years and finally in 1990, I got around to doing what I always intended and that was to publish it in an elegant small edition. This led me to meet Michael Mitchell,[5] a very fine letterpress printer and book designer who ran his *Libanus Press* from an elegant house in Marlborough

When I visited Michael for the first time to ask him if he would design and print my book, he took an immediate warm interest in my project, but also mentioned he was engaged with another Dylan Thomas publication which was to come out presently from his *Libanus Press* which was to be illustrated by Peter Blake. It transpired that he and Peter had been neighbours when Peter had left London in the early 1970's for the countryside and he moved into a railway station made vacant by Beeching's cuts, at Wellow, near Bath. I explained to Michael that I was a huge fan of Peter's art, especially his famous cover for the Beatles Sgt. Pepper album cover which featured Dylan Thomas. Michael responded by finding an off-print of his current Libanus catalogue detailing the work in progress; it was to be a fine press edition of *UNDER MILK WOOD*. And more importantly – he also gave me Peter's address and suggested I write to him. Michael's revelation regarding Peter providing illustrations for *Under Milk Wood* was very exciting news but it was not going to be the first Illustrated *Milk Wood*, so here is a run-down on the previous attempts...

Illustrating Milk Wood

In 1954, the year the book was published, a contemporary artist of Peter's, Paula Rego, made this fine painting entitled *Under Milk Wood*, She was a Portuguese-British visual artist who studied at the Slade. In her painting she seems to have set her scene, which could be in Butcher Beynon's Milk Wood kitchen, but transported back to her native rural Portugal, but she seemed to have been inspired to make just this one painting ...

In the same year John Minton, a fine artist who had taught

Peter at the R.A, made a series of small woodcut illustrations for the first printing of the text over two issues of the *Sunday Observer* newspaper;

The pre-eminent Welsh Artist, Ceri Richards, had met Dylan Thomas just before his last trip to America in 1953. When he heard of his new friend's death from Vernon Watkins the painter assuaged his grief in a frenzy of artistic responses to Dylan's poetry. He systematically embellished at least four copies of Dylan's 1952 *Collected Poems* with spontaneous pen and ink drawings throughout the text in the blank margins and blank half pages. The copy in Swansea Reference Library also has a hand painted coloured original dust jacket. The bookseller and collector, the late Allan Clodd had a copy, which he published through his own Enitharmon Press. Ceri Richards went on to produce numerous huge oil paintings based on Thomas's greatest poems and also produced a suite of large coloured lithographs inspired by his favourite Dylan Thomas poems. Later, in 1966, he made a series of lithographs for an illustrated edition of the text of *Under Milk Wood* for a *Folio Society* edition.[6] When Ceri was asked to do this, which was to be one of his last projects, he heard that *Swansea Little Theatre*, (where Dylan, in his youth, had been a regular performer), were rehearsing a new production of the play, so he called in on their rehearsals, sat in the front row and sketched what he saw in a very immediate, loose, simple flowing style. I have had an original hand-touched, inscribed and signed print of Ceri's Captain Cat which has hung in my house, for many decades, and I still enjoy it.

In 1968 the Welsh publishers Gwasg Gomer, published the first Welsh translation of *Under Milk Wood*; *Dan Y Wenallt*, as it is in Welsh, was translated T. James Jones, or Jim Parc Ness, as he is better known. It was also well illustrated by Gaynor Owen. Herewith the cover of the first edition and Gaynor Owen's image of the three Ogmore Pritchards.

Captain Cat

When this Welsh text was reprinted in 1996 it utilised colour illustrations taken from stills from the animated film version of the play that Cardiff Animation Studios had made in 1992 commissioned by the Welsh language TV channel S4C. This is the cover image and their image of Mae Rose Cottage.

Rosie Probert

In 1987 a large print edition of *Under Milk Wood* was published by *Large Print Books*. It is uncommon and hard to find, as most copies are bought by public libraries (I have kept a copy for when my own sight begins to fail). In this edition the text is just an enlarged off set litho copy of original type-set printing, but it also has a suite of spirited illustrations by Judy Deykin who usually illustrates children's books;[7] herewith the dust-jacket image, and her inebriated Mr Waldo and her saucy Mrs Dia Bread Two;

John Minton's *Milk Wood* woodcuts

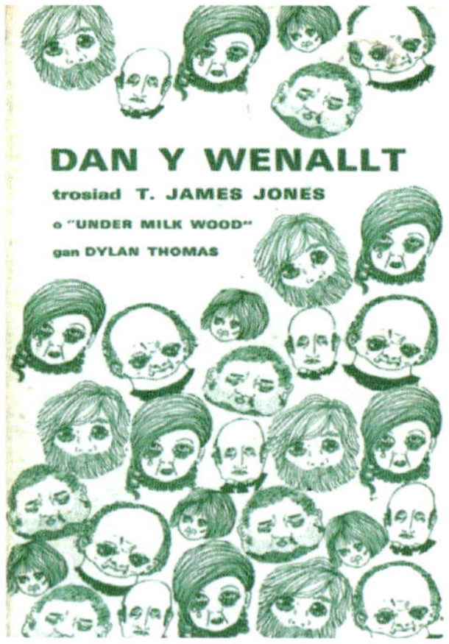

The Welsh *Milk Wood* Gaynor Owen

Mae hi'n gorwedd yn ddwfwn, yn disgwyl i'r gwaetha ddigwydd
:rechwenu a chwyrnu a wna'r geifr.

The animated *Milk Wood*

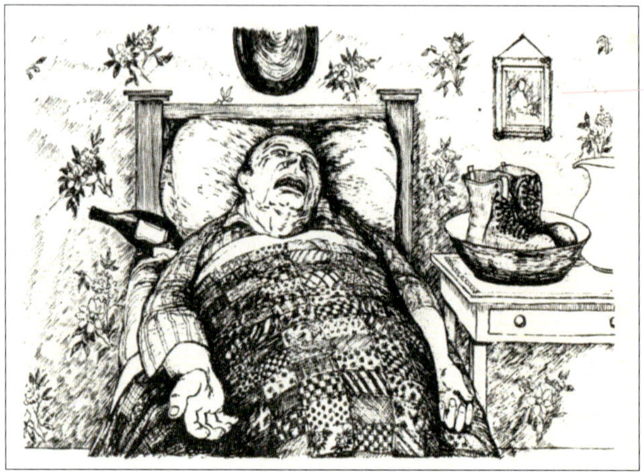

Large print edition illustrated by Judy Deykin

The late Shelia Waters, was an outstanding English calligrapher, who later settled in America, she was commissioned by a great, early 20th century book collector, Edward Homby, when she was still in England in 1961, to create a calligraphic illustrated version of *Under Milk Wood*. It took her 17 years to complete; finishing it in America in 1978. It is now reckoned to be one of the most magnificent calligraphic masterpieces of modern times. The cover of the book is stunning, with an impressive blind embossed panel on ivory paper. The panel is repeated inside the book, with Sheila's typical, magisterial Roman Capitals in black with intricate drawings and vibrant colours.

This panel alone took Sheila a month to design and execute. The original vellum manuscript is now owned by the late Sir Paul Getty's estate. He was an outstanding book collector who's magnificent Library is still in his Wormsley home.[8] Before his death John Paul Getty selected the huge vellum scroll as one of the 100 great treasures from his collection, which were exhibited in London and New York. I was lucky enough to get to see it at Wormsley and to then to make the acquaintance of Shelia Waters – albeit just by mail and e-mail. A full-colour reproduction of the manuscript book was published by International Letter Arts Network in 1989 in a fine trade and limited edition, in which there are 26 illustrations spaced throughout the 76 pages of the book.[9]

And to bring us right up to date, in 2022, Cerys Matthews,[10] musician, writer and broadcaster, brought out a splendid edition of *Under Milk Wood*, aimed at young children, (or for their grandparents to read to them). She worked on the project for over two years, long and hard, and she succeeded. The book is embellished with a charming, very modern, suite of illustrations by a young illustrator, Kate Evans – herewith a typically

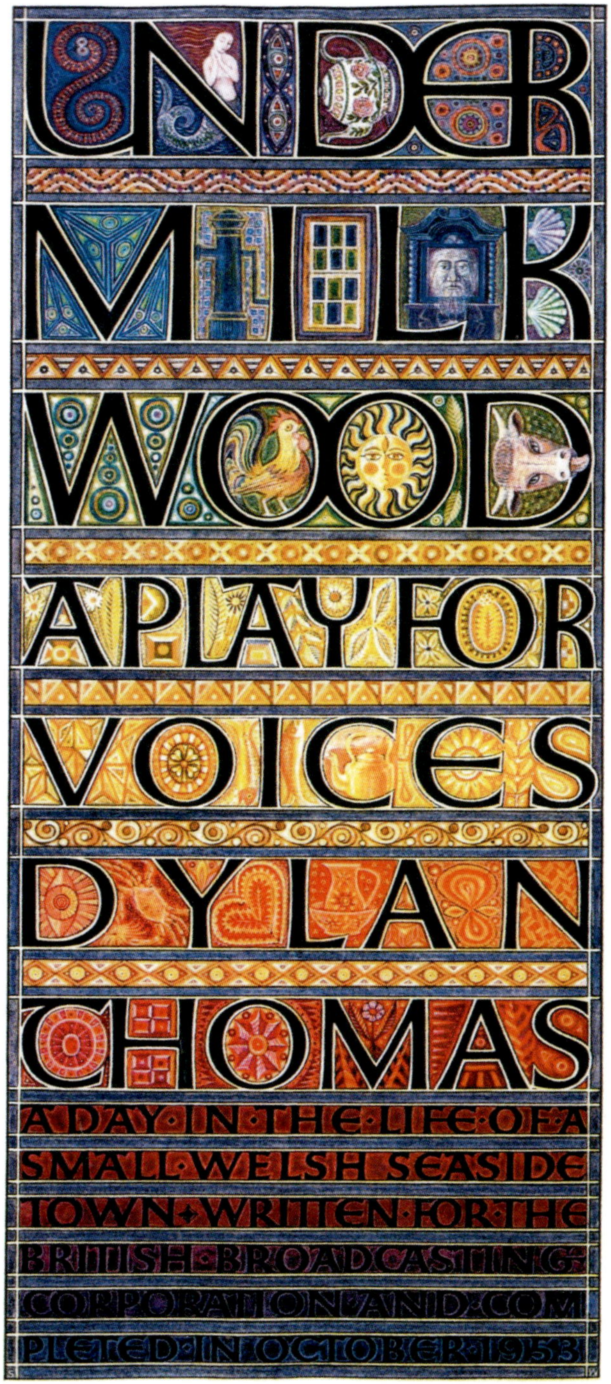

The stunning title page of Shelia Waters Calligraphic *Under Milk Wood*

lively double-page spread...

Cerys also mischievously instructed her illustrator to base certain of her characters on real people. I must admit to being well chuffed to find myself depicted as one of Mrs Ogmore Pritchard's two dead husbands (my co dead husband is based on the actor, comedian and TV presenter, Adil Ray.) Even better still is this – Lord Cut Glass – the obsessive horologist is none other than; Sir Peter Blake!

I wonder who the next artist will be to endeavour to depict Llareggub in pictures[11] but I have to say Peter Blake has set the bar very high. But back to Peter's journey into the woods ...

* * * * *

Michael Mitchell agreed to work on my *Letter to Loren* and he looked forward to me sending him the text and facsimiles of the letter Dylan wrote to Loren. Once back in Swansea I quickly typed up a letter to Peter and by return he invited me to call on him at his West London Home. I was very excited.

I will never forget my first visit to see Peter,[12] some thirty years ago. At that time Peter had a studio in his house. I made my way to West London and approached the front door through an arch of lilac and a front garden bedecked with flowers. I nervously lifted the shining brass knocker on the bright red door. Peter opened the door, welcomed me in and ushered me upstairs to his studio where I was immediately confronted with the life size wax work of Sonny Liston[13] which came originally

Peter Blake as Lord Cut Glass

from Madame Tussaud's London Wax Museum and had featured on the *Sgt Pepper* cover. The wax boxer was surrounded by a cornucopia of wonderful *objet trouvé, objet de curiosité* and all manner of bric-a-brac, amidst which were numerous of Peter's art works in progress. I was given a quick tour of his amazing collection with my eyes out like organ-stops before we settled down to talk. One after the other I asked my questions and Peter patiently and lugubriously answered them all. Most were concerned not with *Sgt Pepper* which had become almost a millstone on Peter's back, such was the band's and that seminal album's fame. I was more interested in Peter and *Under Milk Wood*. Peter explained that he was an art student in London in the early fifties and there were a few budding Welsh artists in his peer group and they were talking about this Welsh poet, Dylan Thomas, who had recently died young in New York. They were very enthusiastic about *Under Milk Wood*, a play of his which had recently been broadcast on BBC radio a few times, with Richard Burton taking the main role. I was later able to surprise Peter by giving him the original pages from the *Observer* Sunday paper from 1954, which had printed, over two weeks, the full text of *Under Milk Wood* with woodcut illustrations by John Minton, his former tutor and friend. Another coincidence I shared with Peter was this later edition of the play, published in

a much more appealing, pictorial dust jacket than the rather dull plain green dust-jacket on the original 1954 edition.

This dust-jacket was designed by another Welsh artist; Neath born, Brian Rees, who also studied art in London but at the Central School of Arts and Crafts and Peter was familiar with his work. I once owned the original art work for this dust jacket[14]. which came out in 1959. I was intrigued that the artist had used various early *LETRASET* transfer sheets for some of the larger areas – a late fifties design tool.

Peter also spoke of how he had come to regard Dylan's *Llareggub* as the first 'soap opera' and the prototype for future radio and TV popular soaps and indeed he noticed that in the opening monologue in which the listeners are urged to;

Listen. It is night moving in the streets, the processional salt-slow musical wind in **Coronation Street**...

I asked Peter if he had a favourite recording of the play and although he admired the Richard Burton version he had become enamoured of the 1987 Spindrift production in which Anthony Hopkins took first voice, surrounded by a host of great Welsh acting and singing talent; with the ambient sound recording and some new music added by his old friend from *Sgt. Pepper* days, George Martin, who produced this version and had enlisted musical contributions by Mark Knopfler, of *Dire Straits* and Elton

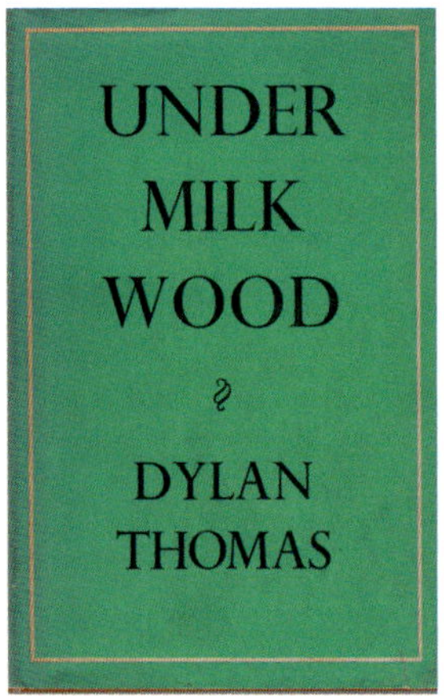

Rather drab first edition DJ

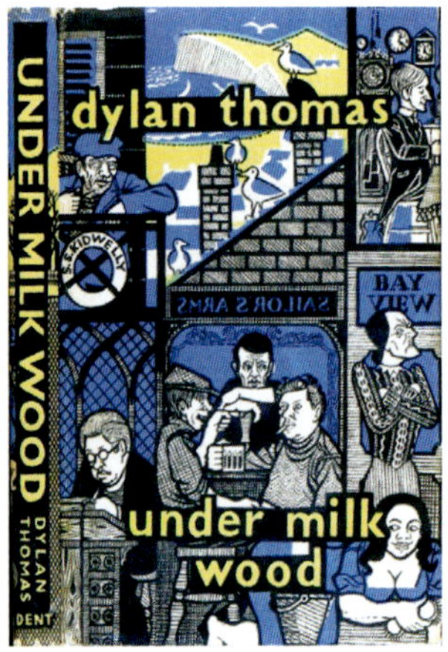

Much livlier reprinted jacket by Brian Rees

Ian Pollocks striking illustration for the LP

John; and he used real Welsh pop-singers – Bonnie Tyler and Sir Tom Jones to sing the key songs. I told Peter how I had been involved with a *Dylan Thomas Summer School* in Aberystwyth back then and had met George Martin, who had given a talk about this recent production and that we had talked about Peter's obsession with the play. It was a much publicised release which came out on all three current platforms – as a double L P, as a double Cassette and as a double CD. I tried to buy the cover art from the artist Ian Pollock whose work I knew as a book illustrator, sadly the cover had gone but I did get the original portrait of Dylan which is on the back cover of the album.

Ian Pollocks portrait of Dylan – a favourite of mine

I also explained to Peter about my bookshop and my obsessive specialisation in Dylan Thomas and all things Welsh and Peter, being an inveterate collector, smiled empathetically. We left the Studio and went downstairs into his magical library room with delightful stained glass windows depicting scenes from classic nursery rhymes and *Alice in Wonderland*.

The shelves were full of illustrated editions of that classic and many other wonderful and rare illustrated children's books. We talked books, booksellers and book-collecting for a while before I steered the conversation back to Dylan Thomas and *Under Milk Wood*. Peter explained that his interest got more serious when, in the early seventies, he tired of London and decided to escape to the country. He went west to Somerset[15] and moved into a disused railway station made vacant by Dr Beeching's cuts, at Wellow, near Bath. One of his neighbours was a very talented dentist who was tiring of dentistry and becoming obsessed with letterpress printing and book design. Shortly after he met, his new neighbour he decided to swap teeth for type full time and established his Libanus press in an elegant house in Marlborough – The very same Michael Mitchell who was to introduce me to Peter.

Michael Mitchell & Peter's Milk Wood

Michael Mitchell was also aware of *Under Milk Wood*, and when he and Peter became friends they began to talk about the play. Michael, seeing how Peter used to play records while working in his studio, recalled;

> At the time he had only vaguely heard of the play. I knew he liked to listen to something while he worked – usually Chuck Berry. So I gave him the 1954 recording of *Under Milk Wood* with Richard Burton and he loved it.

Michael began to suggest a collaboration on a fine limited edition of *Under Milk Wood*: Michael would design and print the text and Peter would make a suite of wood engraving to illustrate it. Peter Blake was no stranger to literary illustration and had already been working on literary subjects including Lewis Carroll and Shakespeare, and was intrigued that no other artist, apart from Swansea-born Ceri Richards had produced a significant illustrated edition of the play. Michael succeeded in inspiring Peter to collaborate on an edition of the text with wood engravings by Peter.

However, it turned out to be an extremely long process. In an early Libanus Press Prospectus Michael Mitchell apologises;

> It may seem to our regular readers, that this production has had a lengthy period of gestation. To us it seems right and necessary to take time over our most ambitious project to date...

He suggests that the book might be ready for Summer 1989.

It would be another twenty-five years before the book was finally published!

At this early stage the book was to be a fine limited edition with maybe just a dozen woodcuts. It would be a small signed limited edition printed on fine hand-made paper in the style of the then flourishing *Golden Cockerel Press*, *Nonesuch Press* and the

UNDER MILK WOOD *In Preparation*

By Dylan Thomas. Wood engravings by Peter Blake. It may seem, to our regular readers, that this production has had a lengthy period of gestation. To us it seems right & necessary to take time over our most ambitious project to date. The type, an exciting combination of Bembo and narrow Bembo, has been set, and the page layout decided. Peter Blake is now working on the wood engravings. Summer 1989

Gregynog Press in Wales, with no more than a dozen fine wood engraved text printed in black ink. The opening first illustration, for the lines '*moonless night... starless and bible-black*' was to be a solid jet-black square. This woodcut[16] is the only one to make it into the final published book.

On my first visit with Peter he had already cut around ten blocks depicting characters and scenes from the text and he showed me these along with a few proof page pulls from the engraved blocks. They were exquisite in design and craftsmanship but it was a very laborious and time consuming process and it appeared that this may have what stalled the project. But Peter never stopped thinking about the play and

The first woodcut

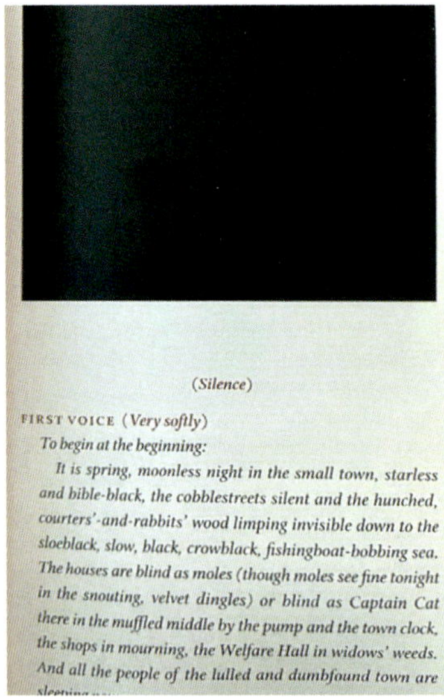

(*Silence*)

FIRST VOICE (*Very softly*)

To begin at the beginning:

It is spring, moonless night in the small town, starless and bible-black, the cobblestreets silent and the hunched, courters'-and-rabbits' wood limping invisible down to the sloeblack, slow, black, crowblack, fishingboat-bobbing sea. The houses are blind as moles (though moles see fine tonight in the snouting, velvet dingles) or blind as Captain Cat there in the muffled middle by the pump and the town clock, the shops in mourning, the Welfare Hall in widows' weeds. And all the people of the lulled and dumbfound town are

illustrating the text, which he began to know intimately and Michael was always gently encouraging him to progress and persevere with the project. To this end, in 1986 he accompanied Peter on a reconnaissance trip down to Laugharne where they explored the town looking for clues and inspiration for characters and landscape, to inform Peter's continuing efforts to illustrate the text of the radio play. They were also armed with a camera and Peter and Michael took photographs of the town and its buildings. They were curious when they were outside *Browns Hotel* to see a small crowd of people and a T.V. camera crew milling around the *Corran Bookshop* opposite; intrigued, they crossed over to investigate. The bookshop was owned and run by George Tremlett[17] who had recently spent a few months staying with Dylan Thomas's widow, Caitlin, in her Italian home, where he recorded many hours of interviews with Caitlin for a projected joint account of her life with Dylan Thomas. The book had just recently been published[18] and Caitlin herself, with her grown up daughter, Aeronwy, were in the book shop at the start of a promotional tour to publicise the book.

Peter and Michael could not believe this amazing coincidence and crossed over and joined the throng of locals and visitors and they even managed a brief meeting with Caitlin, Aeronwy and George; and obtained signed copies.

Peter later spoke about this adventure;

Just walking around the town was good

too. I took a lot of photos, thinking that could have been where Captain Cat lived or maybe Mrs Ogmore Pritchard lived. It helped bring it to life.[19] One of the first photographs Peter took was of Michael walking on the pavement towards Browns, Dylan's favourite watering hole. With the addition of a collaged naked lady, that photograph became an illustration in the finished book; Michael Mitchell undresses Gossamer Beynon with his eyes, Peter's caption uses Dylan's words – *She Blazes Naked...*

The Laugharne trip boosted their enthusiasm for the project but inevitably, some domestic upheavals and other more pressing and urgent work and commissions took precedent, not least was his appointment as *Associate Artist at the National Gallery* for over two-years, between late summer of 1994 and 1996. Peter very kindly invited my wife and I to the special celebration party in the gallery. It was thronged with artists and celebrities so we only got to speak with Peter and Chrissy briefly. The event got well written up in the papers; the illustration is of one of many such cuttings;

And one of my paparazzi shots of the night; Peter with the late punk-rocker, Ian Drury.[20]

Sadly cancer took Ian at just 58. After he passed I watched a very warm portrait of Ian come alive on the easel in Peter's studio. It eventually became the cover art for an amazing tribute album.

Michael and Peter had negotiated an option on the text of *Under Milk Wood* with Dylan Thomas's agents but that ran out; so they negotiated a new one. All these things got in the way; but *Milk Wood* would not go away. In 1995, when I was very involved in Swansea's year-long literature festival, Peter very kindly let me

Peter with Ian Drury

Peter's cover portrait

Pictures: DAVE BENETT

Raising a glass: Rolling Stone Ronnie Wood enjoys the party

Rock meets art at Blake's party

by ROBIN STRINGER Arts Correspondent

THE National Gallery reverberated to the unfamiliar sound of rock music last night when veteran pop artist Peter Blake threw a party to celebrate his two-year residency there.

Rock stars mingled with artists among an estimated 500 guests. Rolling Stone Ronnie Wood was there, as was Pink Floyd's Roger Waters, The Beatles' Sir George Martin and rock maverick Ian Dury. From the art world came painters Ron Kitaj, Howard Hodgkin, Patrick Caulfield and Allen Jones, as well as Tate Gallery director Nicholas Serota.

A practising artist himself, Wood said of Blake: "I'm glad the

Arty party: Peter Blake

Establishment likes him because that means there's hope for me."

Blake's sense of fun runs through his show, which features three abstracts by his friend, Cheeta the chimpanzee from the Tarzan films. Both are 64, hence the show's title, Now We Are 64, with its Beatles references.

Ronnie Wood

exhibit the early wood-cuts in the exhibition I had installed in the city's new Dylan Thomas Centre. This is the catalogue page;

Peter was very keen for me to emphasise the status of these early woodcuts; they came in an envelope inscribed thus;

The project then began to expand into a multi-facetted diverse experiment in book illustration as only Peter could create. He began to see this as a *long-game* project, a project separate from his day-time work and it became almost a hobby project, enjoyed in the evenings at home but an intense and very

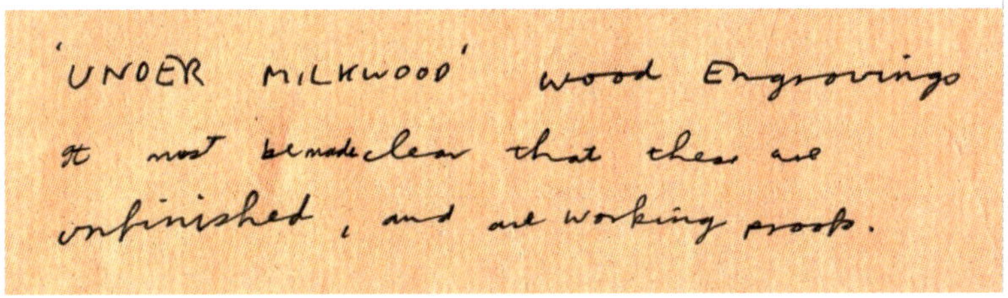

'UNDER MILKWOOD' Wood Engravings
It must be made clear that these are
unfinished, and are working proofs.

The page from *Word and Image* catalogue

PETER BLAKE'S
MILK WOOD

Peter Blake is known as one of the key figures in the development of the British Pop Art movement of the late fifties and early sixties. His paintings and collages, hang in major collections throughout the world. We are most familiar with his big, bold, pictures depicting the Beatles, Bo Diddley, and Elvis Presley (and with his brilliant cover design for the Beatles' 'Sgt. Pepper' album cover.)

In some respects *Under Milk Wood* can be seen as an prototype 'Soap-Opera'. Elements we take for granted in CORONATION STREET, (Thomas had given the main street of his imaginary Llareggub exactly the same name), EAST ENDERS, and POBOL Y CWM, are crucial to the appeal of *Under Milk Wood*. Maybe it is this 'pop-culture' aspect of 'Milk Wood' which make it a favourite of Peter Blake's.

The Arethusa, the curlew and the skylark, Zanzibar, Rhiannon, the Rover, the Cormorant and the Star of Wales tilt ... working proof

In 1988 Peter Blake embarked on a project with his friend Michael Mitchell, a fine printer who runs the Libanus Press in Marlborough, toproduce an edition of 'Milk Wood' which would feature a series of delicate wood-cuts by Peter Blake. The project is still very much a 'work-in-progress' but we are privileged to offer here a preview of the work. Blake's wood-cuts are based on found images and photographs from a variety of sources - magazines and snapshots, postcards and adverts. They have an eerie, timeless quality and they do have the effect of fleshing out the different characters in a new and startling manner. The opening wood-cut is a master-stroke in which the first word of the text, *"(silence)"*, is depicted by a solid black (Bible-black!), rectangle, an effect achieved by printing a totally un-cut wood-block.

It must be stressed that the engravings shown here are a very early trial proofs and one can only look forward with great anticipation to the eventual completion of the project.

serious hobby. He began to make exquisite fine imagined pencil portraits of each and every character mentioned in the text; not just the characters in the cast list but also anyone named, however obliquely, in the text – they amounted to some 70 fine drawings. Some were totally imagined; others were based on random found images from popular magazines and some were recognisable as known celebrities but some of these are jig-saw like amalgamations of two different faces. Peter explained how his fine, benign old Captain Cat was achieved;

> In this instance, this is a picture of the racing driver Sir Tommy Sopwith, who did later go blind, like Captain Cat. I adapted his eyes a little and then drew in my own beard.

So, Peter's beard is depicted in his illustration for Captain Cat – one of the main characters, so, it is fitting that his *First Voice* is based on Michael Mitchell ...

Peter as Captain Cat

In 2002 Peter was knighted and in 2003, which was the 50th anniversary of Dylan's death in New York, The Dylan Thomas Centre was the venue for many commemorative events throughout the year and Peter once again, very kindly loaned us some 20 of his wonderful *MilkWood* pencil portraits, which I hung in the corridor gallery of the Centre. The show was very popular; people were amazed at their fine and imaginative beauty. For the final night of our festival Sir Peter came down to Swansea and I interviewed him in front of a packed auditorium about his love of *Under Milk Wood*.

Over the next few years I followed Peter's career and looked out for any new *Milk Wood* developments. In 2012, he kindly invited me to his 80th birthday party which was held in the rotunda of the Royal Albert Hall. As a special birthday present I gave Peter one of the Caedmon Dylan Thomas Records which was signed by Dylan Thomas while he was on tour in America. Peter loves an autograph and he was very pleased with the record. The party was a dazzling affair. All guests were given a special commemorative enamel badge – I treasure mine and only wear it on special occasions;

On the night of the party Peter's magnificent *Art Bus* was parked up outside; the lifts were all decorated with Peter's Pop art creations. Once up on the rotunda the drinks and canapés were served by roller-skating waiters and waitresses provided by the Groucho Club. A homage to the 60's and J.F.K,'s birthday seemed fitting; and a giant

Michael Mitchell - First Voice

Dear Peter Blake

This is the from Jeff - the Swansea Dylan Thomas nut – I hope this finds you and your family well.

I remember my visits with you and your visit to Swansea with great pleasure. I have followed your life in the press and media – bought all the books that have come out , got all the catalogues of your exhibitions and even managed to put a modest small collection of you work together [mainly prints, but I have one original collage which gives me great and constant pleasure]. Oh and I have your circus/freak woodcuts which I adore

I am moved to write to ask about your ***'Milk Wood'*** project – I know it goes on – I have the ***Ambit*** and ***Dazed*** magazines which reproduced some more of your wonderful illustrations, but what moves me to write at this point in time is that I am becoming involved in a really big push to make 2014 – the centenary of Dylan Thomas's birth, a Wales-wide, even world- wide celebration of his life and work. Already all sorts of interesting projects are being planned – including a very serious new Operatic version of ***Under Milk Wood*** and a restaging/ re-enactment of the original New York production of Milk Wood at the YMHA venue where it was first performed.

Is there any chance that your version might be ready for 2014? Might there be another but major exhibition of your work in progress here in Swansea? Might you want to have some input in the stage designs for the Opera?

Sorry if this seems presumptuous but I do think your illustrations are wonderful and hugely supportive of the text and it would be great if you could be involved again. The Opera is has been commissioned and funded by Taliesin Arts Centre – a fine space on the Swansea University Campus which has a very fine small gallery – Oriel Ceri Richards – and a good Theatre/performance space.

birthday cake was rolled in; out of which emerged a Marilyn Monroe look-alike who proceeded to sing happy birthday to Peter. The musical entertainment was provided by the two-tone group *Madness*, supplemented by the remaining members of the late Ian Drury's band – *The Blockheads*. And at one point in the evening I found myself beside a group made up of One *Beatle* – Paul McCartney; A *Rolling Stone* – Ronnie Wood; and Eric Clapton, late of *Cream*.

And then it was well into 2013 and we were fast approaching 2014 – Dylan's Centenary Year. I felt moved to write to Peter to solicit his involvement. Here is my letter (including typos and errors). Little did I know then what lay ahead...

Peter replied promptly and once more invited me to visit him again at his studio. I was quick to get up to London. I can remember very vividly ringing the bell on his studio and Peter inviting me inside. However, once inside my path was almost totally blocked by a long row of low benches upon which were laid out, like a giant pack of cards, a multitude of art works, all large-page-sized.

Some I recognised; the portraits, and one or two others I had seen as *Milk Wood* works in progress, but there were so, so many. I was dumbfounded. Peter let me catch my breath and then announced;

"I think I've finished"

I responded excitedly;

"Peter do you know that next year is Dylan Thomas' Centenary Year? He was born in 1914!"

Peter was blissfully unaware, but became very enthusiastic about my quickly formulated plan to somehow have this whole, magnificent body of work, exhibited in a prestigious venue in Wales as the opening event of the forthcoming year of Centenary commemorations.

By now there were over 170 pieces of art featuring the portraits drawn in black and white pencil on tinted paper, watercolours illustrating the dream sequences in the play, and 'narratives and locations' in a mix of media including collage, and photographs that Peter had taken himself in Laugharne in the 1970s. Following the sequence of the play, Peter had divided his work into three distinct sections: brightly-coloured watercolours of the characters' dreams, collages which capture scenes and snippets of text from the play and portraits of each character rendered in hard pencil. Later watercolours, added to the series after Blake imposed his 'artificial deadline' on the project in 2013, capture new scenes and moments from the play. Peter said of these later works;

> *When [Dylan Thomas] wrote those sequences, I don't imagine he ever thought of it visually, he would have thought of it as words. So I really enjoyed making something that was never intended to be visual, visual.*

I envisioned a mammoth exhibition of all the original artworks with some extra glass cases with *Under Milk Wood* books and ephemera; some of Peter's and some from my collection. An

"I think I've finished"

exhibition of work made over some three decades! Remarkably, due to a measure of good fortune and the realisation by the powers that be, that this really was a fantastic opportunity to start Dylan's centenary year with a huge and important event. And in a few very busy months the exhibition opened at the National Museum of Wales in Cardiff. The staff at the museum, from the top down really got behind the project once they realised they had a big enough space free for the relevant time frame and with the help of Peter, his wife Chrissy and the Staff of the Waddington Clusot Gallery in London's Cork Street, his long time representatives, they pulled out all the stops to get the huge exhibition installed and ready in just a couple of months. In the meantime Peter and I went up to the Annual Manchester Literature Festival and on Saturday 11 October, at 3pm, in the packed Martin Harris Centre for Music and Drama I interviewed Peter about his love of *Under Milk Wood*, illustrated with a slide-show of his work.

Finally the exhibition opened at Amgueddfa Cymru – National Museum Wales; ***Llareggub: Peter Blake illustrates Dylan Thomas's** Under Milk Wood*, on November 23 2013 and ran until March 16th 2014. It proved to be hugely popular throughout its 4 month run.[21]

On the opening night I interviewed Peter in the packed large auditorium in the adjoining Reardon Smith Lecture Hall. At the end of a wonderful evening some 100 visitors queued to get their copies of the catalogue signed by Peter, who patiently sat for over an hour engaging with each and every one of them and signing his slow measured signature.

In the short run up to the opening, Michael Mitchell at Libanus began to work at great haste with two other prestigious publishers; the *Enitharmon Press* and the *Queen Anne Press*, to produce a large paperback catalogue for the exhibition of works, which also included the full text. It ranged in price quite significantly; £30 for a regular large paperback copy through to £850 for 1/100 signed with one original print and then up to £5,500 for one of just ten copies in a fine designer, full-leather binding, with three prints signed and numbered by Blake. The binding features coloured leather inlays of a pair of Staffordshire pottery dogs either side of a mantel clock; and each binding was to be unique, as each clock will be set at a different time!

Even at this late-stage Peter still regards the project as a work in progress. He managed to meet the deadline for the

The 1/100 copies in Blue slipcase – The 1/10 Special Bindings on the easel

book/catalogue publication, but in the ensuing three months he carried on working on *Milk Wood*, and he continued to add new work and he was still painting in details, such as Mog Edwards's "eyes like blowlamps" at 3 am, just a couple of Sundays back; the day before a van arrived to take everything to Cardiff. But as Peter is only too aware, "*Time passes*", as Thomas, Burton, Hopkins and countless other *First Voices*, played by actors professional and amateur, school-kids and pensioners, the world over have, and will continue to dramatically intone;

"*Time Passes*"

There was to be one final cherry on the cake. While all this was happening a TV Company approached Peter and myself with a view to making a TV Documentary about Peter and his *Under Milk Wood* inspirations. As ever there were the inevitable hurdles to be overcome but when a new Director/Producer was put in place – David Schulman,[22] an American, ex New York City artist, the film went ahead at speed. The final documentary went out on BBC2 on Monday November 25, on BBC One Wales and it was repeated twice more; in April 2024 on BBC2 and again on June 20 on BBC Four. The finished film was very good – especially when one considered the rushed short time that David had, and a rather unspectacular budget! I was happy to be involved, especially as I bathed in the reflective glory of his other, much more famous friends – one Rolling Stone, Ronnie Wood – himself an Artist, Pete Townsend of the *WHO*, discussing Peter's, influence on POP Art and POP Music; Damian Hirst, warmly talking of how Peter influenced the next generation of artists; and an introductory cameo by Dylan Thomas' granddaughter Hannah Ellis Thomas.

I was filmed nervously driving my huge Mobile BookBus around Swansea and adjoining beaches, whilst pontificating to camera; as well as having my tattooed right arm hanging casually out of the window so my Tatt was in view for the camera; as demanded by the director, David Schulman. I was also filmed taking a telephone call from Peter, who asks me to do him a very quick favour and quickly go through the text of *Under Milk Wood*, listing all the sexual innuendos and *double entendres* and slightly more explicit smut, which peppers the text and report back to him A.S.A.P! For the more prurient readers I have attached my response to this request at the end of this chapter.

Since 2014 I have remained good friends with Peter and still follow his work. He has continued to engage with Dylan Thomas. I bought this lenticular print DYLAN THOMAS, KIM NOVAK AND JAMES JOYCE IN NEW YORK. Lenticular – Digital printing on PETG plastic. Signed and numbered by the artist. 68 x 48 cm Edition of 100.

When, in 2015, the Swansea-based film director Kevin Allen, made his new film of *Under Milk Wood*, Peter very quickly put this publicity postcard together featuring the stellar, mainly Welsh cast – led by Rhys Ifans and Charlotte Church;

And then, following on from his long-running collage series, *Marcel Duchamp's World Tour*, Peter has started another series, this time it is another of his artistic heroes, Joseph Cornell, who Peter takes off on a long, collaged, imagined holiday. In a work entitled *Joseph Cornell's Holiday-*

Hastings a Wedding on the Beach; Dylan Thomas is sandwiched amongst the guests!

However my favourite acquisition is my most recent, which came in 2018. Peter and I both have a passion for tattoos, but mainly of a vintage variety. We both view them as a strong strand of folk-art. Over some forty years, I had built up an extensive collection of rare tattoo books and ephemera which I recently sold to a major American art college library. Peter too had a section of his studio full of tattoo ephemera; sheets of original early tattoo Flash and vintage photographs of tattooed men and women. Around 2016/17, Peter made a one off life-size wooden cut out of a boldly collaged tattooed lady, alliteratively named *Tattooed Tina*. I saw it pictured at an exhibition but, much as I coveted it, I could not afford it. So I was delighted when one of Peter's print studios – *Dark Matter* made a full size print of it – a hundred copies only and you could customise your print by mixing and matching the colours of her bikini and head band (a total of 216 permutations were possible – I went for pink hair band/ blue bikini). It was affordable, so I ordered one immediately. When it arrived I was so well pleased and excited that I spontaneously rang Peter to tell him of my joy. He answered and, after I told him how pleased I was, he asked; "Have you seen what I did for you." I had, as yet, hardly examined her and was puzzled, and said I had not noticed.

"Look above her bikini top"

he instructed. I did and lo and behold; there was tattooed;

BOB DYLAN THOMAS

Peter was well aware of my passion for both Bob Dylan and Dylan Thomas. How cool and kind was that gesture by a great artist.

As I mentioned, I recently co-wrote a book about *Bob Dylan and Dylan Thomas – The Two Dylans* and Peter kindly let me use the image as the cover design. When I launched the book and when giving subsequent talks, I always point to Bo Diddley's name tattooed under Tina's bikini and refer to Bo Diddley's great version of the Willie Dixon blues song, *You Can't Judge a Book by Lookin' at the Cover!* and point to our book and say;

In this case you can – Peter's Tina is the best part of the book!

In 2022 Peter celebrated his 90th birthday in his usual style and again I was delighted to be invited. I took my daughter, Kate to his Eightieth and my plus one a decade later was my oldest grand-kid, Rosie. This time Peter had booked out the first row of seats around the edge of *Giffords Victorian Circus* in the Chiswick Gardens with dinner in a trailer restaurant after. As ever we had a splendid time and Peter was on fine form.

I saw him again just a few weeks back (early May 2024) the day after I visited Waddington's to see his Sculpture Exhibition. We had a fine visit, talking mainly about the photographer John Deakin, who took a few great photographs of Dylan Thomas and who, I learned, Peter used to drink with in Soho's legendary French Pub back in the fifties. When I left I gave him a copy of Cerys Matthews recent *Under Milk Wood*[23] adapted for

children – so most of what follows below was gently removed and I must say it still reads with great charm and my younger grandchildren love it.

* * * * *

THE EROTIC & SCATOLOGICAL ELEMENTS IN *UNDER MILK WOOD*

Peter summed up his attitude to sex in the play when he was talking to Andrew Lycett, who was writing an article on Peter for the *Guardian*. Andrew wrote;

> Blake deals confidently with the play's many differing explorations of love. There is a "thinly veiled sexuality", he says, but it's "never pornographic", whether it's Mrs Willy Nilly's bare bottom being spanked, or Myfanwy Price's dream of her lover Mog Edwards "tall as the town clock tower", which shows him priapic alongside a phallic tower, based directly on the one in Laugharne.

However, not everyone agreed with Peter's assessment of this element in the play. David Holbrook, one of Dylan's fiercest critics has this to say in his 1962 book *Llareggub Revisited. Dylan Thomas and the state of modern poetry*. Holbrook, in trying to account on the popularity of the play which he saw as no more than a 'comic radio entertainment' and goes on to describe the play as;

> ... essentially cruel and untender and full of seamy hints and obscenities [with] no moral sense, no compassion, and so no real drama... hard, cruel and childishly dirty about sex.

I'd like to give the great Nobel-Prize-Winning Irish poet, Seamus Heaney, the last few splendid words on the subject, this from his lecture *Dylan The Durable*;[24]

> His 'play for voices', *Under Milk Wood*, is an idyllic romp, as if *The Joy of Sex* were dreamt under the canvas at a Welsh eisteddfod.

Peter's image of Mrs Willy-Nilly's Dream

Peter's image of Myfanwy Price's Dream

Below is my compilation of these *Seamy hints and obscenities*, an enlarged version of the notes I sent, at his request, to Peter as he was completing his Illustrated *Under Milk Wood*.
THE COMMENTS IN *ITALICS* ARE MINE
THE PAGE REFERENCES ARE TO THE STANDARD Dent hardback edition of 1954 onwards.

Page 1. The boys are dreaming wicked of the bucking ranches of the night and jollyrogered sea.
To have sexual intercourse with (someone), especially in a rough manner. He took her home and rogered her
Young girls lie bedded soft or glide on dreams ...down the organ playing wood.
Young Girls dreaming of playing with the male sexual organ.

Page 4. Second Drowned: Do you see me, Captain? the white bone talking I'm Tom Fred the donkeyman... we shared the same girl once ... her name was Mrs Probert...
Donkey man + Hung like a donkey = very well endowed in the sexual organ department.
Shared the same girl – had sex with the same prostitute
Woman's voice: Rosie Probert, thirty three Duck Lane. Come on up boys, I'm dead.
Rosie was obviously a sailor's whore – a 'lady of easy virtue' a dockside prostitute.
Second Drowned: Tell my missus no I never
Third drowned: I never done what she said I never
Fourth drowned: Yes they did
What they did or did not do was surely of a sexual nature.

PAGE 5. Third Drowned is dreaming of 'Bosums and Robins'
Bosums are breasts and Robins have cute red breasts.

Page 6. First Voice ...Miss Price dressmaker and sweetshop-keeper dreams of
Second voice: Her lover tall as a clock-tower, Samson-syrup-gold-maned, whacking thighed and piping hot thuderbolt-bass'd and barnacle breasted, flailing up the cockles with his eyes like blowlamps and scooping low over her lonely hotwaterbottled body.
An erotic dream of desire for a sexual hunk of a man.

Page 7. First voice ... Jack Black sleeps in his nightshirt tied at his ankles with elastic.
This prevents him from the sin of Onan i.e. To prevent him from masturbating.
[HE] dreams of
Chasing the naughty couples down the grassgreen gooseberried double bed of the wood... flogging the tosspots ... driving out the bare bold girls from the sixpenny hops of his nightmares...
Jack is a perverted peeping tom, flogging the toss pots could be masturbation he wants to punish the naked wanton village girls.

Page 8. Jacks shouts out
Ach y fi!
Ach y fi!
The Welsh for – 'dirty, nasty, disgusting, sickening – in a hygiene and sexual connotation.
Jack is feigning puritanical disgust when he is really sexually excited by what he sees.

Page 9. first Neighbour; Poor Mrs Waldo
Second Neighbour: What she puts up with
First Neighbour: Never should of married
Second Neighbour: If she didn't had to
First neighbour: Same as her mother
Mrs Waldo is being chided for getting pregnant before marriage as had her mother before her.

Page 10. *The neighbours on Waldo*:
And carrying on
With that Mrs Beatie Morris
Up in the quarry
And seen her baby
It's got his nose

They are accusing him of impregnating Mrs Beatie Morris a married woman but not married to Waldo.

Page 11. *More on Waldo* Using language [*obviously bad language*] Singing in the w [*obviously singing out loud while in the lavatory*]

Page 12. *More on Waldo's bad behaviour as a child*
Chalking words [*obviously dirty words*]
Saw him in the bushes
Playing mwchins [*mwchin = Welsh for pig – here used to describe sexual capers in the bushes with the opposite sex*].

Page 16. *Gossamer Beynon – the butchers daughter dreams of being in the slaughter house and finding in a carrier bag* a, 'small rough ready man with a bushy tail' who *seems to be winking at her She sighs to him,* 'At last my love' *and his* 'bushy tail wags rude and ginger'
For *'tail' is this his penis?* Organ Morgan = *this is an obvious play on words -= Organ = musical instrument; Organ = penis.*

Page 17. Organ Morgan *describes how* P.C.Attila Rees has got his truncheon out. *A double innuendo on Organ for penis and Truncheon for penis.*

Page 18. *PC Attila urinates in his helmet in his sleep* voice says 'You'll be sorry for this in the morning'
Mrs Willy Nilly postman *is spanked by her husband. She says* Don't spank me, please teacher ...whimpers his wife at his side, but every night of her married life she has been late for school = *she enjoys a bit of gentle Sado-Masochism.*

Page 19.
Mae Rose strips off for Mr Right and temps him like a tramp in a pulp paperback, Call me Dolores like they do in the stories.

Page 21/22. *Mary Ann Sailors in little clothing* 'smock-frock and clogs' *moves through the garden ripe with rich fecund imagery and surely the peas growing up through her skirt has sexual connotations. The first two characters have sexual dreams* Dai Bread *dreams of 'Harems' and* Polly garter *dreams of* 'babies' *which suggests the making of them and the nursing of them as well as caring for them.*

Page 22. First voice says '*This is Llareggub Hill'. This place name was a favourite crude palindromic word – it is BUGGER ALL spelled backwards. Although Bugger-all has become somewhat accepted as a mild description of nothing and negativity it was originally slang for pederasty.*
Lilly Smalls has dreamed of 'royalty' who *she has spent* 'all night long 'larking with her full of sauce in the Milk Wood dark' [= *saucy behaviour in the dark – the larking has a sexual component*].

Page 26/27. *Lilly Smalls examination of her own face in the mirror culminating in her kissing her own image whilst she* 'breathes the name and clouds the shaving glass' has erotic overtones.

Page 28. Straight-laced Mrs Pugh berates the floor scrubbing Lily Smalls; 'She's tucked her dress in her bloomers – oh the baggage'. *Lily is obviously showing too much flesh and her underwear behaving like a Baggage and nasty insult meaning a sexually loose woman.* 351

Page 30. *The self-description of the wanton* Mrs Dai Bread Two, 'Me Mrs Dai Bread two, gypsied to kill in a silky scarlet petticoat above my knees, see my body through my petticoat brown as a berry high-heel shoes with one heel missing, tortoiseshell comb in my bright black slinky hair, nothing else at all but a dab of scent lolling gaudy in the doorway'. *She behaves like a gypsy loose and immoral wearing no underwear only a dab of cheap alluring perfume and ending with the oral erotic* 'lighting up my pipe'
Polly Garter: Me Polly Garter under the washing line giving the breast in the garden to my bonnie baby. Nothing grows in our garden, only washing and babies. *Another loose woman unashamed of breast feeding her baby in the open air and obviously she has had a good few children 'out of wedlock'.*

Page 31. *Polly takes the Lord's name in vain when she declares she has* *no morals* – 'Oh isn't life a terrible thing, thank God?'

Page 32. [*This may be over the top*]
'Captain Cat: Blind and fine –fingered savours his sea-fry.' *The smell of the fishy sea on his fingers make him remember earlier sexual pleasure. Elsewhere Dylan makes a joke about a blind man passing a fish shop and saying 'Hello Ladies' a crude joke of the fishy smell of an excited pudenda/vagina.*

Page 33/34. Mrs Cherry Owen; Then you danced on the table all over again and said you were King Solomon Owen and I was your Mrs Sheba.
Cherry Owen: (softly) And then?
Mrs Cherry Owen: And then I got you into bed and you snored all night like a brewery
Mrs Cherry deflates Cherry Owens when she describes his propensity to suffer 'brewers droop' and falls asleep before making love to her, unable to fulfil his drunken boasts and sexual gestures. Him comparing himself to King Solomon and her to the Queen of Sheba is harking back to this incident in ancient history.[25]

Page 40. *Mrs Ogmore Pritchard tells Willy Nilly that she doesn't want guests 'sleeping in my sheets' meaning in her guest beds but Willy deliberately makes it sexual by commenting* 'he only wants a single bed'. Mrs Ogmore Pritchard slams the door in disgust at such a filthy suggestion.

Page 42. *Blind Captain Cat is sexually aroused by the sounds of some of the towns women walking past his window first it's the obese Mrs Dai Bread One* 'waltzing up the street like a jelly, every time she shakes it's slap, slap, slap.' *of her fleshy thighs and rear cheeks. Then it's Mae Rose Cottage walking by in high heeled shoes..* 'High Heels now, in the morning too, Mrs Rose Cottage's eldest Mae, seventeen and never been kissed ho ho, going young and milking under my window to the field of nannygoats, she reminds me all the way...And then he hears the 'women gabbing round the pump 'Who's having a baby, who blacked whose eye, seen Polly Garter giving her belly an airing, there should be a law...

Page 43. *Captain Cat again day dreams of* 'Polly my love' and imagines 'Who cuddled you when? Which of their gandering hubbies moaned in Milk Wood for your naughty mothering arms and body like a wardrobe, Love? '*He imagines her having sex with a 'gandering hubby' this is a definition of the slang use of gandering which has a sexual connotation; To look at, glance at, as in Will you take a gander at that woman's red hair! This slangy idiom, dating from the early 1900s, presumably came from the verb gander, meaning 'to stretch one's neck' possibly alluding to the long neck of the male goose. Captain Cat then imagines her cleaning the Mother's Union Hall floor and describes her as 'one mother* [*who*] *won't wiggle her roly poly bum ...tonight' or pat her little buttery feet in that wedding-ringed holy tonight*

Page 45. *There is a suggestion throughout that the bird watcher who wants to stay at Mrs Ogmore-Pritchard looks at more than just feathered birds through his telescope and the gossips in Mrs Organ Morgan's general shop remember a previous husband* 'he didn't need a telescope he looked at them undressing through the key hole ...and he used to shout Tallyho.'

Page 46. *The gossips conclude after disrespecting Dai Bread for having* 'two wives one for the daytime one for the night.' *they agree that,* 'Men are brutes on the quiet' *Their gossiping concludes with them chatting with Mrs Morgan...* 'And how's Organ Morgan, Mrs Morgan – You look dead beat – it's organ organ all the time with him up every night until midnight playing the organ, *and Mrs Organ Morgan declares*; 'Oh I'm a martyr to music.' *A passage of innuendo and double entendre worthy of the smutty Music Hall comic Max Miller!*

Page 48. *The sexual deviant and pervert* Jack Black the Cobbler;'cobbles a high heeled shoe for Mrs Dai Bread Two the gypsy' but as he 'hammers it sternly out' *he muses and frets* 'there is no leg belonging to the foot that belongs to this shoe'
Captain Cat still dreams of his past sexual exploits and how he exercised his rights as captain,

Second Voice: The sun and the green breeze ship Captain Cat's sea memory again.

And then probably the most explicit line in the play

Captain Cat: No, *I'll* take the mulatto, by God who's Captain here? Parlez-vous jig jig, Madam?

Masked only by the use of cod French and slang he basically is asking a whore 'shall we fuck' - 'Jig jig' being a fairly common slang term for sexual intercourse.[26]

Page 49. Mog Edwards *relates his last night dream to his love Myfanwy Price* 'I dreamed last night you were all dripping wet and you sat on my lap as the reverend Jenkins went down the street. I see you got a mermaid in your lap and he lifted his hat. He is a proper Christian. Not like Cherry Owen who said you should have thrown her back he said' [*let the Freudians sort that dream out*!]

He also is amazed that 'Polly Garter bought two garters with roses but she never got stockings so what is the use I say. *And next* 'Mr. Waldo tried to sell me a woman's nightie outsize he said he found it and we know where' *For him, sex is in his dreams and in his gossip about other people's sex lives.*

Page 52/53 *The brazen hussy that is Mrs Dai Bread Two cons her opposite number the plain fat Mrs Dai bread One out of money by pretending to see scenes of a sexual nature in her crystal ball*; 'which she holds in the lap of her dirty yellow petticoat, hard against her dark thighs'.

Page 54.

Polly Garters song is rich with innuendos when she describes her lost lovers 'He was strong as a bear and two yards long...He was big as a barrel and three feet thick He was six feet tall sweet as a cherry

Polly is singing about the differing penis size of her past sexual partners. The Rev Eli Jenkins hears none of this innuendo and in his innocence he declares, 'Praise the Lord! We are a musical nation'.

Page 54. *In the pub* Sinbad Sailors *tells his drinking companion Mr Waldo of his love* Gossamer Beynon:

'She's a lady all over'

But Mr. Waldo likes his woman rougher – he thinks of 'a woman soft as Eve and sharp as sciatica to share his bread-pudding bed' [*a play on apple pie bed*] *and counters that* 'No lady I know' *is* 'lady all over'.

Page 56. *Polly Garters song is drowned out by the children's song with erotic innuendo;*

Polly sings: Tom Dick and Harry were three fine men And I'll never have such...Children sing: ding a ding. Polly: again. *This is reminiscent of Chuck Berry's comics song 'my ding-a-ling my ding-a-ling'.*

A childish euphemism for the penis it leaves little to the imagination of the listener.

The children's game that comes next is innocent in where the kisses have to be placed or achieved after payment of a penny-Kiss me in Goosegog Lane, *Kiss on* Llareggub Hill, *but when they are not being watched the game no doubt becomes even more risqué.*

Page 60/61. Gossamer Beynon 'high heels out of school' *and at first is ravished by the sun which*:

'hums down through the cotton flowers of her dress into the bell of her heart and buzzes in the honey there and couches and kisses, lazy loving and boozed in her re-berried breast.' But the 'boozed' *suggests the sun has become her dream love* Sinbad Sailors who's; 'Eyes run from the trees and windows of the street, steaming 'Gossamer' and strip her to the nipples and the bees.' [*the birds and the bees = sex*] *she continues in her revelry* 'She blazes naked past the Sailors Arms, the woman on the Dia-Adamed earth. Sinbad Sailors places on her thighs still dewdamp from the first mangrowing cock-crow garden his reverent goat-bearded hands'

A passage redolent of sexual words and images – blazes, naked, thighs, dewdamp, mangrowing, cock-crow and goat bearded.

Gossamer admits to herself – 'the stripped and mother-of-the-world big-beamed and Eve-hipped spring of herself 'I don't care if he is common. I want to gobble him up. I don't care if he does drop his aitches, So long as he's all cucumber and hooves' *i.e.- all cock and bestial balls! And as poor Sinbad lusts after her but bemoans her pride and education* 'She feels his goat beard tickle her in the middle of the worlds like a tuft of wiry fire, and she turns away from his whips and whiskery conflagration = *rough cunnilingus'*.

Page 63/64. *The repressed Mrs Pugh accuses her hen-pecked husband* "I saw you talking to a saint this morning. Saint Polly Garter. She was martyred again last night. Mrs Organ Morgan had seen her with Mr Waldo' [for 'martyred' read fucked! *this echoes Mrs Organ Morgan's* I'm a Martyr to music' *earlier in the play*] *Mrs Morgan begins to relate her tale of her disturbing the couple engaging in sexual intercourse, to her Husband Organ Morgan*; And when they saw me they pretended they were looking for nests... but you don't go nesting in long combinations, I said to myself, like Mr Waldo was wearing, and your dress nearly over your head like Polly Garter. Oh they didn't fool me ... and when you think of all those babies she's got then all I can say is she'd better give up bird nesting that's all I can say, it isn't the right kind of hobby for a woman that can't say No even to midgets. Remember Bob Spit? He wasn't any bigger than a baby and he gave her two. *When she realises that her music-obsessed husband has been dreaming of Bach she becomes irate and tells him off in no uncertain terms*; Organ Morgan, you haven't been listening to a word I said. Its organ organ all this time with you... *Which is ironic when that is just what she has been talking about!*

Page 65/66. *Lord Cut Glass is obsessed with clocks and time and has no time for sex – he lives 'a life at siege' but he is aware that outside the town is different and any one day*; 'the unknown enemy will loot and savage downhill... The lust and lather and emerald breeze and cackle of bird praise and body of Spring with its Breast full of rivering May-milk... tribes of navies who'll sear and pillage down Armageddon Hill ... the town that has fallen Head over bells in love'

And Polly Garter reiterates her song;

Now when farmer's boys on the first fair day
 Come down from the hills to drink and be gay,
Before the sun sinks I'll lie there in their arms
 for they are good bad boys from the lonely farms
But I always think as we tumble into bed
 of Little WILLY Wee who is dead, dead, dead....

Page 67. *First voice gives us another description of the Town's domestic animals that re-enforces the ambience of fecund sexuality with a string of rich juicy words* –'lolls, laps, idles, sleeping in its lap, goat nap happy lazy, sag, pillow, grunt, wallow-bath, snort dream rooting for pig-fruit, bagpipe dugs, squeal, snuffle of yeses of the women pigs in rut, mud bask, rollick, slobber, snore, smug, after-swill, sleep.

This orgiastic description ends 'Donkey's angelically drowse on Donkey Down' [= *hung like a donkey*].

Page 68/69. Captain Cat *is again described daydreaming of when he was young and virile*:

'when his eyes were blue and bright and he was ear-ringed and rolling, I Love You Rosie Probert tattooed on his belly he brawls...roves with a herd of short good time cows in every naughty port and twines and souses with the ...blowsy breasted dead *He remembers* Lazy early Rosie with the flaxen thatch [= *pubic hair*] whom he shared with Tom-Fred the donkeyman [= *hung like a donkey*]and many other seaman... Rosie Probert from Duck Lane quack twice and ask for Rosie who is the one love of his sea life that was sardined with women

[*what a wonderful and erotic image this phrase conjures.*

Page 69/70. *The duet between the two lovers Captain Cat and Rosie Probert is steeped in sexual images and innuendos* 'When you were my master, you were my bosun, Dear you Tom Cat's tart, My little deck-hand, My honey my daddy with my name on your belly...'

Captain Cat ends,

I'll tell you no lies.
The only sea I saw
Was the seesaw sea
With you riding on it.
Lie down, lie easy, Let me shipwreck in your thighs. [*pure poetic genius!*]

Page 72/73. *Nogood Boyo up to no good, we are told first by a little girl who admits to her mother*

'Nogood Boyo gave me three pennies yesterday but I wouldn't'

This sets the tone for what follows. Nogood is out on his boat lazily fishing, but when he catches a 'whalebone corset' it sets him off on erotic revelry; 'Mrs Dai Bread Two the gypsies up his mind's slow eye, dressed only in a bangle. She's wearing only her nightgown (Pleadingly) Would you like this nice wet corset Mrs Dai Bread Two? And a bite of my apple?... *When she refuses him even in his dream he begins to masturbate anyway thinking of* 'There in the bloodshot centre of his eye [*His 'japs eye + the hole atop his penis*] a geisha girl grins and bows in a kimono of ricepaper. I want to be a good Boy, but nobody'll let me. He sighs as she writhes politely. *He approaches his climax* 'The land fades the sea flocks silently away; and through a warm white cloud where he lies silky, tingling [his ejaculation] uneasy Eastern music undoes him in a Japanese minute. [*To turn Japanese' = a euphemism for the face boys pull when approaching masturbatory climax.*[27]

Next we are treated to Mae Rose Cottages' sexual day dream: 'The afternoon buzzes like lazy bees round the flowers round Mae Rose Cottage. Nearly asleep in the field of nannygoats who hum gently and butt the sun and he blows on a puffball. He loves me, he loves me not he loves me, he loves me not, He loves me! – the dirty old fool. Lazy she lies alone in clover and sweet-grass, seventeen and never been sweet in the grass ho ho'. *Like the earlier* 'never been kissed ho ho' *we are being invited to take this statement with a huge dose of irony and imagine just the opposite.*

Page 74. *We are told that Rev Eli Jenkins's father, also a minister*, was 'undogcollared because of his little weakness'. *But this* 'little weakness' [= *mild paedophilia*] *had even graver consequences because it caused him to be* 'Scythed to the bone one harvest by mistake when sleeping with his little weakness in the corn. He lost all ambition and died, with one leg'. *The ever-innocent Rev Eli Jenkins sums up his grief*
Poor Dad, to die of drink and agriculture

Page 78. *The charmingly explicit description of Mae Rose Cottage who declares*:
'I'm fast. I am a bad lot. God will strike me dead. I'm seventeen. I'll go to hell'
While she is; 'lying in clover, listening to the nannygoats chew' while she 'draws circles of lipstick round her nipples', 'You just wait I'll sin till I blow up!. She lies deep, waiting for the worst to happen. The goats champ and sneer'

Page 79. *After Eli Jenkins sweet and innocent Evening Prayer we are brought back to the reality of Llareggub by Jack Black the cobbler the depraved and perverted peeping-Tom, who*, Prepares once more to meet his Satan in the Wood. He grinds his night teeth, closes his eyes climbs into his religious trousers, their flies sewn up with cobbler's thread [*to prevent self-abuse!*], and pads out, torched and bibled, joyfully, into the shining dusk' *he shouts* 'Off to Gomorrah' comparing Llareggub to the *But he doesn't see*; 'Lily Smalls who is up to Nogood Boyo in the wash-house' [*up to = having sex with*].

Page 81/82. *While the men folk are drinking in the pub the young* 'Unmarried girls' *are* 'alone in their privately bridal bedrooms [*place of virginity loosing first sex*] *where they* 'powder and curl for the Dance of the World' *which involves them making* 'in front of their looking glasses, haughty or come-hithering faces for young men in the street outside at the lamplit leaning corners, who wait the all-in-once wind to wolve and whistle.'

Page 83. *After another dose of Rev Eli Jenkins sweet innocence we are once more brought back to the 'reality' of Llareggub by Mr Waldo's rendition in the Sailors Arm, of a song of a type favoured by the likes Max Miller and later George Formby, who's signature tune was his Window Cleaner song, a ribald music hall style song with the obvious double entendre climactic chorus and refrain.*[28] *It is hard not to think that Formby's song was the inspiration for Dylan's climactic pub song about a* 'kind young woman' *who begs the young* 'chimbley sweep' *to clean her* 'chimbley' *with his* 'chimbley brush' *i.e. to have intercourse with her! Here is the last verse*;
Poor little chimbley sweep she said
Black as the ace of spade
nobody's swept my chimbley
Since my husband went his ways.
Come and sweep my chimbley

Come and sweep my chimbley
She sighed to me with a blush
Come and sweep my chimbley
Come and sweep my chimbley
Bring along your chimbley brush!

Page 85. *One last look at Mr Waldo who;* 'Hugs his lovely Polly Garter under the eyes and rattling tongues of the neighbours and birds, and he does not care. He smacks his live red lips. *She in her turn* 'Lies under the oak and loves him back.' *But she dreams of her all-time best love and lover;*
'But I always think as we tumble into bed
Of little Willy Wee who is dead, dead, dead.[29]

1. In 2022 I wrote the Dylan Thomas half of a Book BOB DYLAN AND DYLAN THOMAS The Two Dylans with an obsessive Bobcat K G Miles. We had a chapter on the Sgt. Pepper cover.

2. This photograph was taken by a fine photographer; Nore Summers, who lived in Hampshire near to Dylan's mother-in law, Yvonne Macnamara and the two had a longstanding lesbian relationship. Dylan sentthis photograph to Vernon Watkins with a note "Here's a photograph, taken by a woman near us, its one of many: this is the toughest. Why I want you to think of me as a tough, I don't Know...

3. Gwen Watkins, in her book *Portrait of a Friend*, on Dylan Thomas' friendship with her husband Vernon, postulates that John Lennon plagiarised a passage from Dylan and Vernon's favourite humourous book; a curious old 19th century English-Italian vocabulary for travellers written by a Prof. Carlo Barone. Dylan and Vernon used to love enacting their go-to favourite chapter which was the scene set at the dentists. Gwen suggests that John Lennon 'transcribed verbatim' the same scene in his book, In *His Own Write*... Lennon too, like Dylan, couldn't resist the Dentist's jibe to his suffering lady patient
"That tooth is black and decayed, besides you have none but old stumps in your mouth."

4. This letter is the subject of Chapter 2.

5. Sadly Michael passed away in 2017. The *Guardian* published an Obituary the headline was, *Typographer and designer who aimed for perfection with his books.*

6. *Dylan Thomas Under Milk Wood: Folio Society. 1972.* With nine two colour lithographs by Ceri Richards, of characters from the play.

7. However she has done another classic – Borges, Jorge Louis: *The Book of Sand* – Large Print Masterwork Series. 1989

8. Shelia Waters: *Under Milk Wood: A Play for Voices: A Reproduction of the Illuminated Manuscript.* International Letter Arts Network, 1989. Issued in a regular trade hardback but also as a fine signed limited edition (100 copies)with a sample fragment of vellum calligraphy tipped in. The leather binding of the specials was designed and executed by Shelia's husband, Peter Waters who was head of Conservation at the Library of Congress, and the typeface is designed by her son Julian.

9. I write about my visit to Wormsley towards the end of my Introduction to this book.

10. More on this topic in Chapter 16.

11. As I was proofing this Chapter a new fine illustrated edition of *Under Milk Wood* has just been published in an elegant large format limited edition. The Illustrator is Bonnie Hawkins.

12. This was the first of many visits but shortly after this visit Peter took on a large, two-story Studio just off Hammersmith High Street which became a fantastic, marvellous, and enchanting Museum of Curiosities, beyond description. I recall; Tom Thumbs tiny leather boots; huge glazed cases containing tableau of stuffed mice and other small mammals playing cricket and enjoying tea; and pinned on a wall; what looked like a genuine Beatles autograph was forged for fun at a dinner party by Damian Hirst...

13. Sonny Liston's inclusion is probably due to Peter having the waxwork. It is curious because the Beatles had recently met Cassius Clay, (as he then was; He later converted to Islam and changed his name to Mohamed Ali). The meeting took place in the boxer's Florida Gym and resulted in a famous photo-shoot. Cassius/Ali would defeat Liston on two occasions. At the time of the Album cover was being constructed Sonny Liston had lost his world crown, and his wax figure was about to be melted down. Peter Blake is a big boxing and wrestling fan and asked Tussaud's whether he could keep it permanently after the photo shoot. Tussaud's readily agreed, and now it has pride of place in his studio.

14. Brian Rees's original art work is now in The National Library of Wales as part of the Jeff Towns/Dylans Bookstore Collection.

15. This was the time of Peter's involvement with the Brotherhood of Ruralists, a British art group founded in 1975 in Wellow, Somerset, to paint nature. Their work is figurative with a strong adherence to 'traditional' skills. Painting in oil and watercolour predominate, with mixed media assemblage, printmaking, ink and pencil drawing also being common. It has been described as "a kind of late twentieth-century reinvention of William Morris's arcadian craft guilds." Peter was a founder member with then wife Jann Haworth and other like-minded artists who wanted to get out of the city and get back into nature.

16. After the Russian Futurist artist KAZIMIR MALEVICH, who made such an image in 1915 and also used by the American Abstract Expressionist, Mark Rothko in the 60's.

17. George was a good colleague and friend of mine. Before entering the book trade George had been a journalist and writer mainly covering pop music for the New Musical Express and writing biographies of Pop stars of the day. But he was also a Dylan Thomas enthusiast and this had brought him and his family out of London to settle Laugharne, open a bookshop and write. George died in 2021.17.

18. Caitlin Thomas with George Tremlett; *Caitlin A Warring Absence*. Secker and Warburg.1986.

19. Like his collage heroes before him, Joseph Cornell and Kurt Schwitters, Peter kept all the photographs ephemera, train tickets, tourist leaflets and stuff from that day, and it made it into the final exhibition as a collage of place.

20. Before he fronted his band the Blockheads and became a rock-star, Ian Drury had been at art school where Peter taught him at and they remained good friends

21. The Exhibition moved on from Cardiff, down to west Wales Oriel Y Parc, in St Davids in Pembrokeshire between May and September 2014. It has subsequently been shown in its entirety, in London, at Peter's Gallery, Waddington Clusot in a special space place across from their main gallery on Cork Street in June July 2022. I was at the opening's of all three big shows, as was Sir Peter. At the Cork St. event, I arranged for Trefor Ellis, Dylan Thomas's son-in law, to sing, *A cappella*, in his rich Welsh tenor voice, the Rev. Eli Jenkins evening prayer. Peter, and the whole room were spellbound ...

22. David is a BAFTA and TV Academy Award-winning, and Grierson-nominated, director. With creative flare and inventiveness, he has produced, directed, and occasionally self-shot many acclaimed arts, science, and history programmes for BBC1, 2, 4, Channel Four, PBS, and Discovery. He has recently published a well-received science fiction novel; AXION The Memory Rights Uprising, I and we are good friends ...

23. See above and also Cerys Mathews features in Chapter 16.

24. I think Seamus' brief summation of *Under Milk Wood* is amazing, but I just hope younger readers can relate to relate to the *Joy of Sex* reference, it was a graphically illustrated sex written by Alex Comfort. It caused quite a stir when it came out back in 1972 and was a benign good influence on society, when it appeared 52 years back. |You can read about it here https://www.bbc.co.uk/news/magazine-15309357

25. Solomon is able to sexually possess the Queen once her hairy legs have been made smooth, in an echo of Samson and Delilah – a story which offers a clear example of hair as a signifier for masculine strength, inappropriate for a woman. However, beauty tends to be described as a power, and the Queen's seductive power is one of the factors that make her so dangerous. But it is perhaps a secondary power, ineffable in contrast to the actual physical strength of men, and and once a woman's beauty is sexually possessed it loses its influence and its threat.

26. It is hard to fathom how this got by the BBC back in 1954. However, I was sad to see it censored and cut, and not even given any more subtle replacement, in the recent Michael Sheen *Under Milk Wood* at the National Theatre. One wonders whether *mulatto* is now too considered derogative or the sexual reference is too harsh?

27. And image well used by *The Vapors* in their Punk anthem 'I think I'm turning Japanese'

28. This is a typical sample verse from Formby's *Window Cleaner* song
In my profession I'll work hard
But I'll never stop
I'll climb this blinkin' ladder
Till I get right to the top
The blushin' bride, she looks divine
The bridegroom he is doin' fine
I'd rather have his job than mine
When I'm cleanin' windows

29. I have just read an essay by Katie Gramich, *Daughters of Darkness: Dylan Thomas and the celebration of the Female*, in which she writes of *Under Milk Wood*;
Phallic anxieties are reflected in the work for example, in the obviously named Little Willie Wee, whose presumably modest endowment is preferred by Polly Garter to Tom, who was, Strong as a bear and two yards long –
It is included in Goodby, John and Wigginton, Chris, eds. Dylan Thomas, New Casebooks. U.W.P. 2001.

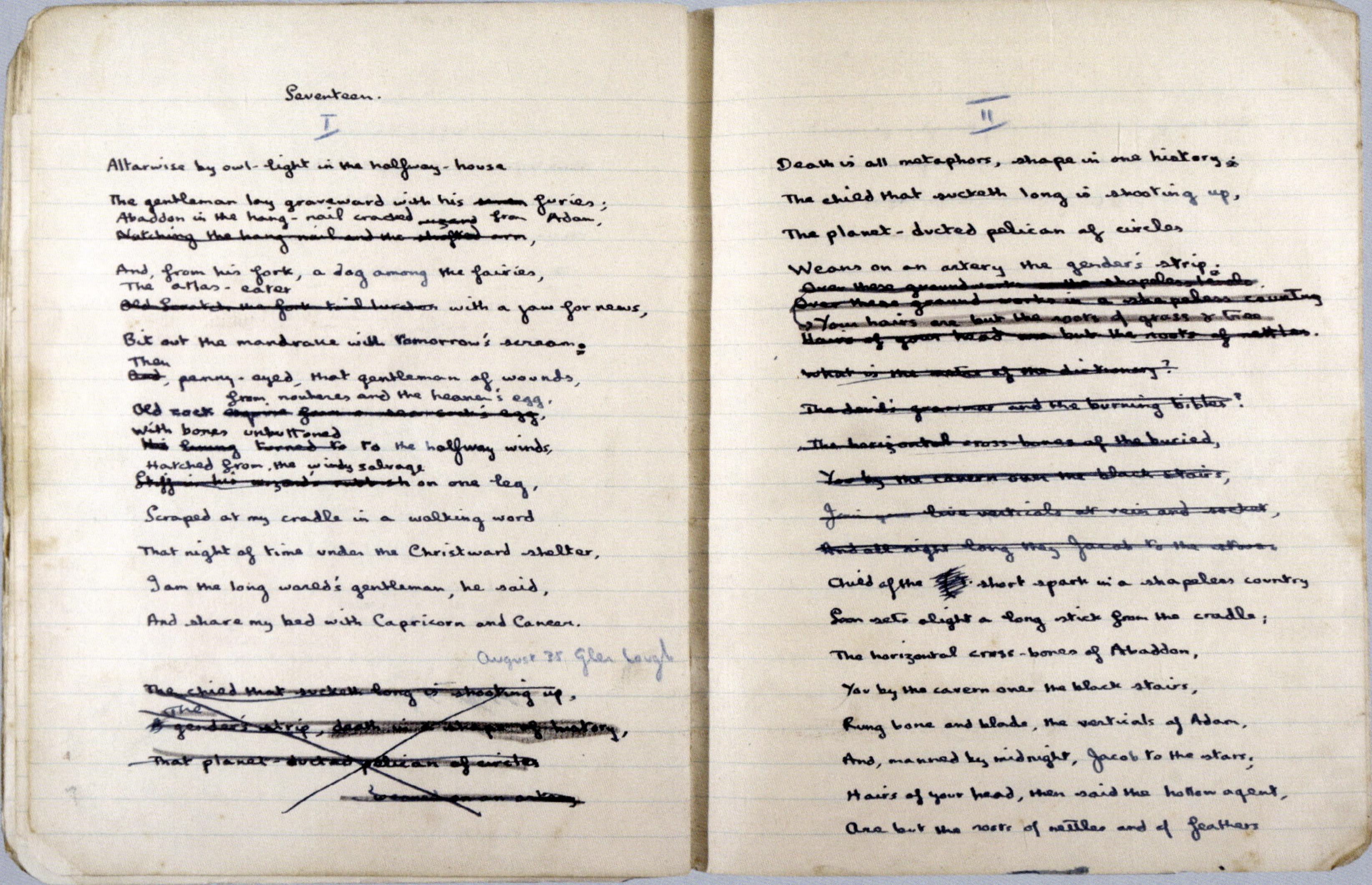

Seventeen.

I

Altarwise by owl-light in the halfway-house
The gentleman lay graveward with his ~~seven~~ furies;
Abaddon in the hang-nail cracked ~~urged~~ from Adam,
~~Watching the hang-nail and the stuffed arm,~~
And, from his fork, a dog among the fairies,
The atlas-eater ~~Old Scratch, the fork-tail hurdler~~ with a jaw for news,
Bit out the mandrake with tomorrow's scream:
Then ~~And~~, penny-eyed, that gentleman of wounds,
Old cock from nowheres and the heaven's egg,
With bones unbuttoned ~~His limey~~ ~~turned to~~ to the halfway winds,
Hatched from the windy salvage ~~Stiff in his wizard's~~ ~~...~~ on one leg,
Scraped at my cradle in a walking word
That night of time under the Christward shelter,
I am the long world's gentleman, he said,
And share my bed with Capricorn and Cancer.

August 35 Glen Lough

~~The child that sucketh long is shooting up,~~
~~The gender's strip, death ... history,~~
~~That planet-ducted pelican of circles~~
~~Weaned on an artery~~

II

Death is all metaphors, shape in one history;
The child that sucketh long is shooting up,
The planet-ducted pelican of circles
Weans on an artery the gender's strip;
~~Over these ground works ... the shapeless lands~~
~~Over these ground works in a shapeless country~~
~~Your hairs are but the roots of grass & tree~~
~~Hairs of your head are but the roots of nettles.~~
~~What is the water of the dictionary?~~
~~The devil's grammar and the burning bibles?~~
~~The horizontal cross-bones of the buried,~~
~~You by the cavern over the black stairs,~~
~~... the vertical of vein and socket,~~
~~And all night long the Jacob to the stars.~~
Child of the short spark in a shapeless country
Soon sets alight a long stick from the cradle;
The horizontal cross-bones of Abaddon,
You by the cavern over the black stairs,
Rung bone and blade, the verticals of Adam,
And, manned by midnight, Jacob to the stars;
Hairs of your head, then said the hollow agent,
Are but the roots of nettles and of feathers

18.

Dylan Thomas:
LOT 125. The Lost Fifth Notebook.

LOT 125, That's yours sir at 85 thousand pounds ...
Thank you very much.
The Sotheby's auctioneer when I bought Dylan's *Lost Notebook*

In his short 1938 story, *The Fight*,[1] DylanThomas writes;

> In the evening... I sat in my bedroom by the boiler and read my exercise-books full of poems.
> There were Danger Dont's on the backs.

As I have already mentioned a few times in these essays, 2014 was Dylan Thomas's Centenary Year. It was taken up by the Welsh Assembly government who appointed a small team of suitable civil servants to oversee the year-long celebrations, and they, in turn, enlisted Hannah Ellis Thomas, Dylan's granddaughter, to keep her and the Dylan Thomas Trust and David Higham Associates, Dylan Thomas' literary agents, involved with all their plans. But once again coincidence/

synchronicity/fate, call it what you will, also played a part in the ensuing proceedings. As the year progressed, various important new books, art projects, films and music came to fruition and were featured in, and added to, an altogether very rich year of great celebrations. To mention a just a few; the year was kick-started by an exhibition at The National Museum of Wales in Cardiff of Sir Peter Blake's ravishing and immense illustrations for *Under Milk Wood*. There was also a proper opera composed by John Metcalf based on *Under Milk Wood*. (The CD used one of Sir Peter Blake' images for the CD cover.)[2] A new film based on Dylan's first visit to America and the time he spent getting to know his 'agent' John Malcolm Brinnin, was made by a fledgling film company *Mad as Birds Films*,. Its title was *Set Fire to the Stars*.[3] It was directed by Andy Goddard, who co-wrote the script with Welsh actor/writer, Celyn Jones, who played Dylan in the film alongside Elijah Wood's portrayal of John Malcolm Brinnin – so Froddo Baggins became J. M. Brinnin.

The BBC also made documentaries and yet another rendition of *Under Milk Wood* with the current crop of Welsh actors and celebrities. And thanks to *Visit Wales* I got to go paddle a canoe out into the estuary at Laugharne and read *Fern Hill* to an intrepid group of poetry loving canoeists, afloat below Dylan's Boathouse.

Reading Fern Hill in Laugharne estuary

The above events were all outstanding, but an unexpected e-mail from *Sotheby and Co*, the prestigious London Auctioneers, which arrived in my inbox in very early November 2014, (very close to the date on which Dylan Thomas died) aged just 39 in New York City, actually took my breath away. I was being alerted to the astounding news that a hitherto lost and unknown, original manuscript notebook of early poems by Dylan Thomas had been brought into their Bond Street salerooms and was to be offered for sale there on December 9 2014. This is how *Fine Books & Collectors Magazine* in America described the announcement;

> **Unknown Dylan Thomas Notebook Discovered,**
> **Estimated to Sell for $150,000-$235,000 at Sotheby's**

As the world celebrates the centenary of the birth of the Dylan

Thomas, Sotheby's announces the most exciting manuscript discovery since his death in 1953. The exercise book, which contains 49 handwritten pages, will be the most important poetical manuscript by Thomas ever to appear at auction when it is offered at Sotheby's London on 9 December.

This previously unknown and unrecorded notebook contains a series of 19 poems written during his urgent burst of creativity in the 1930s. The scratchings-out, doodles and revisions that mark the pages offer a unique insight into the creative process of one of the world's most loved poets. Thomas appears to have left the book behind during one of his many stays at the house of his mother-in-law, Yvonne Macnamara, during the 1930s.

Evidently, Thomas had a fractious relationship with his mother-in-law, illustrated in a letter written by Thomas to a friend[4] while staying at the home:

> This flat English country levels the intelligence, planes down the imagination, narrows the a's, my ears belch up old wax and misremembered passages of misunderstood music, I sit and hate my mother-in-law, glowering at her from corners and grumbling about her in the sad, sticky, quiet of the lavatory...

This letter will also be offered as part of the sale on 9 December (est. £2,000-2,500). Perhaps glad to rid the house everything to do with Thomas, Yvonne Macnamara gave the exercise book to a member of the household staff, Louie King (c.1904-1984), with instructions to incinerate it in the kitchen boiler. King decided against it, sparing the precious book and recording the event in a note attached to the cover:

> *"This Book of Poetry by Dylan Thomas was with a lot of papers given to me to burn in the kitchen boiler. I saved it and forgot all about it until I read of his death..."*

The book has remained with the family of Louie King, hidden in a drawer and unknown to Thomas scholars, only emerging now more than fifty years after his death. Although not consistently dated, the notebook was presumably begun before 20 July 1934, when Thomas sent a copy of the book's first poem, 'All and all', to his lover Pamela Hansford Johnson, and it was completed by August 1935. It was written during a crucial year in Thomas's life and work, when he firmly established a place for himself in the literary world. This period was marked by two major events: his move to London in November 1934 and the publication of his first collection, 18 Poems the following month. The notebook shows that he continued to write consistently through his months in London, but his most intense burst of creativity came when he left the city and its distractions. Firstly, when staying with A.J.P. Taylor and his wife Margaret in Disley, Cheshire, and secondly during an August visit to County Donegal with Geoffrey Grigson. Notable poems from the book include the only known manuscripts for Thomas's famously demanding sonnet sequence, 'Altarwise by owl-light'. Replete with revisions and reworkings, these drafts provide a crucial new insight into Thomas's most challenging work.

What an incredible item, and for it to turn up with such immaculate timing; a spectacular discovery coming at the end of the centenary year. At that time I had no idea just what actually lay in store for me.

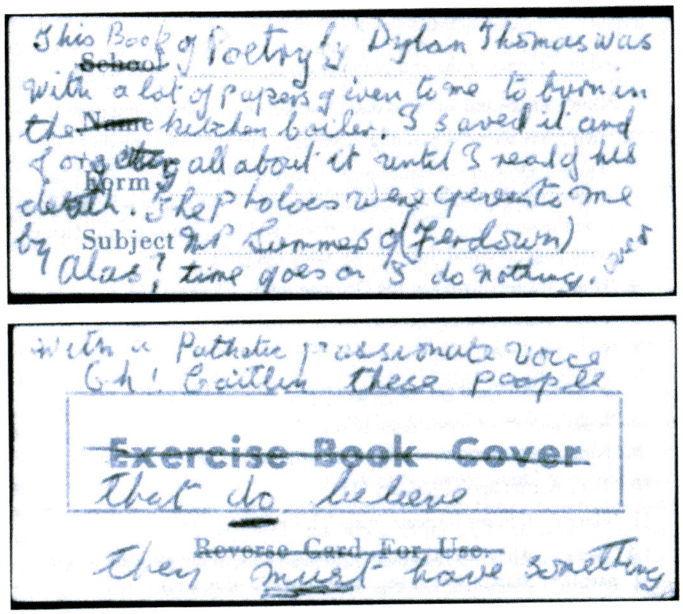

This Book of Poetry by Dylan Thomas was
with a lot of papers given to me to burn in
the kitchen boiler. I saved it and
forgot all about it until I read of his
death. The photoes were presented to me
by Mr Summers (Ferdown)
Alas! time goes on I do nothing.

with a Pathetic passionate voice
Oh! Caitlin these people
~~Exercise Book Cover~~
that do believe
~~Reverse Card For Use.~~
They must have something

Louie King's brief explanation note attached to the notebook[5]

Around the same time Sotheby's notified me in Swansea, as one of the leading booksellers specialising in Dylan Thomas.[6] They also enlisted the services of the current leading specialist Dylan Thomas academic critic, John Goodby,[7] who was based in Swansea in the University's English Department. So, as I was trying to persuade various institutions to take an interest in Lot 125, John was working with Sotheby's in promoting the sale across the media. Along with the Sotheby's PR team John did a good job – the presale publicity went global; it seems that the story captured peoples' imagination not least because the notebook had been kept by the family in a vintage TESCO plastic bag, with DYLAN THOMAS scrawled on it in blue biro, and it was delivered to the auction house still in it, and the infamous bag remained as part of the lot. Such an ignominious pairing; a three-dimensional cultural oxymoron.

However, all the publicity did not aid my cause. I desperately wanted the notebook to stay in Wales; Sotheby's mentioned in their description that Dylan had sold four earlier poetry notebooks via a major London bookstore and that they went to America and are part of the huge collection of literary manuscripts in the Harry Ransome Centre at the University of Texas. I did not want this surprise companion to end up in the States as well. I tried every institution I thought might or should be interested, but got nowhere. This was mainly due to lack of funds, but excuses were also made about 'dubious provenance' or questions about 'ownership and title'. And no matter how I framed it, I could not afford to buy it myself. I was in despair. But then fate stepped in.

Approaching 2014, through the previous year I had been engaged with the English Department at Swansea University. I knew the professor, M. Wynn Thomas, who was the founder and director of CREW[8] and a wonderful writer and scholar of Welsh Literature in both languages, and he was also a respected member of the Gorsedd of the Bards. Alongside him were two younger professors, Daniel G. Williams, also bilingual, and John Goodby, who I've mentioned above. But I was more involved with the Research Institute for Arts and Humanities(RIAH), working with them on the annual *Dylan Thomas Prize*, and on various exhibitions and events to do with Dylan Thomas and Vernon Watkins over the last few years. I worked closely with Dr Elaine Canning, a Spanish specialist who was Head of RIAH and Head of Cultural Engagement and Development, and John Spurr, Professor Emeritus at the Humanities and Social Sciences and History department and at the time he was Head of the College of Arts and Humanities. I was good friends with both of them and we had a very good working relationship.

After the news of the notebook appeared, during our coffee chats and more structured meetings we had talked in general about the forthcoming auction sale and I more than likely mentioned my concerns and lack of success, in a few of our meetings. But I was almost literally bowled over when, out of the blue, John asked me to meet him at a campus coffee bar and calmly asked me to act for the university and bid on the manuscript at the forthcoming sale at Sotheby's. And he went on to coolly inform me that I could bid up to the top end of the estimate. I could hardly believe my ears. How had he conjured this money up. I was astounded but also ecstatically excited and immediately said I would waive the 10% commission booksellers usually charge for executing a commission bid...We were in with a chance.

I went home and let it sink in and began to prepare myself for the big day. The first thing I did was book a train to London for the next day. On arrival, I took the tube to Bond Street straight into Sotheby's. I bought a catalogue at the counter, went straight into the viewing room and spent an hour or so sitting at a table with the actual notebook and ephemera in front of me. It was a hairs-on-back-of-neck moment when it was handed to me – still in the TESCO bag! I was almost too shaky to take it all in. I gingerly, but gently turned the pages and tried my best to concentrate on the task in hand. On the train home I read and then re-read the catalogue, pouring over Lot 125. Sotheby's cataloguers had done a very good job – the description filled two 4to. Pages, with an illustration. This is how it began;

LOT. 125: Description
Thomas, Dylan; Autograph manuscript notebook of poems. Ink on paper.

PREVIOUSLY UNKNOWN AND UNRECORDED, containing a series of numbered poems from "one" to "nineteen", neatly written in Thomas's fair hand, with revisions (including in some cases extensive rewriting) to fourteen of the poems, other poems with variant readings to the subsequent published text, written in a lined exercise book, mostly in blue ink but five works partially written in pencil then overwritten in blue ink, primarily written on the rectos only, 49 pages, with two further pages of pencil jottings including doodles, calculations, addresses and telephone numbers, plus blanks, quarto (c.220 x 165mm), [c.July] 1934 to August 1935, *lacking covers, three leaves partially excised (probably removing rejected drafts), stubs of two further leaves, one leaf loose where the conjugate leaf has been torn away, further tears to an additional four leaves.*

A MAJOR GROUP OF MANUSCRIPT DRAFT POEMS BY DYLAN THOMAS, WRITTEN DURING HIS URGENT BURST OF CREATIVITY IN THE MID-1930S AND CONTAINING VERSIONS OF POEMS PUBLISHED IN HIS FIRST TWO COLLECTIONS. THE MOST SIGNIFICANT POETICAL MANUSCRIPT OF THOMAS KNOWN TO SURVIVE IN PRIVATE HANDS. This remarkable manuscript follows directly on from the sequence of four similar surviving notebooks at the State University of New York at Buffalo. The last of the Buffalo notebooks was completed on 30 April 1934; this notebook is not consistently dated but was presumably begun before 20 July of the same year, when Thomas sent a copy of the first poem in the notebook ('All all and all') to his lover Pamela Hansford Johnson, and was completed in August 1935.

Then the agonising wait for sale day. I can't remember how I got to London on the day, but do remember entering Sotheby's and encountering a small group from Swansea University – including Elaine Canning, John's Spurr and Goodby. I can recall registering to bid and getting my bidding paddle at the same time as two academics from Reading University, who were at the sale to try and secure a fine group of Samuel Beckett manuscripts[9] to add their already substantial collection. We then all trooped into the designated saleroom and took up seats close to the front and settled back to watch and listen to the sale for a couple of hours. The auctioneer Peter Selley, was an old acquaintance of mine who I had known in the book-trade as a young man, before he joined Sotheby's and had worked his way up; and now here he was, on the rostrum, wielding the gavel; would he bring it down for me today?

Just before the sale began there was a bit of a commotion at the back of the room and I spun around to see a small group of large no-good boyos who had travelled up from Laugharne, West Wales up to enjoy the day's action. I knew a few of them from the annual Laugharne Weekend Festival and they were good, but high-spirited lads, indeed some form of alcohol may well have livened then up already.

Things quietened down and Peter Selley got the sale started. I tried to take an interest and made a few cursory scribbled notes in my catalogue, but my mind was in a state of adrenalin-fuelled agitation and I was willing the lots to fly by. Lot 104. The Beckett manuscripts came up and, after some fierce bidding, Reading University beat-off the other bidders in the room and on telephones and made the successful bid. Would we do the same and achieve our goal? I ran over in my head my simple mathematical formula to know when to join the bidding so as not to be wrong footed if I had to go to my maximum.

And then it was the Dylan Thomas lots. Lot 125, the first of four Dylan Thomas lots, was a good letter to Charlie Fisher. I would like to have had a go at it, but I needed to stay focused and it failed to sell at £1500. Was that an omen of some kind? Now it was our turn. The auctioneer began;

Lot 151, Ladies and Gentlemen... The extraordinary Dylan Thomas autograph manuscript poetry note book. Unknown and unrecorded, from a fertile period in the Thirties, there has been lots of interest in this item and publicity...

Where shall we start?
at 60 thousand I have 60...
I waved my paddle.
Thank you sir I have 65 do I see 70?
70 I have 70. Is there 75?
I twitched my paddle again (with sweaty palms).
75. I have 75 Do I see 80?A pause...
80 thousand pounds. I have 80 on the telephone
80 ... do I see 85?

I waved my paddle again, I could not see
my adversary but I was in the zone.
85 I have 85 thousand. Thank you, your bid sir on my
left against the telephone. Looking for 90 thousand.
Anywhere. Last chance at 90.

Small lakes of sweat gathered in the palms of my hands...
Silence in the room

Anywhere. Final chance. Now anywhere...
A resounding knock, the sound of wood hitting down on wood.

And then – with a gesture across to me... ***That's yours sir at 85 thousand ...Thank you very much.***

Hand-clapping broke out, a few Welsh-accented cheers rippled around the room and high fives were exchanged. I had bought it. It was coming home to Swansea. The University team are smiling and hugging. I am smiling, somewhat in disbelief, my hand is pumped and my back is slapped in praise.

From: "Selley, Peter" <peter.selley@sothebys.com>
Date: 11 December 2014 09:28:10 GMT
To: "'jefftowns@dylans.com'" <jefftowns@dylans.com>
Subject: Re: Dylan Letter to Charles Fisher

Jeff thank you many congratulations to you and your team. It isn't every day that you see high fiving in front of you as an auctioneer! It is fantastic that the notebook is going to Swansea - the Beckett archive similarly went to a UK institution. A gratifying change from years ago, though consignors perhaps achieve less with the absence of some US libraries now (and the falling apart of the museum in Paris which was buying mss).
The other Dylan Thomas letter is now sold I'm afraid, so sorry I can't give you a second chance at that one. It has gone overseas to a private collector.
I hope we will have more DT business in the future.
Wishing you all the best for the festive season and 2015
Yours
Peter

We HAD damn well bought it! We all adjourned to the café and had coffee(it should have been exorbitantly priced champagne – but times are tough in further education!) But all was fine in the world at that moment. And then my memory goes blank, but I know I was very happy and very satisfied in the moment of what was, without doubt, the highlight of my bookselling career. Back in Swansea the next day I received an e-mail[10]. from Peter Selley, the Sotheby's Auctioneer, which congratulated us and added

"It isn't every day that you see high fives in front of you as an auctioneer! It is fantastic that the notebook is going back to Swansea"

Our success also garnered strong and TV and press coverage. The BBC carried a news piece on radio and TV quoting this;

Jeff Towns, chairman of the Dylan Thomas Society and owner of Dylan's Bookstore, who bid at the auction on behalf of the university, said:

"I cannot conceive of anything more fitting and purposeful to bring what has been a vibrant year-long celebration of a great writer's centenary to a close, than to bring this lost notebook – so telling and

National

Poetic justice as university saves Dylan Thomas drafts for Wales

Mark Brown
Arts correspondent

A lost notebook containing drafts of some of Dylan Thomas's most challenging poems is to remain in the UK after Swansea University successfully bid £104,500 for it at auction in London.

The previously unknown book emerged earlier this year, with one scholar calling it the most exciting Thomas discovery since the poet's death in 1953. Thomas was born in 1914 and died aged just 39 in New York.

The university's winning bid - £85,000 plus commission - was made by Jeff Towns, chairman of the Dylan Thomas Society. "I'm overwhelmed," he said after the buy. "I've been coming to auctions for 40 years but holding this bidding number at the end of the centenary year is incredible ... it is a sensational coup and a real statement of intent from Swansea University."

The book had lain in a drawer for decades, with its owners unaware of its cultural significance. It is the fifth notebook in which Thomas wrote poems: the others are owned by the State University of New York at Buffalo and are currently on loan to the National Library of Wales.

poignant – back to Swansea. If anybody had suggested such a thing last January I would have said 'impossible' on so many counts. To keep it in Wales for future generations is a huge achievement and I am overwhelmed to have been a small part of it."

The notebook will be kept in the University's archives, which already houses Richard Burton's diaries and other papers bequeathed by his widow Sally Burton...

The sale was very well covered in the National Press; *The Guardian* ran a long piece and *The Independent* had a piece which began thus;

And locally, back in Wales the local press and media gave the Notebook's homecoming a very good reception, and Dylan's granddaughter came down to Swansea for the celebrations.

Hannah Ellis Thomas with her grandfather's note-book in Swansea University's Archives

IN ASSOCIATION WITH NEWSLETTERS
Don't miss the latest health stories in Wales

WalesOnline

Dylan Day: Poet's lost notebook goes on show in Swansea, revealing 'tiny, neat writing of a meticulous craftsman'

One further development occurred quite soon after the London auction. In early December I was contacted by Sotheby's New York; they had recently held a Fine Books and Manuscripts Sale in New York which included one lot made up of a very interesting group of twenty-five original Dylan Thomas, unrecorded manuscript worksheets, for two important poems; *Into your Lying Down Head* and *Unluckily for a Death*, which were both first published in a New Directions book *New Poems*, in 1943. This was their sale description:

THOMAS, DYLAN

Two autograph manuscripts, both working drafts of early poems. Ca. 1940

Autograph manuscript being drafts of the poem "Into your Lying Down head." 11 pages (10 x 8 in.; 254 x 203mm) in ink with 3 ink sketches, Laugharne, Carmarthenshire, Wales, July 1940; minimal wear, central horizontal crease — Autograph manuscript being drafts of "Unluckily for a death" (here titled "Poem"). 14 pages (most approximately 6 x 4 in.; 153 x 102mm) in ink with one ink sketch, Laugharne, Carmarthenshire, Wales, [ca. 1940]; small holes in upper margin of final leaf, affecting one word.

TWO VERY REVEALING WORKING MANUSCRIPTS OF EARLY POEMS BY DYLAN THOMAS. THESE DRAFTS SHOW THOMAS NOT ONLY REVISING IMAGERY AND WORD CHOICE, BUT ALSO GRAPPLING WITH AND WORKING OUT RHYME SCHEMES AND RHYTHMIC STRUCTURES.

"Into your Lying Down head" was published after further revisions as "Into her Lying Down head" in *New Poems, 1940* (1941), an anthology edited by Oscar Williams. It then appeared in Thomas's *New Poems* (1943). The present draft is remarkable for the poet's diagrams of his tentative rhyme scheme. There are also three small drawing in which Thomas appears to be visualizing his imagery. For example, a sketch of an island with trees, ink dots representing a sandy beach and two sailboats at sea illustrates the lines "Two sand grains together in bed / Head to heaven-scraping head" (in the published poem "heaven-scraping" becomes "heaven-circling").

The drafts of "Unluckily for a Death," first published in *New Poems*, are equally revealing. Thomas completes the beginnings and endings of some stanzas and stalls with the middle, drawing horizontal lines to leave space for the words to come. Imagery and vocabulary both go through dramatic transformation from early draft to published poem. Thomas begins and ends the poem with a vision of the phoenix. The earliest draft includes the line "Though the phoenix stir in the rocks" underlined and also a small drawing of a phoenix walking upright and a man riding on a whale. The draft begins with a phoenix under a stone and the finished poem with a phoenix "under / The pyre yet to be lighted of my sins and days." In the final stanza of the published poem, Thomas writes, "Love, my fate got luckily, / Teaches with no telling / That the phoenix' bid for heaven and the desire after / Death in the carved nunnery / Both shall fail if I bow not to your blessing."

These drafts, totaling 25 pages in Dylan Thomas's unmistakable miniscule hand, give an intimate and detailed record of the poet's creative process.

$ 50,000-70,000

It transpired that the lot had failed to sell at the auction sale and, in view of my recent purchase of the Notebook in London, I was being offered them at a post auction bargain price: I could make a significant, reasonable offer which would be looked upon favourably. The auction estimate been $50,000 – $70,000 dollars (around £40,000 – £50,000). I spoke with the University who encouraged me to pursue the worksheets so I requested a catalogue to be sent priority air mail and once we had considered the full catalogue description (they also provided extra scans of the material), I secured them for Swansea University at under half the original estimate and it appeared that everyone was happy with this outcome. Certainly it meant that Swansea University Archives suddenly held a significant and major holding of Dylan Thomas manuscripts.

There were some faint dissenting voices regarding the monies involved but the notebook came in well under the estimate – the price with premium was £104,500 – a reasonable amount, perhaps, since the estimate had been £100,000-150,000. And the additional manuscript poems were also what I would consider a bargain. After the Sotheby's sale one journalist questioned the prices paid and this was my response;

Towns said the figure had to be put in perspective. "I walked here from Green Park and there are millions of pounds changing hands for bangles and baubles on Bond Street and we're in here excited we

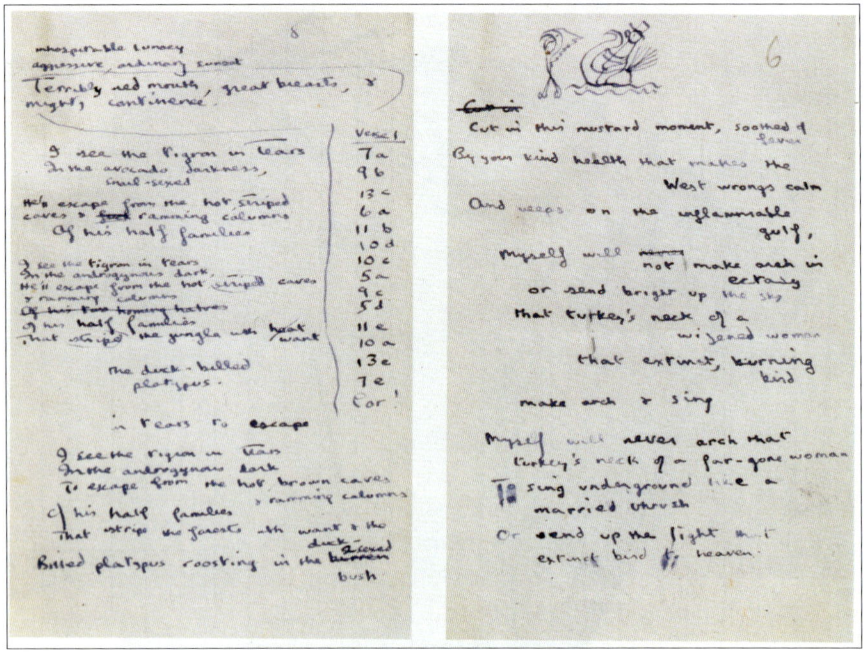

got this for £85,000. I'm not making light of £85,000, it is a lot of money, but in the scheme of things ...

Once all the recent acquisitions were back safely in the hands of Swansea University Library and Archives staff, their first task was to manage the digitalisation of the whole, rather fragile manuscript note book and the worksheets, and to affect any essential conservation work. This coincided with the University's recent partnership with The Harry Ransom Library at the University of Texas in a project in which both libraries would digitise their entire Dylan Thomas archives and make them all available online for all to use. This was very efficiently achieved and the next task was for two of the University English department to prepare the digitised manuscript for publication. John Goodby[11] was the lead, assisted by Adrian Osborne, a postgraduate English student, who had recently gained his PhD and he was also working on the Library's digitisation project. They worked hard together to get as accurate a transcription as possible and John enthused about his younger colleagues' sharper eyesight which greatly helped the transcription and deciphering of Dylan's small and somewhat untidy early handwriting. The book was eventually published by Bloomsbury Academic in 2021, and a very handsome and readable volume it is.

At the end of what had been a very busy and successful Dylan Thomas Centenary Year, Hannah Elis Thomas in particular, was keen for there to be some kind of lasting legacy and it was decided to establish a *World Dylan Thomas Day*. After much discussion and rumination she collaborated with the Welsh government's *Dylan Thomas 100* senior staff and they decided, for various reasons, on May 14th. They wanted a day otherwise uncluttered in terms of established annual events, but with some Dylan Thomas significance, as it was on that day in 1953, that the first full performance of *Under Milk Wood* took place in New York, with Dylan playing *First Voice* and other parts, supported by five American stage actors.

Swansea University used this first ever *Dylan Thomas Day*, in May 2015 to put their recent new, important acquisitions on display for the people of Swansea to visit. They could inspect this literary treasure in his *ugly lovely town* as it then was, when he grew up there back in the early quarter of the century. I helped to curate a small, but powerful Dylan Thomas exhibition in the Library at the University Bay Campus, with the Notebook very much the focus of attention. At the opening various academics and dignitaries said a few words; I spoke

briefly, and the fine Welsh actor, Celyn Jones, who had just played Dylan in *Set Fire to the Stars*, gave a moving reading of some of the notebook poems.

It was a fitting end to a

remarkable journey that the fragile notebook had endured; a journey that could have begun and ended in flames had Louie King, a housemaid, obeyed her mistress, Dylan's mother-in-law Yvonne Macnamara, and burnt it in the household incinerator as instructed. Luckily for us all she chose to preserve it; her accompanying note offers no real explanation;

I saved it and forgot all about it until I read of his death.

So it had remained hidden, languishing in a drawer in a humble TESCO bag for some seventy-five years before being taken to London and dropped off at Sotheby's on Bond Street to begin its journey back to Swansea – where it had originated almost a century ago. The university produced this final flyer;

For me, these acquisitions by Swansea University, were a wonderful climax to a rich and varied *Dylan Thomas Centenary Year*, but I would go even further and say that hearing the gavel go down in my favour in Sotheby's, that day in 2014, that meant that the long-lost Dylan Thomas notebook was coming back to Swansea, was the absolute pinnacle of my fifty-plus years as a Welsh bookdealer.

Rollie McKenna's photographs of Dylan and his New York cast rehearsing.

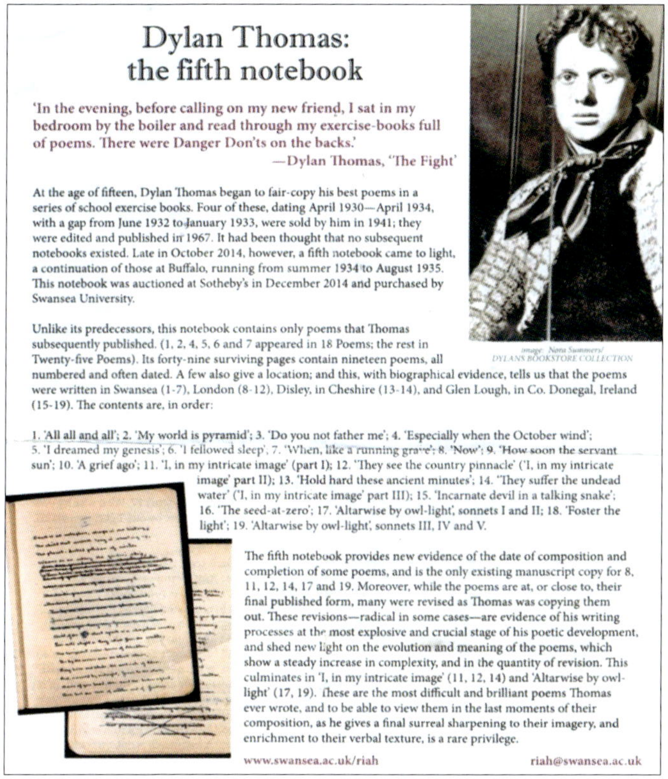

Dylan Thomas: the fifth notebook

'In the evening, before calling on my new friend, I sat in my bedroom by the boiler and read through my exercise-books full of poems. There were Danger Don'ts on the backs.'
—Dylan Thomas, 'The Fight'

At the age of fifteen, Dylan Thomas began to fair-copy his best poems in a series of school exercise books. Four of these, dating April 1930—April 1934, with a gap from June 1932 to January 1933, were sold by him in 1941; they were edited and published in 1967. It had been thought that no subsequent notebooks existed. Late in October 2014, however, a fifth notebook came to light, a continuation of those at Buffalo, running from summer 1934 to August 1935. This notebook was auctioned at Sotheby's in December 2014 and purchased by Swansea University.

image: Nora Summers/
DYLANS BOOKSTORE COLLECTION

Unlike its predecessors, this notebook contains only poems that Thomas subsequently published. (1, 2, 4, 5, 6 and 7 appeared in 18 Poems; the rest in Twenty-five Poems). Its forty-nine surviving pages contain nineteen poems, all numbered and often dated. A few also give a location; and this, with biographical evidence, tells us that the poems were written in Swansea (1-7), London (8-12), Disley, in Cheshire (13-14), and Glen Lough, in Co. Donegal, Ireland (15-19). The contents are, in order:

1. 'All all and all'; 2. 'My world is pyramid'; 3. 'Do you not father me'; 4. 'Especially when the October wind'; 5. 'I dreamed my genesis'; 6. 'I fellowed sleep', 7. 'When, like a running grave'; 8. 'Now'; 9. 'How soon the servant sun'; 10. 'A grief ago'; 11. 'I, in my intricate image' (part I); 12. 'They see the country pinnacle' ('I, in my intricate image' part II); 13. 'Hold hard these ancient minutes'; 14. 'They suffer the undead water' ('I, in my intricate image' part III); 15. 'Incarnate devil in a talking snake'; 16. 'The seed-at-zero'; 17. 'Altarwise by owl-light', sonnets I and II; 18. 'Foster the light'; 19. 'Altarwise by owl-light', sonnets III, IV and V.

The fifth notebook provides new evidence of the date of composition and completion of some poems, and is the only existing manuscript copy for 8, 11, 12, 14, 17 and 19. Moreover, while the poems are at, or close to, their final published form, many were revised as Thomas was copying them out. These revisions—radical in some cases—are evidence of his writing processes at the most explosive and crucial stage of his poetic development, and shed new light on the evolution and meaning of the poems, which show a steady increase in complexity, and in the quantity of revision. This culminates in 'I, in my intricate image' (11, 12, 14) and 'Altarwise by owl-light' (17, 19). These are the most difficult and brilliant poems Thomas ever wrote, and to be able to view them in the last moments of their composition, as he gives a final surreal sharpening to their imagery, and enrichment to their verbal texture, is a rare privilege.

www.swansea.ac.uk/riah riah@swansea.ac.uk

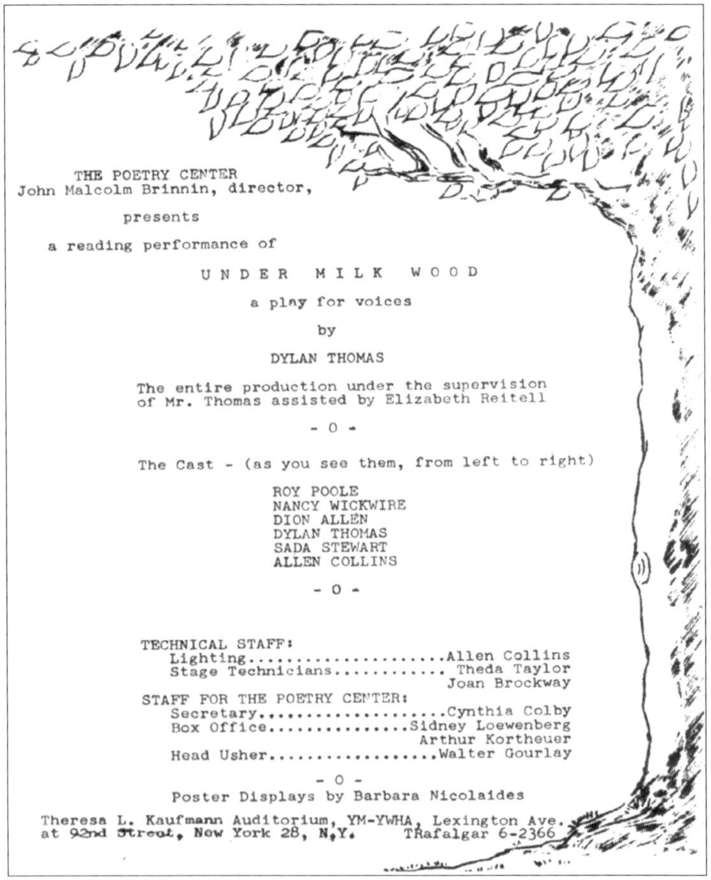

The original poster for the first full cast stage performance of *Under Milk Wood* in New York May 14 1953

1. The story first appeared in *Life and Letters Today* in December 1939 and was later included in *Portrait of the Artist as a Young Dog.*

2. This exhibition and the book of the illustrations is featured in Chapter 17.

3. The title of the film and the Production Company's name are both taken from Dylan's poem *Love In The Asylum*. I was very fortunate to get involved in movie which was filmed mainly in and around Swansea. It is a good honest production and I am proud to have been given a credit as 'Poetry Advisor'. I was also an extra for one night of filming on Swansea's Wind Street, but sadly when I went to the premiere I realised I had been consigned to the cutting room floor. It was a very friendly, lively and passionate cast and crew; it was a pleasure for me to be part of the team.

4. The friend was none other than Charles Fisher – see Chapter 11.

5. The Mrs Summers mentioned in the note is Nora Summers, a friend of the Macnamara's and Augustus John's tribe. She lived nearby in *Ferndown* and was an artist and a fine photographer who took many of the best images of Dylan and Caitlin. I wrote a book about her with her Grandson Gabriel Summers and his wife Leonie: *Dylan Thomas and the Bohemians The Photographs of Nora Summers*. Parthian 2014. No photographs were with the notebook when it came to auction.

6. Over the years I had bought at Sotheby's auctions; lots which included various inscribed Dylan Thomas books and first editions; his only known Watercolour paintings; all his surviving letters to his parents, and his correspondence with Desmond Hawkins. Most all of which are now in The National Library of Wales.

7. John Goodby is an academic specialising in Irish writing, Welsh poetry, and British / US poetry, especially modernist poetry,. He is one of the leading authorities on the work of Dylan Thomas and has written and published many books on his works, most importantly bringing out the most recent annotated edition of *The Collected Poems of Dylan Thomas, – The New Centenary Edition* which appeared early in 2014.

8. Centre for Research into the English Literature and Language.

9. What was on offer was the collection of annotated playscripts and letters from Beckett's favourite actress Billie Whitelaw.

10. I had enquired after the Charles Fisher letter that had not sold. I also received a congratulatory e-mail from the academics from Reading who bought the Beckett they wanted at the same sale; a phenomena that Peter Selley also commented on.

11. As I mentioned above John is a leading academic specialist in the works of Dylan Thomas. He has written critical work on Thomas; *The Poetry of Dylan Thomas: Under the Spelling Wall* (2013). He recently took up a post as Professor of Arts and Culture at Sheffield Hallam University, and with his former Swansea colleague there, past collaborator Chris Wiggington, they have just co-authored and published a new short biography of Dylan Thomas in the Reaktion Critical Lives series.

A GARLAND FOR DYLAN THOMAS
The Life of Dylan Thomas
Constantine FitzGibbon
THE FINAL OBSERVATIONS of a TECHNOSHAMAN GEORGE TIRADO ROAD KILL PRESS
The Dylan Thomas Murders
DYLAN THOMAS'S SWANSEA GOWER AND LAUGHARNE JAMES A DAVIES
Discovering Dylan Thomas John Goodby
Gendering Border Studies Jane Aaron, Henrice Altink and Chris Weedon
Dylan Remembered Volume Two 1935–1953
Dylan Remembered Volume One 1914–1934
Pariah Genius Iain Sinclair
My Friend Dylan Thomas Daniel Jones
LA BD EST CHARLIE
DYLAN THOMAS THE BROADCASTS EDITED BY RALPH MAUD Dent
DYLAN THOMAS BY PAUL FERRIS
DYLAN THOMAS THE NOTEBOOK POEMS EDITED BY RALPH MAUD Dent
DYLAN THOMAS A NEW LIFE ANDREW LYCETT W&N
Dylan Thomas John Goodby · Chris Wigginton palgrave
DYLAN THOMAS The Collected Letters NEW EDITION Edited by Paul Ferris Dent
DYLAN THOMAS THE BIOGRAPHY New Edition Paul Ferris Dent
MARCEL WILLIAMS
BLISTER & OTHER STORIES JK MAZELIS
DYLAN THOMAS JOHN GOODBY AND CHRIS WIGGINTON
REUBEN, REUBEN Peter DeVries
my life with Dylan Thomas: double drink story CAITLIN THOMAS
Mr Mahli's Shed Laura Sheldon
THE MAGICAL DILEMMA OF VICTOR NEUBURG JEAN OVERTON FULLER
Dylan Thomas in Print Ralph Maud
WHEN I WAS DESMOND HAWKINS
After the First Death
LESLEY BLANCH The Sabres of Paradise
TWENTIETH CENTURY POETRY
The Doctor and the Devils
FATAL NEGLECT Who Killed Dylan Thomas?
A GARLAND FOR DYLAN THOMAS
Rebecca's Daughters DYLAN THOMAS
PREACHER BOOK TWO Garth ENNIS Steve DILLON
GLYN JONES · THE DRAGON HAS TWO TONGU
The Collected Poems of Dylan Thomas
The Poetry of Dylan Thomas
A REFERENCE COMPANION TO DYLAN THOMAS

Acknowledgements & Sources.

Acknowledgements

To Ali Anwar at the H'mm Foundation, Jon Gower for his support, advice and enthusiasm, Karl Morgan for his friendship and assistance through the long process. Andy Dark for his sympathetic design. David Cowell for his enthusiasm and proofing efforts. Tim Batcup and Lin Beverley for proofreading (but I take full responsibility for the published text.) To the late Gwen Watkins for years sharing with me her knowledge of Dylan Thomas and his friends. Andrew Lycett for his generous support. Lisa and Leonard Baskin for their friendship and generosity on both sides of the Atlantic. Carol Hughes and Robert Orchard for help and photographic permissions with the Ted Hughes Chapter. Antony Penrose and The Lee Miller Archive, farleyshousenandgallery.co.uk for help and images for the Surrealist Chapter. The National Library of Wales, Aberystwyth and The Harry Ransom Center, Texas. Hilly Janes for help and images in the Charles Fisher Chapter. Sir Peter Blake for his friendship and generous permission to use his magnificent *Under Milk Wood* art-work. Artist Philippa Jacobs for her fine portraits of D T and R S Thomas opening Chapter 9. Photographers Ruth Crafer and Matt Roberts for the front and back, cover images, Bernard Mitchell, Andrew Dally. Lal Hardy of New Wave Tattoo for the ink. Gabriel and Leonnie Summers for Nora's great photographs. Cerys Matthews, and Ralph McTell for sharing their personal enthusiasms for Dylan Thomas. Caitlin Fisher in Toronto. Veronica Watts, Ed Maggs, Sammy Jay, Peter Finch, Elaine Canning, M Wynn Thomas, David Sacks, Enitharmon Press and Iain Sinclair, Geoff Haden at the Dylan Thomas Birthplace; for friendly bibliographic help and advice. Wyn Thomas for his friendship and Illustrations. Huw Davie for constant general life support and chauffeuring.

And my two great kids, Kate and Joe, my 6 grandkids and to my wife Lizzie, who has tolerated and stoically endured 50-plus years of my obsession with books and their writers ...

Bibliography

Details of the most of the books I consulted and quoted from are given in the text or in footnotes. My main aids were the three standard biographies of Dylan Thomas – Fitzgibbon in 1966, Ferris in 1999 and Lycett in 2002. What follows are details of the books I used.

Works by Dylan Thomas

Collected Poems, 1934-1952, Dent. 1952.
Early Prose Writings. Edited by Walford Davies. Dent. 1971.
Under Milk Wood. Preface by Daniel Jones. Dent. 1975.
The Collected Stories. Dent. 1983. Edited by Walford Davies, Introduction by Leslie Norris.
The Broadcasts; Edited by Ralph Maud. Dent 1991.
The Film Scripts; Edited by John Ackerman. Dent. 1995.
The Collected Poems of Dylan Thomas: The New Centenary Edition, edited by John Goodby. Weidenfeld & Nicolson. 2014.

Letters

Letters to Vernon Watkins. Dent/Faber. 1957.
The Collected Letters of Dylan Thomas; Edited by Paul Ferris. Dent New Edition. 2000.
A Pearl of Great Price; The Love Letters of Dylan Thomas to Pearl Kazin, edited by Jeff Towns. Parthian 2014.

Books about Dylan Thomas and some background books

Ackerman, John: *Welsh Dylan*. John Jones Cardiff.
A Dylan Thomas Companion Life, Poetry and Prose. Macmillan. 1991.
Dylan Thomas The Filmscripts. Dent. 1995.
Agar, Eileen: *A Look At My Life*. Methuen. 1988.
Broyard, Anatole: *Kafka was the Rage A Greenwich Village Memoir*. Carol Southern Books. NYC. 1983.
Burke, Carolyn: *Lee Miller A Life*. Knopf. NYC. 2005.
Davies, James A. *A Reference Companion to Dylan Thomas*. Greenwood. 1978.
Deren, Maya: *Divine Horsemen The Living Gods of Haiti*. Document. NYC. 1983.
Maya Deren and the American Avant-Garde, edited by Bill Nichols. U.C.L.A. Press. 2001.

Ferris, Paul: *Caitlin The Life of Caitlin Thomas*. Hutchinson. 1993.
FitzGibbon Constantine: *Through the Minefield An Autobiography*. Bodley Head. 1967.
Fraser, Robert: *Night Thoughts The Surreal life of the poet David Gascoyne*. Oxford. 2012.
Fuller, Jean Overton: *The Magical Dilemma of Victor Neuberg*. W. H. Allen. 1965.
Gascoyne, David: *Journal 1936-1937*. Enitharmon. 1980.
Goodby, John: *Discovering Dylan Thomas*. University of Wales Press. 2017. *The Poetry of Dylan Thomas Under The Spelling Wall*. Liverpool University Press. 2003.
Jones, Daniel: *My Friend Dylan Thomas*. Dent. 1977.
Leader, Zachary: *The Life of Kingsley Amis*. Jonathan Cape. 2006.
Main, Peter: *A Fervent Mind The Life of Ruthven Todd Lomax*. 2018.
Maud, Ralph: *Dylan Thomas The Notebook Poems*. Dent. 1989. *Where Have These Old Words Got Me*.
Montalk, Stephanie: *The Life of Geoffrey Potocki de Montalk*. Victoria University Press N.Z. 2001.
Norris, Leslie [edits]**:** *Vernon Watkins 1906-1967*. Faber. 1970.
Palmer, William: *In Love With Hell Drink in the Lives and Work of Eleven Writers*. Robinson. 2021.
Ramsbotham, Richard: *An Exact Mystery The Poetic Life of Vernon Watkins*. Choir Press. 2020.
Sinclair, Upton: *The Cup of Fury*. Chanel Press New York. 1956.
Smith, K. & Barfoot R: *New Theoretical Perspectives on Dylan Thomas*. University of Wales Press. 2020.
Stanford, Derek: *Dylan Thomas*. Spearman 1954
Stevens, Meic: *Rhys Davies A Writers Life*. Parthian. 2013.
Thomas, M. Wynn: *Corresponding Cultures*. University of Wales Press.1999. *R. S. Thomas Serial Obsessive*. University of Wales Press. 2013. *All That Is Wales Collected Essays*. University of Wales Press. 2017.
Tindall, William York: *A Readers Guide to Dylan Thomas*. Thames & Hudson. 1962. Texas.
Watkins, Gwen: *Portrait of a Friend*. Gomer Press. 1983.
Williams, Robert Coleman: *A Concordance to the Collected Poems of Dylan Thomas*. University of Nebraska Press. 1967.

Original Sources

Some of the contents in this book have appeared in previous varied publications. In most cases the originals have been edited and updated with new materials. Chapter 2. is based on the Introduction to my 1993 book, *Letter to Loren*, published in an edition of 225 copies by my *Salubrious Press*. Chapter 3. is based on the catalogue I compiled for the 1995 Dylan Thomas Exhibition, *Dylan Thomas Word and Image*, which is still open at Swansea's Dylan Thomas Centre. Chapter 5. *Dylan Thomas & Hermaphroditism* is based on an article in a, now defunct, American online periodical publication, *Ralph*. Chapter 6. *Borrowed Plumes – Requiem for a Plagiarist*, was first published in the 2014 collection of Essays, *Dylan Thomas A Centenary Celebration* edited by Dylan Thomas' granddaughter Hannah Ellis, Published by *Bloomsbury*. Chapter 8. *O Rare Dylan Thomas*, has grown over many years and a few publications, the last being the *H'mm Foundations* 2014, *Encounters With Dylan Thomas* edited by Jon Gower. Chapter 14. *Dylan Thomas, Ginsberg & The Beats* was inspired by a chapter I wrote with K. G. Miles in my recent 2022 book *The Two Dylans*. Published by McNidder & Grace.

I have done my best to the best of my ability to track down and acknowledge all the images. Many images accompanied press releases and in many cases we rely on fair usage but should you feel that an image is legally yours do get in touch and we will add an acknowledgement or remove from future editions.

Other publications from the H'mm Foundation

Encounters with Nigel Jenkins
Edited by Jon Gower

CONTRIBUTORS:
Edwina Hart AM, John Barnie, Stevie Davies, Steve Griffiths, Angharad Jenkins and Branwen Jenkins, Noel Witts, Deborah Llewelyn, Robert Minhinnick, Peter Finch, John Davies, Menna Elfyn, Delyth Jenkins, Daniel G. Williams, Dave Hughes, Margo Morgan, Janet Dube, Jane James, Steve Griffiths, Ivor McGregor, Benjamin Palmer, Dave Oprava, Iwan Bala and Twm Morys, Janice Moore Fuller, Mike Parker and Ceri Wyn Jones, Ifor Thomas, Jane Fraser, Martyn Jenkins, Carey Knox, Steve Dube, Humberto Gatica, Tom Jenkins, D.J. Britton, Fflur Dafydd, Anne Lauppe-Dunbar, M. Wynn Thomas, Jon Gower and Peter Gruffydd.

ISBN978-0-9927560-4-8

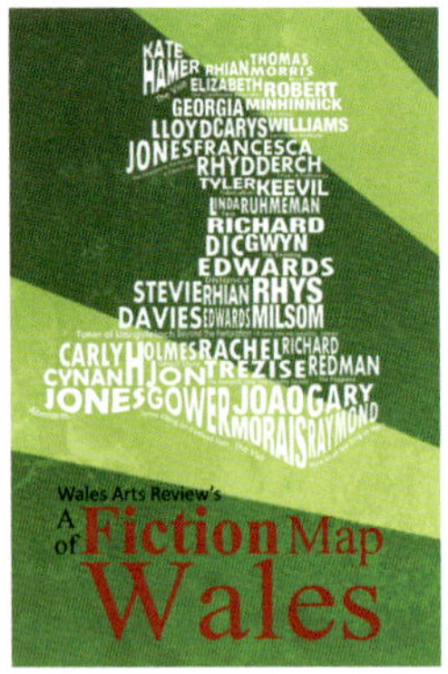

A Fiction Map of Wales
Edited by John Lavin

CONTRIBUTORS:
Rachel Trezise, Thomas Morris, Stevie Davies, Cynan Jones, Francesca Rhydderch, Joao Morais, Jon Gower, Rhian Elizabeth, Carly Holmes, Lloyd Jones, Gary Raymond, Tyler Keevil, Richard Redman, Georgia Carys Williams, Rhian Edwards, Rhys Milsom, Dic Edwards, Linda Ruhmeman, Richard Gwyn, Kate Hamer and Robert Minhinnick.

ISBN 978-0-9927560-6-2

Encounters with R.S. Thomas
Edited by John Barnie

CONTRIBUTORS:
Gillian Clarke, Fflur Dafydd, Grahame Davies, Gwyneth Lewis, Peter Finch, Jon Gower, Menna Elfyn, Osi Rhys Osmond, Jeff Towns, Archbishop of Wales Barry Morgan, M. Wynn Thomas and First Minister of Scotland Alex Salmond.

ISBN 978-0-9927560-0-0

Encounters with Dylan Thomas
Edited by Jon Gower

CONTRIBUTORS:
Rachel Trezise, Michael Bogdanov, Kaite O'Reilly, D.J. Britton, Dafydd Elis-Thomas AM, Dai George, Sarah Gridley, Sarah King, Jeff Towns, George Tremlett, Steve Groves, Gary Raymond, Guy Masterson, Jon Gower, Horatio Clare and Andrew Lycett.

ISBN 978-0-9927560-2-4

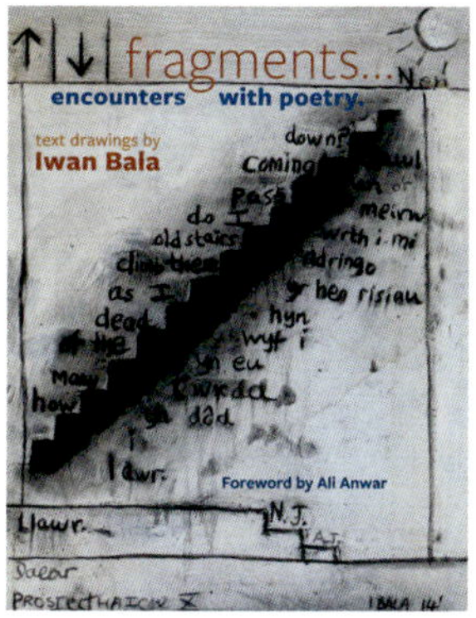

It is as if... fragments
Essays about recent work by Iwan Bala, with images and DVD of the PROsiect hAIcw performances in collaboration with musician Angharad Jenkins, based on the poetry of her father, the late Nigel Jenkins.

CONTRIBUTORS:
Iwan Bala, Dr Anne Price-Owen, Osi Rhys Osmond, Twm Morys, Aneirin Karadog and Angharad Jenkins.

ISBN 978-0-9927560-8-6

Encounters with Osi
Essays about Osi Rhys Osmond, edited by Iwan Bala and Hilary Rhys Osmond.

CONTRIBUTORS:
Iwan Bala, Hilary Rhys Osmond, Ivor Davies, David Alston, M. Wynn Thomas, John Osmond, Christine Kinsey, Dai Smith, Karl Francis, Wyn Morris, David Parfitt, Mick and Thea Arnold, Hedley Jones, Noelle Francis, Susanne Schüeli, Teilo Trimble, Bella Kerr, Steve Wilson, Sam Vicary, Tina Carr, Siân Lewis, Nathan Osmond, Sara Rhys-Martin, Luke Osmond, Simon Thirsk, Lynne Crompton, Gwenan Rhys Price, Linda Sonntag, Rolf Jucker, Ché Osmond, Macsen Osmond, Colin Brewster, Ben Dressel, Megan Crofton, Lesley Davies, Beverley Oosthuizen-Jones, John Barnie, Menna Elfyn, Richard Pawelko and Mary Simmonds, Bethan John, Mererid Hopwood, Ann Oosthuizen,

ISBN 978-0-9927560-9-3

Encounters with John Selway
By Jon Gower

CONTRIBUTORS:
Paul Bowen, Derek Butler, Ivor Davies, Ken Elias, Richard Frame, Karl Francis, Brian Gardiner, Jonathan Glasbrook-Griffiths, Robert Alwyn Hughes, Alison Howard, David Hurn, Julian Meek, Phil Muirden, Osi Rhys Osmond, Brian Rice, Dai Smith, Marion Sprackling, Norman Toynton, Keith Underwood, Peter Wakelin, Phil Watkins, Roger and Den Wolfe.

ISBN 978-1-9999522-0-4

Other publications from the H'mm Foundation

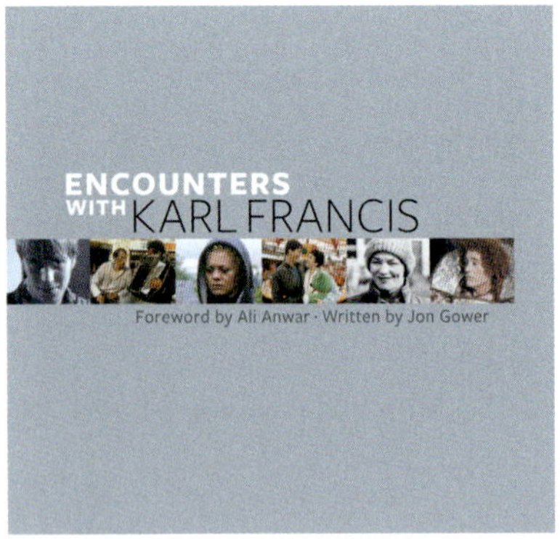

Encounters with Karl Francis

CONTRIBUTORS:
Foreword by Ali Anwar, written by Jon Gower

ISBN 978-1-9999522-1-1

Nigel Jenkins
Damned for Dreaming and other essays

CONTRIBUTORS:
Foreword by Ali Anwar and Jon Gower

ISBN 978-1-9999522-8-0

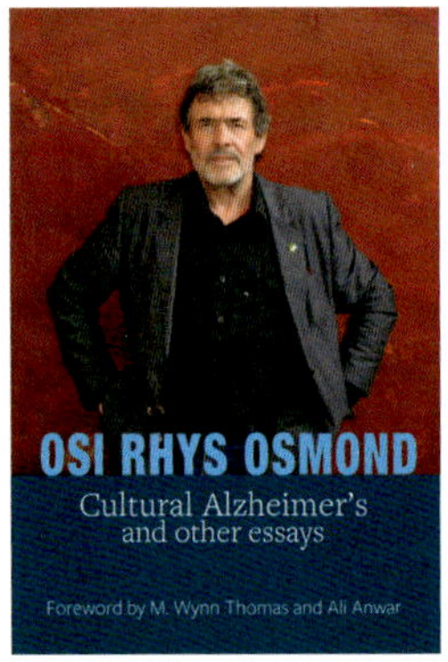

Osi Rhys Osmond
Cultural Alzheimers and other essays

CONTRIBUTORS:
Foreword by M. Wynn Thomas and Ali Anwar

ISBN 978-1-9999522-9-7

Wicked Words
£2.95

In partnership with The Wales Millenium Centre in 2015

ISBN 978-0-9927560-7-9

HON 2022
Artistiaid Benywaidd
Yng Nghymru
Women Artists In Wales

ARTISTIAID/ARTISTS
Marian Delyth
Sadia Pineda Hameed
Angharad Pearce Jones
Julia Griffiths Jones
Christine Kinsey
Sian Parri
Sarah Rhys
Catrin Webster
Sarah Williams
Sarah Younan

Editor Christine Kinsey
Introduction by Menna Elfyn
and Ali Anwar

ISBN 978-1-9999522-6-6

Truth, Lies & Alibis
Encounters with
Christine Kinsey

Foreword by Ali Anwar and
M. Wynn Thomas.
Introduction by Menna Elfyn

ISBN 978-1-9999522-5-9

IMPACT*Ardawiad*
Angharad Pearce Jones

Foreword by Ffion Rhys
Afterword by Ali Anwar

CONTRIBUTORS:
Dylan Huw, Beca Brown

ISBN 978-1-9999522-2-8

Other publications from the H'mm Foundation

Shaping Art in Wales
Ceri Thomas

Foreword by Karen Mackinnon

ISBN 978-1-9999522-3-5

Gaynor Funnell
Penbanc: Notes from a Welsh Farmhouse

Foreword by Jon Gower and Ali Anwar

ISBN 978-1-9999522-4-2

Energy and Power
Our perilous obsessions

R. Gareth Wyn Jones

Foreword by Mark Mansfield

Preface by Robin Grove-White

ISBN 978-1-0685053-0-0

Let the World's People Sing
Menna Elfyn

Foreword: Menna Elfyn and Ali Anwar
Translation to Arabic:
Rawan Sukkar and Lara Matta

ISBN 978-0-9927560-3-1

Published by the H'mm Foundation,
c/o Bevan Buckland,
Langdon House,
Langdon Road,
Swansea SA1 8QY.

The H'mm Foundation is a not-for-profit organisation dedicated to raising the profile of the arts and culture in peoples' lives.

www.thehmmfoundation.co.uk